The Affinities and Antecedents of Medieval Settlement

Topographical perspectives from three of the Somerset hundreds

Nick Corcos

BAR British Series 337
2002

Published in 2016 by
BAR Publishing, Oxford

BAR British Series 337

The Affinities and Antecedents of Medieval Settlement

ISBN 978 1 84171 424 0

BAR Publishing is the trading name of British Archaeological Reports (Oxford) Ltd.
British Archaeological Reports was first incorporated in 1974 to publish the BAR
Series, International and British. In 1992 Hadrian Books Ltd became part of the BAR
group. This volume was originally published by Archaeopress in conjunction with
British Archaeological Reports (Oxford) Ltd / Hadrian Books Ltd, the Series principal
publisher, in 2002. This present volume is published by BAR Publishing, 2016.

Printed in England

BAR titles are available from:

BAR Publishing
122 Banbury Rd, Oxford, OX2 7BP, UK
EMAIL   info@barpublishing.com
PHONE   +44 (0)1865 310431
FAX   +44 (0)1865 316916
www.barpublishing.com

In Memoriam

Dr Michael Geoffrey Corcos, 2nd December 1919-12th December 1996

Bettina Mary Corcos (nee Brooksbank), 27th June 1921-7th January 2002

Acknowledgements and Dedication

In the course of the six years work which has gone into this work, the reader will appreciate that the debts of gratitude which I have accumulated, and can in some cases never repay, are many and various.

The support and encouragement of my entire family, my seven siblings (Jints, Rob, Phil, Chris, Lil, Steve and Sal), my mother and my father, has been unstinting throughout. I cannot imagine having completed this task successfully without their collective strength. If only all families were like this. Two years into the work, we lost Dad, while Mum, who lived to see it successfully completed, submitted for examination and my doctorate awarded in May 2001, died six years later in January 2002. This publication is, therefore, dedicated jointly to the beloved memories of Dr Michael Geoffrey Corcos, LRCP, MRCS, DTM&H, and to Bettina Mary Corcos, without doubt the two most remarkable people I have ever known or am ever *likely* to know. I can say only that I hope they will both approve.

Likewise have my friends and colleagues in the Dept of Archaeology at Bristol provided the kind of empathetic support that only those going through the same or similar work can do, and never doubted me when I frequently doubted myself. Jodie Lewis gave numerous invaluable insights into the more arcane aspects of prehistoric landscape archaeology, especially on the theoretical side; the influence on the present work, brief as it is, will, I hope, be manifest. To Jodie and her partner Dave Mullin I also owe the survey of the newly-discovered Bronze Age barrow on the Woolavington/Puriton boundary (Whitley Hundred), which is included here as part of Appendix 1. Magnus Alexander's groundbreaking study using GIS to inform perspectives on early medieval territorial arrangements, settlement and land-use in North Somerset, has also played its part; this is work of the highest importance, and my debt to both him and Jodie will be clear from the references. In the course of this work I saw Paula Gardiner and Shirley Everden, like me veterans of the first Bristol Archaeology Certificate course, both progress to First Class degrees and in Paula's case, to the research and submission of her own PhD thesis. To both of them, I offer thanks, and likewise to Penny Stokes, another Certificate student of the Class of '91, who by a wonderful irony went on to take the same MA as I had done in the Dept of English Local History at Leicester. Her encyclopaedic knowledge of, especially, the medieval agrarian landscape, has benefited me more often than I care to mention.

It cannot be many people who, doing their best to come to terms with notoriously unforgiving and difficult Domesday evidence, have the benefit of advice and guidance from two leading DB scholars; I was fortunate enough to enjoy exactly that privilege, and to Frank and Caroline Thorn, joint editors of numerous editions of the Phillimore DB series, I am indebted not only for their help with many points of detail in the great survey itself, but also, in their other capacity as teachers of medieval Latin, for an understanding of whatever part of that language I have been able to deploy here. Since their raw material was a Latin scholar perhaps most generously described as a slow-learner, this in itself is a considerable achievement on their part.

My friend Dr Nigel Chaffey and his wife Chris have on untold occasions entertained me royally at their house in Weston and fed me when it is, quite literally, doubtful whether I would have eaten properly myself. Their unwavering moral and practical support throughout the last six years, in so many ways, is, I regret, one of my unpayable debts.

Teresa Hall, whose own MPhil on Dorset minsters, now published, has provided such a rich quarry for my own speculations on that theme, lent a much-needed steadying hand when I began looking at the landscape and phenomenological contexts of my 'own' minsters.

Of my former colleagues at BT, with whom for over eleven years it was a privilege and a pleasure to work, I must mention especially Suzanne Bromme, whose work for her OU degree ran almost exactly in parallel with my own. The mutual support and understanding that came from checking each other's texts was extremely welcome.

Chris Webster, SMR Officer in the Archaeology Section at Somerset County Council, went far beyond the call of duty in supplying me with full printouts from his database of every parish in Whitley and Carhampton hundreds. He always answered the e-mails with which I constantly deluged him patiently and quickly, and kept me advised of any new developments in those hundreds of which he became aware. Chris's kindness meant that I was at no disadvantage when the constraints of a full-time job precluded visits to Taunton to use the SMR in person, and without that information the work simply could not have proceeded.

I am grateful to Mark Corney for reading and commenting on my Roman chapter, and supplying some key references.

Dr Robert Dunning, Editor of the Somerset VCH, gave me pre-publication access to his files for the Whitley hundred parishes, a source of the first importance. Even if we differ over matters of interpretation of the ecclesiastical evidence, his unstinting assistance over many points of historical detail will, again, be clear from the references, and I greatly appreciate his kindness.

The staff of the Somerset Record Office were, as ever, always courteous and efficient in the course of my many visits there, and never less than indulgent with my requests to see *original* documentary material (especially maps) rather than merely microfiches. Figures 32 and 41, and Plate 7, are reproduced here with their kind permission, and by far the majority of the early OS maps upon which many of the figures are based were likewise taken from those kept at the SRO.

Finally, I need to pay a special tribute of thanks to my joint supervisors, Prof Mick Aston and Dr Michael Costen. It was due to their gentle but firm 'badgering' that I embarked on this study in the first place, in November 1994, and their good humour, patience and constant stream of advice, ideas and knowledge were central to the successful completion of the work. The pleasure of inspirational tutorials was in both cases always enhanced by copious quantities of good food and good wine, such that I never left either's house without feeling completely buoyed (in a purely emotional sense, of course). Whatever may be considered 'good' or 'useful' about the present work is firmly underpinned by their faith and confidence in me over the course of the last six years.

Few hearts to mortals given
On earth so wildly pine
Yet none would ask a Heaven
More like this Earth, than thine.

Emily Jane Brontë

Contents

List of Tables

List of Figures

List of Plates

List of Abbreviations

ASSAH: Anglo-Saxon Studies in Archaeology and History

BAA: Bristol and Avon Archaeology

BAR: British Archaeological Reports

BL: British Library

CBA: Council for British Archaeology

EPNS: English Place-Name Society Journal

MSRG: Medieval Settlement Research Group Annual Report

OUCA: Oxford University Committee for Archaeology

PPS: Proceedings of the Prehistoric Society

PRO: Public Record Office

RCHME: Royal Commission on Historical Monuments (England)

SANHS: Somerset Archaeological and Natural History Society Proceedings

SDNQ: Notes and Queries for Somerset and Dorset

SELRC: Severn Estuary Levels Research Committee Annual Report

SMR: Sites and Monuments Record

SRO: Somerset Record Office

SRS: Somerset Record Society

UBSS: University of Bristol Speleological Society Proceedings

VCH: Victoria History of the County of Somerset

Chapter One

Introduction

Historical Background

The search for the origins of rural communities in England as we perceive them in the medieval period has exercised a strong (some might say unhealthy) fascination for scholars since at least the time of Maitland. Until well into this century, such work was almost exclusively the preserve of historians, who by definition tended to deal with the subject very much from a legal and constitutional [Maitland 1897], or social and economic [Seebohm 1883; Homans 1941] perspective. Their sources were overwhelmingly documentary, and ideas about the ways in which medieval society operated, its agrarian practices, legal framework, social relationships, economy and so on, were informed very largely by often highly detailed analyses of the documentary record, especially for the period from the late 12th century onwards.

Problems arose, however, when historians attempted to extrapolate back into the *pre*-Conquest period using for the most part the post-Conquest evidence which was then at their disposal; although it is a mark of the ingenuity of some of these early pioneers, and particularly Maitland, that some of their speculations have since been lent support by the later work of scholars of other, more recently-developed disciplines. Analogies drawn from English society and the nature of its rural settlements and economy in the medieval period were used to explain pre-Conquest developments, in the largely mistaken belief that the situation after 1066 must necessarily be a direct reflection (albeit through more 'developed' or 'advanced' forms) of that obtaining in the countryside in and throughout the Anglo-Saxon period.

This, then, was a perspective that was *document*-driven. And in looking for the first glimmerings of realisation that the landscape *itself* should be admitted as evidence in its own right, one is torn between Maitland and Hoskins.[1] It was Maitland, for example, who first drew attention to the potential significance of the supposed dichotomy in England between nucleated and dispersed patterns of settlement: "as our eyes grow accustomed to the

work we may arrive at some extremely important conclusions.........the outlines of our nucleated villages may have been drawn for us by Germanic settlers, whereas in the land of hamlets and scattered steads old Celtic arrangements may never have been thoroughly effaced. Towards theories of this kind we are slowly winning our way" [Maitland 1897, 39]. Hoskins himself, on more than one occasion, acknowledged the profound debt that he owed his great constitutional predecessor [Hoskins 1982, 17, and 1984, 26]; and would have been the first to admit that (to paraphrase Newton), if he saw further, it was at least in part by standing on Maitland's shoulders. Nonetheless, with the publication, in 1955, of *The Making of the English Landscape*, it was Hoskins above all others who almost single-handedly laid the foundations for the discipline that historic landscape study has now become, including, from the outset, establishing its most fundamental principle: eclectic and all-encompassing, a 'jack of all trades' capable, at its best, of giving us a window on the past that amounts to far more than merely the sum of its constituent parts. And it is *this* aspect of Hoskins's legacy that has been most recently characterised by Richard Muir as the discipline's greatest asset: "because so many different forms of expertise may be called upon for the resolution of a particular problem, the landscape historian is frequently found seeking-out the help of specialists working in other fields. Therefore it can be argued that the complexity of the discipline is its strength. Its span is too wide to be encompassed by any current fad, dogma or dictate which might debilitate a more narrowly-defined discipline.........the width of this span *obliges* enthusiasts and practitioners to exchange information and ideas – it must be an interdisciplinary discipline whether or not one chooses it to be so. With a breadth that makes it tyrant-proof and a composition which dictates cross-fertilisation" [Muir 2000, 20].

The Present Work

This latter view is quoted at length here because it is a perspective which underpins and informs this study in a defining way. I present here a general, synthetic survey of certain aspects of medieval settlement in three contrasting areas of Somerset. The aim has been to give an impression, a broad overview, of the nature of rural occupation, its affinities and antecedents, very much from a topographical perspective. The particular topics with which I deal here are intended to link in with some of the central questions currently occupying other scholars engaged in this kind of work, and, conversely, to make a broad contribution to the general thrust of that work, even if only, at this stage, by asking questions that may not necessarily yet have

---

[1]We need to distinguish here between topographical/landscape writing as *description*, such as we find in the works of William Worcestre, Camden, Fiennes, Defoe and others of this tradition, and as *explanation*, whereby pertinent questions are asked of what is observed; see for example the collection of essays edited by Mark Brayshay, 1996. Although not necessarily able to provide answers at that time, Maitland was arguably the first to recognise that the landscape was actually capable of being interrogated in this way. The 'prehistory' of landscape history has been brilliantly surveyed recently by John Chandler, who identifies three key figures before Maitland as contributing in seminal ways to laying the foundations of the subject as it is understood and practised today. These are Thomas Burton (15th century), John Leland (16th century), and John Aubrey (17th century). Chandler 2000.

answers, at least, in Somerset. It is, I hope, as wide-ranging in its use of the basic kinds of evidence such that Hoskins himself would have approved [Hoskins in Taylor 1988, 18]. However, I have also attempted, where appropriate, to inject an element of the more abstract, theoretical approach that has been espoused by some prehistorians since the mid 1990s, and to apply certain elements of those ideas in a pre-Conquest topographical context; specifically, in Chapter Four. Having said this, there are missing from this account two topics, one chronological, the other thematic, which might reasonably have been expected in a topographical analysis of this kind: on place-names and on the post-Roman period. Both, in fact, were quite fully written up, and originally formed the basis of two separate chapters in their own right, but constraints of length imposed some very painful editing decisions, and these chapters were eventually sacrificed so that other material that I perceived as being more directly relevant could remain. Some place-name material was salvaged to be inserted into the thematic chapters, but this was a highly subjective and personal exercise; I can only hope that readers will not regard the loss as terminally disastrous.

As a synthetic work, the study by definition leans heavily on secondary material, but I have also made use here, for the first time in a coherent way, of a whole series of unpublished archaeological and landscape reports that are currently only available in the Somerset SMR or the RCHM archives; notably (and respectively) the Hollinrakes' work on the Polden pipeline, and the various surveys conducted on Exmoor recently by Hazel Riley and Rob Wilson–North of the Royal Commission. Many other sources have at one time or another been consulted, and these are detailed in the textual references, but among the most important are:

- A range of historic maps for all three hundreds, most notably tithe and estate maps, and early editions of the OS, at various scales, chiefly in the Somerset Record Office and Somerset Local Studies Library at Taunton.
- The Somerset and BANES SMRs.
- Other documentary evidence, both published and unpublished – the former include the volumes of the Somerset Record Society and a range of state records printed by the PRO, and the latter include glebe terriers (SRO), and various Glastonbury Abbey records, especially the great early 14th century survey that for the most part now forms British Library Egerton 3321.
- Fieldwork. Within the constraints of the study, fieldwork was carried out as often as possible, a direct consequence of which was the recognition of two previously unrecorded monuments, one of which, a Bronze Age barrow, has direct implications for certain of my arguments[2]. The theoretical, 'phenomenological' theme outlined in Chapter Four arose almost entirely out of extended field visits to the church sites involved,

and a recognition of the significance of topography in shaping the psychological response of the viewer.
- Some limited and non-systematic fieldwalking was conducted on several sites, and at Chew Magna, south of Rattledown farm, this revealed that a previously known Roman site was actually larger than previously thought, and suggested the existence of another farmstead close by.

The Choice of Hundreds

The choice of hundreds rather than some other unit of investigation may require some justification. Hundreds are primarily administrative rather than economic entities and are probably late (ie late Saxon) in date [Thorn 1989, 35-36; Loyn 1974]. It is, of course, possible that they have some underlying economic basis, such as relationships to different kinds of *pays* or countrysides, natural topography, agricultural potential (often but not always dictated by local soil fertility: *cf* Harvey in Campbell 1991, 9-11), and so on. It is suggested, however, that the hundred offers itself as a valid and convenient area for study because, by virtue of its size, it is likely to encompass a range of variables affecting the nature of settlement within its bounds; while at the same time not being so large as to make detailed study, with limited time and resources available, impracticable. Also, many ancient hundreds, where their bounds can be restored with confidence (and leaving aside the question of the effects of post-Conquest interference), do tend to possess an essential geographical unity that may well give hints of far earlier origins. Whitley itself, for example, is essentially 'held together' and defined topographically by the Polden Hills. Where hundred bounds follow obvious natural features, or ancient man-made ones such as prehistoric earthworks or Roman roads, it is possible that they represent at least the partial adaptation of older units. And Howard Williams has recently observed that the hundred of Chalk in Wiltshire "may represent an earlier territorial unit defined by natural frontiers formed by the downs long before it was recorded in a charter of AD 955" [Williams 1999, 78]. The hundred is also often of a size which is sufficient to provide a usefully large sample of settlement types, whether surviving or deserted, which allow valuable comparisons to be drawn at a high level of detail. A variety of reasons, therefore, combine to make the hundred a convenient unit for the study of the origins and development of medieval settlement [eg Wade-Martins 1980 (Launditch); Prosser 1995 (Keynsham); Bowman 1996 (Langton)]. And if not the hundred itself, the idea of both unity and contrast suggested by the examination of a group of contiguous parishes, is highly attractive. It is this unit of study which some years ago was proposed in outline plans to find an area suitable to become the 'Wharram' for the next millennium [MSRG 8, 1993, 27-35].

Somerset (Figure 1) is a county of striking topographical contrasts, and the study hundreds were chosen with considerable care to reflect this. This has been achieved by choosing three hundreds at widely spaced

---

[2] My fellow doctoral student Ian Powlesland, having examined the other feature, advises me that it *may* be a barrow, but is rather more likely to be a farm midden.

intervals, two in the northern (Chew) and western (Carhampton) extremes of the county, and one, Whitley, occupying the central position (Figure 2). Nearly twenty years ago, Harold Fox noted that 'transitional' areas, which seem to straddle the very diffuse and somewhat notional boundary between the classic Midland open-field systems, and the more irregular systems east and west of it, might hold the key to the evolution and development of *both* types of field arrangement [Fox 1981, 101]. Somerset is such a place, and Fox's observation might usefully be extended to *settlement* patterns, the subject of the present study, since the two seem so often to march hand in hand, and in this context a recent attempt to map intensity of settlement dispersion in the 19th century seems strongly to confirm western Somerset's 'frontier' character [Roberts and Wrathmell 1994, esp figs 2 and 3]. It will become apparent that a wide range of settlement patterns and forms is encompassed both within and between the three hundreds of the present study, and this allows us to draw illuminating comparisons and contrasts in terms of the topographical themes which define the work.

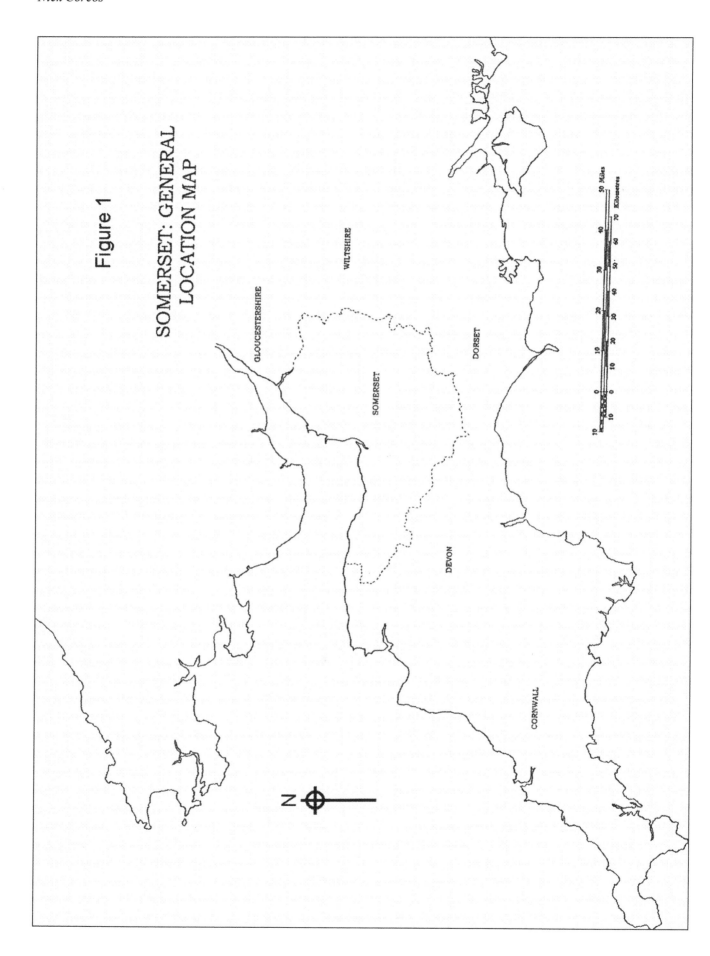

Figure 1

SOMERSET: GENERAL
LOCATION MAP

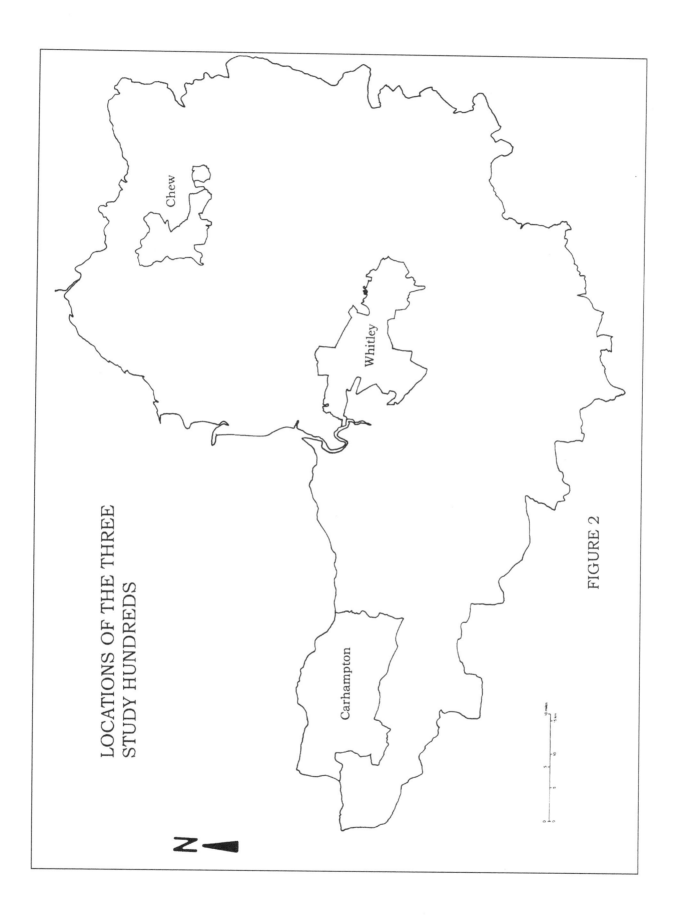

LOCATIONS OF THE THREE
STUDY HUNDREDS

N

Chew

Whitley

Carhampton

FIGURE 2

Chapter Two

The Roman Background

Introduction

The pattern of medieval rural settlement in at least the lowland zone of England takes much of its cue from, and owes much of its character to the Romano-British phase which preceded it; and which in its turn grows to a large extent from Iron Age roots. So much is now an accepted fact of the development of the human landscape in this country, and the point was well made in Somerset as long ago as 1977 by Roger Leech [Leech 1977; for more summary, published accounts, see Leech 1982a and b]. To the authors of the most recent regional survey of the subject: "an awareness of pre-medieval exploitation is an important precondition to our understanding the settlements and landscapes of the middle ages" [Lewis *et al* 1997, 77]. The implications of this tie the experience of the British province firmly into that of its neighbours across the English Channel. It is certainly true that continental post-Roman developments in many respects diverged strikingly from those in Britain. Nonetheless, it is also becoming increasingly clear that over large parts of Romanised western Europe, the broad fabric of at least the *early* medieval settlement pattern, if not the finer detail of its weave, has a *Roman* basis. In Picardy, in north-eastern France, a recent landscape survey has revealed a significant, although by no means homogeneous or static Roman element underlying the region's medieval rural settlement pattern [Haselgrove and Scull 1995]. A programme of intensive fieldwalking, selective excavation and detailed topographical survey in the Redon area of Brittany led to the conclusion that "in view of the intensity of use of this landscape in both the first and second centuries and the ninth century, the region cannot have been deserted. There is no hint of any post-Roman (or later) cataclysm.........the likelihood is that the land continued to be worked throughout this period in a largely self-sufficient way" [Astill and Davies 1997, 110]; and at the heart of the old empire, on the Italian peninsula itself, "the transition from Roman to medieval can never be adequately understood without first considering the Late Roman background. This.........provides the foundations for analysing how far Roman society, administration and settlement survived the transition or indeed how far they were transformed even before the break-up of Roman rule" [Christie 1995, 99]. The importance, therefore, of conducting at least a broad overview of the probable Romano-British settlement pattern in the three study hundreds is implicit, and requires no further justification.

The Conceptual Background which follows summarises some of the key themes which currently exercise scholars looking at the nature of Roman rural settlement in this country, and reinforces the importance of conducting at least a broad overview of the probable Romano-British settlement pattern in the three study hundreds.

Conceptual Background

Following the publication of Finberg's ground-breaking reconstruction of the supposed villa estate at Withington [Finberg 1955], the notion of continuity of Roman (and even earlier) economic units, sometimes to become the parishes of the middle ages, passed into received orthodoxy[1]. Since then, similar attempts have occasionally been made, based for the most part on considerations of natural topography and the availability of a wide-ranging resource-base [Applebaum 1975, for Bignor; Branigan 1977, 192-197, for Gatcombe.][2]. More recently, however, one discerns a growing disquiet on the part of scholars from a variety of disciplines, firstly that all villas invariably had estates attached to them (ie that they were essentially productive farming concerns); and secondly, in the case of villas for which the archaeological evidence might suggest at least a partly agrarian function, that it should in any case be possible to recreate the extent of its farmland with any degree of certainty. The focus had until very recently shifted away from the attempted reconstruction of villa 'estates', now seen, at least at the present state of knowledge, as a task strewn with pitfalls, to looking at the very varied ways in which both the villas *and* other types of settlement, exploited their hinterlands; on which archaeology, and especially the environmental evidence, has a great deal to say [Branigan and Miles 1989; Dark 1999, and 2000, 81-129]. Richard Hingley states blankly that "there is very little direct evidence for villa estates in Britain" [Hingley 1991, 75, 78]. Hill and Ireland echo this sentiment [Hill and Ireland 1996, 86], as does de la Bedoyere [1999, 94], and in the east midlands, past suggestions of direct continuity of Roman land units are now discredited [Lewis *et al* 1997, 106]. The most recent overview of the Romano-British countryside is equally sceptical [Dark 1997, 73-74], and indeed, as long ago as 1987, Stephen Bird was expressing similar doubts [Bird 1987, 63]. However, the discoveries in the Swale Valley in Kent, outlined further below, have now given fresh vigour to the 'villa estate' controversy, and provide a sound empirical basis for ideas outlined in this study

---

[1] A more modern study along similar lines has been conducted by Michael Costen, again using charter evidence. He concludes that the group of Anglo-Saxon estates around the Iron Age hillfort of Stantonbury near Bath "had bounds of great antiquity and the nature of those bounds points to origins for the estates which lie in the Roman period". Costen 1983, 33.
[2] For an attempt to trace a direct line of continuity from a large Romano-British estate to an Anglo-Saxon and medieval federate manor based on the Forest of Bernwood, Bucks, see Baines 1993.

relating to the extent and nature of Roman land division on the Polden Hills, in Whitley hundred.

Our perceptions of the relationships between high-status Roman rural sites may also sometimes be misguided; for in presenting idealised models, there is a danger that we will see patterns that exist only on paper and have no basis in reality. As Bird has warned us, "while two closely-sited villas may be explained as a working farm next to a country house, the gaps that appear in the distribution pattern cannot be explained so easily. Moreover such an argument assumes that each villa estate occupied roughly the same amount of land or exploited a similar range of resources, which may not be true" [Bird 1987, 63-65]. The last point is a particularly crucial one and I would tend to go further, to suggest that, in terms of their structures, extents and economies, it is highly unlikely that villa estates were homogeneous, *except* perhaps within the Imperial domain. This crucial exception may be precisely the context underpinning the Swale Valley discoveries. Indeed, Malcolm Todd comments that "the single consolidated *fundus* was probably comparatively rare. Those that did exist were probably always subject to division by inheritance" [Todd 1989, 17]. This has implications for two of our hundreds, Chew and Whitley.

Bird describes one recent paradigm which we might usefully consider here: "it is possible that some villas were tenurially related to others and that a landowner based at one of the large, well-appointed villas owned a number of satellite villas which contributed to the economy of the larger estate and which may even have concentrated on particular aspects of farming" [Bird 1987, 65]. Percival, by contrast, is cautious about the idea of dependency [Percival 1989, 11], but more recent accounts do accept that direct, tenurial links between landlords and tenants may well be reflected in the clear differences in status revealed in some villa/'peasant' settlement relationships, especially from the late 3rd century onwards [Faulkner 2000, 131-149; de la Bedoyere 1999, 77-98, esp at 94][3].

Yet a further area of contention is the question of the economies of Romano-British villas, a debate in which Branigan, again, takes a sceptical view. The case for specialisation, although extremely difficult to prove archaeologically, is not disputed; but rather its nature, extent, and the particular circumstances, primarily economic, which might trigger its development. Branigan is especially pessimistic about precisely those activities for which the environmental evidence at Chew Park appears so telling (below), and is even less convinced by the bone evidence [Branigan 1989, 42-44].

These views are cited here because I would contend that Branigan and Percival's uncertainties, although understandable, are misplaced. Branigan is right to emphasise present difficulties, mainly methodological, surrounding the whole question of the identification of any

type of villa economy, let alone specialist ones. But he also talks of villa economies being designed to "[seize] specific opportunities", which I understand to mean that he believes such opportunities to have been chance occurrences, very much secondary to the (supposedly) dominant *raison d'etre* of most villas, that of running a mixed economy [Branigan, *ibid*]. I would approach the issue from the other direction: I would suggest that in fact, relying ultimately on the complexity and sophistication of what was essentially an international economy, many villa estates were probably created, and their 'demesne' villas sited, with the specific aim of exploiting as efficiently as possible a particular type of environment, in a particular way, to produce a specific product or products.

By this view, the apparently overwhelming importance of the mixed economy, so much to the fore in Branigan's arguments, needs to be balanced carefully against the known diosyncrasies, imperfections and misinterpretations of the archaeological record. We need not for one moment doubt its existence, indeed perhaps even ubiquity, on British villas as a whole, and indeed the requirement for access to a spread of resources, a perceived *sine qua non* for economic viability, is an assumption which underpins virtually all of the more recent attempts to reconstruct their economies and estates, including my own, very basic effort presented later on in this chapter. But we should also allow that for some, and perhaps many villas, it should be relegated to a secondary, and chiefly subsistence role, its output flowing for the most part back into the villa estates to feed workers and villa owners, and generally maintain the internal, day to day operation of the villa estate. The fact that we know many villas to have grown from Iron Age predecessors, as, for example, Chew Park itself and several of the Whitley examples did, may simply indicate that by the late pre-Roman Iron Age, agrarian regimes were already becoming influenced by, and increasingly embedded in, the more market-oriented economies of both the continental Roman empire, and the growing population centres of the British lowland *oppida* [Macready and Thompson 1984; Collis 1984; Miles 1989, 63].

A further hindrance to our understanding of villa 'estates' is the known fluidity of settlement. Changes in settlement patterns, both within the Roman period and afterwards, together with a concomitant realignment of boundaries, would, as Dark suggests, negate the use of later evidence to reconstruct Romano-British economic units. In Somerset for example, Gerrard, building on earlier work by Wool, Leech and Fowler, has suggested that the tendency of many villa sites to lie on or close to parish boundaries, is explained satisfactorily only by models "which require a shift in emphasis from villa sites to [Romano-British] settlement sites, and imply that continuity of settlement location is more likely over Romano-British settlements than it is over villas" [Gerrard 1987, 42]. Only does one of these models [fig 2.29] allow for partial continuity of the original boundary. However, the increasing rate at which substantial Roman buildings are being discovered, in Somerset and elsewhere, directly under or very close to the parish churches which frequently

---

[3] Faulkner's view is that "most men on good land were likely to be obliged to a lord", and that the most intensively exploited southern and eastern part of Roman Britain was "a controlled countryside.........where most land and labour were held in lordship" [Faulkner 2000, 140].

lie at the medieval cores of present-day villages, may no longer make it entirely safe to assert that "continuity on villa sites can only be hinted at in a very few examples, such as Cheddar" [Gerrard 1987, 43].

Gerrard also suggests that "it is the economic rather than the administrative boundaries which tend to be preserved.....villas stand on the edge of combinations of economic units because their own administrative units have not survived.....so, is it Romano-British economic units that survive as modern parishes?" [*ibid*, 43]. It seems equally likely, however, that any perceived distinction between an 'administrative' unit and an 'economic' one probably had little basis in reality. It is doubtful whether such a dichotomy was recognised either by the villa owners or by the people who lived and worked on the villa estate, and in any event it is likely that in many cases villas combined the tripartite functions of amenity, administration and some kind of economic activity, whether agricultural or industrial, or a combination of both. We can probably equate many villas with Gerrard's 'Romano-British economic units' precisely because they would have stood at the centres of fully productive estates, of whatever nature.

Roman Settlement and the Evidence of -*wics*

Credit for the recognition of the importance of this word rests not with our own age of scholarship: for it was known, or suspected, at the latest by the early 18th century. Such is clear from a remark made by the eminent Somerset antiquarian John Strachey, of Sutton Court in Stowey (Chew hundred), and relating to Sutton Wick; the latter word, he says, "w.ch generally speaking denotes A Roman Vicus & giving Strong Marks of a Roman Work....." [quoted in Williams 1986, 41]. Modern toponymic thinking would agree precisely with this view [*cf* Gelling 1978, 67].

The nature of *wic* has been discussed at length elsewhere[4]. However, Richard Coates, who has reviewed the linguistic evidence for what *wic* actually meant to English-speakers, concludes that "the central root historical meaning.........is 'dependent economic unit'" [Coates 1999, 98]. Logically, this must in turn suggest at least a partial survival, and recognition of, antecedent 'estate' *structures*, something which is not necessarily in conflict with Coates's view that "the majority, and probably the overwhelming majority, of *wic* names have no Roman archaeological significance" [Coates 1999, 110-111]. He is persuaded, however, that "*wic* as the *first* element [my italics] in a compound word is an indicator to be taken seriously of Roman connections, even if not one of absolute reliability" [Coates 1999, 111]. Curiously, Coates does not consider *field* names in his analysis, and although a sample of one can hardly be taken as conclusive, nonetheless these views receive little support from archaeological evidence from at least one of the field

names at Shapwick in Whitley hundred. This is a point to which we will return in the context of this word's implications for post-Roman settlement. Gerrard, however, notes that many *wics* "appear to be closer to villa sites than a random distribution might be". Whether or not they had their own formalised boundaries [Gerrard 1987, 43] is, however, quite unknown, and it is significant that, in Somerset at least, few *wics* became parish centres: most survive only as minor names or field names [Costen 1992, 66]: out of a total of a little over 70 *wics* which are known in the county, either identified on the ground or mentioned in documentary sources, only six are parish names [*ex inf* Susan Fitton]. It seems unlikely, therefore, that *wics* can *by themselves* be used to indicate continuity of villa 'estates'.

Notwithstanding the difficulties of recreating exact boundaries, it is more reasonable to suggest that in many cases villa complexes, although not necessarily their estates, persisted in traditional memory for long enough, as places of earlier importance, to attract later settlement and church foundation on or very close to their sites (Gerrard's model H, fig 2.29); a memory aided no doubt by the long survival of substantial stone buildings, impressive even in decay. In these cases, the villa site might be found close to the centre of the later parish, the latter representing the formation of a later estate, or combination of estates, which may or may not be coterminous with the original villa lands, depending on the various imperatives behind its creation. There seems no good reason why, if obvious physical boundaries remained in the landscape, a villa estate should not, after an interval of abandonment, be reconstituted, in whole or part, at a later period. Alternatively, for villas at or close to a parish boundary, later subdivision of a larger estate (rejected by Gerrard, his model F, fig 2.29), seems perfectly plausible and indeed the Shapwick/Ashcott split may provide a concrete example of this. The potential importance of *wic* sites, emphasised by Gerrard, we need not dispute, but it is, I would suggest, a late (ie post-Roman) development, and to a large extent the result of differential survival. Some *vici* may well have been independent self-supporting economic units, in the fullest sense, in the Roman period. As we have seen however, Richard Coates's view, from the linguistic perspective, is that to English-speakers, a *vicus* or a *wic* was characterised by economic and/or administrative dependence, and this also seems to have been the dominant sense in which the term was understood during the Roman period itself [Coates 1999]. If, therefore, an abandoned villa site, surrounded by a few now autonomous *vici*, was marginalised by the division of its once large estate, a rearrangement of the settlement pattern may well have been necessary to place subsequent communities occupying the new estates at the centres of their farmlands; it is perfectly possible that one or more existing *wic* sites, finding themselves by chance in convenient positions, might be used for this purpose and be elevated to the status of *caput*. This is what may have happened at Shapwick, and some degree of continuity at a much reduced level in a scatter of minor farmsteads, is more likely in the post-Roman period in Somerset than further east, where economic and social displacement was much greater. Indeed, there may well be a wider pattern here: we may find that, overwhelmingly, only

---

[4] See Gelling 1997, 67-74 and 245-250; Coates 1999; Newman 1999 for -*wics* as *emporia*; Balkwill 1993 for *wīc* as applied to Romano-British land units surviving as later hundreds; for Somerset, Costen 1992a, 66, and 1993, 94-100; and Fitton 1997.

estates subject to later fission produced *wics* which became parish centres (eg Shapwick/Ashcott, Wick St Lawrence/Congresbury), and as such they may be no older than the 10th or 11th centuries, for reasons already stated. Where possibly very early estates remain at least partly intact (eg Chew?), the *wics* tend to remain peripheral, sub-parochial places (North Wick, Sutton *Wic*), or field-names. I wonder, therefore, whether it might be possible to use 'parochial' *wics* as predictive tools to alert us to the likelihood of fragmentation, and to look for other signs of it.

On balance, the suggestion that *wic* sites may indeed be indicative of a type of Romano-British settlement is a highly plausible one and has been adopted for the purposes of this study; but the point is that they are likely to have been peripheral, subsidiary places, perhaps bond villages for estate workers, dependent on the main villa site. If this is so, then the connotation of 'dependency', and therefore the wider administrative/economic context of the *wics*, must have been at least partially understood by the Anglo-Saxons, since the word passed into English with this as one of its meanings [Gelling 1978, 67-74; Smith 1956, 257-263].

Chew Hundred

It is fairly clear that the sources we have to hand must represent only the absolute minimum picture of Roman settlement, and it is likely that at least some of the major lacunæ in the two northernmost hundreds are more apparent than real. Major settlement names in -*wick* for which medieval spellings are extant, such as Northwick and Sutton Wick in Chew Magna, are included, and I outline the rationale behind this in the next chapter. Other sources are indicated where appropriate, but Timsbury and Clutton, for example, are almost devoid of evidence, perhaps partly as a result of disturbance wrought by later coal-mining activity, and partly through a lack of previous fieldwork, landscape and documentary study. Neither can there be any concession to chronological depth in this approach. Sites are mapped as either Roman or medieval, or both. No distinction is made between evidence for Roman activity of different periods, although in any case, such evidence is by no means always available. Nonetheless, if the relative density of sites shown here is accepted as a fair reflection of reality, it becomes possible to make broad inferences about the nature of the Roman settlement pattern, and perhaps also about some of the major imperatives informing it. In this respect then, Chew hundred offers intriguing possibilities, especially in terms of the relationship of its *wick* place-names to the known Roman sites, and the evidence of the parish boundaries and known or suspected resources.

Figure 3 depicts all the known Roman sites in Chew hundred, and those which may reasonably be conjectured. Two of the main centres are represented by the Chew Park and Gold's Cross villas, although the latter is not included in Scott's listings [Scott 1993]. Additionally, I have placed another villa at Chew Magna itself. The resulting pattern somewhat expands on the work of Kemp, in roughly the same area, with the difference that

I have taken account of place-name evidence: Northwick and the various *wick* names around Sutton, since they show medieval spellings, are presumed to represent Anglo-Saxon *wics*, and are therefore also included as Romano-British settlement sites (Chapter 3).

Within the main Chew Valley body of the study area, Kemp provides a useful overview of settlement [Kemp 1983, summarised in Kemp 1984]. His conclusion is that "Roman settlements were very evenly spaced at intervals of *c.*1 km forming a lattice of settlements that include sites that became medieval villages" [Kemp 1983, 76-77].

The idea that Roman farmsteads were regularly spaced in the landscape has long been a working hypothesis for describing rural settlement in that period; at Shapwick a density of 0.7 sites per sq km has been proposed on the basis of extensive fieldwork [Aston and Gerrard 1999, 15-23; see also Aston 1994, 230; fig 11.7, 231]. It may be worth noting that such models do not at present appear to take account of the effects of natural topography, relief, drainage, soils and a whole host of other possible influences, and we cannot expect that even in relatively flat or gentle, featureless terrain, the true Roman settlement pattern, if it could be fully reconstructed, would bear more than a passing resemblance to the idealised 1 km lattice. Recent work in the Rockingham Forest area of Northants has, for example, revealed a density of Romano-British settlement of about 0.5 to 0.6 km [Bellamy 1994, 35]. Current models do not seem to take account of the *type* of site that may be represented: in the Cotswolds for example, "large houses of fourth-century date seem to appear very roughly at distances of 4-8 miles (6.5-13km) apart.........with a more unpredictable scattering of smaller houses and settlements around them" [de la Bedoyere 1999, 96]. It is reasonable to suggest, on the basis of work carried out on I/A hillforts, that even highly localised hinterlands and areas of influence will vary greatly according to the nature of the individual site in terms of its size, importance and functional diversity (the latter determined only by excavation) [Grant 1986].

Having said this, the inclusion here of the *wic* names gives some substance to Kemp's suggestion, based on his analysis of the likely spacing and distribution of Roman settlement sites in the area, that gaps in the pattern await the discovery of new Roman sites [Kemp1983, 55-59][5]. I have recovered significant amounts of pottery from the ploughed surface of a field at about NGR ST576648, consisting mainly of grey, black burnished and Congresbury wares, with two pieces of flint, and, perhaps crucially, a single sherd identified as either Iron Age or post-Roman [Vince Russett, *pers comm*]. This suggests that the site extends underneath the present field boundary; and dense but highly localised spreads of pennant sandstone, lying on the crest of the small ridge in the same field and perhaps the remains of roofing tiles, may reveal

---

[5] This has, indeed, been borne out to some extent even in the relatively short interval since 1983, for the Roman sites west of Norton Hawkfield [SMR 3189], at Double House [SMR 716], and north-west of Blacklands [SMR 704] were unknown to Kemp.

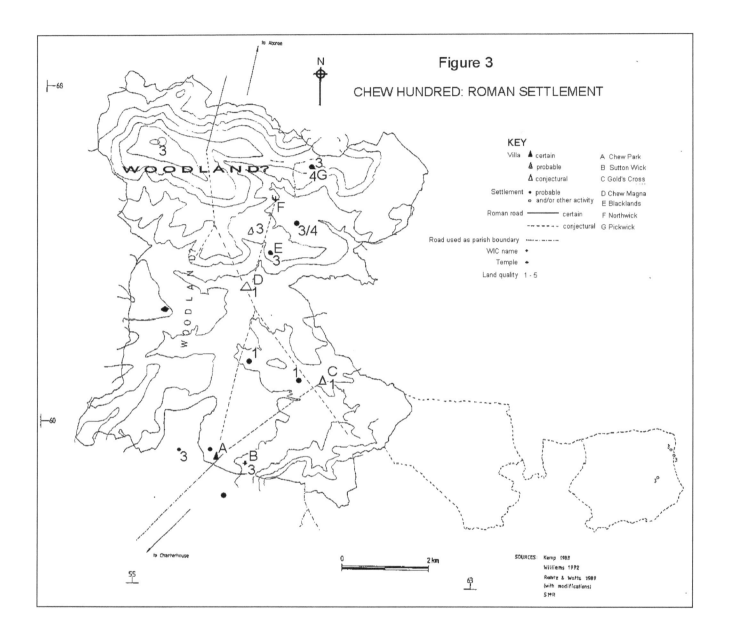

Figure 3

CHEW HUNDRED: ROMAN SETTLEMENT

KEY

Villa	▲ certain	A Chew Park
	▲ probable	B Sutton Wick
	Δ conjectural	C Gold's Cross
Settlement	● probable	D Chew Magna
	○ and/or other activity	E Blacklands
Roman road	—— certain	F Northwick
	- - - - conjectural	G Pickwick
Road used as parish boundary	—·—·—·—	
WIC name	✦	
Temple	✦	
Land quality	1 - 5	

SOURCES: Kemp 1983
Williams 1992
Rahtz & Watts 1989
(with modifications)
SMR

the presence of a former Roman building. The site lies on the northern edge of an expanse of relatively level ground, sloping away very gently to the south; while immediately to the north, the ground rises sharply towards Rattledown Farm. The land quality in this area is only Grade 3, according to MAFF; but if there is indeed a Roman farmstead here, perhaps somehow related to the site suspected in the field adjacent to the east, its existence may be explained at least in part by the minor resource interface, level ground for arable and slopes for grazing, which it occupies.

While Dundry is known to have been exploited as a source of freestone in the Roman, as indeed it was in the medieval period [Bird 1987, 66; Williams 1983, 12-20, esp at 18], nothing is known of any Roman settlement in the immediate area, although the SMR [644] notes a 'possible Roman enclosure' on Dundry Down. The date and nature of this feature is actually problematic, but if there is at least the possibility that it is indeed Roman, a suggestion that it might have been used for stock control perhaps reinforces the impression (below), that those parts of the later parish which did not still support woodland by the end of the

Roman period, were used largely as upland pasture, perhaps managed from seasonal shielings, by communities to the south.

These sites together contribute to a localised density of settlement which sees some sites considerably closer together than the 'optimal' 1 km [*cf* Aston 1994a, 153-154, esp fig 17.1 B]. Blacklands, for example, is now only about 700m away from its nearest neighbour, although the question of whether or not the sites depicted here were actually in simultaneous occupation will remain an imponderable without detailed fieldwork and selective excavation. There is certainly precedent for settlement density of this order, as for example in the Somme Basin of northern France [Percival 1989, 10], and elsewhere in Somerset, in the Somerton area [Leech and Leach 1982, 63]. The inclusion of our theoretical Chew Magna villa as well as the two additional *wics* appears to provide at least a localised pattern rather closer to the idealised 1 km distribution. For all the sites shown on the map here, there is archaeological, topographical or toponymic evidence of one kind or another, even though the nature of individual sites remains in considerable doubt.

On the basis of the pattern presented here, and developing the work of Kemp, we can perhaps draw certain broad conclusions. Firstly, we must consider the position of the putative villa and/or settlement at Chew Magna itself, occupying topographically the most favourable site, in the midst of the most agriculturally productive land. It is certainly true that the existence of a villa, either at Chew Magna itself or in its immediate vicinity, remains to be proven; those at Chew Park and Gold's Cross both lie some distance away [Kemp 1984; Hanley 1990, 156], as does the somewhat more enigmatic site, a little north-west of Blacklands, of a probable Roman stone building of indeterminate nature [Scott 1993, 15]. However, recent archaeological work in the centre of the village may provide a crucial pointer. The discovery of a worn cobbled surface, dated by sealed pottery and passing close to the west wall of the churchyard, has confirmed the line of a known north-south Roman road long suspected to have passed through Chew, fording the river Chew near the site of Tun Bridge, but not previously located within the village itself [Tratman 1963, 170-171]. An early bridge at or close to this location seems equally likely. The excavator reports that the road "appeared to follow the same alignment as the churchyard wall which ran along its east side......there may be Roman occupation in the area or even a roadside settlement. This.....discovery.....might help to explain the location of the church.....only 30m east of the road. Pottery dating from the late 11th/12th century and a wall were also found, indicating the likelihood of early medieval occupation....." [Anon 1997, 20-21]. Most importantly however, "it is possible that [the church] stands on or close to the site of either a Roman villa or else an early Christian roadside mausoleum" [Bell 1996, 7].

It is surely significant that it is this site, and not that at Chew Park, which retained its 'centrality' in terms of the later administrative boundaries of hundred and parish. A recent survey of the Leicestershire evidence found that medieval market towns there were closely correspondent, although never exactly coincident with, the sites of Roman small towns. This is potentially important for our general view of perpetuation of function, and the ability of certain locally-paramount sites to weather periods of temporary social and economic displacement, to re-emerge with their 'central-place' position essentially intact although perhaps changed in nature. More specifically, if Chew Magna was indeed a quasi-town in the middle ages, we may now plausibly ask whether it may not also have been one by, say, the later Roman period. It may be significant that Chew satisfies all the topographical criteria put forward by Liddle for possible 'small-town' status [Liddle 1995, 91].

This is not to go so far as to suggest that the present hundred or parish boundaries necessarily encapsulate, in whole or part, the boundary of any estate or *territorium* which may have been attached to a villa or small town at Chew Magna, although of course they may do. What is important is that, while later boundaries had the effect of marginalising and sidelining Chew Park, the reverse was true at Chew, whose status as a nodal point in the landscape was confirmed, reinforced and perpetuated into the early medieval period.

In terms of its economy, Chew Park certainly appears to have sustained at least an element of arable: large numbers of quernstones, environmental evidence for the presence of grain, and the discovery of a large corn-drying furnace, are frequently cited to support this [Bird 1987, 63; Rahtz and Greenfield 1977, 56-57]. But it was hard-won, at the cost of an apparently massive campaign of drainage, the excavators estimating the prize at a minimum of 20 acres of farmable land [Rahtz and Greenfield 1977, 35-65]. This is not much, and anyway it seems rather to miss the point to assert that the Chew Park quernstones "emphasise the importance and intensity of cereal *production*" (my italics) [Bird 1987, 63]. They do not necessarily do any such thing: what they actually emphasise is the importance and intensity of cereal *processing* at Chew Park; the distinction is crucial, because there seems to be an unwarranted assumption that all the grain which undoubtedly passed through the Chew Park mills must also have been grown on land directly associated with the villa. Conversely, other environmental evidence shows a strong pastoral component, coupled with some small-scale industrial activity, part of which may have been related to its construction. It seems, then, quite possible that a villa at Chew Magna, and the nature of its relationship with the Chew Park site, would fit well with Massey's summary of the evidence from North Oxfordshire: "successful integration into the market economy and profit generation are likely to have depended largely on the capacity to produce grain surpluses on the better soils of the valley sides, with livestock production concentrated on the poorly drained valley floors and poorer soils of the hill-tops" [Massey 1999, 164].

We can suggest then that the basis of Chew Park was predominantly pastoral, with a semi-industrial element based at least partly on the working of lead from the Charterhouse mines [Rahtz and Greenfield 1977, 78-79], and that some, perhaps most of the grain processed there may actually have been brought in from elsewhere. The 'villa' was poorly endowed for arable husbandry, and instead looked south, to the high grazing grounds of the Mendips, for by far the greater part of its livelihood - eschewing the word 'marginal', its agriculture may merely have been different from that of the suggested Chew Magna villa, exploiting different types of resources. Indeed, Chew Park's position in itself argues strongly for some kind of major Roman site further north, since it seems very unlikely that a tract of high-grade arable such as surrounds Chew Magna would not have attracted settlement very early on in the Roman period, or merely have developed from existing Iron Age occupation, as certainly happened at Chew Park. Perhaps the situation there in the late Roman period, in terms of both its own economy and of its relationship to our proposed Chew Magna villa, is perhaps best summarised by Todd's more general views: "I.....think of villa-estates as essentially and normally agricultural units, but with industrialised crafts being developed where local raw materials or initiative allowed.....when a concentration of such activities is found at one place, we may well suspect that the settlement formed part of a larger organism, probably an estate" [Todd 1989, 20].

Whatever its economic basis, Chew Park was hardly a high status site, and did not even make an appearance until around AD 270, following a succession of earlier timber buildings. Its form was small, prosaic, and spartan - no bath-house, or hypocaust system of any form, is known, and still less the existence of tessellated floors [*cf* Bird 1987, fig 5.6, 61]. If the proposed Chew Magna villa be allowed, might there have been a relationship between it and Chew Park? North and east of Rome, the authors of the Ager Veientanus project have drawn a distinction in their findings between 'villas' and 'farms'. And it seems clear that, by their criteria, Chew Park was probably not a villa, but instead, lacking as it does even the most basic villa-type amenities, looks decidedly farm-like [Percival 1989, 6-8]. A further comparison may be drawn here with the Ager Veientanus project, which found that villas were related directly to the Roman road network (as both Chew Park and Chew Magna are), and that they were also frequently provided with paved approach roads [*ibid*, 7-8], a feature now proven archaeologically at Chew Magna. Indeed, closer to home, Bird notices the same relationship [Bird 1987, 63], and it is likely that Chew Park was linked to Chew Magna by road (see map).

From what evidence there is, we can reasonably infer that the putative Chew Magna villa/settlement was the chief focus in the Roman period, and that it was concerned with the intense exploitation of the high quality arable land which lay, and lies, immediately around it. I see no difference in principle between this suggestion for economic specialisation at the Chew Magna villa, and the Saxo-Norman farmers of Northamptonshire tailoring their open-field systems and cropping regimes to reflect, almost precisely, variations in the quality of the land available to them [Fox 1988][6].

By this view, then, the economies of the two villas are seen as complementary rather than conflicting, based on a high degree of agrarian, and perhaps even industrial specialisation: with Chew Park acting as a dependent, subsidiary, pastoral 'outstation', but at the same time being part of the same overall estate, of whatever extent that may have been, centred on Chew Magna.

The existence of a possible relationship between Charterhouse and the Chew Valley communities was first postulated by Rahtz and Greenfield, who observed that "a connection between the [Stratford Lane] road and the lead-mining settlements seems reasonable and it may be that it served a double purpose. Mendip soil is notoriously poor, and the corn needs of the miners could perhaps hardly be met by local farming. The soils of the Chew Valley would, however, be fertile if properly drained and this is precisely what has taken place at the sites excavated there. It is suggested that the road was partly for the transport of this corn from the valley to the lead miners.....Another possible use for the road is for the transport of lead.....the journey to the river Chew is short, perhaps the daily capacity of a horse or mule with two pigs" [Rahtz and Greenfield 1977, 159]. This is certainly a very plausible idea, and is very likely to be correct in its essentials. We may wonder, however, whether it was not in fact *processed* grain which flowed from the Chew Valley to Charterhouse? Although the presence of grain storage facilities at Chew Park was suggested by Rahtz and Greenfield, nonetheless their existence there is entirely unproven, and no building or feature was found to which a function as a granary could be unequivocally attributed.

The question of storage apart, however, this need not conflict with the evidence, already noted, that grain was certainly processed there; because it seems perfectly possible that grain brought in from elsewhere was simply milled at Chew Park, and the flour produced rapidly 'turned round' and despatched to other destinations, or stored for a time on site, which would not have required granary-type buildings. This introduces the concept of the 'value-added' product, where profit margins are likely to be higher if transport involves finished goods rather than raw materials. In this case, rather than incur heavy transport costs on a high-bulk, low value product (grain), value is added by milling close to the point of production, and the resulting flour transported as a high-bulk, but now also high-value product. Indeed, for Chew Park, this model may be doubly useful in terms of that farm's potentially very close links with the mining settlement at Charterhouse; since it would have made far better economic sense, in terms of both profits and transport costs, to haul milled flour, rather than raw grain, up the difficult, steep northern flank of Mendip, even given the assistance of a decent road in the form of Stratford Lane [Rahtz and Greenfield 1977, 154-158; Williams 1992].

---

[6]In much the same way, indeed, as James Russell has shown recently that the medieval field system of the parish of Clifton, west of Bristol, was so

---

disposed that the "central zone of arable land coincided almost precisely with an area of Triassic marls and breccias, producing relatively fertile red clayey soils. To the north and west, where these Triassic deposits gave way to outcrops of Carboniferous limestone with a much thinner soil cover, lay Clifton down, the main common grazing area in the parish"; Russell 1999, 79.

This suggestion should also be viewed in the context of the well-known lack of reliable surface-water streams across the Carboniferous Limestone of the Mendip plateau, which would have mitigated against the use of water-powered milling without extensive hydraulic engineering, for which there is (as yet) no archaeological evidence (I am grateful to Mrs Suzanne Bromme for suggesting this to me). If the proposed Chew Magna villa also possessed large-scale milling facilities, the logical destination for its output would be northwards, to the port at Sea Mills (*Abonæ*), and thence, perhaps, to south Wales [Rahtz and Greenfield 1977, 159].

In any event, the evidence for lead processing found at Chew Park might make us wonder whether the relationship ultimately became a symbiotic one, with flour and other agricultural produce flowing south to Charterhouse, and quantities of lead flowing north to Chew Park. The latter may have had Iron Age antecedents, but it would be interesting to know whether its later development exactly mirrored that of the mining settlement, and whether, indeed, the whole *raison d'etre* of Chew Park in its later phases was as the main supply 'depot' for the Charterhouse mining boomtown. Rahtz and Greenfield have certainly noted what appear to be parallel chronologies in the early phases of both Charterhouse and Chew Park: "The *flourit* of the Chew valley ditch-systems has been shown to be from the middle to late years of the first century AD to the later part of the second century AD, a period similar to that covered by the inscriptions from lead pigs on Mendip" [Rahtz and Greenfield 1977, 159]. It is worth remembering, though, that the main villa complex at Chew Park dates from the later third century [Rahtz and Greenfield 1977, 64], well over a century *after* military involvement at Charterhouse had finally ceased, probably in the 160s.

Unlike Chew Park, however, the Charterhouse settlement has never been subjected to modern, systematic area excavation, and its chronology is, consequently, highly problematic. The general view of a subsequent decline in Charterhouse's fortunes after the withdrawal of the military is based chiefly on the lack of large, stamped lead pigs from the third quarter of the second century onwards [Burnham and Wacher 1990, 208-211]. But this is an assumption: there are hints of individual enterprise on Mendip from as early as Nero's reign [Frere 1987, 276-277], and as Frere observes, "it seems possible that government interest in direct working of the more southerly [lead] fields was relaxed in the second half of the second century, and that the industry was allowed to fall more and more into private hands, which no longer produced large inscribed ingots" [Frere 1987, 278]. Like the other major Roman lead-working centres on Mendip [Williams 1998] the site continued in existence, and probably in full operation, at least into the early 4th century. The progressive transfer of its operation into private hands may, on the contrary, have marked a new and prosperous phase, perhaps partly characterised by a change in the nature of the products being made there, and the apogee of which may be represented at least in part by

the final and most pretentious phase at Chew Park. Massive, inscribed lead ingots are impressive, easy to provenance and difficult to misinterpret when found. The same might not be true, however, of the kinds of items coming out of Charterhouse after the late second century, and it seems perfectly possible that products from this later period have simply been missed or misconstrued in the local archaeological record; indeed, in this respect, the recently-discovered MINNIVS ingot, from a (probably) 4th century context at the Roman roadside settlement at Fosse Lane, Shepton Mallet, may represent merely the tip of a significant iceberg [Hassall and Tomlin 1993, 319-320].

If a close, possibly dependent relationship between Chew Park and a possible Chew Magna villa be allowed, how would it have worked in practice? I think it at least possible that by, say, the end of the 3rd century AD, Chew Park functioned chiefly as a grain-processing plant, for an agrarian estate centred on Chew Magna. Most production from the rich arable lands around Chew would have been sent by road southwards to Chew Park, processed, and sent onwards as flour to the town at Charterhouse. Some, if not most of the Roman sites within Chew hundred which we know today, would have been subsidiary farms centred on the Chew Magna villa, perhaps operating different specialisms but all bound together in an integrated economic whole, along the lines already suggested by Bird. The sites north-west of Blacklands, at Blacklands itself, west of Knowle Hill, at Double House, and west of Norton Hawkfield, all of them on or close to the central tract of first-quality plough land, were probably predominantly arable concerns. The two northern *wic* sites, at North Wick and Pickwick, could have had some arable: a field system identified at Pickwick may be Roman or earlier [Williams 1982, 55-56]. By virtue of their more difficult topography and less attractive land, both sites seem rather better suited to a pastoral role, although this is perhaps rather less true for the southern *wic* site.

There seems to be a noticeable absence of Roman sites to the west of the supposed north-south road system. Part of this gap may, as we have already suggested, eventually be filled by further discoveries. However, it is equally possible that, in the area of the Chew Magna/Chew Stoke boundary, pre-Conquest woodland cover, the existence of which we can infer from toponymic evidence, may also have been a feature of the Roman landscape. Indeed, it may be significant that only the major temple site of Pagan's Hill is known in this western half of Chew Hundred. Evidence for activity there dates from at least the late Neolithic [Rahtz and Watts 1989], a clear indication that this locally prominent spur, a typically characteristic site for this class of late Romano-British rural temple in Somerset, had been cleared of woodland long before the Roman period [Bird 1987, 67-68; Leech and Leach 1982, 74-75].

TABLE 1: PARISH SIZE IN THE THREE HUNDREDS[7]

	Parish	Date	Acres	Hectares
CHEW HUNDRED	Chew Magna	1840	5006	2027
	Dundry	1841	2800	1134
	Chew Stoke	1839	2092	847
	Clutton	1838	1637	663
	Timsbury	1838	1149	465
	Norton Malreward	1839	1068	432
	Stowey	1839	815	330
	Norton Hawkfield	1839	620	251
		TOTALS	15,187	6,149

	Parish	Date	Acres	Hectares
WHITLEY HUNDRED	Butleigh	1843	4467	1809
	Ham	1832/38	4229	1713
	Shapwick	1839	3781	1531
	Street	1842	2914	1180
	Westonzoyland	1836/40	2730	1106
	Compton Dundon	1842	2571	1041
	Middlezoy	1853/93	2520	1020
	Walton	1843	2502	1013
	Ashcott	1838	2272	920
	Catcott	1841	2256	914
	Edington	1838	2167	878
	Chilton	1839	1857	752
	Othery	1840	1821	738
	Woolavington	1842	1725	699
	Puriton	1842	1632	661
	Cossington	1839	1381	559
	Moorlinch	1836/41	1122	454
	Stawell	1833	974	394
	Sutton Mallet	1837	879	356
	Greinton	1841	845	342
		TOTALS	44,645	18,080

	Parish	Date	Acres	Hectares
CARHAMPTON HUNDRED	Cutcombe	1841	7231	2929
	Carhampton	1839	5724	2318
	Exford	1840	5699	2308
	Porlock	1841	5665	2294
	Minehead	1842	4581	1855
	Luccombe	1841	4126	1671
	Luxborough	1843	3740	1514
	Dunster	1842	3455	1399
	Stoke Pero	1841	3423	1386
	Wootton Courtenay	1844	3145	1274
	Oare	1842	3100	1255
	Selworthy	1841	2219	899
	Timberscombe	1843	1902	770
	Treborough	1841	1799	729
	Withycombe	1839	1788	724
	Culbone	1838	1502	608
		TOTALS	59,099	23,933

[7] All parish areas taken from the tithe information contained in Kain and Oliver 1995. The date given is that of the Tithe Map, *not* the Apportionment. Where Kain & Oliver provide two acreage figures, usually the difference between the extent of land actually subject to tithe, and the area of the administrative tithe district in 1851, the larger figure is always given here. For an explanation of the acreages of tithe districts, see *ibid*, 21. Hectares are rounded to the nearest whole figure.

Whitley Hundred

It will become apparent that of the three areas under scrutiny in this study, it is Whitley which, for the period of the Roman occupation, is seen to be clearly pre-eminent in terms of the known density of settlement it supported, if not necessarily in the quality of the archaeological record which informs our knowledge of both that settlement itself and any associated land use. In one major respect, this is perhaps only to be expected; since, while in terms of bare size, it is second to Carhampton (Table 1), conversely it encompasses within it land which always was some of the most favourable and productive in Somerset, with access to a significant range of resources. The natural physical environment of Whitley is one of great variety. But it is probably true to say that if a single, overriding and recurring theme can be identified, it is surely the presence and the seemingly all-pervading influence of the Levels, to which virtually the entire hundred looks inward, from all directions, on the southern, King's Sedgemoor side, and outward, to the Brue Valley, on the northern Polden flank. The almost magnetic attraction of the marshland margin for settlement and exploitation from at least the early fourth millennium BC laid down an indelible pattern that, where it can be traced, is repeated time and again in the landscape of Polden itself, and the surrounding moors and islands [Caseldine 1988; Coles 1978; Coles 1982; Coles and Coles 1986; Coles and Coles *et al* 1990]. So that on the eve of the Roman occupation, a framework of wetland exploitation of considerable antiquity was already in operation, linked to a settlement pattern from the basic characteristics of which much of what was to follow took its cue [Miles and Miles 1969; Coles and Minnitt 1995; Creighton *et al* 1997, 156-157].

What follows is essentially an overview of the current level of knowledge. Nonetheless, the background sketched here will provide a sound basis for a consideration of the settlement pattern of Whitley hundred as it emerges into the historic period.

The Nature of the Evidence

On first acquaintance, Whitley seems to suffer badly by comparison with Chew; since, leaving aside the work of the Somerset Levels Project, which was overwhelmingly concerned with pre-Roman archaeology [Coles and Coles 1986], there has been no systematic campaign of excavation, over such a large area, as was possible through the exceptionally thorough Chew Valley Lake campaign [Rahtz and Greenfield 1977]. This, however, is to do scant justice to the accumulated years of rather less systematic work which characterises archaeology and other field studies in or including Whitley, and which has resulted in a dichotomy between general surveys over larger areas, and geographically-restricted, but more concentrated and detailed work. Roger Leech's review of all aspects of Romano-British settlement in south Somerset and north Dorset included large parts of the hundred [Leech 1977 and 1982], to some extent building upon the Miles' earlier work for the Iron Age [1969]. Whitley has its fair share of

high-status Roman buildings (below), some known from a relatively early date, a fact doubtless reflecting the interests of early antiquarians. A number of villas or other significant structures and complexes are known or suspected, at Edington, Shapwick (two, one definitely a villa), Compton Dundon (Littleton), probably two and possibly even three at Street, one each in Woolavington [Taylor 1967, 67] and Puriton, and two in Ham parish, the group culminating, of course, in the strikingly opulent complex at Low Ham [Scott 1993, 165-172]. Finds of *tesseræ* from a site immediately south of Cossington village, apparently unknown to the SMR, are noted by Rippon as suggesting a villa there as well [Rippon 1997, 78]. These are referenced more fully later on, but Whitley is also exceptional in that one of its parishes has over the past decade provided the focus for a sustained and detailed study of the historical development of a landscape: the work of the Shapwick Project, apart from adding the high-status building at Old Church [Gerrard 1995, 108], has considerably improved our understanding of the nature of Romano-British rural settlement rather further down the social scale within the study area [Gater and Gaffney 1993, 30-32; Aston 1994a, 153-154; Aston and Gerrard 1999, esp at 15-23]; although in fact it is looking increasingly unlikely that the Old Church site *is* actually a villa. Part of the reason for this lies in the very recent discovery, at another location in Shapwick, of a previously unsuspected building complex which (as yet unpublished) geophysical survey and exploratory excavation show clearly to be an extremely substantial Roman courtyard villa (below). A survey of Compton Dundon to modern standards, also pending publication, provides a comprehensive level of detailed information, archaeological and documentary, relating to that parish [*ex inf* C and N Hollinrake]; and work by the same authors for a watching brief on a pipeline extending east-west along the northern slope of Polden has added greatly to the overall picture of settlement development in the parishes west of Shapwick [Hollinrakes 1994a]. It is possible also, although as yet unproven, that Whitley may also match Chew hundred in possessing evidence of Romano-British religious activity, in the site of a suspected temple on Pedwell Hill in Ashcott [Poyntz-Wright and Barlow 1967, 16]. The identification is highly problematic and rests solely on the nature of the finds from the site: no buildings are known at present. However, lying as it does at the western end, and on or close to the crest of a narrow, sharply-defined ridge commanding extensive prospects on all sides except the east, "the location is hardly suitable for anything else" [Rahtz, *pers comm*]; in which case the topographical parallel would be entirely consistent with the now well-established hilltop distribution of other (late?) Roman temples elsewhere in Somerset, including, of course, Pagan's Hill [Rahtz 1982]. And in terms of the markedly constricted nature of the site, the similarity to the location of the temple on Lamyatt Beacon is striking [Leech 1986; de la Bedoyere 1991, 191, and colour plate 12]. We have already seen that the 'high status' Roman occupation known from Chew hundred, even the so-called villas at Chew Park and Gold's Cross, gives an impression of distinct austerity, lacking as it does either hypocaust systems or tessellated floors; and this despite the fact that, at Chew Park, "the owner was comparatively wealthy, to judge by the number of coins and other finds" [Rahtz and Greenfield 1977, 18]. Leach and Leech have warned that "for the larger villas the evidence for most is so inadequate that what may appear in print as fairly complete ground plans should be treated with the utmost caution, with regard to their chronology, detail and overall extent" [Leach and Leech 1982, 67]; the clear implication being that, leaving aside exceptional instances of total excavation or geophysical survey, published plans should be regarded as representing only *minimum* extents of villa complexes. Even allowing this however, in comparison to Chew, some of the Whitley villas are altogether of a different order in terms of both size and elaboration: hypocaust systems are known or suspected at Low Ham [Scott 1993, 168], and Edington [Hollinrakes 1994a, 37-44], and at the high-status (but probably *non*-villa) site at Shapwick Old Church [Gutierrez 1997]. The detailed internal archaeology of the 'new', very large courtyard villa at Shapwick (Nidon) is at present a complete unknown. Mosaic floors existed at the Littleton villa, in Compton Dundon [SMR 53765; Hollinrakes 1994], which site has been subjected to (only partially-successful) geophysical survey [Gater *et al* 1993]; and at High Ham (Wood Road) and Low Ham (Hext Hill) [Scott 1993, 168], the latter being the source of the famous Dido and Aeneas pavement [Leach and Leech 1982, 62]. The poorly-recorded but apparently very large Marshall's Elm complex at Street [Scott 1993, 171], should also be included here on the basis of known finds from the site, as should the probable villa at Holy Trinity churchyard, Street, on the same grounds [Hollinrakes 1994b, 11-14]. The recent discovery of Roman occupation sites at both Greinton and Stawell has begun to fill in something of the settlement picture on Polden's southern flank, otherwise something of a lacuna.

It is clear that a significant proportion of Roman settlements in Whitley had in fact been occupied since at least the preceding period, with much of the dating evidence indicating continued occupation during the transition between the two cultural horizons. The Roman site in the northern part of Walton is closely associated with large quantities of Iron Age pottery [SMR 24770]; and a potentially important Iron Age settlement has been located immediately north of the Hotel at Shapwick, also associated with Roman occupation of unknown extent and nature [Creighton *et al* 1997, 152-165]. In both cases where the Polden pipeline campaign revealed evidence for substantial Roman settlement (Little Parks, Chilton; and Edington, Holy Well), it was associated with evidence of Iron Age occupation [Hollinrakes 1994a, and Reports numbers 61 and 71]. Significantly, this was also true of the other, lower status, isolated farmstead-type site within Edington, at Clover Close [Hollinrakes 1994e]. Likewise the probably large Romano-British settlement at Crockland and Bannick in Puriton seems to have directly succeeded Iron Age habitation on the same site [SMR 10702]. The other, much more substantial Roman site at Puriton, east of Downend, produced both pottery and stratigraphical

relationships indicating an Iron Age precursor [Fowler 1971, 7; SMR 10705], and the Roman villa at Littleton (Compton Dundon) lay on an Iron Age occupation site [SMR 53765].

Villas, Farms, Environment and Economy

The starting point is a seminal palynological study of the area of Meare Heath, in the Brue Valley [Beckett and Hibbert 1979], which can be used to illuminate landscape development on the wetland fringes.[8] It seems that while the Heath itself was undergoing a marked decline of hazel by the Bronze Age, the "dry land areas apparently remained wooded until well after this phase.........and there was no major increase of clearance until the latter half of the Iron Age.........cereals seem to have been cultivated locally from this date, but much woodland remained" [Dark 2000, 49]. In the Roman period, these trends were confirmed and reinforced, and something of an ecological balance seems to have been achieved, if only temporarily, with the pollen evidence indicating "a mixture of woodland and open land.........with cereal cultivation of dryland areas" [*ibid*, 98]. This, then, was the environmental background against which developed the framework of rural settlement, at least on the Polden Hills, in the Roman period.

Figure 4 maps the sites already outlined above, and its main sources are: OS 1"-scale Index to the Tithe Survey, sheets 19 and 20 (British Library); Rippon 1997, 67, fig 16; Somerset SMR (various); Hollinrakes 1994a and 1994b; Gray 1939; Gater *et al* 1993; Creighton *et al* 1997; Miles and Miles 1969; Coles 1989; and information for Compton Dundon supplied in advance of publication by Nancy Hollinrake. Figure 4 expands slightly the impression of Iron Age settlement shown on two previous published maps [Miles and Miles 1969, 52; Rippon 1997, 48. Information for Shapwick is scattered throughout the series of Annual Reports between 1988 and 1999, but is conveniently summarised in Aston and Gerrard 1999, 15-23.

In sketching the Roman background in Whitley, it is worth highlighting a clear contrast in the status of some of the buildings within the hundred, as revealed by the archaeological evidence, compared to the situation in Chew. In what terms it should be explained is problematic, and the great discrepancy in the respective areas of the two hundreds may partially invalidate the comparison, since at the simplest level one might expect a better chance of locating a larger number of structures within a wider compass. On first acquaintance, it seems as though at least basic economics should favour Chew. The point can be made by a crude comparison of land values in the late 11th century, using the manorial values given in Domesday. The calculation was made by simple addition of the acreages of all the parishes known to be in the respective hundreds in 1086, and their values at that date. As we will see later on, some of the marshland manors in Whitley had already experienced significant increases in value since 1066, probably as a result of drainage and reclamation, but the main thrust of this movement was yet to come

---

[8] I am grateful to Prof M Aston for drawing my attention to the significance of this work.

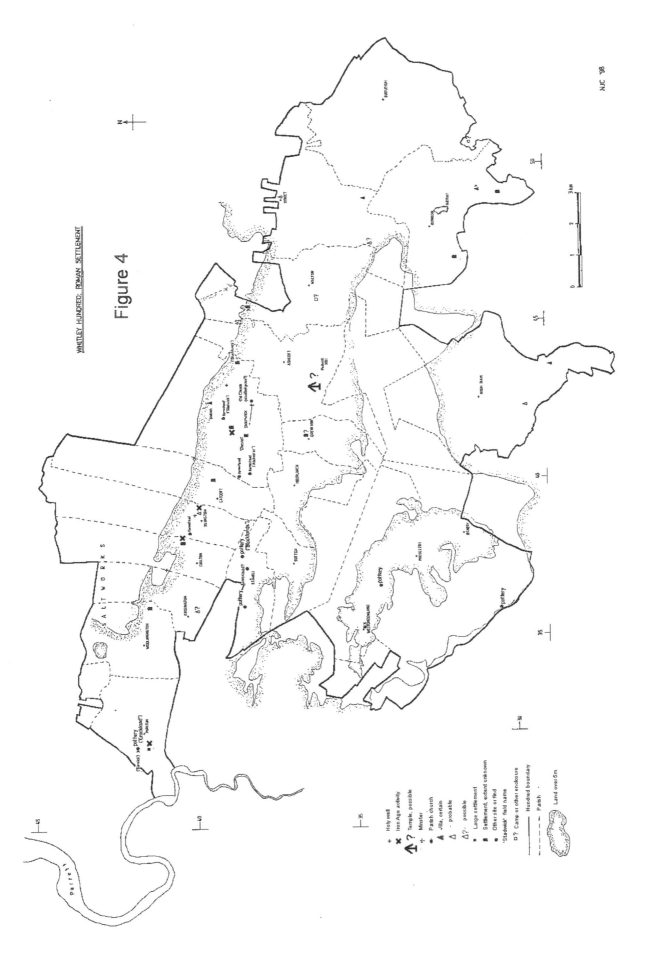

WHITLEY HUNDRED: ROMAN SETTLEMENT

Figure 4

[Musgrove, 1999]. At the time of Domesday, then, increases in the values of individual manors had probably not yet made much impact on land values in the hundred as a whole. In 1086, the value of land per acre in Chew, at 0.948d, was nearly twice that in Whitley, at 0.552d.

I do not, of course, suggest that the detail of late 11th century land values can be extrapolated back into the Roman period. However, it may be possible to speculate that the basis of a discrepancy of this general order may be of some antiquity, and may prompt us to ask why, apparently, the area which was later perceived as containing the more valuable land should actually prove less attractive to high-status Roman settlement. It is certain that a combination of forces is at work here, particularly those bearing upon economy, territorial arrange-ments and land-holding, with only the first of these allowing any possibility of recovery at present. But without doubt the main consideration is the difference in the resource-base available to communities in the two hundreds, in turn directly related to the natural environment, a point we have already stressed. Chiefly from the results of the Chew Valley Lake campaign of excavations, we can speculate that Chew hundred in the Roman period possessed (probably) woodland, arable, a small amount of meadow, and grazing on those slopes around Dundry which had been cleared of woodland [Rahtz and Greenfield 1977, 14-19].We can argue quite reasonably though, that Whitley's ability to support Roman occupation at an apparently far higher level than that of Chew, derives ultimately not from its size advantage, but from its far greater diversity of exploitable economic resources, and specifically from the presence of extensive wetlands to north and south of Polden. As Massey has observed recently of the apparent success or failure of villas in North Oxfordshire, "land quality may be an issue……as may be the extent to which villas were able to diversify their economies" [Massey 1999, 163].

The economic significance of the marshes turns upon their versatility in terms of land-use, and, crucially, this is not something which, historically, has always been quantifiable in terms of crude land values, since the contribution of the wetland element in integrated, fen-edge economies is often 'invisible' to us. To accept this at face-value, however, would be completely to misjudge the significance of their role in the subsistence regimes of communities close by. The Somerset wetland has always been an extremely dynamic natural environment, subject to often marked changes in and differences between drainage regimes over very short periods and distances [Aalbersberg 1996]; a tendency strongly influencing the nature of, but also in turn exacerbated by man's growing engagement and interference with this remarkable landscape probably from the Mesolithic onwards [Caseldine 1988; Coles 1989; Druce 1998; Wilkinson 1998; Housley *et al* 1999]. However, in general, it is true to say that the wetlands provided a wide range of constantly-available 'background' resources, particularly fish, fowl, reeds and probably peat-digging, for the latter of which there now appears to be direct archaeological evidence [Brunning 1994, 51], to add to the environmental clues to its use as

fuel in the salt-making process [Rippon 1997, 119]; and on the more elevated margins, arable, pasture, and woodland, for both coppice and timber [Coles and Minnitt 1995, 192-193].

Further, the great raised bog extending westwards from the Glastonbury area, and occupying much of the Brue Valley north of Polden, probably provided additional grazing grounds, local variations in the vegetational composition of the bog providing year-round access to fodder from at least the Bronze Age [Caseldine 1988, 255-257]. Housley, looking at the evidence in the vicinity of the Glastonbury and Meare Lake Villages, has concluded that "by the Iron Age the diversity of environment in the Brue Valley was probably very high, in part due to the actions of humans but in part due to sea-level changes and the amount of time the environment had had to develop differing ecological niches" [Housley 1995, 135]. This persistent attraction can only be understood in the context of a finely-balanced system in which the roles of upland and wetland were fully integrated, a characteristic also noted, for example, by Alan Everitt, of the Stour and North Kent Levels [Everitt 1986, 57-58].

The probable reasons for this in the Levels have been summarised by Rippon: "firstly, being situated on a geological and ecological boundary enabled the community to exploit the resources of two distinct environments. Secondly, soils of the foothills adjacent to the Levels tend to be the most suited to arable farming. A third factor that applied in a number of cases was that a fen-edge location enabled settlements to lie closer to rivers which were an important means of communication....." [Rippon 1997, 78].

The economies of marshland-fringe communities represented, therefore, in a very real sense, far more than merely the sum of their constituent parts. As Rippon has observed, "the predominance of fen-edge settlements ever since prehistory, ideally located to exploit both wetland and upland environments, strongly suggests that both areas must be considered as one economic system" [Rippon 1993, 34].

This, then, was the blueprint for exploitation that was inherited, developed and intensified by the Roman incomers. While it may be true, as Miles has suggested, that "in the countryside AD 43 rarely registers" [Miles 1989, 125], it nevertheless seems quite clear that eventually, at least the principle of the 'concave landscape' model developed by Coles as a model for resource exploitation in the Iron Age [Coles and Minnitt 1995, 192-193], was adopted, whether consciously or otherwise, in the Roman centuries. Fundamentally this model favours settlement at or close to, and exploitation of, 'ecotones', or resource-interfaces [Aston and Gerrard 1999, 8]; and it is noticeable that all the Whitley villas, although occupying sites, for the most part between about 10m-40m OD, also lie either immediately adjacent to, or within easy striking distance of open moor, on the fringes of surrounding uplands.

The substantial villa at Shapwick Nidons, discovered only in 1998, is a case in point. A large and internationally-important hoard of silver *denarii*, deposited under a floor probably shortly before the mid 3rd century, attests to the wealth and status of those who owned this building [Abdy 2000; Brunning and Webster, 2000; Abdy, Brunning and Webster 2001; Minnitt 2001]. At present the ground-plan is known only partially, from geophysical survey and preliminary excavations carried out in the summer of 1999, and there is not yet enough evidence to allow us to dwell on Dark's distinction between 'courtyard villas' and 'villas with courtyards' [Dark 1997, 44-45]; but the south-facing site which it occupies atop one of the Nidons in the north of the parish, although lying at only 18m OD, is locally very prominent, and with the southern fringe of the Brue Valley wetlands only a few hundred metres away to the north. The Old Church complex in the same parish, by contrast, some 1.5km away from the same resource, is not as advantageously sited for its exploitation on an economic basis; and notwithstanding questions over dating, it is pertinent to ask whether two such apparently large concerns could co-exist so close together if the economies of *both* were solely or even partially agricultural in nature.

Fieldwalking and excavation data from Old Church have led to the idea that the site carried "a suite of buildings with different functions, possibly a well-appointed courtyard villa with ancillary agricultural buildings stretching westwards" [Gerrard and Gutierrez 1997, 50], and the extent and importance of Old Church in the Roman period cannot be doubted. However, since the affinities of the Nidons site, so far as they are known, appear to fit easily with those of a well-attested villa type [de la Bedoyere 1991, 125-141; Dark 1997, 44-47], I would argue that this diminishes the likelihood of Old Church itself *also* being a villa, at least in the sense in which that word is usually understood [Dark 1997, 43-44][9].

This in turn raises the question of the nature of the Old Church site, and although the evidence is circumstantial, some kind of religious/ritual complex associated with the adjacent spring is looking an increasingly plausible interpretation. The suggestion that its affinities are religious rather than 'secular' may well gain support from the fact that, faced with the choice of *two* substantial Roman complexes within easy distance of each other, it was Old Church, rather than the Nidons villa site, which drew to itself the later (?minster) church of St Andrew. This idea is developed further in Chapter Four.

None of this, however, is to suggest that the buildings each existed in isolation. Indeed far from it: the two sites are clearly intervisible, and the geophysics shows that the villa, which lies precisely north of Old Church, is oriented to look south, perhaps partly to catch the sun, as one might expect, but partly also perhaps revealing a deeper and quite deliberate relationship between the two.

Was the villa owner also the builder and owner of the putative 'shrine' at Old Church?[10]

Be that as it may, for Old Church itself, an intriguing parallel suggests itself, since elsewhere in the county there is *another* church with proven late-Roman antecedents, an Andrew dedication and strongly associated with, indeed, directly aligned upon, a major spring [Aston, Bond and Ingle 1994a; Rodwell 1996]. This is of course the pre-Conquest cathedral church at Wells, and it is yet another clue that may point towards an early relationship between Wells and Shapwick.

There is of course no suggestion that Old Church was anything other than a fairly modest rural shrine, but nonetheless, we might seek potentially instructive analogies in the wide range of ancillary structures, with a variety of interpreted functions, associated with the temple precincts at both Uley and Lydney [Woodward 1992, 47-50]; and the recovery of flue tile from Old Church [Gutierrez 1997] raises the prospect of high-status, hypocaust-equipped residential occupation, perhaps for visitors, and/or an officiating priest. If the dominant function of the Old Church site in the Roman period *was* religious/ritual, then perhaps a context for its fate in the post-Roman period, and for the relationship between Shapwick Old Church itself and its Roman predecessor, may be provided in the construction of a building interpreted as a Christian church directly on top of the temple of Mercury at Uley, Glos, "in the late sixth or early seventh century" [Woodward 1992, 117][11].

The one Whitley villa seemingly lacking a 'wetland fringe' location is the probably very large Marshall's Elm site at Street, the economy of which may have been rather different. Its *raison d'etre* may not even have been entirely that of an agricultural entity; Rippon himself reinforces the point already made for both Whitley and Chew hundreds, relating to the varying functions of buildings that can tend misleadingly to be lumped together under the catch-all heading of 'villas': "not all villas need have been estate centres. Some of the smaller 'cottage-type' houses may represent the 'popularization of the villa idea' as the 'taste for *Romanitas* had moved down the social and economic scale.....'. Other examples could have been the residences of bailiffs, which.....might not have been any less opulent than those occupied by landowners themselves" [Rippon 1997, 115, and quote there cited; and *cf* Dark 1997, 74]. Even in this case though, Sedgemoor lay only a km to the south-west down Polden's steep southern scarp, and any estate attached to this villa might

---

[9] Although we need to note that Steve Minnitt [*pers comm*], who has been closely involved with Nidons and its exploration ever since its discovery, has reservations about the exact nature of the site, and suggests that its complex, multi-phase development may actually make its very villa-like affinities more apparent than real.

[10] We may wonder then whether Old Church conforms to that category of Roman ritual sites categorised by Rodwell as 'estate temples', that is, a private religious focus having a direct, *proprietorial* relationship with a villa but lying at a little distance from it. Cited in Hopkins 1998. Hopkins [105-107] quotes previously published church/villa relationships which could be of this type, and from his own studies further suggests that the major Anglo-Saxon church at Brixworth, Northants, may have exactly this connection with a substantial and wealthy villa some 400m to the north. It is interesting that, as at Brixworth, the Old Church/Nidons relationship also has the villa to the north, and the religious focus to the south.

[11] I am grateful to Teresa Hall for making me aware of the possible parallels with Uley.

easily have included access to the wetland. One observer has drawn attention to the apparent concentration of villas in this area, and commented on "the consequent shortage of farming land available to each" [SMR 24708]. But this seems to miss the point that, firstly, some of these complexes may not have been farms at all; and secondly, that the very nature of wetland-edge economies was one in which arable may have been merely one element, and not necessarily even the most important one, in agrarian regimes which, as we have already seen, integrated resources available from both marsh and upland.

We have already noted scholarly concern over the idea of villas being involved in economic specialisation. In Whitley however, this may indeed be hinted at to some degree in the results of recent fieldwalking in the area of Lollover Hill (NGR ST474325) at Compton Dundon. This produced but a single sherd of Roman pottery; a fact leading to the suggestion that at least this part of the parish was used as permanent pasture in the Roman period[12]. Outside Somerset, similar conclusions arose from a study of the Sutton Coldfield area carried out by Hodder [Hodder 1992, 180]. Our knowledge of the general distribution and nature of Romano-British settlement within the main body of Whitley hundred, is steadily increasing [*cf* Coles 1989, figs 10 and 25, for Sedgemoor and the Brue Valley; and Rippon 1997, 117, for the Somerset Levels in general]; and consideration of this aspect introduces us to a level of occupation different from or below that of the villas. We have already noted that of those villas known or suspected in Whitley, the majority lie very close to the margins of the wetlands. Within the hundred there have as yet been no discoveries of villas of the same type as Wemberham near Congresbury [Leech and Leach 1982, 71], or Lake House Farm near Brent Knoll [Rippon 1996a, 109-112], on sites actually in the marsh, requiring their own flood protection measures. The same general pattern is seen for the non-villa settlements [*cf* Rippon 1997, 67, fig 16], and we can envisage a relationship between the two, perhaps along the same lines as that already proposed between the putative Chew Magna villa, and the complex at Chew Park; in other words, major, high-status structures (the 'true' villas), with those lying at the centres of estates controlling dependent, outlying farms and/or 'bond' settlements. We will return briefly to this theme again later on; for now, though, it will be useful to note two possible examples of this kind of relationship in the Polden area.

At Compton Dundon, Nancy Hollinrake [*pers comm*] proposes that the settlement lying to the south of the Littleton villa was related to it, and was perhaps a community of people living and working on the villa estate[13]. And as part of the Polden pipeline campaign, a site at Edington, Clover Close, was identified as being a low-status family farmstead, with Iron Age origins, and the siting of which is specifically related by the excavators to

"the exploitation of the differing habitats available in the area. These are considerations eminently suitable to mixed farming, probably as part of an estate rather than as an independent unit" [Hollinrakes 1994e, 18]. A direct, possibly tenurial relationship to the 'villa' site at Edington Holy Well, half a km or so to the east, seems a strong possibility.

In terms of land-use during the Roman period, Rippon would exclude any significant creation of arable through drainage and reclamation by communities around the Brue Valley fen edge. His view is that this area, lacking systematic flood defences, "was probably exploited seasonally" [Rippon 1997, 77, and 73, fig 18]. Instead, the western Brue Valley was deliberately left as tidal saltmarsh "because its wetland resources were more highly valued than the arable/pasture that would result from drainage", particularly in regard to its overriding importance for salt-production [Rippon 1997, 121, and 67, fig 16].

The Pattern of Romano-British Settlement

As we have already seen, there are numerous difficulties inherent in trying to suggest even the crudest and most basic model of villa estate size and structure, and the place of the lesser settlements within the overall framework. Were *all* the villas necessarily farming establishments with their own estates? To what extent *did* specialist units exist, needing different types of land, and so skewing the distribution of the natural resource from what we might expect? And most seriously, how, if at all, are we to make allowance for the gaps in the archaeological record relating to settlements and villas as yet undiscovered?

It is likely that models constructed as an answer to this last problem will be applicable only where intense fieldwork over a small area has already given some indication of the nature and density of settlement [Aston 1994a, 153-154]. Here, as with Chew Hundred, detailed analysis lies outside the scope of this study, and a straightforward distribution map such as Figure 4, for all its shortcomings in terms of the misinterpretation of known sites, or the obvious omission of sites as yet unlocated, must nonetheless serve to provide the necessary context for consideration of the period itself and of subsequent developments.

Figure 4 immediately reveals a certain regularity in the distribution of sites in some parts of the hundred, and most notably on the north Polden slope. Almost every parish from Puriton in the west to Walton in the east can show at least one villa, or a settlement whose extent and nature is not yet certain.

The two exceptions to this generalisation, Cossington and Butleigh, the latter devoid of any proven evidence at all for Roman occupation of whatever kind, are clearly anomalous, and their lack can be confidently ascribed to the deficiency of the archaeological record. For the parishes west of and including Shapwick, the picture is one of remarkable conformity. A regularly-spaced line of sites marches roughly north-west/south-east, the last one of this series being the settlement in the northern part of Walton (below). The authors of the Polden pipeline survey

---

[12] I am indebted to Charlie and Nancy Hollinrake for allowing me sight of their unpublished survey report in advance of publication, and for discussing with me at length their data, and problems surrounding its interpretation.

[13] *ex inf* Nancy Hollinrake, to whom I am grateful for giving me sight of her map of this area for the Roman period, in advance of publication.

have stressed the concentration of Romano-British settlements within a relatively narrow range of elevations: all except Walton lie at between 10-20m; Catcott, although rather higher, at 25-30m, is probably also a member of this group [Hollinrakes 1994a, 5]. Indeed so uniform is the arrangement that discrepancies become obvious, the most notable example being Cossington. Here, the identification of a villa, and the supposed position of its site, rests solely on the testimony of some poorly-located *tesseræ*. If, though, the surviving pattern is a reliable guide, we would reasonably expect a Roman site to lie about 1km north-east of Cossington church, not far from its eastern boundary with Chilton; an area not, unfortunately, traversed by the Polden pipeline [Hollinrakes 1994a].

Likewise at both Woolavington and Puriton, it is probable that the break-down in the regularity of this pattern represented at these places is more apparent than real, and that the existence of Roman sites can be predicted at roughly similar elevations on this northern slope. So also for Ashcott, the known settlements immediately adjacent east and west, in Walton and Shapwick, strongly suggest a suspicious 'hole' in the overall pattern on or slightly above the 5m contour in the northern part of the parish. The site on Pedwell Hill in Ashcott is clearly exceptional, and its relationship to the nearby communities problematic. And although obviously an element *in* the surrounding settlement framework, its character is palpably different, and its location alone seems obviously to lift it out of conformity with its associated occupation sites.

We might reasonably caution that the Polden pipeline work may have produced an undue bias in the record towards this part of the northern slope; in fact though, the work of the Shapwick Project, with its far greater breadth and depth and coverage, has to a large degree confirmed the importance of the 10-20m contour, with the sites at Blacklands and Sladwick [Figure 5 and Plate 1], while at the same time having revealed the existence of two further sites, perhaps, like Sladwick, individual farmsteads, at Abchester, further upslope to the south between 50-60m OD[14]. Indeed, the intensive fieldwalking regime at Shapwick has suggested the existence there of an 'arable core' lying between the 10m and 60m contours [Gerrard 1995a, 24], which can probably be extended east and west right along the northern flank of the Polden ridge proper. For Shapwick itself, as we have already noted, a theoretical framework for the total settlement pattern in the Roman period, based on discoveries thus far, has been proposed [Aston 1994a, 153-154]. And even given Shapwick's large size (within the hundred only Butleigh and Ham are larger) the implications for the parishes west, east and south are clear: allowance must be made, and ideas formulated, on the basis that the evidence we have is partial. Unlike the parishes sketched briefly above, evidence for Roman

settlement in the rest of the hundred is not yet good enough to enable us to discern any particular patterns, nor, by extension, to form in most cases any meaningful views on a possible Roman influence on the medieval settlement pattern.

From the point of view of topographical affinities, it seems clear from Figure 4 that Walton should properly be included with the group of parishes to its west lying on Polden's northern slope, and should be regarded as the most easterly member of that group; since Walton is the last parish to occupy a position on the Polden ridge proper, which immediately eastwards becomes lost in the higher, more broken terrain occupied by the three easternmost parishes of the hundred, Butleigh, Compton Dundon, and Street. The complete lacuna at Butleigh is unfortunate; the minor name Wickham's Cross, on the south-western boundary with Compton Dundon, might well have given a clue to at least one Roman site in its vicinity awaiting discovery [Costen 1992a, 58-60], except for its almost certain origin as a late personal name [Costen, *pers comm*]. An unidentified cropmark enclosure in the southern part of the parish, from its configuration may, according to the SMR [23189], indicate a Roman marching camp, but the site has not been systematically investigated. And the two, possibly three villas at Street (two of them in fen-edge positions) prompt questions, as yet lacking answers, about the likely location(s) of associated settlements of lower status.

Although both Ham and Sowy island fall within the area of the later hundred, topographically they are quite distinct, something which is, of course, especially true for Sowy, unique in the hundred in representing a completely geographically-bounded entity, something that cannot be said even of the Polden ridge. The major evidence from Sowy comes in the form of what is thought to be a large settlement at Westonzoyland whose status is problematic. It appears, like the indeterminate complex at Shapwick Old Church, and the villas at Street and possibly Edington, to be distinguished by a relationship to the site of the medieval parish church, but unlike those places there is as yet no evidence at Westonzoyland that there was a specifically villa-type building on or close to the church. The Westonzoyland site was certainly occupied in the late pre-Roman Iron Age and perhaps earlier [Miles and Miles 1969, 17-26], and because of its extent in the Roman period its apparent propinquity to the church may be merely coincidental. It is also significant that although large, it seems also to have been comparatively humble [Miles and Miles 1969, 26]. Apart from this site, the only other notable signs of a Romano-British presence on Sowy island are represented by isolated pottery scatters from Westonzoyland airfield, and the recent discovery of extensive scatters of both worked flint and Roman pottery from a site just above the 5m contour, "on the north and north-western margins of Weston Zoyland....." [Hollinrake 1991, 142]. Pottery has also come from the yard of the (19th century) chapel of St Michael, at the foot of Burrow Mump, on the extreme western edge of Othery parish [Gray 1939, 98; Additions 1921, lxxv; Adkins and Adkins 1992, 32-33].

---

[14] We should note, however, that the *nature* of Sladwick is now open to question, since preliminary analysis of the pottery assemblage from the site seems to suggest affinities far more akin to those of "a villa or well-appointed Roman establishment with a moderately good complement of fine tablewares and mortaria" [Jane Timby, unpublished report, *pers comm* Chris Gerrard to M A Aston].

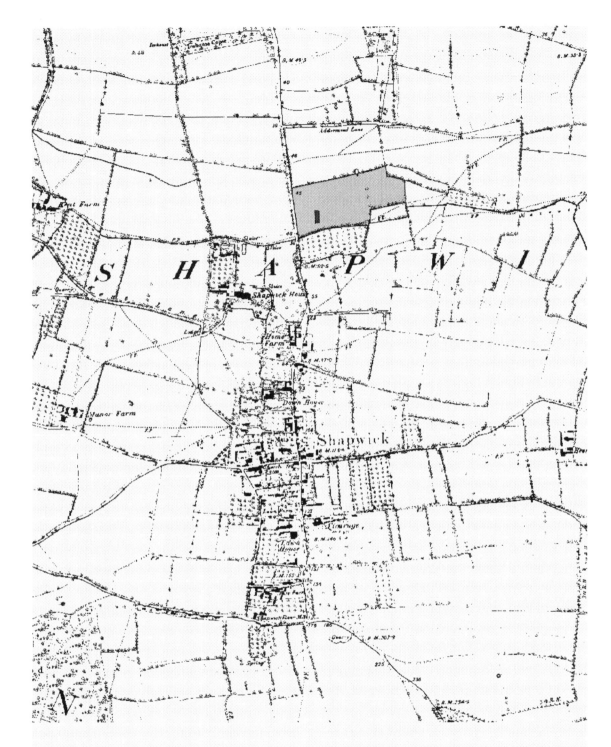

Figure 5

Extract from First Edition 6" OS map (1885), showing (shaded) the location of Sladwick field at Shapwick, the subject of the archaeological excavation depicted in Plate 1. The approximate position of the excavation trench is shown. Adapted from Aston *et al*, 1998d.

Plate 1: The Roman building (field barn?) at Sladwick field, Shapwick, under excavation. On the left, the east of wall of the building is emerging from the trench. Looking approximately south.

As for Street, so also for Ham, do the two villas there suggest the presence of associated but as yet unlocated dependent settlements; a probability heightened by the almost certainly misleading impression of a complete lack of Romano-British occupation in the northern half of the parish, covering by far the greater proportion of its area.

The impression of both regularity and density, in terms of settlement distribution in the Roman period, on the northern slope of Polden, presents a striking contrast to the picture on the steeper, southern slope, overlooking King's Sedgemoor. At present, Moorlinch cannot show even a basic level of evidence for a Romano-British presence. Settlements known or suspected through pottery from both surface scatters and excavations, and possibly associated enclosures at Stawell and Sutton (on the SMR, counted together under the modern civil parish of Stawell), might hint at the existence of further sites in the other parishes [SMR 10023, 10837, 11896, 11897, 11903; Croft 1991, 153]. Indeed, this suspicion has been given substance very recently by two separate discoveries. Limited trial excavations at Stawell, on a site in an orchard a few hundred metres east of the church, have confirmed the presence there of a stone building of Roman date, from which wall plaster has been recovered [SMR 11903][15]. And at Greinton, the excavation of foundations for a new house close to the village core, revealed beam slots, a boundary ditch, and a burial, all dated by associated pottery to the Roman period. The SMR infers the existence of "a settlement in the immediate area" [44866; see also records 44864 and 44865]. How far this suggestion will be borne out by future work is impossible to say. We might think that Greinton lends some credence to the view that the apparent sparseness of Roman occupation on this southern side of the Polden ridge does stem at least in part from a lack of systematic fieldwork, and limited opportunities for discovery afforded by the nature of local ploughing practices. However, the site does not at this early stage appear to represent high-status settlement, and may rather in fact reinforce the impression that what occupation there was may have been relatively limited and austere, leaving behind few vestiges of its material culture.

It is also clear that a significant proportion of Roman settlements in Whitley had in fact been occupied since at least the preceding period, with much of the dating evidence indicating continued occupation during the transition between the two cultural horizons. The Roman site in the northern part of Walton is closely associated with large quantities of Iron Age pottery [SMR 24770]; and as we have already noted, a potentially important Iron Age settlement has been located immediately north of the Hotel at Shapwick, also associated with Roman occupation of unknown extent and nature [Creighton *et al* 1997, 152-165]. In both cases where the Polden pipeline campaign revealed evidence for substantial Roman settlement (Little Parks, Chilton; and Edington, Holy Well), it was associated with evidence of Iron Age occupation [Hollinrakes 1994a, and Reports numbers 61 and 71]. Significantly, this was also true of the other, lower status, isolated farmstead-type site within Edington, at Clover Close [Hollinrakes 1994e]. Likewise the probably large Romano-British settlement at Crockland and Bannick in Puriton seems to have directly succeeded Iron Age habitation on the same site [SMR 10702]. The significance of these particular names is a question to which we will return later on. However, the other, much more substantial Roman site at Puriton, east of Downend, produced both pottery and stratigraphical relationships indicating an Iron Age precursor [Fowler 1971, 7; SMR 10705], and the Roman villa at Littleton (Compton Dundon) lay on an Iron Age occupation site [SMR 53765].

As with the Roman evidence itself, so should this picture of Iron Age activity be regarded as the very

minimum. High-status Roman occupation and/or 'cult' sites in particular might be expected to produce such evidence (as at Holy Well, Chilton), and it was presumably on this basis that the excavator of the Old Church at Shapwick, occupying a Roman site of high-status close to a (?sacred) spring, observed that "there was no evidence of any prehistoric activity on the site but [it] may not survive well in the ploughsoil and the trenches were rarely excavated deeply enough to expose pre-Roman stratigraphy" [Gerrard 1995, 107].

Settlement Location: Some Possible Influences

Even though imperfect, it seems clear, then, that what evidence we have points strongly towards Polden's northern slope as a primary focus for Romano-British settlement within the area of Whitley hundred. The possible reasons for this are problematic, but probably amount to a combination of factors relating to the physical environment and availability of resources, developing and expanding, as already suggested, an existing late prehistoric framework. The natural relief, for example, presumably played a prominent role; and while, as we have already noted in relation to villa economies, arable cultivation may not invariably have been the most important activity, nonetheless the short, steep southern slope, with its far more broken topography, would have been at a distinct disadvantage, in terms of ease of working, compared to the long, gentle and relatively smooth gradients on Polden's northern flank. This dip and scarp slope topography is directly related to the trend of the underlying geology [Hardy 1990, fig 8.8], and in this respect, there is a striking contrast between the northern and southern slopes. All the southern settlements, from Stawell in the west to Greinton in the east, lie on beds composed of the Mercia Mudstone (formerly called the Keuper Marl) group. The northern villages, east to west from Puriton to Butleigh (and, indeed, beyond), are underlain chiefly by beds of the Blue Lias group, a locally highly variable lithology of clays and limestones, the complexity of which has only recently been highlighted by detailed fieldwork carried out as part of the Shapwick Project [Hardy 1989 and 1990]. These lithologies have naturally had their effect on the nature of the Polden soils, and such matters are central to any consideration of farming practices at this period. Indeed, Keith Branigan, in his suggested reconstruction of the economy of the Gatcombe villa estate, took as his starting point the nature of the soils and the underlying geology, and largely on that basis put forward calculations for the suggested positions of and area occupied by each type of land-use (arable, meadow, pasture and woodland) [Branigan 1977, 192-197]. His proposals are doubly relevant here because of the appearance on Polden of a variety of soil groups similar to some of those found around Gatcombe, particularly the Mercia Mudstone (formerly Keuper Marl).

Polden's northern slope is dominated by and large by calcareous soils, the most important being the Somerton/Sherborne series, a free-draining group with a generally neutral or alkaline character [Avery 1955, 25-31

---

[15] *pers comm* Chris Webster.

and 37-43; Findlay *et al* 1984, 271-274 and 319-321].[16] Avery notes that "the soils are stiff and dry out rather slowly in the spring, but will work down to a good, stable, granular tilth in most seasons" [Avery 1955, 39]. On the southern slopes, the Mercia Mudstone has given rise to soils classified as brown earths, and here the Worcester series is the most extensive. They are slightly acidic, but their chief drawback is their heaviness. Avery observes that "drainage is restricted by heavy-textured parent materials, so that some seasonal waterlogging occurs in the surface horizons or in a zone immediately above the unweathered sub-stratum" [Avery 1955, 25]. These problems are echoed and developed by Findlay *et al*: "the water retentive nature of these soils and their relatively large clay contents make any structural damage difficult to rectify. The risk of poaching [the tendency to become spongy and sodden] is appreciable not only during spring and autumn but also during wet summer spells. Cultivated land is common only in drier parts of the region and is normally restricted to slopes of less than 8 degrees. The very slowly permeable subsoil horizons and water retentive topsoils cause severe surface wetness" [Findlay *et al* 1984, 321].

In this context, it is fortunate that the soils of the Glastonbury district in general, and their possible influence on settlement and agriculture in the Roman period, have been the subject of a valuable, but little-known study by Alan Kosse. As long ago as 1963 he noted the tendency for "the [Roman] sites in general [to] cluster on or near two soil series, the Somerton and Evesham.....with more of the sites located on the Somerton series" [Kosse 1963, 11]; and an accumulation of new information over the past 35 years, rather than refuting this view, has in fact gone far towards confirming it, although not without some qualification. We have already noted the potential attraction of soils suitable for intensive cultivation as an important consideration for Roman period settlement in Chew Magna (above). And in her study of the possible survival into the early medieval period of Roman estates in south-east Wales, Wendy Davies has emphasised the significance of land quality, pointing out that "the best land was exploited and.....the [Roman] settlement pattern bears some relation to land use" [Davies 1978, 154; also at 156]. A further parallel elsewhere is offered by Hodder's study of settlement in the Sutton Coldfield area in the Roman and medieval periods, "which suggests that the pattern of land-use in both.....periods was strongly influenced by physical factors.....[and] exhibits a dichotomy which corresponds to the physical division of the region into upland and lowland parts" [Hodder 1992, 178-181]. For the Glastonbury district as a whole, Kosse argued that "it seems unlikely.....that the area in the immediate vicinity of the villas was devoted primarily to pasture during Roman times". Where he can now be seen to have been mistaken is in proposing a relatively even density of settlement across the whole breadth of the Polden ridge: "it seems reasonable to assume.....then as now, that the Poldens and the Somerton plateau (those areas marked by the Evesham

and Somerton soil series), were intensively cultivated" [Kosse 1963, 15-16]; a fair conclusion given the state of knowledge at the time he was writing.

In terms of arable viability alone, then, Polden's southern flank from the outset lay at a disadvantage compared to the northern, hindered as it was by relatively heavy, poorly-draining soils on steep slopes. The shorter, more abrupt southern scarp slope also means that the potential arable land on this side is restricted to a much narrower band than is the case on the north, and during episodes of serious flooding, not only would a far greater proportion of the soils here have been adversely affected than on the northern dip-slope, but they would also have taken far longer to dry out. We can, then, suggest that soils did play a role in providing a part at least of the overall environmental framework within which patterns of both settlement and land use had developed by the Iron Age at the latest, certainly in this part of Whitley hundred if not elsewhere. It can, indeed, hardly be coincidence that one of Whitley's most persistent blocks of ancient woodland, Loxley, appearing in 1086, and well into the 19th century, as fifty acres, and from which the old western part of the hundred took its name, lay exactly on top of a small patch of soils of the Denchworth group (formerly Charlton Bank) [*cf* Hill *et al*, 1994, 121]. It is, of course, quite possible that Loxley as it survives is at least in part the result of post-Roman regeneration [but *cf* Aston and Gerrard 1999, 27]. However, amidst a small sea of the better-drained Sherborne series to the north in Shapwick, it seems quite clear that the wood is where it is because, as early medieval clearance progressed in other parts of the locality, in those areas of primary woodland or of old Roman arable that had fallen down to woodland, it was recognised that the Denchworth soils, "slowly permeable and.....waterlogged for prolonged periods in winter and at times in the growing season", would be far more usefully left for managed woodland rather than be pressed into service only to produce a very inferior quality of ploughland [Findlay *et al* 1984, 151-154; Aston and Costen 1994a, 7, fig 1.3].

The idea of a predominantly arable component in the Romano-British farming of Polden's northern slope is further strengthened by the presence of the saltworkings immediately to the north in the Brue valley, and it is likely that the relationship between the two land-uses may be based on far more than mere coincidental contiguity; since a growing body of evidence from saltmarsh fringes around the North Sea basin in both this country and in Germany has established that, where saltworking and arable husbandry occur side by side, there is probably a positive link between the two. At Hullbridge Basin in Essex, for example, "the coarse seivings from the agricultural processing of spelt wheat were used to temper clay in the salt-working process" [Jones 1989, 130]. These findings are certainly supported from the limited investigations of briquetage mounds that have been carried out in the Brue Valley, from which impressions of spelt wheat, barley and rye grains, and indeed examples of the grains themselves, have been reported from clay hearths in at least one of the salterns there [Leech, Bell and Evans 1983, 74-78; I am

---

[16] The soil lithology on Polden's northern flank trends roughly east/west. For the example of Shapwick, see Aston 1994c, Fig 1.3, 7.

grateful to Dr Stephen Rippon for drawing this work to my attention]. There may be sound ecological and economic reasons behind this relationship; since, as Jim Jones has recently pointed out, "the best time of year for salt production would appear to be between March and June............production would therefore take place in the period between ploughing and sowing spring crops and harvesting the winter crop, [and] would.........fit in well with the agricultural cycle as a whole.........emphasising the essentially seasonal nature of the salt production process" [Jones 1998, unpaginated].

A reappraisal of the environmental potential of the Brue Valley Romano-British salterns, through systematic archaeological examination of a larger sample of briquetage mounds, might, then, throw valuable light on contemporary agrarian regimes in operation on the higher land of north Polden immediately to the south [*cf* Grove and Brunning 1998]. Polden's northern slope, far more than the southern, is characterised by a series of major springs, issuing at various heights along the long axis of the main ridge, and the result of faulting in the underlying geological structure [Hardy 1990, 29]. The ready availability of a pure water supply, together with the other considerations already noted, may certainly have played a role in preferred settlement location in the late pre-Roman Iron Age and later. It is also, however, becoming quite clear that it is crucial to admit less rigidly functional elements into the settlement equation, and to try to restore to the landscape something of the more spiritual 'otherness' which, as modern studies are increasingly showing, were rooted so deeply in the everyday thought-world of pre-industrial, and particularly of prehistoric societies both in Europe and far beyond [Darvill 1997, 74-78 and 81-86; Nash 1997; Tilley 1994]. In the specific case of north Polden, it may, therefore, be as or more significant than the purely functional consideration of water supply that certain of the springs, namely at Shapwick [Aston and Costen 1990, 39-40 and Aston 1993, 13], Edington [Hollinrakes 1994a and Report No 71], and on the Cossington/Chilton boundary [Hollinrakes 1994a], are sulphurous to varying degrees and have emerged into modern understanding and usage as 'holy' wells [*cf* Scherr 1986, 82-84]. A detailed examination of the origins and development of this attribution lies outside the scope of this study; it is worth noting, however, that the high status Romano-British (?villa) site at Edington is closely associated with the 'holy' well there, and that at Shapwick, already suggested as a ritual focus in the Roman period, although divorced from the known 'holy' well at Northbrook became the site of a minster church and may be directly related to the spring hard by to the north-east [Aston 1993, 13; Gerrard 1995, 104-105; Aston, Bond and Ingle 1994a]. Further, the well on Cossington's western boundary with Chilton lies close to the point at which, as already noted (above) a gap in the known settlement pattern might suggest the location of an undiscovered Roman site. Certainly in Edington's case the possibility of a cult function is implicit in the excavators' assertion that "the well is highly sulphurous and can never have been used purely as a drinking water supply so it is unlikely that

any settlement, Iron Age or Romano-British, would have chosen this spot because of that aspect" [Hollinrakes 1994a, Report 71, 35; and *cf* Woodward 1992, 53].

Communications

In considering the economic viability of Roman settlements on Polden, and in looking for the reasons behind the area's apparent attractiveness in this respect, it is probably safe to assign an important role to the routeway which runs north-west/south-east along the crest of the ridge. It is virtually certain that although the present line of the Polden road was fixed in the Roman period with a properly engineered surface [Fowler 1971, 7; Costen 1992, 29], its origins are far earlier, as a prehistoric ridgeway. During winter flooding, Polden would have become effectively a peninsula, and for the Roman period, the year-round access from both east and west afforded by the ridge route would have been central to the effective, intensive exploitation of the Polden slopes, if the movement of large and regular shipments of agricultural surpluses was involved, as it probably was.

David Miles has recently cautioned that "the presence of a local and regional network of roads should not be allowed to hide a fact of life in the ancient world: overland transport was slow and expensive.....nevertheless, the location of villas, usually set back from but close to main roads, emphasizes the importance of communica-tion with the local market....." [Miles 1986, 43]. This last point describes exactly Romano-British settlement on north Polden in relation to the road, just as it does the Chew Park villa and the putative villa at Chew Magna. It is also worth noting in this context Martin Jones's forceful warning against the assumption, in his view unwarranted, "that the evident wealth of villas automatically implies the stimulation of agricultural production to support it" [Jones 1989, 129]. Nevertheless, it seems likely that such wealth as produced the three high-status sites at Edington Holy Well, and Shapwick Old Church and Nidons, was based at least partly on the external disposal of agricultural surpluses. This in turn presupposes the existence of both adequate transport links, and access to suitable markets. Ian Hodder's theoretical modelling of marketing networks in southern England has demonstrated the central importance of the road system, particularly in relation to towns, in shaping the known distribution patterns of various types of Romano-British coarse pottery [Hodder 1974, esp at 349]; and there is every reason to suppose that, although far more difficult to corroborate, the effects on the nature of both agricultural produce and practices may have been similar. Historians have shown that in the late 18th and 19th centuries, the incidence of parliamentary enclosure was in some areas directly related to the presence of a high-quality, pre-existing road, usually a turnpike [Szostak 1991, 29 and refs there cited; Aldcroft and Freeman 1983, 58]. More generally, Aldcroft and Freeman describe how "improved roads which offered easier, cheaper and more reliable access to markets, and to inputs such as lime or marl, were.....important in the process of agricultural transformation.....by improving market access the turnpikes helped to break down local and regional marketing patterns and self-sufficiency, and so give an added spur to the commercialisation of agriculture" [Aldcroft and Freeman 1983, 57]. Indeed, following precisely this argument, albeit at a rather later period, Dallimore *et al* have suggested that the construction of the Central Somerset Railway along Shapwick's northern boundary in about 1858, had the direct effect of moving the parish's agricultural economy even further away from arable, and reinforcing the already predominant emphasis on dairy production, grazing and stock-rearing; since the railway "afforded an important link for the dispatch of animals to distant markets and, on a daily basis, milk to nearby urban areas and processing dairies" [Dallimore *et al* 1994, 104]. An analogy here with the new and improved roads of Roman Britain seems to me entirely appropriate, for these are precisely the processes which Hodder has adduced for Roman pottery [Hodder 1974]; and it raises the distinct possibility that the Polden road had an indirect, as well as a direct landscape impact in the Roman period, perhaps even to the extent of influencing agricultural practices and field layouts, and promoting specialisation.

In any event, both Shapwick Nidons and Edington must by definition have lain above the economic threshold identified by Black in his study of villas in south-east England, below which their construction does not seem to have been viable [Black 1987, 67-72]. To the east, we need look no further than the major regional centre at Ilchester, located on the Fosse Way and into whose hinterland Polden was integrated by virtue of its ridgeway road which joined the Fosse immediately north of the town [Leach and Leech 1982, 76-80]; although it must be said that, for Ilchester, the results of a study attempting to define statistically the relationship between the town and the surrounding villas were inconclusive [Hodder and Millett 1980, 75]. To the west lay potentially even better possibilities, for in that direction the course of the road brought it down to the port at Crandon Bridge, "significantly the most easterly point at which a port could be situated on the Parrett and still have access inland along the Polden ridge". However, the road continued further west still, now off the ridge and across lower-lying terrain, to the other riverside site at Combwich. Both these ports seem to have been occupied throughout the Roman period [Leach and Leech 1982, 72].

The importance of this link for the Polden economy in the Romano-British period is clear, and is highlighted by Miles's observation that "it was cheaper to send a shipment of grain from one end of the Mediterranean to the other than to cart it overland 75 miles" [Miles 1986, 43]; for the Parrett ports were the gateway to the western sea-lanes, and gave villa-owners access to the coast of south Wales, to the financial opportunities presented by the significant military presence at Caerleon, and probably even to Ireland and Spain. Indeed, a recent study of the Dorset black burnished pottery industry has identified Crandon Bridge as potentially "of exceptional importance in the Roman economy of southern Britain", probably acting as a major distribution point for Dorset pottery, sent thence along the Polden ridge road, via Ilchester [Allen and Fulford 1996, 258-259; I am grateful to Mark Corney for this reference]. Since it now seems that the Dorset BB pottery industry was among those which continued to operate, albeit on a reduced scale, well into the 5th century [*pers comm* Mark Corney; Dark 1996, 58-61; Sparey-Green 1996, 123-126], it may be that the Polden road also maintained a role in any associated, even if far more restricted distribution network until at least a similar period.

The road's function as a significant boundary in the landscape should also be noted briefly at this point, providing as it did virtually the entire length of the southern boundaries of all the parishes from Cossington eastwards to Shapwick. Further east, Roger Leech suggested that the boundaries of some of those parishes adjacent to the Fosse Way, and which follow the road for long stretches, date from a reorganisation of Roman estates which took place in that area in the late first century [Leech 1982, 234-236]. However, the use of the Polden road as a boundary is, I would suggest, different, and is far more likely to be associated with the progressive break up, probably from the late Saxon period, of the old *Pouelt* estate into smaller entities far more like the later medieval parishes. The main road on the crest of the ridge may, though, be only the most important and obvious in use on Polden in the Roman period, for lower down the slope to the north its east-west course is almost exactly paralleled by at least one other routeway, surviving as a combination of minor road, tracks and footpaths, running roughly between the 35m and 45m contours and joining all the north Polden villages from Woolavington eastwards to Shapwick. Its line is lost east of Shapwick, but can probably be projected west of Woolavington, where parish boundaries follow a surviving trackway on a secondary ridge down to the Parrett; and it may well be significant that its course passes only a few hundred metres or so to the south of the major Roman, and probably Iron Age site near Downend in Puriton, the unknown extent of which may in fact make the association between settlement and routeway far more intimate than at first appears [Fowler 1971, 7]. It is likely that this route at least pre-dates the laying out of the northern cells of the Shapwick village plan, which its line clearly influenced [Aston and Penoyre 1994, 27-44, esp at 43, fig 4.12], and a continuation east of the village aligns it directly on the ?ritual/minster site in Old Church.

The existence of yet another east-west parallel route, slightly further north still between roughly 10m and 20m OD, is a distinct possibility. At Shapwick, the northern part of the village plan clearly lies on top of it, completely disrupting its line, and it is also close to the line of this route that the Roman settlements strung out along the northern slope for the most part lie. The villa at Edington, for example, would lie almost directly on its course, which, with few gaps, it is possible to trace as, again, a combination of minor road, field boundaries and tracks, from Puriton (probably serving the 'Crockland' Romano-British settlement there) eastwards, at least as far as Shapwick's eastern boundary.

The notion of at least one route of Roman date following a 'dedicated' alignment terminating at the putative Old Church 'ritual complex', raises intriguing possibilities in the light of recent suggestions by Miranda Aldhouse-Green. Working on the finds from the isolated rural spring-shrine at *Fontes Sequanae* in Burgundy, which flourished between the first and third centuries AD, Dr Alhouse-Green has proposed that it, and sites like it all over Gaul and Britain, was the focus of a pilgrimage movement underpinned by a potent belief in the healing and restorative powers of the spring. She argues that such sites gave rise to a widespread and dynamic fervour for pilgrimage that was as intense and as vigorous as anything found in the medieval period. Further, she notes how in the post-Roman period, the pagan goddess of the spring at *Fontes Sequanae* was deliberately and systematically appropriated into the *Christian* canon, and also that, in Britain, the great medieval shrine and pilgrimage centre at Walsingham in Norfolk appears to have a Roman predecessor [Smith 1999; I am grateful to Dr Aldhouse-Green for this reference]; both facts offering at least the possibility of a mechanism for some degree of ritual continuity into the medieval period [Aldhouse-Green, 1999 and 2000]. On the basis of what we have already suggested earlier in this section, the reconstruction of *Fontes Sequanae* published by Dr Aldhouse-Green seems far too large and elaborate to answer for Old Church, but in its essential principles, it may provide some idea at least of the nature of the Shapwick site. If, in the Roman period, the Old Church spring-shrine attained any degree of celebrity, we can perhaps imagine the establishment of pilgrimage routes from both west and east, with that from the west involving the pilgrims travelling by sea from south Wales, and from further up the southern coast of the Severn Estuary. This is not to suggest that these routes necessarily owe their existence to the Old Church complex, but rather, perhaps, that something akin to a wayside shrine centred on the spring there developed beside an existing (?prehistoric) routes, and once established, became progressively more elaborate (I am indebted to Teresa Hall for her advice on this latter point). After disembarking at the port at Combwich, the pilgrims would then make their way eastwards on the Polden ridge road towards Shapwick before dropping down the northern slope onto one of the minor routes leading to the shrine complex itself. Can Shapwick show any tradition to parallel that of St Sequanus, the direct Christian embodiment of the pagan *Sequana*? [Aldhouse-Green 2000, 15]. With the focus shifted to Glastonbury, perhaps there are, nonetheless, elements in the purportedly 8th century story of the murder of St Indract and his companions, while travelling as pilgrims on this same route, that might recall a far earlier tradition, one with a different destination as its objective [Costen 1991, 50 and 55, and refs there cited].

In any event, our perspective on Polden's early routes has become even more complex with the very recent discovery (1999) that an excavated ditch which exactly follows the line of a modern hedge, parallel to and immediately beside the course of a medieval and later road (now a footpath), is probably Bronze Age in date [Plate 11,

Fig 40]. It may be possible to trace this line westwards to a point about halfway between Catcott and Shapwick, and part of its course may then be marked here by the 'medieval' Lippett's Way (below). In any event, it seems as though this is a clear-cut case of a prehistoric boundary feature exercising a tenacious and controlling influence on subsequent boundary and communications alignments in this locality. If other boundary/communications features could be investigated systematically, the implications for our understanding of the chronology of these fundamental landscape elements could be far-reaching.

Roman Polden: Estates and Settlement Relationships

We have already seen that by virtue of a relatively substantial body of archaeological evidence, Polden offers an opportunity, unique in Whitley hundred and rare enough in Somerset as whole, for speculation on the nature of the Roman settlement hierarchy and of land-holding. The natural topography is again central to this theme, and it is an interesting question whether the emergence in the medieval period of a territorial entity of some description, covering very roughly the area of the later hundred, could actually have been predicted given only a base map of the area to work from showing relief and drainage. Recent work by historians is beginning to suggest the possibility that at least some of the defining characteristics of regional societies tended to develop within areas of landscape, dubbed 'cultural provinces', bounded by features of natural topography. It was within such 'primary' areas that, among many other things, resource exploitation and the development of early (ie at least early medieval) polities took place, and the physical definition of these units, so the argument runs, most commonly relied on river basins and watersheds [Phythian-Adams 1993]. Phythian-Adams has recently used this concept to help explain the origins, and many of the characteristics, of early medieval society in Cumberland [Phythian-Adams 1996], and in both west Somerset and west Cornwall has also identified distinct 'topographies of superstition', which as late as the early modern period were quite clearly defined by reference to major river basins and watersheds [Phythian-Adams 2000, 134-142]. Likewise in this context, in North Yorkshire, Andrew Fleming has identified a distinctive late Roman and early medieval polity centred on the valley of the River Swale [Fleming 1994a, 1998a and 1999a].

Similar themes are now being adopted by archaeologists in their attempts to identify and characterise 'historic' landscapes. Thus Darvill *et al* [1993, 565], consider that "a relict cultural landscape is...........likely to possess geographical or topographical coherence as a macro-region, perhaps a range of hills, a river valley, a peninsula or a plateau. Geographical integrity occurs in the sense that it is a continuous area rather than a collection of discrete, unconnected topographic units, although its extent need not coincide with present land-use."

It is probable that some later landscape arrangements may well have developed around the existing frameworks provided by these primary territories. In south-east Scotland for example, a recent study has suggested that territorial arrangements discernable in the medieval period may take their cue, at least in part, from antecedent entities based on late prehistoric, *oppida*-like centres "significantly sited on watersheds" [Proudfoot and Aliaga-Kelly 1997, 33]; and in Dorset, Teresa Hall's study of the origins and development of the minster system there has shown that "the boundaries of the *parochiæ* use more major topographical features than the internal boundaries of the later parishes into which the *parochiæ* split and it is very noticeable that some of the *parochiæ* consist of natural land units such as river basins" [Hall 2000, 77-83, quote at 83 and refs there cited]. As with the Dorset minster territories so also with the hundreds, for it seems that the largely tenurial arrangement of hundreds we see in operation by 1086 was the result of the break-down of an earlier system that was originally rooted firmly in the natural topography [Hall 2000, 89-96]. Hall's conclusions for Dorset, very much in tune with the Phythian-Adams model, are clear about the geographical basis of cultural development there: "the division of the county into royal demesne/*parochiæ* units based on topographical components presents a picture of society operating against this background at a local level as well as a regional one, albeit at an earlier date" [Hall 2000, 101]. This is very much along the lines suggested by Klingelhofer for the development of the early medieval estate structure in the valley of the Upper Itchen, Hampshire, except that the topography is inverted, and on Polden we are dealing with a watershed rather than a river basin [Klingelhofer 1990].

These ideas are sketched here because it seems to me that Polden presents a parallel example, and displays some of those characteristics which may in the past have marked it out, if not as a cultural province in its own right, then at least as a recognisably distinct, partially 'bounded', and regionally significant territorial entity, probably by the Roman period at the latest. With the exceptions of the original foundation endowment of Glastonbury itself [Abrams 1996, 123-131], and the acquisition of Brent, which came to the Abbey as a distant estate at the end of the 7th century [Abrams 1996, 69-72], it is probably significant that among the very earliest grants to Glastonbury of which we are aware, from the early 8th century, is a group which seem to involve the transfer of rights over various blocks of precisely this 'core' area south-west of the abbey, so far as the considerable difficulties of the historical evidence allow us to identify the areas concerned [Abrams 1996, 204-211]; and the notion that the various *Pouelt* documents represent nothing more or less than the piecemeal acquisition of a recognised, pre-existing, ancient land unit, flows directly from the realisation that what was taking place was in fact the progressive alienation of royal demesne.

The exact extent of this putative Polden territory as it may have existed in the Roman period is highly problematic, although elsewhere, Wendy Davies would argue for a considerable degree of stability between the fourth and sixth-seventh centuries: of early medieval estates in south-east Wales as revealed by the Llandaff charters and other sources, she observes that "there must be a strong probability that some estates retained their

fourth-century shape, and that many of the others were the direct successors of fourth-century properties.....it is historically improbable that there was a total change in the units in which the property rights were held in the late fourth or fifth century.....we should expect, therefore that some estates had a continuous physical existence, though methods of working and intensity of exploitation might well have changed" [Davies 1979, 158]. A possible parallel example from the midlands is cited by Faith, who describes how "the 'core estates' of Evesham Abbey were 'originally a single estate granted to the abbey in the early 8th century, [and] may itself have been made up from a nucleus of one or more estates of Roman origin'" [quoted in Faith 1992, 26-27]. In any event, the settlement pattern already described can be set in the context of the natural topography, and later territorial arrangements, to produce a crude model of one possible arrangement of Roman estates on Polden. Despite the probable pre-English antiquity of its name [Ekwall 1960, 70], it would be rash to suggest that the present line of the River Brue was necessarily a recognised northern boundary. It is more likely that the area drained by its predecessor, dubbed the 'proto-Brue' by Rippon [Rippon 1997, 73, fig 18], was undemarcated internally and subject to some kind of intercommoning arrangement between settlements on the surrounding higher ground. Likewise on the southern flank, intercommoning for the settlements on the northern slope may have precluded the need for any formal boundary in Sedgemoor.

The distribution and nature of settlement may be indicative of a basic dichotomy, as between north and south, in the land-use pattern, if we envisage, as I think we can, a fundamental north-south alignment of estates calculated to give each one access to the maximum possible range of resources. It seems that the signal lack of a dense settlement pattern on the southern flank gives a strong indication that the proposed estates, centred on the northern settlements, would have extended from the putative Brue valley 'commons' all the way southwards to the fringes of Sedgemoor. Further, we can suggest that the northern part of the estates, roughly from the crest of the ridge northwards down to perhaps the 10m contour, was given over predominantly, although by no means exclusively, to cereal production, on those soils best suited to that purpose[17]. Northwards, the Brue Valley yielded the usual range of wetland resources, as well as being involved in the more specialist production of salt; as we have already intimated, the latter was probably run from the north Polden settlements, a suggestion supported by the survival of a trackway, which may well be Roman, running directly out to an extensive area of saltworks, and now forming at least the northern stretch of the parish boundary between Cossington and Chilton [Hollinrakes 1994a].

---

[17] Keil's analysis of land values from the Glastonbury Abbey medieval *compotus* rolls, together with a comparison between the physical disposition of open-field furlongs and modern soil maps, led him to conclude that "the abbey distinguished between the relative merits of the land for agriculture". Keil 1964, 82-83.

The model goes on to propose that the southern Polden slope was given over largely to pastoralism, the effective grazing area being extended out onto Sedgemoor during the drier summer months. The small, poor, lower status settlements suggested for the southern flank were part of, and would have acted as secondary pastoral outstations for, the main estates to the north.

Much is talked by modern historians about multiple estates in the early medieval period, and the idea of economic specialisation of the various component settlements within them [Faith 1997, 11-14 and refs there cited]. We simply do not yet know how, in terms of size, and the complexity of their social, settlement and tenurial organisation, the estate units proposed for Polden in the Roman period compared to the 'classic', theoretical multiple estate model of current literature. But there is no good reason why they should not have shared at least one characteristic in common, and that is in the possession of an integrated economy. The Polden model outlined here, for example, provides each linear estate with both pastoral and cultivation elements which, although physically separate and distinct, were nonetheless mutually dependent, combined in an essentially mixed economy, intended both to support the communities of the estate itself and to produce a surplus for 'export'. And the relatively small distances involved within this structure meant that the flocks and herds of the pastoralists could be easily taken north to be folded on the cultivators' land, thereby maintaining soil fertility.

How any arable regime on the northern slope would have operated in practice is difficult to say. Certainly, the fieldwalking results from Shapwick are beginning to bring into sharper focus a picture that was already emerging from the more sporadic, less systematic work of earlier years, namely that the settlement pattern was based on a framework of relatively evenly-spaced, individual, probably ring-fence farms sitting amidst their own fields [Gerrard and Gutierrez 1997, 50, and fig 6.24, 81].

Even within such a small compass as Shapwick however, the picture is really far more complex, for a three-tier settlement hierarchy is beginning to emerge with the identification of certainly one, and perhaps two hamlet or village-type settlements occupying a niche intermediate between the lone farmsteads and the high-status site [Gater and Gaffney 1993, 30-32; Aston and Gerrard 1999; Gerrard *pers comm*]. Again though, problems of dating at present preclude concrete statements about the contemporaneity or otherwise of these different forms.

The nature of Romano-British field arrangements at Shapwick is also problematic, although two models immediately suggest themselves. The first would involve a series of 'Celtic' type, enclosed fields, using a flexible and adaptable system of rotational cropping incorporating a fallow and perhaps even the use of nitrogen-fixing crops [Kosse 1963, 20-24]. Arable husbandry based on this kind of rotation has, for example, been suggested by Barker and Webley [1977, 198-200] for the large establishment at Gatcombe near Bristol, and included among the farming models proposed by Jones for the putative villa estate at Barton Court Farm, Oxfordshire [Jones 1986, 40-42]. Some form of infield-outfield arrangement might have been an alternative possibility. David Miles, citing work by Tom Williamson, has described how "in north-west Essex detailed field survey and the plotting of pottery scatters have generated a pattern of dispersed farmsteads close to the better quality soil surrounded by manured infield and less frequently ploughed outfield" [Miles 1989, 125]. On balance, environmental conditions may well have favoured the former, since with careful management to maintain fertility there seems no good reason why the north Polden soils should not have supported fairly intensive cropping [Dark 1997, 104-105].

How this problem could be resolved archaeologically is not yet clear. Environmental evidence can suggest which crops were grown, but not necessarily how. Detailed field survey, and the continuing programme of intensive fieldwalking, may yet, as in Essex, indicate the nature of field systems in operation at Shapwick in the Romano-British period; but it is possible also that at least part of the answer could lie in soil phosphate/heavy metal analysis around the sites of Romano-British farmsteads: marked differentiation in the results might suggest the existence of a boundary between an intensively cropped infield, and a far less intensively cultivated outfield. A relatively homogenous pattern, by contrast, could be a clue to the existence of a regime in which the cropping 'load' was much more evenly spread throughout. At present, however, while promising considerable potential, it seems that soil chemistry techniques are not yet sufficiently refined to be able to answer such specific questions [for the scientific basis of this approach, Aston *et al*, 1998a; for the historical and archaeological implications, idem, 1998b; both relate specifically to the results from Shapwick]. On our ability to identify, for example, infield/outfield boundaries, work in progress by Andrew Jackson in the North Somerset Levels leads him to doubt that "even with the best results.....any such demarcation will present a clear cut boundary". So also for nitrogen-fixing crops, on which he observes that "as to the historic time scale we are considering.....it is very unlikely" that soil chemistry will be able to reveal their use [Jackson, *pers comm*.]. [18]

The suggestion of the existence of dependent relationships between settlements, put forward for Chew hundred and proposed by Nancy Hollinrake for the area west of the Fosse Way in south-east Somerset, should at least be considered as a possible element in the overall pattern of Romano-British settlement on the Polden ridge. We have already noted some objections to this idea, to which we can add Dark's recent caveat [Dark 1997, 72-73]. In the final analysis, although differences in status can be recovered archaeologically, it will probably never be possible actually to prove the existence of dependent relationships between Romano-British settlement sites, and the best we can do is to suggest affinities on the basis of a balance of probabilities. At Shapwick for example, Gerrard has tentatively proposed that the Romano-British

---

[18] I am indebted to Andrew Jackson for his detailed guidance relating to the technique of soil chemistry analysis, its problems, and applications in archaeological contexts.

occupation known in Field 2736 was in fact part of a more extensive village-type roadside settlement dependent on the high-status site immediately to the south in Old Church field [Gerrard *pers comm*]. If the Old Church site was indeed a rural shrine complex, we can easily envisage, I think, a small, partly agricultural 'vicus' growing up nearby to service it. We must also remind ourselves that such arrangements would certainly have been highly fluid, and characterised by dynamism rather than stasis. Settlements (although not necessarily territories: below) would have been subject to often abrupt changes in their economic fortunes, so that formerly dominant places could lose out to settlements originally much lower in the hierarchy. Tenurial changes would have been another element, with formerly subservient and dependent farms or settlements gaining their independence and perhaps gradually assimilating their own estates.

A further complexity, giving rise to much debate, is the question of exactly how the application of Roman land law, inheritance customs of the period, the interests of the state, and the nature of Romano-British kin structure, would have affected the changing framework of rural settlement on the ground, the transmission of land through successive generations, and the progressive fragmentation or amalgamation of estates [Hingley 1991, 77-79; Dark 1997, 71-72; Smith 1997; Miles 1986, 50-51; Black 1987, 67-72; Faith 1997, 2-3 and notes 7, 8 and 9; de la Bedoyere 1999, 77-83]; and an important element of which, although one fraught with difficulties, is the whole question of the survival of Roman administrative and taxation structures into subsequent periods, whether in whole or part [de la Bedoyere 1999, 57-60; Faulkner 2000, 111-114]. This latter debate has been enlivened recently by Barnwell's suggestion that the ultimate origin of the hide lies in the Roman system of land division by centuriation. Barnwell further contends that, in the post-Roman period, "while there may have been a discontinuity in terms of settlement in many places, there was a broad continuity of territories and, perhaps, of some of the fundamental ways in which they were organised" [Barnwell 1996, 58]; a view which is relevant for the model of Roman estates on Polden proposed below.

In Whitley as a whole then, we have, as yet, little detailed idea about the chronology of rural settlement, its dynamic, its nature and function, apart from drawing crude and subjective distinctions between 'high-status', 'low-status', and possibly 'cult', or 'religious' sites. Still less, then, can we be expected to know anything concrete about relationships between settlements. Yet again, Shapwick is an honourable exception, and here at least it seems as though the fieldwalking and excavation data are beginning to resolve themselves to present an impression of Romano-British settlement that was either long-lived (1st-4th centuries) or late (2nd/3rd-4th centuries) [Gerrard and Gutierrez 1997, 50; Aston 1998, 240, fig 1; Aston and Gerrard 1999, Table 1, 18-19]. Of course, that such results may reflect more upon incomplete information rather than genuine discontinuity is a major caveat here.

However, even at this stage, the preliminary analysis of the full pottery assemblage from Shapwick has thrown up distinct and probably highly significant chronological trends: "the number of Roman sites [increases] to a peak density in the 3rd century. There are double the number of sites in the 3rd than there were in the 1st century.........gradually the lights go out on many of these sites, Shapwick Hotel and the villa are the first to go and don't go beyond the 3rd century. [There is] no pottery evidence for the rest beyond the early/mid-4th century". Perhaps most intriguingly of all, however, is that it is *precisely* those sites which emerge in the medieval record with archaeologically-indicative fieldnames (Blacklands, Chestell, Sladwick, Abchester) that are the longest lived [*pers comm* Chris Gerrard to M A Aston].

It is probable that within the Roman period, perhaps in the late 2nd/early 3rd century, there was a (?major) change in the settlement pattern, one possible model being the replacement of at least some of the smaller, low-status, isolated farms by the Nidons villa, amounting effectively to a form of nucleation, and perhaps even involving a degree of deliberate planning. The highly regular, ladder-like layout of the Romano-British settlement in Field 7078 at Shapwick may, indeed, be an example of exactly this development [Gater and Gaffney 1993, 30-32; Aston and Gerrard 1999, Table 1, 19]. A major discovery at Shapwick in 1999, again through geophysical survey, was an extensive occupation site immediately to the west of the present village at about 35m OD, roughly the same distance (about 1.5km) to the south of the Brue Valley marshland fringe as the Old Church complex. In this case, at the suggestion of Teresa Hall, the geophysics was specifically targeted on an indicative field name ('Chestell'), an approach spectacularly vindicated when it revealed a very large rectilinear enclosure surrounded by a mass of boundary 'features', some showing indications of regularity [Figures 6 and 7; Aston and Gerrard 1999, Fig 9, 17]. Although the nature of this intriguing site is as yet problematic, trial excavation confirmed at least a Roman date, the evidence including a child burial dating probably to the 4th century. However, it is almost certain that the site is actually multiperiod, the Roman phase perhaps representing a nucleated (planned?), hamlet-type settlement engaged in the exploitation of the arable and woodland resources of these upper slopes.

One possible context which may have implications for both these Shapwick sites has been proposed by Roger Leech: "it might be expected that villa owners, farming their land with a view to maximum profits, might reorganise the smaller tenant farms on.....an estate. Particularly where a Roman military road ran through the estate some movement and replanning of farms close to the road might be expected, with earlier settlements being abandoned and their replacements having regular layouts indicative of a deliberate planned decision" [Leech 1982, 225].

The evidence from Shapwick may, then, conform to that elsewhere, a recent survey of which by Michael Fulford has led him to observe that "the combination of successful settlements and the evidence for a minor reordering of the landscape setting of the failed sites seem to imply a reorganisation of estates, where successful

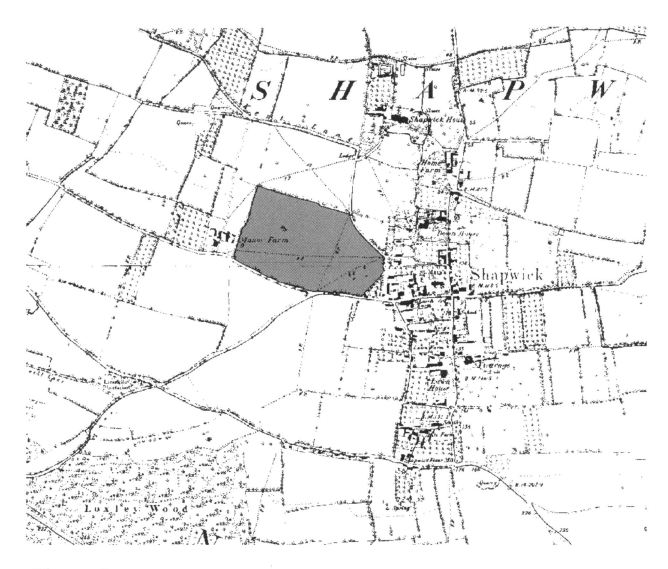

Figure 6

Extract from First Edition OS 6" map (1885), showing (shaded) the position of Chestells field at Shapwick, which produced the geophysical survey results shown in Figure 7.

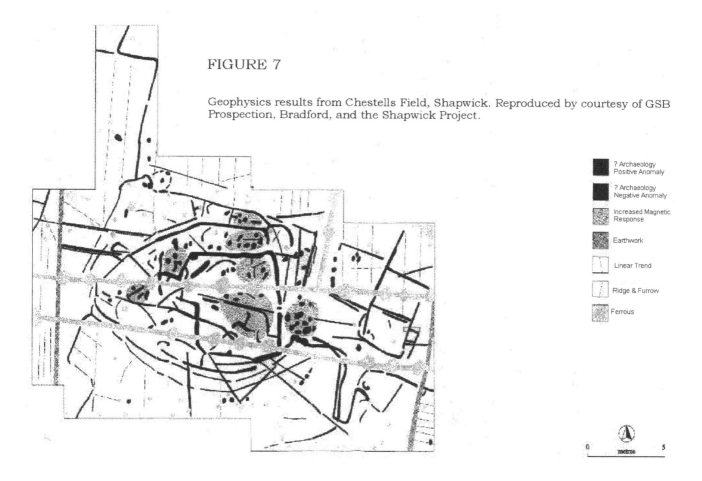

FIGURE 7

Geophysics results from Chestells Field, Shapwick. Reproduced by courtesy of GSB Prospection, Bradford, and the Shapwick Project.

farms perhaps absorbed the land of the deserted sites" [Fulford 1990, 28]. Neither may this trend have been unique to Shapwick among the Polden settlements, for the Hollinrakes' work at Edington Holy Well strongly suggests that the villa site there succeeded a sequence of short-lived "superimposed timber and stone structures.....[displaying] distinct changes in their orientations" [Hollinrakes 1994c, 38]. The phasing of a major ditch seems to date the villa building to the late 3rd/early 4th century, and it would be interesting to know whether, for both Edington and Shapwick, this period also signalled a change in the agricultural regimes which these villas operated. At Holy Well's possibly associated, lower status farmstead of Clover Close, occupation appears to have been continuous: the site "survived into and throughout the Roman administration of this part of Britain, despite any changes brought about in.........tenurial arrangements after the conquest". Although throughout its entire life its level of material culture seems always to have remained distinctly poor [Hollinrakes 1994e, 18].

Carhampton

The hundred of Carhampton stands in stark contrast to its two more northerly neighbours, since what evidence there is leads us irrevocably to the view that if its pattern of medieval settlement has inherited anything from an earlier period, then it has done so directly from late prehistoric

foundations. It is almost axiomatic of Somerset archaeology that the Roman interlude had little or no settlement impact west of the Parrett/Chard line. The most westerly villa known in the county is at Spaxton in Cannington hundred [Leach and Leech 1982, 65; Langdon 1992, 168-169]. A systematic trawl through the county SMR entries for each individual parish in the hundred produced only three stray finds of Roman coins (at Selworthy, Carhampton and Luxborough), a stray quern stone at Timberscombe, and evidence of Roman occupation at Bats Castle (Carhampton). In 1977, Leach knew of no Romano-British settlement sites in Carhampton, although more recently a possible Roman fort has been identified from aerial photographs immediately south-east of the tor at Dunster [Gathercole 1996, 5-6]. This is not the whole picture, however: recent discoveries of an arc of Roman military sites around the southern fringe of Exmoor (ie outside the hundred) have prompted the suggestion of imperial involvement, or at least interest in, the iron ore mining which is now suspected to have been taking place from the previous period [Wilson North and Riley 2001, 76-81]. No evidence of rural settlement of a characteristically Romano-British type has yet been identified in this area, as distinct from the widespread evidence of Iron Age occupation sites, mainly in the form of hill-slope enclosures, at least some of which would certainly have persisted into the Roman period. Dating, however, is highly problematic, and these sites are viewed as being "the single most important area for further research on Exmoor" [Wilson-North and Riley 2001, 55-75, at 70]. In any event, the clear inference must be that at least the nature of *settlement* here was unaffected by developments in the more Romanised lowlands east of the Parrett/Chard line. For we must be clear about our terms of reference here: what we can say with some confidence, at the present state of knowledge, is that in Carhampton there is a singular absence of those attributes of *material* culture that we normally use to identify and define communities with characteristically Romano-British affinities. However, this is palpably *not* the same as saying that the Roman period had effectively no landscape implications, and the question of whether or not land-use also remained unchanged is entirely another matter.

The Prehistoric and its Environmental Context

Like the Brue Valley fringes and the Chew Park villa, what Carhampton *can* show is a comprehensive body of environmental evidence, which allows us to assign some degree of time-depth to landscape change in the interval straddling the late prehistoric and Roman periods.

West of a line between Chard and the mouth of the Parrett, evidence for pre-medieval settlement, once considered sparse at best, is steadily increasing; and recent pollen evidence from Hoar Moor in Exford parish has been crucial in demonstrating that arable activity on Exmoor had begun at the latest by the early Bronze Age, locally intermittent with pastoral interludes but generally increasing in intensity throughout that period and into the Iron Age and early Romano-British phases [Francis and Slater 1990, 18; Straker and Crabtree 1995]. Likewise does the palynolgy indicate that The Chains "was predominantly open by the mid Bronze Age" [Dark 2000, 50-51]. Large areas of co-axial field systems with associated settlement sites have been identified south of Dunkery Beacon [SMR 33531; Francis and Slater 1990, 19]. As Preece observes, "it seems that a similar episode of large-scale land allotment to that seen on Dartmoor also occurred.....on Exmoor, though perhaps based on the individual farmstead.....[and] settlement seems to have continued through Roman times and probably beyond" [Preece 1993, 131-132].

For the earlier part of the period between about the mid third and the very early seventh centuries AD, "the pollen profile.....suggests continuance and probable intensification of clearance and agricultural activities", while by contrast, "toward the end of the zone.....there is every indication of a shift away from arable land use" [Francis and Slater 1990, 20]. This last trend the authors attribute partly to economic and political dislocation following the collapse of the Roman province, the resulting disappearance of markets within Britain and the blocking of access to those abroad; and partly to the constraints on cereal production imposed by a rising water table and consequent soil acidification and peat formation [*ibid*, 21].

Significantly however, as Petra Dark emphasises, while much of the pollen evidence from Exmoor seems to indicate a general contraction of arable cultivation in the post-Roman period, as on Hoar Moor, it was by no means ubiquitous. On The Chains for example, "some cereal pollen occurred throughout the Dark Age deposits.........suggesting that the area was not totally abandoned" [Dark 2000, 143]. This may well provide the environmental context for the survival of a tenacious thread of settlement forming at least the skeletal structure of the pattern of dispersal that emerges into our sight in the medieval period.

The Iron Age provides somewhat better evidence in Carhampton both for major centres, in the form of hillforts, which may or may not have been permanently occupied, and other earthwork sites, generally undefended, sub-circular and less than 1 hectare in size, which are likely to have been domestic settlements [Burrow 1982, 84-86; Wilson-North and Riley 2001, 56-64]. The most important of the hillforts are Bats Castle (about 1 hectare, and the only one of the Carhampton sites in Burrow's Group I), just over 2km west of Carhampton, and Gallox Hill or Black Ball Camp (0.3 hectare), 600m away to the north-west [Adkins 1992, 23-24 and 26]. It is likely that these sites are associated and together form a key Iron Age central-place 'complex' in the landscape. The precise nature of any putative territory associated with such features is problematic, and some archaeologists, arguing that closely-defined hillfort 'estates' may in fact be more apparent than real, warn against the too-ready assumption of their existence [Haselgrove 1986, 10]. Certainly, the Thiessen polygon which Burrow draws around Bats Castle bears little resemblance to either the hundred or the parish of Carhampton [Burrow 1979, fig 5, 36], although the analogy may not be entirely valid, for two reasons: the medieval parish may not be reflecting accurately the original (ie late Saxon) extent of the Carhampton estate, possibly having undergone some fragmentation since that time; and secondly, the use of Thiessen polygons would not now be regarded as acceptable, being too crude and taking no account of terrain and little account of the varying sizes and relative contemporaneity of hillforts. More sophisticated analytical tools are now being used for this purpose [Grant 1986].

Nonetheless, the idea of some kind of continuity of central-place function between the prehistoric and medieval periods, as I am suggesting here for Bats Castle/Black Ball and Carhampton, is both a tenacious and an attractive one; and elsewhere in Somerset, the apparent relationship between similar groups of sites has been remarked upon [Aston 1986, 53].

Burrow himself [1982] includes Bats Castle in his list of hillforts "re-used [in the post-Roman period] or in continuous occupation since the Iron Age" [95 and 96], and tentatively suggests a connection between that site as a power-centre of continuing importance in the post-Roman period, and the close proximity of the putative 'early' Christian foundation, associated with the Welsh saint Carantoc, at Carhampton itself [Burrow 1981, 58-59, and 60]. Indeed, the tenacity of far lower status Iron Age sites is well known, such as that at Bagley, which continued long enough, whether or not in continuous occupation, to appear as a manor identified by name in 1086 [Aston 1983,

83 and 94], and nearby Sweetworthy, which was certainly the site of at least one medieval farmstead and which the place-name suggests must have originated before the Norman Conquest [Aston 1988, 70; Wilson-North and Riley 1996]. Within the hundred, at least two examples are known of medieval farmsteads "actually situated within.....a [prehistoric] ringwork", namely at Spangate in Wootton Courtenay, and Twitchen in Oare [Aston 1989, 24-25]. Although the relationship is not so clear cut, another case in point may be the very recently discovered late prehistoric hilltop enclosure on Ley Hill, Horner Wood, Luccombe parish, and the deserted medieval settlement of Lower Wells, just under a kilometre away to the north [Veryan Heal, *pers comm*, and 1995, 173 and 179; Wilson-North and Riley 1997]. Such discoveries may point the way to future research into possible later occupation in, or close to, prehistoric enclosures *not* yet known to be associated with medieval settlement. The Ley Hill site, for example, is paralleled by the identification in 1992 of another previously unrecorded (and again, probably Iron Age) rectilinear enclosure, about a hectare in extent, within Timberscombe Wood [Heal 1999, 35]. One could also quote, among others, examples at Harwood Brakes, in Timberscombe [SMR 34132], and within Long Wood in Carhampton [SMR 33446] [Wilson-North and Riley 2001, Appendix 1: Site Gazetteer, 180-181]. Further instances from Devon suggest that more such sites might reasonably be expected from west Somerset; perhaps the most notable has been the identification of a medieval longhouse, dating from the 12th century at the earliest, sitting inside a previously unrecorded circular Iron Age enclosure in the precinct of Buckland Abbey [Gaskell-Brown 1995]. The implication of continuity, or at least, of the re-use of older sites, is something to which we will return later on in discussing medieval settlement.

Conclusion

The work of attempting to draw some kind of overall meaning, in spatial terms, from this general survey earns its best rewards when directed towards the main study area of Whitley hundred, and specifically to the Polden ridge. For reasons we have briefly explored, Carhampton, as in so many other respects, stands in striking contrast to the other two hundreds, and the affinities of its pre-medieval human landscape make it rightly the province of the prehistorian rather than the Romanist. However, it is crucial to note that in this context, Carhampton's contribution may in one respect prove to be far more significant than either of the other two hundreds. For while the resolution of broad patterns and chronological relationships must await better field data, at the level of the individual *site*, there appears in Carhampton to be exciting potential for investigating archaeologically the question of unbroken continuity (or otherwise) of occupation, and possibly land-use, from the pre-Roman Iron Age into the early medieval period.

For Chew, we can suggest patterns of distribution related to natural topography, available resources and toponymy; and in view of the likely existence in the early medieval period of a river territory based on the Chew valley, with Chew Magna at its centre (Chapter Four), further, more detailed work might enable us to point to pre-English origins for at least certain elements in the overall structure of pre-Conquest territorial arrangements. Chew also reveals indications of sometimes quite distant economic relationships and a distinct settlement hierarchy in the Roman period. It is certainly probable, given the high arable quality of the surrounding farmland, that any villa at Chew Magna would have lain at the centre of an agrarian estate; and indeed we suggested that the Chew Park complex operated as a major grain-processing outstation *within* that putative unit. But there does not seem to be, within Chew hundred, the same overall regularity of distribution in the Roman settlement pattern that one discerns on Polden. And while we must be constantly mindful of the constraints of incomplete information, I would argue that, at least in part because of the more broken, less 'regular' character of the natural topography, it is therefore less easy within Chew to propose territorial divisions encompassing a range of resources to which we might assign the term 'estate'. It seems clear, in fact, that the *nature* of settlement in Chew was different to that on Polden, with a lower density of generally lower-status sites. We can cite, as material considerations here, the advantages bestowed by Polden's more 'versatile' and resilient fen-edge economy, and its position astride a major communications artery giving access both eastwards, inland, and westwards to the Severn Estuary. There may well also have been major dissimilarities in the ownership and tenurial circumstances obtaining in the two areas, matters which are nigh on completely unrecoverable to us now.

To suggest that inter-settlement relationships on Romano-British Polden can actually be demonstrated would certainly be placing an unsustainable burden on the available evidence. What we can say, however, is that archaeology very strongly favours the existence of a marked settlement hierarchy [Aston and Gerrard 1999, 20], and that it is probable that some settlements of palpably different status were closely linked. Indeed, the evidence for this here is actually far better than that for Chew Magna/Chew Park, where the argument was largely speculative.

We have already touched upon the idea of a regular division of the Polden ridge into a series of estates in the Romano-British period. The suggestion is based on a model which sees the settlement structure developing within the context of well-defined agrarian units, each of them focussed on a centre of demonstrably superior status, and by which the Polden ridge proper came to be divided into a series of linear, north-south territories, each one extending from the valley of the proto-Brue in the north to Sedgemoor in the south. The major problem with this model is that it lacks both chronological precision and time depth − it is static, not dynamic, and makes the major assumption that at least the estate centres were in simultaneous operation and occupation. There is no solution to this at present, for apart from Shapwick and those sites investigated as part of the Polden pipeline campaign, the archaeological picture is not yet detailed enough to allow close dating across as wide an area as we would wish. And even at Shapwick, the totally unexpected appearance of the Nidons villa, and the striking confirmation of the suspected site west of the village, are sobering reminders that our *perceptions* of the settlement pattern are likely to bear only a nodding acquaintance with reality. On balance, however, we would probably not be too wide of the mark to suggest a date around the late 3rd/early 4th century for the outline depicted on Figure 4, at least as far as the Polden Ridge is concerned (for a summary of the Shapwick dates see Aston and Gerrard 1999, Table 1, 18-19).

Aston and Gerrard have proposed recently that "by the end of the fourth century, villagers in small nucleated agricultural settlements with highly regular linear plans......provided customary service to the owners of 'villas' on a series of estates along the northern flank of the Poldens" [Aston and Gerrard 1999, 20]. If we are intended to infer from this that the putative estates probably did not extend *south* of the main Roman road along the ridge top, I would take a different view. I suggest that we can identify four estates, based on topography and on the locations of the high-status Romano-British sites (probably villas) known or suspected to date. These are shown on Figure 8. The model is proposed partly on the basis of topography: each estate is made roughly the same size, and to each is apportioned a roughly equal share of available resources, especially of the high-quality ploughland on the northern slope. As we have already noted, the wetlands north and south of the ridge may have been regarded for the most part as intercommonable, as they certainly were later on. Charlie Hollinrake observes [*pers comm*], that between Ashcott, Walton, Street and Butleigh, boundaries are formed from natural stream courses, but that "it is the western Polden group that has less obvious natural boundaries".

It has recently been suggested that *within* the area which later included Shapwick, a series of minor north-south streams, had, by the Bronze Age if not earlier, "major significance in mapping out social and cultural differences. They were important reference points in the landscape and doubtless could be named and identified, perhaps even invested with mythological associations" [Aston and Gerrard 1999, 11-14]. However, west of Shapwick, in the absence of any significant features of natural topography, aligned north-south, which could have been pressed into service as boundary lines, a significant reliance has been placed on later administrative arrangements when considering the structure of the model. We must concede the potential pitfalls of this kind of highly subjective, retrospective extrapolation, and the brief critique that was applied in the discussion on Chew Magna carries equal force here. To those voices choosing to emphasise the difficulties we should also add that of Della Hooke, whose view, based on an apparent lack of really firm evidence, is that "not one villa-estate has yet been successfully identified.....[and] there are indeed persuasive arguments for rejecting the hypothesis that the boundaries of minor estate units can be traced back into Roman times" [Hooke 1998, 63 and 65]. This seems to me both overly

pessimistic and an unwarranted generalisation, since the amount, nature and quality of the evidence will vary greatly and it would be more helpful to treat each individual case on its own merits. Neither does this take any account of new developments currently taking place in techniques of historic landscape analysis, particularly GIS, which may help to cast completely new light on precisely those kinds of spatial relationships that could reveal the existence of Roman villa estates; so that perhaps even despite ourselves, modern historic landscape methodologies may be carrying us almost inevitably towards their recovery *on the ground*. On the peripheries of Salisbury Plain, for example, Mark Corney and his co-workers have revealed "a considerable number of villa-based 'estate centres' along the Avon Valley, Wylye Valley and the Vale of Pewsey, occupying the same general locations as the medieval and modern villages.........comparison of the villas and their associated settlements [on the high Plain] when overlain onto a map of the post-Roman parishes and estates shows a close correlation" [Corney 2000, 35]. And most excitingly, in north Kent, the Swale Archaeological Survey has recently identified systematic early Roman land division on a massive scale, with a series of (probably contemporary) villas "arranged with a near-mathematical regularity" forming the centres of land-blocks of about 2,500 acres each, and 'cast off' either side of the Watling Street [Denison 2000, 7]. Linear bank and ditch systems almost certainly representing the contemporary boundaries of these estates, later followed by both parish and lathe boundaries, have also been located [*pers comm* Dr Paul Wilkinson; and Wilkinson 2000].

It is of course impossible to say, at the present state of knowledge, whether the boundaries later delimiting the various ancient parishes have any relevance, in part or in whole, to the administrative geography of the Romano-British period. However, failing any other known territorial framework, it seems to me that the parish bounds provide as good a topographical basis as any for conjecture, and among other, more theoretical criteria, they were certainly regarded as admissible evidence by Martin Jones in his suggested reconstruction of the Barton Court Farm villa estate [Jones 1986, 40]. More locally, of the palatial villa at Durley near Keynsham in north Somerset, and its associated nucleated settlement, Lee Prosser considers it probable that at least some "modern parish boundaries may preserve a semblance of the shape and form of the later Roman estate" [Prosser 1995, 50]. Again, the Swale Survey has now given this conjecture a firm basis in reality. On Polden, the Chilton/Edington/Catcott block, for example, with the villa site lying virtually at the centre, probably comes closest to the theoretical ideal, although the Shapwick/Ashcott unit also displays a high degree of regularity. The boundary between these two blocks is that which now divides Shapwick and Catcott, and of which Aston and Gerrard have remarked [1999, 14] that "the northern stretch..............defined by Mill Brook, may still follow a prehistoric division in the landscape". If the Marshall's Elm villa in Street did indeed lie close to an estate boundary, as suggested by the model, this would

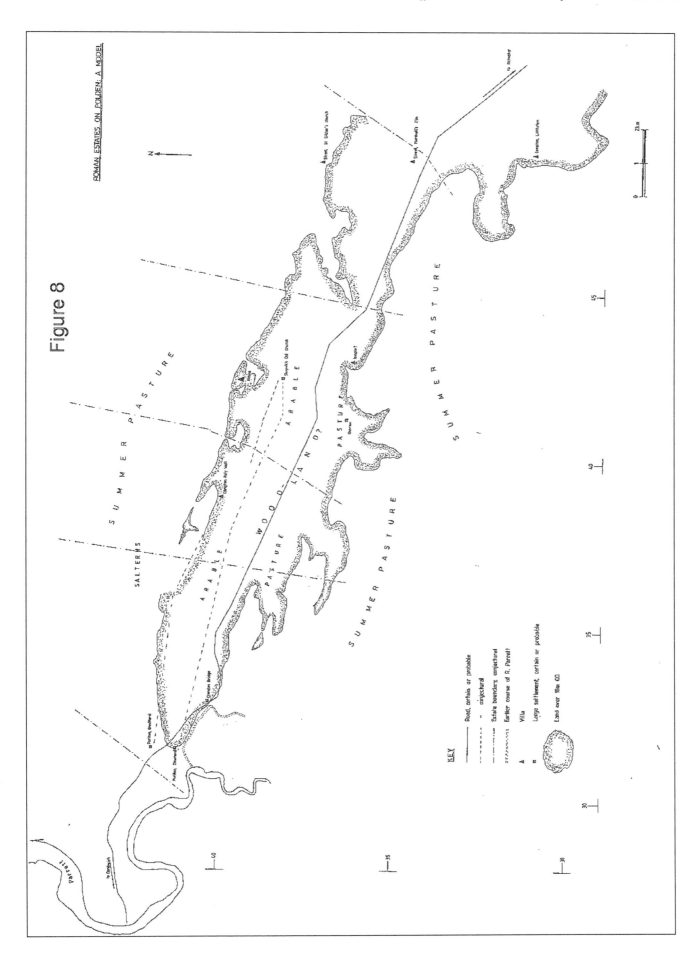

Figure 8

ROMAN ESTATES ON POLDEN: A MODEL

KEY

——— Road, certain or probable
—·— conjectural
—··— Estate boundary, conjectural
·········· Earlier course of R. Parrett
▲ Villa
◼ Large settlement, certain or probable
Land over 10m OD

tend to support the idea that, whatever its role, it was largely non-agricultural - the estate centre in that respect being revealed as the St Gildas villa to the north.

The lack of any known high-status building in the Puriton/Woolavington/Cossington unit, the westernmost of the putative estates proposed here, indicates that such a site yet awaits discovery, probably roughly in the centre of this area. In the absence of GIS modelling, at least parish bounds probably have some basis in economic realities, and are here preferred to the use of Thiessen polygons, a technique presenting its own difficulties, recently characterised by Harvey [1996, 34; and *cf* Grant 1986; Gerrard 1987, 117; Jones 1986, 38]. The later evidence of parish relationships has also been taken as one element in the affinities reconstructed here: so that, for example, the model depicts an estate based roughly on Street/Walton, and another on Shapwick/Ashcott. The former we can argue for topographically, since it would have been the most easterly of the suggested estates enjoying access to the wetlands both north and south, the natural topography changing abruptly further eastwards and the Polden ridge proper becoming lost in the much more broken terrain around Butleigh. There may also be tenuous indications on Polden (Chapter Six) that certain stretches of parish boundary were established while some Roman settlements still existed, if not as working farms, then at least as features in the sub/post-Roman landscape significant enough to take into consideration in the laying out, or re-use, of boundaries.

Chapter Three

Obscuritas or *Lucerna*?: Roman Echoes in a 'Dark Age' Landscape

Introduction

The subject of this chapter confronts us with a whole series of difficulties that over the past decade or so have moved centre stage to become the focus of intense debate among archaeologists, historians and toponymists. By its very nature, it is certainly the least satisfactory of the separate chronological sections of this study, from the point of view of the evidential basis of the discussion; but it is an unavoidable irony that a period which marks such a crucial and dynamic phase in the development of society, landscape, religion, institutions and territorial arrangements in lowland Britain, is in so many respects simply transparent to us. What follows, therefore, is necessarily a survey drawn on a very broad canvas.[1].

We will look again at specific questions as we deal with the individual hundreds in turn. Evidence for this period from Carhampton hundred is perhaps even more tenuous than that from Chew and Whitley, although what there is, chiefly from the village of Carhampton itself, is highly intriguing. However, in view of the very particular character of these recent discoveries, which may suggest the existence there of a pre-English 'monastic' site associated with a planned (and possibly urban) settlement, and also because their dating as yet remains somewhat fluid, it seems best to discuss their implications under a more appropriate, thematic heading. This we will do in the next chapter, which deals with Ecclesiastical Relationships.

Archaeologists and historians dealing with this period find themselves besieged by conceptual and methodological problems, and these have recently been the subject of a wide-ranging study by Ken Dark [2000]. However, it is probably true to say that at their core lies our fundamental inability to identify and characterise, from its material remains, the society which, from the early 5th century down to at least the early 7th in our area, replaced that which had been based on the all-powerful Roman economic machine [Rahtz 1982, 1987 and 1991]. Prosser has surveyed the main points in this debate both in general terms, and as they may apply specifically to the area of the Keynsham hundred in north Somerset [Prosser 1995, 50]; and the Somerset evidence as a whole is summarised by Webster [2000]. But it is certainly the case that by far the greater part of what we *think* we know about this period comes from burial evidence and high-status occupation

sites. The increasing number of 'Dark Age' cemeteries which are coming to light in Somerset, a high proportion with coastal or near-coastal locations, coupled with intensive work on high-status settlements such as South Cadbury, Cannington, Glastonbury and Cadbury-Congresbury, is crucial in this respect, although at present "only Cannington exhibits clear indications of continuity of use from [the 4th century]" [Rahtz, *pers comm*; Snyder 1997, 11-13, 16-17, and 21-23 for references to these four sites, including cemeteries; the full report on Cannington, too late to be included by Snyder, is in Rahtz *et al* 2000. See also Rahtz 1982a, 102-103; Rahtz 1987, 77. For Lamyatt Beacon, Leech 1986; for Henley Wood, Watts and Leach 1996. For Carhampton, Hollinrakes 1993, 1994, 1995 and McCrone 1993, 1994, 247, and 1995. For Bradley Hill, Leech 1981; for Portishead, Rogers and Ponsford 1979. The small but important cemetery at Wembdon Hill, SMR 12470, remains unpublished apart from a series of interim notes: Langdon 1986, 151; Croft and Woods 1987, 215; Croft 1988, 221; Hollinrake C and N 1989, 171, and Woods 1990, 222. I am grateful to Chris Webster for these latter references. Further references to some of these sites, and to another one at Langford Budville, are given by O'Brien, who provides the most up to date review and gazetteer of post-Roman and Anglo-Saxon cemeteries in Britain [O'Brien 1999, see esp 30-44].

However, the task of tying the cemetery communities to specific settlements, or even of identifying exactly who these people were and what their changing social, political and economic affinities may have been through time, has highlighted the severe limitations of our knowledge outside the highly localised, elite centres [Rahtz 1982, 101; Dark 1994]. Indeed, Philip Rahtz has remarked that "we are largely ignorant about the exact processes of land ownership and management for the whole of the post-Roman centuries until the late Anglo-Saxon period" [Rahtz 1987, 77]. It is precisely these shortcomings, among other objectives, that the South Cadbury Environs Project is designed to address as part of a total landscape survey across all periods [Leach and Tabor 1996; Leach 2000]. What happened to the indigenous people in the countryside between, say, 400 and 900 AD is a question whose apparent simplicity belies the methodological problems which at present preclude clear answers. Powlesland, for example, complains that, even with Migration Period settlements in eastern England, "we seem to be without any clear model which covers the transition from Roman to Saxon at the overall population level; the concept of a largely-depopulated post-Roman landscape taken over by an overwhelming immigrant population seems unsupportable" [Powlesland 1997, 103].

It seems fair to say that we cannot, then, as yet, people our 5th, 6th and 7th century rural landscapes with 'ordinary' peasant farmers, and observe them changing it,

---

[1] The problem of the identification and characterisation of post-Roman cultures is one of the most intractable currently facing scholars working in this field. There is an already large, and rapidly growing body of literature attempting to confront this question, from a variety of different perspectives. Current views, with extensive bibliography, are usefully surveyed in Rippon 2000, to which we can add Aston and Martin 1998a, b and c; and Ward-Perkins 2000. Other key references are cited in the main text of this Introduction.

and it shaping them [Reynolds 1999, 38-41]. Cleary suggests that "given the high suggested population levels for late Roman Britain and the evidence for the landscape remaining open and worked in the fifth century, what we are facing is surely a population that archaeologists find difficult to locate, rather than a population that was not there in the first place" [Cleary 1995, 19]. A clear consensus is emerging that the problem is far more one of methodology rather than of actual absence, and Philip Rahtz expresses optimism about the future: "the settlements will be found (or recognised) when all the sites with [4th century] material have been re-interpreted or dug more precisely" [*pers comm*]. Powlesland seems tacitly to agree with this, noting of Yorkshire that although "by the early 6th century Anglian communities were well-established in the region............there is little evidence to allow us to interpret the transition from Late Roman to early Anglo-Saxon. There is little archaeological evidence for the native British population during the 5th century, reflecting an almost complete lack of research into Roman rural sites in the region such that we are unable to establish clearly the context of the emerging Anglian communities" [Powlesland 1998, 2.3.1.1.].

Certainly in Somerset, the view has been expressed that, shielded as they were from the early phases of the English migration, 'indigenous' sub-Roman communities proved themselves highly tenacious, and there simply *were* no English-speaking peasant farmers tilling the land until well into the late Anglo-Saxon period. The eventual ubiquity of English place- and field names, it is suggested, arises from the *social* dominance of a very small number of high-status Anglo-Saxon landholders, *not* a numerical superiority of English-speaking peasants [*pers comm* Michael Costen]. Views such as this are gaining increasing credibility, in part as a result of very recent studies combining the evidence of linguistics and genetics, and tellingly summarised by Martin Evison. He observes that "becoming 'English' may have been a conscious choice for many native communities; a limited one perhaps, but one where adopting the linguistic and cultural trappings was a stepping-stone to benefiting from and influencing new economic and political activity, and an alternative to prolonged conflict or attrition...............the British survived, essentially, by becoming English...............biological kinship was not a requirement for being 'English'" [Evison 1997, 9]. Reassessment of the purely *archaeological* evidence is beginning to bear similar fruit; and an extensive study of early Anglo-Saxon cemeteries involving both grave goods and the palaeopathology of the burials themselves, leads Heinrich Härke to conclude that "about half the men............were of native British rather than immigrant German origin, with further Britons living in separate enclaves............there must have been a substantial immigration by Continental Germani into post-Roman Britain (as suggested by the traditional, migrationist model), *but*............there was also a substantial survival of the native population (as advocated by more recent, revisionist writers)" [Härke 1998, 19, and refs there cited;

see also Härke 1995; James 1999, 109-113, esp at 112; and Snyder 1998, 225-252].

A major part of our difficulty with this period lies in the sudden removal, from the early 5th century, of the economic base under-pinning and shaping the character of the *material* culture. The economy of Britain in this period, and its response to the massive disruption to which it was subjected, have recently been reviewed by Dark [1996]. However, Michael Jones, in a radical departure from received orthodoxy, has recently suggested that the final collapse of the province owed as much, if not more, to internal insurrection by an essentially un-romanised majority of the lower social order, as to the economic reasons normally at the centre of this debate. Jones maintains that "concentration on archaeological evidence, the economy, and the wider imperial context does not explain satisfactorily why the ending of Roman rule and culture in Britain was so early, so rapid, so complete - and so unlike the experience of the rest of the western empire" [Jones 1996, 8]. More recently, Faulkner has adduced arguments along similar lines, maintaining that British *romanitas* was inherently unstable, a thin veneer won at the expense of an over-taxed and exploited peasantry, and that with its collapse "the mass of British people could.........enjoy a short golden age free from landlords and tax-collectors" [Faulkner 2000].

However much one may agree with this, Jones's argument about a society trying strenuously to throw off every last vestige of the taint of Rome seems perhaps less credible when considered in the light of the latest evidence from, among other places, sub-Roman Wroxeter [Barker and White 1998; and *cf* Wacher 1995, 408-421]. However, what we are concerned with here are the overall effects on settlement and territorial arrangements, and on our ability to perceive, or not, the dynamics of landscape change, and the social, economic and political forces which were its main imperatives. No matter what the ultimate cause(s), the economic effects are not disputed. And no matter how little or how much, in the west at least, the inhabitants may have continued to think of themselves as 'Roman', however much they tried to conceptualise and to cocoon themselves in a built environment that was as Roman as resources and techniques would allow, nonetheless the imported material paraphernalia of *romanitas* could by definition be acquired, exist and be replaced only within the stable economic framework of the wider empire. Once this was removed, the effects on two of our central archaeological indicators, coinage and pottery series, were almost immediate: both rapidly cease [Cleary 1989, 131-161]; "by the mid to later fifth century in the British areas, archaeology almost entirely fails us" [Cleary 1995, 18]. The same writer has evocatively summarised the situation in the first half of the 5th century: "the generality of the archaeological evidence points to a sudden and total collapse of the romanised way of life.....the villas, the industries and the other material evidence diagnostic of Roman Britain disappeared. There was no slow drawing-down of blinds: the end was nasty, brutish and short" [Cleary 1989, 161; and *cf* Evans 1990].

But herein lies the central, and frustrating paradox of this period; for Cleary himself, citing literary and epigraphic evidence, goes on to make the point that "despite the material poverty there was a rich social and cultural formation" in the sub-Roman west [ibid, 187; and cf Dixon 1984, 21-25]. Dark has more recently echoed this sentiment: "Fifth- and sixth-century British society and culture retained far more of the Late Roman past than has usually been supposed, and did so within a political framework inherited from the fourth century" [Dark 2000, 57]. This is a view which gains support from a detailed linguistic and literary survey of the epigraphic evidence, and which leads David Howlett to infer the existence of a class of Britons who could readily understand spoken Latin and construe written Latin in the centuries after the departure of Roman civilian and military administrators" [Howlett 1998, 11]. Is this the social class represented so strikingly in the Lamyatt Beacon cemetery? (below).

That there was marked regional variation in terms of Anglo-Saxon settlement has long been clear, with the country dividing roughly between the early-settled east, and the late-conquered west. Of the former, Powlesland emphasises the fact that "by the end of the fifth century the material culture of a large part of former Roman Britain had effectively been completely displaced by the distinctive mix that is early Anglo-Saxon in character" [Powlesland 1997, 103; and cf Dark 2000, 58-104].

In the west, the material trappings of *romanitas*, although becoming progressively debased, display much greater tenacity, and scholars working in this field are now far more inclined to characterise the period as one of change and transmutation rather than collapse and chaos [cf Prosser 1995, 50; Dark 2000, 105-149]. Again though, and as with the settlements, Rahtz tends to the view that our difficulties here are methodological and conceptual: "there is no shortage of [5th-6th century] material culture - the problem is that it is still Late Roman. The [material culture] of Late Roman Britain goes on as residual material - or close copy.....[and] the cessation of coinage does not coincide with the end of [material culture]" [Rahtz, *pers comm*].

Chew Hundred

As we have seen in Chapter Two, we are fortunate, in Chew Hundred, to have a range of Roman sites to which, as a result of the Chew Valley Lake campaign of excavations in the early 50s, and the separate work at Pagan's Hill, we can assign chronological depth, and also make informed guesses about their nature, and the kinds of activities carried on there [Rahtz and Greenfield 1977; Rahtz and Watts 1989]. The other side of this coin is that despite this abundance of data, the post-Roman period offers a striking example of precisely those difficulties which we have already briefly reviewed: "extensive excavations in *c* 500 ha of the Chew Valley Lake area failed to find any evidence of occupation there between the fourth and eleventh centuries" [Rahtz and Watts 1989, 337].

A remark such as this serves only to emphasise the striking contrast between the relatively sudden demise of these places as settlement sites, that is (presumably), where people had actually once lived, and the situation at the ritual site of Pagan's Hill temple. Extensive archaeological work at the latter has revealed intermittent activity at the site from the Neolithic at least into the 7th century AD [Rahtz 1987, 74-75]. The nature of that activity is problematic. The archaeological evidence, shows clearly that the temple, built probably in the decades either side of AD 300, retained its roof into the 13th century [Rahtz and Watts 1989, 330, 333]. From this it was inferred that "not only was some use made of the temple at this time, but also.....the building was substantially intact, with at least some roofing in position" [Rahtz and Watts 1989, 333]. Rahtz and Watts have discussed at length the possible implications of the temple's survival, and whether there is anything that provides unequivocal evidence of a Christian presence there in the post-Roman period [Rahtz and Watts 1989, 360-366]. The conclusion is that there is not, although it is certainly possible quite plausibly to interpret much of the archaeology in that light.

Rahtz had earlier talked about the temple's "*survival* (my italics) to at least the 13th century.........." [Rahtz 1987, 75]. Indeed, even by the early 19th century, enough rubble, roof slates, stone footings and other general debris survived on the site to make stone robbing worthwhile, an activity witnessed by the Revd Skinner [Rahtz and Watts 1989, 333; Rahtz, *pers comm*]. The implication is that the building had simply stood uncared for in the landscape for the whole of that time. Although, as Rahtz [*pers comm*] points out, foundations as massive as those at Pagan's Hill will tend to persist, it is difficult to see how even a well-built structure could last that long without at least intermittent intervention by human agency. This would be particularly true in the case of the roof: once damaged or removed, the rest of the building above ground level, no matter how massive its foundations, would quickly decay.[2]

An alternative approach would be to suggest that for a continuous period of nigh on a thousand years (over 30 generations, in historical terms), from the late 3rd or early 4th century AD to the 13th, the Pagan's Hill temple, although not necessarily the rest of its associated complex, had been subjected to some degree of regular and systematic maintenance, with all that implies for organisation in terms of resources and manpower; although of the eastern range, Rahtz and Watts comment that even it "continued in use at least into the earlier fifth century and possibly much later" [Rahtz and Watts 1989, 333]. By whom, and for what reasons, this putative maintenance was carried out, it is not yet possible to say, but such tenacity among Roman rural temples in Britain is not entirely without precedent. The remarkable beehive temple known as Arthur's O'on, at Carron near Falkirk, was even longer-lived than Pagan's Hill, having been built probably

---

[2] *cf* Morris's striking account of the rapid degeneration of church fabrics as the result of a lack of maintenance in general, but on the roof in particular; Morris 1986, 316-320.

by the Roman army around the mid 2nd century, and surviving intact until its deliberate demolition in 1743 [de la Bedoyere 1991, 204-205; *pers comm* Miles Russell; and *cf* Blagg 1986]. I must concede that both the inherently-stable design and the robust, high-quality construction of Arthur's O'on, entirely in stone, made its survival more likely in the absence of human intervention. Nonetheless, if this proposal for Pagan's Hill is correct, it offers up the intriguing possibility that the temple was important to successive communities, an importance which clearly transcended perhaps rapidly changing patterns of ethnicity, land-ownership, settlement, agrarian practice and 'religious' ritual and belief. The overriding significance can probably be attributed to a persistent thread of supernatural associations, for the clear psychological appeal of ancient sites as centres of unworldly forces is a recurring theme in landscape history, with communities in successive periods constantly reinventing the particular imperatives which informed their reverence for and fascination with monuments of older times. What seems to have been important is the simple *belief* that a given site, for whatever reason(s), had supernatural or religious/ritual associations, marking the perpetuation of a collective folk memory that did not necessarily depend on the survival of standing structures. At the two Roman temples at Wanborough in Surrey, for example, it is very doubtful whether anything survived above ground much beyond the late Roman period; but this seems not to have mattered to the depositor of what might be interpreted as a votive coin hoard on the site at the turn of the 13th century [Williams 2000, 437].

At Pagan's Hill, apparently anomalous 19th century finds from the temple site, the figurine lid-knob of a Wedgewood teapot and a Victorian half sovereign, may themselves be explicable in terms of 'votive' offerings [Rahtz, *pers comm*]. Howard Williams has recently highlighted the re-use of Neolithic and Bronze Age sites for burials by both Romano-Britons and Anglo-Saxons. He argues "that ancient monuments were re-used because their antiquity encouraged their association with supernatural and ancestral powers, and.....they became the focus of new local cults to these ancestors and deities" [Williams 1997, 6]. And in rhythm with the literary evidence, mainly from Bede [eg HE I, 30], there are indications to suggest that the 'Christianisation' of ancient monuments may have formed the basis of a conscious policy against pagan practices and sites on the part of the early church [Grinsell 1986; Holtorf 1997].

If, therefore, at least the possibility of conscious intervention be allowed, the successive communities responsible for the longevity of Pagan's Hill can presumably be placed living, working in, and continuing to mould its immediate hinterland. Rahtz and Watts make the important point that in the Roman period, and "although a religious site, [Pagan's Hill] must have been closely integrated into the local communications network, and the social and economic systems of the area" [Rahtz and Watts 1989, 335]. If the temple continued to function as a ritual centre, of whatever nature, in the 5th and 6th centuries, presumably its importance as a focal point in the wider

landscape persisted as well, if perhaps at a lower level than before.

Although giving us little direct information about settlement in the area in the centuries preceding 1066, nonetheless the temple may well provide strong circumstantial evidence that in the 5th and 6th centuries, we should emphatically not envisage an unpeopled landscape in terminal crisis. On the contrary, an increasing corpus of, particularly, environmental evidence, highlighted by Cleary and reinforced in a more recent study by Dark, suggests a rather different picture in many places: "far from there having been an agrarian collapse and a relapse to forest, the immediate post-Roman period sees no significant increase in the amount of tree pollen and maintained levels of pollen of the plants of deforested land. The inescapable conclusion is that the landscape of England which had been largely deforested by the late Iron Age remained that way.....[and] in agricultural use, though not necessarily in precisely the same ways as it had been in the Roman period. There was also both continuity and change in the agrarian use, though not perhaps in the expected contexts" [Cleary 1995, 14-16; Dark 2000, 130-156]. This new perspective on the early medieval landscape, which we will also consider for Whitley hundred, has been quoted at length here to point up its contrast to the present state of knowledge about this period in this area, as viewed by Professor Rahtz: "what is remarkable about Chew is the lack of Anglo-Saxon evidence; [there is] really nothing between [the 7th century] and [the 10th/11th] (except sculpture in Chew Stoke)" [Rahtz, *pers comm.*; Foster 1987]. If, though, we can plausibly suggest the survival of at least some vestige of post-Roman society up to, say, the late 7th century, with its particular institutions, customs, language and pattern of land-holding, it also seems reasonable to expect that these same distinctive traits may have left their own mark on later settlement patterns, land use, and territorial arrangements; although how far we can actually identify this earlier framework is entirely another matter.

Whitley Hundred

Most of the evidence we have in Whitley comes, of necessity, from Shapwick, but even here, it is still extremely difficult to assess developments in the post-Roman period. Even at the coarsest level of analysis, however, it seems clear that the picture is one of mixed fortunes, with some settlement sites eventually becoming lost relatively quickly as visible landscape features, and others surviving at least as upstanding remains perhaps for centuries [Aston 1998]. The extensive Roman site which probably gave rise to the medieval furlong name Blacklands, in the extreme north-eastern part of the parish [Costen 1993, 98], may also have fallen within those areas of probable pre-Conquest woodland which emerge in the medieval documents as Catterwood and Hurst [Costen 1993, 88-89; Aston 1994a, 154, fig 17.1]. Abandonment of this settlement early on in the Roman period (above) may have made its site susceptible to woodland recolonisation if by, say, AD 400 it was being used for cultivation rather than occupation. Certainly the name Blacklands, although a recognition of the distinctive character of the soil, does not suggest that even severely decayed ruins recognisable as built structures survived to greet the first English speakers here (this is *contra* Aston and Gerrard 1999, 26]. If as seems likely minor Old English toponyms later applied to furlongs actually pre-date the laying out of its open-field system, it looks as though the woodland regeneration (or, at least in the case of Loxley, survival) suggested by Broad Wood, Hurst and Catterwood, was confined to the peripheries of what had probably been the Romano-British core arable area. Aston and Gerrard also note "that most of the woodland area [except Loxley] must be post-Roman", but incline more to the view that "arable may have been far less extensive than the area covered by the later open fields and may have excluded.........the area of Eastfield by Northbrook on the eastern fringe of the parish" [Aston and Gerrard 1999, 27, and Fig 11, 24; for the most recent survey of palynological evidence from Roman Britain as a whole, Dark 1999]. Abandoned agricultural land in lowland Britain is susceptible to vigorous and rapid woodland recolonisation [Rackham 1990, 18-19]; the logical inference, therefore, is that continuing agricultural activity prevented extensive regeneration right through from, say, the 5th century to the point at which English had become the dominant linguistic force in the landscape [Hooke 1997, esp at 65-72]. In this part of Somerset, the period in the last quarter of the 7th, and the first quarter of the 8th century may be suggested for this event, although, as revealed by some early charters, there certainly seems to have been a 'transitional' period, albeit short, in which British toponyms continued to be used alongside English ones [Costen 1992a, 60-62].

We have already considered the place-name element –*wick*, at the beginning of the previous chapter. Landscape historians continue to draw attention to the potential significance of this toponym: in Hertfordshire for example, Hunn has recently highlighted two cases in the St Albans area where he discerns a close correlation between Roman villa sites and medieval manors containing -*wick* in their place-names [Hunn 1994, 318]. The implications of -*wick* for Whitley as a whole are problematic. Apart from the place-name Shapwick itself, only three other certain, and one probable example of this toponym are known from the hundred, all as field-names. Two of them, Sladwick and Snadwick, are, rather ironically, also from Shapwick [Costen 1993, 92 and 97; Ecclestone 1998, 215-216], another, Whitewick, is from High Ham [Costen 1993, 96], and Bannick, almost certainly a -*wick* name, is found on the Puriton tithe map [Costen, *pers comm.*; and SRO D/D/Rt 384, 1842], where it refers to a group of contiguous enclosures to the north-west of the village, and is still remembered in the house name 'Bannock' on the modern 2½" map [Figure 42]. The line of the Great Western Railway drives straight through the middle of these fields, the M5 motorway brushes their eastern side, and it is precisely in this area where lies one of the known extensive but ill-explored Roman settlements close to Puriton. The toponymic evidence is further strengthened by the appearance, immediately to the south of Bannick, of

a group of fields called 'Crocklands' in 1842, which we can now reasonably interpret as arising from a long tradition of the appearance of significant amounts of Roman pottery turned up during ploughing [SMR 10702; and *cf* Field 1993, 212, 218].

It is open to argument whether, as Ross Samson would maintain, archaeologists (but *not* historians!) have indeed been guilty of misrepresenting, misunderstanding and misusing the term *emporium* [Samson 1999]. But such problems of definition aside, it may well be that Combwich, the probable Roman port at the mouth of the Parrett and lying outside the hundred, finds its closest affinities in this period, at least in terms of function, with the eighth-century so-called *emporia* such as Lundenwic and Quentovic, although of course on a much smaller scale; since Alan Morton has recently shown that contemporary use of that term seems to have been quite strictly applied only to the very largest, most important and most 'cosmopolitan' centres [Morton 1999; Costen 1992a, 100; Yorke 1995, 302-309; Russo 1998, 137-167, and Scull 1997; *cf* Dornier 1987 for the linguistic basis of this form of the name]. In terms of the present question, that of occupation, if not actual continuity of settlement, in the early post-Roman period, only Sladwick at present has anything to tell us: nothing of either the archaeology, or the history of the toponym, is known about Snadwick, which did not, apparently, survive into the 16th century [Aston *et al* 1998d], and whose location can be narrowed down from a late 13th century reference only as far as the East Field [Ecclestone 1998, 215-216]. The same is true of Whitewick in High Ham, except that there at least, a specific field is identifiable from the tithe map [*ex inf* Sue Fitton]; indeed, "we do not as yet have a clear idea of where the original 'Shapwick' was", although it may of course lie under the present village [Aston *et al* 1998b, 54; Aston and Gerrard 1999, 26; and see further below].

Sladwick, by contrast, proved the value of taking toponymy into account in the planning of archaeological strategies. Because of its -*wick* epithet, the field was made the target of fieldwalking [Thompson *et al*, 1997], geophysical survey [Ely *et al*, 1995; Andrews *et al*, 1997], and two seasons of excavation, with the result that it is now known to contain surviving foundations of at least one substantial and well-constructed Roman stone building [Plate 1]; a discovery, as we noted in the previous chapter, somewhat at odds with Richard Coates's views on the connection between –*wicks* and Roman archaeology, coming as it does from a minor name with –*wick* as the *second* element [Coates 1999, 110-111].

The attribution of function to the Sladwick structure is at present problematic: it may be a simple field-barn, and several hearths may relate to 'squatter' occupation at a time when it had gone out of use [Aston and Gerrard 1999, 25]. Can Sladwick, therefore, tell us anything about whether people continued to live in the immediate vicinity after the end of the Roman period, and if so, what was the nature both of the occupation and the economy on which it was based? The overwhelming problem remains that we are still unsure exactly how to interpret this word. *Pace* Richard Coates, a direct spatial relationship with Roman sites is now generally accepted [Costen 1992a, 66], and we may now add to the growing list of examples a fascinating and perhaps highly significant discovery which may have implications here; for building upon earlier chance finds and the results of aerial survey, recent geophysical work and trial excavation at Shapwick's namesake in Dorset has revealed the existence of an extensive, and probably defended Roman settlement that may well in fact be a small town [Papworth 1997, 354-358]. Quite apart from the (?)coincidence of the name, perhaps this work might usefully inform our own views about the nature of the Chestell site to the west of the Somerset Shapwick. This was also disclosed by geophysical survey, and although on a smaller scale than the Dorset example, nonetheless in some of its elements shows at least a superficial resemblance to it.

It is, though, still the case that, archaeologically, we do not actually know what a *-wīc* looked like, and even in those cases where we can demonstrate a relationship between a *-wīc* name and a Roman site, continuity of occupation is not yet proven. Presumably, initially at least, the English did not apply *-wīc* names to their own settlements, but to places which they recognised as having distinctively Roman antecedents. But it is a fundamental gap in our knowledge that we are not yet able to say whether or not at least some *wīcs* represent working, occupied farmsteads, surrounded by an appendant estate of whatever size, at the time that they were seen, and perhaps taken over, by the first English farmers. At Sladwick, for example, pottery series from the Roman building itself do not extend beyond the 4th century [Chris Gerrard, *pers comm*]. Indeed, in the course of fieldwalking, the site yielded not a single sherd that could be identified as either early medieval or post-Conquest fabric [Thompson *et al*, 1997]. This does not mean that occupation on or close to the site did not persist into the 5th or 6th centuries or even later, if environmental conditions allowed (below), since we have already seen the difficulties of recognising early post-Roman material culture. If *-wic* is merely a reference to the known Roman site, it is possible that there still may have been subsequent occupation elsewhere in Sladwick field, but at least partly on pragmatic grounds there may also have been perfectly good reasons why English-speaking incomers, at whatever date they arrived and in whatever numbers, should have wished to avoid altogether the low-lying, crumbling Roman settlement or farmstead, if such it had become. It is unlikely that such people would have had the necessary skills, even had they the inclination, to repair and re-roof ruinous stone buildings even for storage purposes, let alone occupation. And the fieldname itself, with its connotation of dampness [Costen 1993, 92 and 97], may suggest that by the time the English arrived, the site had actually become too wet to occupy [*cf* Rippon 1997, 124-127]; a possibility carrying with it a disquieting association even in the Christian mind that made fens and wetlands the haunts of demons and monsters: it is worth remembering that Beowulf's dreadful adversaries, Grendel and his mother, were marsh-dwellers [Stenton 1971, 194-195; Wilkinson 1998, 9]. And of the experiences of St Guthlac in the East Anglian wetlands at

Crowland, Lennard has reminded us that the evil spirits by whom he was tormented are made by the saint's *vita* to talk specifically in the *British* tongue; a fact which he takes to indicate "an actual survival of un-Saxonised Britons in the fens down to the beginning of the 8th century" [Lennard 1938, 63-64]. This is a psychological perspective on the landscape the power of which we should not underestimate [Wormald 1982, 82; Williams 1997, 28, n19; Semple 1998, 112-114].

Indeed, we may question whether, in those cases like Sladwick where the Roman settlement that originally gave rise to the name can actually be identified on the ground, we have a right to expect traces of early medieval occupation directly on top of the site itself? It is completely problematic whether or not the *-wic* at Sladwick remained at the centre of a working British farm, with its own lands: its function in the Roman period is obscure enough; but even if abandoned by, say, the 7th century, enough of its 'resource-base' might have remained recognisable in the landscape to be at least partially reconstituted into a viable estate, worked from an Anglo-Saxon farmstead on a new (higher and drier?) site somewhere hard by. In this context, Michael Costen has noted, for Wessex as a whole, that *-wics*, among other Anglo-Saxon habitative toponyms, indicate "almost certainly.....the territory of these places, not.....buildings" [Costen 1994, 99]; although examples such as Sladwick itself must surely indicate that at least some of these names *were* indeed intended to be quite deliberate and precise references to Roman built structures.

Wics may, then, represent specific cases of short-distance shift in the settlement pattern in the mid-Saxon period, but differing from the so-called 'shuffle' described elsewhere [Hamerow 1991; but *cf* Hooke 1997, 94-95, for a critique of the concept of the mid-Saxon 'shuffle'], in that it was not merely a random, unplanned and apparently 'aimless' drift, but rather, a quite conscious process based on pragmatism, expediency and perhaps also for cultural reasons, designed deliberately to eschew the surviving material remnants of Roman settlement, while at the same time recognising the advantage of taking over functioning or at least recognisable agrarian estates. The likelihood of this is explicit in Costen's remark that "it would be absurd to suggest that the English failed to utilise the pre-existing structure which they found" [Costen 1992a, 86]. It is settlement shift of this kind that has been used in the Fens to explain why, apparently, "very few of the numerous Romano-British sites had Saxon pottery on them. Iron Age to Roman continuity appears to be much commoner than Roman to Saxon" [Hayes 1988, 324]. If then, *-wics* do represent an older, underlying settlement pattern bearing a close relationship to Roman precursors [Costen 1993, 97], it is possible that Shapwick itself has already been found, but not identified, in the form of one of the several potential pre-Conquest occupation sites now known or suspected in the parish [Gerrard and Gutierrez 1997, Fig 6.10, 68-69, and Fig 6.23, 80].

Yet again, however, we are brought full-circle back to the basic problem, namely that even in an area as well-studied as Shapwick, even the most circumstantial of conventional archaeological evidence fails us, and leaves us with a chronological vacuum of several centuries during which we are effectively blind; although new techniques of settlement detection, especially soil phosphate and heavy metal analysis, pioneered at Shapwick, promise significant results [Aston *et al*, 1998a, b and c]. In Somerset we have as yet, so far as we know, nothing to compare with the pottery fabrics from further east identifiable from about the mid 7th century and typified by the series known generically as Ipswich ware (mid Saxon) and Thetford ware (late Saxon) [Rogerson 1996]. The occurrence of pre-Conquest pottery even directly on top of, or very close to, known Roman occupation, as at Shapwick Old Church, does not, unfortunately, *prove* continuity of occupation; if not merely manuring scatters, the best we may infer from it at present is possible re-use of a site [Gerrard and Gutierrez 1997, 50, Fig 6.17, 77; Fig 6.23, 80; Fig 6.24, 81]. The uncertain dating of (supposedly) late pre-Conquest pottery series lies at the centre of the dilemma, and indeed in the opinion of at least one authority, it is possible that up to now the dates assigned to some of this material may be too late. The fabrics designated Cheddar A, for example, "are pre-Conquest at Cheddar and dated there to.....[the] early 10th to later 10th century. This dating stands.....[but] any new.....excavation could change [it]. It would only push the dates back though....." [*pers comm* Chris Gerrard]. It seems in fact as though even now there is still no clear cut answer to the question of what inferences we should make about occupation sites from pottery scatters. At Shapwick itself, others have observed that "clearly there is no simple correlation to be made between high densities of material on the surface of the ploughsoil and what lies beneath" [Gerrard and Gutierrez 1997, 51]. Conversely however, in Northamptonshire, it is precisely this correlation that has been made, by which occupation structures have been identified beneath scatters of early/middle Saxon pottery, and to the extent that specific thresholds of recovery are suggested as being indicative of likely occupation[3]. Even here though, the actual dating of the fabrics lacks chronological precision, the best that can be managed being a range of four centuries between 450-850 AD [Shaw 1993-4]. Likewise at Rendlesham in south-eastern Suffolk, archaeological investigation of an area indicated through fieldwalking by scatters of mid-Saxon Ipswich Ware pottery, revealed the presence of contemporary occupation structures directly underneath [Newman 1992, 36-37]. Indeed, closer to home there are indications that such may yet prove to be the case in central Somerset, since recent fieldwork in the Brue valley to identify Roman period salt workings, and which included very limited trial excavation, has led to the

conclusion that "briquetage scatters do actually represent saltern sites rather than unstratified debris" [Grove and Brunning 1998, 66]. Although relating to industrial rather than to occupation sites, this at least establishes in principle the potential significance of positive fieldwalking results.

It is worth pointing out that the dating dilemma is a widespread one; fieldwork for the Fenland Project, for example, has thrown up exactly the same problem, with one writer noting recently that while broad categorisation of post-Roman fabrics is possible, "unfortunately a large proportion can at present only be classed as 'Early or Middle Saxon' (c 450-850AD)" [Hayes 1988, 324]. These waters have been muddied even further by the recent discovery at St Neot's, Cambs, of late Roman pottery on a post-Roman site all of whose other cultural affinities are Anglo-Saxon, *not* Roman [*pers comm* Dr Lee Prosser]. The implication is clear: that Roman pottery could be somehow 'inherited' by English incomers and could remain in practical use for some three centuries after manufacture. Availability of a ready supply of stockpiled Roman fabrics may go some way towards explaining why, in some areas at least, diagnostically Anglo-Saxon wares do not appear until the 7th century [Prosser 1995, 57], and henceforth, it seems as though Roman pottery from clearly post-Roman contexts cannot automatically be taken to indicate continued occupation by an indigenous Romano-British population.

The work of the Shapwick Project has cast a welcome shaft of light on the landscape within its bounds, and after ten years work it is now possible for the Directors to state quite firmly that "however we arrange our data, more than half of the tenth-century settlement pattern is a relict of the late Roman pattern of farms, villages and villas" [Aston and Gerrard 1999, 27]. This in itself is a considerable achievement. But if by comparison the other parishes within Whitley as a whole are not necessarily cloaked in darkness, it is nonetheless the case that the level of available evidence makes inference extremely hazardous. It is true that things do not all go Shapwick's way; indeed, it is three of the other estates (Ham, Sowy and Butleigh), that give us a glimpse of the landscape in these contrasting parts of the hundred in the late Anglo-Saxon period, through the survival of detailed bounds attached to charters. However, excluding the excavation of specific, individual sites, archaeological fieldwork to modern standards has been applied to any meaningful extent only twice elsewhere in the hundred: during the work on the Polden pipeline, and in the parish survey of Compton Dundon, both campaigns being directed by Charlie and Nancy Hollinrake. The results from the pipeline serve merely to highlight the problems surrounding the early post-Roman period that have already been described. None of the important Roman sites ascribed to this campaign (see preceding section for refs) produced evidence of material culture that could be securely dated beyond the 4th century AD, and indeed, neither element of the work, fieldwalking or excavation, produced a single sherd of fabric that could be confidently ascribed to even a late pre-Conquest date [Hollinrakes

---

[3] In this respect it seems as though the *nature* of the material found in the course of fieldwalking is as important, if not more so, as its *density*: "our more detailed analyses suggest that we should take more account of pottery abrasion and rounding and of sherd size.......large 'platy' objects......can be carried surprising distances, smaller more friable objects travel less far and may be more reliable indicators to the location of buried archaeology". Gerrard 2000, 33. Preliminary fieldwalking and excavation results from the Whittlewod Project in the Midlands have suggested that even extremely low densities of early medieval pottery may be directly related to contemporary sub-surface occupation remains.

1994a]. At Edington Holy Well, stratigraphical evidence may indicate activity dating "to Phase IV, the post-Roman period", although "the lack of medieval pottery suggests that activity on the site ceased before the 10th century". In conclusion, the excavators are understandably reluctant to venture any more for one particular feature here than that "the evidence available suggests it is part of an important late Romano-British settlement site which *might* [my italics] extend into the 5th century....." [Hollinrakes 1994c, 40-41]. At Compton, the same workers have recovered evidence which may cast light on the origins of the nucleated village there: since their parish survey, involving fieldwalking and limited excavation, has recovered pottery dated by them to the 10th century from a bank and ditch system surrounding what is probably a pre-Conquest 'manorial' complex in the centre of the village [Hollinrakes 1989, 172-173; I am indebted to Charlie and Nancy Hollinrake for giving me sight of a draft of their survey, and for discussing its contents with me, in advance of publication]. Again, though, the post-Roman evidence is seemingly non-existent and allows us to say effectively nothing about what was going on in the area between the late 4th century and the 10th.

But if not, for the time being at least, archaeology, are there any other threads of evidence, however few and tenuous, which may suggest that something of the past survived in Whitley's landscape to be recognised and even used by English-speaking peoples probably from the late 7th century onwards? We can identify two main examples, one unequivocal and rather obvious, the other more speculative. To take the latter first: Cossington's western boundary, with Woolavington, has potentially intriguing implications. It exhibits a marked eastwards 'bulge' (ie towards Cossington) that stands out in an otherwise relatively straight course. There is a distinct impression that the bound here is going around a landscape feature that is no longer visible. We may wonder, however, whether it is entirely coincidence that the diversion occurs in the general area of the known, and probably extensive, Roman site that lies in this eastern part of Woolavington parish [Figure 4; SMR 10947; Taylor 1967, 67]. Although, as far as I can see, this is the only obvious relationship in Whitley hundred between Roman occupation and a boundary detour, I strongly suggest that it is causal, and that at the time the boundary was established, built structures of Roman date survived well enough to influence its course. Indeed one wonders whether there was rather more than just ruins involved. Substantial heaps of rubble might have been regarded as a useful marker, in which case we might expect the boundary to go right through the site [*cf* Hooke 1998, 64, fig 21]. There may, however, have been a deliberate effort to include this small additional piece of land within the bounds of Woolavington, and there must presumably have been a good reason for doing so; it seems, then, at least possible that the boundary here may take the line it does because it is respecting the site of a former Romano-British farmstead that had continued in occupation (or whose site had been reoccupied), perhaps even as a working unit, when the boundary was drawn. If so, the Woolavington site may offer crucial evidence about the nature of any post-Roman occupation in its immediate area, and a programme of fieldwalking and geophysical survey here would be effort well spent.

There is another possibility for the Woolavington site, and it is related to the ownership of Roman ruins as valuable sources of worked stone. In the early medieval period, the use of freshly-quarried stone before the 11th century was extremely rare. The majority of surviving pre-Conquest churches, for example, are probably constructed largely or wholly from re-used Roman ashlar [Parsons 1990, 5-8; Everson and Stocker 1990; Eaton 2000]. This being so, it is conceivable that the course of the Woolavington boundary is actually designed to 'lay claim' to Roman buildings in that area which, although themselves ruinous, would have provided a useful ready supply of worked stone. It is also possible that the possession of Roman stone buildings was considered in some way to bestow status on the owner[4]. We may actually catch an intriguing glimpse of this in the mid 14th century at Shapwick, in a court roll reference to the theft of stone, by night, from Abchester, in the West Field, formerly the site of extensive Roman occupation [Ecclestone 1998, 213]. The thief, John Sherp, was accused of taking the stone "to his own house at Glastonbury Abbey", a distance of over 10km, measured from the modern 2½" map along roads that are likely to have been in existence at that time. This is a long way to come, to an obscure corner of Shapwick, merely to collect ordinary field stone. However, the very nature of the act, by stealth, and the fact that it was serious enough to have been considered an offence, suggests that the material involved was something considerably more valuable and useful, and the possession of which was regarded as an important manorial prerogative. Sherp is even said to have beaten the Abbot's *famulus*, causing him serious injury, for refusing to have anything to do with the removal of the stone. Was Sherp carting away collapsed Roman ashlar, and are there still, embedded somewhere in the fabric of one of Glastonbury's medieval houses, fragments of one of the Roman buildings that once stood in Abchester field, re-used for illegal repairs in the mid 14th century?

With the second example, we are on far surer ground. The east-west route along the top of the Polden ridge, probably re-engineered in the Roman period from a prehistoric trackway, provides in whole or part the boundaries between the northern parishes, from Cossington in the west to Shapwick in the east; and those (I would argue, secondary settlements) immediately to the south, from Bawdrip (although outside the hundred) in the west, to Greinton in the east. The implications of this for estate development, its chronology and nature, in the pre-Conquest period, I will examine further in Chapter Six. It is enough for now to note that by definition, for at least part of its length the road must have remained a significant landscape feature in the post-Roman period, and indeed its usefulness as a dry, direct east-west route between the

---

[4]*pers comm* Tim Eaton, to whom I am indebted for these references, and for his general advice on the question of re-use of Roman building materials in England in the early medieval period.

Glastonbury/Street area and the Parrett estuary, is likely to have ensured its survival through constant use even through periods of economic and social displacement [*cf* Rackham 1986, 257].

Conclusion

The sheer obscurities of the period, perhaps understandably, seem sometimes to lead to apparent contradictions in the views expressed by those engaged in its study. Thus Dark, on the one hand, observes that "in politics, culture, society and rural economy.........Roman Britain survived in the West for centuries after AD410" [Dark 1998, 9]; and on the other, that "it would be incorrect.....to claim that the landscape of Roman Britain formed the usual structure of the medieval landscape, but it is true that it formed part of its basis - a partial skeleton of boundaries and site locations.....what we lack.....is clear evidence that functions and uses of the landscape continued into the Middle Ages.....in Anglo-Saxon England, farms established on villa sites were, for instance, usually deserted in the seventh century, while in the same century evidence for rural settlement continuity in social and economic terms ends in western Britain" [Dark 1997, 145-146].

This 'partial skeleton' is presumably a reference to those Roman features which are most likely to have remained in use for a period from the 5th century onwards, even if that use was both much reduced in intensity and changed in nature, and which therefore survived long enough to influence subsequent developments in the landscape. We have already suggested a possible context for this. We have also noted the growing body of evidence that even in those areas further east which bore the initial brunt of the Germanic incursions, there was probably a far more significant British presence than orthodox views allow for. The current general view among archaeologists and historians is that in Somerset, not only was there a high degree of cultural continuity among the surviving Romano-British community, but it was tenacious, long-lived and in the early part of the period at least, sophisticated. Certainly the economic circumstances of the upper echelons of this society exceeded those of mere subsistence. This last point is brought strongly home by the results from the excavation of the post-Roman (6th-8th centuries) cemetery hard by the late Romano-British rural temple at Lamyatt Beacon; for skeletal pathology revealed that the occupants of the excavated graves, chiefly women, had enjoyed good health in life, had suffered no nutritional deficiencies or extreme and repetitive physical exertions, and were exceptionally tall, even by modern standards [Leech 1986; for the palaeopathology, 326-328. I am grateful to Penny Stokes for alerting me to the wider implications of these findings].

Chapter Four

Hundredal Structure and Ecclesiastical Relationships

Introduction

I define hundredal structure here as the way that the hundred as a unit is built up from the parishes which it contains, the nature of the relationships between the parishes, and the evidence of the hundred's internal and external boundaries. The ecclesiastical framework is also dealt with here since its testimony is crucial in helping to impose a fundamental order on other, somewhat more disparate and amorphous strands of evidence. Economic links, showing evidence of transhumance or the exploitation of detached and/or distant resources, may be closely related to ecclesiastical development: recent studies have indicated that sometimes ancient transhumance/resource links to outlying areas may have preceded church foundation in those places when seasonal sheilings developed into permanent settlements [Everitt 1986, 155-162, 181-224; Fox 1996]. In Somerset, for example, Penny Stokes has drawn attention to the probable settlement and economic significance of such links in Whitstone Hundred and the north-eastern part of the county [Stokes 1996]. It is possible that similar relationships played an important role in underpinning the internal cohesiveness of virtually all of Chew hundred, and of extensive parts of Whitley; Carhampton, as we shall see, presents the most striking contrast in this respect, but in all three areas, this kind of evidence can be used to cast light of varying intensity on the development of the respective medieval settlement patterns.

However, this suggestion should also be seen in the context of an increasing unease on the part of scholars working in this field about the way in which, hitherto, there has tended to be an assumption that large, ancient, 'primary' estates followed a straightforward, linear path towards progressive fragmentation through time. Recent detailed regional studies have countenanced caution against the current, widely accepted orthodoxy that the fission of larger land units into smaller ones, in a straightforward linear progression through time, was invariably the main dynamic behind the development of pre-Conquest settlement patterns. Thus Sawyer: "the main development in the settlement history of Anglo-Saxon England was.....the fragmentation of large multiple estates which were themselves of great antiquity" [Sawyer 1974, 108]. The chief objector to this idea, Dawn Hadley, as part of a wider critique of both the 'minster' model of ecclesiastical development, and the multiple estate model of territorial, social and tenurial structure, accepts that in some cases this is certainly true; but her work in the northern Danelaw has revealed, by contrast, a situation of almost bewildering variety and complexity in pre-Conquest patterns of both tenure and territories, with overlapping and interlocking structures of lordship, and a constantly fluid, fluctuating territorial framework characterised by a dynamic interaction between units at every level of the hierarchy. Land units could fragment and reform, producing completely new entities, in totally irregular, unpredictable and non-linear cycles of change. Not all land was necessarily neatly divided and allotted, unitary estates and multi-vill manors were not mutually exclusive, and there were no fixed rules, because early medieval society was itself an organism of infinite complexity [Hadley 1996 and 1996a; and further below]. Indeed, this fundamental characteristic was evident at all levels of the territorial hierarchy, up to and including the kingdoms themselves; as Barbara Yorke has recently remarked, "the history of Anglo-Saxon kingdoms in the seventh and eighth centuries was not one of simple linear growth" [Yorke 1999, 27].

The authors of a recent survey of four counties in the east midlands are similarly sceptical about the general applicability of the multiple estate model, and, like Hadley, regard its inability to account for the complexity and dynamism of early medieval land units as a serious flaw [Lewis et al 1997, 108-110]. Large territories need not, it transpires, necessarily be 'early'. From his Surrey evidence, John Blair argues strongly that the apparent primacy of multiple estates is to some extent illusory, the result of the fact that "initial grants to sees and great minsters were especially liable to take this form"; so that ultimately they were "as estates, essentially a product of early Christian England". Conversely, Blair lays far more stress on the importance of much *smaller* units which appear as autonomous entities at an early date. Territories of the order of a few hides, appearing in the documents as early as the 7th century, from the outset apparently fully-formed and self-contained, are not always merely the result of centuries of progressive fission of larger entities [Blair 1991, 23-24]. Rather, they probably "belong to the same stage of development as the primary territories............multi-vill manors may thus have been founded on an existing organisational structure" [Blair 1991, 27; and Faith 1997, 11-14]. A review of the pre-Conquest charter evidence leads Bond to similar conclusions for Worcestershire, at least for those "large composite estates [consisting] of several separately names places from an early date". He observes that "these charters are describing estates which appear to represent an accumulation of formerly separate properties, perhaps over a period, in the hands of one individual or institution, *and their later division into parishes need not represent their subdivision so much as a partial re-establishment of earlier bounds*" [my emphasis; Bond 1988, 137]. Even the Welsh basis upon which Glanville-Jones founded his original multiple-estate thesis, chiefly in the form of a series of medieval law codes, is no longer immune from critical scrutiny [Jones 1998]. A major part of the difficulty seems to be a simple problem of definition; and in this context, a recent contribution by Alexander is probably one of the more effective attempts yet to produce a pragmatic, empirically-derived checklist of criteria, which endeavours to reconcile at least some of the often conflicting approaches currently informing our perspectives on the multiple-estate model [Alexander 1997, 14].

Despite certain doubts, however, it is clear that in some respects Hadley's scepticism regarding the evidence of mother-daughter church relationships is by no means complete; for she is prepared to admit that while, in her study area, "the later medieval hierarchy of mother churches and dependent chapels is unlikely to have existed as such at an early date [ie before the 9th/10th centuries].....the vills in which chapels were later founded may well have long looked to the respective mother church for pastoral care" [Hadley 1996a, 13 n20]. Criticism of some elements of the minster model, particularly the use of later evidence to cast light on earlier arrangements, has also been robustly dismissed by Palliser, in the course of his attempt to reconstruct the *parochia* around Beverley minster in Yorkshire [Palliser 1996]. The case for using ecclesiastical relationships as one of a range of criteria to establish the extent of pre-Conquest territories still, therefore, seems strong. Hadley's findings in the Danelaw are supported by the work of Chris Wickham, from which we may infer that complexity of territorial organisation is in fact entirely to be expected, since it is merely a reflection of the true nature of early medieval society across western Europe; a society to which, Wickham argues, we have thus far been guilty of attributing a degree of both homogeneity and stasis directly conflicting with evidence that seems clearly to demonstrate the precise opposite [Wickham 1992]. That we should expect some parts of Somerset to display at least elements of the Hadley/Wickham view is implicit in Stokes's observation, of Ditcheat in Whitstone hundred, that "we see [there].....the fluid tenurial circumstances of an ancient entity devoted to the limited-term provision of land for retainers of various ranks" [Stokes 1996, 35].

Notwithstanding these misgivings, an approach which includes a consideration of ecclesiastical relationships is still seen by many as at least a useful starting point in the examination of pre-Conquest territorial arrangements [eg Gittos 1989; Hall 2000, 68-69]. For Somerset in general, these relationships have been mapped, tabulated and briefly discussed by Aston [1986, 54-58, and 74-76] and re-examined from a more specifically topographical and spatial perspective by Gerrard [1987, 12-23].

The question of *groupings* of churches, to the possible significance of which attention was first drawn by Warwick Rodwell [1984], has been more recently reviewed at length by Blair [1992, 246-258]. While observing that "common though they are, the purpose of these groups is still not fully understood" [247], nonetheless Blair is clear that in this respect England ultimately took its cue from continental practice [250]; and where such groupings survive or can be reconstructed, especially those aligned longitudinally east-west, he believes they provide telling evidence of *early* origins

[250]. While skirting round the question of how exactly we should define 'early', Blair cites examples to show that the older, primary church within any given grouping will "sometimes [be] pre-English in origin" [250-251, at 250]. These comments are particularly significant for it seems to describe precisely the situation at both Carhampton and Chew Magna; and on this basis, this Chapter discusses how the antiquity of the various 'superior' churches in the three hundreds may in part be suggested by their possible disposition as planned groups.

Another of Blair's topographical criteria for minster status is closeness to water, and applies particularly to slightly elevated sites constricted on several sides by water, giving an impression of promontory-like isolation [Blair 1996, 9-12]. There is some pre-Conquest literary evidence to suggest that a girdle of water was indeed a sought-after topographical attribute in the siting of early minsters, as, for example, in the case of the church founded by St Cuthman at Steyning, Sussex, in the 7th or 8th century, where the saint's *vita* describes the precinct as being bounded by two streams [Blair 1997]. Similar characteristics have been identified by Silvester in Clwyd and Powys as being associated with "most indisputable early Welsh churches" in these areas [Silvester 1997, 117]. For the church at Chew this is an important consideration, and for those at Shapwick and Moorlinch in Whitley hundred, these affinities may help to explain at least in part the nature of their very particular relationship.

Likewise has the existence of systematic spatial links between churches and Roman villas long been suspected; Morris and Roxan's examination of the subject nearly 20 years ago, in which they concluded that there was indeed, in many cases, a direct and probably causal relationship was given substance by the results of the Rodwells' seminal studies at Rivenhall (Essex) [Morris and Roxan 1980[1]; Rodwell and Rodwell 1985 and 1993]; although as these authors further point out, any church-villa link "is likely to reflect the relationship between manor and villa as *estate* centres (my italics), and that churches, most of which are proprietary in nature, are incidental to the equation" [noted by Hall 2000, 58-59]. The strong inference, of at least the possibility of a degree of continuity of territorial arrangements, is discussed briefly below.

In Somerset it is possible that we can attribute the correlation at least in part to a preference by evangelists from the British church infiltrating from Wales for the re-use of high-status Roman sites. This view does not allow for an unbroken thread of continuity from late Roman Christianity. But it does at least suggest that some, perhaps many, Somerset minsters will have a continuous history of Christian use from the 6th and 7th centuries [Teresa Hall, *pers comm*]. We should recognise, however, that this pattern is by no means ubiquitous. Teresa Hall's recent important study of Dorset has shown, for example, that overall there is no significant correlation between the two types of site in that county [Hall 2000, 52-59]. It is possible though, as Hall suggests, that this might be

---

[1] I am grateful to Jenni Butterworth for this reference.

accounted for by very particular circumstances, arising partly from the Theodorian reforms in the second half of the 7th century, carried through in the Diocese of Sherborne by Theodore's pupil, Aldhelm of Malmesbury; and partly as a result of Dorset having been little affected by the influence of British missionaries, the Welsh evangelistic movement having 'burned itself out' before reaching Dorset [Hall, *pers comm*].

Dorset may therefore be unusual in these respects; it has certainly become usual to highlight the later centrality and importance of places where, in purely spatial terms at least, a church/villa relationship can be clearly discerned. Their status as hundred and estate centres, the sites of royal residences and ancient minster churches, and perhaps early (ie pre-Conquest) towns, are all elements of this general theme. However, although Dorset seems to be an extreme case of non-conformity, nonetheless, even in Somerset, where there does not appear to be the same evidence for conscious meddling in ecclesiastical arrangements, the correlation of minster church/villa is by no means an invariable one. The mere presence of Roman occupation did not by any means automatically bestow importance on any successor religious building on or near the same site; the relationship was clearly both fluid and hierarchical, its exact nature probably depending on the complex interaction of many influences. At Priddy, for example, a high-status Roman building has been found at a location about 300m east of the church [Barlow 1967], and to argue for a direct relationship in this case would clearly be stretching a point. Also, while the unusual survival of what appears to be a British habitative place-name [Mills 1991, 264] may be evidence of some degree of continuity of either settlement and/or land use, the church there, far from becoming a minster, in fact originated as a chapelry of Westbury-sub-Mendip [Torr 1974-79, 88]. Neither did Priddy become either a hundredal centre, royal vill or town.

Despite these caveats, it remains true that known minster church/villa 'complexes' in Somerset are appearing at an increasing rate: the location of the putative minster church at Shapwick on or adjacent to the site of a Roman (?ritual) complex [Aston 1994, 230-232] is noted in Chapter Two, and we will return to it here. At Wrington, also a probable minster, a short stretch of Roman walling with box-flue tiles *in situ* has been found "in the garden of the Court House, adjacent to the church on its west side. This was the manor house of the abbots of Glastonbury Abbey....." [Russett, *pers comm*]. The clear inference is that this was a hypocaust system belonging to a high-status residence. John Blair has highlighted the similar propinquity between his putative minster at Cheddar and the large Roman structure there [Blair 1996, 112-113], and at East Pennard, perhaps the site of a pre-Conquest minster [Stokes 1996, 25-27], "there may have been a villa close to the church, as Roman brick has been found beneath the floor" [*ibid*, 56]; Gay lists further examples of villas on, next to, or near church sites in North Somerset [1995, 3.3 and 4.3], but was unable to include the very recent discovery of a substantial Roman building close to the church at the hundredal centre of Portbury [Alexander 1997, 17-18].

Hundreds, then, were far from stable entities. For a variety of reasons, and especially the administrative convenience of great landlords, they were subject to constant change and interference [Thorn 1989a, 36-37]. For this reason it seems most useful to define the study hundreds in terms of their composition at the earliest date for which we have the most complete evidence, which not surprisingly is provided by Domesday Book and its associated texts. Tables 2, 4 and 5, Chapter Five, give an indication, for each hundred, of the manors of which they are thought to have been composed in 1086, the ownership at that date and in 1066, and which of the manors later appear as parishes in their own right.

It is against this background of fluidity, and the often conflicting demands of tenurial, economic and ecclesiastical expediency, that we need briefly to examine, in turn, the composition of, and relationships within, our three hundreds. We will begin in the north with Chew, and since, as I hope to show later on, the history of this entity is inextricably bound to that of Chewton, its hundredal neighbour immediately to the south, we will need occasionally to consider the evidence from Chewton if we are properly to understand the nature of that relationship.

Chew and Chewton Hundreds: Composition

The composition of Chew hundred at the time of Domesday seems to have been straightforward: administratively and geographically it formed a compact unit with no outlying dependencies, or inclusions within its own boundaries of detached parts of other hundreds (Figure 9). With Chewton however, the situation is complicated by the existence both of a large block of detached land to the west and the inclusion of detachments of the hundreds of Winterstoke and Wells Forum. As Table 2 and Figures 10 and 11 both show, the western detachment consists of the parishes of Brockley, Yatton and Kingston Seymour[2]. Unlike the main body of the hundred, the parishes of Brockley, Yatton and Kingston Seymour occupy for the most part very low-lying land which is properly part of the northern extension of the Somerset Levels. Nowhere in Kingston Seymour, for example, is much above 20ft OD, and some areas are effectively at or below OD. As I will argue elsewhere, this western outlier may be crucial to our understanding of territorial developments affecting Chew and Chewton in the late Anglo-Saxon period, and it is the only part of Chewton which we need consider for present purposes.

---

[2] Dr Thorn's recent map of the Somerset hundreds shows Yatton at the centre of its own 'manorial hundred' [Thorn 1989], but this probably reflects a then-recent administrative expedient on the part of the Bishop of Bath and Wells. There are strong indications that before this, Yatton had been a detached member of Chewton hundred, although later on it was in Winterstoke [Thorn (ed), 1980, 375].

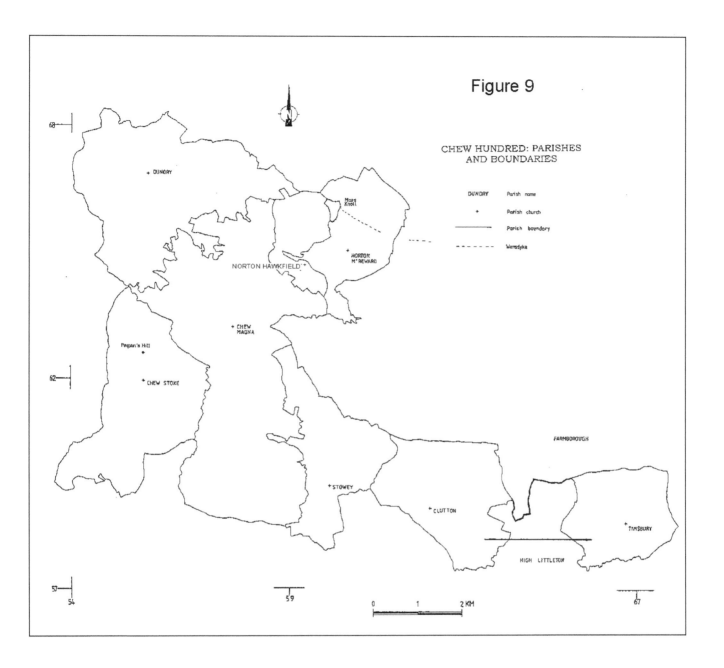

Figure 9

CHEW HUNDRED: PARISHES
AND BOUNDARIES

DUNDRY	Parish name
+	Parish church
——	Parish boundary
– – –	Wansdyke

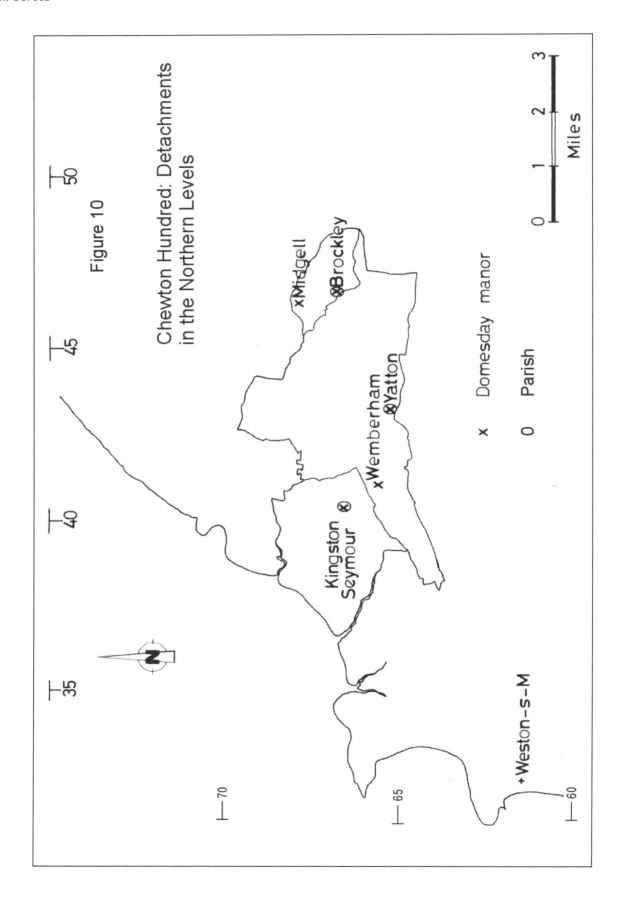

Figure 10

Chewton Hundred: Detachments
in the Northern Levels

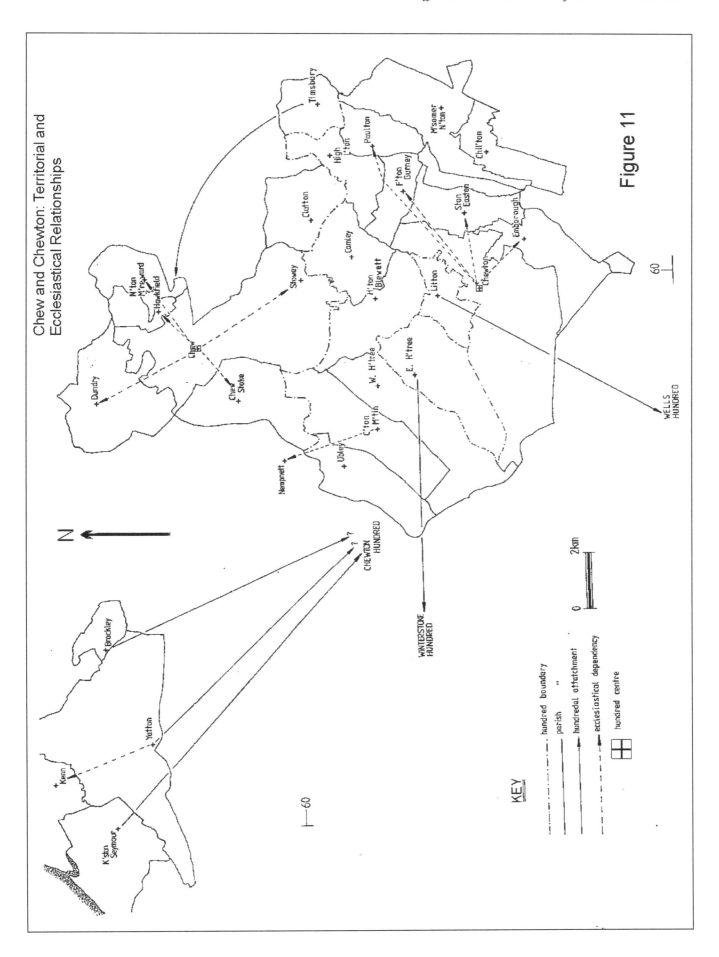

Chew and Chewton: Territorial and Ecclesiastical Relationships

Figure 11

KEY

hundred boundary
parish
hundredal attachment
ecclesiastical dependency
hundred centre

Chew and its Churches: Internal Relationships

One of the most important indicators of capital status for a church is the existence of 'daughters' which can be shown to have been dependent on it, to whatever degree. Such evidence exists for Chew Magna (Figure 11). The only church in the rest of the hundred that is recorded in historic times as originating as a full dependent chapelry to Chew is Dundry [*cf* Greenwood 1822, 88; Collinson 1791, II, 105]. It is probably very significant, however, that three of the other churches in the hundred, namely Chew Stoke, Norton (Hawkfield) and Stowey, also give indications of former dependence on Chew Magna [Collinson 1791, II, 96; Aston 1986, 58]. In the 17th century, all these places were paying tithes of one sort or another to the vicar of Chew [Dunning 1968, 77-78], who also claimed mortuary fees from the inhabitants of Dundry, Chew Stoke, Stowey and Norton Hawkfield, and half the offerings of newly weds from Chew Stoke. And in the same period, the vicar of Chew was responsible for the maintenance of the chancel of Stowey church [glebe terrier for Chew Magna 1638, SRO D/D/Rg 26/2]. Under the circumstances it is highly improbable that the other Norton manor, Malreward, was not also originally dependent on Chew. The evidence of its place-name, and its topographical relationship to its neighbours within a putative Chew 'proto-hundred', speak very strongly of this. However, ultimately giving its name to the parish containing both it and Hawkfield, it seems by the 17th century at the latest to have freed itself from any tithe obligations it may once have owed to the superior church [glebe terriers for Norton Malreward 1628 and 1634, SRO D/D/Rg 44/1 and 2][3].

The glebe documents provide further evidence of Chew's likely primacy, especially when considered against similar evidence from Chewton. Teresa Hall's study of Dorset identifies a recurrent characteristic of what she calls the 'primary' minsters there, in that they are consistently those churches possessing the largest glebes [Hall 2000, 63-66]. In this respect, comparison of the figures for glebe from Chew Magna and Chewton reveals a striking dichotomy. The earliest surviving terrier for Chewton, dated 1623 [SRO D/D/Rg 152], records a mere 5 acres of land, a tiny amount considering that Chewton parish itself ran to nearly 6,000 acres and its church possessed no fewer than four parochial dependencies (below). At Chew Magna, by contrast, the glebe in 1614 amounted to at least 100 acres [SRO D/D/Rg 26/1]. We will look again at the question of Chew and Chewton's respective affinities, but this seems to be another telling element in the overall picture of Chew's dominant position in the relationship.

The Structure of Chew Hundred

Even at the most superficial level, Chew shows signs of accretion, whereby a 'core' entity has been added to at some point before 1066. The main evidence for this, as we have already seen, comes from the ecclesiastical pattern within the hundred; however, the physical disposition of the constituent parishes also provides clues. From both these strands of evidence it is clear that Clutton and Timsbury are interlopers; whether they were attached to Chew actually at the time of hundredation, or later on, it seems likely that some special, but now unrecoverable circumstance of ownership was involved (Figure 9). We have already noted evidence relating both to Chew Magna's position as a hundredal centre, and its status as a capital, and probably a minster church. The latter point we will return to again later on. While I would argue that the north *tūn* almost certainly once had an existence as a distinct sub-unit within a larger entity, it is clear that at some point before 1066 the original unit was split under divided ownership: Malreward was held by the Bishop of Coutances in 1086 and a Saxon lord before the Conquest. In the medieval period it emerges as an independent secular manor [Collinson 1791, II, 108-110], while Hawkfield, by contrast, appears with its ties to the episcopal estate still evident; indeed it is likely that Hawkfield's non-appearance in Domesday is due to its assessment being included under that for Chew Magna [Thorn and Thorn 1980, 352].

It is clear that, by the time Chew Hundred emerges into historical record in the late Saxon/early Norman period, its substance was considerably greater than merely the episcopal manor of Chew Magna alone; and the holdings making up the Bishop's manor account for only a part of the area of the later hundred [Thorn and Thorn 1980, 354, note 6,13]. For despite its obvious linkages to the mother church of Chew, at least elements of Chew Stoke were tenurially independent, the possessions of secular lords since at least 1066 (see Domesday Tables). Dundry, although later claimed by the See of Wells (below), is not recorded in Domesday and both its ownership and the manor under which it was taxed, are problematic.

We must, though, ask whether an original grant to the See (in or after 909?) had included these two estates, subsequently lost, and if so, whether also this was effectively a grant of a minster church and its *parochia*? The just over 6 hides of what is apparently royal land noted at Chew Stoke in the Geld Inquest of 1084, but ignored by Domesday, may at least hint at both the royal antecedents already suggested and, as significantly, its former extent [Morland 1990, 110]; so that "it may be that.....the king's villans [there] are working a tiny rump of the once royal estate" [Frank Thorn, *pers comm*]. The general confirmation S1042 [Sawyer 1968] includes among holdings claimed by the Bishop, land in Dundry, naming *Hæsele* (modern Hazel Farm) separately. This charter may, as we have already noted, be palpably fraudulent in terms of its purported date of 1065; but as Abrams has recently reminded us of items of similarly dubious provenance among the Glastonbury Abbey archive, "a forged document does not necessarily indicate a false claim. Charters can have been fabricated for a variety of reasons, not all of them dishonest" [Abrams 1996, 319]. If S1042 is at the least recording a claim which long tradition

---

[3] Indeed a century earlier Leland himself, without naming them, had remarked how "there be dyvers paroche chirches there aboute that ons a yere do homage onto Chute theyr mother chyrche". Toulmin-Smith 1910, V, 103.

considered rightful at the time of its production, then Dundry can probably be seen as a member of a putative Chew *parochia*. The fact that the claim amounts to 50 hides rather than the 30 of 1086 [Harmer 1952, 488], might have suggested a retrospective attempt by the See to annexe all those estates which lay in the medieval hundred of Chew; except that, significantly, both Timsbury and Clutton are excluded from the list of lands rehearsed in S1042, suggesting strongly that, although they were both part of Chew hundred, the See knew it could not by right claim them for its own precisely *because* neither had been part of the original grant. The hundred of Chew in 1086 amounted to 65½ hides, but Timsbury and Clutton together accounted for 20; excluding these two estates takes us very close to the 50 hides claimed by the See in S1042. Likewise for Chew Stoke, for whose membership of the same estate the secondary, dependent nature of its toponym, combined with the ecclesiastical evidence, seems to be powerful evidence. In any event, Morland [1990, 98] is unlikely to be correct in suggesting that the See came into the possession of the entire hundred, for the first time, only after the 1084 Geld Inquest; at that time, Chew Magna itself was indeed, as Morland notes, a member of Bishop Giso's private hundred. But the arrangement seems to have been merely a temporary administrative expedient, the clear implication being that, prior to the Bishop's meddling, in or shortly before 1084, Chew had long been at the head of its own hundred, as it certainly was two years later [Thorn 1989a, 36; and *pers comm*]. While Anderson was strictly incorrect to say that "the *hundred* (my italics) belonged to the See of Wells" [Anderson 1939, 39], there is a sense in which, in principle, he may not be far wide of the mark. In his recent study of Portbury, Alexander, following Helen Cam, has reiterated the significance of the so-called "manorial hundred", whereby included implicitly in the grant of a manor which was also a hundred centre, was the lordship of the entire hundred in which that manor lay [Alexander 1997, 7]. We can agree with Michael Costen that the See of Wells acquired the manor of Chew very early on in the 10th century. If so, it is quite possible that it also acquired a block of surrounding land which was already identified as, or which was later to become, the core area of Chew hundred. Together the four estates of Chew Stoke, Dundry, Stowey and Norton, form a tight cluster around Chew itself, and topographically the resulting territorial entity has an appearance of unity and cohesion. This area, I suggest, is the original Chew 'proto-hundred' which was ceded to Wells.

Timsbury and Clutton seem altogether different. Timsbury's geographical detachment from the hundred, separated from it by Farmborough to the north and High Littleton to the south, seems merely to heighten the impression in both parishes of 'non-belonging': in historical times neither had any ecclesiastical connection with Chew Magna parish, and both are physically isolated from it, Clutton sharing a common boundary (its westernmost) only with Stowey. While not an infallible guide to either dependency or superiority, as the case of Norton Malreward has already shown, nonetheless glebe terriers for both places give no indication of tithes or other

dues owed either to or from other parishes [Clutton, SRO D/D/Rg 30; Timsbury, 54/1 and 2]. Even when considered only in relationship to each other, links are not immediately obvious. In 1086 both were in the common ownership of the Bishop of Coutances, but only to an extent: while Clutton in its entirety belonged to the Bishop, only half of Timsbury did. Indeed the same tenurial distinction extends to the sub-tenant level, since the Bishop of Countance's interest in both manors was leased to (probably) the same man, William, while Odo of Flanders had kept his half of Timsbury in hand, in chief of the king. Before 1066 even these tenuous threads break down, for the four pre-Conquest manors recorded by Domesday for these two places were held by four separate owners [Thorn and Thorn 1980]. Shadowy records of two Anglo-Saxon charters suggest designs on Clutton by Glastonbury Abbey Abbey, the first attributed to the gift of a layman probably in the 9th century, the second, perhaps a lease, to King Edmund in the first half of the tenth [Abrams 1996, 92-93]. It does not seem likely, even from this dubious evidence, that Glastonbury Abbey's apparently short-lived and tenuous claim on Clutton could have played any role in its 'anamalous' membership of Chew hundred, still less that of Timsbury.

Topographically, these two estates would have sat far more comfortably with either Chewton hundred to the south, or Keynsham to the north. Indeed, having already stressed the fluidity of territorial and administrative arrangements throughout the early middle ages in England, it is perfectly possible that before they first become visible to us in the late 11th century as members of Chew hundred, this may in fact have been the case. Neither do they have any known link of any kind with each other. That leaves the possibility that they became attached to Chew, at the time of formal hundredation, perhaps rather later in the 10th century [Yorke 1995, 124-129], by which time they were almost certainly fully-functioning, self-contained and autonomous economic units in their own right. This is, in fact, the explanation favoured by Prosser, who has surveyed the north Somerset hundreds as part of his more detailed study of the Keynsham Hundred. He sees the anomalous inclusion of Timsbury and Clutton in Chew Hundred as the result of administrative expediency, and of adjustments made in assessments "in order to 'top up' the hidation of a slightly smaller estate which was transformed into a hundred" [Prosser 1995, 123]; and we might consider that the suspiciously 'rounded' nature of the 20-hide Domesday assessment for Clutton and Timsbury together does give some support to this view.

Antecedents: Chew Hundred and its *Tūn*

There may be wider implications here, and perhaps at least part of the answer lies in the possibility that the area which later became Chew hundred had itself originated as an element in a larger entity, from which it had subsequently been carved. The evidence pointing to this conclusion is perhaps circumstantial, but nonetheless telling, and turns mainly upon our interpretation of the relationship between Chew Magna and Chewton Mendip.

In the past the tendency has been to emphasise the primacy of Chewton Mendip rather than Chew Magna, but there is a danger that this perception may be, I think, misleading, and the stress on Chewton's royal ownership, a natural consequence of the unbalanced perspective of the historical record, obscures its true status as very much a secondary estate to Chew Magna [*cf* Costen 1992a, 88, and Fig 4.8, 108, map of suggested primary churches, which includes Chewton as a possible minster but omits Chew completely]. So much becomes clear from an examination of the topographical, toponymic and archaeological evidence. Chewton was indeed a royal estate; but should we, therefore, be looking there for the site of a mid Saxon royal complex? I do not consider so.

We have already noted that the toponym Chew is derived from a simplex pre-English river name, and Michael Costen has stressed the royal associations of places with a river name plus *tūn* [Costen 1992a, 87-88]. Sawyer has also highlighted the royal implications of some *tūn* names [Sawyer 1983]. However, we might also consider those cases in which clearly linked pairs of names, one a topographical simplex and the other combining the same element with a habitative word, indicate the existence of a dependent relationship between the two [*cf* Aston 1985a, 34-35]. Chardstock, until 1896 lying in the hundred of Beaminster in Dorset, for example, clearly originated as an outlying dependency of Chard in Somerset's East Kingsbury hundred, four km away to the north-east and just over the county boundary [VCH Dorset 1988, III, 132; and map of Domesday Dorset]. Chard is not a river name, but rivers do figure prominently in such relationships. Wellow near Bath carries a pre-English river name, was the site of a major Roman villa [Scott 1993, 18] and a hundredal centre [Anderson 1939, 42-43], with (non-parochial) chapelries at Shoscombe and Peasedown [Aston 1986, 76]. It is linked toponymically, upstream of the Wellow Brook, to Radstock in Kilmersdon hundred. Radstock was originally *Welewestoce*, at once revealing its genesis as an outlying farmstead, secondary or dependent settlement of Wellow [Costen 1979, 15; Sawyer 1968, S854][4]. The existence of such early estates centered on rivers was first mooted by Hoskins, based on his work in Devon [Hoskins 1952][5]. However, the idea has since been adopted and elaborated by, among others, Alan Everitt in Kent, who suggests, on the basis of examples from other counties, that names in *stoc* which are compounded in linked groups with pre-English river names may in some instances indicate former membership of large, ancient 'river estates' centred around early-established (or so-called 'seminal') settlements [Everitt 1986, 73 and refs there cited]. Wellow's 'seminal' status (hundredal centre + villa), its simplex river name, and its relationship with *Welewestoce* may hint at a former status as the *caput* of just such an estate. The antiquity of the Somerset examples quoted is suggested by the fact that the putative estates

both cross hundred boundaries, and therefore probably pre-date not only hundredation, but in the case of Chard/Chardstock, the shiring of Dorset and Somerset[6].

Following the example of Hoskins's work in Devon, Teresa Hall has shown recently in Dorset how, in terms of the relative chronology of X/X*tūn* relationships, the early (ie British) simplex river name X is likely to be the senior partner [Hall 2000, 62]; the primary territorial entity in a given area will have acquired the same name, will have probably at least originated as a royal estate, and will be the site of an early, high-value minster church at the centre of a large *parochia* containing a network of dependent churches [Hall 2000, 18-67]. The X estate will also have given its name to the hundred in which it lies, and in some areas, probably in Somerset but not, apparently, in Dorset, is likely to possess Roman antecedents. I would suggest that this model precisely describes the relationship between Chew and Chewton.

Topographically, Chewton makes little sense as a 'seminal' settlement: it occupies an awkward and constricted site in the upper Chew valley, on high ground well up the northern slope of Mendip (the church lies just above the 150m contour). The modern land-quality map shows clearly that Chewton's immediate hinterland, categorised as Grade 3, is not what would be regarded as good arable, and was probably not subjected to regular ploughing until the late 18th century, when large-scale enclosure went hand in hand with attempts to improve soil-quality; Michael Williams makes the point that both of the main soil types found on the Mendip plateau itself "presented problems, and a great deal of preparatory labour and capital investment were needed before they could be cultivated successfully" [Williams 1971, 69]. Indeed even by 1801, when such work had already been under way for at least a decade in some areas, and only a year after the granting of Chewton's own Enclosure Award [Tate 1948, 47], still only about 190 hectares of its 2,608 hectare parish area (about 7.3%) were actually under the plough [Williams 1971, 71, Table 1].

A large parish is often taken to indicate both antiquity and importance; however, in this instance I would argue that the bare figures do not accurately reflect Chew's primacy in relation to Chewton. For although, in the mid-19th century, Chew parish contained a little over 5,000 acres, against Chewton's 5,800 [Kain and Oliver 1995, 437], we should bear in mind that nearly 40% of the latter's area was not considered fit for any form of agriculture other than rough grazing[7]. By contrast, in the whole of Chew hundred (including Timsbury and Clutton) only some 236 acres around Dundry Hill were ever subject to parliamentary enclosure, by an award of 1819 [Tate 1948, 53 and 79]. As far as the 'core entities', the parishes of Chew and Chewton themselves, are concerned, the point here is that proportionately, Chew contained a far greater extent of potentially productive land, and there was

---

[4] This important point goes unremarked, and its possible significance is therefore unfortunately missed, by a recent survey which otherwise provides a useful summary of early (ie early medieval) territorial and settlement patterns in and around Wellow hundred. See Ford 1998.
[5] I am grateful to Teresa Hall for this reference.

[6] A possible context for this split perhaps being provided by a grant by King Æthelwulf, in the first half of the 9th century, probably of Chardstock, to the see of Sherborne; O'Donovan 1988, xlvii.
[7] If we can judge from the 2,266 acres of "Commons or Waste Lands" included in the Chewton Enclosure Award of 1800; Tate 1948, 47.

probably little of it that could not have been pressed into service for arable should the need arise.

In common with other Mendip-flank settlements, Chewton's true economic *raison d'être* was as a rough-grazing sheepwalk [Neale 1976, 88, and 94-95], a point made by Domesday Book, which records a flock of 800 sheep there, and pasture 2 leagues by 1 league (about 1,166 hectares by Rackham's formula for the Domesday league [Rackham 1988, 20]). And while, again, we may doubt whether the one square league (about 583 hectares) of woodland recorded in 1086 all actually lay at Chewton, nonetheless it is the pastoral role of woodland in the pre-Conquest period which has recently been re-emphasised by Harold Fox [Fox 1996, 7-9].

What, then, of Chewton's royal credentials? It seems very likely that Chew and Chewton once formed part of the same 'early' (ie at least 7th-8th century) river estate, an economic and territorial centred on Chew. Chewton, I suggest, has a higher 'royal profile' than Chew, in historical terms, precisely *because* it remained in royal hands, not because it had originally been the more important place. Significantly, it is Chewton, not Chew, which is granted to Edward the Elder in King Alfred's will [Keynes and Lapidge 1983, 173-178], which descends, probably through Edward the Confessor, to his widow Eadgyth and thence, by 1086, to William the Conqueror [Meyer 1993, esp at 81; Costen 1992a, 88]. Sawyer draws a distinction between those estates which were in the personal possession of the King, and those which belonged to the institution of the crown and which would have been regarded as inalienable except under exceptional circumstances [Sawyer 1983, 279]. The inference here must be that Alfred did not bequeath Chew because he was not entitled and perhaps anyway not inclined to do so; it belonged in the latter, non-personal category of royal estates, probably because of its 'central-place status', value, productivity and early origins. We have already noted clear royal antecedents in Chew hundred in the 1084 Geld Accounts. However, Sawyer also makes the point that it would have been easier for a king to alienate part of an estate only [*ibid*, 280]; which is exactly what Edward the Elder did when endowing Wells with Chew, splitting the old Chew 'river estate' and retaining Chewton to himself. How this process may have been related to the emergence of the two hundreds, Chew and Chewton, it is difficult to say; there can be little doubt, however, that certainly in Chew's case, the split resulted in a 'core' entity very close in extent to the later hundred.

The 'fracture lines' within the Chew river estate structure were probably well-defined long before 909: the very fact that Alfred was able to identify a Chewton entity for inclusion in his will suggests strongly that it had already been defined territorially, and had probably existed as an important semi-autonomous unit for some time. So much is further implied by Chewton's status as a mother church, and its possession of a series of dependent churches[8]. John Blair makes the point that "minsters are not identified on individual criteria, but on recurrent

combinations" [Blair 1995, 200], few of which are satisfied by Chewton. If it was indeed a minster by, say, 1086, it was presumably only elevated to that position after the loss of Chew Magna, the early *caput* of the estate. It seems likely that Chewton falls into that category of 'late' minsters described, again, by John Blair [1995, 197]. It is Chew, not Chewton, which was the 'primary minster' of the two. How the area delimited by Chewton's dependencies relates to the extent of the later hundred, King Alfred's bequest, and the Domesday estate, is not clear. A possible context may, however, be provided by Teresa Hall's work in Dorset, which has highlighted at least one example where a probable late minster seems to have had a *parochia*, containing pre-existing churches, specially created for it [Hall 2000, 67]. Hall suggests that such artificial arrangements can be spotted by considering, particularly, the degree of dependency of daughter churches, and the general topography of the parochia itself. In this light, a church which has been elevated to minster status at a later date will betray its 'secondary' origins by a low degree of both dependency on the part of its subsidiary churches, and topographical cohesiveness within its own *parochia*. This may well describe the background to Chewton's status, and would fit with a suggested formalisation of Chewton Hundred in the early 10th century. There may, indeed, be telling indications of artificiality in at least the initial stages of the break-up of the putative Chew river estate, and it is possible that an attempt was made to make the split a roughly equal one in terms of the land area allocated to the new, smaller territories. The parishes within Chew hundred, excluding Timsbury and Clutton, and counting only those places whose churches can be shown to have had some degree of dependence on Chew, covered an area of some 11,200 acres (4,536 ha) in the mid 19th century; while Chewton and its direct ecclesiastical dependencies amounted to some 12,400 acres (5,022 ha) at the same period [Kain and Oliver 1995; and glebe terrier for Chewton Mendip, 1638, SRO D/D/Rg 152/2][9]. Although this can at best offer only a crude comparison, the general order of the similarity seems too close to be accounted for by coincidence alone. This may then provide yet another piece of circumstantial evidence that Clutton and Timsbury were not originally part of the Chew 'proto' hundred, and indeed that Chewton hundred also, before it emerges fully-formed in the post-Conquest period, had probably passed through at least two and possibly more stages of growth by the accretion of additional lands around an original early core.

Later on I will try to explain at least one aspect of the composition of Chewton hundred as it emerges in the post-Conquest period, and to relate this to the fission of the putative Chew river estate. However, in terms of the current general debate regarding the relative dates of origin of 'multiple' estates and hundreds [*cf* Alexander 1997, 8-14], it is beginning increasingly to look as though, in Somerset, at least some of the hundreds in their early form were created by the division of larger, pre-existing territories. If Chewton, for all its royal interest, is

---

[8] Paulton, Emborough, Farrington and Ston Easton [Torr 1974-79, 88], the last three all recorded as manors in 1086.

[9] The terrier shows that the vicar of Chewton had jurisdiction over the churchyards at these places.

secondary, it is Chew which emerges as very much the centre of gravity in the local landscape, by almost every criterion which modern scholarship regards as significant.

Topographically, Chew's site and situation are far more amenable than those of Chewton. Although the core area around the church occupies a small peninsula, the Chew valley at this point is far less constricted, offering plenty of room for expansion especially towards the valley floor immediately to the south, and gradients are altogether gentler. Archaeological confirmation of Chew's position on the local network of Roman roads (Chapter Two) reinforces the already strong impression that it lay at a communications nodal point of some antiquity, just above a convenient crossing of the river from which it takes its name [Costen 1987, 84, fig 7.2; Tratman 1963]. Where the modern land quality map highlights Chewton's deficiences, by contrast it very much emphasises Chew's advantages: for an extensive tract around the village, as far as Stanton Drew to the east, Sutton and Stowey to the south-east, and Chew Stoke to the south-west, is classed as the best quality (Grade 1) agricultural land [MAFF 1" Agricultural Land Classification, 1972, Sheet 166]. This is reflected directly in the attraction which the area has had for human activity since at least the Neolithic, most spectacularly at Stanton Drew, and Gerrard's detailed statistical work on the locations of a large sample of Somerset villas has confirmed an overwhelming preference for sites on high-grade agricultural land [Gerrard 1987, 102-104; and *cf* Chapter Two].

We need to ask why a king should feel Chew Magna, rather than Chewton, to be an appropriate inaugural gift to a nascent diocese. Perhaps value was at least partly a factor: Chew's potential agricultural productivity has already been noted. In 1086 its 30 hides were worth £30 as opposed to Chewton's £50 on its 29 hides, but Chewton's assessment, including as it would have done a high proportion of Mendip plateau, related to a far larger, but much less productive geographical area. As a 'flagship' element of Edward's reorganisation of dioceses in the Wessex royal heartlands [Yorke 1995, 210], there may certainly have been a desire to set the nascent See of Wells off on a firm economic footing. If so, however, and as Stenton makes clear, any early stability was short-lived [Stenton 1971, 439]. By 1066, in fact, the Bishop's writ ran in only some 221 hides of his own, less than half that pertaining to Glastonbury Abbey [Loud 1989, 15-16].

It seems far more likely that it was chiefly for other reasons that Chew was chosen as a prestige gift to the new see, to form a prominent part of its 'core' estate, suitable to the dignity of a diocesan bishop; specifically, because it already enjoyed a role as a seminal and central place in the landscape. The disparate antecedent elements already noted came together at Chew: a probable early minster site with strong royal associations, a communications focus, and a position at the centre of an intensively-settled and exploited Roman countryside, now with archaeological

proof of Roman activity within Chew itself. If Chew's status as an important mid-Saxon minster be accepted, and the balance of what evidence there is must allow it to be, the questions which follow relate logically to the extent of the minster site, and the additional possibility of a permanent and significant royal presence close by. John Blair has, admittedly, warned recently of a too-easy assumption that the supposed affinity between royal 'palace' and minster was both ubiquitous and geographically intimate: "the normal relationship.....seems to have been one of proximity rather than absolute contiguity". Especially from the mid 7th century, Blair suggests, "though often 'twinned' with a royal centre no more than 2 or 3 miles away, a minster was normally set amid its own lands and housed within its own enclosure" [Blair 1992, 231]. Yet relationship there clearly was, and in his later study of Cheddar and Northampton, one detects a distinct shift in his perspective, concluding as he does that it was the minsters which should probably be regarded as primary [Blair 1996, 120-121].

On this basis, at Chew it would be by no means unreasonable to look for topographical and archaeological evidence of a possible precinct boundary. From here it is a logical step to speculate that an as yet unidentified royal residence of some kind lies in proximity to the minster; the site of the bishop's mansion would be the most likely candidate: we have already seen that an episcopal seat was located at Chew certainly by the late 12th century, and probably by 1086. With Cheddar as a useful model for a possible sequence of developments, we might imagine an 'early' minster site (present by the 7th century but with British Christian antecedents?) and its dependent *parochia*, being annexed to the nascent Wessex royal demesne by, say, 700. By perhaps 900, the religious enceinte, bounded or at least dissected on the west by the Roman road, encompassed certainly the minster itself, and had perhaps also drawn to it an associated villa *regalis* of indeterminate nature. If royal presence there were, the exact nature of its relationship with the minster would be difficult now to recover; indeed even of Cheddar, far better documented both historically and archaeologically, Blair is constrained to admit that it is "unclear whether or not [the] minster was itself part of the royal property" [Blair 1996, 117; Yorke 1995, 194-195]. Nonetheless, when the estate's link with royalty was for the most part severed in or around 909, it would surely have been rational for the new bishop to have appropriated any pre-existing high-status residence for his personal use, perhaps perpetuating its site into the post-Conquest period. The fate of any surviving community serving the minster at the time of the transition to the see is likewise problematic; although it is possible, as happened elsewhere during the course of the monastic reforms from the mid 10th century, that any remaining secular clergy were simply evicted [Yorke 1995, 210-213], thereby curtailing the pastoral function of the minster in the wider lay community. Alternatively, the putative Chew religious community could have been removed to Wells to form the core of a body of secular canons serving the new cathedral.

Chew: Minster, Chapel and Town

We have looked briefly at Chew's wider, *territorial* claim to local supremacy, and as an element of that argument have also noted the probable minster status of its church. We can turn now to consider this latter aspect in rather more detail, and to try to develop and reconcile a number of different strands of evidence.

Chew Magna lies at the centre of both its own parish and of its hundred, with its mother church and hundred meeting place; the latter, on the western slope of Knowle Hill according to Wood [1903, 3] was Moote Hills in 1614 [SRO D/D/Rg 26/1; Aston 1986, p63]. Because of the present lack of evidence of a community there, we cannot yet say with certainty that Chew was a minster [*cf* Foot 1992]. However, we have seen that it may well have formed part of the original endowment of the newly-founded diocese in 909, from which we may infer prior royal ownership, and royal connections would make minster status more likely.

Within the churchyard at Chew there stood, until at least the mid 16th century, a chapel dedicated to the Virgin Mary [Wood 1903, 231-234]. Its exact site is now lost, although Wood notes anecdotal accounts of probable wall footings found outside the church on the eastern side of the chancel [Wood 1903, 234]. It seems always to have been assumed to be a chantry chapel founded in the post-Conquest period [Ashley 1978, 14], but it is significant that, while many of the 15th and 16th century wills noted by Wood mention bequests of money or animals to St Mary's chapel, not one explicitly includes money for a priest to say masses for the deceased. The few bequests for chantries or lights which are noted in this period can all be safely assigned to chapels or to the altar within the main body of St Andrew's church itself [Wood 1903, 231-233; Colvin 2000, 172, n45]; and Wood further observes that the chapel appears not to have been among the chantries dissolved by the Commissioners appointed to that task under Edward VI [*ibid*, 233-234; Green 1888]. Neither is there any record of land or other property pertaining to a chantry chapel at Chew Magna itself being bought or sold [Woodward 1982; Colvin 2000, 164-165]. If, then, the chapel could indeed be shown to have lain either directly east or west of the main church (Figure 12), the dedication would take on a greater significance, since the Virgin is especially well-attested within minster-status church groupings, in longitudinal alignment, of known early (ie early-mid Anglo-Saxon) foundation [Blair 1992, 246-258][10]: "it was usual for one of the churches to be that of St Mary's………sometimes it was the older, more westerly church, as at Glastonbury Abbey………but more often St Mary's was both the later and the eastern building, as at Canterbury and at Wells" [Jones 1996, 214]. It is possible

that we should also assign Chew Magna to this latter category.

A very strong 'water' element, the significance of which we have noted in the Introduction to this section, is present at Chew. The church sits on a low bluff overlooking the River Chew about 300m to the south, which is flowing east-west where the Tun Bridge crosses it. In addition, a much smaller stream, flowing west-east, curves around the northern and eastern flanks of the bluff to join the Chew about 300m east of Tun Bridge. The bluff is indeed, therefore, a peninsula, surrounded on three sides by water, the only 'open' approach being from the west. In Dorset a relationship between proven minster sites and early, simplex river names, such as Chew itself is, has been identified by Teresa Hall [Hall 2000, 59-63], and the territorial implications of this for Chew I will discuss briefly below.

One diagnostic element which was until recently missing in the overall picture of Chew Magna as a seminal place displaying a continuous thread of settlement, was any evidence, on a significant level, of activity in the Roman period. The case for suggesting the existence of a villa on or close to the site of St Andrew's church was outlined in Chapter Two; and it certainly seems very clear, from that evidence, that at least the surviving western boundary of the churchyard took its cue from the line of the archaeologically-attested Roman road [Anon 1997; Bell 1996]. It seems perfectly possible that a larger, antecedent enclosure could have extended west of the road, bringing the latter within its compass. As to whether there is any direct causal, as opposed to topographical relationship between church and road, the evidence is inconclusive; a road, after all, is not a settlement site, and could not on its own be considered to support a case either for the presence of Roman occupation, or for its continuity into subsequent periods [Costen *pers comm*].

Nonetheless, the now-proven existence of Roman archaeology so close to what was clearly an important (?early) church, even in the absence of evidence for actual occupation, must give at least some prospect that Chew Magna may eventually be shown to satisfy this particular criterion of 'seminal' status. No indications of burials were found during either this excavation or, indeed, in the course of the only other modern archaeological work to have taken place in the vicinity of the churchyard, in a garden close to the eastern boundary. It is, though, doubtful whether any firm conclusions can be drawn from this regarding the existence or otherwise of an older and formerly much larger graveyard, since both excavations were extremely small-scale, and in the case of the work on the eastern side of the church, had to contend with ground "heavily disturbed by the construction of [an] equestrian ring". [Beaton and Lewcun 1994]. This still does not fully discount the possibility that burials could simply have been missed, destroyed by later construction work, or even systematically re-interred within the area of the present graveyard.

---

[10] A resistivity survey of the eastern end of the churchyard was carried out on my behalf by Dr Jenni Butterworth of Bristol University, and the data assessed and analysed by Mr Alex Turner of King Alfred's College, Winchester. The results (now deposited in the SMR at Bath and North-East Somerset District Council, Bath) were inconclusive, probably, as one might expect of a cemetery, because of a very high degree of disturbance, and this should by no means be taken to prove the absence of St Mary's chapel from that part of the churchyard.

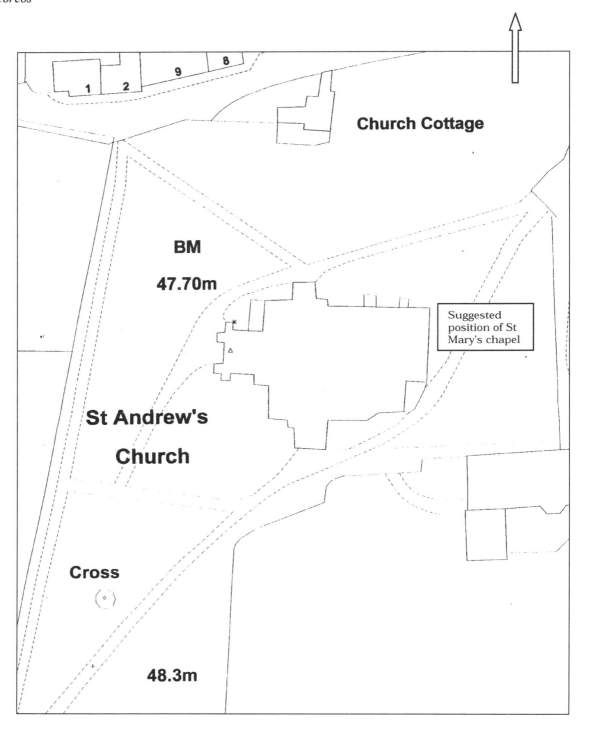

Figure 12: Large scale plan of St Andrew's church, Chew Magna, showing the suggested position of the so-called 'chantry' chapel of St Mary the Virgin, outside the eastern end of the chancel. Adapted from its SMR digital mapping data by courtesy of Bath and North-East Somerset District Council.

An instructive parallel comes from Wroxeter, and may suggest a possible late-/sub-Roman context for the new discovery at Chew; there, "the Anglo-Saxon minster church of St Andrew founded in the 7th century is located in the south-west corner of the town aligned upon an earlier Roman road leading down to the Severn crossing……this may indicate the church was founded 'not in a long-deserted urban wasteland, but a living settlement of some importance'" [quoted in Edwards 1996, 50]. Another potential example with strikingly similar affinities, but much closer to home, is at Ilchester, where the minster church of St Andrew at Northover seems to lie on top of an extra-mural Roman cemetery, on an elevated site to the north of the town, and adjacent to the Foss Way which leads south to a crossing of the River Yeo or Ivel. The church of St Mary Major, which probably has Saxon antecedents, lies in the centre of the walled town, and Dunning has suggested that some parishes in the Ilchester area, namely Bearley, the two parts of Sock Dennis and Northover itself, may have Romano-British boundaries

[Dunning 1974-5, 44-46 and 48; Gathercole 1997, 11; Aston and Leech 1977, 67-75 and Map 28].

The coincidence of the church dedications in these cases is intriguing but its significance is not clear. It is of course possible that at Chew it represents merely a renaming in honour of the mother church of the diocese, and dates only to the time of its likely acquisition by the new see of Wells after 909; although it should also be said that neither Nicholas Orme's survey of dedications in Devon and Cornwall, nor Graham Jones's seminal work on the same theme in the diocese of Worcester, have revealed any significant indications that those recorded by the later medieval period had been subjected to much interference either at that time or after the Reformation [Orme 1996, 11-24; Jones 1996, 30]. Consideration of all the other evidence relating to Chew's status as a capital church makes it likely that its dedication is indeed genuinely ancient, that is, perhaps of the 8th century or earlier. Certainly, it seems rather more than coincidence that Andrew dedications are overwhelmingly prominent in Somerset among that group of places with 'early', and largely topographical, simplex toponyms, such as those, like Chew, derived from river names [*ex inf* Graham Jones]. In terms of the relative chronology of ecclesiastical foundation in the hundred, it may also be significant that Chew's dedication to St Andrew is shared by its dependency of Chew Stoke; territorially secondary perhaps, but the antiquity of whose own church may be revealed in the survival there of pieces of an important late Saxon carved cross-shaft (Plate 2)[Foster 1987, 56, 59-60, 72][11]. On the basis of this discussion, Figures 13, 14 and 15 represent an attempt to trace a basic sequence of development for the area around the minster, from the Roman period to the beginning of the 14th century. While largely speculative, this model seems at present to reconcile most of what little hard evidence we have, and provides a foundation for amendment or elaboration should future work require it.

While we can probably regard Chew's minster status as secure, by contrast an *urban* role there remains unproven on any formal level, and in the mid 50s Savage felt able categorically to state that "in the absence of definite records I find no evidence of a town" [Savage 1955, 71]. In her seminal study of social and economic developments affecting the see of Bath and Wells in the century after the Reformation, Hembry asserts that "Chew.....held the dignity of a borough", but does not state the basis for this suggestion. She adds that "it had a market and was a busy clothing town, but it is doubtful whether the bishop drew any profits from its trade". Again, the evidence for the former is not explicitly stated; certainly the *Valor Ecclesiasticus* contains no reference to either a borough at Chew or to revenues accruing to the bishop from a market there, although a cursory reading might lead one to infer that the *Valor* was the source of these remarks [Caley and Hunter 1810-1834]. While Hembry does go on to say that a borough at Chew "does not appear among the

list of boroughs and hundreds owned by [the bishop] in 1535.....", she clearly believes that in this case at least, it is safe to argue from the silence of the documentary record [Hembry 1967, 20].

In any event, Chew was clearly a 'focal place' in the landscape; incipient urbanism there has been hinted at [Aston 1986, 71], and there is enough anecdotal evidence, dismissed out of hand by Savage, to give the firm impression of a past perception that this was indeed the case [cf Collinson 1791, II, 94; Toulmin-Smith 1910, V, 103]. This includes Collinson's frustratingly cryptic remark that "Subsequent Monarchs [to William I] enriched the burgh of Chew with many and great privileges" [Collinson 1791, II, 95][12]. It is possible that Chew conforms to the town/minster paradigm, for there does indeed seem to be a link between early administrative centres, such as those in the Thames Valley recently described by John Blair, and minsters [Blair 1996a]. Blair's remark that "the towns are there because the minsters were there first" [Blair 1996a, 12], has thrown wide open the question of urban origins in the mid-Saxon period. It is certainly true that, in simple chronological terms, many of the early-founded minsters, dating from the 7th or 8th centuries and of which Chew may be one, preceded urban growth at the same locations, because to use the term 'town' at this period is an anachronism. Noting the transience and instability of the early *wics* or *emporia*, David Palliser has stressed recently that "permanent English towns on their present sites started to be created (or re-established on former Roman sites) in the eighth, ninth and tenth centuries" [Palliser 1992, 177]. Indeed, Tom Saunders shifts the focus to an even later phase, observing that "the formative period in the process of urbanisation in early medieval England occurred in the late 9th and 10th centuries, as is clearly illustrated in the documentary and archaeological record" [Saunders 1995, 40; cf Anderton 1999, Russo 1998].

But even given the likely chronological primacy of the minsters, it would be disingenuous to claim that we yet understand, and still less can explain their frequent coincidence with towns. Whatever the nature of the relationship, it seems unlikely *always* to have been a straightforward causal one of minster = town. Rather, it was probably complex and fluid, an outcome of the interaction between a bewildering hierarchy of factors, not all of them now recoverable to us, operating at varying intensities at different times and in different places. I will return to another aspect of this same problem below, and we confront similar questions at Carhampton, later on in the Chapter; but for now, it is sufficient to note that the only really clear common denominator at present is the fact that both towns and minsters frequently co-habited at sites which earlier periods had already marked out as important points in the landscape, showing a variety of recurring characteristics; indeed, Blair himself makes precisely this

---

[11]For the specific significance of Andrew+Mary dedicatory relationships as indicators of early foundation, see below the discussion of Shapwick and Moorlinch.

[12]Writing in the late 1730s, Collinson's often more thorough, but unfortunately unpublished predecessor, John Strachey, the great antiquary of Sutton Court at Stowey, remains silent on the matter of Chew's problematic urban status. Strachey 1867, 82-100. I am grateful to Naomi Payne for this reference.

point [Blair 1995, *passim*]. But conversely, it is legitimate to ask why numerous early churches, some of them minster/villa 'complexes' (in Somerset, Shapwick is a good example) failed to attract urban growth; and why, both before and after 1066, the absence of an ancient minster apparently did little to prevent some places (Somerset examples include Axbridge, Dunster and Bridgwater) from becoming towns, and subsequently flourishing in their new-found urban role? [Aston 1986, 74-76; Beresford and Finberg 1973, 154-155; Costen 1992a, 105-107].

Neither should the existence of a market of itself be taken as a certain guide to urban status, for exchange was by no means the sole prerogative of the towns; on the contrary: Schofield and Vince point out that "in some counties.....there were more markets in villages than in towns. There were also many communities on the borderline between villages and towns, so the distinction cannot be forced" [Schofield and Vince 1994, 51-52]. And in the West Midlands, Dyer has identified an entire sub-stratum of rural settlements which seem to possess quasi-urban characteristics, and which probably played a central role in local exchange and trading networks, despite the fact that any marketing function at such places is to a large extent historically 'invisible' to us [Dyer 1992]. Nonetheless, when considered in conjunction with a range of other evidence, the operation or otherwise of a market may help to point us either towards or away from an urban perspective.

While there is no known formal grant for Chew, this does not mean that an ancient prescriptive market did not operate: speaking of Sevenoaks in Kent, for example, Everitt observes that although "it was not a 'primary town' in the sense of an old caput.....archaeological evidence indicates a pre-Conquest market at this point, and the fact that this market was a prescriptive or traditional one, and never acquired a formal charter from the crown, tends to confirm its Old English origin" [Everitt 1986, 268-269]. Indeed, a blanket grant to Jocelin, Bishop of Bath and Glastonbury, in 1227, of markets and fairs on all his manors to be held at his discretion, is more likley to have been actually exercised at Chew, where it may have had the effect of merely confirming existing practice, than elsewhere [Cal Charter Rolls I, 1903, 16]; a suggestion supported by Britnell's emphasis on the importance of hundredal centres in market networks before the 13th century, proposing as he does a pre-Conquest origin for many ancient prescriptive markets that are documented in the high middle ages, but which possess no formal charter [Britnell 1978]; such a market has, for example, recently been proposed by Alexander at the hundred, minster and royal centre of Portbury [Alexander 1997, 7].

Neither need the economic or social viability of any market at Chew have been compromised by the relatively very late (and probably retrospective) grant of a weekly market and annual fair at Chewton in 1348 [Cal Charter Rolls V, 1916, 72]: since, as Gerrard observes, "it is clear that contemporary exchange centres.....need not always have competed for trade. They drew their potential vendors and purchasers from the same areas: each fair did not

control its 'economic territory' autonomously, as might have been assumed had we drawn Thiessen polygons and argued that each fair commanded a different territory from the next" [Gerrard 1987, 117]. At Chew, the name 'Tun' ('town'?) Bridge adds to the body of circumstantial evidence, and the existence of Port Bridge a kilometre or so to the west [OS 1st edn 6" map (1884), Somerset, XII SW] assumes an even greater significance in the light of the suggestion that some 'port' names are related to the collection of tolls [Gerrard 1987, 120]. It may be that Port Bridge is so named not from any reference to Chew, but from its position on a major route between Wells and the regional centre of gravity in commercial terms, Bristol. However, in this context we might also consider the appearance of a man taxed under one of the Chew Stoke manors in 1327, whose name, *Philip le Portreve*, strongly suggests that he was a market official, living a suspiciously long way from Bristol [Dickinson 1889, 138].

Chew Magna certainly does not look like a village. Especially in terms of many of its private buildings, the general impression is overwhelmingly like that of a small but thriving market town. The main east-west road into Chew is lined on both sides with a succession of large, impressive and clearly wealthy 18th and 19th century houses that would sit quite comfortably in an urban setting. What they may tell us of Chew's medieval face is quite another matter. Discussing the profound economic changes which came about in the wake of the various population crises from the mid 14th century, and their implications for towns and trade, Gerrard observes that "after the 15th century, there.....seems to be a shift in wealth within regions, from the towns into the countryside. Rural clothiers became wealthy....." [Gerrard 1987, 244]. If this is what happened at Chew, then the evidence of its surviving, very town-like, but relatively late houses, can be used only to elucidate the history of the period which produced them.

Map evidence gives no hint of a 'conventional' burgage-plot layout, and traces of a former central open space which might have held a market are restricted to a small area of possible infill south of the church, and another one a short distance to the west. On balance I favour the latter location, since it is larger than the 'church' site, its position is such that its activities would not have interfered unduly with the flow of traffic along the main east-west road through the village, and it occupies a relatively level position: the 'church' site sits awkwardly astride a marked break of slope where the main road swings sharply southwards, downslope towards the river crossing at Tun Bridge. The eastern side of the western site is also bounded by Silver Street, which may perhaps be a memory of activities in that area involving relatively large quantities of coin, and/or of the presence of silversmiths attracted there by flourishing and profitable trade [Room 1992, 95-96]. In any event, topographical indications of urban status at Chew certainly appear to be limited. Appearances alone, however, can be deceptive. It is worth noting, for example, Christopher Taylor's recent strictures against a too-easy assumption that the topographical attributes so characteristic of large, planned medieval towns will also be found in that class of settlement which he describes as 'market villages', and of which Chew Magna may have been one. When such rural centres acquired markets, "the physical changes which may have occurred are not likely to be those which are so obvious in planted towns with their neat grid plans, well-marked market-places, and equal-sized burgage plots. Further, with the growing realisation of the complexity of the origins and development of the English medieval village, it is obvious that the identification of such features which might relate to a market grant is going to be very difficult" [Taylor 1983, 21]. This rather pessimistic view is, though, reassessed in a recent short survey by Lilley, in which, building on Taylor's own work, he concludes that "there exists the opportunity to use settlement plans to further explore cases where villages functioned as centres for commercial exchange, but received no formal market charter.....[and] for rethinking the distinctions that are so often drawn between 'town' and 'village' in medieval settlement studies" [Lilley 1996, 24].

Certainly, none of this is to suggest that Chew's topography has not been interfered with. On the contrary: it is quite clear that the line taken by the present main east-west road marks a very distinct and deliberate southerly diversion around the site of the Bishop's mansion, perhaps originally to accommodate a small emparking scheme; it seems to have been this existing line which was reinforced by turnpiking at the end of the 18th century [Ashley 1978, 9]. Air photographic evidence [NMR CPE/UK 1869, 4/12/46, frame 3244] seems clearly to indicate the course of a former road running immediately south of the Bishop's mansion, a feature first noted on the ground by Roger Ashley [Ashley 1978, 9], and probably forming part of an antecedent east-west route directly through the middle of the settlement.

John Blair's recent development of an earlier suggestion by Christopher Dyer establishes a possible relationship between the presence of bordars and cottars in 1086, minster status, and indications of urban characteristics [Blair 1996a, 13-14]. This may be worth considering for Chew: although DB records 9 bordars on the Bishop's 4 demesne hides, and a total of 27 on the remaining 26 subinfuedated hides, the ratio of bordars per hide on the demesne, at 2.25, is over twice that on the rest of the estate (just under 1.04) [Thorn and Thorn 1980]. This relative concentration of smallholders and cottagers on the demesne, which would presumably have encompassed the settlement of Chew Magna itself, prompts the suggestion that they may been involved in activities closely related to a developing proto-urban centre [Dyer 1985]. We might also note that the 14 slaves recorded in 1086 on the demesne seems a disproportionately large number, producing a ratio of 3.5 slaves per hide, as opposed to the 8 slaves on the subinfuedated estate, a ratio of about 0.31 slaves per hide. Following Penny Stokes's suggestion for Ditcheat, it is possible that the demesne slaves had been settled on land close to the lord's hall at Chew and had the specific task of servicing a large manorial curia [Stokes 1996, 67]. If so,

such a settlement may have left traces in the topography around the site of the Bishop's house.

Dyer, re-examining recently the whole question of the place of small towns in the medieval English economy, defines them as "permanent settlement[s] in which a very high proportion of the population lived by a variety of trades, crafts and other non-agricultural activities. The town had a distinct appearance, as it was compact and had a high density of structures and people, with building plots arranged closely in rows along streets and around market places" [Dyer 2002, 2]. It is difficult to avoid the impression that applying these criteria, and on the basis of the evidence currently available, Chew could not by default be admitted as a town, but the case against can by no means be said to be absolutely proven.

The following is an attempt briefly to summarise points both for and against Chew's possible historic status as a town:

FOR
1. Anecdotal and antiquarian accounts (Leland, Collinson, Wood).
2. ?General 'townlike' appearance: wealthy 'town' houses.
3. Apparent concentration of cottars on demesne estate in 1086.
4. Probable minster church.
5. *Possible base of market cross now in churchyard [Wood 1903, 231].
6. *Possession of stocks [*ibid*].
7. Oblique antiquarian suggestion of a relict market place [*op cit*].
8. Port Bridge and Tun Bridge.
9. Hundred centre.
10. Evidence of infill of a once larger open (market?) space south of the church, and another one slightly further west.
11. Portreeve personal name at Chew Stoke.
12. Silver Street(?)

AGAINST
1. No topographical evidence of burgage plots.
2. No unequivocal evidence from street names within Chew suggestive of either a market place or urban status.
3. No burgesses in 1086.
4. No known formal market, fair or borough charter grant (excluding 'blanket' grant of 1227).
5. *No corporation or mayor[13].
6. *No particular importance emphasised on early maps, eg Johan Blaeu's map of Somerset, 1648; compare, for example, with Axbridge.
7. *Urban function inherently unlikely due to distortion of local trading networks by the massive economic influence of Bristol.
8. No current evidence for the range of economic activities taking place.

---

[13]Although in this context we should note Dyer's assertion that "few small towns had mayors". Dyer 2002, 10.

*Suggested by Vince Russett

On balance, I consider it extremely unlikely that Chew was ever a town in any formal, legalistic sense. There is nothing known in the documentary record which even hints that at any period it ever enjoyed that status, and it is extremely difficult to imagine that had this been the case, there would not have been some indication of it among the massive archive of so financially-assiduous a landlord as a major diocesan bishop. If, after all, the see was so careful, in the late 12th century, to obtain charters of borough privileges for its tiny and ultimately doomed wharf site at Rackley, on the River Axe [Beresford and Finberg 1973, 157-158], how much more might we have expected it to apply the same zeal to one of its most important and lucrative estates? By the end of the 12th century at the latest, many lords, secular and ecclesiastical, could claim the same rights in boroughs under their control that the king enjoyed from royal centres, especially "rents and other charges paid by tenants.....an income from penalties imposed by borough courts, tolls on trade and traders, the profits of local mints, and perhaps other traditional payments" [Miller and Hatcher 1995, 285]. None of these are apparent at Chew Magna, and it is difficult to escape the conclusion that, for reasons which are not clear, the see felt no necessity to obtain formal borough instruments for it, and indeed may have operated a deliberate policy of avoiding doing so. This may perhaps be at least partly related to the use of Chew as one of the bishop's capital residences outside Wells, and a perception that the bustle, noise and worldliness of a thriving borough was incompatible with, and would disturb, the calm, reflective atmosphere of an essentially rural mansion; which was presumably one of the reasons why successive bishops chose to withdraw to it.

Equally however, formal borough status would have been irrelevant if the bishop, as manorial lord, already enjoyed rights and privileges in Chew Magna similar or equal to those normally associated with it. We have already seen (above) that even by the late 11th century, Chew may have been displaying certain attributes of incipient urbanism. We must of course be cautious in extrapolating backwards from later evidence, and the recorded anecdotal perceptions of Chew's 'town-like' qualities are indeed both late (beginning only with Leland) and sporadic. However, we have also noted that trade and exchange functions were by no means the sole prerogatives of towns and legal boroughs, and likewise it is becoming clear, as for example in the case of Ipswich, that regularity of plan may not necessarily be as diagnostic of urban attributes as was once thought [Palliser 1992, 180-181]. The profound effect on settlement of the existence of resource-interfaces (below) is emphasised by Dyer's comment that in the medieval period, "a great deal of long-distance trade helped to redress imbalances between the resources of different regions. This helps to explain the location of many towns on or near the frontier of farming regions" [Dyer 1988, 32-33]. Trade of any distance requires communications routes, and one wonders whether it is entirely coincidence that the former main road south

from Bristol, over Dundry Hill and into Chew Magna, enters the village at just that point where the plan opens out into the more westerly of the two possible market places. Further, to contend that "no village could hope to grow into a town without acquiring both a market and borough status" [Gerrard 1987, 123] may not be invariably true; in the east midlands, for example, "while not all boroughs became towns, there were a number of other settlements which developed into towns apparently without the aid of borough status" [Dyer *et al* 1997, 191]. Chew's reputation as a cloth town may represent merely a late specialisation; but the proximity of the sheepwalks of Mendip and Dundry, and the fact, as we have already seen, of Chew's own situation amidst a large tract of high-quality arable, the two land uses together forming an agrarian sub-region, might at least in part underpin a rôle in its rural hinterland that was urban in all but name

Whitley Hundred

While by 1086 the Bishop of Wells had lost his grip on all but the core estate of Chew hundred, Whitley remained by that time *par excellence* a manorial hundred; that is, virtually all of the estates within it had at some point belonged to a single lord, namely Glastonbury Abbey Abbey. Indeed, Whitley represents the heartland of the abbey's possessions in central Somerset. Excluding detachments, the evidence of Domesday Book and its satellites suggests that of the 18 named manors which lay within the main body of the hundred in 1086, only one, Puriton, did not at that time belong to Glastonbury Abbey. In addition, a few manors within the hundred which Domesday does not mention, all of them parish centres later on, can readily be shown also to have been Glastonbury Abbey estates: these are Othery, Moorlinch, Street and Weston Zoyland [Thorn and Thorn 1980; Morland 1986, 66 (map)]. Even Puriton's inclusion in the old Loxley Hundred may be explicable in terms of its probable membership of a large (28 hides in total) estate in the area of the Polden Hills granted to Glastonbury Abbey in the mid-8th century [Morland 1986, 96], although the Abbey had clearly lost the manor before 1066, when it was among the possessions of Queen Edith. Likewise the seven certain detached parts of Whitley, which we will not consider further here, owe their membership to the fact that in 1086 they were all, in whole or part, Glastonbury Abbey manors [Thorn and Thorn 1980].

The Constituent Manors

Table 4 (Chapter Seven) gives basic details of the manors of which Whitley was composed in 1086. The approximate sizes of the ecclesiastical parishes are shown in Table 1, and their spatial relationships are mapped in Figure 16. While Whitley had detachments in south-east and west Somerset, it does not itself seem to have 'suffered' from detached parts of other hundreds being included within its own bounds. This may have much to do with the way in which a large proportion of this land was acquired by Glastonbury Abbey, in the form of early (ie pre-Conquest)

Plate 2: Anglo-Saxon sculptural work set into the jambs of a doorway in the churchyard wall at Chew Stoke.

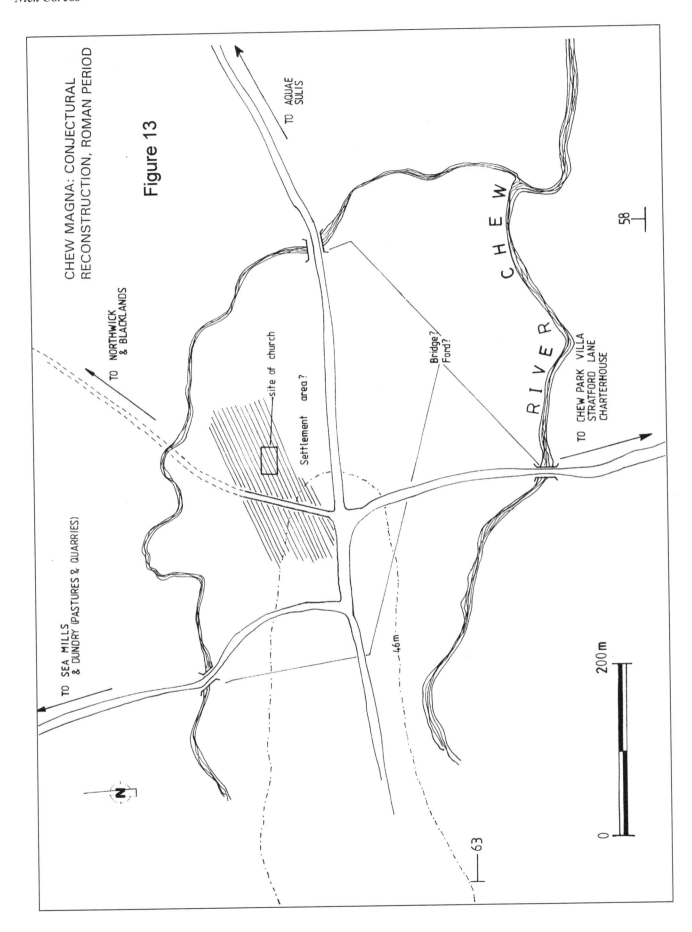

CHEW MAGNA: CONJECTURAL
RECONSTRUCTION, ROMAN PERIOD

Figure 13

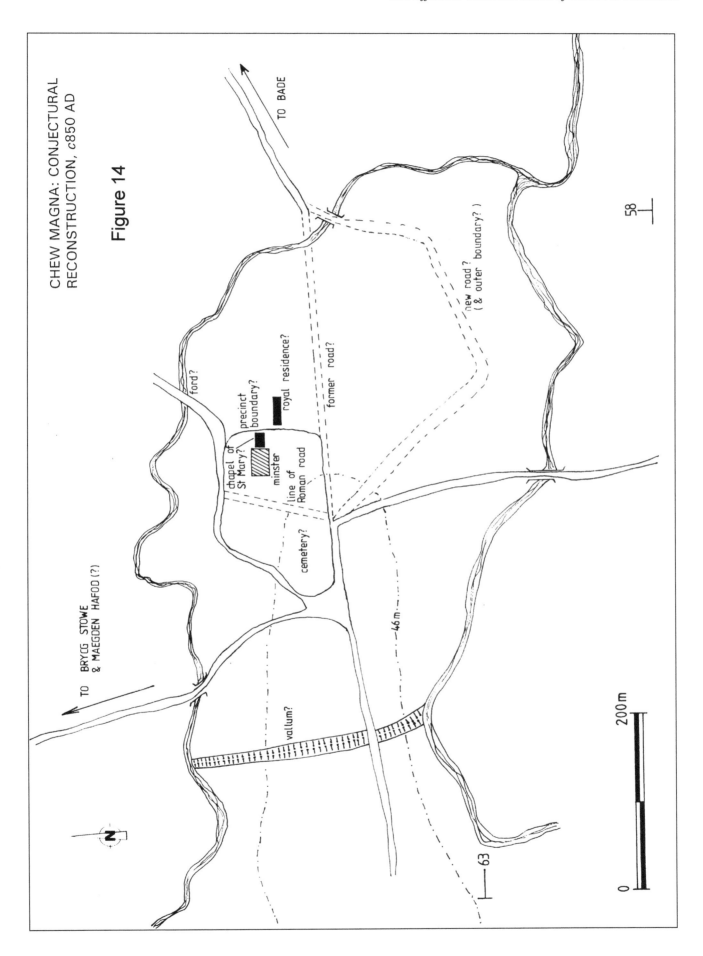

CHEW MAGNA: CONJECTURAL RECONSTRUCTION, c850 AD

Figure 14

TO BADE

new road?
(& outer boundary?)

former road?

ford?

precinct boundary?

royal residence?

chapel of St Mary?

minster

line of Roman road

cemetery?

vallum?

TO BRYCG STOWE & MAEGDEN HAFOD (?)

N

46 m

58

63

200 m

0

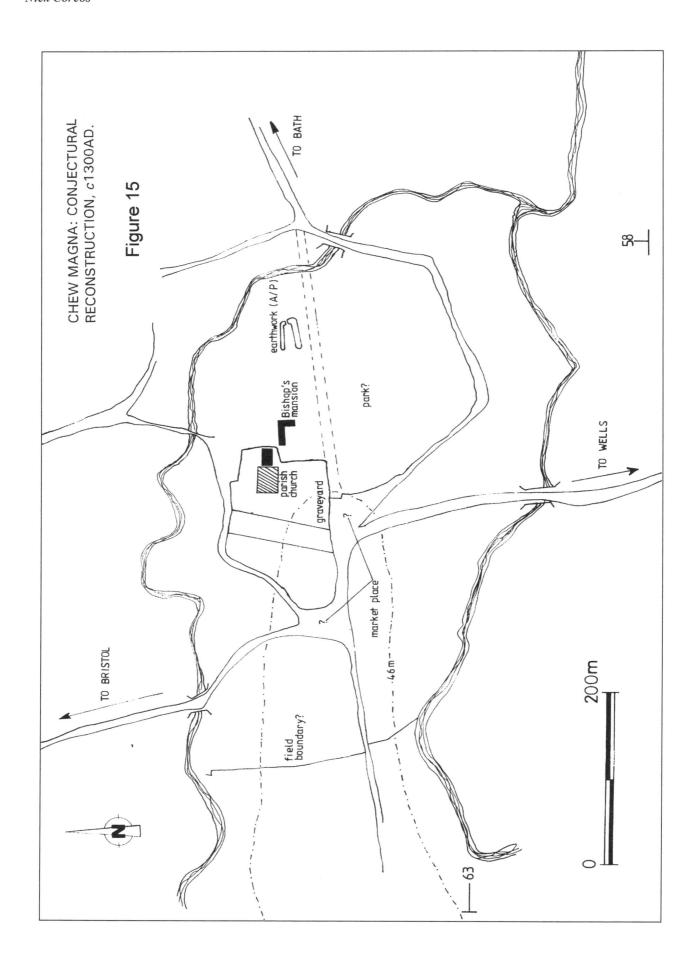

CHEW MAGNA: CONJECTURAL RECONSTRUCTION, *c*1300AD.

Figure 15

TO BATH

earthwork (A/P)

Bishop's mansion

park?

parish church

graveyard

?

market place

·46m·

?

field boundary?

TO BRISTOL

N

TO WELLS

58

63

200m

0

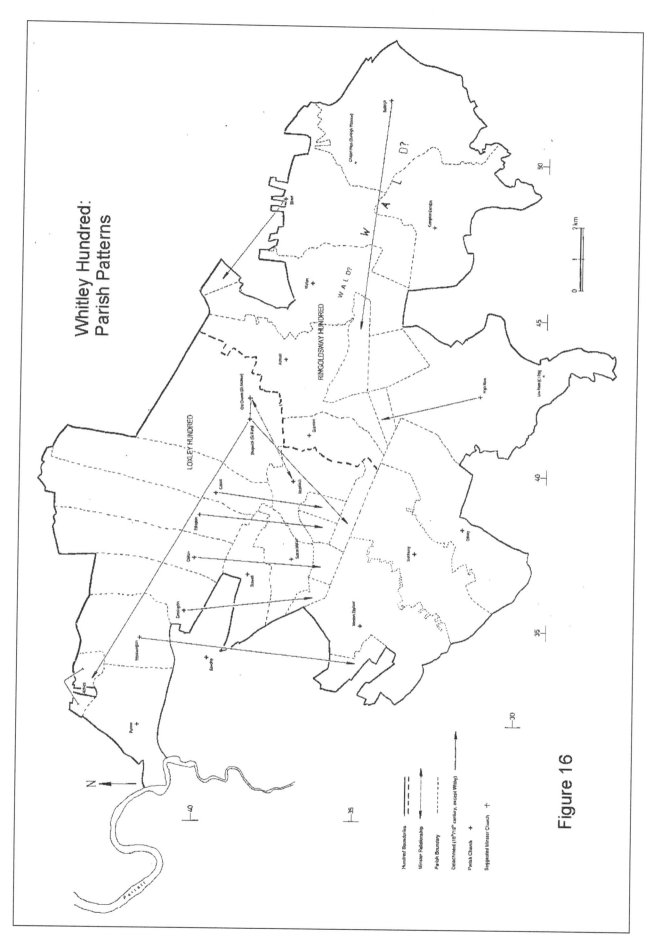

Whitley Hundred:
Parish Patterns

Figure 16

grants of a succession of large tracts of territory, with the core estates stretching westwards from Glastonbury Abbey itself and embracing effectively the whole of the Polden ridge. This early and tenacious domination of such a large area presumably had the effect of 'locking out' competing landlords, although Michael Costen emphasises the distinctly fluid nature of land ownership in the *late* Anglo-Saxon period [Costen 1992, 28]. Against this background, the early tenurial integrity of this area is all the more impressive, and taking even the most sceptical view, the evidence of surviving Saxon charters, when mapped, shows that the core of what was later to become the hundred of Whitley appears in the mid tenth century to have remained intact from the time of the earliest recorded grants relating to land here in the early 8th century [Costen 1992, Fig 1; and 41, 1.14, 'Poholt'].

The Territorial Background

As we have already suggested, the particular topographical attributes of the hundred may hint at least at a partial origin in a territorial entity of some antiquity. On the face of it, Whitley stands out from the other two study hundreds as being the only one to which we can attribute an approximate date of origin, namely, the late 12th century. It is also distinguished by the nature of its toponym (below), and by its 'artificial' creation from the fusion, in the late 12th century, of two pre-existing, smaller hundreds, Loxley and Ringoldsway [Thorn & Thorn 1980, 376; Anderson 1939, 51-52; Morland 1990, 116-117 and 122]. The origins of these two antecedent units are generally regarded as obscure, but Frank Thorn draws attention to the fact that most ancient hundreds take their names generally from either the chief vills or moot sites within their bounds, for which it is usually possible to establish some kind of link with royal ownership suspected [Thorn, *pers comm*, and 1989, 36]. Although in itself a routeway, Ringoldsway lay in Butleigh, and a charter of the very early 9th century [S270a] survives showing the king granting away the Butleigh estate to one of his officials. Likewise, Loxley hundred took its name from a wood where presumably the moot site was, but Loxley itself lay largely, as it still does, within Shapwick, whose pre-eminent status within its original hundred (its first church may have been a minster) is strongly suspected [Aston 1994, 230, and fig 11.8; Costen 1992a, 105-109, and 156; and see further below]. Again, royal antecedents are evident: it is likely that Shapwick was a member of a 20-hide estate on Polden granted to Glastonbury Abbey by the king in the first decade of the 8th century; as it certainly was part of a much larger (60 hides) royal grant to the abbey somewhat later, in 729 [Abrams 1991, 124-127]. This ties in well with Richard Morris's argument "that most minster churches probably began life on royal estates as chapels for the use of the king and his household" [cited in Costen 1992a, 105]. We might, then, reasonably conclude that, at least from the late pre-Conquest period, it is to Loxley and Ringoldsway, and not Whitley, that we should attach chronological and administrative primacy. An echo of this has been highlighted by Michael Costen, who has observed

how, even after the creation of Whitley brought some measure of administrative unity to what had essentially long been a massive Glastonbury Abbey manorial hundred, the tenacity of the old division between Ringoldsway and Loxley continued to be reflected in the customary obligations of the Abbey's tenantry. For in the early 14th century, the larger Shapwick tenants were required to discharge part of their service to the Abbot by accompanying the bailiff into the *western* part of the hundred (ie Loxley), for summoning and distraint, a clear indication that, in some respects, the old hundredal boundaries were still a reality even at this relatively very late date [Costen *pers comm*; and 1989, 80]. It is possible, though, that this picture is more apparent than real, and that Whitley hundred may in fact represent at least in part no more than the reconstitution, conscious or otherwise, of an older territory *pre-dating* the two smaller hundreds; by this argument, the fragmentation of the larger unit into the two smaller is seen as merely a temporary phase lasting perhaps a couple of centuries between the 10th century and the 12th. The evidence pointing towards this conclusion emerges from the discussion below, under various sub-headings; but it turns fundamentally on a number of internal inconsistencies in ecclesiastical and parish boundary relationships, which seem explicable only in terms of territorial and administrative arrangements from a time before formal hundredation, probably in the 10th century [Loyn 1974; Yorke 1995, 124-125]. And it seems increasingly likely that in many areas, the establishment of a hundred marked simply the formal recognition of existing practice, often based on far older, pre-existing territories *and* their institutional mechanisms, such as law courts and assemblies: "hundred names derived from meeting-place names away from royal vills suggest a more ancient origin for the district court and imply some form of administrative unit on which the hundred was later based.........it is probable that the territories of [early Anglo-Saxon folk] groups roughly correspond to the areas of later hundreds.........the (proto) hundred and the hundred court have considerably earlier origins than previously thought" [Turner 2000, 3-4].

The very early series of acquisitions by Glastonbury Abbey of lands identified with an estate called *Pouelt*, or variations thereof, present enormous difficulties of interpretation, and have been analysed in exhaustive detail by Dr Abrams [1996, 204-211]. Whatever their exact extent however, one is left with the distinct impression of an attempt to preserve the territorial integrity of a pre-existing entity, as far as possible, by transfer from the royal fisc in a succession of large grants. Morland considered, and Abrams allows as at least a plausible suggestion [1996, 206], that the 60 hides of the *Pouelt* charter of 729, can be traced in 1086 as the sum of two 30-hide estates based on Shapwick and Walton respectively. If this is the case, we have here a block of land which palpably ignored the later Ringoldsway/Loxley division, and which was at least partially reborn with the creation of Whitley in the late 12th century, probably to allow Glastonbury Abbey to administer its core estate more expediently, through its operation as a 'manorial' hundred [Anderson 1939, xv]. It seems very likely, indeed, that the origin of the two 30-hide units is linked directly to hundredation, and is the result of a straightforward equal allocation of tax liability upon the two 'new' hundreds, made on purely administrative grounds and heedless of former territorial affinities.

Church and Chapel: The Medieval Ritual Landscape

For Chew hundred, an attempt was made to reconstruct, on the basis of the relationship between Chew minster and its known daughter churches, the *parochia* of the minster, which in turn, I suggested, formed the core unit upon which the later and somewhat larger hundred of Chew was based. For Whitley, a similar exercise has already been attempted for the area thought to fall within the pre-Conquest estate of *Pouelt* [Aston and Costen 1994a, 75]. A few general observations will serve to highlight some problems and questions arising from this last reference, beginning, necessarily, with Shapwick.

Certain 'classic' minster affinities are missing at Shapwick; for example, there is nothing topographically distinctive about the site of the old church, such as a location on a promontory surrounded on three sides by water, as at Chew Magna; no river passes through Shapwick, and as a corollary, the place-name itself is a rather 'ordinary' habitative one (although important enough in its own right), and not a simplex pre-English river name.

Part of the problem is that we cannot yet say with any certainty exactly where any *caput* for *Pouelt* may have lain, or how it may have been related to any early mother church. In the Vale of Evesham, Bond has shown how a series of chapelries there were directly dependent on Evesham Abbey itself, and we may wonder whether this was not also the case in the early history of Glastonbury Abbey's ownership of *Pouelt* [Bond 1988, 128-138; Cox 1975][14]. Although the site of Shapwick Old Church is unprepossessing [*cf* Blair 1992], we might also consider that if a particular location were deemed important enough for other reasons, it would be perfectly possible for purely topographical considerations to be overidden. Shapwick's claim to early importance, revealed by a variety of strands of evidence, has considerable merit, and the balance of probabilities appears to favour those who support its likely status as a capital church at the centre of a large estate [Costen 1992a, 106, 119 and 156]. One indication of this comes from Shapwick's inclusion in a brief list of churches which in the medieval period were directly subject to the Abbey church, and outside the control of the Bishop, and which is contained in a privilege attributed to Ine [Sawyer 1968, no 250; Costen 1992a, 144-145; Scott 1981, 99-103; Finberg 1964, 113-114], to which Abrams assigns a *terminus ante quem* of the early 12th century. Even allowing that the charter itself is a palpable fabrication, it may well have implications about the ancient status of Shapwick church as it was perceived by that date, and Abrams herself concedes that it "has something to tell us

about the development of the concept of a core estate and privileged zone……" [Abrams 1996, 127-128]. We have already noted Abrams's caution that forged charters may well contain perfectly legitimate claims, and she has suggested that the very earliest surviving *Pouelt* grant, purportedly from the first decade of the 8th century and involving some 20 hides, may actually refer to Shapwick [Abrams 1994]. This was clearly land which the Abbey was anxious to acquire, not only for its agricultural potential and proximity to Glastonbury Abbey, but also perhaps for what lay on it from previous ages, bearing in mind what I will say later on (in Chapter Six) about Roman sites bestowing prestige on their owner, and doubly so if that at Old Church was thought to possess ancient ritual or religious connotations.

There is here, however, an intriguing anomaly, for by the post-Conquest period, Shapwick itself was *not* the mother-church of the estate: it had only a single chapelry, at Ashcott immediately to the east, with Ashcott itself, in turn, the mother church of a chapel in the hamlet of Pedwell [Thomson 1994, 11-12]. Instead, it is Moorlinch which emerges into the medieval period acting as mother to at least five of the churches lying within the Greater Shapwick estate. These were Sutton Mallet, Chilton, Catcott, Stawell and Edington [Torr 1974-79, 86]. The simplest explanation is that it was indeed Moorlinch, and not Shapwick, which had always been the capitular church of *Pouelt* [15]. This model would be based on the premise that Moorlinch had probably been founded first and took precedence, with Shapwick as a secondary, dependent church perhaps established with the specific object of christianising a Roman (and perhaps earlier) site.

We cannot, though, be sure whether or not Moorlinch's apparent ecclesiastical superiority in the post Conquest period represents the original arrangement (ie 10th century or earlier). Of the five dependent chapelries, all were tenurial dependencies of Shapwick in 1086 except Stawell [Abrams 1996, 209], and one inference might be that, for a time at least, ecclesiastical and tenurial development had run hand in hand, with Shapwick as the mother church, until some point at which Moorlinch was elevated to this status and in the process 'inherited' Shapwick's dependent churches. Moorlinch itself is not mentioned is 1086 and its assessment is almost certainly included with that of Shapwick [Costen 1994b, 76-78; Abrams 1996, 179]; and it is interesting that as late as the second quarter of the 13th century, it was the Abbot's *curia* at Shapwick at which his Moorlinch tenants were required to discharge their service obligations [Hobhouse 1891, 155-156; Costen 1994c, 80]. In the early 14th century, the *Nomina Villarum* recorded "Shapewyk, cum suis hamel", one of which was Moorlinch [Dickinson 1889, 53], and indeed even two centuries later, Moorlinch was still being described in these terms [Corcos 1982, 28].

Moorlinch might then appear to defy both the clear evidence for its *de facto*, secular, administrative subservience, and also the logic of what we might

---

[14] I am grateful to James Bond for these references.

[15] I am indebted to Teresa Hall for discussing with me her views on the nature of these two churches, which do not necessarily agree with my own.

reasonably have *expected* to find, namely Shapwick acting as the ecclesiastical hub of its area throughout its history. One possible explanation turns upon the progressive break-up of the old estate. Michael Costen has suggested [*pers comm*] that increasingly assertive and independent-minded manorial tenants, perhaps having founded proprietorial churches of their own, may have placed pressure on Glastonbury Abbey to relinquish its traditional claims to ecclesiastical jurisdiction over the *Pouelt* churches [*cf* Costen 1992a, 147-148]. This control, with far-reaching implications for the flow of ecclesiastical revenues to the Abbey, it exercised by keeping a firm grip on Shapwick and its church, as part of its core demesnes. When change could no longer be resisted, the Abbey compromised by making Moorlinch the notional minster for the 'independent' manors, thereby giving the impression to manorial tenants that they were no longer so tightly bound in to the restrictive and financially-disadvantageous ecclesiastical framework of the old *Pouelt* estate. It is though, significant that the choice fell on Moorlinch, since it was hardly a 'neutral' candidate. With its intimate ties to Shapwick, it seems very likely that the Abbey, reluctant to relinquish jurisdiction completely, was minded to retain at least a degree of authority, however notional, through their continued relationship; for despite the loss of so many daughters, Glastonbury Abbey still clearly regarded Shapwick as one of its paramount churches, a concern attested, as we have already seen, in the post-Conquest forged privilege of Ine[16].

It may, though, be possible to explain this difficulty in the form of an alternative, and somewhat more radical model of ecclesiastical development which attempts to reconcile the apparently conflicting strands of evidence relating to the churches at Shapwick (Old Church) and Moorlinch. This turns upon a consideration of the exact nature of their relationship, and itseems worthwhile to explore this link in rather more depth.

In complete contrast to the topographically uninspiring situation at Shapwick, the site of the church of St Mary the Virgin at Moorlinch is spectacular. It sits perched on the eastern end of a narrow but steeply-sided ridge which juts out like a promontory outlier from the main mass of the southern flank of Polden[17]. It is to all and intents and purposes a peninsula, approachable only from the east, and surrounded on the remaining three sides by sharp slopes to the dry, open coombes below. The northern side of the ridge is cut by a series of clearly artificial broad terraces which curve around its western end [Plates 3 and 4]. The very striking nature of these features is especially apparent on aerial photographs [*eg* RAF, CPE/UK 1924, 16/1/47, frame 4056].

With the sole exception of Stawell, Moorlinch is also the only parish centre in western Polden whose place-name is purely topographical in nature, and therefore probably to be included in the earliest stratum of English

toponyms [Gelling 1984, 1-9, and 1998]; although *contra* Gelling [1984, 163-164], I would suggest that the *hlinc* element here is likely to be a reference to the terracing, a corollary of which would be that it was in existence *before* the toponym was coined. The most obvious, and initially convincing explanation of these terraces is that they are *medieval* (ie post-Conquest) cultivation lynchets; and certainly this may at least in part explain why they are absent from the *southern* flank of the 'promontory', since the slope on that side is rather less steep. However, such features are notoriously difficult to date [Astill 1988, 79-80] except on crude morphological grounds or in relation to associated earthworks; and while they may indeed arise from cultivation on a slope, they need not necessarily be post-Conquest in date. The question of the date of the Moorlinch terraces is a matter to which we will return shortly. For now though, we can make two further points: firstly, that Margaret Gelling herself observes that *hlinc* "is fairly frequent in charter-boundaries, and in some instances there......can be shown to refer to the cultivation terraces on hill-sides which are known to modern students of landscape history as strip lynchets" [Gelling 1984, 163]; so clearly, cultivation terracing was *not* a post-Conquest development, and there seems no reason why the Moorlinch examples should not have been in existence early enough to have inspired the second element of the place-name. Indeed, Dr Gelling's explanation of *hlinc* in this specific context has found its way onto the back cover of the latest edition of her book on topographical place-names, in the form of a photograph of a contour-track in Moorlinch. [Gelling and Cole, 2000]. She also appears to leave the way open for the alternative interpretation offered here in her remark that "man-made terraces can sometimes be seen at farms with names derived from *hlinc*" [*ibid* 182]. However, the implication seems to be that she is talking about countour routeways cut into hillslopes, rather than, as at Moorlinch, a *series* of clearly-bounded terraces whose function is palpably *not* communications.

Secondly, the position of the terraces on the north and north-western side of the church peninsula means that they are most immediately striking to a traveller approaching from the north, going south; in other words, coming over the ridge top from the direction of Shapwick and descending the southern slope towards Sedgemoor. This may not be coincidental, and perhaps, then, an explanation that goes *beyond* the purely functional may be needed to account for these features? We will return to this point in Chapter Six, in looking at the nature of the communications system on the Polden ridge.

Moorlinch church is in a locally dominant position, looking uninterruptedly south across Sedgemoor, and west, along the southern flank of the hill[18]. However, significantly, St Mary's *cannot* look eastwards, its prospect being comprehensively blocked by the rather higher, broken terrain in that direction. The parish boundary with Greinton, which also forms the old Loxley/Rigoldsway

---

[16] I am grateful to Dr Costen for discussing with me the difficult interpretational problems surrounding these two churches.

[17] I am grateful to Penny Stokes both for her guidance relating to the architectural history of Moorlinch church, and on the nature and function of medieval hill-slope cultivation.

[18] Sir Stephen Glynne, in the mid 19th century, was moved explicitly to observe that St Mary's occupied a site that was "elevated and striking, commanding an extensive view" [McGarvie 1994, 242].

Plate 3: St Mary's church, Moorlinch, sitting at the eastern end of its promontory and showing the series of terraces cut into the northern slope. Looking roughly south-east.

Plate 4: Looking down on St Mary's church, Moorlinch, from the top of Knoll Hill, to show the wider landscape context. View roughly south-west, out across Sedgemoor. The striking set of terraces west of the church are again very apparent.

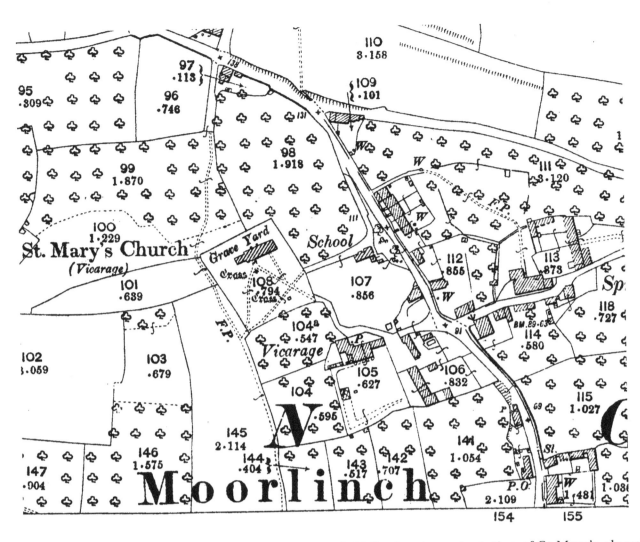

Figure 17: Extract from OS second edition 25" map (1904), showing orientation of St Mary's church, Moorlinch, about 30° north of grid east.

hundred boundary in this area, runs north/south a km or so to the east of the church.

It seems very clear that the site of Moorlinch church was carefully and quite deliberately chosen, for there is no good reason why it should not instead have been built in a lower and probably more convenient location at the foot of the southern slope, where the village of Moorlinch itself for the most part lies[19]. It is obvious that the position of St

Mary's is designed to impress, and to make a statement about status that would have been clearly understood by contemporaries. Moorlinch church seems strongly to reinforce Altenberg's recent observation, arising from her work on the late medieval landscape of Dartmoor viewed very much from a phenomenological perspective, that "the religious elements in the landscape were dependant on and appealed to the visual sense. A direct visual impact was needed in the landscape if Christianity was to be perceived as superior to nature and therefore convincing and comforting" [Altenberg 1999, 28]. In seeking both context and precedent, one does not need to look very far, for leaving aside only the lack of a girdle of water around its 'peninsula', the topographical affinities displayed by Moorlinch church are exactly those so closely associated by John Blair with mother churches of early foundation [Blair 1992; 1996a].

The apparent absence of both a high-status (ie royal) secular site close by and obviously pre-English

---

[19] We might add that a lower, roomier site would have allowed a far more liturgically correct orientation. Bearing in mind the post-Conquest propensity for correcting such defects [Morris 1989, 208-209], it may be significant that the Norman re-build of which there are clear indications in the fabric of the church itself, left the building on its original site, and presumably alignment, offset some 30° north of grid east as measured from the 2nd edn OS 25" map (1904). Hoare and Sweet have recently shown that while in some cases the Anglo-Saxon approach to orientation appears somewhat cavalier, nonetheless in general "the early medieval ideal *was* to obtain a liturgically-correct alignment" [Hoare and Sweet 2000, 169]. They also suggest that anything in excess of an error of ± 10° should be attributed to reasons *other* than merely "an inaccurate knowledge of the time of day and a variety of indeterminate causes" [167]. At Moorlinch the particularly idiosyncratic degree of misalignment (Figure 17) was clearly a constraint imposed by the very restricted nature

of the site, and may imply that in this case, more important considerations relating to its use over-rode the requirement for strict liturgical accuracy.

place-names, and the fact that neither place gave its name to the old Hundred, might all be seen as compromising Shapwick and Moorlinch's claims to superioity. Even these points have answers, for we have already seen that before passing to Glastonbury Abbey the Polden lands were part of the royal fisc; likewise the likely relative primacy of the toponym Moorlinch. Indeed, we do not yet know exactly how, in spatial terms, the British name *Pouelt* was applied, and whether it ever became associated with a particular place, or remained merely a district name [Abrams 1996, 204-211, and esp 210, n117; Aston 1998]. And we may wonder whether it is entirely coincidence that Loxley Hundred takes its name from a wood that straddles the Shapwick/Moorlinch boundary, perhaps yet further evidence of a certain unity of existence. There can be little doubt that those significant affinities associated with Shapwick Old Church that we can identify do appear to be characteristically early. One recent view is that before 1066, Shapwick Old Church had probably been endowed with a large estate which, described in suspiciously archaic terms, emerges in the post-Conquest period as effectively a sub-manor appropriated by Glastonbury Abbey for the use of its almoner [Costen 1989a; and *pers comm*].

Nonetheless, it does seem questionable whether, considered on its own, Shapwick's case as an important, ancient mother church would necessarily be any stronger than any one of its immediate neighbours. However, between them, it is possible to see that Shapwick Old Church and Moorlinch, St Mary, satisfy most of the criteria of primary status that modern scholarship would regard as important; and it is this realisation about the significance of their *combined* attributes which, if applied to an individual church would place its primary status beyond reasonable doubt, that allows us to approach the problem of their relationship from a perspective that might appear at first somewhat radical, but which is in fact no more than an extension and development of current orthodoxy.

We have seen already that throughout their respective recorded histories, the ties between Shapwick and Moorlinch were intimate. However, what distinguishes them when they emerge in the post-Conquest period, the first time that we can really discern their relationship with any clarity, is a palpable demarcation of function, that was at the same time complementary and mutually dependent. By this time, Shapwick had assumed an overwhelmingly secular mantle at the centre of the old estate's developing 'manorial' and economic administration, so clearly attested in 1086 [Costen 1994b], while Moorlinch acted as the ecclesiastical hub. And herein lies the key to understanding the fundamental basis of this duality, for the problem up to now is that, no matter how close their ties, the understandable tendency has been to see Shapwick and Moorlinch as separate entities. I would suggest instead that they represent merely two sides of the same coin: they were, on one level, both minsters, indeed, they were one and the same minster. They should be treated as effectively one unit, and one church, albeit on different sites. The dedications may provide a crucial clue here, and Dr Blair considers them "quite suggestive. It is absolutely standard practice for the two main churches of a minster group to be dedicated to an apostle and to the Virgin; Wells itself is an 'Andrew + Mary' group......[we] might like to think of Shapwick and Moorlinch forming a liturgical pair"[20].

By this view, we can regard Moorlinch as Shapwick's *alter ego*, a physical extension of itself and a kind of sub- or proxy-minster *through which* it exercised its primary ecclesiastical prerogatives over its dependent chapels, having been founded for that specific purpose. John Blair's own discussions relating to *groups* of churches on minster sites provides a basis for this idea, the only major difference here being one of degree in terms of the physical distance between the associated churches [Blair 1992; 1998]. And while he acknowledges that "the distance between Shapwick and Moorlinch is a bit much", Dr Blair also allows that he is "very receptive to the idea of a single minster complex comprising churches some way apart" [*pers comm* Dr John Blair]. This idea may also confirm what we might already suspect regarding contemporary attitudes towards the topographical context of primary churches, and the perceived appropriateness or otherwise of different kinds of site.

Although dating is highly problematic, it may be possible to propose a model for an approximate relative sequence of events. At some time in the second half of the 7th century, a royal church, perhaps taking its dedication from the already important mother church at Wells [Rodwell 1996], was founded at Shapwick Old Church, drawn there by the presence of a substantial, high-status Roman complex, the ruins of which may still at that time have been standing to a considerable height. This is in contrast to the situation at Chew Magna, for which we could only suggest the presence of major Roman structures

---

[20] *pers comm* Dr John Blair, to whom I am very grateful for his guidance in this respect. The dedication of Shapwick Old Church to Andrew is perhaps best attested in a document which Watkin [GC II, 1948, cxxxii and 376] dates to the mid 13th century. This is a grant, explicitly naming Andrew as patron, of an area "of reed-bed for a light......in the church there" [*ibid*, cxxxii]. This record is doubly interesting since not only is the grant given "in puram et perpetuam elemosinam Deo et Beate Marie et ecclesie Beati Andree de Schapwyk'", but it also requires that the light is to burn "coram altare Beate Virginis quod est in eadem ecclesia" [376]. It is possible that this is a reference not to the high altar itself, but to a *separate*, Marian altar [*pers comm* Helen Gittos], although whether contained in a projecting side chapel is problematic. The archaeological evidence (Plate 5) does not *at present* suggest it [Gerrard 1995, 108-109; Turner 1998, 42 and 50]. In any event, this seems almost to presage the later change of dedication when the new church at Shapwick was built in the early 14th century, and Andrew was abandoned in favour of the Virgin. The twin dedications of the Old Church, therefore, reinforce the intimate and *early* relationship that seems to have existed between these two figures. Is it possible that Moorlinch owes *its* dedication to the deliberate transference of the patron of the altar at Shapwick Old Church, so emphasising the insoluble bond between the two churches? A blocked-up, round-headed arch is visible in the external south nave wall of Moorlinch church, with remnants of projecting footings. However, there is no such indicative architecture in the opposing, north wall of the nave, and *contra* Sir Stephen Glynne, it is likely that this is a simple relieving arch rather than marking the site of a transeptal chapel [McGarvie 1994, 242]. *Ex inf* Brian and Moira Gittos *via* Helen Gittos. For a note of caution against the assumption that certain architectural forms (but particularly cruciform types) are invariably indicative of minster status, see Franklin 1984, 74.

Plate 5: The Old Church of St Andrew, Shapwick, under excavation. Looking roughly north-west, towards the Brue Valley and Mendip.

under or in the immediate vicinity of the minster church of St Andrew. At Shapwick Old Church, it is possible that the spring nearby also figured largely in the perceptions of those making the choice, who may have associated the juxtaposition of Roman structures and spring with notions of 'ritual' significance stretching back into antiquity, and perhaps even attested by the remnants of a prehistoric barrow cemetery [Aston 1993a, 12-13; Aston and Gerrard 1999, 23-25; Blair 1998; Field 1999; Bell 1998, 4-8 and 9-11; Aldhouse-Green 1999 and 2000]. Andrew Reynolds has also suggested that springs, wells, ponds and other water sources associated with important churches and/or royal centres may have been involved in the procedure of judicial ordeal [Reynolds 1999, 102], and because of the special nature of the site it seems perfectly possible that its Christian affinities are rooted in *pre-English* origins. In this context we may wonder, with John Blair, "how many minsters in western England may have a British past? Certain types of minor cult foci, notably cemeteries and holy wells, could have been maintained within a broad continuum between Romano-Celtic paganism, sub-Roman Christianity, and Anglo-Saxon religious activity both pagan and Christian" [Blair 1996b, 6].

A similar relationship between the late Roman and early Anglo-Saxon activity at West Heslerton, north Yorkshire, has recently been proposed by Powlesland [1999, 55-56], who considers the survival of a probable shrine or temple complex as having a formative influence on the earliest phase of Anglian activity on the same site. His general conclusions for West Heslerton present an intriguing basis for comparison with Shapwick Old Church: "the data collected offer a remarkable potential for examining the interface between Roman and Saxon, and may indicate continuity of use of a ritual landscape defined, and in fact completely re-worked, by the middle of the 4th century AD at the latest, and apparently still in use until the middle of the 9th century............although the frequency of Roman material is very high, evidence for housing during this period is negligible and it would appear that the site operated as some sort of sanctuary, supporting a large, but short term, visiting population............both the stratigraphic sequence and the ceramic evidence point towards continuity of use of parts of the Roman 'ritual landscape' and some degree of continuity of population.........sherds of Anglo-Saxon vessels in Roman fabric offer pointers towards addressing this fundamentally important issue" [Powlesland 1998, 6.3 – 6.4].

At Shapwick, the obvious connotations of status attached to the Roman building, would also have reinforced the site's claim as a suitable location to be re-used for a primary royal church. Even more significant though would be a continuing local tradition of a religious and ritual focus here, whether or not any actual *activities* related to that function had continued from the late Roman period. It is possibly *this* distinction which marked out the Old Church site as suitable for conversion to Christian use, rather than the extensive, topographically much more impressive, but perhaps too 'secular' courtyard villa site on the Nidons. We have already noted (Chapter Two), possible parallels with the former temple of Mercury at Uley. The spring could have been adapted if necessary to provide a ready-made baptistry [Woodward 1992, 100-105]. It is likely that, initially, Shapwick Old Church itself dominated the then royal estate of *Pouelt,* of whatever extent that may have been [Abrams 1996, 204-211][21].

---

[21] It is possible that the significance of the Old Church site can only be understood in terms of its relationship with the Nidons villa, for if the latter was indeed at the centre of an extensive estate encompassing the western part of Polden, there seems no reason why it should not have been *this* entity, initially taken over as *royal* property, which was progressively transferred to Glastonbury Abbey in that series of grants, to which I have already alluded, in the first half the 8th century.

We can have no idea of the nature of the church building which Glastonbury Abbey, presumably, inherited from its royal benefactors. We can, though, suggest that the Abbey would have been keen to assert its authority over what was to become one of its most important and productive 'core' estates; one means of achieving that was through the endowment of churches and, particularly, through the promotion of a suitably prestigious mother church for at least part of the estate. While Shapwick (or rather, its predecessor) seems to have been allowed to remain the *administrative* centre of the estate, the old church, with its inherited dedication to St Andrew, was found wanting. Its low-lying, unprepossessing site did not conform to the Abbey's requirement for a highly-visible church in a dominant position which made a clear public statement about the ancient dignity and authority of its patron. Shapwick Old Church was simply no longer regarded as suitable material for this purpose, and this may be an indication that perceptions of what attributes such a church *ought* to have were changing, and beginning to crystallise out into something approaching the model of topographical development that has been outlined by John Blair [1992; 1996]. The Abbey, therefore, cast about for a suitable location close by for a church that could, in effect, 'deputise' for Shapwick while at the same time providing both a liturgical partner for it, and the appropriately impressive public face of ecclesiastical provision that Shapwick could not.

In these circumstances, the choice of the site at Moorlinch was almost inevitable, and may have been made all the more attractive if the massive lynchets which probably gave the place its name were already in existence. A Romano-British or prehistoric origin for these features is by no means impossible, and if so, then even in the 8th century, they would have lent the site an air of 'utter antiquity'. Indeed, in looking closely at this location, and especially at the terraces, it is difficult to avoid the speculation that a major part of its attraction, whether consciously or otherwise, lay in its remarkable resemblance to Glastonbury Tor, whose own system of terraces may date from the Neolithic [Rahtz 1993, 51-54]; and viewed from certain angles, the form of the Moorlinch promontory as a miniature version of the Tor is indeed striking (Plates 3 and 4). Considered in this light, there could hardly be a more appropriate location for Shapwick's new confederate in this ecclesiastical partnership, and in Chapter Four, I shall suggest that the terraces may even have been created or at least modified specifically to this end.

As the western part of the old estate began to fragment, probably from the 9th and 10th centuries, Moorlinch retained its position as the notional mother church of the increasingly independent chapelries at the centres of the new manorial territories; although its lack of control over those places in the westernmost part of the hundred, Cossington, Woolavington and Puriton, suggests their loss from the old estate at an early date (below). But it seems that Shapwick itself continued to be associated with at least a tradition of antiquity and precedence. Why otherwise was it even mentioned in the forged privilege of

Ine, which whatever its provenance, cannot be ascribed a purpose relating to *secular* (ie manorial) administration; on the contrary, its importance in this context arises precisely from its self-proclaimed concern with *ecclesiastical* jurisdiction[22].

Against this background, we might reasonably have expected Shapwick to have ceded notional ecclesiastical authority over *all* its dependent territories to Moorlinch; so there remains the question of why, apparently, the church at Ashcott remained attached to Shapwick as its only chapelry. The answer may lie in the chronology of the processes at work, and relates to Shapwick/Ashcott having originated as a single entity, which then managed to retain its integrity. It is only possible to talk in relative terms, but Shapwick/Ashcott may still have been joined long after Shapwick had relinquished ecclesiastical supremacy to Moorlinch, and perhaps while the internal cohesion of at least the western part of the old estate progressively collapsed around them. They were probably still joined at the time of hundredation: we will consider this point further later on, but there seems no other way to explain why that process should place them in different hundreds, with total disregard for their clear integrity as a unit. When Ashcott finally did split off from its parent estate, it is logical that any church already there, or constructed afterwards to serve the newly independent unit, would inherit and continue the long-established *secular* links with the parent estate that may also be evident in the place-name itself. It may be significant that *both* of Shapwick's parochial neighbours immediately adjacent east and west, *and* the hamlet of Buscott, in Ashcott but close to the Shapwick boundary, carry names in *–cot*; since in other contexts this word is considered to have specific connotations of a subordinate, minor, dependent status, to

the extent that it may only survive attached to furlongs or fields [*cf* Dyer 1985a; Brown and Foard 1998, 76][23].

Pedwell, in Ashcott, is a settlement that would repay closer examination than can be accorded here, for like Tivington in Selworthy parish, Carhampton hundred (below), it displays distinct signs of a latent parochial independence which it never in fact achieved. Although Pedwell was a dependency of Ashcott, a chapel had been established there perhaps in the mid 13th century as a manorial prerogative, and by the early 14th century was being used as a chantry [Thomson 1994, 11-12]. As a Domesday holding of three hides, Pedwell is very likely to have been the estate of one or more low-status thegns who in 1066 were bound to the church at Glastonbury Abbey by military service [Thorn and Thorn 1980; Yorke 1995, 243-255, esp at 246]. There is unfortunately no direct documentary link, but if Geoffrey of Langley's chapel *was* that of St Martin at Pedwell, then in the mid 13th century it served a holding that was described as half a knight's fee [Weaver 1910, 70]. It is also unfortunate that the site of this chapel is unknown, since it would have indicated the location of the manor with which it was clearly associated; but presumably, Geoffrey's case for the construction of his own chapel, set out in his petition to the Abbot, would have lost a great deal of its force if his manorial *curia* had lain close to the church at Ashcott [Watkin 1952, 392-393][24]. A good candidate must, however, be the site now occupied by Pedwell Farm, halfway down the southern Polden flank at a place where the slope becomes temporarily more gentle, providing a relatively level platform. Hill Farm immediately to the south sits on a steeper, more difficult gradient, and Eastern Farm is on an even lower site fringing the edge of Sedgemoor. A crucial topographical clue is the survival of a lane running east-west along the contour, connecting Pedwell Farm directly with Ashcott, on which church it is exactly aligned. This route, known today as Pedwell Lane, was in existence at least by the late 18th century [Dunning and Harley 1981], and at that time, Day and Masters depicted settlement at Pedwell as for the most part strung out along what is now the main A361 road, skirting the foot of southern Polden, with Pedwell Farm the only other dwelling shown. The Ashcott tithe map shows that the field boundaries abutting onto the lane at both its western and eastern ends, clearly enclosed from open arable strips, respected its course – they run up to it but saving possibly a single exception, they do not cross it [SRO D/D/Rt 218, 1838]. There is not today, nor does there ever seem to have been, any westward extension beyond Pedwell Farm, and the strong inference must be that the lane therefore represents a 'dedicated' medieval route between Ashcott and the putative sub-manor (Figure 18).

The site of Pedwell Farm is traversed north to south by an elaborate system of substantial, stone-built drainage culverts, probably of 17th or 18th century date, and one spring in particular, rising immediately to the north of

---

[22] Evidence for both the former extent of the *Pouelt* estate, and Shapwick's prominent position in it, comes from a record among the Glastonbury Abbey archive dated 1242, when the rector of Bawdrip church was formally censured by episcopal officials for non-payment of tithes to Glastonbury Abbey [GC I, 1944, xxxii and 40]. This document is important because it states explicitly that the tithes were due in right of the Abbey's church of Shapwick, rather than being owed *directly* to it. There is no mention of Moorlinch. It is of course possible that Glastonbury Abbey Abbey had acquired the tithes, and nothing else, after 1066, but if so I can find no record of it, or indeed of any other relationship between Glastonbury Abbey and this manor. VCH is similarly unaware of any such connection [Dunning 1992, 184-191]. Neither does the incumbent's status as rector, rather than vicar, give any clue to prior appropriation by an 'external' collegiate or conventual institution such as Glastonbury Abbey. At least by 1086, Bawdrip lay outside Whitley, in North Petherton Hundred, and was held by secular tenants both at that time and in 1066 [Thorn and Thorn 1980]. I would suggest, however, that this case reveals the existence of a relict link of Bawdrip's former dependency on Shapwick, and that it goes back to a time *before* Moorlinch was elevated to the status of joint mother church of the old estate. It may also provide confirmation that *Pouelt* did originally include Bawdrip, whose geographical position would anyway make its *exclusion* somewhat anomalous [*cf* Abrams 1996, 209]. This is a further example of almost certainly later hundredal (ie administrative) arrangements being imposed upon and cutting across an earlier *ecclesiastical* relationship. Bawdrip's early loss from *Pouelt*, and later annexation to another hundred, might explain why its link to Shapwick remained intact and was never dissolved in favour of Moorlinch.

[23] The dependent, subsidiary nature of names in *–cot* is lent strong support by a recent survey of the Buckinghamshire evidence. See Bailey 1999, and *cf* Watts 2000, 60 and 70.

[24] I am grateful to Dr Robert Dunning and Mary Siraut for this reference.

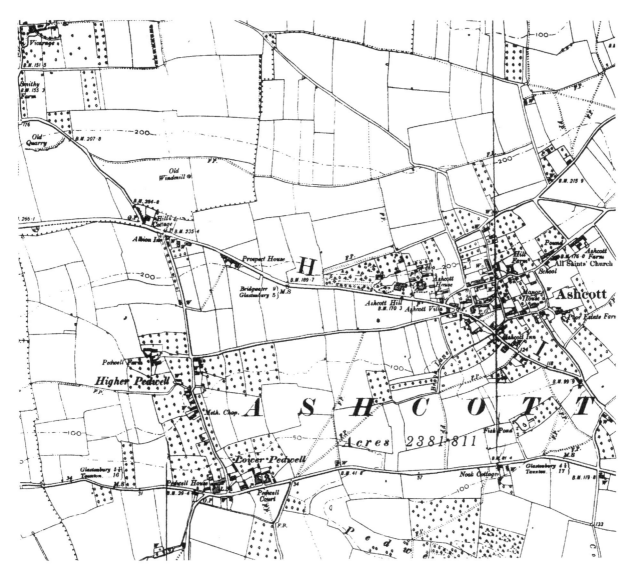

Figure 18: Reduced extract from OS second edition 6" map (1904) showing probable 'dedicated' routeway and associated field boundaries between Ashcott and Pedwell Farm.

the present house, is fed into a substantial stone well-head before being culverted directly under the house. The potential significance of the water supply here may be seen in the context of the place-name, which is from OE and means 'Pēoda's stream or spring' [Ekwall 1960, 360]. Notwithstanding the present, probably largely 18th century house and farm buildings, the size of Pedwell Farm, and the nature of the site, give every indication that this was always a holding of considerable importance and, I suggest, it marks the site of Domesday *Pedewelle*[25]. A single small sherd of medieval pottery (?11th-13th century; *pers comm* Dr Chris Gerrard) was found on a building spoil-heap immediately to the west of the farm buildings by the writer during fieldwork, but it may be merely the result of manuring and cannot be said to add to the evidence for medieval occupation on the site. It

nonetheless remains likely that Pedwell Farm represents a pre-Conquest thegnage holding, which in the medieval period developed a role as a small but significant manorial *curia* and demesne farm. It is also probably a vestige of a more dispersed pattern of settlement in the late Saxon period which may have been eradicated in those estates immediately to the west. Within the territory that was later to be defined as the parish of Ashcott, therefore, the experience of settlement change appears to have been different, and the forces driving nucleation, not as vigorous. Woolavington and Cossington had almost certainly been part of the original *Pouelt* estate acquired perhaps in stages by Glastonbury Abbey at various points in the 8th century [Abrams 1996, 204-211; Costen 1992, 41]. Neither of these churches, however, are known to have any relationship, or to owe any suit or dues to either Shapwick or Moorlinch; and it cannot be coincidence that it was precisely these estates which were the earliest tenurial losses from *Pouelt*, Cossington certainly breaking

---

[25] I am very grateful to the present owner of Pedwell Farm, Mr John Tilt, for his permission to conduct fieldwork on the site.

away before 1066, and Woolavington showing strong signs of independence, although still technically within Greater Shapwick, by 1086 [Costen 1992, 41, and 1994, 77; Abrams 1996, 98]. It may be that either the churches at these places, having once been subject to Shapwick (or to Moorlinch, depending on how one interprets the evidence), had completely shaken themselves free of those bonds at a date early enough such that no vestige of former links survives (9th/early 10th century?), or perhaps were both founded at a time (?late 10th/11th century) when their respective tenants had won the right to construct on their land proprietorial churches which from the outset were fully independent. Puriton is an even more extreme case. If Glastonbury Abbey had acquired it by purchase in the mid 8th century [Morland 1986, 78-79, and 96], it had certainly been absorbed into the royal fisc before 1066, perhaps for strategic reasons [Abrams 1996, 208-209], and by Domesday is found in the hands of St Peter's at Rome, although held in chief of the king [Thorn and Thorn 1980]. Della Hooke has recently emphasised that the early stages of estate fragmentation, particularly as seen in the process of daughter churches asserting their independence, tended to affect those blocks of land most geographically remote from the estate centre [Hooke 1998, 70-71]. It may then be significant that together, Cossington, Woolavington and Puriton occupy the westernmost extremity of the original *Pouelt* estate, the area most physically isolated from Glastonbury Abbey itself. A further clue that this was the case is provided by the relationship between Shapwick and its tiny sub-manor of Withy, a kilometre or so north of Puriton and today represented by Withy Farm. Withy had been regarded as a detached part of Shapwick long before it was depicted as such on the tithe map of 1839 [SRO D/D/Rt 361, 1839], and had paid tithes to Shapwick since at least the early 13th century [Costen 1989, 77; GC II, 1948, 376-380]. Rippon has identified Withy as the location of an 'infield' complex indicative of early (ie pre-Conquest) settlement and exploitation, and the site also possesses earthwork traces of medieval and later occupation [Rippon 1994, 244-245; and *cf* Costen 1989, 85-86]. Further, the legend of St Indract suggests strongly that the Shapwick-Withy link may extend as far back as the 8th century, to which period the story, mentioning as it does King Ine, is usually attributed [Costen 1991, 55]. It is, then, likely that Withy, as a detached outlier of Shapwick probably before 1066, can be characterised as one of those "parcels [lying] within the boundaries of the larger initial unit and within the holding of the overall lord", [Hooke 1998, 120], and provides further evidence that Greater Shapwick's westward extent did indeed originally include both Withy itself and probably Puriton too. This fact of distance may have influenced Glastonbury Abbey's management policies relating to these estates, manifested in a preference for leasing rather than direct stewardship, and in so doing, have unwittingly lain the foundations for the subsequent dilemma of retaining control [Gilchrist and Morris 1993, 116]. Indeed it is likely that both Cossington and Woolavington had been involved in leasing arrangements at various times before 1066 [Costen 1994b, 77].

Taking a much wider perspective, it is possible that ecclesiastical arrangements within this part of Whitley may allow us to say something, in very general terms, about the relative chronologies of both these and the secular administrative pattern. These relationships become very clear when mapped [Aston and Costen 1994a, 75]. It is notable that Shapwick's only known chapelry, Ashcott lies immediately to its east, while the five dependent churches of Moorlinch all lie to its west. The north-south boundary between the old Ringoldsway and Loxley hundreds is represented by the parish boundaries between Shapwick and Moorlinch to the west, and Ashcott and Greinton to the east. It is apparent that while the ecclesiastical arrangements centred on Moorlinch respect this boundary, and therefore must post-date it, the relationship between Shapwick and Ashcott palpably ignores it. Moorlinch looks *only* west - Shapwick looks both west and east. I suggest from this evidence that the Shapwick-Ashcott link takes us back to a time before the formal hundredal arrangements had crystallised, that is, probably before the tenth century [Loyn 1974; Yorke 1995, 124-125], and can be used to support my earlier argument that at least the Polden 'core' of the later Whitley hundred may in fact represent far more closely the extent of the territorial unit that preceded the 'earlier', smaller hundreds of Loxley and Ringoldsway. It is also likely, on the same basis, that the elevation of Moorlinch to the status of mother church of those parishes west of it, is therefore either closely associated with, or must *post-date*, hundredation.

Similar relationships, on a somewhat smaller scale, occur in the parts of Whitley we might consider to lie outside this 'core' area. At the eastern extremity for example, the church at Baltonsborough, although beyond the hundred and at various times in either Glaston Twelve Hides or Whitstone Hundred [Thorn and Thorn 1980, 356; Greenwood 1822, 8-9; Glasscock 1975, 267; Morland 1984], actually originated as a chapelry of Butleigh [Aston 1986, 74; Torr 1974-79, 86][26]. This is yet another case where I would argue that ecclesiastical relationships reveal an older structure of territorial arrangements *preceding* hundredation (see fn 29, above); and it seems likely that Glastonbury Abbey's acquisition of lands at Baltonsborough in the mid 8th century [Abrams 1996, 53-54], and Butleigh purportedly in the early 9th [*ibid*, 76-77], may represent the beginnings of fragmentation affecting an earlier unit consisting of at least these two areas.

In this context, the case of Sowy island is particularly interesting. Topographically Sowi forms a discrete unit, and one might therefore expect it to be possible to establish relationships between the churches of the three major settlements on the island, namely Othery, Middlezoy and Weston Zoyland. In fact, only between Othery and its chapelry at Burrow Bridge, away from the island about 2½ km to the south-west, can we easily demonstrate such a link [Torr 1974-79, 94]. Nonetheless, references to the payment of tithes and other dues, and its

---

[26] As late as the early 17th century, an annuity was being paid by the churchwardens of Baltonsborough to the vicar of Butleigh, for "the finding of a curatt to be resident att Baltonsburrow" [SRO D/D/Rg 186, 1627].

inclusion in the list of 'mother' churches directly subject to Glastonbury Abbey in the medieval period, contained in S250, the forged charter of Ine [Costen 1992, 144-145], strongly support Middlezoy's pre-eminence as the mother church of the island [GC I, 1944, xxviii-xxix and 24-26][27]. Topographically, this is no surprise: Middlezoy occupies the highest part of the island, with, in turn, the church of the Holy Cross dominating the highest part of the village, at its northern end, close to the 25m contour[28]. There are also strong indications, in terms of the overall regularity of layout and the arrangement of the street pattern, that Middlezoy is a planned village (Chapter Eight). The notional division of the island into three parishes in the early 16th century should probably be taken as no more than a formal confirmation, for purely for administrative purposes, of existing arrangements [n19; and Costen 1992, 41-42]. There is certainly persuasive incidental evidence that the three places were effectively separate units, in terms of ecclesiastical provision certainly and agrarian regimes probably, at least by the 13th century: presumably the chapels at Othery and Weston Zoyland, even if technically dependent on Middlezoy, were needed to serve communities at those places, and Weston was an independent parish by the very early 14th century (Chapter Eight). Again, this is almost certainly a reference merely to the formalisation of existing practice [*pers comm* Dr R W Dunning].

Although a (probably 10th century) charter bound exists for Ham, other, somewhat conflicting documentary sources make it problematic whether it encompasses all or merely a part of the area occupied by the later High Ham parish [Abrams 1996, 134-135; Morland 1986, 73]. However, both the proximity of the place names High Ham and Low Ham, and the link between the two churches at these places, together confirm that they should indeed be regarded as a single estate [Gelling 1997, 124-125; Costen 1992a, 119]. Low Ham never became an independent parish in its own right, and its church, in existence by the 13th century [GC I, 1944, x-xi][29], remained a chapelry of its larger neighbour [Torr 1974-79, 88]. The topographical prefixes here are to be taken literally and, as at Middlezoy, attest to High Ham's superiority, occupying a favourable, expansive, promontory site at about 100m atop a broad plateau; it has also clearly undergone some degree of planning [Ellison 1983, 38-39]. Low Ham, by contrast sits on much lower ground to the south, at the base of the plateau slope at between about 20-30m; it gives all the appearance of a secondary, dependent settlement, although even here a rather straggling, hamlet-like appearance may in fact represent the degeneration of an earlier, much more regular layout [Ellison 1983, 59-61].

In sum, then, we can see that the tenurial division of the old *Pouelt* estate between Shapwick and Walton, as revealed by Domesday, is essentially a reflection of its division between the two hundreds of Loxley and Ringoldsway. It seems likely, therefore, that administrative developments within the estate as we see them in the early medieval period, in terms of the creation of the two hundreds and the distribution of tax liability (ie hidation) between the places within them, were intimately related, and must post-date the earliest ecclesiastical pattern in which, before the 10th century, Shapwick and Moorlinch together may have provided the pastoral focus for at least the western part of the estate.

We must also note the relationship between the possibly very ancient church at Street, with its pre-English associations [Abrams 1996, 153-154; McGarvie 1987, 25-32, esp at 27], curvilinear churchyard containing evidence of high-status Roman occupation [Hollinrakes 1994b], and chapelry at Walton[30]. This is only one respect in which, in stark contrast to Shapwick, the latter gives no indication whatsoever that it had ever been a place of any significance; so that its position at the head of a 30-hide unit in 1086 [Thorn and Thorn 1980; Abrams 1986, 208] is revealed clearly as nothing more than an administrative and accounting expedient, probably arising from Glastonbury Abbey's deliberate allocation of an equal hidage between the eastern and western halves of the old *Pouelt* estate, when Loxley and Ringoldsway were created at the time of hundredation.

---

[27] In 1268, when the Bishop, at the behest of Glastonbury Abbey, instituted the first perpetual vicar to Middlezoy church, it was recorded that the tithes from Weston, Othery and Middlezoy itself, and the glebe at all three places, were rightfully his. I am grateful to Dr R W Dunning for this reference. By the early 16th century however, it is clear that the ecclesiastical focus had shifted to Weston Zoyland, since the vicar there, in petitioning the Bishop to have the 'parish' of Sowy (ie Weston) divided into three parts, underlines the perceived subsidiary status of the churches at Othery and Middlezoy by referring to them as "two fair chapels" [Maxwell-Lyte 1939, 176-177].

[28] The dedication of Middlezoy church has changed certainly once, and possibly twice. In *c*1220 the patron was St Lawrence [GC II, 1948, clxxiii and 501], but at least by the mid 18th century, he had been abandoned in favour of the Holy Cross, which remains the dedication today [Ecton and Browne Willis 1742, 25]. Intriguingly however, Bates includes Middlezoy in his list of churches dedicated to the Virgin, on the basis of a mid-16th century will which purportedly refers to the "Churchyard of oure Lady of Mydelsowey" [Bates 1905, 112-113 and 128;]. Bates gives as his only reference for this vital document some ms notes made by Weaver from sources in the Wells District Probate Registry [*ibid*, 115], and it is extremely unfortunate that for whatever reason(s) it has not found its way into Weaver's own published volume of Somerset medieval wills for the relevant date [Weaver 1905], or indeed into any of the other usual printed sources of county wills [Weaver 1890; Shilton and Holworthy 1925]. The adoption of the Virgin as patron would be far more likely before the Reformation than after it [*pers comm.* Dr M D Costen]. A second re-dedication between the mid 16th century and the late 18th is certainly possible, although in view of Middlezoy's primary status (above, n35) in the medieval period, there is just a chance this may be a cryptic reference to a subsidiary churchyard chapel not otherwise recorded. Unlike that at Shapwick, the context and significance of the re-dedication(s) at Middlezoy are not clear. Another possibility, bearing in mind Weston's apparent superiority by the early 16th century (above, n35) is that somehow its dedication to the Virgin [Bates 1905, 113 and 134; Ecton and Browne Willis 1742, 25] has become confused with that of Middlezoy.

---

[29] I should warn the reader wishing to check this reference that GC is uncharacteristically unhelpful here. The Roman numerals actually refer to the section headed 'Introductory Documents', *not* to the 'Descriptive Analysis' which precedes it and which, confusingly, *also* uses Roman pagination.
[30] But see the note of caution sounded below, in the discussion on Carhampton, regarding the supposed chronological primacy of curvilinear churchyard enclosures.

Carhampton Hundred

In almost every important respect which bears on the nature of settlement within its borders, Carhampton stands in stark contrast to the Hundred of Whitley. In terms of size alone, Carhampton fell in about the middle range in comparison to the rest of the county [Aston 1986, 55], extending from Carhampton itself in the east, to Oare, close to the Somerset/Devon border on Exmoor, in the west, and taking in Exford to the south. In the post-Conquest period it eventually came to include the former, smaller hundreds of Cutcombe and Minehead, both of which had come into being as manorial entities [Thorn and Thorn 1980, 376; Thorn 1988]. Including these later additions, the total area of the hundred in the 19th century, by simple additon of all the parishes within its boundaries, was 59,099 acres (Table 1; Figure 19). Carhampton is not notable for any great variation in parish size, the smallest, Culbone, being exceptional, and it does not contain any larger parishes such as occur immediately to the south, Winsford (8656 acres, 3506 ha), Dulverton (8339 acres, 3377 ha) and Brompton Regis (9080 acres, 3677 ha) being examples. This perhaps bears out Roberts's view, citing work by Winchester, that the oft-quoted vastness of upland parishes is actually more apparent than real [Roberts 1987, 168]. Carhampton parish itself, as it emerges in the 19th century, at 2,318 ha compares quite favourably with other parishes in Somerset which originated as royal manors; places such as Wedmore (at least 5778 acres, 2340 ha), Somerton (6924 acres, 2804 ha) and Cheddar (7000 acres, 2835 ha). North Petherton, with 10336 acres (4186 ha), was clearly exceptional (parish areas taken from the Somerset section of Kain and Oliver 1995, 434-449). And as I hope to show, Carhampton's minster credentials are as sound as those of any major church in the county.

Carhampton hundred also shows a different aspect to Whitley in terms of tenure. Whereas Whitley, in the late 11th century, fell almost entirely under the aegis of a single lord, the various manors of which Carhampton was composed were for the most part divided between two secular lords, namely William of Mohun, whose estates in the area later formed the core of the Honour of Dunster; and Roger of Courseulles (Table 5). The sizes of Carhampton holdings in 1086 were also tiny compared to those in Whitley, a point to which we will return elsewhere.

Ecclesiastical Development in Carhampton

The only realistic candidate for minster status within the hundred is Carhampton itself. However, its only known chapelry, at Rodhuish, was never a parish in its own right but merely a detached part of Carhampton. It, though, at least had a clearly defined boundary and as a Domesday manor and a toponym containing OE *hiwisc*, was probably recognised as a discrete entity by the late Anglo-Saxon period [Costen 1992b, 65]. Such was still the case in the mid 19th century [Aston 1983, 74], and Rodhuish can perhaps be characterised as a 'proto-parish' which never quite attained independence.

At an even lower level of the ecclesiastical hierarchy are the two chapels of Lynch and Tivington, both within Selworthy parish, and indeed it appears that these are merely the survivors of the four that were known in this parish in the early 18th century [Chadwyck Healey 1901, 23-24]. Lynch cannot at this stage be associated with a defined unit, although it is thought to have been attached to the manor of Bossington, in existence by 1086, and Tivington similarly served the manor of Blackford [Bush 1994, 177; Selworthy PCC 1987]. It seems probable that Bossington manor included land in both Porlock and Selworthy, since Lynch chapel is separated from Bossington, lying in a detached piece of Porlock parish, by the boundary between the two parishes. While the surviving chapel at Lynch (Plate 6) dates only from the early 16th century, opinion on the date of Tivington is divided between the mid 14th [Selworthy PCC] and the 15th century [Bush 1994, 177]. The map evidence, however, is also important here, for it shows Tivington lying in the centre of what appears to be a peninsular-like enclave on the south-eastern side of Selworthy parish. One wonders, again, whether this unit, possibly representing the extent of Blackford manor, did not originate as a pre-Conquest addition to the original area of Selworthy, and like Rodhuish, had at least begun the process of splitting away from its parent estate as a first step to attaining parochial status. Other examples of intra-parochial chapels are that at the manor of Doverhay, noted in Pope Nicholas's taxation of 1291 under the assessment for Luccombe church, in whose parish it lay; its site is now apparently lost, but if a proprietary church it is likely to have lain in the vicinity of the present 15th century house known as Doverhay Court, now in the civil parish of Porlock [Savage 1830, 170; SMR 35128]; another probable proprietary chapel adjacent to a manorial curia in the hamlet of Horner [Chadwyck Healey 1901, 101; SMR 33663], and the ruined chapel of St Andrew, both in Luccombe parish but the latter in an isolated location [SMR 34584]; the 16th century chapel at Porlock Weir, demolished in the late 19th century but with fragments preserved in the walls of the cottage now occupying the site [SMR 33926]; and the so-called Burgundy Chapel in Minehead Without, the surviving fabric of which dates to the late medieval period, probably the late 14th or 15th century [Burrow 1985, 22-23; Huish 1941; Bryant 1984; Osborn 1983, 28; SMR 34487; Francis nd].

Indeed, it seems as though the only easily-discernable example in Carhampton hundred of a chapelry eventually gaining full independence is Luxborough, although at present the date by which the mother church of Cutcombe had 'lost' its daughter is uncertain. Even in the mid 19th century, Cutcombe, at nearly 7,000 acres, was the largest parish in Carhampton, perhaps as much as a third of its area, to the north and west, consisting of unenclosed rough grazing land on high Exmoor. Possibly Cutcombe's large parish, and its position as a lowly mother church, is due at least in part to its short-lived status as a manorial hundred within the Mohun barony, part of a group of demesne manors withdrawn by William of Mohun from Carhampton hundred in 1084, and restored to it when

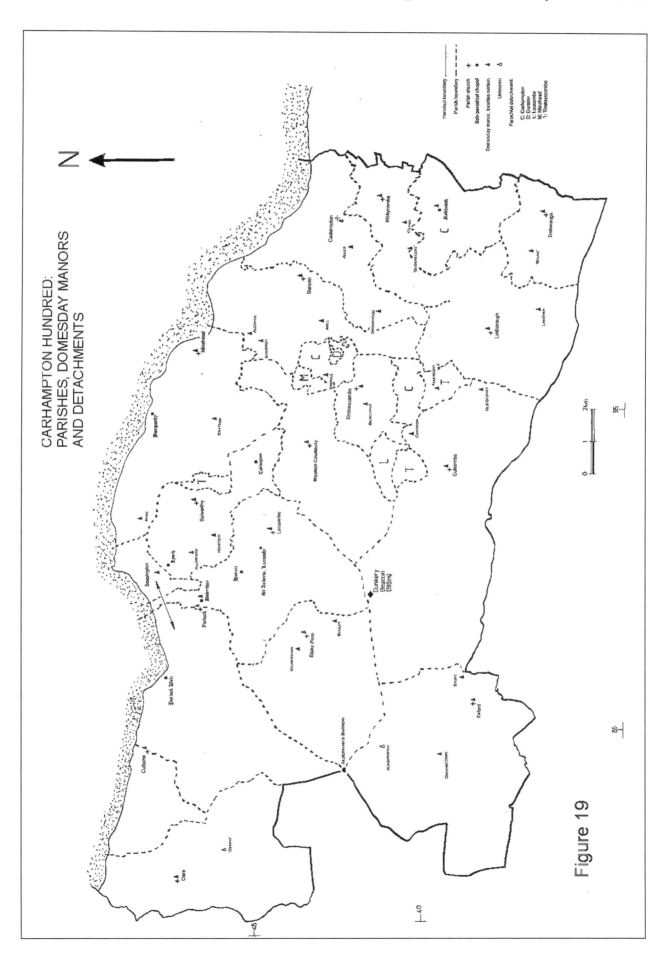

CARHAMPTON HUNDRED:
PARISHES, DOMESDAY MANORS
AND DETACHMENTS

Figure 19

Plate 6: Lynch Chapel, Bossington (formerly part of Porlock parish). Existing fabric of the 16th century but perhaps occupying a far earlier site, and originating as a manorial/proprietorial chapel.

he obtained its lordship [Morland 1990, 98 and 110; Thorn 1988a, 36-37]. If one then asks why William should particularly choose Cutcombe for this purpose, it may be relevant to note the four-fold increase in Cutcombe's tax assessment between 1066 and 1086, from 3 hides to 15 ploughlands, the latter making it the single most heavily-burdened of the hidated manors within the later area of Carhampton hundred, and with an annual value at Domesday, £6, equalled only by Minehead and Withycombe; Minehead, we should note, like Cutcombe, also enjoyed a temporary existence as a small manorial hundred created by William [Morland 1990, 110; Thorn & Thorn 1980, 376], although unlike Cutcombe does not seem to have given rise to any extra-parochial churches. Cutcombe's pre-Conquest hidation may be a further example of a favourable assessment, and perhaps an indication of a status such as to set it apart from other manors in the hundred. An estate consisting of both it and Luxborough together must have been vast, amounting to well over 10,000 acres, and perhaps more detailed work in the future would elucidate both their relationship and the chronology of Luxborough's boundaries.

In reviewing the evidence for ecclesiastical development in Carhampton, it may be possible to discern a relationship between place-names and the physical locations of the chapels we have already noted. Excluding the supposed chapel at Horner, now lost, the latter divide quite sharply into two distinct categories: those associated with, and actually sited in, settlements with habitative elements in their place-names; and those sited away from settlements and associated with topographical and/or descriptive names. In the former category are Tivington, Bossington (Lynch), Doverhay, and probably Rodhuish; in the latter, Porlock Weir, St Andrew's Luccombe, and Burgundy, Minehead Without. In drawing this distinction, it may be possible to suggest that what we are seeing is a relative chronology of foundation. The chapels associated with habitative place-name elements seem to represent a later, secondary phase of the ecclesiastical framework, perhaps of a 'manorial' or 'proprietorial' nature; this explains why they are located in or close to settlements. The cases of Bossington (Lynch) and Tivington are particularly telling in this respect; Bossington, *contra* Ekwall [1960, 54], is almost certainly Bosa's *tūn* (farmstead, estate, settlement); and while at this stage no early spelling can be found for Tivington, it is likely to be of the same personal name+*tūn* formula. These names can be directly compared to the series of similar forms along the north side of the Poldens in Whitley hundred (Woolavington, Cossington and Edington), which preserve the names of their respective late Saxon 'lords'. The second element of Doverhay appears to be one of the OE words for an enclosure of some kind, and Rodhuish contains the distinctive word *hiwisc*, 'land for the support of a family' [Costen 1992b, 65]. All of these places except Tivington were Domesday manors, and continued to be so into the later post-Conquest period, Tivington being associated with the manor of Blackford in Selworthy.

If these places do indeed represent a later, intrusive element into an older-established settlement and ecclesiastical pattern, then conversely it is reasonable that the remaining chapels should be seen as surviving vestiges of that earlier structure. The nature of the chapels of Burgundy, Luccombe and Porlock Weir, the latter apparently attributed to a guild and dedicated to St Olave [SMR 33926], may be at least partially explained by the clear Celtic undercurrent discernible in the religious development of the hundred. Dedications to pre-English saints are to be found at Carhampton itself (St Carantoc), Timberscombe (St Petroc), Porlock (St Dubricius) and Culbone (St Bueno). The coastal or near-coastal distribution of these sites is part of a wider pattern of similar dedications, with a strong preponderance of the names of attested Welsh saints, or at least, of names with clearly Welsh forms, stretching westwards along the northern coasts of Devon and Cornwall. Neither are the cults involved those of minor, 'second division' figures. Dubricius (Dyfrig), and Carantoc were both leading saints of the Welsh canon [Bowen 1956, 36-39; Pearce 1978, 195-197], men for whom Preston-Jones has coined the term 'inter-Celtic' saints [1992, 109][31].

Against this background, the three known isolated chapels of Carhampton seem to sit most easily within the eremitic tradition of the early church in western Britain. They are best explained as originating as hermitages, the dwelling-places of lone religious ascetics, however 'developed' they may have become later. Dating is highly tenuous; none appears to contain pre-Conquest fabric. But the topographical and structural parallels with other areas of northern and western Britain are at least suggestive [Thomas 1971, 85]. Thomas draws attention to the layout of some of these sites, where an oratory is associated with a living cell, either combined in a single, two-cell structure, or as separate buildings close together [*ibid*, 86-87]. This is precisely the arrangement, albeit in a more elaborate form, found at Burgundy chapel, although there is some doubt whether there the surviving fabric is all contemporary [Burrow 1985, 22-23]. Closer study may show that we can presume certain of Carhampton's parish centres to be eremitic sites, the prime example being Culbone, in its secluded valley location close to the coast. Preston-Jones [1992, 109], Pearce [1978, 136-137] and Burrow [1981, 59] all warn against the presumption that pre-English dedications must necessarily be early (ie relate to a time shortly after the *floruit* of the saint himself). Nonetheless, the dedication here should be considered alongside both a surviving late Saxon/early post-Conquest window [Grinsell 1970, 119], and the suggestion that "a blocked doorway is supposed to have communicated with a priest's or an anchorite's cell, the foundations of which were at one time to be found" [Porter 1971, 100]. On topographical grounds we may also, perhaps, suggest an eremitic origin for Oare, whose church sits at the bottom of a gentle, sheltered valley within easy distance of the coast;

although at present only the place-name, which is a British river-name, gives any hint of a possible pre-English existence [Ekwall 1960].

The topographical isolation of these places does not, however, necessarily mean that they existed *in vacuo*. On the contrary, although their *raison d'etre* was as places of refuge from the turmoil of the 'outer', temporal world, to which the religious could occasionally withdraw to experience a deeper level of spiritual contemplation, it was often the case that a hermitage was connected with some 'mother' house[32]. Parallel relationships occur in Ireland where, in the south-west at least, hermitages, minor churches and island retreats were affiliated to, and regarded as extensions of, specific monasteries [Hurley 1982]. There are, therefore, clear affinities here with the very earliest roots of western European monasticism, as exemplified by the island community of Lerins off the Mediterranean coast of southern France, founded in the early 5th century [Aston 1993b, 25-26].

Carhampton cannot claim any of the early personal and Christian inscribed stones apparently so characteristic of the 'Celtic' regions of western Britain, and recently the subject of a detailed survey by Charles Thomas [1994]. Nonetheless, a stone marked with an incised ring-cross on the hillside above Culbone church, and probably related to it in some way, is dated rather vaguely between the 7th and 9th centuries and said to have Welsh affinities [Grinsell 1970, 106 and 126; Quinnell and Dunn 1992, 61]; and Anglo-Saxon sculptural work survives at Porlock [Foster 1987, 77]. Current opinion views Wales, and specifically Welsh monastic foundations, as the ultimate source of the vigorous evangelising activity occurring in Cornwall in the 5th and 6th centuries, and that those involved were either men of Welsh birth or members of Irish Christian émigré communities living in Wales [Olson 1989, 48-50; Preston-Jones 1992, 119-120]. Doubtless the same is true of those sites on the north Somerset coast, and other parts of the southern shore of the Bristol Channel, where we may suspect the presence of pre-English cults: in Carhampton, Culbone may be a case in point. If, however, we accept arguments for a pre-English monastic presence in Carhampton itself, then we also raise the prospect that what hermitages and early secondary chapels there were in the area of the later hundred, were founded as offshoots of that mother house.

Carhampton: Town, Crown and Minster

One of the major ways in which both Chew and Carhampton hundreds differ from Whitley is in the fact that they take their names from settlements. As for Chew Magna, so also for Carhampton is it possible to discern affinities which seem to go beyond those we would expect from a purely rural place with an overwhelmingly agrarian economy; and time and again, just as at Chew, it is the *church* at Carhampton to which we to return as the element

---

[31] For the most recent summary biographies of Carantoc, Olave and Petroc, see Orme 2000. Such was Dubricius's reputation in the 12th century that the possession of his relics, removed from their resting place on Bardsey Island to his cathedral by the first Bishop of Llandaff in 1120, was considered central to that church's claim to be the leading foundation in Wales by virtue of antiquity [Porter 1971, 98-99]. Some modern authorities argue that the term 'Celtic church' is now best avoided [*eg* Davies 1992].

[32] For the Scillies, Aston 1993b, 34; for Lundy/Hartland, Pearce 1978, 82; for Beckery/Glastonbury Abbey Abbey, Rahtz 1993, 118-127; and for dependent hermitages in the Somerset wetlands in general, Aston 1995, 372.

which above all others seems to inform our perspective of developments there in the early medieval and post-Conquest period.

A church at Carhampton was noted in 1086, and by at least the end of the medieval period it had a chapel at Rodhuish [Torr 1974-79, 91], now in Withycombe parish [Aston 1983, 102]. Carhampton was a royal possession both before and after the Conquest (with a brief interval in the hands of the religious community at Cheddar: S806 [Sawyer 1968]), having been acquired by the crown at some unknown date before the end of the 9th century, since it is mentioned in King Alfred's will (S1507). A church of some status might therefore be expected, and the potential importance of the site as a focus of early Christian activity has been greatly increased by the recent discovery of a cemetery a few hundred metres east of the present church, with "radiocarbon determinations [suggesting] a 12th-16th century date....." [McCrone 1993, 144]. In fact, discoveries made during further, subsequent evaluation work in the same area have now raised the possibility that there was at Carhampton an early (5th-6th centuries AD) Dark Age centre comparable in status even if not in size to places such as Tintagel, South Cadbury and Cadbury Congresbury. Part of the evidence consists of indications of industrial activity, including metalworking [McCrone 1995, 177]. Parallels from the Middle Saxon high-status site at Flixborough suggest themselves, and Reynolds remarks on how "there is a tendency for industrial production to be linked to high-status sites" [Reynolds 1999, 122, 155; and see further below]. These elements take on an added weight in the light of Paul Blinkhorn's recent observation that in the Middle Saxon period, "the role of ecclesiastical communities in production, trade and redistribution appears to have been highly significant......it appears that most ecclesiastical sites had the capability of manufacturing surplus goods for trade" [Blinkhorn 1999, 18-19]. In this same context, we may also wonder whether the renders of iron blooms flowing into Carhampton from various manors in the hundred, recorded in 1086 (Chapter Seven, and below), are a relic of the early medieval industrial activity attested so clearly in the archaeological record.

Taken together, we might consider the balance of this evidence to elevate Carhampton to the status of one of Charles Thomas's 'primary coastal sites' of this period [Thomas 1971, 24-25]. Medieval documentary references to two churches at Carhampton have prompted the suggestion that the cemetery is associated with the chapel dedicated to St Carantoc which was in use in the Middle Ages [Bush 1994, 56], and which survived into the mid 16th century to be described by Leland [Toulmin Smith, I, 1907, 167]. There does not, as Collinson astutely points out [1791, II, 2], appear to be any independent support for Leland's assertion about the original parochial status of St Carantock's, and it is the other church, St John's, which from before the Conquest has been pre-eminent [Bush 1994, 56]. This does not, though, fully exclude the possibility of a shift in status between the two at some point before 1066, something which might be highlighted

by close topographical study and a reassessment of the documentary evidence.

At present Carhampton itself, whether St John's or St Carantoc's, appears to be the only church in the hundred with attributes which might indicate an origin as a minster church of early foundation. The status of Carhampton as a royal vill and an early centre of importance is further supported by the facts, firstly, that it gave its name to the hundred in which it lies; secondly, that it was still, in 1086, receiving customary dues from several other manors in the hundred; thirdly, it had not been hidated (ie rated for geld); fourthly, "the suggestion.....that the word tun had a special sense referring to the functions of a royal vill as a local centre" [Sawyer 1983, 282-283, and 292], an argument supported in the case of Carhampton by the fact of one and possibly two battles (in 836 and/or 843) being fought there by the men of Wessex, under royal leadership, against Viking raiding parties [below; and Sawyer 1983, 283-284; Pearce 1978, 114]; and lastly (Michael Costen, *pers comm*), the possession by its church in the late 11th century of its own large (1½ hides) estate. An indication of the original extent of the royal estate centred on Carhampton is given by the tithe map, which shows detached pieces of the parish surrounding "a series of isolated farmsteads and hamlets on the Brendon Hills and Exmoor.....with other settlements intruded between parts of Carhampton where they expanded at a later date" [Costen 1992a, 98-99].

So far as it relates to Carhampton, a recent paper by John Blair is of interest. Blair has suggested that the obviously-planned, ladder-like grid layout to be found at Cheddar, immediately north of the Saxon 'palace' site, "is a form of topography which can be recognised in the environs of many minsters, where it can be ascribed to the formation of a lay settlement on the periphery of a pre-urban monastic zone" [Blair 1996, 14]. This is part of a wider review of evidence from which Blair concludes that certain high-status sites previously regarded as purely secular in nature, and particularly the Saxon 'palaces' at Northampton and Cheddar, are in fact monastic establishments. In Somerset, Blair cites parallels to the Cheddar grid-plan at Dundon, Shapwick, Carhampton and Hardington Mandeville [note 51].

The Hollinrakes have proposed the existence of two possible 'compartmental' plans at Carhampton, the first with its long axis aligned roughly east-west and containing three 'cells', with the present church sited on the northern edge of the easternmost cell; and a second grid running roughly north-south, again containing three main compartments [Hollinrakes 1994, plan 15]. This latter seems to me rather less convincing: there is no surviving lane or road forming its western side, the road pattern appears to bear a far more intimate relationship to the east-west grid, and it was not, in the late 19th century at least [OS 1st edn. 25" map], a settlement focus, although of course it is possible that settlement has shifted and that the present arrangement, stressing the primacy of the east-west grid, is not the original one. The dates of such layouts are problematic, although it is becoming increasingly apparent that at least some are manifestly pre-Conquest: at

Shapwick the more compact, northern grid was probably in place by the 10th century [Hollinrakes 1995b, 183-184], and in Dorset Saxo-Norman pottery recovered from fieldwalking suggests a pre-Conquest origin for a number of regular village plans there [*pers comm* Teresa Hall]. At Carhampton, the context in which the plan took shape, whether under a 'monastic' aegis (below), or a secular (royal) one, is at present unclear.

The putative 'monastic' site is placed by the Hollinrakes outside the east-west grid, at its north-eastern corner, on or close to the site of Eastbury Farm. Furthermore, they propose an ovoid monastic precinct boundary with its long axis aligned roughly east-west [Hollinrakes 1993, fig 1]. The inference appears to be that the chapel of St Carantoc described by Leland in the mid 16th century was, if not itself a surviving monastic church, at least in some way related to the monastic site, perhaps as a subsidiary chapel, with the present parish church a later provision for an expanding lay population [Hollinrakes 1994, para. 8.2].

The Hollinrakes are rightly cautious about making their site's 'monastic' attributes bear more weight than the present evidence can sustain and at present, the idea is made no more than "a good working hypothesis" [Hollinrakes 1995a, 30]. Nonetheless, the suggestion of "a dispersed burial ground pre-dating the enclosed medieval graveyard....." [Hollinrakes 1994, para. 8.3], is interesting in the light of Charles Thomas's views on the primacy of cemeteries in northern and western Britain as frequently the earliest features on sites which later contained monasteries [Thomas 1971, 50]. Thomas sees a clear sequential path from 'undeveloped', unenclosed, possibly pre-Christian (Roman, sub-Roman or even prehistoric) cemeteries, with increasing preference for alignment of burials; through to supposedly overt Christian burials perhaps focussed on certain 'special' graves of particular significance [58-64]; to so-called 'developed' cemeteries with circular or rectangular ditched and/or embanked boundaries, with the final phase including buildings of various kinds, churches or chapels in wood or stone which later still would have progressed to a function that was either monastic or parochial, or both [Thomas 1971, 68]. Thomas's stress on the high antiquity of the circular groundplan is a central theme of his argument [51-53].

The evidence from Carhampton, however, is at best ambiguous. We have already stressed the dangers of assuming that a cult bearing a pre-English name must invariably be early [Burrow 1981, 63], the dedication to Carantoc himself being unattested before the early 14th century [Porter 1971, 88]. The connection may arise from nothing more than a back-formation from the place-name by the author(s) of the extant lives of the saint, which, although containing earlier material, date probably to the late 11th or 12th centuries in the form in which they survive [Pearce 1978, 195-197].

We can present arguments both for and against a monastic, or at the least early Christian, origin for Carhampton. Perhaps one of the more promising is the presence of the name Eastbury on the eastern boundary of the Hollinrakes' putative enceinte. The relationship of -bury names to sites with monastic connotations is well attested, and seems to represent a development in meaning of OE *byrig*, 'a fortified place', so that eventually -bury acquired the specific sense of 'a monastic site'. The massive size of some early *valla monasteriorum* might, through their highly defensive appearance, have attracted the -bury epithet [Burrow 1981, 50-51; Sims-Williams 1990, 92-93, and 107-109; Blair 1992, 233-234], and the etymology of its association with monasteries has recently been discussed in detail by Margaret Gelling with specific reference to Cadbury-Congresbury [Gelling 1992, 5]. It is perhaps in this light that Eastbury is best considered. Teresa Hall's painstaking topographical survey of the Dorset evidence, largely superseding earlier reviews by Barker [1982 and 1984], has shown clearly that there, planned elements of some towns and villages are related to the presence of monastic houses. At Sherborne, regular blocks called Westbury and Eastbury lay respectively south and east of the Abbey precinct, probably as additions to a much earlier, curvilinear boundary [Hall 2000, 110-113]. And at Bradford Abbas, another apparently planned block, called Westbury, lies immediately north of the minster church [*ibid*, 155-156]. While the date at which these areas were laid out is uncertain, it is likely that in both cases it was the religious house which was responsible. And the suggestion that by the mid 11th century Wimborne may have supported "both a defended royal residence and a monastic precinct" [Barker 1982, 104], raises the question of whether at Carhampton we must consider a similar duality of function[33]. Against this background, John Blair's views on the nature of the regular plan at Cheddar, and the Hollinrakes' western grid, one wonders whether the Eastbury name has anything to tell us about monastic influence in the settlement topography of Carhampton.

A closer consideration of both the topography and the toponymy of this enigmatic site, and of its wider context, might allow us to synthesise, if only in outline, a model for development which reconciles at least some of these diverse strands of evidence. At first glance it may appear that the parish church is an intrusive and disruptive element in what must originally, as the Hollinrakes suggest, have been a highly regular settlement plan. One gets a good sense of this if the church is removed from the plan and the road which used to run east-west, immediately to its south, through the churchyard, is restored to its original line (Figure 20). Stratigraphically, it looks very much as though the church takes its cue from a pre-existing road pattern. It seems likely that St John's was originally placed to abut directly on to the northern side of the east-west road, and that subsequently its churchyard was extended southwards, across the road, giving the *appearance* of an intrusive element. This would make the church either contemporary with or later than the putative village plan. Figure 20 also suggests very strongly that the Hollinrakes' proposed 'primary' curvilinear enclosure is disrupted and cut across by Carhampton's putative grid plan layout, which on this model must, then, be a

[33] But see also Hall 2000, 109 and n22 for a correction to part of Barker's suggested plan layout at Wimborne.

subsequent feature. If so, we could argue that the curvilinear enclosure had been at least partially abandoned either before or at the time of the later phase of planning.

The diagonal NW/SE road cutting through the centre of the village did not exist before the first half of the 19th century [tithe map, SRO D/D/Rt 277, 1839; Luttrell Estate Plan 1827, SRO DD/L 297/3 s562; and Plate 7]. For the moment, while accepting as a reasonable model the general extent and outline of the Hollinrakes' putative primary enclosure, based as it is on detailed map and fieldwork, I would offer an alternative layout, differing somewhat in its form and in the interpretation of its *nature*. Figure 20 indicates this divergent view. A possible criticism might be the use of a clearly 'canalised' water system to form the northern and north-eastern boundaries of the enclosure which I propose, probably to service a mill site on the eastern side of the Eastbury Farm complex. Some might regard this as too late a development to allow it to be used as the boundary of an early medieval plan. This is by no means necessarily the case, however, and in support I would cite John Blair's demonstration that the royal/monastic complex at Cheddar was in part bounded

by a diverted and canalised stretch of the Axe (Blair 1996).

In any event, it is noticeable that *both* models produce enclosures which exactly straddle the main east-west road through the village, linking Dunster with Watchet. Eastbury Farm is located on the road frontage on the eastern side of this unit, so that it could be said almost to form a gateway 'guarding' the through route. Some kind of military/strategic relationship with the known *burh* at Watchet would allow us to admit the possibility that the function of this primary cell at Carhampton was, or at least *became*, partially defensive [McAvoy 1986]. And to the west, the existence of a Dark Age hilltop site, of whatever nature, on Castle Hill, cannot be discounted [*pers comm* M Aston]. The history of this area, as we have already seen from Susan Pearce's suggestion, might, for the later 9th and 10th centuries, allow Carhampton to fit into the context of one of a line of defensive positions along this insecure coast, which included Dunster and Watchet; and we may here remind ourselves of the Chronicle entry for 914 recording how Edward the Elder "arranged that men were stationed against them [ie the Danes] on the south side of the Severn estuary" [quoted in McAvoy 1986, 59].

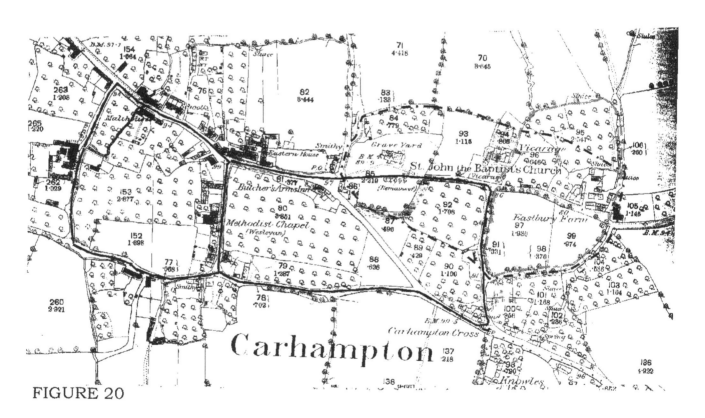

FIGURE 20

Reduced extract from OS first edition 25" map of Carhampton (1885), showing outline of settlement grid plan (black line), and 'primary' curvilinear (?monastic) enclosure proposed by the Hollinrakes (black dashed line). Adapted from Hollinrakes 1993 and 1994. A possible alternative form is represented here by the grey dashed line, and has the advantage of allowing both the grid plan and the curvilinear enclosure to co-exist as mutually complementary elements.

Plate 7: Plan of Carhampton, from a general manorial survey of 1827, SRO DD/L 297/3. An east-west road originally ran through the churchyard, which has subsequently been extended southwards forcing the road into a dog-leg diversion. If the road is restored to its original position the church can be seen to occupy a site abutting the northern side of what is apparently a highly regular grid plan.

Is it possible, then, that the *burh* of Eastbury is really defensive rather than monastic? The question is extremely problematic because at Carhampton the meaning of the word may be blurred, and John Blair has recently reminded us that the affinities embodied in the idea of the 'monastic city' allow us to view large, collegiate or conventual religious complexes in the early medieval period as essentially *urban* in nature. These places, he remarks, "were bigger, more populous and more permanent than any lay settlements: the closest thing to

towns that the early insular societies knew" [Blair 1996b, 9].

My suggested model is that the proposed Eastbury enceinte did indeed start life, perhaps in the 6th/7th century, as the focus of pre-English monastic activity, but was later adapted, perhaps with strengthened defences, to an at least partially military use, when the crown recognised its potential strategic importance. There seems no reason why, in principle, ecclesiastical and military/royal functions should not have shared the same space, as we know they did, on an altogether larger scale, at Cheddar [Blair 1996].

This leaves open the question of which of the two institutions, church or state, was responsible for the grid plan layout, in my own model (Figure 20) lying exactly where we would expect it to be: butted hard up against one side of the primary enclosure. This is another reason why I think it unlikely that the latter ever extended as far west as the parish church; as we have seen, the new layout would have to be superimposed upon it, greatly reducing the area within the enclosure. It is difficult to imagine either Church or Crown allowing this to happen, and still less the establishment of a 'secular' pre-Conquest church (which St John's probably is), *inside* the *vallum* of a working monastery. A relative sequence of development might then be: 1) the establishment in the 6th or 7th century of a pre-English monastic enclosure; 2) in the late 9th or 10th century, the adaptation by the state of the original enclosure for defensive purposes, associated with the laying out of a planned settlement. Whether or not the monastery itself was still in operation at this point is uncertain; but if the state was responsible for the regular plan, an awareness of Carhampton's strategic significance may have brought with it a realisation of its economic potential, and the planned element may have been intended from the outset to have, or ultimately to develop, *urban* attributes. Up to this point, pastoral care was supplied by the putative monastic church, St Carantoc's original foundation or its successor, which we know to have been functioning at least till the end of the 12th century [Hollinrakes 1994, para 2.5]; 3) in the 10th or 11th century, the foundation of St John's church presumably, as the Hollinrakes suggest, to serve a growing lay population, on a central site *outside* what I would regard as the primary enclosure, and immediately to the north of the settlement grid.

A further model for Carhampton, attempting to place these developments in a wider landscape context, is offered later on. But there are also implications in this scheme for the relationship between St John's and the supposed church of St Carantoc. While the exact location of the latter remains uncertain, from what has already been said, a site in the vicinity of Eastbury Farm seems most likely. While we know that St Carantoc's was still standing in Leland's day, until recently its fate thereafter was obscure. However, we can now say with certainty that it continued to survive at least down to the early 17th century and probably much later, from a reference in a glebe terrier that is as frustrating as it is intriguing. The terrier is undated but is probably from the first decade of the 17th century, and records a tenement consisting of "on[e] other house called Quormes Hayes being [in] former tyme the church............" [SRO D/D/Rg 335/1]. Quormes is also noted in a later terrier of 1634 [SRO D/D/Rg 335/2], but by that time its earlier function went unmentioned. This cannot be the parish church and it is far too early for any of the dissenting denominations. It can only be an account of the conversion of St Carantoc's church to a dwelling, the fact that the churchwardens considered it worthy of note implying that the conversion had occurred shortly before the earlier terrier had been drawn up. I have regrettably not

been able to trace the subsequent history of this crucial tenement in later records.

However, supposing both a position immediately north of the farm buildings depicted on the 1st edn. 25" OS map, and a 'normal' east-west orientation, the chapel must, when standing, have been on a close, if not exact east-west alignment to the present church. This raises the possibility of the two churches at Carhampton eventually forming a deliberately-planned 'group', and again, there may be striking parallels here with the known chapel of St Mary the Virgin in the churchyard at Chew Magna, and with the relationship that has been suggested for Shapwick and Moorlinch in Whitley hundred.

Dr Blair's suggestions about the significance of church groups relate to series of *contemporary* churches, but at Carhampton the suggested chronology precludes this. However, whether or not, by the 10th or 11th century, there was still a functioning monastery within the primary enclosure, there seems no reason why the original early church should not have continued to exercise a lasting liturgical influence that was a material consideration for those choosing the later site of St John's; a site for the 'new' church slightly to the north, *outside* the planned framework, would surely have served just as well. This is clearly a matter needing closer study, but the circumstantial evidence suggests strongly that the relationship between St Carantoc and St John's, and the possibly monastic nature of the arrangement, may be best explained in this way.

However, a note of caution perhaps needs to be sounded against an overly easy presumption that the correct interpretation of Carhampton necessarily depends even partially on a monastic function. Even if Carantoc's chapel should eventually be found, attributing purpose and use to it may prove problematic. For example, in Wales for the pre-Conquest period, we can note the apparent difficulty of distinguishing between truly monastic churches and 'ordinary' secular ones [Edwards and Lane, 1992, 4; Edwards 1996]. While preferring a religious explanation, we have already noted the reticence of the site's excavators in this respect, and the nature of the burials found at Carhampton thus far illustrates the need for a careful approach. From the point at which burials first began to turn up in the early 19th century, in the vicinity of the Vicarage garden and orchard, to the most recent campaign of controlled excavations, a relationship with either St John's or the lost chapel of Carantoc has always been assumed [SMR 33449]. Certainly so far as the burials from the latest work are concerned, some 200m east of the present churchyard, this is completely reasonable, since they are clearly Christian; quite apart from an E-W orientation, they date to between the 12th century and the 16th [34].

However, while the specifically Christian nature of an E-W alignment is still regarded by many as unambiguously diagnostic, the experience of both Wales and elsewhere in the 'Celtic' fringes leads Edwards and

---

[34] I am grateful to Chris Webster for his advice on this point.

Lane to argue that this is no longer a safe position [Edwards and Lane 1992, 6]. At Carhampton this is not yet an issue because of the relatively late dates and secure contexts of the burials so far recovered. However, if work continues, and reveals far *earlier* inhumations, these are matters which will need to be considered.

Carhampton has not yet yielded any 'special' grave(s), of the kind described by Thomas, although, again, these may yet materialise if future work pushes down to pre-Conquest levels. Likewise, the existence of an ovoid enclosure, suggested by the Hollinrakes, and modified here, cannot *per se* be taken as an indicator of either antiquity or function. While, as we have already seen, Thomas regards the circular ground-plan as primary, he also demonstrates that rectilinear enclosures were in use in the earliest period of Christian activity in western and northern Britain [Thomas 1971, 30-32]. It is certainly true that, especially in the 'Celtic' provinces, curvilinearity continues to be deployed regularly as the 'acid' test of early foundation; as, for example, in the cases of Silvester's study of churchyard morphology in Clwyd and Powys [Silvester 1997, 114-118], and Brook's similar work on either side of Offa's Dyke [Brook 1992]. However, on the supposed primacy of curvilinear enclosures, Morris expresses scepticism [Morris 1986, 455], and John Blair has forcefully refuted the widespread belief that circular enceintes, when found at sites which are demonstrably monastic in nature, are in some sense diagnostically pre-English [Blair 1992, 235 and 260]. The merits of these views are underlined by an increasing body of evidence from a range of regional studies. Preston-Jones's detailed analysis of the topography of Cornish churchyards allows her to state with confidence that not all curvilinear enclosures are necessarily either early in date (ie $5^{th}/6^{th}$ century), or monastic in nature [Preston-Jones 1992, 105]; and in Dorset, Teresa Hall suggests that of 18 churchyards of either wholly or partially curvilinear form, only four are likely to have originated as pre-English enclosures, and *none* of these "was associated with a high-status church" [Hall 2000, 157 n91, and Appendix 4, 205][35].

The final element which we can consider relates not to the site of the putative Carhampton monastery, but to the estate which may have been attached to it, namely the 1½ hides recorded in 1086. In Cornwall, Olson, collating the evidence of both Domesday Book and other sources, has shown that estates of small hidages attached to churches in the late 11th century are usually an indication of collegiate status [Olson 1989, 86-97]. For Michael Costen the estate attached to it, and the fact of its location on ancient

demesne, suggests that the church at Carhampton was "probably a minster" [Costen 1992a, 154]. So also for Sawyer, the evidence of a church "with property that was separately assessed for the geld" in 1086 is seen as a diagnostic attribute of formerly royal minsters [Sawyer 1983, 278]. The most promising candidate may, yet again, be the manor of Eastbury. Eastbury's existence by the late 13th century, the possible 'monastic' connotations of the name, and its location adjacent to the area of the most recent archaeological discoveries, we have already noted: the key here may prove to be the transfer, in the later 12th century, of the Carhampton churches first to the cathedral of Wells, for the use of the canons there, and subsequently to Bath Abbey [Maxwell Lyte 1931, 104; Hollinrakes 1994, para 2.5].

The whole question of the exact nature of the site at Carhampton must yet remain open. The alleged historical associations with St Carantoc and the estate attached to 'the church' in 1086 are the two most important strands of evidence which might suggest a religious use. There has, however, been a realisation recently that it is extremely difficult to attribute function, as between religious (monastic) or secular, to many of the known high-status sites of the 5th-6th centuries known in western Britain, and which have been dated primarily by imported Mediterranean pottery types. Thus, in the most telling reappraisal to date, the so-called monastery at Tintagel in Cornwall has now become the seasonally-occupied stronghold of a post-Roman warlord and his entourage [Thomas 1994, 214; Morris 2000], although a monastic use in the late Anglo-Saxon/early Norman period has also been suggested [Dark 1994, 50-51]; and the excavator of the Dark Age settlement on Glastonbury Abbey Tor prefers on balance a monastic attribution, but with some hesitancy [Rahtz 1993, 59-60].

Comparisons are not, unfortunately, helped by the fact that the discovery of early medieval evidence at Carhampton came too late to be included in either published version of the most recent survey of British sites with potentially similar affinities [Snyder 1996, 1997]. However, more positively, the problem of assigning function to high-status Dark Age centres in western Britain has recently been subjected to detailed reassessment by Dark [1994]. Dark's rejection of the notion of duality of function (as between monastic/royal) on *early*, high-status, pre-English sites [15], does nothing to undermine the case that has already been outlined for the possibility of just such a development at Carhampton, since that proposal turns upon a *late* (9th-10th century) royal involvement.

Dark's general conclusions may have important implications for Carhampton, but the nature of the evidence gathered so far might be considered still to leave wide open the problem of the exact nature of the site: are we dealing, in the pre-English period, with a secular (royal?) centre, a monastic one, or both, separate but in close proximity? Dark does not seem to consider the possibility, as I have suggested, that sites might *change* their function through time, in the case of Carhampton from religious to military/defensive/strategic; although ultimately such changes would be impossible to trace

---

[35] These doubts make all the more surprising Edwards's recent claim that "a number of studies have shown.............the likely antiquity of curvilinear churchyard enclosures" [Edwards 1996, 56]. Indeed, one of the references cited in support of this is Preston-Jones's Cornish study, which I have also cited here precisely *because* it is by no means conclusive, as the author herself concedes. Until a clearer picture emerges from further detailed regional studies about the likely chronological affinities of curvilinear churchyards, each case should be taken on its own merits, and in the absence of other 'diagnostic' criteria, curvilinearity should not *by itself* be used to underpin a firm conclusion of *either* early foundation *or* pre-English origin.

effectively without intrusive archaeology. The point is an important one for our correct understanding of the nature of this type of occupation, and the case of the Middle-Saxon 'high-status' site at Flixborough, Lincs, may suggest affinities for places like Carhampton; since, as Reynolds describes, it is the excavator's view that functional dynamism was an inherent characteristic of such sites [work cited by Reynolds 1999, 113 and 123].

Dark's main criteria seem strongly to support the Hollinrakes' preference for a religious use. However, bearing in mind the uncertainties, an attempt is made here to represent a simple path of development for the Carhampton site, integrating both monastic and secular functions, and based on the framework offered by Edwards and Lane in the form of nine possible models "for the origin and initial development of early medieval ecclesiastical sites in Wales" [Edwards and Lane 1992, 10]. The similar model given here as Figure 21 adapts and combines elements of those authors' 3, 4, 5 and 8, since none of their sequences seem to answer more than approximately to the situation at Carhampton.

Parishes and Early Territories

The tithe maps of Carhampton hundred reveal an often complex pattern of parochial detachments embedded in other parishes [Aston 1983, 74; Figure 19]. There may a number of reasons behind this: as a remnant of a former link with distant resources belonging to a parish, perhaps as the foundation of new settlements and their territories 'cut off' older communities from resources to which the latter traditionally had access; as the result of a link by ownership (ie a manorial relationship); as a vestige of a former multi-vill estate which subsequently fragmented, as perhaps in the case of Carhampton, already noted; or from the payment of tithes from land shared with another parish [Winchester 1990, 11-15, and 47-48]. Some parishes seem to present clear signs of having been created by the fission of larger units. Stoke Pero/Luccombe is the most obvious example, the outer boundary taking the form of an ovoid which has been split almost exactly down the middle. Indeed the modern civil parish of Luccombe has now absorbed Stoke Pero and may represent something like the shape and extent of the original unit. A further striking feature of this entity is the way that the north-western quarter of Luccombe is extended in a narrow, tongue-like corridor all the way to the sea (Figure 22), giving an otherwise landlocked 'estate' access to the coast and in the process splitting Porlock parish into two parts, an occurrence unusual enough to prompt both Collinson and Chadwyck Healey to remark upon it [Collinson 1791, II, 22; Chadwyck Healey 1901, 42]. It seems clear that at the time that Luccombe's boundaries were fixed, coastal access was at least perceived as being of considerable importance, and may be related to the need to include a particular resource which lay in that area within the Luccombe/Stoke Pero estate; perhaps, at least in part, seaweed, whose use as a valuable restorative of soil fertility was, as we have already noted for Chew, well known in the medieval period and long before [Bell

1981][36]; or as a device to bestow fishing and other rights associated with littoral access on what would otherwise have been a landlocked estate. We do not know of any settlement at the point where this parochial extension strikes the coast; but perhaps fishing privileges exercised here by Luccombe manor found expression in ephemeral seasonal shielings such as those lying on the coast of south Devon in the later Middle Ages recently described by Harold Fox [Fox 1996a]. In that county, coastal detachments of landlocked parishes have been shown conclusively to relate to the possession of fishing and other littoral privileges, and Luccombe's coastal 'corridor' seems very likely to be merely a logical development of this [Fox 2001, 47-51][37]. The recent discovery of 18th century references to a herring house attached to Luccombe parish seems strongly to support this suggestion [Richardson 2000, 15].

It is also generally true that, for the hundred as a whole, the constituent parishes tend to increase in size to the west, with the smaller parishes to the east. Two factors particularly may have played a role: the eastern area may, for reasons which are not yet clear, have been subjected to more intense fragmentation of the larger, pre-Conquest estates of which it was once doubtless composed; and probably closely related to this is the fact that the western parishes include within their boundaries a far greater proportion of upland commonable pasture. Very small areas around the margins of Exmoor were ploughed from at least the 13th century [Hallam 1978, 44], but the restricted commonable nature of grazing lands within the Forest is well-known from documentary evidence [Macdermott 1911, 196], and outside the Forest a more extensive system of communal use of the moor seems to be hinted at by some of the parish boundaries in the west of the hundred. The best example of this is the radial pattern of boundaries which emanates from Alderman's Barrow (SS 837423), marking the meeting-point of Porlock, Stoke Pero and Exford parishes (Figure 19). Such an arrangement 195-probably arises from "the division of an area of rough grazing land between the communities around its edge in such a way as to allot a share to each", the area having originally been intercommonable. The date that such division may have taken place is open to question, although, citing Rackham, Winchester states that one of several similar boundaries converging on a point on Goonhilly Down, Cornwall, was probably in place by the mid 10th century [Winchester 1990, 56-57]. Alderman's Barrow is a corruption of *Osmundesburgh*, and the site was noted as a boundary point in the earliest surviving example of the many medieval perambulations of the Exmoor Forest bounds, dating to the early 13th century [Macdermott 1911, 117; Grinsell 1970, 62 and 129-130]. It is tempting to equate this Osmund with the Edmund who gave his name to the Domesday farmstead of

---

[36] I am grateful to Paul Cope-Faulkner for this reference.
[37] I am grateful to Harold Fox for drawing my attention to the very similar cases at Stoke Fleming in Devon, and Towednack in Cornwall, both involving long, narrow parochial extensions to the respective coasts; Fox 2001, 77 n9.

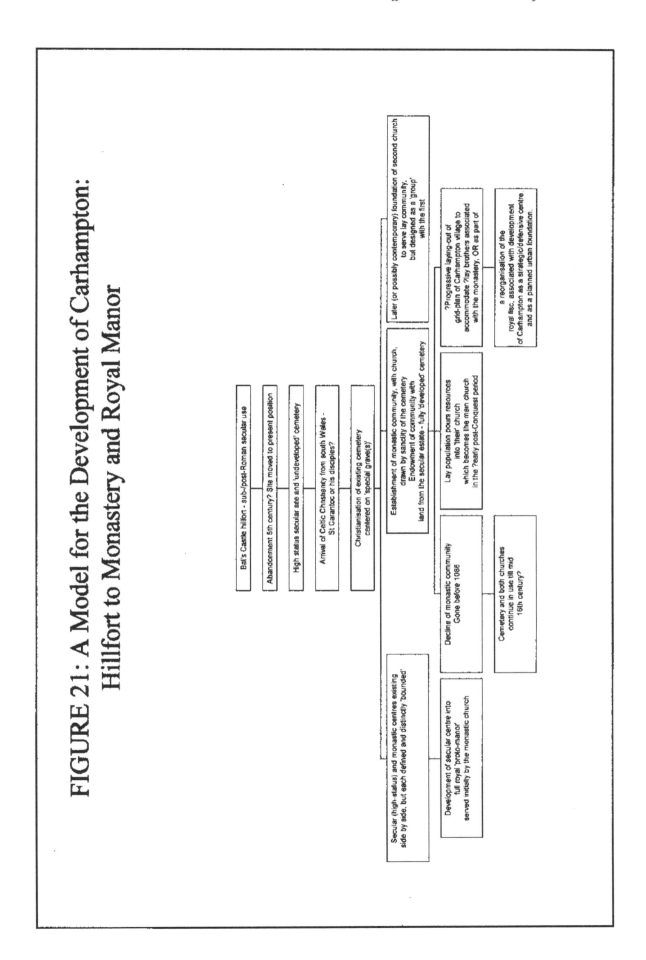

FIGURE 21: A Model for the Development of Carhampton: Hillfort to Monastery and Royal Manor

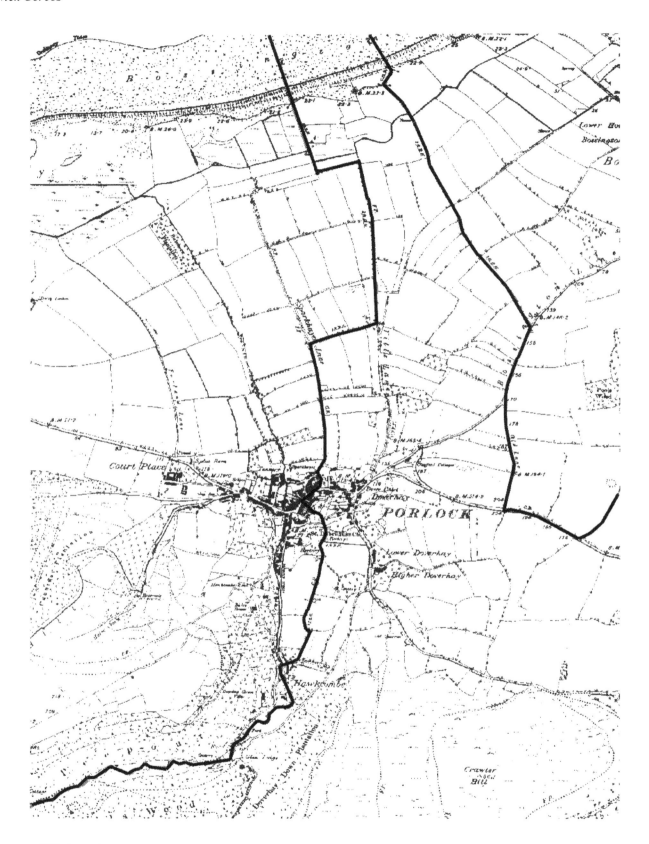

FIGURE 22

Extract from OS first edition 6" map (1885), showing, as a black line,
detail of Luccombe's parochial extension which runs northwards down to the
coast, splitting Porlock parish in two.

Edmundesworde in Exford parish that later became Almsworthy. In any event, the use of a major Bronze Age barrow, associated with an Old English personal name, as an important boundary marker, similarly suggests a pre-Conquest division of the commons in this western part of Carhampton hundred, and by extension the existence of earlier territorial arrangements.

Administrative as well as ecclesiastical relationships can be used to reconstruct antecedent (ie pre-Conquest) territories, and in Carhampton vestiges of such links survived long enough to be recorded in 1086. As we have already briefly noted, Domesday Book contains several examples of manors which owed customary dues to the head manor of the hundred, that is, Carhampton itself. These places were Oare, Allerford and Bossington [Welldon Finn and Wheatley 1967, 212]. Because of the inconsistencies of the recording process in 1086, it is likely that the number of manors owing similar dues in Carhampton was actually greater than this [Frank Thorn, *pers comm*][38]. The significance of these dues is that they may well be relict features of an older 'multiple estate' type arrangement, from a time when the capitular manor, Carhampton, lay at the centre of a single, large, estate, before the process of disintegration into parish-sized units had begun [Aston 1985a, 34-35]. The nature of the dues in Carhampton, as elsewhere in Somerset, overwhelmingly in the form of animals (chiefly sheep) rather than cash, is notably antiquated and may carry some hint of an origin in a framework of agrarian specialisation, which is one of the key components of the multiple estate model. Sawyer observes that where Domesday records such obligations, they relate almost invariably to royal manors, and represent vestiges of the pre-Conquest food-rents which previously flowed from the surrounding, subsidiary estates to the central *villa regalis* [Sawyer 1983, 280-281]; although Timberscombe is the sole surviving example of a specialist place-name among the parish centres in Carhampton. If this be allowed, the render from Oare may be of particular interest, for Oare was the westernmost manor in the hundred (and, indeed, in Somerset), while Carhampton was one of the three easternmost. We of course have no way of knowing whether all the settlements in between formerly owed dues similar to that recorded for Oare, but on that basis, past interpretations of the nature of early medieval territorial units would have allowed us speculate that, before it broke up, the putative Carhampton estate could have extended as far west as the later boundary with Devon. However, this is no longer a safe position even, it seems, for conjecture, and Dawn Hadley specifically countenances against it [Hadley 1996a, 12][39]. It *is*, though, inherently likely, from all the other evidence that we have relating to Carhampton's focal place in the landscape, that it *did* lie at the hub of a dependent 'estate'; but for now, both the nature and the extent of that entity remain unclear.

Conclusion

In terms of their early development, the two northernmost hundreds, Chew and Whitley, share the same kind of internal cohesiveness that allows us to say with some confidence that either in whole or in part, arrangements discernible in the early medieval and post-Conquest periods reflect far earlier territorial patterns, dominated by large antecedent entities based on either a river basin (Chew/Chewton) or a watershed (Whitley). The clear survival of these vestiges in Chew and Whitley is probably due in part to their early, *en bloc* acquisition by powerful and inherently conservative ecclesiastical overlords; whose natural tendency vigorously to protect and reinforce their dominance over at least the *outer* boundaries of their lands might also have the effect of slowing down the disintegration of antecedent *internal* relationships. But it also perhaps owes much to the tenacious quality of cohesiveness lent by the natural topography which so closely underpinned both the administrative and the economic rationales of these early territories.

In Carhampton, there are hints of a larger, antecedent unit perhaps based on Carhampton itself, but the indications are far more shadowy, and the topographical basis not as clear cut. For this reason, and in the absence of a single, overarching lordship, we get the distinct impression that internally Carhampton is likely to have been inherently far more unstable, and far more prone to disintegration if indeed any degree of *in*tegration had ever existed, than either Chew or Whitley.

This is probably also closely associated with the apparent absence of a dense framework of links between mother and daughter churches in Carhampton hundred, another area of striking contrast between it and both Chew and Whitley. It seems difficult to avoid the conclusion that the natural topography of Carhampton played a major role in these developments; since the often difficult nature of the terrain, its ruggedness, elevation and isolation, especially on and around Exmoor, must have lent a considerable degree of independence in terms of both tenure *and* of church foundation, with those mother-daughter ecclesiastical links that *did* exist, disintegrating relatively early on (below).

At the level of the minster churches themselves, Chew and Carhampton seem very likely to share a distinctive characteristic in the probable existence of *groupings* of churches. Within Whitley, and specifically in regards to Shapwick and Moorlinch, the evidence is as yet less clear, and the level of argument needed to sustain the idea somewhat more radical. Developing this line further into the realms of outright speculation, we may simply ask whether it is entirely coincidence that Chew and Carhampton, with probable church groupings, bestowed their names on their respective hundreds, while Shapwick did not; although this may say as much about the tenurial and ownership history of the lands west of Glastonbury Abbey as about the still very enigmatic and equivocal position and influence within them of Shapwick Old Church. The pre-Whitley hundredal 'naming' imperative seems to have been overwhelmingly based on

---

[38] For example, in Cornwall, Domesday Book records an apparently similar customary due (although in cash) paid to the dean of St Piran's, in Perranzabuloe parish, from various detached manors [Olson 1989, 88-89].

[39] I am grateful to Magnus Alexander for this reference.

communications; we have seen that Loxley Wood stood on the main Roman east-west road along the Polden ridge, and Ringoldsway was actually named from the road itself. Is this exactly what we should expect? The road effectively tied together, into a cohesive, integrated whole, Glastonbury Abbey's vast and ancient Polden estate, an economic unit of the first importance to the Abbey – a consideration which might easily have taken precedence over the use of the name of a single, relatively isolated church, no matter what its ancient status and dignity.

It is yet too early to be able to identify the forces to which we should attribute the particular nature of the ecclesiastical pattern in Carhampton. In Whitley, it was probably the proprietorial and manorial imperatives which were chiefly responsible for the foundation of churches, especially on Polden, driven by Glastonbury Abbey's need to create small estates on which to settle the thegns it had to provide to meet its military obligations, and by a desire to run its estates with greater economic efficiency. It seems very likely that large-scale estate re-organisation in Whitley, perhaps in the 10th century, swept away existing settlement patterns and field systems, but it is also possible that an earlier stratum of ecclesiastical organisation was lost as well, perhaps a pre-English pattern of hermitages, small field chapels and occasional higher-status churches like Shapwick Old Church, dependent on Glastonbury Abbey, and looking far more like the arrangements in Carhampton of which vestiges survived into the post-Conquest period. Recent geophysical work in the area to the east of Shapwick old church has, for example, thrown up a highly complex network of boundaries and structures which rightly or wrongly have already attracted 'monastic' attributes. Glastonbury Abbey itself was, after all, always highly conscious, and vigorous in the promulgation of, the tradition of its own 'Celtic' antiquity [Finberg 1969]; and it is possible that such lore had a basis in fact and was not entirely the work of post-Conquest myth-makers. In Carhampton before 1066, underdeveloped [Costen 1992a, 124-125] and with a far lower population density, the unity of ownership and therefore the economic imperatives which might have given rise to the same or similar developments, were entirely lacking.

Whatever the processes involved, it seems clear that those churches which did eventually become the centres of their own parishes must have been independent either from the outset, or from a stage so early in their existence that any evidence of former dependence on a superior church has been lost. The sole example of Cutcombe/Luxborough may, therefore, suggest a relatively late split.

Chapter Five

Place-Names: Language and Landscape

Introduction

It is important that a sound corpus of place-names, their provenances and probable meanings, be established to provide a reliable toponymic reference that can be used to illuminate or extend discussions of related questions. In this context, the work of Magnus Alexander, on the parishes of north Somerset, provides an ideal model, cast as it is in the form of a searchable database of names and provenances, based on painstaking study of a wide variety of sources both primary and secondary. The result is a meticulous analytical corpus consisting of numerous fieldnames and every major toponym on the modern 2½" map [I am grateful to Magnus Alexander for allowing me sight of his database in advance of its inclusion in his own doctoral dissertation].

In the case of the present study however, constraints of time and practicality have imposed certain limitations, and have dictated an approach which, quite apart from the necessity of being highly selective, is also overwhelmingly qualitative and descriptive rather than statistical and analytical. Matters are not helped by the fact that as yet, the English Place-Name Society's series of detailed county surveys has not reached Somerset. The same restrictions have meant that it is also rooted chiefly in secondary material. The basic sources are the relevant sheets of the modern 2½" map, and the search has included both settlement and topographical names. Field names, of fundamental significance in the elucidation of antecedent settlement patterns, will, because of the mass of evidence available (mainly from the tithe survey) have to be used selectively, in discussions of individual settlements. Where possible, the map evidence is supplemented by that from other, published sources, such as the Lay Subsidies of 1327 and 1334. For the meaning of major (ie usually parish) names, Ekwall 1960 and Mills 1991 are the chief authorities. Because practical considerations unfortunately precluded detailed documentary research, by far the majority of the hamlet, farm and minor names taken from the 1:25,000 map lack what would be regarded by toponymists as 'safe' (ie at least medieval) early spellings; although for some, meanings have been inferred from analogues quoted by Ekwall, or where a plausible suggestion can be offered even from just the 'modern' form of the name. This chapter presents merely a short sketch of the most prominent toponymic patterns, and it should be said that we will return to specific themes drawn and developed from this survey as and when they arise in later chapters. An example is the OE word *wyrðig*, which is mentioned briefly here, but the settlement connotations of which are held back for consideration later on. Finally, the reader should note that because of the very specific implications they hold for the nature and physical form of medieval settlement, there are two name types which will

not be found in this section, but which form the subjects of separate reviews, under more appropriate headings, elsewhere. The much-discussed element *−wick* has already been dealt with in previous chapters. The name *Ga(r)ston* appears in Chapter Eight, where, in the context of examples found in our study areas, we will briefly develop and apply ideas about its potential significance first put forward by Chris Thornton.

Chew Hundred

As we shall also see for Carhampton, it seems as though the toponymic landscape of Chew is overwhelmingly a natural one, dominated as it is by elements describing hills, valleys, woods, rivers and so on. It is accepted that there may exist a few names containing a personal element, although this would be difficult to quantify without a larger corpus of medieval spellings. Of the very small number of possible candidates in Chew for the use of a personal name to form a toponym, one of the more likely seems to be Pickwick (*Pepwyk* in 1327) in Norton Malreward; not because the first element has yet been identified, but because the name is attached to an isolated medieval farmstead which also shows evidence of Roman (and, indeed, Iron Age) activity, and which therefore seems, as we have already seen (Chapter Three), to conform to recent views regarding the coincidence of the element *-wic* with Roman sites [Williams 1982, 55; Costen 1992, 66; Gelling 1978, 67-74]. A further suggestion, that many compound names containing -wic may represent the centres of large, pre-hundredal (Romano-British?) estates, does not, though, seem correctly to answer the occurrence of the small group of such names in Chew hundred [Balkwill 1993]. While it is possible that Lescomb (1327), in Dundry, has a personal name as a first element, it seems more likely to be an adjectival prefix describing this particular cumb (a short or broad valley). And as names containing *leah*, a woodland clearing, both Chilly and Walley, both in Chew Stoke, may have personal prefixes. The name *Doddyngmed* (1327) in Chew Magna may contain the genitival connective particle *-ing-*, so that perhaps the first element is a personal name.

These few scattered examples probably represent the maximum of what Chew hundred may be able to offer in the way of personal toponyms, and from this fact alone we can draw certain inferences. Chew was palpably not a personalised landscape in the sense that settlement sites or particular landscape features had become associated with named individuals, in the way that has clearly happened in such spectacular fashion within Whitley (below). Unlike the latter for instance, all the parish centres in Chew are topographical names; there does not, at this stage, appear to have been that same systematic and regularised carving up of the landscape, and subsequent allocation of the resulting estates to named individuals, that is so characteristic of Whitley's Polden backbone, and the like of which Chew can nowhere display. The point is emphasised by the sole example (at an unlocated site in Chew Magna parish) yet found in the hundred of that most 'several' of habitative elements, *wyrðig*, used as a field-name in its simplex form and appearing as merely *le Worthe* in the late 16th century [Wood 1903, 34-35]; the absence of a personal prefix perhaps suggesting that this pre-Conquest farmstead, if such it really was, had been abandoned probably before 1066 [Costen 1992a, 80]. This is in stark contrast to the situation we find in Carhampton, with its hierarchical arrangement of toponyms headed by the parish names, based overwhelmingly on topographical elements, dominating a substratum of habitative and personal names attached to numerous scattered farmsteads and hamlets, both abandoned and still occupied [Aston 1983]. We ought then to ask whether the same kind of organisational upheaval which appears to have had such a profound effect on the toponymic landscape of Whitley, also operated in Chew. The evidence of other types of place-names must now be brought into the equation.

Personal names aside, by far the majority of the toponyms of Chew hundred fall broadly into the two chief categories of habitative and topographical. The habitative names are confined to the sub-parish level, with three notable exceptions, Chew Stoke, Norton (Malreward and Hawkfield) and Clutton. It seems clear that the latter does not sit easily with the first two, and should not be counted with them. Its first element, a topographical term referring to a rocky hill, must be describing a landscape feature particular to the immediate locality; despite the habitative second element, therefore, Clutton looks inward, to its own landscape, as the source of its toponym, an independence confirmed by other aspects of its (and Timsbury's) ambiguous relationship with the main body of the hundred (below). Chew Stoke and Norton, even though both parish centres are, by contrast, outward-looking names, taking their cue from a superior centre and with strong connotations of dependency and secondary status. Chew Stoke can only reasonably be interpreted as the *stoc* (outlying or dependent farmstead, estate or settlement) of Chew Magna, since it does not itself stand on the river Chew. If, as some authorities would suggest, we are to attribute to stoc a specifically pastoral connotation, there may, like Timsbury (below), be echoes here of former agrarian specialisation within a larger entity, perhaps connected with an early regime of initially seasonal use by communities at some distance [Fox 1996, 6-7, and 20, n14]. Likewise, it seems clear, again bearing in mind other relationships, that Norton must be Chew's north *tūn*, just as Sutton, straddling both Stowey parish and the southern part of Chew Magna, was the south *tūn*; the significant difference being that Sutton did not attain parochial status. Indeed, apart from Clutton itself, all the other *tūn* names in the hundred seem to be describing relationships to other settlements, or in terms of position in the landscape. Littleton, a name apparently applied to an area at the meeting point of the boundaries of Chew Magna, Chew Stoke and Dundry, is 'the little farmstead or estate'. Upton

is 'the higher or upper farmstead or estate', not inappropriate given its position at 200m on the southern slope of Dundry, but perhaps the allusion here is more than purely topographical, for it too may signify a relationship with some 'parent' estate. A 1327 place-name *Buttone*, probably in Norton Hawkfield, almost certainly contains *tūn*, but the first element cannot yet be identified.

The potential general significance of -*wic*, and one example (Pepwyk or Pickwick), have already been noted, but others in Chew hundred may be added. Northwick survives as a hamlet in the extreme north of Chew parish and is noted in both 1327 and 1334. At the opposite end of the parish, a group of -*wic* names is attached to surviving farms in Sutton: Wick, Sutton Wick and Wick Green. The toponymic credentials of these examples are supported by the appearance in 1327 of a Johanne de Wyk listed under Bishop Sutton. So far the only certain evidence of Roman activity at any of these places has come from Pepwyk (above), but the medieval spellings available allow us to say with some certainty that all of them must represent pre-Conquest *wics*.

Somewhat more revealing in terms of our perception of the dynamic of landscape development in Chew are the woodland names. Names in Chew hundred with connotations of woodland (major names only; no field names; spellings not yet attested from the medieval, late medieval or early modern periods asterisked; see place-name tables for details) are: Chilly, Walley, Breach, Woodford (C/Stoke); Hazel (Dundry); Beche, Wode, Grove, Rode (Chew/M); Timsbury, Ridings (Timsbury); *Hartley, *Hazeldene, Nassh (Clutton); Curl's Wood, Dowling's Wood [Chapman *et al*, 1992]; Whitewood, *Whistley (Norton Malreward/Hawkfield).

With the exception of Breach, the group of names in Chew Stoke form a distinct arc from north to south on the eastern side of the parish. While in some cases *leah* can have a meaning of 'pasture' or 'meadow' [Gelling 1984, 199], I would suggest that the presence of the name 'Woodford' within this group, attested in the early 15th century [BL Harl. 112D.54], shows that we would be correct to infer a woodland derivation. While the field shapes around these places appear generally regular and rectilinear, it seems probable that they arise from pre-Conquest clearance at the edge of the parish.

If this belt represented the last vestiges of woodland fringing an area of open-field land, it is possible that formerly irregular assart fields around the *leah* farmsteads were gradually and progressively recast into more regular form, for incorporation into the open field system, as clearance continued. It seems clear that Chew Stoke did operate open fields in the middle ages: in the early 17th century, the glebe holding remained for the most part scattered in small parcels, whose locations are described by reference to the immediately adjoining lands of other tenements; there is also a reference to an East Field [SRO D/D/Rg 28/1]. In 1086, the assessment for Chew Stoke was included, for the most part, in that for Chew Magna. Nonetheless, DB still lists four small subsidiary manors in Chew Stoke, three of them called simply Stoke, with a fourth at Chillyhill. Although ostensibly in origin a woodland name, the latter had no recorded woodland in 1086; and while at present I would favour pre-Conquest clearance as the explanation, the 1½ acres of meadow noted as this small (0.75 hides) manor's only other resource at that date, apart from a little arable, may instead suggest that in this case *leah* was applied in its late OE sense of 'pasture, meadow'. Determination of the meaning of the first element might resolve the question [Gelling 1984, 199]. One of the Stoke manors, rated at half a hide, had woodland 4x1 furlongs, another, rated at 1.75 hides, had 3x2 furlongs. These seem relatively large figures for such small holdings, and together with the *leah* names already noted, I suggest that this woodland was not elsewhere but was actually within the bounds of the Chew Stoke estate. The 1 square league of woodland (just under 583 hectares based on Rackham's calculation that a league = 1.5 miles; [Rackham 1988, 20]) assigned to Chew Magna itself in 1086 I cannot yet plausibly allocate to the few as yet unlocated woodland names associated with the manor in 1327 (above); but if, as is likely, it was by that time a peripheral resource, it is possible that at least part of it was common to its boundary with Chew Stoke. As in the case of Clutton though (below), this is such a large amount of wood compared to the size of Chew parish itself (about 2025 hectares in the mid 19th century), that much of it was probably detached, distributed among Chew's adjacent dependent manors.

Breach in Chew Stoke is palpably a 'colonising' name, as a simplex used generally of the intaking of new arable from open waste [Gelling 1984, 233-234, and *pers comm.*; and *cf* Costen 1987a, 24, for further local examples]. We should, though, note that it could be used in conjunction with another word to take on the specific meaning of a woodland assart: thus *La Wudebrech* at Ditcheat [Stokes 1996, 59]. In the case of Chew Stoke, there is no evidence to show that the name is not being used in its usual sense, and refers to what is probably post-Conquest intaking activity on a small, elevated plateau just above the 130m contour, in an isolated position in the extreme south-western corner of the parish. Breach was in existence by 1327; the field pattern around Breach Farm is one of small, highly irregular enclosures, and the earthworks of possible house-platforms have been noted in the area of Breach Hill [Kemp 1983, 67-68]. This also leads me to infer a date for Breach relatively later than the *leah* farmsteads already noted, since their lack of a regular disposition indicates that the Breach fields may never have been incorporated into any existing open-field land. Did they operate as an independent field system surrounding the farmstead?

In Dundry, Hazel was certainly in existence by 1327, and as we noted in Chapter Four, it is likely to be this place which was recorded as *Hæsele* in the forged general confirmation charter of the Bishop of Wells attributed to Edward the Confessor (S1042). Hazel lies in the south-west corner of Dundry parish, close to Littleton, also a 1327 settlement; it may represent a pre-Conquest assart within a small pocket of remaining parish-edge woodland, a later medieval woodland offshoot from Littleton, or perhaps even a farmstead involved in, and

originating from, specialist management of a particular type of woodland (perhaps as part of a larger estate), as the name might suggest [*cf* Gelling 1984, 218, *ac*, 'an oak tree']. However, it may also be that Hazel may simply take its name from a particularly prominent and noteworthy single example of that kind of tree [Gelling 1984, 218], a suggestion perhaps lent support by the apparent lack of early-attested woodland toponyms in the rest of Dundry.

Timsbury is a major settlement name deriving wholly from a woodland context. It is the 'grove where timber is obtained' [Mills 1991, 330], and direct comparison with the parish name Timberscombe in Carhampton is unavoidable; it is possible, but remains to be proven, that both names may carry wider implications about the potentially specialist economic function of their respective estates within a larger unit. The lack of other woodland names within the parish is therefore surprising, but its reality seems to be borne out by the entries for both of the Domesday manors here, for in 1086 neither contained any woodland, not even *silvae minutae*. Only Ridings can at present be given at least plausibly early credentials, as Ridens (probably OE *rodu*, 'a clearing') in 1634 [SRO D/D/Rg 54/2; Field 1993, 67; Gelling 1984, 208; Rackham 1990, 48].

In Clutton the only early-attested 'woodland' name so far is Nassh, 1327, which is 'the place at the ash tree' [*cf* Mills 1991, 238]. Since this is probably a literal reference to a solitary tree of that kind, it cannot of itself be used to indicate surviving woodland; notwithstanding a Domesday reference to woodland covering an area of half a league square (about 146 hectares) [Rackham 1988, 20], which is commensurate with its large 10-hide assessment. Since Clutton parish today is only about 632 hectares in extent, this must raise the likelihood that at least part of its DB woodland lay detached elsewhere. The names Hartley (Wood) and Hazeldene, from the 2½" map, as yet lack early provenances.

Whitley: The Names of the Hundreds

Whitley differs from both Carhampton and Chew in that its own hundred name derives not from the name of its major settlement (or more strictly, in the case of Chew, from a river name that became attached to the chief place), but from a topographical term referring to a woodland within the hundred. Whitley is also unique among this group in that it is, as we have already seen, composed of an amalgam of two smaller, *pre-existing* hundreds, both of which were themselves also named from topographical features, namely a wood and a road. This being so, it seems useful and logical briefly to review here the toponymic basis of the three 'Whitley' hundreds, before passing on to deal with their 'internal' place-names, since, as I hope to show, there as certain respects in which the two levels of naming are mutually dependent and are best understood when considered together.

[I am indebted to Charlie Hollinrake for his advice relating to the various meanings usually proposed for the name Ringoldswey]. The toponymy of Whitley and its two antecessors was treated in detail by Anderson [1939, 51-

52], and although there is little in his account that can be usefully amended or added to, nonetheless some general observations may prove helpful, and in the case of Ringoldswey at least, a new interpretation offered here casts some light on the appearance of the late Anglo-Saxon landscape in this area. Loxley and Ringoldswey, and their successor, Whitley, present an interesting contrast to Chew hundred in a number of respects. We have already seen that Chew conforms closely to the model of an ancient 'river estate'; it is at a communications nodal point, geographically it lies centrally within its hundred, its church is certainly an important minster, and its simplex pre-English place-name is that of a river; although it is worth remembering that even given all this, the historically-recorded moot site was not at Chew itself, but on a small knoll well outside the village to the south. In the three Glastonbury hundreds however, there is no obvious place that compares with Chew Magna itself in terms of 'central place' attributes. The closest thing to Chew in Whitley is probably Shapwick, or Street, both of which satisfy some, but not all of the same seminal criteria that can be applied to Chew (below). But it is surely significant that when it came to naming the hundreds, in all three cases nowhere that emerges in the medieval period as a settlement site with its own estate attached, was considered important enough, in either the 10th century or the late 12th, for its toponym to be transferred to an entire hundred. Why we do not see a hundred of Shapwick in the west, and perhaps a hundred of Walton or Street in the east, is at present problematic. What we have are two woodland names (Loxley and Whitley), and a road name. Leaving aside Whitley for the time being, it seems that Loxley and Ringoldswey fall clearly into that category of hundreds recently characterised by Audrey Meaney as being "named from places which never became settlements, and which therefore must surely have been the original assembly sites" [Meaney 1995, 35]. Part of Meaney's argument turns upon the likelihood that some hundred moots originated as pagan sanctuaries. In Somerset, while there are certainly toponymic indications of tenacious Anglo-Saxon paganism [Costen 1992a, 100-101], none of the county's hundred names are considered to contain overtly 'pagan' elements [cf Anderson 1939, ix-xvii]. However, Meaney goes on to suggest a tripartite division of toponyms as they apply to hundred meeting sites, and her remarks are worth noting in relation to the three names under scrutiny here: "I regard as primary those where people would have encountered each other in the course of their journeys, usually at some kind of bottleneck.....and which (later) became formalized as assembly sites.....There are good practical reasons for the choice of these sites as Hundred meeting-places, and there is no need to postulate an earlier sanctuary as the reason for it.....Secondary meeting places I consider to be those named after natural landmarks.....Tertiary meeting-place names are where the landmarks are man made, deliberately to mark the site or to play a part in the assembly" [Meaney 1995, 35]. The road-name Ringoldswey would by this definition presumably be a primary meeting place, and Loxley, a woodland name, would be secondary. How helpful this is for our understanding of these names is,

though, open to question, since on closer examination, each of them shows attributes which might fit comfortably in either the primary or secondary role. It seems rather more than coincidence that both names are related closely to important routeways, Ringoldswey directly, and Loxley in so far as the wood from which the hundred takes its name straddles the Polden ridge Roman road. However, conversely, the relationship of both with woodland is also intimate. Loxley contains a first-element personal name (probably *Locc*), while the second element is straightforwardly *leah* [Anderson 1939, 52]. The meaning is therefore 'Locc's wood' or 'Locc's woodland clearing' [Costen 1994, 70]. Ringwoldswey is more problematic, but it is the central element which is of most interest here. The early spellings cited by Anderson [1939, 51-52], *weald* and *wolde*, seem clearly to show a derivation from *wald*, a word originally with a general sense of 'woodland on higher ground' [Gelling 1984, 222-227; and *cf* Everitt 1986, 25-31 and 52-57]. It seems strange then, that Anderson does not draw the obvious conclusion that the name contains a reference to a tract of *wald* exactly where we might expect it (below). Dr Gelling [*pers comm*] likes "the idea of a 'wold' on the eastern part of the Polden Hills". She also points out that as well as Ringoldswey itself, the Butleigh charter S270a, whose bounds are probably 10th century in date [Costen 1992, 43], mentions another weald name, *woldespath* [GC II, 1952, 426]. As for the first element of Ringoldswey, it is "OE hring, 'circle', perhaps a reference to Windmill Hill" [Gelling, *pers comm*]. The latter is a prominent, steep-sided eminence on the northern stretch of Butleigh's western boundary with Compton Dundon, with extensive prospects on every hand and now the site of the Hood Monument [Bush 1994, 54]. Topographically, Windmill Hill might present an ideal location for folk moots. Any wood crowning the summit of this hill would by definition have been circular, and a meaning "the road next to the circular wood" is certainly possible. This was, indeed, the meaning favoured by Grundy as long ago as 1935 [Grundy 1935, 11] in his discussion of the occurrences of this name elsewhere in the bounds of two other (contiguous) Somerset estates; namely in two Winchester charters for the Taunton area, S310 and 311 [Grundy 1935, 7-28], and in the bounds of the three extant Pitminster charters, S440, 475 and 1006 [Grundy 1935, 30-36, esp at 33, boundary point 17]. In the case of S440 for example, an almost exactly cognate term, *wealdenes weg*, was applied in the mid 10th century to "'the forest road', which ran into Neroche" [Costen 1992a, 96]. Since, though, the most usual sense of *wald* is of woodland of some size (below), its application just to a relatively small area of wood on top of a hill does not seem satisfactory. We can perhaps suggest instead that the element *hring* is a reference to the semi-circular shape of the entire *wald* in this area, clinging to the abrupt, curving, south-westerly facing scarp, and the dip slope behind it, which is such a major feature of the natural landscape between Butleigh and Compton Dundon; a suggestion that takes nothing away from the likelihood that, if we are looking for the site of the Ringoldswey hundred moot itself, we need probably look no further than

Windmill Hill. However we are to interpret the detail of the hundredal toponomy, the impression of a heavily-wooded landscape in this part of Whitley which it, and indeed other kinds of evidence, convey, is quite clear; and as a direct consequence of this conclusion we are almost certainly correct to dismiss as misleading Welldon-Finn's map of Domesday woodland, insofar as it records hardly any woodland at all precisely where, I suggest, the pre-Conquest *wald* lay. This, though, we can attribute directly to the almost intractable difficulties presented by the obscurity of DB woodland statistics, a point emphatically stated by Welldon-Finn himself [Welldon-Finn 1967, 173-179].

The question of probable land-use in the pre-Conquest period we will review more closely later on, and of course woodland will be an important element in this. Because of its specific remit to focus chiefly on the wetlands, very little of the mass of environmental data arising from the Somerset Levels Project casts light on either the post-Roman period or on Polden itself. We have only a general statement that pollen evidence from the Brue Valley indicates "large increases in herb pollen.....for the Polden slopes and the Burtle and other islands. The period, from about 300 BC to at least [my italics] AD 400, was one of ever-wider forest clearance, the establishment of pasture and the cultivation of cereal" [Coles 1989, 30; see also Dark 1999]. However, I have also already suggested (above) that at least parts of the Polden ridge may have remained wooded in the Roman period. And in the absence of detailed palynological studies targeted specifically on the Polden ridge, it is impossible to know how much of what existed by, say, the late Anglo-Saxon period, was attributable to post-Roman regeneration, and how much had survived from the Roman period or before. In this case, then, toponymy may be more promising than environmental archaeology. Dr Gelling observes that "the use of *wald* for large stretches of ancient woodland is likely to have been relatively early, and the term would not be sufficiently fasionable after *c.* AD 750 to acquire the developed senses which characterise *leah*" [Gelling 1984, 225]; and this suggested chronology of *wald*, and its occurrence in this part of Whitley, is therefore an indication of extensive woodland cover here, at the latest, by the end of the 8th century, whatever its origin may have been [*cf* Cox 1976, 51].

Whitley: Toponymy Inside the Hundred

We will look again at individual place-names throughout the various discussions to follow as and when they arise, and an examination of the hundred's field names I have thought best to incorporate in the final chapter of the study (Chapter Eight), on settlement patterns and morphology, to which it is closely related and where it forms an important element of the overall discussion. For immediate purposes though, it will be useful to consider in very broad terms the general toponymic background against which patterns of settlement and estates developed in Whitley hundred. We have already seen that one of the most important names from Whitley, that of the wood of Loxley from which one

of the old hundred names was taken, contains a personal name. Despite this, like Chew hundred, Whitley does not, for the most part, present a highly *personalised* toponymic landscape (in its major names at least), but this fact serves merely to heighten the significance of that tight-knit group of major north Polden toponyms based on personal names which stretches westwards from Shapwick, and the small but significant set of *–cott* names around Shapwick, to both of which points we will return. Indeed, even at the level of minor names, and particularly of field names, the evidence from Shapwick, the only place in the hundred for which a systematic survey is available, suggests that personal names have only a minor presence. Habitative elements, as we shall see, there are aplenty, but they do not seem in most cases to have become associated with the names of particular owners in the pre-Conquest period. Of the 123 Shapwick field names from both medieval and more recent sources which are analysed in Costen 1993, only three, Abchester, Catterwood and Enworthy, show any sign of containing Anglo-Saxon personal names, and one of these (Catterwood) is not even linked with a habitative term. Othery contains a late example of a *wyrðig* field-name which *may* be compounded with a personal name, but this is by no means certain [Costen 1992b, 76], and the point is made by the appearance, in the only other known examples in Whitley, of the non-personal compound *worthyhyll* in Street [Costen 1992b, 77], and of *wyrðig* field-names in Butleigh in their simplex form, without any personal qualifier. Field-name *wyrðigan* in Somerset tend to be concentrated in the lower-lying areas east of the Parrett, and the implication, it has been suggested, is that large-scale landscape re-organisation of some description in these parts made these isolated farmsteads redundant before they had a chance to become associated with the names of any specific owners [Costen 1992b].

Elsewhere, names of parish centres, sub-parochial settlements and farmsteads/hamlets, again rather like those of Chew, are based on personal, topographical or 'descriptive' elements, either on their own or in combination with 'settlement' epithets, specifically *tūn* and *cot*. The latter form a particularly interesting group around Shapwick: Catcott, a personal name, and Ashcott, both as parish names, and Buscott, with almost certainly another personal first element, as a farmstead (below). Loxley aside, of the major *settlement* names in Whitley, only Butleigh and Pedwell (the latter in Ashcott) combine personal names with topographical elements. The distribution of elements between north and south Polden may be suggestive. Stawell's 'stony stream' fits in well with the rest of the southern Polden group, such as Moorlinch and Sutton, which tend towards non-personal, descriptive/topographical terms. Here, only Greinton and Pedwell contain personal names [Ekwall 1960, 204], and this slight bias may have implications for our understanding of the nature of the relationship between the settlements on Polden's northern and southern slopes, an idea which I have already outlined in Chapter Two and which I will develop further later on.

Outside the main Polden group, *tūn* is found combined with 'descriptive' words, in Walton and

Littleton (in Compton Dundon), all fairly self-explanatory, although Ekwall considers that this Walton probably does not contain OE *W(e)ala*, 'Britons or Welsh', but rather *W(e)ald*, 'a large wood' [Ekwall 1960, 494-495][1]. Bearing in mind what I have already said about the origins of the hundred name Ringoldsway, and what follows later in the discussion of the evidence of the Butleigh Anglo-Saxon charter, the balance of probability does seem to lie with Ekwall; the existence of a surviving enclave of indigenous Britons here is not out of the question, but is certainly almost impossible to prove. It is easy, by contrast, to imagine the area around Walton as the westward extension of a large tract of woodland running east-west along the top of the south Polden scarp, and for which the evidence further east, around Butleigh, is pretty secure. Indeed, a sound context for this suggestion is provided by the major toponym Leigh, which was the original name for Street [McGarvie 1987, 29; *cf* Gelling 1984, 203; Abrams 1996, 153-154]: it was was *Lega* in 1086, and in landscape terms it provides a continuous woodland link between Butleigh and Walton, lying as it does between those two estates.

In Compton, *tūn* is combined with a topographical element. Ekwall's explanation of Dundon, 'the valley by the hill' [Ekwall 1960, 153], is acceptable only to a degree, since it seems impossible to believe that we should not take the first element, which seems to be OE *dūn*, as a specific reference to the massive Iron Age hillfort which dominates the village to its east. However, it should also be said that this suggestion would be vigorously denied by Dr Gelling [1984, 140-141]. Dr Gelling's discussion includes a note on a small corpus of examples where *dūn* appears as a *first* element [1984, 149]. In the case of Dundon, however, which must otherwise surely have been a candidate for a name in OE *byrig*, it is reasonable to consider James's observation, based on a recent review of the British toponymic evidence from south-west Wales, that "in the context of hillforts........the *din* element is almost universally placed first or qualified by an adjective" [James 1998, 106].

As we shall see later, the west *tūn* on Sowy island should perhaps not be included in this group, since its function was probably different, arising not from the outset as the name attached to an individual estate, but rather being applied subsequently to distinguish between the fragmented parts, the others being Middlezoy and Othery, of a former, more ancient unit. Early spellings of the simplex name Ham show clearly that it is from OE *hamme* [Ekwall 1960, 214]. The many possible uses of this word are discussed at length by Dr Gelling [1984, 41-50], but the basic thrust of the argument is that its connotations are overwhelmingly topographical. Looking at Ham's topographical setting it is difficult to see how a sense of 'land in a river-bend/river-meadow' could be applied to it, and Dr Gelling's own favoured explanation is 'promontory jutting out into marshland' [1984, 43]. The settlement of High Ham itself is actually a kilometre from the nearest marsh edge, to the north, but this need not be an objection since obviously the pre-Conquest name would have been applied to the whole estate: such is clear from Ham's 10th century charter (below). However, bearing in mind what I will say later about Ham's heavily-wooded pre-Conquest landscape, we might also note Dr Gelling's observation that "study of major place-names containing *hamm* suggests that there was a sense-development from meanings associated with water and marsh to meanings appropriate to enclosures in wooded country or moorland" [Gelling 1984, 42]. An alternative model might, therefore, be that an antecedent *hamm*, enclosed from woodland on or near the site of the present village of High Ham, formed a focus for the progressive extension of settlement, and of cultivation through assarting, to the extent that the name came eventually to be applied to the whole estate. This is perhaps less likely though, firstly since we might expect the topographical, 'promontory' sense to be applied to such a major feature as the Ham plateau, and secondly because, as with Butleigh, it is probable that an origin in an isolated, ring-fenced woodland farmstead would be indicated by the presence of a *personal* name as a first element.

In standing back and attempting to gain a wider perspective on Whitley's toponyms, it seems as though the area is distinguished by the very absence of significant patterns. There are no certain examples of *surviving* British names, and although the now-lost *Lantokay* in Street, 'the church of St Cai', is attested in one of the earliest Glastonbury charters [Abrams 1996, 153-154], this is an exception, recorded probably because of its claim to antiquity, and the linguistic landscape of the hundred is overwhelmingly Old English. Consequently, unlike Chew hundred, there is no 'neat' coincidence between hundredal centre and pre-English place-name based on a simplex river name. Certainly the name of the Brue, the only likely candidate for this purpose [Ekwall 1960, 70] did not become transferred to the estate(s) to its south. Indeed, in Street, Whitley even contains one almost certain example of a *post-Conquest* coining, the chronology of which can be pinned down to quite close limits in the late 12th/early 13th century [McGarvie 1987, 36-37].

Patterns, however, there are, and as we have already seen, they enable us, for example, to discern significant pre-Conquest woodland in the landscapes of Butleigh and Ham (and probably Walton as well). There is also the question of the one surviving name denoting, apparently, an economic specialism, namely Shapwick itself. However circumstantial, Shapwick's survival as a toponym, probably because it was always kept tightly in hand by Glastonbury abbey, is an important indication that it may once have been part of a wider estate, at least some of whose members carried out specific economic roles and which were welded into a coherent, mutually dependent and integrated whole [*cf* Faith 1997, 11-14; Hooke 1998, 52; Dyer *et al* 1997, 108-110]. Shapwick allows us to speculate that other specialist names may very well have been lost through their replacement with personal, 'manorial'-type forms. The group of *cot* names surrounding Shapwick may represent the last stage in this process, indicating the existence, for a time at least, of a small northern 'rump' estate consisting of Catcott, Ashcott (with Buscott) and Shapwick. If, then, we are to look for

---

[1]There is a similar difficulty relating to the interpretation of a 'Walton' place-name near Aylesbury, Bucks. Baines 1993, n46, 29.

potential successors to our putative specialist toponyms in this area, we need look no further than the north Polden ridge west of Shapwick. Uniquely in Whitley, we are presented here with what appears to be a coherent grouping of three heavily-personalised *major* place-names of virtually identical form. Each of these settlements, Edington, Cossington and Woolavington, consists of a personal name combined with the affix *–ingtūn*. Identifying two other similar groupings, around Frome and Ilminster, Michael Costen argues that these are "some of the earliest portions detached from the great multiple estates". Such distinctive toponymy in the midst of such variety, together with, as we have seen, the highly regular shapes of both parishes and settlements, here and elsewhere in the county, leads him to conclude that "they represent estates made from new, complete with new villages, founded in order to supply a dependent thegn with a benefice which would support him, in return for his service to his lord, the owner of the land", at some point, he thinks, between the mid 10th century and the mid 11th [Costen 1992a, 115, 119 and 121]. This reasoning informs our ideas about why and to some extent how the process operated, but it is also important to consider, at least in a general way, how we can add to it a *spatial* element as well. Later on, I will review various strands of evidence, and will then make an attempt to synthesise and reconcile their sometimes conflicting testimonies in order to suggest why north Polden in particular seems to have provided such a strong focus for these or similar developments.

Carhampton Hundred

We have already seen how some of Carhampton's habitative toponyms might provide clues to both the nature and at least the relative chronology of ecclesiastical provision within the hundred. A brief review of the place-names of Carhampton's parish centres reveals interesting contrasts with those of Whitley. The Glastonbury hundred, although having what is probably best described as a 'mixed' toponymy, is dominated by the 'settlement' epithet *-tun*, some in combination with an OE personal name, and with other settlement elements (*wick*, *-cott*) making up part of the remainder. There are, as we have seen, names containing topographical words, but only the Zoys show a vestigial pre-English influence, from a river name [Ekwall, 1928, 375-376]. In Carhampton the situation is different to the extent that by far the greater part of the parish names there are composed of 'topographical' and/or 'descriptive' elements. There are very few 'settlement' words, only two *-tun* names (Carhampton itself, and Wootton), and none in *-ington*, an ending which in Whitley, as has been suggested, denotes a late Anglo-Saxon 'manorial' origin connected with a named holder. I have already argued that the two *-ington* names that do exist, Bossington and Tivington, arrived too late on the scene to become parish centres. British elements are more to the fore in Carhampton, but not perhaps as much as might have been expected. Exford and Oare both contain pre-English river names; Dunster seems to have OE *torr*, originally a British loan-word into

English; and the first element of Minehead is probably Welsh *mynydd*, 'a mountain, hill' [Gelling 1984, p172]. Timberscombe contains a specialist reference to timber production and can be directly compared to Timsbury in Chew. Selworthy is the only parish-level *wyrðig* in the entire hundred, and is not even combined with a personal name, but with a topographical word. Conversely, Carhampton supports a relatively large corpus of *wyrðig* names attached to surviving hamlets and farmsteads at the *sub*-parochial level. And it is notable that the hundred's few toponyms which include OE personal names (Luccombe, Luxborough and Cutcombe) are also combined with topographical, rather than 'settlement' nouns. Even Stoke Pero, with OE *stoc*, 'dependent farmstead, secondary settlement', occurred originally as a simplex word, to which a 13th century 'manorial' epithet became attached.

Conclusion

The one, tenuous thread which links all three hundreds together is the appearance in each of a single 'specialist' toponym. In Whitley it is Shapwick, and the first elements of Timsbury in Chew, and Timberscombe in Carhampton, are cognate, and refer to wood production for timber.

In Chew, topographical words provide not only by far the majority of the parish names; they can also be subdivided into two further broad categories: hills and woodland. The numerous references to hills and eminences is hardly surprising bearing in mind the highly broken nature of the hundred's natural landscape. What is perhaps less expected is the notable lack of a British influence: as yet we can only point with certainty to the river name Chew itself, which seems to suggest that the advent of the English language here heralded an especially thoroughgoing displacement of existing British toponyms. The reasons for this are not yet clear, but from it we might at least infer an intensity of control (not necessarily the same as occupation) of the landscape by the English that permeated every level of the toponymic hierarchy, and which touched even those major features of the natural landscape, probably formerly bearing British names, which were frequently immune from renaming.

By the time of Domesday Book, the landscape of Carhampton was less 'personalised' than that of either Whitley or Chew; there was little tradition of ownership of specific places by individuals to the extent that the name of a particular person became associated with a particular estate. And it may be possible to demonstrate that those few examples which do occur are late (ie late Saxon) in origin. This must mean that before 1066, 'manorialisation' in Carhampton had made little headway. The overwhelmingly topographical nature of the Carhampton parish names hints at an altogether earlier stratum of landscape organisation than is discerned in Whitley in 1086. The probability that, within a given area, such names will represent the primary phase of the English settlement, has been stressed by Margaret Gelling [1984, 1-9], and it may be significant that, with the sole exception of Selworthy, none of the other known *wyrðig* names became a parish centre; they occur instead at a far lower level of the settlement hierarchy, a point to which we will return, and develop, in Chapter Eight. The clear implication however is that by, say, the 10th century, the Carhampton landscape was being colonised and exploited from settlement which was too small-scale, scattered and insignificant to make much of an impact on the development of the toponymy, in some areas a still relatively empty terrain where the larger units, the 'proto-parishes', took their names instead from natural features. This may, indeed, simply have been a continuation of a pre-English framework of which names like Minehead and Oare are merely the survivors, with originally pre-English names for major landscape features being replaced by their nearest English equivalents after a period of parallel use. The example of Creechbarrow Hill near Taunton actually demonstrates this process in operation [Costen 1992, 60-61].

The question then arises of why even these later English names were able to survive at all levels of the settlement hierarchy, attached to both parish centres, and pre-Conquest farmsteads alike. Following Michael Costen, I have already suggested that in Whitley, for a variety of reasons, there was, probably from the 10th century, a major hiatus and dislocation in the way that the landscape was organised and settled (above). Many villages appeared for the first time, some with highly regular plans, associated with series of small estates of equal size and, indeed, similar, regular rectilinear shape, an arrangement best seen along the north Polden slope. Part and parcel of this process was the annihilation of many minor settlement names as they were subsumed beneath the new open fields laid out around the villages. By contrast, the situation in Carhampton is one of irregularity; there are no series of parishes of similar size and regular shape, giving almost the impression that the landscape has been partitioned on the drawing board [Gerrard 1987, 28-33, and Appendix 2.2]. Minor settlement names survive, and even the names of parish centres are noticeably topographical and 'apersonal' compared to those of Whitley. Field systems remained, generally, irregular both in operation and layout, with arrangements conforming most closely to the classic 'Midland' open-field model confined to limited areas of the coastal strip [Aston 1988a, 91-93; and see further below]. In short, Carhampton does not appear to have been affected to the same extent, if at all, by those forces of change which so profoundly affected its eastern neighbour in the late pre-Conquest period; and an attempt to determine the origins of these differences will form a central theme of subsequent chapters.

Chapter Six

Boundaries, Charters and Communications

Introduction

For these themes more than perhaps for any of the others we have so far examined in the earlier chapters, it is the hundred of Whitley which overwhelmingly takes centre stage, with the other two very much in supporting roles. There are good reasons for this. It is really only for Whitley that a sound foundation of previous work, in certain areas, allows some exploration beyond mere description, although the physical compactness and clear territorial unity of Chew hundred do provide reasonable scope for an attempt at explanation in that area as well. In addition, of our three hundreds, it is *only* the landscape of Whitley which can be viewed from the perspective of a small corpus of Anglo-Saxon charters with bounds, and this additional topographical perspective, although by definition partial and imperfect, we should exploit as far as the remit of the study allows. On Polden, Whitley also contains the most striking example here of parochial boundaries being systematically 'laid off' from a major routeway, and again, it seemed that appropriate weight should be given to an examination of this circumstance (Figures 8 and 16). Carhampton does not appear here, but the reader is referred back to the section under that hundred in Chapter Three headed 'Parishes and Early Territories'. This contains material which is very relevant here but which after careful consideration seemed to fit best into the context of territorial and ecclesiastical relationships. And from that discussion, I hope I have been able at least to suggest that Carhampton emerges as an area of considerable potential for future, more systematic examination of the nature of its hundredal and parochial boundaries.

Chew Hundred

We have already noted the topographical coherence and unity of the original Chew 'proto-hundred'. This impression is reinforced by the disposition of the Roman road pattern within the hundred, and particularly with regard to its relationship with parish boundaries. The known and conjectural Roman roads in the area are shown on Figure 3, and it is surely significant that within the main body of the hundred, not one of these roads is followed by a parish boundary. Two very short stretches of road tracing parts of the boundaries between Norton Malreward, Dundry and Chew, may or may not be Roman or earlier in origin. This situation is in contrast to that outside the hundred, where to the south, the Stratford Lane Road, leaving the hundred by crossing the boundary between Chew and West Harptree, almost immediately becomes the parish boundary between the latter and Compton Martin. Gerrard's general analysis of Roman roads and parish

boundaries in Somerset has shown that boundaries are likely to follow roads only where the road is a major routeway, which may then form the basis of a reorganisation of adjacent estates in the Roman period or later, and that many boundaries are probably pre-Roman in origin [Gerrard 1987, 35-38]. This work may cast light on the situation in Chew, for the Roman road pattern in the area suggests just such a reorganisation and splitting of estates immediately outside the 'core' hundred, while inside it, the likely presence of long stretches of road apparently did little to compromise its territorial integrity. Since this appears particularly true to the south of the hundred, it would also tend to support our earlier suggestion that Chew was probably once a single unit with its southern neighbour, Chewton.

There is certainly some evidence that at least stretches of the hundred's external boundary are of some antiquity, most notably in the signal failure of any part of Norton Malreward's boundary to follow the course of the western Wansdyke; a fact also noted from very close by along the course of the monument, around Keynsham [Whittock 1987, 9]. While we must concede that the dating of Wansdyke remains problematic, and it is unlikely to be a single-phase monument [Rahtz 1987, 77; Yorke 1995, 26-27; Erskine and Young 1994/95, 68; Gardner 1998], nonetheless, Gerrard's brief review of the available evidence leads him to conclude that those parish boundaries which ignore West Wansdyke are at least Roman in origin [Gerrard 1987, 38-40].

As to parish boundaries within the hundred, I do not suggest that they are necessarily prehistoric in origin, although they may be, at least in part; since some 'frontiers of interest' may have been recognised long before they became fossilised as parish boundaries [Gerrard 1987, 24-28]. However, the general impression in Chew is that cohesion remained strong, and that internal boundary formalisation was generally probably late (ie late Anglo-Saxon) in date and ignored Roman roads which may have fallen largely into disuse. There are reasons for thinking this, and in this respect it may be possible to discern a very basic relative chronology, notwithstanding Gerrard's concerns about the difficulties of assigning *absolute* dates to bounds of any category [Gerrard 1987, 33-34]. The boundary between Chew Magna and Chew Stoke, in particular, follows for the most part a clear topographical route, namely a minor stream and the course of the River Chew itself (Figure 9). This, and the fact that the place-name Stoke defines a clear, and probably intimate (although subordinate) relationship with the capital estate, might suggest that this boundary came early in the sequence. Certain stretches between Chew and Norton seem to take a clearly rectilinear course, suggesting that it was at least partially mirroring the disposition of strips or furlongs in an open-field system. This might incline us to look to a formalisation date at any point between the later 9th and the 11th century [Fox 1981; Lewis *et al* 1997, 175-177]. The intimacy of Stowey's territorial relationship with Chew is reflected in the course of its bounds, the complexity of which resulted in large blocks, and some smaller fragments of detachments of Chew parish becoming embedded within Stowey, a development related closely to the local landholding pattern [Chapman *et al*, 1992]. Again, though, a general angularity in the shape of the northern stretch of bounds (the southern stretch follows the course of a minor stream) suggests formalisation after, or perhaps contemporary with, the emergence of strip-based open-field agriculture.

Most intriguing is the highly tortuous boundary between Chew and Dundry. Dundry was, I think, probably the last parochial fragment to be detached from the old Chew 'proto-hundred', on the basis that, unlike the other parishes (Stowey, Norton and Stoke), Chew retained direct ecclesiastical control of Dundry, which always remained a dependent chapelry. It is possible that this may have some bearing on the course of the boundary between the two. It trends roughly north-east/south-west, along the southern flank of Dundry Hill, and in view of the very steep slopes here it seems unlikely that its convolutions are the result of the intervening headlands, furlongs and strips of an open field system. Apart from anything else, the boundary contains few of the regular, right-angled turns that one might otherwise expect. Rather, it takes an incredibly twisting, almost random line, with protruding 'bulges' taking portions of either parish deep into the territory of the other. A shape such as this is far more characteristic of late 'colonisation', from opposite directions, of an area of woodland or waste which intervenes between the land of two settlements, the boundary between which had not yet been clearly defined [Winchester 1990, 24-26]. The field pattern in this area is highly suggestive in this respect: on the very steepest slopes, in the southwestern part of Dundry parish, the 1st edn. 6" OS map reveals a patchwork of small, highly irregular enclosures strongly redolent of woodland assart [Taylor 1975, 95-99], and this is a pattern continued eastwards and over the parish boundary into Chew, for example in the area around North Wick (Figure 23). It is very likely that Bitham's Wood [NCC 1988, Map 7], abutting the boundary on the Dundry side and containing internal woodbanks and pre-1600 woodland, is merely a remnant of a once much more extensive swathe of woodland, cleared early (perhaps by the Roman period) on the gentler gradients, but surviving longest on the more difficult, steeper slopes[1]. Indeed, it is possible that this area was itself formerly a part of the much larger tract of woodland, a southern extension of Kingswood Forest later known misleadingly as Filwood, which in 1086 seems to have lain north of Mendip, immediately south of Bristol [Iles 1987, 117; Rackham 1988, 27; Bond 1994, 117; Welldon Finn and Wheatley 1967, 176 and 178-179].

In any event, it seems clear from this that before its formal demarcation, which would have involved the definition of a boundary, Dundry already had an existence in some form or another, probably as a recognised agrarian unit with an associated settlement and perhaps (above) with Roman antecedents, but within and dependent upon the main Chew estate. We can suggest that Dundry perhaps originated as a seasonal settlement, whose place-name clearly reflects the wearysome climb up the "steep ascent" of the hill [Ekwall 1960, 153] to its ridge-top position; and was later made permanent, as a grazing and stock-rearing 'outstation' for the more systematic exploitation of the upland pastures around it by the sheep flocks and cattle herds of the parent estate [*cf* Campbell 1990, 74; and see further, Chapter Seven]. It may well be that Dundry's genesis is closely related to an increase in the area of land under cultivation on the parent estate, and the need to find additional sources of grazing somewhere at a distance to which stock could be removed during the growing season to prevent damage to crops by straying animals [Fox 1996, 3-4].

Whitley Hundred

1. Boundaries

Various strands of evidence, apart from the ecclesiastical, point strongly towards Shapwick-Ashcott formerly being a single unit, which did not split until a relatively late (ie 11th–12th century?) date. It is notable that Shapwick's western boundary with Catcott, and all the boundaries west of that as far as the eastern boundary of Cossington, are highly regular, running as they do in almost straight lines north-south [*cf* Abrams 1996, 207-208; Figure 16, and below]. This might be expected on the featureless, low-lying moors to the north, which land forms the greater part of the parishes of Chilton, Edington and Catcott, and virtually half the area of Cossington and Shapwick respectively. On the higher ground further south, however, towards the Polden ridge itself, one might have expected to see rather more irregularity, with occasional right-angled turns around the edges of furlongs, if the boundaries had been laid out at a time when open fields were already in existence. This suggests that these boundaries either pre-date any open fields which existed, or that administrative and accounting criteria, requiring the creation of a series of regularly-shaped units of roughly equal size, took precedence and existing field arrangements were recast to constrain them within predetermined boundaries. Alternatively, and probably more likely, this may have been done actually at the time that open fields were first laid out. Dead-straight Landshire Lane (OE *landscearu*, 'a boundary', probably a reference to a man-made, physical marker such as a hedge, bank or ditch; *ex inf* Dr R W Dunning) [Field 1993, 144], marking part of the boundary between Cossington and Chilton, may hint at the latter, and open fields divided into strips certainly existed in all these parishes: for example, Chilton had west and south common fields; Catcott had three common fields by the early 17th

---

[1] John Knight advises me (*pers comm.*) that Bithams contains "approximately 20 Ancient Woodland Indicator Species". I am very grateful to him for allowing me sight of his own botanical and earthwork survey of Bithams in advance of its inclusion in his own doctoral thesis.

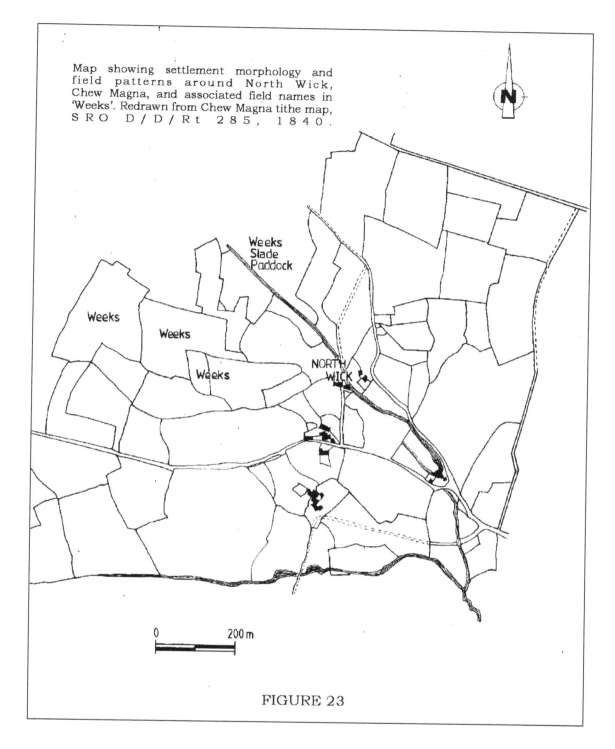

Map showing settlement morphology and field patterns around North Wick, Chew Magna, and associated field names in 'Weeks'. Redrawn from Chew Magna tithe map, SRO D/D/Rt 285, 1840.

Weeks Slade Paddock

Weeks

Weeks

Weeks

NORTH WICK

0   200 m

FIGURE 23

century; and Edington had east and west fields [VCH, Whitley Hundred, forthcoming; and see further below, Chapter Seven].

We have already noted, in Chapter Four, the nature of Woolavington's eastern boundary, with Cossington, and some possible reasons behind the very distinctive course which it follows. In the southern, highest part of Woolavington's western boundary, with Puriton, a previously unrecorded Bronze Age barrow, discovered by the writer in the course of fieldwork, has been subjected to

both geophysical and earthwork survey for this study (Appendix 1; Figure 24]. It has clearly been used as a marker. The point is made by the existence of another mound on the Shapwick/Ashcott boundary, which although listed in the SMR as post-medieval [SMR 10743], is probably in fact a barrow [Aston 1993a, 12-13; Ashbee 1998]. Like the Woolavington/Puriton example, its significance is that of a marker on a straight boundary carved through relatively featureless terrain, a situation which may be contrasted with the much more irregular

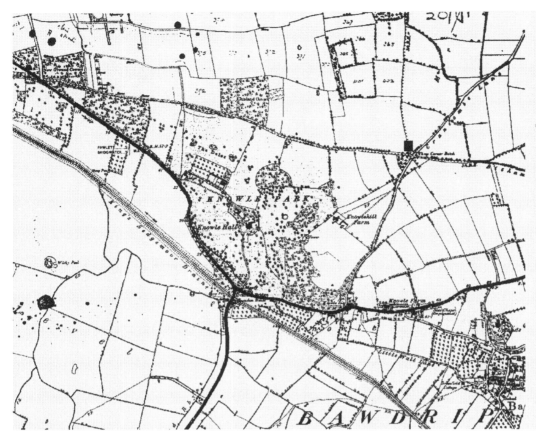

FIGURE 24

Extract from OS first edition 6" map (1885), showing location (marked by a black rectangle) of the newly- discovered Bronze Age barrow lying on the parish boundary between Puriton (west) and Woolavington (east). The Bawdrip boundary lies immediately to the south, and the barrow is therefore sited very close to the meeting point of no fewer than three parishes.

Romano-British or (and therefore probably later) boundary between Shapwick and Ashcott (below).

We have already seen that the Polden pipeline campaign, which looked at sections running east-west across this series of parishes, revealed that the boundaries between them were very minor features, archaeologically barely discernible [Hollinrakes 1994a]. The possible significance of this has yet to be fully assessed, but might suggest that these bounds originated as internal divisions of a pre-existing unit, and whose function, to provide clearly recognisable, agreed demarcations in featureless terrain, did not necessarily require them to be very substantial. An upstanding boundary such as a hedgeline would answer the purpose very well, and at Shapwick, the only location in Whitley where hedgerows have been examined botanically in detail, Hill *et al* have observed that "the hedges with the more positive scores [ie greater number of ancient woodland indicator species] were to be found in more distant parts of the parish....." [1994, 121], that is, on or close to the parish bounds.

By contrast, Shapwick's eastern boundary with Ashcott appears to follow just that kind of zig-zag line, with right-angled bends, that might suggest it was laid out through the furlongs and strips of an already fully-operational open-field system from which the boundary had to take its cue, and which indeed, in some areas elsewhere, are known to be underlain and influenced by Iron Age field arrangements [Hooke 1998, 124-126]. This raises the possibility that before the putative Shapwick-

Ashcott unit split, it consisted of a single field system. Further evidence points to a degree of 'commonality' along the Shapwick-Ashcott boundary. Abbot Bere's terrier of 1515 provides clear indications that some tenants, in both manors, also held land in both, and that much of this lay along the parish boundary, presumably to produce more conveniently-worked, compact blocks of land. Most significant, however, is the fact that some of the furlongs where this trans-manorial landholding was occurring, in Shapwick's East Field and Ashcott's North Field, had identical names, a feature explicable only in terms of the division of pre-existing open-field furlongs. Elsewhere in Shapwick lay small detached parcels belonging to Ashcott, Greinton and Moorlinch, held by the tenants of those manors who may also have been tenants of Shapwick [Corcos 1982, 27-28]. Part of this may be explained merely by the pattern of medieval landholding, so that small areas held by tenants of other parishes, perhaps in the 13th and 14th centuries, may have paid tithe to the tenant's 'home' church rather than to that in the parish where the land physically lay, and eventually came to be counted as part of the tenant's parish. In the case of Ashcott, however, it is possible that this is further evidence that it may once have shared a field system with Shapwick, some small parcels remaining intermixed with the Shapwick lands at the time that the division to form two separate field systems occurred [Winchester 1990, 13-15].

In attempting briefly to draw these threads together, it is, for Polden at least, instructive to take a wider perspective, and in doing so it is yet again the recurring theme of the dichotomy between north and south that immediately strikes home. On the southern side of the ridge, the parish boundaries dividing, in particular, Stawell and Sutton, have clearly been laid out around a pre-existing field-system, displaying as they do a zig-zag of tight, right-angled turns. Moorlinch's western boundary, by contrast, with Catcott in the north and Sutton to the south, follows a relatively smooth, curving alignment, and is therefore far more akin to those of its northern neighbours which, as we have already seen appear for the most part to been established through open, featureless terrain; or at least, through terrain where pre-existing boundaries were either ignored, *or* were used selectively to produce the highly regular pattern that emerged in the medieval period. A further possibility, and perhaps the most likely one at present, is that a larger, pre-existing unit with clear boundaries was systematically sub-divided with newly-established *landsceara*[2] [*cf* Abrams 1996, 207-208]. This argument follows on from what has already been suggested for territorial arrangements in the Roman period.

While it is true that the southern settlements for the most part use the Roman road as a common northern boundary, there are also slight anomalies which give hints at earlier arrangements. Shapwick's southern boundary with Moorlinch, for example, crosses the road, and returns to it, twice, to take in two separate areas on its southern side. Likewise Edington's south-eastern boundary crosses the road for a short distance, to take in a small triangular piece of ground on its southern side. So also for Catcott, except that in its case the extension south of the road takes in a far larger area of land, on Billicombe Hill. In the south-easternmost part of this extension lies Loxley Farm, lying now nearly 1km to the west of the present position of Loxley Wood's westernmost point. The most likely explanation for these aberrations is that they represent an allocation to these parishes of formerly commonable woodland, and that Loxley Wood formerly extended further west along the ridge than it does today. We have already noted the position of Loxley in relation to the underlying Charlton Bank soil type, and Knight has observed recently that "this soil series continues a little to the west of the present day woodland" [Knight 1998, 10]. He further points out how "woodland resources would be shared between settlements providing wood for estates in the same ownership, some of which may be some distance away" [Knight 1998, 13]. Knight found no evidence for this in surviving field names in the immediate vicinity [1998, 25], but it seems perfectly possible that while boundary arrangements in this area betray the former presence of woodland, much of it may have been cleared at a date early enough such that this fact is not reflected in the field-name record. Further east, and probably, as we have already seen, for the same reason, Butleigh's boundary extends south-west across the road and into the *wald* in this area.

In sum, then, we can see that the tenurial division of the old *Pouelt* estate between Shapwick and Walton, as

revealed by Domesday, is essentially a reflection of its division between the two hundreds of Loxley and Ringoldsway. It seems likely, therefore, that administrative developments within the estate as we see them in the early medieval period, in terms of the creation of the two hundreds and the internal distribution of tax liability (ie hidation), were intimately related. They very probably post-date the earliest ecclesiastical pattern in which, before the 10th century, Shapwick and Moorlinch either together, or, at different times, independently, may have taken on the role of mother church of at least the western part of the estate (Chapter Four).

As for the situation in 'greater' Whitley, *outside* Polden, we can look briefly at the example of Sowy Island. The progress of wetland reclamation around the island on either side of 1066 (Chapter Seven) means it is unlikely that the bounds of the Sowy Anglo-Saxon charter correspond exactly with those of the three modern parishes. However one defines their exact course (below), it is clear that this external limit of the estate was a relatively simple one; there are only five points to define an area of considerable extent, and we get the clear impression that the bounds took as straight a line as possible between the points: this is not a boundary of numerous minor twists and turns that needed to be identified by the most insignificant landscape features. In turning to Sowy's internal boundaries, ie. those between Othery and Middlezoy, and between Middlezoy and Westonzoyland, we find a complete contrast. Grundy, in his elucidation of the Saxon charter, believed he was dealing only with those of Middlezoy. He was struck by the contortions displayed by the Othery/Middlezoy boundary, observing that "the curiously in and out nature of the SE b[oundar]y. looks very much as if ploughland had come down to that part of the b[oundar]y. at the time the b[oundar]y. was last defined" [Grundy 1935, 116-117]. His suggestion that the boundary was following the sharp changes of direction that would be necessary to take it round the edges of furlongs and strips in an open field system is understandable; for it here displays just those characteristics which one would expect in such a landscape. This is, however, only true of the western part of the boundary, on Earlake Moor. Where it strikes the higher ground around Othery itself, just north of the village, the present parish boundary follows the 25ft contour along a relatively smooth, curvilinear course to Greylake, just beyond the northern extremity of Othery parish. Even more striking is the Middlezoy/Westonzoyland section. For almost its entire length along a roughly north-east/south-westerly line, this boundary follows a tortuous course in a rapid succession of numerous right-angled turns across Weston Level and Langmead, until it too strikes the 25ft contour marking the higher ground north of Middlezoy. There, and subsequently, the shape of the boundary noticeably changes: it is still indented, but the bends appear to be much less regular in shape; they are no longer all right-angles. Again, we should note that by far the greater part of this boundary lies on low-lying moor ground which historically was probably

---

[2] Old English usage *ex inf* Dr M Costen.

never under the plough. How, then, is the nature of these two boundaries to be explained?

Whenever the external limit of Sowy island was defined, it seems clear that the internal divisions are later, perhaps much later. The heavily indented boundaries between Othery, Middlezoy and Westonzoyland are, for the most part at least, carried round not the divisions within a subdivided arable field system, but around the highly rectilinear, tightly-packed network of drainage ditches or rhynes which cover the moors west of Sowy. Although the question of date must remain open for the present, these boundaries can only, it seems to me, have been laid down either at a time when drainage and reclamation activity had reached an advanced stage in the post-medieval period; or, it is possible that enough survived of a pre-existing (Roman?), although probably relict drainage system to allow it to be used for the purposes of marking boundaries in the pre-Conquest period[3].

2. Charters

The physical sites of human occupation did not exist *in vacuo*, and before attempting to consider the nature of pre-Conquest settlement patterns within Whitley, and the detailed form of individual settlements, it is important to think about the landscape context within which communities became established, grew, developed and declined. In Chew Hundred, evidence for the nature of the pre-Conquest landscape is confined overwhelmingly to place- and field-names, sources which are also available in Whitley. The latter, however, furnishes an extremely useful additional perspective in the form of three Anglo-Saxon charters containing boundary clauses in Old English, of varying degrees of detail. By definition, the viewpoint in which we are placed by these documents, at the edge of an estate, can only ever be imperfect; but as Della Hooke remarks, "such information can be interpreted to give a much fuller picture" [Hooke 1998, 93][4]. Except in the case of Butleigh, I have made no systematic attempt to

'solve' these documents in the accepted sense, although occasionally I have tried to indicate the likely relative positions of the various boundary points. My chief concern here is the topographical light which this evidence casts on the respective estates in the 10th century, to which period, it is generally agreed, we should attribute all three sets of bounds [*cf* Costen 1988, 33-35].

Butleigh[5]

It is indeed unfortunate that a potentially very important cross-check on any proposed solution to the charter bounds of this grant, in fact comes to nought. For Baltonsborough, the estate immediately adjacent to the north-east across the River Brue, is also described in a charter with bounds of apparently early (ie mid-8th century) form, but the boundary points given therein are few and there are seemingly no features which are common to both sources [Abrams 1996, 53-54; Grundy 1935, 61-64; Costen 1992, 42]. This is doubly disappointing when, as we have already noted, there is a possibility that Butleigh/Baltonsborough may originally have formed a single unit, probably as itself a component of an even larger entity. Even given this though, there are still valuable insights which we can gain from the Butleigh bounds about the nature of the landscape in this area (Figure 25). Probably the main point that emerges most strongly from S270a is the predominance of the woodland term, *leah*. On balance it seems unlikely that any of the Butleigh examples need be ascribed to the later Old English sense of 'pasture, meadow' [Gelling 1984, 199]. Given the undoubted occurrence of *wald* in the old hundred name, repeated in this charter, and the likelihood that the *leah* terms here congregate on the higher ground in the southern part of the estate, in the area of the ridge road, a woodland context is certainly indicated. Indeed, remarkably, the *leah* name by which the estate, and then later the parish and the medieval village became known, *Bodekaleye*, appears here as a boundary feature. This might suggest that this was a tract of wood of some size and at the time these bounds were surveyed still extended from well inside the estate to the edges or beyond, probably as itself part of the larger *wald*. There is, though, an alternative possibility. If as Ekwall suggests the first element is derived from a personal name [Ekwall 1960, 79], an association, perhaps denoting ownership, with the man commemorated may partially explain the subsequent transfer of this essentially topographical name to the main settlement [Gelling 1998; Johansson 1975, 55; Costen 1992a, 96-98]. The original association was perhaps between the woodland and an isolated farmstead, that of the eponymous *Budeca* [Ekwall 1960, 79], on its edge or in a cleared area within it; certainly some woodland toponyms, and especially those recorded as estate-names in 1086, are likely to have been associated with settlement [Costen 1988, 41]. This suggestion clearly has implications for the nature of the settlement pattern at the time that the

---

[3] Extensive archaeological fieldwork in the northern Somerset Levels by teams under Dr Steve Rippon has clearly demonstrated the potential for this development. For recent summaries see Rippon 1996, 1997a and 2000a.

[4] Questions surrounding the dating and reliability of these sources, for Butleigh, Ham and Sowi, have been tackled at length by Costen and, latterly, Abrams [Costen 1992, 41-42 and 43; Abrams 1996, 76-77, 134-135 and 218-220], and a new edition of the texts of all the Glastonbury Abbey charters is in preparation by Abrams. The charter texts are printed by Watkin, and are all in GC II (SRS 63, 1948): Butleigh, 426; Ham, 493; Sowy, 495. The bounds for Ham and Sowy have been analysed by Grundy [1935, 118-125 and 116-118], with subsequent revision of the latter by Morland [1982], although Grundy omitted the Butleigh charter. The texts and translations followed here, however, are those prepared by Dr Costen based largely on a new appraisal of the manuscript of the 14th century Great Cartulary at Longleat House. I am grateful to him for allowing me to use this material in advance of publication, and for his guidance and advice relating to its interpretation. Those cases where I differ from his own explanations are indicated. A mid-10th century charter, S721, appears in GC under Othery [II, 1948, 496] among Glastonbury Abbey's Somerset lands, but at least its bounds, if not the whole document, are generally thought to relate in fact to Ottery St Mary in Devon. It is not considered further here. For a detailed discussion of the likely geographical affinities of this anomalous charter, and full references, see Abrams 1996, 189-191.

---

[5] I am indebted to Charlie and Nancy Hollinrake for allowing me sight of their own map of the Butleigh charter in advance of publication, which differs in detail from my own, particularly in the position of those points which lie probably on the southern and western sides of the estate.

Butleigh boundary was surveyed (below). One wonders, therefore, whether the site of this putative farmstead not only survived at that time, but continued in occupation and provided a convenient marker on this part of the boundary? Indeed, the question of earlier antecedents raises the prospect that Budeca's woodland farmstead may be English in name only; for Dr Gelling has proposed that "clusters of settlement names containing *leah*.....may contain the word in a quasi-habitative sense, used by English speakers to denote sites where settlements in forest clearings were flourishing when they arrived" [Gelling 1984, 199]. Only a single point on the Butleigh bound has survived into recoverable documentation, and we can be confident in following the Revd Synge's view that *Coppanleye* is represented today by Copley [Synge 1974, 4], which remains part of an extensive wooded area on the high ground in the southern part of the parish south of the main Roman road; it appears as a group of field names in this area in the mid 19th century [tithe map here, as indeed it did in the western part of this southern boundary; and I would differ slightly from Dr Costen here in interpreting *stret* of the charter as a reference to 'the street', rather than the place-name Street. The point seems clearly to be in the wrong position, on the estate's *eastern* boundary, for the latter explanation, and in any event Street as a toponym does not make an appearance before the 12th century (Chapter Eight). We need hardly doubt that the extension of Butleigh parish south of the Roman road was intended as Butleigh's allocation of the valuable woodland resource, and almost certainly dates from at least the time of the S270a charter. Although Domesday records woodland at Butleigh in two separate entries, of 100 acres and 2x1 furlongs respectively (with an additional 12 acres of underwood), it was nonetheless probably all at Copley or the other woods here noted in S270a. However one is to interpret these figures, it is clear that from them we should infer a relatively large area of woodland, since in 1086 "the great majority [of Somerset woods did] not rise above 30 acres" [Welldon-Finn 1967, 175]; and Rackham observes that "some 30% of settlements did not have any [woodland]" [Rackham 1988, 21]. But neither, almost certainly, does this represent the full extent of the wood in 1086; and it is likely that most or all of Kingweston's 3 furlongs x 1 acre, perhaps some of Dundon's 10 acres, and even of Somerton's 1 league x 1 furlong, were also part of the Copley 'complex' of woodland [Thorn & Thorn 1980].

In this context also, the link between the churches of Baltonsborough and Butleigh may mask a deeper, economic relationship. In 1086, woodland of no less than 1½ x ½ leagues was recorded for Baltonsborough, which converting from Rackham's formula of 1 league = 1½ miles gives an area of just over 290 hectares (2.9 sq km) [Rackham 1980, 113-115]. Even allowing a ± 10% margin of error [Rackham, *pers comm*], this is a very large tract of woodland for one manor, especially since the ancient parish of Baltonsborough amounted only to just over 1000 hectares [Kain and Oliver 1995, 434]. Probably most of this can be accounted for within Baltons-borough itself: in the early 14th century, two woods are recorded there, containing 100 acres at *Northwode*, and 120 acres at

Southwode [BL Egerton 3321 f89v]. Both survive as settlement names on the modern 2½" map. However, even if we were to apply Rackham's Domesday woodland multiplier of 1.2 to these acreages (and it is problematic whether by this relatively late date it would be correct to do so), it is difficult to reconcile the resulting figure of 264 acres (just under 107 ha) with the far greater area of woodland apparently recorded at Baltonsborough in 1086 [Rackham 1990, 48]. Neither would Rackham's suggested general 5% decrease in the area of woodland in England between Domesday and 1350 account for the discrepancy [Rackham 1986, 88]. C Hollinrake remarks [*pers comm*] that "Baltonsborough itself was heavily wooded, with large woods at Southwood and Norwood much larger than [the 14th survey might suggest, and] not really fully cleared until the18th century. Norwood might have extended as far as Glastonbury Abbey, hence the area later known as Norwood Park". It nonetheless still seems very likely that at least some of Baltonsborough's Domesday, and by extension pre-Conquest woodland, lay within the scarpland *wald* to the south, beyond Butleigh. The allocation of a specific block of woodland attached to Baltonsborough probably dates to the time of the fission of the putative Butleigh/Baltonsborough estate, which process would otherwise have severed Baltonsborough from its woodland resource. This had clearly happened before 1086, and as we have already noted, the Anglo-Saxon charters for Butleigh, and Baltonsborough (S1410), may point to a date at some point in the second half of the 8th century.

The 'orthodox' explanation of Copley is given by Johansson [1975, 63], who argues for a derivation from an OE personal name, Coppa[6]. This was certainly a managed wood at some point in its history and probably by the high middle ages at the latest, since even today, Copley can show extensive lengths of surviving woodbanks, some with ditches [fieldwork, 1/11/98], perhaps representing compartmentation associated with its use for coppice and other purposes [Rackham 1986, 125-126; for woodland earthworks see also 98-101]. For *Dryganlegh'*, Johansson suggests an origin in OE *dryge*, 'dry or dried up' [Johansson 1975, 67]. After *Dryganlegh'*, the next point on the charter bound is *Wrynwoldeswey*, the main road; and, although unlike Butleigh itself (the *Bodekaleye* of S270a), neither Copley nor *Dryganlegh'* were recorded as estate-names in 1086, it is quite possible that these names had also by the time of the charter become associated with colonising woodland farmsteads [Costen 1988, 41]. While it is likely that together, *Coppanleye, Bodekaleye* and *Dryganlegh'* represent an unbroken tract of wood here in the early medieval period, the use of separate names, by definition, suggests that distinct areas within it were recognised, perhaps identified by different management regimes or by ownership, as perhaps, for example, with *Bodekaleye* itself. Goldwey and *Cranhuntereston'* are

---

[6] More recently however, Hough [1998], has suggested that all those toponyms previously explained as compounds with a personal name *Coppa*, including the Butleigh example, actually contain an inferred OE word *coppe*, 'spider', but in place-names used in the far wider sense of 'insect'. The (implied) meaning for Copley would therefore be something like 'the wood/woodland clearing characterised by many different types of insect'.

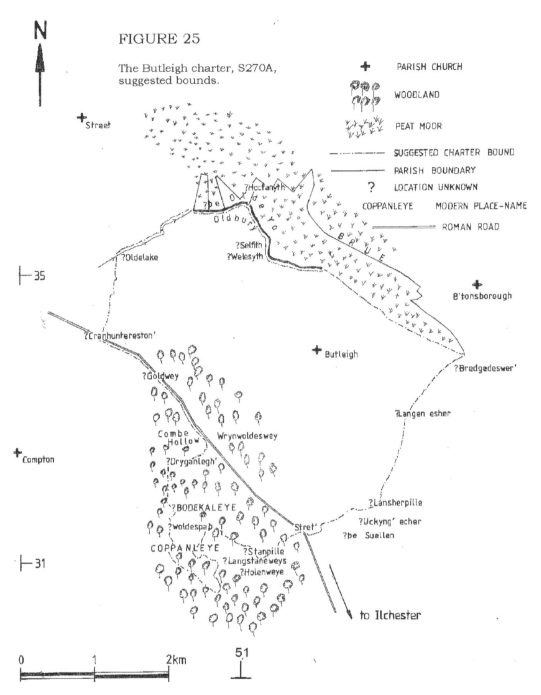

FIGURE 25

The Butleigh charter, S270A,
suggested bounds.

PARISH CHURCH
WOODLAND
PEAT MOOR
SUGGESTED CHARTER BOUND
PARISH BOUNDARY
?   LOCATION UNKNOWN
COPPANLEYE   MODERN PLACE-NAME
ROMAN ROAD

to Ilchester

unlocated, although the latter name, in particular, is intriguing: C and N Hollinrake [*pers comm*] identify the last element as 'stone', giving a meaning 'the stone of the crane hunters'. It seems as likely, however, as Dr Costen suggests, that we can infer a 'tun' name, giving 'the farmstead/settlement of the crane-hunters'. This may be a reference to an isolated farmstead or hamlet, somewhere close to the main road in the western part of Butleigh's southern bound, perhaps at the point where the ancient parish bound swings abruptly northwards to the next putative marker; and whose occupants had become associated with some kind of fowling activity [*cf* Hooke 1998, 179-181]? The settlement's position may imply roadside 'squatter' occupation within the width of the Roman road [Rackham 1986, 278], probably close to the

fringes of woodland, in a location where, as in many woodland areas, territorial rights may have been ill-defined before the advent of formal boundaries [Hooke 1998, 160-162; Winchester 1990, 25; Everitt 1986, 278-292]; only subsequently did the occupants find their settlement relegated to a boundary point on the western extremity of the Butleigh estate. Northward from the main road and the suggested position of Cranhunterston', the parish boundary on the western side of Butleigh strikes a small, north-easterly flowing stream at a point where the First Edition 6" OS map (1886) marks a "stone", presumably a bound stone. I suggest that this is the 'Oldelake', the 'old slow stream' of S270a. I would make this marker a distinctly separate entity rather than, as Dr Costen prefers, being physically contiguous or connected to *hoccanyth*.

The next three bounds all seem to be 'hithe' names [Gelling, *pers comm*], apparently denoting a series of river landing places [Gelling 1984, 76-78], and the probable topographical and archaeological contexts of which in Somerset have been discussed by Russett [1991, 64-66]. These sites are described in the charter as lying on "the old yo", from OE *ea*, a term generally applied to "watercourses of greater size than those denoted by broc and burna" [Gelling 1984, 20][7]. Dr Gelling [*pers comm*], considers that the watercourse referred to here is the River Brue. However, the course of the Brue in this area has been extensively modified [Williams 1970, 62-71; Rippon 1997, 212-214], and at the time of the charter, long before the advent of systematic, widespread and effective drainage, the Brue valley would have been subject to extended periods of flooding; it is unlikely that boundaries had begun to be defined on the featureless peat moors by the early 9th century; we can safely assume a use for intercommunal pasture in the summer, and the exploitation of other wetland resources including, of course, the peat itself. There are in any event, indications of this in the post-Conquest period, at a time when copious Glastonbury Abbey documentation reveals the progressive, and frequently contentious, piecemeal enclosure and 'improvement' of formerly commonable moorland at locations all over the Levels controlled both by the Abbey and by the Bishop [Williams 1970, 32-38, and Fig 13, 90; Rippon 1997, 207-209; Hallam 1988, 218-222, and 364-365 for pasture stints in the moors]. Those few pre-Conquest references we have which might suggest the presence of embryonic drainage and reclamation activity in the Levels, seem to relate chiefly to the area of the coastal claylands, and not to this more easterly part of the back-fen [Rippon 1997, 174-175]. For a wetland-fringe manor of 20 hides, we should regard with suspicion the complete lack of any mention of pasture at Butleigh in 1086, as indeed also for Baltonsborough [Thorn and Thorn 1980]. This strongly supports the view that the peat moors in this area remained open and commonable at this date, and had not yet been systematically partitioned between adjacent manors. Magnus Alexander's detailed statistical application of GIS techniques to the Domesday data in north Somerset has likewise suggested that sometimes very large areas of pasture were simply not recorded in 1086 probably because it was inter-manorial common [*pers comm*, work in progress].

All this being so, I suggest that for the 'old yo' and its hithes of the Butleigh charter, we must look not to the Brue, but elsewhere. The north-easterly flowing stream which I have suggested is the 'old stream' of the charter, flows down to the main road linking Butleigh to Glastonbury Abbey, and turns north. However, on the other side of the road, its line is precisely taken up by a larger stream known to this day as the Old Rhyne, and which is marked as such on the First Edition 6" OS map. In at least the western part of its length, it is clear that the rhyne has not been in any way canalised or straightened, and its winding, roughly northwest-southeasterly course follows the 10m contour very closely. It seems to me that this substantial feature is the likeliest candidate for the "old yo", and that at the time of the charter it marked the formal boundary between the higher, cultivable land to the south, and the floodable, unenclosed and commonable peat moors to the north in the Brue Valley. If, as Russett has suggested, structural vestiges of hythe sites "should be detectable in the archaeological record" [Russett 1991, 66], then for the Butleigh examples, it is the Old Rhyne on which such remains probably lie. *Selfith*, perhaps from OE *sele*, may refer to willows here [Smith 1956, II, 117], while welesyth may contain *wel*, "a deep pool, a deep place in a river, a whirlpool" [Smith 1956, II, 249]. Dr Costen prefers 'slope' for the former and 'spring' for the latter. However, while these explanations are topographically plausible, they do not help in locating the sites on the ground. *Hoccanyth* may offer more hope, since a derivation from OE *hoc* is likely: "a hook, an angle, a bend in a river, a spit of land in a river bend, a corner or bend in a hill" [Smith 1956, I, 255]. This is essentially the meaning favoured by Dr Costen ('the projecting hythe'). It is the first of this group of hythe names mentioned in the charter, and probably, therefore, the westernmost, if, as seems virtually certain, the surveyors were following the usual practice of tracing a clockwise course round the bounds [Grinsell 1991, 51; Hooke 1998, 95]. A likely candidate for *hoccanyth*, then, immediately suggests itself as the point at which the Old Rhyne makes an almost right-angled bend to the south-east about 700m east of the Glastonbury Abbey road. It is precisely within the southern (ie inner) angle of this bend that field names in Oldbury occur (below). At a superficial level it seems obvious that the charter's specific use of the word 'old' to describe both this feature and the 'old stream' suggest their prior existence when English-speakers first arrived in the area. We might consider, however, in what sense exactly this term was applied here. At present, although their respective courses today do not seem straight enough for entirely artificial channels, especially in the case of *oldelake* which is a very minor stream, only detailed archaeological and topographical work would reveal whether these watercourses might at any time have been subjected at least to modification. In any event, the appellation 'old' might reasonably seem superfluous in the case of ancient natural watercourses, unless we are to seek the reason for its use here, and indeed in other cases, in a far more specific context; and we would probably be correct to infer from these instances a meaning of 'the old boundary stream', and 'the old boundary yo'. Admittedly, the chronology of 'old' is highly problematic; although as Peter Kitson has recently reminded us, "we are often told by historical geographers and landscape historians that England in Anglo-Saxon times was already an 'ancient landscape'. The enormous frequency of *ealdan*, 'old', two and a half times as common as the next most frequent qualifier, shows that the Anglo-Saxons themselves were well aware of it" [Kitson 1993, 34]. This being so, it is

---

[7] This word is, for example, almost certainly cognate with the 'Old Ea', a substantial watercourse forming a major element in the largely artificial drainage system used to reclaim extensive tracts of Elloe Wapentake, south of Holbeach in Lincolnshire, in the medieval period; Hallam 1954, frontispiece map.

certainly possible that in these specific cases, 'old' is explicable in terms of the survival of boundaries of pre-existing (ie Romano-British) land units which were recognised as such in the early medieval period. This reading of the charter evidence receives at least circumstantial support from the occurrence of the tithe field names Old Bury at a point abutting directly onto the southern side of the rhyne at its western end [SRO D/D/Rt 434, 1843]. Depending on the vicissitudes of its passage from OE *burh* or *byrig* to modern -bury, this word most often has connotations of either defence or high status settlement, or both [Gelling 1997, 143-146; Field 1972, 154; Faith 1997, 164]. A relationship to prehistoric burial sites, such as Bronze Age barrows, is also known to give rise to names in or derived from -bury [*cf* Griffiths 1986]. Aerial photographs [NMR, Swindon], do not reveal any obviously artificial features in the area; however, the toponymic credentials of the present example are strongly supported by respectable early 14th century spellings [BL Egerton 3321, f109v], and its position at a clear ecological and topographical interface, on a minor promontory jutting out into the surrounding marsh, has obvious archaeological implications, offering as it does the prospect that some kind of potentially high-status occupation, or ritual focus, awaits discovery in this area.

In summary then, the landscape seen through the eyes of the surveyors of the Butleigh charter would have presented a sharp contrast between the heavily wooded *wald* occupying the higher ground in the southern part of the estate, and the low-lying terrain fringing the Brue Valley wetlands to the north. Between these two extremes it is safe to assume the presence of arable land, and while it is not entirely satisfactory to do so, it is possible to argue from the negative evidence of the charter as to its extent. At no point along the Butleigh bound is there mention of any example from that category of Old English toponyms which might reveal the presence of ploughland [Costen 1992a, 125-129]. It seems, then, quite likely that by the early 9th century, the arable land at Butleigh did not yet extend to the boundaries of the estate, although exactly how, at this period, its physical disposition was arranged is impossible to say.

Sowy

Problems surrounding the elucidation of the bounds of the Sowy charter, S251, and references thereto, are fully discussed by Abrams [1996, 218-220], and indeed in landscape terms there seems little useful that can be added here. It now seems generally agreed that, *contra* Grundy [1935, 116-118], S251 deals with the whole of Sowy island as a unit, and includes the three main settlements of Westonzoyland, Middlezoy and Othery. It is disappointingly short on topographical detail, and in particular, indications of settlement and land-use are completely absent. There are only five bounds given, and the general picture that emerges is hardly a revelation. The terms used to describe the bounds are overwhelmingly those of wetland, and the reason for the lack of detail immediately becomes apparent: the surveyors, faced with

the task of defining boundaries across a largely featureless marsh, had of necessity to follow watercourses; at least three, and possibly four of the bounds relate to streams, rivers or static water, the fifth to a pathway. Indeed, it is a strong possibility that in such an environment, the extent of the estate was actually dictated by the need to use suitably distinctive stretches of the pre-existing local drainage pattern. However, we may suggest a rationale on the part of the surveyors in that, although undoubtedly inconvenient, demarcating the estate in this way, rather than withdrawing the bounds to the higher and more easily 'definable' land of Sowy island (and Othery) itself, reinforced its claim to a share in the surrounding summer grazing commensurate to its size.

High Ham

In terms of topographical detail and the number and nature of the boundary points noted, the charter for High Ham, S791, stands in stark contrast to that for Sowy [Abrams 1996, 134-135; Grundy 1935, 118-126]. Part of the reason for this undoubtedly lies in the nature of the physical geography here, for Ham, unlike Sowy, is not a clearly bounded topographical entity; and although wetland may be included in the estate, for the most part the bounds of S791 are essentially those of a fairly typical 'dryland' perambulation, with all that means in terms of the kinds of features utilised as boundary markers. It will be enough here to note a few salient points. At least two toponyms appearing on the modern 2½" map, Henley and Rushley, have counterparts in the charter, but Abrams notes how "the bounds attached to S791 caused Grundy some difficulty" [Abrams 1996, 135], and such is their general obscurity it is not at all certain that we should interpret these as the same names. The overwhelming majority of the markers arise from the natural topography. However, the mention of an enclosure, (?*F*)*autesham*, perhaps associated with a personal name, is a strong hint that the settlement pattern on this estate remained partly dispersed by the 10th century, at least towards the periphery. Likewise the apparent reference to a twelve acre 'hewish', with its connotation of an isolated, ring-fenced family farm [Costen 1992b, 72-73]. Michael Costen has suggested elsewhere that, although the 30 acres of the king may indicate arable land, it was unlikely to have been part of a full-blown open field system [Costen 1992, 126]. The river-name Wearne, appearing in the charter, has probably become attached to the hamlet of that name lying just outside the present Ham parish boundary to the south-west [Ekwall 1960, 502-503], and which according to Collinson was historically a detached part of Pitney parish [Collinson 1791, III, 129-131]. Wearne no longer survives as a river-name, however, having most likely been supplanted by the present Mill Brook. It is interesting to note that there is indeed a point on this south-western side where the parish boundary leaves the Mill Brook and then returns to it, leaving a triangular piece of land in the adjacent parish of Huish Episcopi (Figure 26). As Grundy himself speculated [1935, 122], this presents a plausible candidate for the king's 30 acres which the boundary was clearly intended to avoid and place outside the Ham estate. Grundy did not note, however, that the Domesday evidence may lend some support to this suggestion. Can we, perhaps, equate this small pocket of royal land with the half ploughland which in 1086 is recorded as part of the small manor of Wearne, by then held by a royal servant in chief of the king and never having paid geld? [Thorn and Thorn 1980].

3. Communications on Medieval Polden

That the Roman road along the top of the Polden ridge had, probably by the 11th century at the latest, reasserted its importance as a major through route, cannot be doubted. Whether its use had been continuous since the end of the Roman period is another matter, but its landscape significance alone is clear enough from the fact of its being pressed into service as a common boundary between the northern and southern estates west of Shapwick. East of Shapwick, however, the situation immediately changes; between Shapwick and Ashcott the road ceases to be the boundary, and between Ashcott and Street the emphasis shifts from an east/west, to a north/south orientation in the pattern of parish boundaries. It is striking, and, as I will argue later on, highly significant, that it is precisely this point of change in the orientation of the parish boundary pattern that also marks the division between the former hundreds of Loxley and Ringoldsway.

Further east, the road again serves as a boundary, this time for Compton Dundon, but only for a short distance, between Marshall's Elm, on Street's southern boundary, and Wickham's Cross, halfway along Butleigh's southern boundary. It was this stretch of road which gave its name to the eastern hundred [McGarvie 1987, 32-33]. South-east of Butleigh, to the point at which the road leaves the hundred, the boundary again ignores it, probably, as we have already seen, to take a large swathe of woodland into Butleigh on its south-western side; indeed as the road continues south-eastwards through Kingweston and the Charltons (Adam and Mackrell), to its junction with the Fosse Way, the parish boundaries in this area give it a wide berth [Margary 1967, 84 and 124-125].

While the ridge-top road was clearly the backbone of the communications network on Polden, it was certainly not the only element in it, and particularly on the northern flank of the hill at least two other east-west routes played a role in later times as they most probably did from at least the Roman period. The line of the southernmost can be traced along lanes, field and parish boundaries, virtually from Dunball on the western side of Puriton to a point close to the site of the Old Church at Shapwick, with very few interruptions, and keeping pretty closely for most of this length to the 40m contour. It is first noted in the early 13th century [Watkin 1947, 118][8]. In the medieval period it was "known as the Broadway from Catcott westwards, [and] was diverted to the south in its course to Shapwick along a second route named Lippett's Way" [VCH Somerset, forthcoming]. The original line can still be traced between Shapwick and Catcott as a substantial

green lane, and it enters Shapwick from the west to become a major element in the layout of its highly regular grid plan [Aston and Penoyre 1994].

Indeed there is a common thread here, for it is quite clear that the Broadway also played an important role in shaping the plans of the settlements *west* of Shapwick. Catcott "is an irregular grid formed by three east-west routes", of which the Broadway is the most southerly [VCH Somerset, forthcoming]. At Edington, Broadway provides the southern boundary of the southernmost cell in a grid plan almost as regular as Shapwick's. The picture at Chilton is less clear, but the tithe map suggests that the modern alignment, which carries the road through the centre of the village, may not be the original one, and that the course of the Broadway east-west has been shifted to the north. If so, then as at Edington, its original line would have marked the southernmost limit of the village plan. West of Chilton, the modern road passes into Cossington and stops, forming the southern boundary of the village plan there. However, it may not be this line that represents the medieval Broadway, since field boundaries west of Chilton appear to respect what appears to be a primary boundary running westwards into Cossington, becoming east/west lanes which form the *northern* terminal of the village plan, and then continuing westwards as a track as far as Dunball, providing the southern parish boundaries of Woolavington and Puriton (Plate 8, Figure 27). It seems very likely that this track represents a fork off the main Roman road at some point between these two places, to provide a direct route to the Roman settlements at Puriton, and bypassing the port at Crandon Bridge which was served by the main road probably along much the same course that it takes today.

Further north, we can trace the line of a second east/west routeway, the western destination of which seems, again, to have been the Roman settlements at Puriton, where it starts (Figure 27). At Woolavington it forms the southern side of the village plan, the layout of which is different from those of its eastern neighbours in that its long axis is aligned east/west instead of north/south. Its probable line through Cossington and Chilton can be traced in field boundaries and lanes, but it strikes too far north to play any role in the plan structure of these places. At Edington, though, it forms the northern limit of what has already been suggested is the *original* extent of the plan layout, although its course through Catcott is uncertain and it seems as though, unusually, the intrusion of the settlement plan here has completely disrupted the line of a pre-existing routeway. It is, therefore, by no means certain that the continuation of its course is represented by the track that runs eastwards into Shapwick, becoming Kent Lane, and the line of which was blocked by the laying out of the now-truncated northern part of the village plan [Aston 1994b, 42, Fig 4.11]. The line is continued east of Shapwick by field boundaries and then a track, north of Old Church and Beerway Farm, to stop short at the Ashcott parish boundary.

---

[8] I am grateful to the editors of the Somerset VCH for this reference.

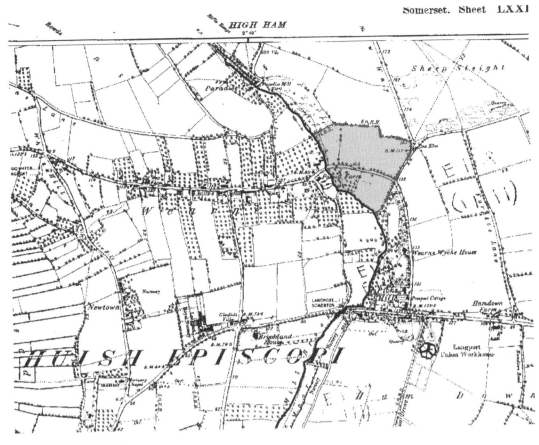

FIGURE 26

Extract from OS First Edition 6" map (1886), showing possible extent and location of the 'King's 30 Acres' mentioned in the bound of the Anglo-Saxon charter for Ham of 973 (S791). The shaded area lies on the eastern boundary of Huish Episcopi, and marks the point at which the parish boundary with Ham (greydashed line), almost certainly marking the course of the charter bound, for no apparent reason temporarily leaves the line of the Wearne Brook (black) to take in a loop of land to its east protruding into Ham parish.

Notwithstanding the detail of these various routes, what is immediately striking is that, with the exception of the main ridge road itself, neither of the subsidiary minor routes can be traced east of Shapwick, whose parish boundary with Ashcott, marking also the old hundred boundary, seems to represent a sharp discontinuity in the local east-west communications network. An exception may be the minor lane which joins Shapwick and Ashcott; while it certainly *appears* that this route "cuts across the old field boundaries" [VCH Somerset, Ashcott, forthcoming], there are no surviving boundaries which actually *cross* it, and the fact that it straddles the parish boundary with no hint whatsoever of a kink or detour of any kind, suggests that it may even pre-date it. Bearing in mind what has already been said about the close topographical and ecclesiastical relationship between Shapwick and Ashcott, a route between the two of some antiquity might be expected; the lane was certainly in place by the mid 18th century [Aston 1994, 25, fig 3.6] and it may not be entirely coincidence that its course north-west out of Ashcott, and before it turns due west just over the Shapwick boundary, is aligned

almost exactly on the site of Shapwick Old Church. The point is made by the road between Buscott and Shapwick. That this was *not* part of an older and continuous east-west through route along the lower flanks of north Polden is suggested by late 18th and early 19th century map evidence [Dunning and Harley 1981]. However, topographical confirmation comes from the fact that Buscott Lane, the road eastwards out of Shapwick, makes a sharp right-angled bend to the south as soon as it strikes the Ashcott parish boundary, so as to join up with the lane running westwards from Buscott, which arrives at the boundary a short distance to the south. Such a discordant arrangement is normally linked to different enclosure histories in adjacent parishes, when the establishment of new farms and field layouts provided the opportunity, or gave rise to the need for new minor routes, even if very often it was not possible to ensure that their alignments were direct [Hindle 1993, 134-135]. Certainly Buscott Lane did not exist in the mid 18th century, except perhaps as an access way into Shapwick's still partially-unenclosed Northbrook common field [Aston 1994b, 25, fig 3.6].

Plate 8: A routeway, now an unmade lane, probably at least of Roman date, south-west of Woolavington following the Polden ridge top, marking the parish boundary between Bawdrip (south) and Puriton (north), and heading west towards the known large Roman settlements near Puriton. Looking west.

It is clear, then, that not only was the most important 'grain' of the communications network on Polden oriented overwhelmingly east/west, but that also it is yet another element in the overall topographical structure which reinforces the pre-eminence of the northern flank. The way in which, as we have seen, the layouts of at least some of the north Polden village plans appear to have been conditioned, or at least influenced, by the various courses of these routes, is strong evidence that they *pre-date* those settlements in their present forms. The real significance of these east-west routes may lie in their use as stock droves, by which the disparate elements of at least the western half of the old *Pouelt* estate were linked and welded into a cohesive and possibly integrated economic entity focussed on Shapwick. This is a theme which we will explore and develop in the overall Conclusion to this study.

There *are* east/west routes following the contours on the southern flank: so much we might expect, if only to connect Moorlinch with its daughter chapels, and indeed this may be the most likely explanation for the two most obvious links in this respect (Figure 28). Billicombe Lane provides an almost direct access between Stawell and Moorlinch, and is quite clearly respected by field boundaries. Tapmoor Road is less convincing as Sutton's medieval link to Moorlinch; although a short stretch is utilised as a parish boundary, it takes a very indirect course, and seems to pay scant heed to the orientation of some of the field boundaries through which it passes. Indeed, Tapmoor itself seems to have originated as a major field boundary part of which was later made into a lane. It seems more likely that the main way between Sutton and Moorlinch in the medieval period lay further south, along what is now a bridle path for its entire length between the 30 and 40m contours, taking a much shorter, almost direct line into the lower part of Moorlinch from right outside the church at Sutton.

While an east/west trend is clearly the pre-eminent characteristic of communications routes in western Polden, so also, however, is it important to consider the secondary system of minor ways running north/south which provides links in western Polden between those settlements on the northern side of the ridge and those on the southern side. We can have no idea about the absolute dates of these routes, although some are probably of considerable antiquity (below). However, bearing in mind what has already been said about the probable nature of this

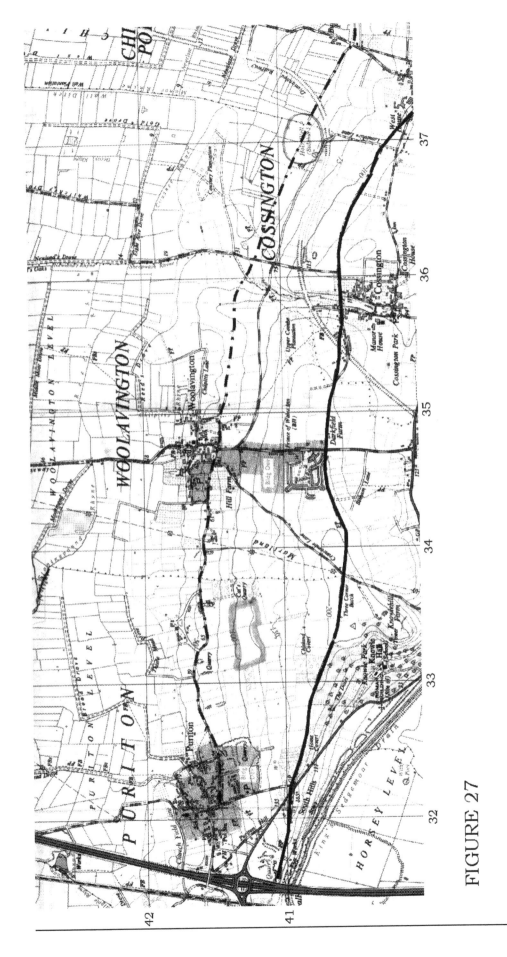

FIGURE 27

Extract from OS 1:25,000 map, showing (dashed line) suggested line of the Broadway west of Chilton, and (black line), secondary route forming the southern side of the Woolavington village plan. Stratigraphically, both seem to have been in existence *before* either Cossington or Woolavington were laid out.

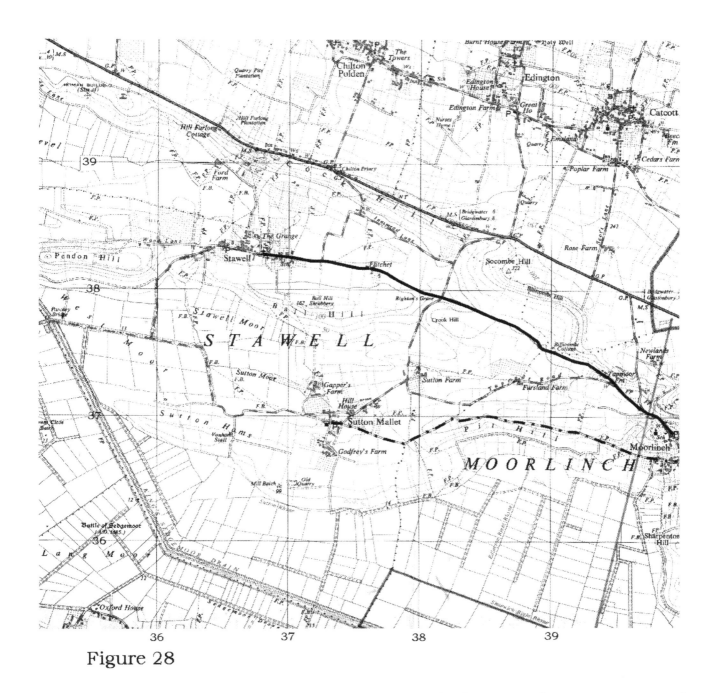

Figure 28

Extract from OS 1:25,000 map, showing suggested primary east/west routes on south Polden, between Stawell and Moorlinch (black line, Billicombe Lane), and Sutton and Moorlinch (black dashed line).

relationship, it would be logical to suppose that they represent a further expression of the subservient, dependent status of the southern communities in relation to their northern neighbours. This is strictly going beyond what the direct evidence will support, but it is a line of argument worth pursuing. Leading from each of the northern villages is one or more routes, be it a lane or track, heading southwards over the Roman road and down the southwards over the Roman road and down the southern flank. Some of these routes appear to reveal a direct relationship between individual settlements; so that, for example, a track south from Edington, shown on modern maps as a footpath but on the OS 1st edn 1" sheet as an embanked lane, proceeds straight down the other side of the hill where it joins the now-metalled Moor Lane which runs into Sutton. Likewise is Chilton linked to Stawell, Woolavington to Bawdrip, Shapwick to both Moorlinch and Greinton, and Catcott, by an indirect route, to Moorlinch. The position of Sutton is especially interesting since it appears to 'funnel' towards itself tracks

Plate 9: The apparently cobbled surface of the lane immediately south of Loxley Wood and the main Polden ridge road, forming an extension of Wood Lane and forming one of the north/south routes between Shapwick and Moorlinch.

coming into it from the north, but there is only a single route leaving it to the south, heading straight out onto Sedgemoor, which significantly is marked on the First Edition 1" OS map (1817) with the name 'Sutton Door' [Harley and O'Donoghue 1981, 17]. Indeed, it is notable that none of the southern settlements, up to and including Greinton, south of Shapwick, actually marks the termination point of these routes, and there is a distinct impression that these links were merely passing through

them on their way to Sedgemoor (Figure 28).

Shapwick's link to Moorlinch arouses particular curiosity. Eastwards towards Shapwick its course is aligned directly on the site of the Old Church. Westwards, it becomes Wood Lane, an old route probably related to access into Loxley Wood [Knight 1998, 51], before crossing straight over the Roman road into a substantial but now very overgrown green lane which still in places shows remnants of cobble metalling [Plate 9]. It is certainly this route which was depicted as a still-usable road even by the late 18th century [Dunning and Harley 1981]. The antiquity of the *entire* route at present is problematic, since there is a middle section whose relationship with adjacent field boundaries might suggest a relatively late date (Figure 29)[9]. What is important here though is its subsequent course, for the lane eventually skirts the flank of Knoll Hill via a deeply cut hollow way and descends into Moorlinch by a track that passes through the present churchyard, but which then continues southwards down the southern slope, its line again marked by a prominent but now very overgrown sunken trackway. The churchyard has been extended westwards, and originally the route would have passed immediately to its west.

Although disrupted by house plots in the lower part of Moorlinch, its general course is continued by paths and tracks which fan out south of the settlement towards Sedgemoor. This particular route may have had a dual purpose. From what has already been suggested, in Chapter Three, about the possible nature of the relationship between Shapwick and Moorlinch churches it may, firstly, represent a direct link between the two. Although this yet remains to be proved, it is a possibility further reinforced by the strong impression that this northern approach to Moorlinch church seems calculated to place the traveller moving towards it in a closely-defined spatial relationship with it, and in doing so allowing him a particularly striking appreciation of the church in its topographical setting[10]. This is especially so, as we have already noted, in relation to the terraces cut into the northern and north-western flank of the peninsula. An approach from the eastern side, as today, would have been easier and more convenient. Perhaps we can draw a parallel from an entirely different cultural milieu to inform our perspective on these features? For the role of the famous artificial terraces created by the Incas of western South America, may be underpinned above all by that society's strongly developed spiritual and semiotic sense of the natural landscape. Implicit in recent accounts of Inca practice is the clear view that functionalist, *economic* explanations are far from being the complete answer; on the contrary, "terrace construction was used 'to sculpt existing hillocks or open areas into new forms and [as such, was] conceptually intermediate between obeying the contours of a valley and imposing a pleasing form on the landscape'" [quoted in

van de Guchte 1999, 152]. May we, then, go so far as to suggest that the Moorlinch terraces, and indeed the entirety of St Mary's topographical context, represent in their startling resemblance to a miniature Glastonbury Abbey Tor a deliberate attempt to manipulate the psychological perspective of the viewer, and to provoke a very specific emotional and cognitive response?

Such ideas about the nature of people's relationship with their environment, with sites of special status whether natural or man-made, their movement through it, and their awareness and perceptions of their place in it, are now common currency among archaeologists attempting to explain the spatial and psychological implications of prehistoric ritual monuments [Tilley 1994; Darvill 1997; Fowler 1998;]. Massey's conclusion from the Iron Age evidence from Britain and Gaul provides a useful general summary of this perspective: "the entire territory assumes a sacred character, emphasised by the divinely-ordained nature of its boundaries. These in turn were reinforced by strategically-placed shrines, which also became contact points with neighbouring polities. Within these limits, natural phenomena assumed the character of a sacred geography, in which the characterisation of places, waters, even of vegetation, created the theatre in which the relationship of the community with its gods was enacted" [Massey 1999, 106]. It is ironic that Tilley's own pioneering work in this field has been recently criticised as conceptually one-dimensional [McGlade 1995, 1999], lacking in critical rigour [Fleming 1999], inaccessible, dull and downright pretentious [Lynch 1996, 84-85]. More recently, Ian Hodder has complained that although potentially a highly illuminating approach, too much of recent phenomenological conjecture has been extrapolated uncritically into accepted orthodoxy on the basis of little or no hard evidence [Hodder 2000][11]. Indeed, the 'phenomenological' perspective as a whole has recently been subjected to a brilliant and robust summary critique by Jodie Lewis, who highlights, among other problems, the singular lack of tightly-provenanced, systematic and rigorous data collection underpinning these views, and their highly subjective nature, relying as they do on *20th century* perceptions of landscape to infer *prehistoric* mental constructs of meaning and symbolism[12]. The lead

---

[9] The earliest available large-scale map of Moorlinch, dated 1797 and depicting only scattered plots for the purposes of a parliamentary enclosure, appears to confirm the existence of the problematic 'connecting' stretch of lane at least by that date. SRO Q/RDe 169, Moorlinch Enclosure.

[10] The nature of this link may be associated at least in part with a use as a formal processional route, as an element of the liturgical relationship between the two churches that was suggested in Chapter Four. I am grateful to Helen Gittos for drawing my attention to this possibility. We can draw direct parallels here with Howard Williams's recent study of the topographical context of the (probably 7th century) Anglo-Saxon burial mound on Lowbury Hill, on the Oxfordshire/Berkshire boundary: "the main axes of movement through the landscape would have been important for the builders of the Lowbury barrow, since they structured the ways in which the barrow would be seen, experienced and interpreted. Perhaps such routes were incorporated into the funeral procession in some way". Williams 1999, 75.

[11] I am grateful to Dave Mullin for these latter two references.

[12] I am very grateful to Jodie Lewis for giving me sight of her own doctoral text in advance of its publication by BAR. Similar sentiments have been echoed strongly in print recently by Richard Muir, who argues forcefully that while we might usefully seek to develop a coherent body of theory for historic landscape studies, it can be effective *only* if grounded firmly in the kind of rigorous, systematic and empirical data collection so passionately espoused by Lewis: "in scores of current projects, theory is used to illuminate the particular, and if landscape history begins to prioritise theory rather than localities and sites it may be surrendering the basis of its individuality" [Muir 2000, 20]. An important start in the process of addressing these very justified criticisms has, however, been made recently by Howard Williams, who explicitly bases his discussion of the phenomenology of 7th century Anglo-Saxon burial mounds on a range of specific, empirical criteria that are both repeatable and testable; Williams 1999, esp at 58-59. Likewise, work in progress by Karin Altenberg, which adopts phenomenological *elements* in a comparative study of the medieval (ie post-Conquest) landscapes of Dartmoor and Bodmin Moor, is a further demonstration that this approach offers significant potential for periods *other* than the prehistoric.

given by Lewis in this respect gives hope, however, that with a suitably critical and empirical approach, founded on the systematic collection of extensive datasets, there need not necessarily be a danger of throwing the baby out with the bathwater. For the prehistorians, an attempt to rescue the debate from ideological impasse by reconciling and integrating its two main opposing themes, has recently been made by Bradley [2000]. A suggestion is made in Appendix 2 as to how a start might be made on this task with specific reference to the topographical affinities of church sites in Somerset. The application of *certain* aspects of these views in a medieval context is undeniably thought-provoking, and with properly rigorous controls firmly based on hard data of *all* kinds, they might at least encourage us to think more about how people perceived their own relationships, both as individuals and collectively, with the ritual sites that churches essentially were[13].

Secondly, however, the Shapwick/Moorlinch route fits squarely into the context of the other north-south ways traversing western Polden, in that its ultimate goal was undoubtedly Sedgemoor. The interest right into the modern period which the northern settlements continued to have in terms of their access to Sedgemoor, is clear from the fact that they were systematically allocated allotments there at the time of the completion of its reclamation and enclosure in the late 18th century [Tate 1948, 44 and 86; Figure 16]. By the early medieval period, and perhaps with far earlier antecedents, at least some of these routes may well have represented short-distance droves by which stock was taken out onto the summer grazing of Sedgemoor, and that although they appear to link the northern and southern settlements, they may in fact, like the east-west routes along the northern flank, pre-date them, at least in their present form. The Shapwick/Moorlinch route, at its eastern end, joins with the Broadway from Catcott which, as we have already seen, forms a major element in the layout of the Shapwick village plan. Sutton may be located where it is as the most southerly outlier of higher land on that side of the main ridge, having its origins perhaps as a convenient 'gateway', or intermediate station, to the grazing grounds to which stock could be easily and quickly withdrawn if necessary.

Altenberg 1999. Also relevant here is a recent attempt to use phenomenological approaches to address questions about the nature and affinities of Roman roads in the landscape. See Witcher 1998.

[13] I am grateful to my brother, Dr Christopher Corcos, for his guidance on the strict clinical and psychological aspects of landscape perception. A full phenomenological perspective is surely only a logical development of the already widely-accepted idea that the richness of the Anglo-Saxon toponymic vocabulary springs directly from a profound acuity of topographical awareness. The early medieval traveller was guided by a detailed 'mind map' underpinned by an intricate and highly specific structure of place-names rooted in direct experience and observation of natural topography. See Cole 1994, and Gelling and Cole 2000, xii-xxiv. With specific reference to Shapwick and Moorlinch, see Corcos 2001 for a developed and expanded version of the ideas presented here.

Conclusion

Chew and Whitley hundreds provide both contrasts and similarities in their respective use of roads and tracks as *internal* boundaries. As the physically smaller entity, with a shorter total length of boundaries, Chew might not by definition be expected necessarily to follow the same pattern as its larger neighbour. But it is striking how Stratford Lane, the one obvious Roman road traversing the hundred, is totally ignored by parish boundaries, and only short, discontinuous and problematic stretches of boundary can be proposed as *possibly* having a Roman basis. Road/boundary evidence from immediately *outside* the hundred shows that while external territorial dynamics saw boundaries of neighbouring parishes being drawn along Stratford Lane, Chew hundred failed to conform and managed to retain a degree of internal cohesiveness. This seems, as we have seen, to have been the result of a deliberate and conscious 'policy'. When internal division *did* come to Chew hundred, I have suggested that it was relatively late, and took its cue largely from natural features, from the various types of boundary provided by sub-divided field systems, or, in the case of Chew/Dundry, as the result of assarting of commonable woodland between the two places. There may be tenurial implications here: Chew's status as a royal estate until its donation to the newly-founded bishopric of Wells in the early 10th century, may have imparted a degree of inertia, in terms of its *internal* economic dynamics, that only began to be broken down *after* the change of ownership. The crown would have had an interest in keeping the putative ancient estate together, in order for it to function efficiently in its role as an *integrated* entity. The management concerns of the new see, however, may have been different, and like any other major landholder with increasing economic and military obligations to the crown through the 10th century, a policy of leasing and 'manorial' subinfeudation may have presented the only course. Some of these boundaries, such as between Stowey and Chew, may well have been newly-drawn at this time, while others could merely have crystallised and formally defined existing divisions.

On western Polden, in stark contrast to Chew, the Roman road has been used as a 'base line' from which the north flank parishes have been systematically 'laid off'. East of Shapwick, however, the road suddenly becomes ignored for boundary purposes, exactly as Stratford Lane does as it *enters* Chew hundred. We will examine this observation further when we look at settlement patterns (Chapter Eight), but for now we can note that, just as we suggested for Chew, there seems clearly to have been conscious interference in the pattern of boundaries west of and including Shapwick, but not (or at least, not to the same extent) east of it. The same is true of other parish boundaries, apart from those using the road – their disposition on western Polden indicates a high degree of artificiality. But we should again bear in mind here that Whitley was originally *two* hundreds; and I will suggest later on that it is no coincidence that this change occurs precisely at the old boundary between Ringoldswey and Loxley. It is likely that the same forces which prompted

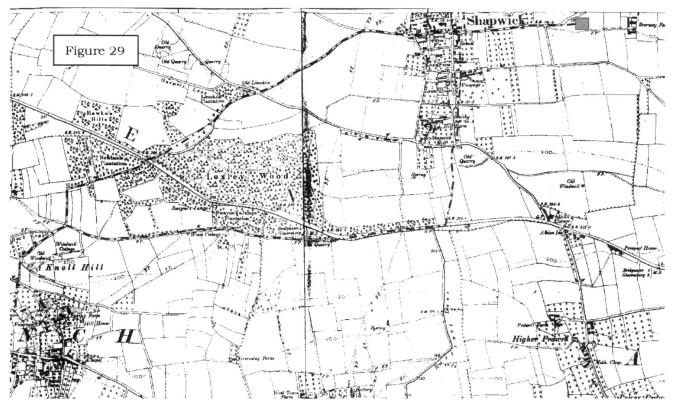

Extract from OS 2nd Edition 6″ map (1904), showing suggestion for two possible routes between Shapwick Old Church (grey square) and Moorlinch St Mary's.

the See of Wells to break up its Chew estate were responsible at least in part for Glastonbury Abbey's systematic subdivision of western Polden.

Turning for a moment to look *outside* Polden, one can draw similar comparisons, and Sowy island is a case in point. The highly indented boundary between Middlezoy and Westonzoyland finds a parallel in that between Dundry and Chew Magna. Their formal demarcation probably occurred at different dates (I would suggest the former in the Middle Ages, the latter either in the late Anglo-Saxon or early post-Conquest period); but *both* are associated with 'frontier zones' of reclamation and colonisation – of

ridge-top woodland in the case of Chew/Dundry, and wetland on Sowy. However, unlike Chew, on Polden we are given the chance to make *internal* comparisons – why were not settlements and boundaries manipulated along the *entire* ridge, and not just the western part? Why do the boundaries of those settlements in western Polden on the *southern* side of the ridge, show the same irregular pattern as those *east* of Shapwick? The evidence from this chapter will later on play an important role in the construction of an explanatory synthesis which attempts to address these questions.

Chapter Seven

Domesday, Fields and Transhumance: The Economic Dimension

Introduction

In this chapter, I attempt an analysis of the evidence found in the folios of Domesday Book, for all three hundreds, but at varying levels of detail. Whitley, forming the core of the study, figures most prominently in the discussion, but the other themes of the chapter, fields and transhumance, devolve mainly upon Carhampton and Chew/Chewton hundreds respectively. Carhampton is the only hundred here to have a separate section on its field systems. Likewise, the 'Transhumance' element centres chiefly around Chew/Chewton, for based upon it is the model presented here to explain the origins of the very particular economic relationship between Chew, Chewton and the latter's detached areas to the west, in the northern enclave of the Somerset Levels. This is not to say that transhumance was not a consideration in the internal economy of Whitley hundred, and specifically of Whitley's core entity, the *Pouelt* estate; indeed, quite the reverse. But since I will argue later on that the practice was intimately linked to the development of the medieval settlement pattern on the Polden ridge, it seemed best not to develop these essentially mutually-dependent ideas in isolation from each other, and they have been used to provide the basis of my concluding chapter. Likewise, for Whitley as a whole, discussion of its field systems is held over to Chapter Eight; since as an area by and large characterised by nucleated settlement it is difficult, and would certainly be counter-productive, to attempt to analyse settlement morphology without also invoking the evidence of associated field arrangements, so closely do the two themes interlock in this area. For these reasons also, this section diverges slightly from the format of the preceding chapters, in that there is no separate heading for 'Conclusion'. Rather, the narrative presented contributes towards the ideas which are worked out in the next, and final, full chapter, and which in turn are further developed, along more specific lines, as a model for the evolution of medieval settlement on the Polden ridge in the main study area of Whitley hundred, which forms the overall Conclusion to this study.

Chew and Chewton Hundreds[1]

The basic Domesday data are summarised in Tables 2 (for Chew only), and 3, and an analysis of the assessments for tax allow some provisional conclusions to be drawn about the state of landholding and estate size in the two hundreds in 1086. Note that in this context the term holding is used in preference to estate, since a large named estate (Chew itself is the obvious example here) could consist of several

smaller individual holdings, unnamed but separately assessed, and probably to be regarded as essentially 'sub-estates' in their own right (I am grateful to Magnus Alexander for his advice on this point).

It is clear that in terms of assessment for taxation purposes, Chew and Chewton were dominated by larger holdings: although they comprise only about half the total number of holdings, those of 5H and over account for over 80% of the hidated land. Smaller holdings, those under 5H, made up only just under 20% of the total, and although the smallest ones, 2H and under, contributed nearly half of this, by themselves they were under 10% of the total hidation. We may also note the relatively high (over a third) proportion of the total hidage made up of holdings of exactly 5H. The significance of the 5H unit in Domesday has been much-debated - surveying the evidence, Welldon Finn and Wheatley dismiss it as "largely artificial in character, and [bearing] no relation to the agricultural resources of a vill" [in Darby & Welldon Finn (eds), 1967, 154-155). It seems likely that this highly regularised regime may be a remnant of the tenth century practice of landlords of dividing their estates "to reward their own followers and to provide for the military service now demanded of them by the kings of the English" [Costen 1992, 118]. How far this was true within the study area remains to be seen. It has, certainly, been noted recently that the Anglo-Saxon hidation system was probably so obsolete by 1086 that it was superseded by a scheme based on the ploughland. Following Nick Higham, Michael Costen observes that the ploughland "is a record of the actual amount of ploughland in use in each of the manors surveyed. It is, therefore, a real measure of the economic activity of each community where it is recorded" [Costen, 123]. Analysis of discrepancies between ploughland and hidage assessments across the county as a whole leads Dr Costen to the conclusion "that the tenth century saw a dramatic expansion in the economy.....but that the biggest expansion was in the relatively underdeveloped west. In the south-east, the old heartland of the county, growth, although not absent, was relatively less impressive. Some estates even slipped back" [Costen, 125].

Another point arising within the study area from an examination of the Domesday evidence is the incidence of cases where it is clear that a number of individual pre-Conquest holdings have by 1086 been brought together under a single landowner. See Tables 1 and 2. Only in one case, that of Moreton, is it specified that the 5H belonging to Serlo of Burcy in 1086 were held as three manors before 1066. Nonetheless it is likely that this was the case elsewhere. At Timsbury for example, a 5H estate held as one by the Bishop of Coutances in 1086 was clearly made up of two pre-Conquest holdings, of 3H and 2H, under two separate, named owners. The 5H holding at Hallatrow, divided among four thanes before the Conquest, was

---

[1] I am very grateful to Dr Frank Thorn for his invaluable and detailed advice relating to the Somerset Domesday in general, and on Chew and Chewton hundreds in particular.

TABLE 2   CHEW HUNDRED IN DOMESDAY BOOK

Place	Domesday Manor	Parish	Geld	Plough-lands	Ploughs	Holder 1066	Holder 1086	Sub-tenant 1086	Value 1066	Value 1086
Chew Magna	Yes	Yes	30H	50	47	Bp of Wells	Bp of Wells	Richard (5H) Roghard (6H) Stephen (5H) Aelfric (7V) Wulfric (2H)		£43
Chillyhill	Yes	No (in Chew Stoke)	3V	2	2	Everwacer	Serlo of Burcy			15s
Chillyhill	Yes	No	½H (added from Chew Stoke)	1	1	Aelfric	Serlo of Burcy		20s	10s
Clutton	Yes	Yes	10H	8	9	Thorkell	Bp of Coutances	William	£3	£6
Norton M'reward	Yes	Yes	5H	8	4	Alfwold	Bp of Coutances	Wulfeva	100s	60s
Chew Stoke	Yes	Yes	½H	1	1	Everwacer	Bp of Coutances			10s
Chew Stoke	Yes	Yes	1¾H	2	1	Aldwin	Aldwin (a 'king's thegn')			25s
Timsbury	Yes	Yes	3H 2H	3 2	2 2	Ape Sibbi	Bp of Coutances	William (both holdings)	26s 14s	50s 30s
Timsbury	Yes	Yes	5H	4	2	Gunfrid	Odo of Flanders (from the K.)			£3
DETACHED MANORS IN THE NORTHERN LEVELS										
Yatton	Yes	Yes	20H	22	22	John the Dane	Bp of Wells	Fastrad (5H) Hildebert (4H) Benzelin (the church with 1H)		£15
Wemberham	No (pasture only)	No (part of Yatton)				The King	Bp of Wells			
Brockley	Yes	Yes	4H	4	4	Aldred	Aldred			30s
Kingston Seymour	Yes	Yes	1H 4½H	17 7	14 6½	Aldred 4 thegns	Bp of Coutances	Wm of Monceux	£6 60s	£6 60s
Midgell	Yes	No (in Brock-ley parish)	1H	2	2	Aelmer	Bp of Coutances	Leofwin	4s	20s
Claverham	Yes	No (in Yatton parish)	2H	3	3	Gunhilda	Bp of Coutances	Fulcran	20s	30s

125

TABLE 3: SUMMARY OF BASIC DOMESDAY STATISTICS FOR CHEW AND CHEWTON HUNDREDS COMBINED

	Hidage	No. of holdings	% of total assessment
Total for study area	218.75	44	
Under 5H	42.5	21	19.43 (of which 2H & under: 45.88%)
2H & under	19.5	15	8.91
Exactly 5H	75	15	34.29
5H and over	176.25	23	80.57

treated as a unitary estate, held by the Bishop of Coutances, in 1086. Likewise at Emborough (3H divided between two thanes in 1066), and Ston Easton, where one of the three pre-Conquest estates, of 4½H, held by the Bishop as one manor in 1086, was shared between threethanes twenty years earlier. Such examples could easily be multiplied within the study area, although it is also clear that agglomeration was not the invariable rule and that smaller pre-Conquest holdings could survive right through to 1086. The other two 1066 holdings at Ston Easton, of only 1H and 1H 1V, are a case in point: both appear intact in 1086 under different chief tenants. This makes a possibly significant point, for it seems as though the tendency towards agglomeration was most marked on those Domesday manors held by very powerful lords, and in the study area, excluding the King and the Bishop of Wells, the greatest landowner was the Bishop of Coutances. This view is, however, 'impressionistic' and based on a relatively small sample of estates. More detailed and systematic work would need to be done to determine exactly how far the Domesday evidence is to be trusted, how it should be interpreted, and what the landscape implications may be.

This is important because elsewhere in Somerset, Aston has suggested that in some cases, details about the pre-Conquest division of holdings in Domesday entries, where perhaps only one estate survives by 1086, may imply a drive towards settlement nucleation in the years between 1066 and 1086. If mapped, the Domesday figures for agglomeration indicate that it was most strongly marked in the southern and eastern parts of the county outside the boundaries of the great lay and ecclesiastical estates. On the larger estates, Domesday apparently reveals little discernable change in landholding patterns, suggesting that a move to larger, nucleated settlements had already occurred in these areas, or had yet to take place. Whatever the chronology, the coincidence of a high density of generally nucleated settlement lying within the great Somerset estates by 1086 is highly suggestive [Aston 1985, 84-85, and 89-92]. The overall impression from within Chew and Chewton is that these suggestions may need to be modified, with at least one of the large secular fiefs, that of the Bishop of Coutances, displaying distinct signs of widespread agglomeration [Table 2].

Conversely though, the pattern is complicated by the clear indications from Domesday that the largest single estate in the study area, that of Chew (Magna), at 30H, held by the Bishop of Wells, had by 1086 been subjected

to extensive fragmentation. The Bishop himself held only 10H 1V directly (the odd virgate may not be real: the Domesday figures do not strictly add up); the remainder was distributed between separate holdings of 5H, 5H, 6H, 2H and 1H 3V, each held by a named individual as sub-tenant of the Bishop. The extent to which this development manifests itself on the ground, in terms of the settlement pattern (whether dispersed, nucleated, or a combination of the two), is a point to which we will return in the next chapter.

An attempt has been made elsewhere to discern indications of change (whether expansion or contraction) in the agrarian economies of manors between the original hidations made in the late Saxon period, and 1086 (Rippon 1994, 242-244). We should be cautious in the interpretation of the figures, and there is at least one important respect in which I depart somewhat from Rippon, namely in the case of Kingston Seymour, which Rippon includes in his table 12.1. It is clear from Domesday that before 1066, Kingston Seymour contained two manors (see Table 2); although this was still the case by 1086, by that time the Bishop of Coutances had acquired both. In 1066 one of the manors was rated at a single hide, but twenty years later was assessed at 17 ploughlands. Rippon attributes this apparently massive increase in the taxable capacity of this manor to an associated expansion of agriculture through reclamation in this part of the North Marsh. It is far more likely, though, that the 'increase' is an illusion, an idiosyncrasy of the Domesday record. It seems deeply suspicious that, despite such a striking 'expansion', the *value* of this manor remained exactly the same, £6, between 1066 and 1086. I think that the 1 hide pre-Conquest assessment was a notional value, and not a reflection of the true value of the manor. It seems to be one of those examples of a 'favourable' assessment which represents, effectively, a tax exemption. Such exemptions are, according to Michael Costen, "rare in Somerset" [Costen 1992, 123], but he is here referring to examples where this is explicitly noted by Domesday, as at Chewton itself, owned by Queen Edith before 1066, and rated at 29 hides but taxed on only 14 of them. We may wonder, though, whether the Somerset Domesday does not contain more instances like Kingston Seymour, where the increase from hides to ploughlands between 1066 and 1086 is so large that it can really only be accounted for by a 'silent' pre-Conquest exemption? I would contend that the real capacity of this holding, in terms of a late Saxon hidation, is not and never can be known, and any calculations based on the Domesday figures for 1066 must by definition be suspect. The reason(s) behind the low value of the pre-Conquest geld are open to question. This was not and never had been church land, and no special circumstances appear to surround the 1066 owner, Aldred. At this stage therefore, one can only speculate from the place-name that Kingston's strikingly trivial tax burden arises from its status as a royal manor at some unknown point before Aldred acquired it [Gelling 1997, 184]. Perhaps this in turn may be related to its position as a detachment of Chewton, which, as we have already noted, was a royal manor with a recorded 1086 tax exemption? In this respect it is interesting to note that the other manor at Kingston, rated at 4½ hides in Exchequer Domesday, is revealed by Exon Domesday to have been the subject of a formal exemption, paying geld on only a single hide before the Conquest [DB Somerset f89, col a; Thorn & Thorn 1980, 316, 5.64]. Here, unlike Aldred's manor in 1066, Exchequer Domesday at least gives us an unexempted hidation which if taken at face value gives some indication of economic change between 1066 and 1086. This may take us back to a time when this was a single estate, a *cyninges tūn*, subject to a blanket exemption which remained in force in the separate parts even when it became split into two before 1066. Again, this may have implications for the settlement pattern.

This being said however, it does appear at present that in broad terms the Domesday evidence from the study area bears out Rippon's findings that away from the Somerset Levels, on the surrounding higher ground, agrarian expansion since the original late Saxon hidation was limited, due primarily, but not wholly, to the lack of land reserves available in the Levels through drainage and reclamation [Rippon 1994]. In some cases there seems actually to have been contraction of cultivation, again as indicated by Rippon from other examples, in those places where the number of recorded Domesday ploughs exceed the available ploughlands. If the ratio of ploughs to ploughlands can be taken as an indication of the extent to which the land was actually being exploited in 1086 (and this is a moot point among historians - the arguments are reviewed in Higham 1990), Table 2 shows that within the study area there were many places where cultivation had reached a maximum and the potential for expansion was, apparently, zero. These are estates where the number of ploughs equals the number of ploughlands. At a small number of places, such as Chewton, Hallatrow, West Harptree, Norton Malreward and Timsbury, there seems to be significant potential for increasing the cultivable area, in some cases by 100%; elsewhere, a surfeit of ploughs over ploughlands, as at Clutton, may indicate places where the frontier of cultivation had attained its maximum extent, although this is by no means to suggest that any kind of agrarian 'crisis' obtained here: "in the Wiltshire Domesday, more ploughs than ploughlands are ten a penny, but I don't think Wiltshire was in terminal decline" [Costen, *pers comm.*].

Detachments, Transhumance and the Chew/Chewton 'Estate': A Suggestion

In her study of the Ditcheat and Pennard estates, Penny Stokes has stressed the consequences for territorial arrangements of the severing of ancient economic links between 'parent' manors and outlying resources [Stokes 1996, 46-53], usually in the form of pasture of one kind or another, be it woodland, rough upland grazing, or low-lying moor and marsh. The processes involved are normally seen as very much related to the loss of resources, with parent estates being forced back onto their own 'internal' reserves; indeed, this development is now viewed as one of the primary driving forces behind the emergence of Midland-type open-field systems [Fox 1981; 1984; 1996, 8-9; Lewis, Mitchell-Fox and Dyer 1997, 175].

However, it is possible that, conversely, there may also have been instances where adjustments, in the form of *attachments* of land, were made as 'compensation' to those places which had lost valuable external resources as a result of estate fragmentation. This may have been especially so where the process occurred as a single, deliberate and controlled act of alienation, when the putative compensatory element could be 'built-in' as an integral part of the overall scheme. Such developments in the pre-Conquest period might well emerge in medieval arrangements in the form of a territory with otherwise inexplicable links to detached areas, perhaps distinguishable from ancient transhumance relationships by the general lack of a dense droveway infrastructure such as Everitt has described for Kent [Everitt 1986, 267-270; Fox 1996, 16], or the complete absence of mother-daughter church dependencies. The possession by Chewton hundred of its detached block in the northern Somerset levels, consisting of the parishes of Kingston Seymour, Brockley, and probably Yatton, may well be an example of this [Thorn and Thorn 1980, 375].

I have suggested, developing Michael Costen's proposal, that the estate at Chew granted to the see of Wells as part of its original endowment, was carved out of an ancient, royal 'river-estate' centred on Chew, but extending before this alienation to cover most of the area later represented by the hundreds of Chew and Chewton. By extension therefore, it seems likely that within this putative Chew estate, resources would have been shared, and imbalances in the availability of pasture countered, by intercommoning and the short-distance movement of animals [Fox 1996, 5-6]; the place-name Chew Stoke we have already noted in this respect.

The Mendip plateau above Chewton was, as we have already seen, part of an extensive tract of traditional intercommoning for the summer grazing of livestock, but especially for sheep [Neale 1976, 94-95]. It was also, and still is, notoriously inhospitable in winter: virtually treeless before the systematic planting of windbreaks and with few artificial boundaries before the enclosure movement in the late 18th and early 19th centuries, and so with little or no protection for stock. Not surprisingly, the quality of grazing at that season was very poor [Williams 1976, 102-

104]. However, while the putative Chew/Chewton estate retained its integrity, there was also available to the communities within it the extensive pastures of the area immediately north of Chew Magna (around Chew Hill and North Wick), north-west of Norton Malreward, and especially the steeply-sloping flanks of Dundry Hill. If one allows that the exposed plateau top around Chewton lies generally in the range about 230-260m OD, the north Chew/Dundry pastures at their most elevated attain only just over 230m, immediately south-west of Dundry, but for the most part are considerably lower. Equally important is the fact that owing to the very broken nature of the natural topography in this area, they are far less exposed than the Mendip tableland.

This argument is somewhat speculative, but at least a vestige of a possible use of the Dundry slopes as traditional (I mean by this pre-Conquest) transhumance pastures may come in the form of a place-name in the southern part of Dundry parish. Harold Fox has proposed recently that toponyms containing the word 'maiden' (OE *mægden*), may be a manifestation of a traditional practice of girls and young women being assigned to guard livestock, and specifically stock which had been brought to that place from somewhere else [Fox 1996, 13]. The name Maidenhead occurs in a central position on the Dundry/north Chew pastures. No early spellings of this word are yet available, but it is certainly possible that the first element is *mægden*. The second element is problematic; it may be OE heafod, 'head, headland, end of a ridge, river-source' [Gelling 1984, 159-162], which might be thought to suit the topography: the place lies on the northern flank of a pronounced ridge. However, Penny Stokes has alternatively suggested [*pers comm*] that at least some instances of 'head' in modern place-names may be accounted for ultimately by the Welsh word *hafod*, possibly taken into English as the nearest-sounding word in that language, *heafod*, without any knowledge of its original meaning of 'summer dwelling'. Assimilation may have been helped by the coincidental fact that many summer pastures, such as Mendip itself, tended to be upland regions, where the natural topography might lead one to expect OE *heafod* to occur anyway. Tacit support for Stokes's suggestion comes from Cornwall, where Peter Herring has highlighted the close relationship between the (cognate) *havos* settlements, and those with names in *hendre* ('winter or home settlement'); evidence, he suggests, of an extremely ancient system of transhumance fully integrated into the more arable economies of the lowland estate centres. Very similar social, economic and toponymic linkages, arising from transhumant economies, have been described from Wales and most other parts of upland Britain, as well as Ireland [Herring 1996, 35-41, and refs there cited; for Wales, Ward 1997, esp at 105-107].

In the case of Maidenhead in Dundry, we might also suspect that something more than coincidence accounts for its position on the Roman road running north from Chew Magna, over Dundry Hill and on into the modern Bishopsworth area of south Bristol [Tratman, 1963]. Indeed, perhaps the very reason for the survival of

this route arises from its use, through long tradition, as a drove. Penny Stokes, for example [*pers comm*], has suggested a similar rationale behind the acquisition, by the Carthusian priory at Witham, of the area around Charterhouse on Mendip as a grange farm.

If 'head' here is indeed rooted in Welsh *hafod*, questions arise concerning both the antiquity and possible continuity of husbandry traditions which may take us back at least to the pre-Roman Iron Age, if not earlier; for in the fenlands of eastern England, Francis Pryor has emphasised that from at least the Bronze Age, stock management regimes were built very much around what he describes as 'structured mobility', the incessant, seasonal droving of animals through the landscape, a practice taking its cue from the cyclical availability of grazing resources at different locations [Pryor 1998, 89-108]. There may well, therefore, be a parallel here with the very similar kind of economic link between Shapwick, in Whitley hundred, and its western neighbours, which, as we have already noted in the Introduction, forms a central theme of this study's overall Conclusion.

One effect of alienating a large area of the former Chew river estate would be the loss of its grazing grounds to those communities which now found themselves outside the new entity which had Chew Magna (I recognise the anachronistic use of the epithet) at its centre. It is at this stage, I suggest, at some point in the early 10th century, that the new Chewton territory somehow acquired its detached lands to the west. We have already noted the Domesday and toponymic evidence for Kingston's links with Chewton. It would certainly have provided high-quality grazing in the summer, and possibly by this time in the winter as well. The work of Steve Rippon in this area of the northern Somerset Levels is increasingly producing a picture of extensive reclamation, and intensive settlement and exploitation in the Roman period. Thereafter, a marine incursion, the full extent of which is not yet clear, may have been partially responsible for the abandonment of certain areas of lower-lying land which had previously been reclaimed. The discontinuity was only temporary however, and by 1086 "the higher coastal parts of the Somerset and Avonmouth Levels were certainly extensively settled and partly reclaimed.....although the evidence is fragmentary, it appears that recolonisation of these previously flooded areas had begun by the ninth century or earlier" [Rippon 1997, 126-127].

Chronologically, Kingston Seymour itself seems to represent relatively late colonisation. Unlike estate centres such as Yatton and Congresbury, it does not lie on a junction between the low-lying levels and surrounding higher ground. Such 'ecotones' represent resource interfaces and are regarded as primary settlement foci; settlements in them are likely to be earlier than those where the range of economic resources is more limited [*pers comm* Vince Russett; Aston and Gerrard 1999, 8]. Rippon, for example, observes that "there were a series of major post-Roman estate centres on the fen-edge, many coincident with hillforts and villas, controlling large estates which included areas of upland, foothills and the Levels" [Rippon 1997, 133]. It is, *prima facie*, probable that

Kingston, on a low-lying, isolated site well out into the North Somerset levels, surrounded on all sides by reclaimed marshland, was a 'colonising' settlement. Its superficially anomalous position may, though, be explicable in terms of a very slight height advantage; for Gilbert points out that whereas "on the North Somerset Levels the majority of the clay belt is approximately 5.5m OD with areas close to the coast rising to 6.0m.....in Kingston Seymour the present land-surface averages at between 5.5 and 6.4m OD" [Gilbert 1996, 23]. There are also no fewer than five probable 'infield' sites at Kingston; that is, enclosures of varying size, characterised by curvilinear boundaries, and suggested by Rippon to represent the earliest phase of the Saxon recolonisation of the Levels [Gilbert 1996, 23-24; Rippon 1997, 172]. It is, though, problematic whether, at the time of its foundation, the area around Kingston was suitable for anything but the most limited arable cultivation, and it is possible that initially at least its intended function was as a source of pasture. If so, the progress of reclamation and drainage may have tipped the economic balance away from the original *raison d'etre*, and certainly by the late 11th century a large reserve of arable was recorded there, producing a pattern of mixed farming that was probably not dissimilar to that practised by the late Roman period, when reclamation of this area was well advanced [Rippon 1997, 117-118; 177-178]. It is notable that other settlements hard by, with names in *tūn*, occupy topographically similar positions; citing especially Puxton, Icelton and Bourton, Rippon comments that "their date of foundation is not known, though a late Saxon date cannot be ruled out....." [Rippon 1997, 172].

Although a king's *tūn*, Kingston Seymour is palpably not a seminal or primary settlement, even given that some kind of tenurial link with royalty is obviously understood; in this respect, it conforms closely to the pattern revealed by the majority of those places in England with the same name. Jill Bourne, in a recent survey, has concluded that the majority are attached to places which are "small and peripheral", that, again in most cases, it is likely "the name is not of an early coinage", and that "far from being settlements which were centres of political importance they are remarkable by their very lack of significance" [Bourne 1987-88, 29, 36].

It is possible, indeed likely, that before the early 10th century, settlement of some description had occurred in the vicinity of what was later to become Kingston Seymour; exactly what form it may have taken is problematic, but an impression of dispersal is implicit in what has already been said (above) about the number of infield sites to be found at various locations in the parish. I suggest, however, on the basis of the evidence available, that royal interest in the estate was late, and that the acquisition, and perhaps renaming, of Kingston by the crown, to be used specifically as detached, high-quality grazing, was related directly to its loss of the northern part of the old Chew river estate to the new See of Wells after 909. In one respect, the attachment to Chewton is unexpected since it was by no means the nearest royal centre to Kingston; Cheddar is considerably closer.

However, it was Chewton which was suffering the loss of resources, and it is therefore reasonable to ask why the crown did not instead obtain somewhere closer to it, an adjacent holding for example, that could have been brought physically and more conveniently within the bounds of the royal estate. The reason for this is unclear, and we can only speculate; however, one possible answer, related to land ownership, may also explain how the process was carried out.

Both Rippon [1997, 134-138] and Broomhead [*pers comm*] propose that by the early 8th century, Kingston was part of a large estate centred on Congresbury, which in turn was the successor of an Iron Age territory whose focus had been the hillfort at Cadbury/Congresbury. Ownership at this time is unclear: it is likely that a religious community was ensconced at Congresbury long before the time of Ine, whose charter, now lost, purportedly granting land there to the church of Sherborne, is known only from a brief note in a late fourteenth century ms [O'Donovan 1988, xlvi-xlvii; Edwards 1988, 243-251]. However, crucially, it seems clear that Alfred's oft-quoted 'gift' in the late ninth century to his priest Asser, of the *monasteria* of Banwell and Congresbury, amounted merely to the exercise of the royal prerogative in what was effectively the appointment of an abbot, and did *not* involve a transfer of rights over land, from the crown, to the church; indeed, we can suggest that at the time of Alfred's intervention, the community at Congresbury already owned extensive lands in the area, and perhaps the greater part of the CadCong successor estate, including 'Kingston'. The central question here is 'who owned Congresbury and its satellites by the end of 909', to which an answer is suggested by Keynes and Lapidge: "both places [ie Congresbury and Banwell] were apparently given to Asser as his personal property, but when he died in 909 they were probably assigned.....to the new bishopric of Wells" [1983, 264, n192; and *cf* O'Donovan 1988, xlvi].

I think it a reasonable inference, therefore, that Kingston's attachment to Chewton arises from a straightforward exchange, in or after 909, by which, to compensate the crown for its gift of Chew Magna, the new See of Wells carved out of its recently-acquired Congresbury lands, and handed over into royal possession, a tract of low-lying, probably relatively under-developed and sparsely settled moor which nonetheless could have been recognised as having considerable potential as rich pasture. Both Yatton and Brockley may have been part of the same accommodation (below). Figure 30 represents a basic attempt to represent this process diagrammatically. The estate subsequently became a king's *tūn*, and it may have been from this point that recolonisation, drainage and improvement gained momentum, under royal encouragement. Developing this argument still further, one wonders whether royal ownership was also a cue, perhaps later in the 10th century, for a move towards nucleation of settlement, a development perhaps to be associated with a desire to exploit more efficiently an increasing area of arable being progressively won from the moor. Certainly field name evidence suggests some abandonment of pre-Conquest isolated farmstead sites, but conditions could not

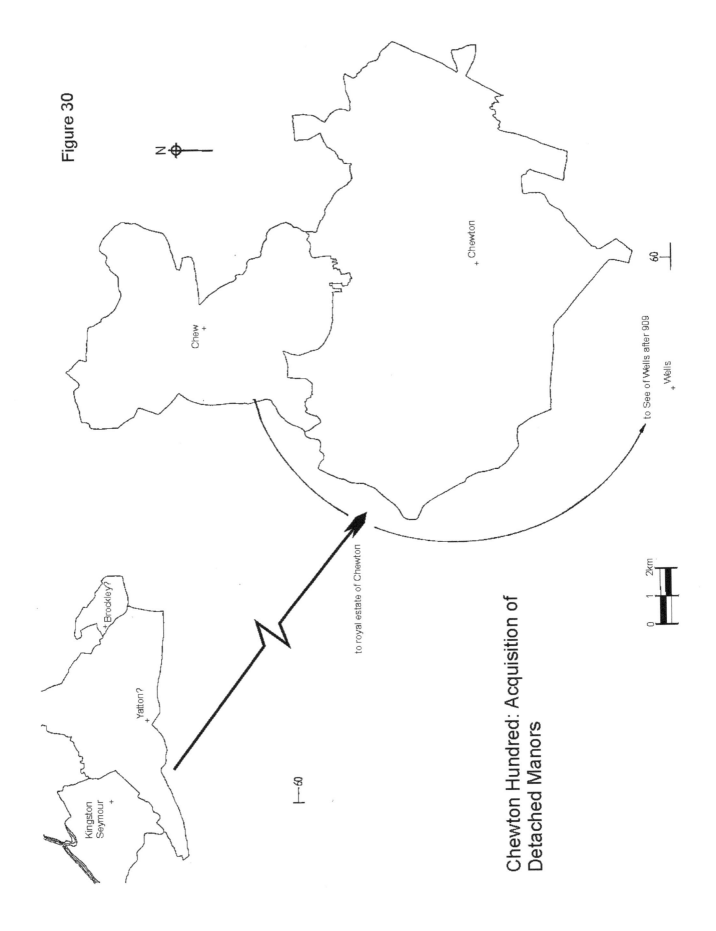

Figure 30

Chew

Chewton

+ Brockley?

Yatton?
+

Kingston
Seymour
+

to royal estate of Chewton

to See of Wells after 909

+ Wells

Chewton Hundred: Acquisition of
Detached Manors

have been entirely favourable to full nucleation since, as probably combined the main, central settlement with a persistent scatter of isolated farms [Gilbert 1996, 16-24]. One reason for this may be that, by the very nature of the way in which its arable evolved, in a piecemeal, somewhat haphazard fashion, Kingston may never have developed a fully-fledged Midland-type open-field system, despite the probably extensive area of arable under cultivation during the high middle ages [Rippon 1997, 225, 226-227]. Indeed, a dispersed or partially-dispersed settlement pattern was often a corollary of this kind of 'colonising' area, where intaking was often carried out an individual basis, and social cohesiveness, as reflected in agrarian regimes, tended to be weaker than in older-settled places with extensive arable where communal farming systems had evolved [*cf* Lewis *et al* 1997, 213-216]. However, it is open to question how far this might apply to moor settlements like Kingston, where historically, maintenance of sea and river defences was accepted as very much a responsibility devolving upon entire communities. It is possible, in fact, to argue with equal conviction the *other* way, and in the next chapter I will outline a case for royal ownership having a *centrifugal*, rather than a centripetal effect on the settlement pattern in Kingston. Gilbert also wonders about the nature of the pre-Conquest settlement sites revealed by field names such as worth, *huish* and *wic*: her comment that "whether they were occupied on a seasonal or permanent basis is unclear" [Gilbert 1996, 19], brings us full circle, and is a useful reminder of my basic premise here, namely that Kingston may have seen its most rapid development only after a period as little more than a glorified royal shieling [*cf* Everitt's description of the overwhelmingly transhumant economy of Romney Marsh in Kent; Everitt 1986, 57-65].

Yatton's attachment to Chewton Hundred in and before 1086 might be explained in the same way, although if so, in that case the estate had been lost by the crown to secular lords before 1066 (as, indeed, had Kingston itself), and regained by the church, in the form of the see of Wells, between the Conquest and Domesday. Yatton's very much higher status may ultimately have made its loss to the See unsustainable: it was rated at 20 hides in 1086, and its church, with a chapelry at Kenn [Torr 1974-79, 89] and a hide of land separately rated in Domesday, may at some point have been a minster [Costen 1992, 105-107]. Topographically, it certainly seems clear that Kenn parish has been carved out of a once-larger Yatton estate [*pers comm* Magnus Alexander]. Brockley's inclusion in the Chewton detachment may, as the name suggests, be related to its use as a woodland resource; and as the Thorns point out, Kingston Seymour, Yatton and Brockley would together "have formed a large single detachment" [Thorn and Thorn 1980, 375].

Whitley Hundred in Domesday Book

Table 4 presents the basic Domesday statistics for Whitley. As we have already seen (Chapter Four), it is strictly speaking anachronistic to talk of 'Whitley' hundred in 1086. This aside though, we have also already noted the

Gilbert has shown, the medieval settlement pattern fact that, at that date, only Puriton, of all the later Whitley manors, did not belong to Glastonbury, and it is possible that at least part of it lay in a different hundred at that date [DB Somerset f91, col b; Thorn and Thorn 1980, 357, 11,1]. Domesday to some extent reflects the former division of the old *Pouholt* estate between Loxley and Ringoldsway hundreds. Morland has suggested that the 30 hides centred on Shapwick in 1086, and the 30 centred on Walton, together make up the 60 hides granted to Glastonbury in 729 by charter S253, although this is not to say that the constituent estates remained the same between 729 and 1086 [Morland 1990, 35-36]. Morland's own reconstruction of Greater Shapwick in 1086 may be open to amendment since he makes up the estate's 30H by including the 3H in Cossington and 2½H in Stawell. In fact neither was part of Shapwick at that time, and the 'missing' 5H is probably to be found at Moorlinch (below). Since we know that *Pouholt* formed the 'core' abbey estate, it can be no coincidence that all the manors listed under Shapwick in Domesday were in Loxley hundred at that time (Edington, Catcott, Chilton, Sutton and Woolavington), while all those listed under Walton were in Ringoldsway (Compton, Ashcott and Pedwell). The importance of Shapwick is becoming increasingly apparent: not only did it contain the western moot site of Loxley Wood, but, perhaps somehow linked to Moorlinch (Chapters Four and Six) its church was probably a minster, on or adjacent to a site that had been occupied by a substantial Roman complex. In addition, Domesday notes that Shapwick itself was free of geld, and Michael Costen has suggested that the 5-hide tax burden which should ostensibly be allocated to Shapwick in fact devolved on Moorlinch [Costen 1994b, 77]. At the rate of 0.75 hides per ploughland of taxable land, the 20 tax-free ploughlands noted in Domesday at Shapwick would amount to some 15 hides, a substantial holding in its own right [Costen, *pers comm*]. In these circumstances, Shapwick's position in Domesday, at the head of the western half of the former *Pouholt* estate, appears logical; and indeed Abrams, observing that "very ancient holdings often did not pay tax", has gone so far as tentatively to suggest that the very early grant of 20 cassati in *Pouelt* by Ine in 705 or 706 (S248) may be represented in Domesday by Shapwick's untaxed 20 ploughlands [Abrams 1994, 74].

Walton's corresponding position is, however, rather more difficult to explain. Walton itself gives no outward indication that it was a manor of anything more than ordinary status; certainly its church was neither a minster nor a mother: on the contrary, it was no more than a dependent chapelry of Street [Aston 1986, 75; Torr 1974-79, 86 and 94]; and unlike Shapwick, Walton contained no geld-free land. Butleigh, however, as we have already seen, was a large royal estate before passing to Glastonbury, it contained the Ringoldsway moot site within its bounds, and if not a minster, was at least the mother church of a chapelry at Baltonsborough [Aston 1986, 74]. We might reasonably have expected these facts to be reflected in the Domesday entry for that manor. However, it seems clear that Butleigh, the subject of its

TABLE 4   WHITLEY HUNDRED IN DOMESDAY BOOK

Place	Domesday Manor	Parish	Geld	Plough-lands	Ploughs	Holder 1066	Holder 1086	Sub-tenant(s) 1066	Sub-tenant 1086	Value 1066	Value 1086
Shapwick	Yes	Yes	30H in total	40	16	G'bury	G'bury		See sub-manors	Not given	£12
Shapwick	Yes	Yes	5H[2]	20 geld-free		G'bury	G'bury	Demesne			
Sutton Mallet	Yes	Yes (but now in Stawell parish)	5H (part of S'wick)		5	G'bury	G'bury	5 thegns	Roger of Courseilles	100s	£4
Edington	Yes	Yes	5H (part of S'wick)		3	G'bury	G'bury	3 thegns	Roger of Courseilles	100s	60s
Chilton	Yes	Yes	5H (part of S'wick)		4½	G'bury	G'bury	2 thegns	Roger of Courseilles	£4	£4
Catcott	Yes	Yes	5H (part of S'wick)		5	G'bury	G'bury	3 thegns	Roger of Courseilles	100s	100s
Woolaving-ton[3]	Yes	Yes	5H (part of S'wick)		8	G'bury	G'bury	Alwi Banneson	Alfred of Spain	£7	£7
Walton	Yes	Yes	19H	40	22	G'bury	G'bury		Demesne	15s	£15
Ashcott	Yes	Yes	2H (part of Walton)	3	2	G'bury	G'bury	Alwi Banneson	Roger of Courseilles	40s	40s
Ashcott	Yes	Yes	3H (part of Walton)			G'bury	G'bury	Could not be sep. from the church	Walter of Douai		
Pedwell	Yes	No (in Ashcott)	3H (part of Walton)		11	G'bury	G'bury	Could not be sep. from the church	Walter of Douai		£8
Compton	Yes	No (in Dundon)	5H (part of Walton)			G'bury	G'bury	Could not be sep. from the church	Roger of Courseilles		
Dundon	Yes	Yes	5H	4	5	G'bury	G'bury	Algar	Roger of Courseilles	£6	100s
Cossington	Yes	Yes	3H	6	6	G'bury	G'bury	Alwin Pike	Walter of Douai	£6	£6
Greinton	Yes	Yes	2½H	2½	2	G'bury	G'bury	Wulfmer	Gerard 'Fossarius'	50s	50s
Stawell	Yes	Yes	2½H	2½	2	G'bury	G'bury	Alfward	Godescal	5s	40s
Butleigh	Yes	Yes	3V	1½	1½	G'bury	G'bury	Winegot the Priest	Roger of Courseilles	6s	10s
Butleigh	Yes	Yes	10H		11	G'bury	G'bury	Two thegns	Demesne	60s	£10
Butleigh	Yes	Yes	8H			G'bury	G'bury		Thurstan		
Butleigh	Yes	Yes	2H	20	7	G'bury	G'bury		Roger of Courseilles	£7	£7
Butleigh	Yes	Yes	½H		1	G'bury	G'bury		Alstan	5s	10s
Overleigh	Yes	No (in Street)	4H	10	9	G'bury	G'bury	1H of thegnland	Demesne	60s	£8
Ham	Yes	Yes	17H	20	11	G'bury	G'bury		Demesne	£4	£10
Ham	Yes	Yes	1¼H			G'bury	G'bury		Robert of Auberville		
Ham	Yes	Yes	5H		4	G'bury	G'bury	Leofric, Alfwold, Aelmer	Serlo de Burcy		110s
Ham	Yes	Yes	¾H			G'bury	G'bury		Gerard 'Fossarius'		

---

[2] The geld of 5H for Shapwick itself may in fact have been levied on Moorlinch. Costen 1994b.
[3] The Woolavington return includes an even smaller sub-manor of ½ hide held by Warmund, valued at 10s in 1086 and with a single plough.

own charter at the beginning of the 9th century (Chapter Six), was not part of the original *Pouholt* estate. Possibly a continuing importance from an earlier period may be the reason behind the location of the Ringoldsway moot site here: such sites appear frequently to be associated with central places in the landscape and in many cases probably pre-date the hundredal system [Aston 1986, 53-54; Gelling 1992, 142-145; Pantos 1999]. At present it seems best to explain Walton's apparently pre-eminent position in Domesday simply as the result of administrative expediency arising from a knowledge of Walton's membership of the former *Pouholt* estate. By 1086 *Pouholt* had become split in two, and the requirement of the compilers of Domesday was for a manor to which they could allocate the easternmost half of 30 hides. They would have been aware that Butleigh, although containing the hundred moot site, lay outside *Pouholt*, and was not, therefore, suitable for their purposes [Corcos 1983]. Apart from its former inclusion within *Pouholt*, Walton may have suggested itself as being a more conveniently central location than Butleigh, which lay at the eastern extremity of Ringoldsway hundred. The choice may, indeed, have been a conscious foreshadowing of the later hundredal rearrangement which created Whitley out of Loxley and Ringoldsway, for the moot site of the later hundred lay within Walton parish, on its western side hard by the eastern boundary of Ashcott, as the place-name (*leah*) might suggest, in the vicinity of Whitley Wood [Gelling 1984, 205]. In the late 19th century, the ruins of the Whitley hundred house were still visible here [Dickinson 1889, xi]. Indeed since at least the early 14th century, a building used "for the pleas of the hundred" had stood on the site, being recorded as a boundary mark in a perambulation of the manor of Ashcott in 1325 (BL Egerton 3321, f52v, survey of Abbot Sodbury) and of both Ashcott and Walton in 1515 (survey of Abbot Beere; *ex inf* Mike Thompson). Even as late as 1086, it seems clear that Walton still retained vestiges of its former affinities, looking as it did west, to the old estate, since two of its three manorial appendages at that date, Ashcott and Pedwell, seem also to have lain in *Pouholt*. Only Compton, lying outside it, appears anomalous in this respect, its attachment to Walton probably arising from a link of common ownership with one of the two Ashcott manors, held by Roger of Courseuilles [DB Somerset f90, col b; Aston 1994, 232, fig 11.8].

The perpetuation of vestiges of the former estate structure, at least in outline, means that by its very nature, Domesday is not as useful a source for those manors lying within the former *Pouholt* estate as it otherwise might have been. The two 'head' *Pouholt* manors in 1086 were Shapwick and Walton. Under these places, the various subordinate vills are identified individually by name, and Exon Domesday, rectifying deficiencies in the Exchequer text, gives an account of the pre-Conquest holder(s), the annual value in 1066 and 1086, and the number of ploughs in operation on each manor [Costen 1994b; Table 4]. Critically though, not even the Exon book gives the number of ploughlands attached to each place: we are told only that the Greater Shapwick estate had 40 ploughlands,

and that a further 20 ploughlands were tax-free. Costen, who has examined the Shapwick Domesday entry in detail, considers that Exon, in locating "both demesne and tenant land.....on the untaxed twenty hides", is the more reliable account [Costen 1994b, 77]. Without ploughland figures for the individual appendant manors there are, then, for Shapwick and Walton, clear difficulties in carrying out even a crude exercise into both the degree of arable expansion since the time of the original hidation (probably in the early 10th century; Costen 1992, 117 and 123), as expressed by the ratio of ploughlands to hides; for there is no way of knowing how the assessment of 40 ploughlands was distributed. To the untaxed 20 ploughlands it seems reasonable to assign the total of 16 ploughs which Domesday notes for Shapwick itself. This represents a notional potential for expansion of some 20% in this core, and possibly ancient area of the Greater Shapwick estate; perhaps even by 1086 there were areas in the northern part of the manor, on the fringes of the levels, which although low-lying might have been perceived as a useful reserve of arable. It is possible that this picture holds true for the Greater Shapwick estate as a whole: the 40 taxed ploughlands carried a total of only 26½ ploughs, allowing an increase of nearly 34% distributed across all the appendant manors. All the Shapwick 'satellites', with the exception of Sutton Mallet, lie on the north side of Polden, and their lands extend into the levels surrounding the Brue Valley. To the south, the lands of Sutton, now in Stawell parish, would have reached onto Sedgemoor, as do those of Moorlinch, unnamed in Domesday. How much weight we can give to the hidage values of these places as an indication of agricultural capacity is questionable. The regularity of the assessments, at 5H each, invites suspicion and seems to betray the hand of the monastic accountant. So Michael Costen implies when he suggests "that Greater Shapwick was assessed as a unit for geld and the abbey then apportioned the tax liabilities onto its tenants....." [Costen 1994b, 77].

A similar problem is encountered at Ham, which in 1086 consisted of a large manor held directly by the Abbot, and three smaller holdings, assessed altogether at 17H. Collectively these are assigned 20 ploughlands, worked by a total of 15 ploughs (11 on the Abbot's estate and 4 on the others), so that in general terms we can suggest both that there had been some expansion since the original hidation (in the order of just under 18%), and also that there was some potential for further growth in the arable capacity (around 33%). Since, however, the ploughlands figures are not broken down in detail, it is impossible to say whether this also holds true for any or all of the smaller holdings (Table 4). A similar exercise carried out for a selection of Polden vills by Dr Rippon may stand in need of some revision, to take more account of the nature of the Domesday assessments, especially those in which some places are treated as appendant to head manors, like Shapwick and Walton [Rippon 1994, 242, Table 12.1]. At Ashcott, for example, there were two manors in 1086, both part of the Walton estate. Rippon notes the total of 5H for both, but assigns to them only the 3 ploughlands of Roger of Courseuilles's 2H holding which is given under a separate heading. Walter of Douai held a further 3H at Ashcott, but to this holding it is impossible to assign a figure for ploughlands since the 40 noted in Domesday devolved upon the rest of the Walton estate, consisting of Walter's Ashcott manor, Compton and Pedwell. There is no way of knowing how this figure was distributed among these constituent manors, but in any event, the total ploughland figure for both Ashcott manors should certainly be greater than 3.

Use of the term 'upland' to characterise Shapwick's economy is perhaps also somewhat questionable [Rippon 1994, 250]. The word is reasonable if being used in a relative sense, since from a purely topographical perspective the Poldens are indeed upland when compared to the surrounding terrain north and south, much of it lying at or below OD. However, while it is true that in the medieval period Shapwick contained a high proportion of open-field arable land, its economy was nonetheless intimately interwoven with the resources provided by its commonable share of the Brue Valley moors to the north and also, I would argue, in the pre-Conquest period, of Sedgemoor to the south. The Brue Valley lands account for all the 1,015 acres enclosed at Shapwick in the years after 1784 by parliamentary act [Tate 1948, 41], a proportion of about a third of the area of the modern parish (just under 3,000 acres, excluding historical detachments; Aston 1989, 5). This could hardly be described as an 'upland' manor.

Even away from the former *Pouholt* estate, it seems that the evidence of Domesday needs to be treated with equal care, although it may be useful for indicating general trends. At Sowi, for example, we have already noted that the estate included Weston Zoyland, Middlezoy and Othery, and here there appears by 1086 to have been a fairly emphatic increase in the assessment compared to that of the original hidation (Table 4). In 1086 the number of ploughlands in Sowi reveals a liability 67% greater than it was before 1066. In the short space between the Conquest and Domesday, the value of the manor more than doubled, from £10 to £24, and a potential for even further expansion may be revealed by the fact that ploughlands exceeded the number of ploughs actually in operation at Domesday by a factor of 25%. Bearing in mind Sowi's topographical context, increases of this order, if real, can only reasonably be accounted for by vigorous reclamation activity on the surrounding levels and moors, which, from the work of David Musgrove (cited in Chapter Eight), we know was certainly characteristic of this area in the post-Conquest period. This should come as no surprise, for elsewhere within Whitley, on the southern side of the Poldens, Domesday provides further, if rather indirect clues about the progress of drainage in this part of the Levels. In 1086, the manor of Greinton was held from the Abbot of Glastonbury by one Girard "the ditcher", and although a marshland estate it certainly had some arable, for two ploughteams were in operation there. Girard also held smaller manors at Ham (also in Whitley) and Lopen, and his presence in the levels may be highly significant, since it is quite possible, as Hoskins has suggested, that he had "been brought in by the first Norman Abbot.....to undertake

a large-scale drainage programme". In support of this, Hoskins cites the sometimes spectacular increases in the value of some of the Abbey's marshland estates between 1066 and 1086 [Hoskins 1982, 167]. Darby also notes this feature, but is more cautious about the possible reasons for it [Darby 1967, 170-171]. If, however, Hoskins is correct, it means, as Rippon has also intimated [Rippon 1994, 242], that Domesday provides us with the first well-documented and systematic, if somewhat oblique evidence that by the late 11th century, drainage activity on the levels was once more being undertaken on a scale and with an energy unmatched since the Roman period [Leach and Leech 1982, 71; Rippon 1992, 1994a].

Carhampton Hundred in Domesday Book

By the most perceptive of its early scholars it was recognised that, interrogated correctly, Domesday might have much to reveal about the nature of settlement patterns in areas dominated by isolated farmsteads and hamlets, where manors were small, and large, nucleated villages rare [eg Maitland 1897, 38-39]. However, the first serious attempt to investigate this question empirically was made by W G Hoskins, who demonstrated beyond all doubt, in a seminal study whose short length belies its importance, that in areas of dispersed settlement it was possible in many cases to relate Domesday holdings directly to the sites of surviving farmsteads [Hoskins 1963]. Hoskins drew his evidence from Devon. There has been no similar, systematic study of the upland regions of west Somerset using specifically the Domesday evidence as a starting point, although Susanna Everett [1967/68] attempted a limited exercise along the same lines for the parishes of Culbone, Porlock and Stoke Pero. Although a pioneering study, a major drawback with Hoskins's work, as with Everett's later on, was that it took little account of deserted farmsteads no longer surviving in the present landscape, a source of evidence which if anything would have strengthened the arguments of both authors for an ancient and continuous pattern of dispersion.

However, even Hoskins himself was well aware of the dangers of assuming an invariable and inevitable coincidence between the detail of the modern settlement pattern and that of the late 11th century; and commenting specifically on Hoskins's findings, Welldon Finn acknowledges the difficulties of reconciling the Domesday figures [Welldon Finn 1967, 235]. This problem of lack of balance in the sources being used to examine dispersed settlement was addressed in Somerset by Aston's study of a large group of Exmoor parishes, which combined an archaeological perspective with a reassessment of a range of documentary evidence [Aston 1983]. The value of such an integrated approach is well evinced in the case of the Domesday manor of Wilmersham in Stoke Pero parish. Everett equates the five villeins recorded in 1086 with five isolated farmsteads surviving to the present day [Everett 1967/68, 57]. However, apart from the farms which she identifies, the later study records at least two other sites which were probably also the locations of medieval farms, now deserted (specifically Prickslade and Nutscale; Aston

1983, 94). There seems no good reason why these also should not be regarded as possible Domesday farms. In areas of dispersed settlement generally, "it is important to realise that many……surviving farms are the result of shrinkage from a small cluster" [Aston 1985, 25]. In Carhampton itself, for example, this process has been demonstrated at Codsend in Cutcombe parish [Aston 1985,

25-26], which was certainly in existence by the late 13th century when two Williams of *Coddesende*, presumably father and son, were recorded in the proceedings of the Exmoor Forest Court [Macdermot 1911, 85]. The chief limitation of documentation is that it will only record the latest date by which a farmstead was in existence, and questions of contemporaneity and relative chronology will

TABLE 5 CARHAMPTON HUNDRED IN DOMESDAY BOOK

Place	Domesday Manor	Parish	Geld	Plough-lands	Ploughs	Holder 1066	Holder 1086	Sub-tenant 1086	Value 1066	Value 1086
Carhampton (with Williton & Cannington)	Yes	Yes	Not rated	100	49	Royal demesne	Royal demesne		Farm of One Night	£100 116s 16½d.
Carhampton (church)			1½H		1½	The church(?)	A priest			30s
Oare	Yes	Yes	1H	6	6	Edric	Ralph of Pomeroy		20s	30s +12 sheep per year due to C'hamp-ton
Luccombe	Yes	Yes	2H	8	7	Qn Edith	Ralph of Limesey		£3	£4
Selworthy	Yes	Yes	1H	5	5	Qn Edith	Ralph of Limesey		20s	25s
Allerford	Yes	No (in Selworthy)	1H	5	3	Edric	Ralph of Limesey		15s	20s +12 sheep per year to C'hampton
Bossington	Yes	No (in Porlock)	1H	5	2	Athelney church	Ralph of Limesey		20s	20s
Treborough	Yes	Yes	½H	5	1 (in demesne, with all of the land save 10 acres).	Edric	Ralph of Limesey			£7 ('laid waste')
Aller	Yes	No (in Carhamp-ton)	2H	4	4	Wulfward	Ralph of Limesey		100s	£6
Aller	Yes	No (in Carhamp-ton)	½H	1½	1½	Brictmer Edmer	Roger of Courseulles	Ogis	5s	8s
'Stowey'	Yes	No (probably in Oare)[4]	1V	3	2 (both in demesne)	Aelmer	Ralph of Pomeroy	Beatrix	20s	20s
Culbone	Yes	Yes	1H 1V	2	1 (customary only)	Osmund Stramin	Bp of Coutances	Drogo	5s	15s
Wilmersham	Yes	No (in Stoke Pero)	1H 1V	5	2		Bp of Coutances	Drogo		30s
Withycombe	Yes	Yes	3H	10	10	Alnoth	Bp of Coutances	Edmer	£4	£6
Almsworthy	Yes	No (location unknown – probably in Exford)	1V	6	4	Edric	Roger of Courseulles		Waste	25s

[4] See Thorn and Thorn 1980, 365, 30.1

Place	Domesday Manor	Parish	Geld	Plough-lands	Ploughs	Holder 1066	Holder 1086	Sub-tenant 1086	Value 1066	Value 1086
Downscombe	Yes	No (in Exford)	1 'Furlong'	1	½	Leofmer	Roger of Courseulles	Aeleva	Waste	2s
Stone	Yes	No (in Exford)	½V	2		Brictric	Roger of Courseulles			Waste
Exford	Yes	Yes	½V	2	½	Aiulf	Roger of Courseulles		Waste	3s
Exford	Yes	Yes	1 'Furlong'	1	½	Edric	Roger of Courseulles	Ednoth	2s	30d
Exford	Yes	Yes	1 'Furlong'	1	½	Wulfwin	Roger of Courseulles	William	30d	30d
Exford	Yes	Yes	1 'Furlong'	'Land for 2 oxen'		Dunn	Wm of Mohun		15d	15d
Exford	Yes	Yes	1½ 'Furlongs'	½ ('but it lies in the pasture')		Sharp	Wm of Mohun		12d	12d
Broadwood	Yes	No (in Carhampton)	½H	1	2	Alric	Wm of Mohun		10s	15s
Avill	Yes	No (in Dunster)	½H	2	1½	Aelfric	Wm of Mohun	Ralph	10s	10s
Staunton	Yes	No (in Minehead)	3V	2	1 (customary only)	Wallo	Wm of Mohun		7s 6d	15s
			1V added	1	–	Held by a thegn as one manor			3s	3s
Old Stowey	Yes	No (in Cutcombe)	1V	1 (demesne only)		Leofing	Wm of Mohun	Durand	3s	10s
Oaktrow	Yes	No (in Cutcombe)	½V	1	1	Manni	Wm of Mohun	Durand	4s	6s
Allercott	Yes	No (in Timberscombe)	½V	2	1	Leofwin	Wm of Mohun	Durand	6s	6s
Myne	Yes	No (in Minehead Without)	½H	2	2 (both in demesne)	Leofwin	Wm of Mohun	Geoffrey	10s	15s
Bratton	Yes	No (in Minehead)	3V	4	4	Aelfric	Wm of Mohun	Roger	5s	30s
Knowle	Yes	No (in Timberscombe)	1H	3	2½	Paulinus	Wm of Mohun	Roger	5s	25s
Lux-borough	Yes	Yes	1H	4	4	Two thegns	Wm of Mohun	Ranulf	15s	20s
Lux-borough	Yes	Yes	1H	3	2	Brictmer	Wm of Mohun	Nigel	15s	15s
Bagley	Yes	No (in Stoke Pero)	½V	1	½	Kafli	Roger of Courseulles	Kafli	12d	40d
Combe	Yes	No (in Withycombe)	1V	1	½	Alric	Roger of Courseulles		5s	5s
Gilcott	Yes	No (probably in Withycombe)	½H	1½	1	Edwin	Roger of Courseulles	Alric	3s	10s
Holnicote	Yes	No (in Selworthy)	½H and ½V	2½	2	Aelfric Brictwin	Roger of Courseulles	William	22s	22s
Holnicote			2½V	2	1 (demesne only)		The King	Two nuns, in alms	10s	5s
Doverhay	Yes	No (in Porlock)	1V	1		Edeva	Roger of Courseulles	Alric	10s	8s
Langham	Yes	No (in Lux-borough)	1H	6	6½	3 thegns	Wm of Mohun	3 men-at-arms	30s	30s
Minehead	Yes	Yes	5H	12	13	Algar	Wm of Mohun		100s	£6

Place	Domesday Manor	Parish	Geld	Plough-lands	Ploughs	Holder 1066	Holder 1086	Sub-tenant 1086	Value 1066	Value 1086
'Brown'	Yes	No (in Tre-borough)	1H	6	6½	Edwald	Wm of Mohun	Durand	20s	40s
Bickham	Yes	No (in Timbers-combe)	1V	2	1½	2 thegns	Wm of Mohun	Richard	6s	15s
Rodhuish	Yes	No (in Carhamp-ton)	1V	1	1 (demesne only)	Alfwy	Alfred of Spain	Hugh	2s	6s
Dunster	Yes	Yes	½H	1		Aelfric	Wm of Mohun ('his castle is there')		5s	15s

only be resolved by detailed field survey or, preferably, excavation of individual farmstead sites. Until this (unlikely) event, Everett's case, although thought-provoking, must be regarded as unproven.

Table 5 gives basic details of the manors within Carhampton hundred in 1086, and from it we may note a few general points. Domesday settlement appears relatively sparse in two of Somerset's three topographical extremes: the low marshlands in the centre of the county, and Mendip in the east [Wheatley 1967, 146]. Wheatley attributes this largely to factors relating to the physical environment [147], a perspective about which some scholars now express some unease [Aston 1985, 81; Taylor 1983, 147-8]. The paradox of an apparently higher density in the west, around Quantock and Exmoor, is explained by the nature of settlement in those areas. Because it tended towards dispersal, with isolated, individual farmsteads, the "actual density of population was far smaller than that of the east" [Havinden 1981, 99]. Wheatley [147] makes the same point, citing several examples of western manors with tiny, and almost certainly dispersed populations in 1086. Also, even such a coarse analysis of ploughteam density as that mapped by Wheatley [158], gives hints of regional bias in Somerset, with consistently higher densities in the south and east. The far greater pastoral emphasis in the west, a region of early enclosure displaying little evidence of the fully-fledged, classic Midland open-field system and the probable widespread use of infield/outfield regimes farmed in severalty [Aston 1988, 91-94], is suggested by this map, and confirmed when Somerset's Domesday pasture is also mapped [Wheatley 1967, 183]. In Carhampton hundred, as elsewhere in west Somerset, small, indeed often tiny estates were worked from scattered, isolated farmsteads and hamlets. The Domesday evidence alone suggests very strongly that the framework of settlement in this region was already ancient by 1086, and archaeological evidence, some of it already noted, is tending increasingly to confirm this. Population density was low and the economy predominantly pastoral, a long-held view now supported by the palaeoenvironmental evidence [Straker and Crabtree 1995, and below].

In assessing the Domesday evidence for the whole of Somerset, Michael Costen took Carhampton as one of his case-study areas, observing that, apart from Carhampton itself (at around 20H), "the other thirty-five estates [in the hundred] averaged only 0.94H each and many were only virgates. It seems that these represented very small land units.........which had started as settlements amidst the waste of the slopes of Exmoor and the Brendon Hills. These units could not be subdivided into estates which would support dependent thegns" [Costen 1992, 123]. Costen has also used ploughland/hidage imbalances to gauge the degree of change in the extent of cultivation in Carhampton between the early 10th century and the late 11th, remarking that "there had been a dramatic expansion of agriculture, and by implication of population, in the district" [Costen 1992, 124]. Contrasting this situation with that in the generally low-lying south and east of the county, he concludes that "the tenth century saw a dramatic expansion in the economy of the county as a whole, but the biggest expansion was in the relatively underdeveloped west" [Costen 1992, 125]. We need to set these comments against the perhaps rather more dispassionate, environmental evidence from Exmoor relating to this period, already noted in Chapter Two. While it could not be taken as a firm rebuttal, this data does not at present seem to give much support to the idea of such a rapid expansion of a specifically arable economy in this area within such a relatively short space of time, a matter of less than two centuries. We will return briefly to this theme again a little later on.

From the Domesday evidence on its own, one can make certain observations. Elsewhere in Somerset, in areas of predominantly nucleated settlement, Aston has suggested that where multiple tenure in 1066 (for example, a vill held jointly by a number of thanes), is recorded as having been replaced twenty years later by perhaps one or two manors, this may be reflected on the ground by a number of separate, identifiable settlement foci within a village [Aston 1985, 84; and Ellison 1983, 130-131, and 133, for the example of Stoke-sub-Hamdon]. It is noticeable, however, how very few of the Domesday vills in Carhampton hundred were in multiple tenure in 1066, so that scope for agglomeration of settlement form would anyway have been extremely limited; and twenty years later, multiple manors were equally scarce, Exford being the prime example with five recorded holdings. The inference must be that the vast majority of tenures in 1066 were small farmsteads capable of supporting only tiny populations, in many cases perhaps no more than a single household. In any case, since Domesday records five separate, named holders at Exford in 1066, it seems highly unlikely that in the succeeding twenty years there had been any appreciable change in the settlement pattern; it is certainly possible that of the eight Domesday holdings within the later Exford parish [Bush 1994, 97], the five called Exford in 1086 were all within Exford itself: the tithe map does suggest the existence of at least two foci within the village. However, this seems inherently unlikely, especially since three other named Domesday manors, Almsworthy, Downscombe and Stone, were isolated farms in other parts of the parish [*cf* Aston 1983, 92-93].

Table 5 also shows that, in general, it was those places which later emerged as parish centres which Domesday records as showing the most spectacular increases in their assessment between 1066 and 1086, in terms of the difference between the numbers of hides and ploughlands (see esp Cutcombe, Luccombe, Luxborough, Minehead, Oare, Porlock, Selworthy, Stoke Pero, Timberscombe, Treborough, Withycombe and Wootton Courtenay). Perhaps this is not unexpected, since it is also generally these places which, against a background of tiny holdings sometimes as small as a furlong (¼ of a virgate), stand out in 1066 as having a hide or multiples thereof, and it seems as though the ploughland reassessment is merely confirming the continuing primacy of these places. This is further supported by the fact that many of the later parish centres, in 1086, were kept back in the hands of the chief tenant as demesne (Cutcombe, Dunster, three of the Exford holdings, the larger of the two Luccombe manors, Minehead, Oare, Selworthy, Stoke Pero, Treborough, Wootton Courtenay). Dunster is a somewhat special case in this respect, its latent importance scarcely reflected in its Domesday taxable capacity: its assessment between 1066 and 1086 increased from half a hide to only a single ploughland. But Dunster was the site of the Mohun castle and the administrative centre of their barony, and was almost certainly already showing indications of incipient urbanism (I am grateful to Mick Aston for this latter point). The increase in the annual value from 5s to 15s may, therefore, derive more from the profits of both manorial jurisdiction and from Dunster's development as a town, than from an expansion of agricultural production [Aston and Leech 1977, 45-47; Gathercole 1996].

Particularly notable in the Domesday entries are those places which are recorded as waste in 1066, but which are assigned a value and a ploughland rating twenty years later [Welldon Finn and Wheatley 1967, 188-190]. Almsworthy, Downscombe and the largest of the five Exford manors all fall into this category. Treborough is rather different in that it is assigned a value, which remains unchanged between 1066 and 1086, and is described as having "been laid waste". Its five ploughlands in 1086 were worked by only one (demesne) plough. The inference is that the manor was at the latter date still relatively unproductive, possibly after a period of complete stagnation, but that its potential for arable expansion was recognised. Perhaps the most interesting case is that of Almsworthy, which in the space of twenty years went from waste to an assessment of six ploughlands, over half of which potential was actually realised by the four ploughs

in operation there in 1086. We might initially think that these 'waste' places in 1086 indicate farms which were new at that time, having been founded at some point since the Conquest. However, this cannot be the case, since all were rated for geld in 1066, and while, as Barbara Yorke observes, "it would appear that a system of hidage assessments must have been in place before our written records begin" [Yorke 1995, 73], the systematic hidage ratings of Domesday, applying to individual estates, had probably become fixed by the early 10th century [Costen 1992, 117 and 123]. Welldon Finn and Wheatley may therefore be correct to conclude that "the waste of these entries was presumably.....land that had gone out of cultivation.....it seems as though there had been some local tragedy or as if marginal land had gone out of cultivation" [Welldon Finn and Wheatley 1967, 190]; although we should also be mindful of David Palliser's strictures on our general ignorance of the nature of Domesday Book 'waste', arising from his reassessment of the Yorkshire folios and their oft-cited 'evidence' for the Harrying of the North in 1069-70 [Palliser 1993].

Nonetheless, the implications for the dynamics of settlement in these areas of Carhampton are intriguing, for it suggests that there was a constant 'background turnover', with farms falling out of use, their sites lying abandoned for a period and then perhaps either being re-occupied or replaced by habitation sites elsewhere. It is suggested that the evidence of Domesday Book is merely scratching the surface of this process.

Carhampton: Economy, Fields, Problems and Possibilities

We can hardly doubt that the character of the terrain and, within historic times at least, the climate of much of Carhampton hundred had a significant role to play in moulding a 'background' economy that was always largely pastoral in nature, with parts of high Exmoor receiving an annual average precipitation in excess of 1500mm or 59ins [Fullard and Darby 1978, 24; OS 1996]. The *extent* of that influence may, though, need to be reconsidered. Until relatively recently, the orthodox view on the relationship between climate and settlement in upland regions was informed largely by the work of Parry, based on studies in the Lammermuir Hills in south-east Scotland. Parry suggested that the altitude frontier for viable cereal cultivation is highly sensitive to climatic variability [Parry 1985, 45], and if accepted, the implications for medieval settlement in the higher parts of Carhampton are clear. Indeed Parry counts Exmoor in general as one of a number of regions where, to a large extent in response to cyclical climatic shifts, "an upward advance of cultivation reached its peak between AD 1100-1300 and was converted into a movement of widespread retreat in the fourteenth century" [Parry 1985, 47].

But is this perspective a correct, or at the least, a helpful one? Much more recently, this work has been subjected to reassessment, and a consideration of new environmental evidence has undermined the fundamental basis of Parry's argument. Using chiefly pollen analysis, and taking as his study area the Cheviot Hills, somewhat further south than the Lammermuirs, Tipping has demonstrated that, *contra* Parry, evidence for abandonment of both settlement and arable agriculture is in fact ambiguous and indeed probably illusory [cited in Coles and Mills 1998, x; Tipping 1998, esp at 46].

This is merely part of a radical reappraisal of the whole problem of exactly what we mean by 'marginality', and it is rapidly becoming apparent that the issue is a far more complex and difficult one than the 'Parry thesis' might suggest. Recently, dissenting voices have begun to question the idea of the 'margin' and whether it has any real meaning in the light of increasing knowledge about the ways in which past societies manipulated their environment and managed the resources which they found within it. For the prehistorians, Young and Simmonds stress the resilience of late Bronze Age society in the north of England, dismissing earlier suggestions of widespread desertions of upland sites as a result of climatic deterioration, and arguing instead that communities merely adjusted their agrarian regimes to take account of changed conditions, with considerable success. The northern uplands in the Iron Age were characterised by stability and continuity, not displacement [Young and Simmonds, 1995].

Of more immediate relevance for present purposes is the fact that this question of 'marginality' has also recently been subjected to increasing scrutiny by scholars of the medieval period, such as Astill and Grant [1988, 230-232]. The most sustained and damaging attack has come from Mark Bailey, who in a seminal paper argues strongly that the whole concept needs far tighter definition, and that current orthodoxy relies much too heavily on the misguided belief that medieval English agriculture was above all a *subsistence* economy, whose every aspect was geared to providing cereals for consumption by the producers at the point of production. His suggestion is that 'marginality' was controlled chiefly not by the dictates of subsistence and soil quality, but by a whole range of external factors, particularly the influence of markets, the level of technology being applied in agrarian regimes, and the strength or otherwise of seigneurial authority. Depending on the complex interaction of these circumstances, it was perfectly possible for an area of notionally 'poor' soil-quality to be less 'marginal' *economically* than an area where the soil-quality was high. Like his prehistorian colleagues, Bailey specifically stresses the flexibility and sophistication of medieval agriculture and its ability to react and adapt to changing conditions, making the best and most appropriate use of available resources, and taking decisions in which environmental considerations such as soil-quality played a very minor role [Bailey 1989]. Such views seem now to be working their way steadily towards received orthodoxy; Ward, for example, explicitly rejects the idea of "a static frontier for settlement on what are today perceived as marginal landscapes", and prefers instead to see "a broader zone within which the extent of settlement can fluctuate according to the interaction of social, political, economic, technical and environmental factors" [Ward 1997, 107].

The publication recently of a series of papers delivered at a major conference devoted entirely to this issue, marks a growing awareness of the inadequacies of our present conceptual frameworks [Mills and Coles 1998]. The authors of one of those papers give a telling summary of the current dilemma: "marginality can only be a meaningful idea in relation to a particular economic and social system – places are not innately marginal even in the geographical sense, since marginality is a relative and scale-dependent concept. Places are only marginal in relation to social and economic pressures, whether or not they are impacted by physical stresses or risks" [Brown *et al* 1998, 147][5].

These arguments have profound implications for historians of landscape, for they mean that no longer can upland areas like Carhampton be viewed merely as entirely discrete 'emergency reserves' for the purposes of settlement and land-use; rather, they should be seen as contributing equally in a balanced and mutually-advantageous relationship with the surrounding lowlands. By this view, the landscape becomes a spatial continuity for the purposes of settlement, and medievalists should perhaps take heed of Tolan-Smith's recent observation on the British Neolithic "that human behaviour is distributed continuously across the landscape - not just in free-floating 'sites' - and that it simply varies in intensity from one location to another" [Tolan-Smith 1996, 7]. As Malcolm Todd has recently observed of Mendip and the Somerset Levels in the Iron Age and Roman periods, "that upland and lowland formed separate ecosystems is inherently unlikely" [Todd 1995, 78].

In the light of these concerns, it is becoming increasingly apparent that far from settlement and agricultural abandonment invariably being the knee-jerk response to climatic deterioration and other environmental crises, it is equally likely that so-called 'marginal' communities under stress attempted to increase their resource base by actually extending the area under cultivation; a development perhaps associated with a shift in the settlement pattern rather than its outright collapse [Coles and Mills 1998, xi-xii]. While far more detailed work than is possible here would be needed even to begin to investigate some of these issues with specific respect to Carhampton hundred, it must now be clear that a proper understanding of their role in the settlement dynamics of its upland margins should be a central element of any future research design. The major problem, and at present it is an insurmountable one, is the almost total lack of

---

[5] Additional *empirical* support for Bailey's views is implicit in Harold Fox's recent comments relating to what conventional wisdom might otherwise characterise as the 'marginal' fringes of Dartmoor. While acknowledging widespread and calamitous abandonment of upland farmsteads and hamlets in many parts of Devon and Cornwall after the mid 14th century, Fox is careful to stress that this was by no means the invariable rule. For he also observes that "not all of the regions of poorer land fell down to grass. Dartmoor is a good example, for there was little decline in arable farming on the moorland border farms and relatively little desertion of settlement during the fourteenth and fifteenth centuries: in this case late colonisation in the more expansive centuries of the early Middle Ages was not followed by widespread contraction and desertion after 1350, for the 'commercialisation' of the moor helped to bolster demand for farm products" [Fox 1989, 63-64].

secure dating evidence for the chronologies of individual medieval settlement sites not only in Carhampton, but from Exmoor generally; a question which we will consider again in the following chapter.

As we have already noted though, Carhampton's pastoral basis seems clear at least from the Domesday evidence, which shows the upland (ie southern and western) parts of the hundred sustaining one of the lowest plough-team densities in the county, and conversely returning some of the highest figures for areas of pasture [Welldon Finn and Wheatley 1967, 157-160, and 181-185]. And as for earlier periods (Chapter Two) so also does the environmental evidence from Hoar Moor provide a firm antecedent context for the Domesday picture. Between the early 7th century and the mid 9th, the decline of arable use in favour of an increasingly pastoral economy, established in the previous phase, became even more marked, and was probably associated with severely depressed levels of human activity. Between the mid 9th century and the mid 16th, a period obviously critical in any assessment of the medieval settlement pattern, while pastoralism continued to dominate, sustained attempts at arable cultivation once more become discernible in the pollen record, although there were "no apparent clearances of the surviving marginal woodlands", which recovered to 3rd-7th century levels. It is likely that at least part of the reason for the limited evidence of arable activity in this period was the designation by the Norman kings of an extensive tract of central Exmoor as Royal Forest [Francis and Slater 1990, 21], although the first documentary reference to the Forest does not occur until 1204 [Rackham 1988, 22-23; Bond 1994, 121-123]. *Contra* Francis and Slater, however, there is no direct evidence that the Saxon kings of Wessex had set the precedent by establishing a formal hunting reserve on the moor.

Against this generally clear pastoral background, by contrast, the nature of medieval field systems in Carhampton is problematic, to a large extent because the systematic and highly detailed terriers available for the Glastonbury estates in Whitley are simply absent for its western neighbour.[6] An extensive and detailed assessment of the far thinner and more scattered range of sources that would need to be used for Carhampton is beyond the scope of this study, but we can at least gain a broad overview by looking at a form of documentation that is easily available and often survives in series. Although relatively very late in date (usually late 16th or 17th century), glebe terriers deal with estates which by their very nature, as church endowments, tended to be conservative in nature, and this is especially true in areas of early, piecemeal enclosure or where arable land had *never* lain in the form of open fields [Edwards 1991, 77-78 and refs there cited].

What emerges from this exercise in Carhampton is the absence of any but the most circumstantial evidence for the existence of classic, Midland type open field arrangements, in contrast to large areas of Whitley (Chapter Eight) and indeed in the Chew hundred

communities. At Minehead in 1633, there were eight acres of arable in two *closes* of four acres each [SRO D/D/Rg 349/2]. Even earlier, in 1606, there had been seven and a half acres in *three* closes [SRO D/D/Rg 349/1], giving evidence of consolidation in the intervening period. But there were also nine glebe tenements which were let out, of which five had some arable, but none more than an acre, and all of it was apparently enclosed. At this earlier date we might reasonably expect remnant open-field land to reveal itself. At Oare in 1613 the terrier refers only to 'ground' which may or may not be arable, but all of it was anyway, enclosed [SRO D/D/Rg 352/2]. At Carhampton itself there is no mention of arable land by name, although it clearly existed as the terrier of 1634 there is careful to record parishioners' obligations to pay tithes of grain [SRO D/D/Rg 335/2]; again though, all the tithable arable was held in closes, some of it, apparently, forming part of or being attached to the parishioners' individual tofts:

> "Tithe of all kind of graine belonginge to the vicarage and in what ground it is [due?]. It[em] the third shefe of the tith in the widdow hills her crufte liinge on the East sid of Agis hodges dwellinge house. It[em] the wholl tith in Estberrie Orchard. It[em] halfe the tith in the widdow h[ills?] her crufte liinge on the south side of the churchyard. It[em] the tith in the weste side of the widdow hils her cruft commonly caled the Title cruft".

And so on. At Carhampton, later topographical evidence highlighted by Janet Dixon certainly suggests the previous existence of strip-like enclosures in the north-western part of the parish [Dixon 1980, Map 5b]; however, it is significant that in the mid 19th century this very low-lying area adjacent to the coast was given over to meadow [Map 6], and the strips are therefore more likely to be part of a 'dole' system of annual redistribution among tenants [*cf* Edwards 1991, Plate 5; Gardiner 1985]. Outside these areas, there is little in the 19th century field pattern at Carhampton, such as long, reverse 'S' boundaries, to suggest the former existence of open-field arable strips [Dixon 1980, Map 4].

The glebe at Exford in 1603 was contained in a series of 'pieces' of ground or closes [D/D/Rg 342/2]. No field-names are given probably because it was considered by the surveyors (ie the churchwardens) unnecessary to do so. At Culbone in 1606 there is a cryptic reference in the terrier to "tow great fields containing by estimation eight akers" [SRO D/D/Rg 346/1], but their small size and the lack of cardinal orientations attached to these fields probably indicates that they were simply large arable enclosures with no internal boundaries. Remnant open-field strips should not be of this order of size.

Elsewhere in the hundred a similar picture emerges. At Treborough the author of the parish survey there notes the likelihood "that there were never any open fields but that land was enclosed as it was cleared" [Williams 1990, 4]. In parts of Minehead Without, Osborn is probably mistaken automatically to equate the identification of ridge and furrow with the existence of 'open fields' [Osborn

---

[6] For the most recent summary account of the *archaeological* evidence for medieval field systems on Exmoor, see Wilson-North and Riley 2001, 97-102.

1983, 7, and Map 3]. With one of her quoted examples lying at around 250m OD, it is far more likely that such cases actually represent a highly dynamic, ebb and flow of viable arable exploitation along an alternately farmed and abandoned 'cultivation frontier'. We have already noted that at this altitude, environmental and topographical factors alone might lead us to expect exactly this, and reasonably to conclude that the operation of fully-fledged midland-type field systems seems unlikely in this area. Osborn herself implies as much, but this activity would have taken place within a framework of *several* fields, enclosed from the outset, probably over a long period of time from the high middle ages perhaps into at least the early modern period or later. While we may not doubt the former existence of strip cultivation in the area around North Hill, to the west of Minehead [Binding 1995, 60], dating, and the *nature* of the cultivation itself, is extremely problematic: ridge and furrow can only be dated in relative terms, by reference to associated features. No systematic study of arable ridging systems has yet been carried out in the Exmoor area, so we are obliged to look elsewhere for comparative material. And in this respect it is surely significant that Andrew Fleming's detailed work on the nature of 'rig' cultivation on Dartmoor, and its historical and archaeological affinities, is set entirely within the context of infield-outfield arrangements, and variations thereof, associated with isolated farmsteads and hamlets [Fleming 1994]; the fully-fledged, Midland open-field system was unknown on and around Dartmoor, just as it almost certainly was on the higher parts of Exmoor and its fringes.

Notwithstanding the name 'Northfield' cited by Binding, it is far more probable, therefore, that the Minehead examples, extensive though they are, represent arable fields enclosed from the outset and attached in coherent blocks to individual farms. This certainly seems to have been the case with the two deserted farmstead sites in Grexy and Bramble Combes on North Hill [Wilson-North and Riley 1997a, 8-9], with the field blocks representing an area of infield cultivated either permanently or by rotation. Elsewhere, the intermittent and sporadic ploughing of upland commons is well attested from other parts of Exmoor, and, indeed, from within Carhampton hundred itself, as for example at Wootton Courtenay in the 16th century [Aston 1988a, 85-87]. And in the early 19th century, traces of (probably) spade-dug cultivation ridging were still to be seen on the upland commons around Withycombe [quoted in Aston 1988a, 85].

Conversely, at Lynch in Selworthy, a grant of about the middle of the 13th century *does* give some indication that, in parts of Carhampton's coastal lowlands at least, arable farming could and did take place in scattered strips organised in furlongs. Among a list of small, dispersed parcels (a few perches up to several acres), a key entry refers to "three acres in that *cultura* which is called Crowewelle, each of them containing six and a half perches of land in breadth" [Weaver 1909, 60]. In theory this would make each of the acre strips, and presumably also the furlong itself, about 135 yds long.

The case of Lynch, however, serves merely to emphasise a fundamental point about Carhampton field systems that mark them out as different from the tightly regular, midland-type arrangements so characteristic of north Polden in Whitley hundred. Even where, as here, some individual elements of open-field arable are clearly present in the medieval period, perhaps the single most 'diagnostic' one is manifestly absent: that is, the equal division of the arable into two or more large, unenclosed and subdivided fields. Medieval extents from other parts of the hundred reinforce this impression. A demesne messuage in Porlock surveyed for an *inquisition post mortem* in the very early 14th century contained a total of at least 191 acres of arable, of which 40 acres lay in closes and the rest distributed among various named *culturæ*, but with no indication whatsoever that they lay in two or three large fields with cardinal nomenclature [Chadwyck Healey 1901, 409-410].

Indeed, in the sources that have been reviewed, albeit briefly, nowhere in Carhampton does one encounter medieval or early modern references to fields named for the cardinal points of the compass. Had they been a feature of arable arrangements at either Lynch or Porlock, the surveys noted above are surely early enough to have recorded them, but they do not, and for the reasons already outlined, the sole (probably late) example from Minehead can be safely discounted. We have long known that open strips and furlongs do not necessarily betray the invariable existence of the classic Midland field system, a point reiterated recently by Nancy Edwards in a brief but telling review of the evidence from Wales [Edwards 1997, 8]. There are also instructive parallels here with the situation in Devon, highlighted by Finberg's classic work in that county [Finberg 1969a, 146].

However, even in places such as Lynch, it seems that what strip arable *did* exist in the middle ages conformed far more closely to Finberg's Devon examples than to those regimes operating in, say, Leicestershire. This is not to say that units of arable land regarded from an *operational* point of view as 'common fields' did not exist in Carhampton, because they certainly did; so much is clear from the 16th century rental of Porlock which we have already noted, and which refers to "common fields" by names which are anything *other* than cardinal ones: "le Nether londe, le Cow lease, le Uatstyle, le Pownde Parke". What is most notable however, is the diminutive scale of the arrangements when compared to what we might expect in a 'typical' midland common-field regime. Only three tenants are noted as holding at least part of their arable in this way, with a total of 48 acres between them, consisting of 40 acres in these named fields, and 8 acres identified as merely "in the common fields"; at 12d an acre, this represents a mere £2 8s of the £41 13s 11d that was the sum of the rentals for the entire manor. The other tenants held arable but it apparently lay entirely in closes [Chadwyck Healey 1901, 414 and 420]. If this does indeed represent the extent of 'common field' arable in Porlock in the 16th century, then each of the four fields held only twelve acres, even if the land was equally distributed between them. It may certainly be possible to argue that enclosure before the 16th century had taken its toll on an originally much more extensive system: the amount of arable land lying in open-field *culturæ* in the medieval period, as we have already seen, seems greatly to exceed that surviving by Henry VIII's time. And by the early 17th century this process may have been complete, for nowhere in a terrier of 1606 recording some 40 acres of glebe arable distributed among various tenants, is there any mention of 'common fields'; the land is described merely as "grounde" [printed in Chadwyck Healey 1901, 474-475]. Early enclosure may also be suggested by the survival, well into the 19th century, of field boundaries around Porlock (for example, to its north-east), whose clear origin in some form of arable strip farming is betrayed by their 'classic' reverse-S curves (Figure 22). Subsequent rationalisation may have straightened other such boundaries that formerly existed [Williamson 2000, 59-61].

But the overwhelming impression, supported by the medieval material from Lynch and Porlock itself, is that, perhaps operationally, and certainly in morphological terms, even in the medieval period, these arrangements were at variance with the classic midland field system.

Finberg suggests that in Devon, fields which have all the appearance of the classic midland model, could actually be operated on a basis that was far more akin to an occasionally-cultivated outfield [Finberg 1969a, 148-149]. Here, then, is a paradigm which might usefully be applied to those places in Carhampton, such as Lynch, which seems to have possessed the kind of scheme probably best characterised as an 'irregular multifield' system [Astill 1988, 68]. Far more detailed documentary and topographical work than is possible here would be needed effectively to elaborate on this idea; although Finberg is clear that the critical element lying behind the emergence of these West Country 'hybrid' systems was the presence of large areas of pasture [Finberg 1969a, 150-151].

Perhaps surprisingly, scholarly opinion about the controlling influence of pasture on both medieval settlement patterns and agrarian regimes has not fundamentally changed since Finberg originally made his suggestion nearly 50 years ago [*eg* Faith 1997, 148]; and a more recent review of medieval field arrangements remarks of *non*-Midland type systems that they "do not have such a large element of communal participation, and probably reflect the greater amount of waste and pasture that was available for grazing" [Astill 1988, 68]. The coastal fringe of Carhampton hundred can certainly be included with those other areas of south-west England where abundant upland pasture had the effect of modifying partially-communal arable field regimes into something "much more haphazard than in the midlands" [Astill 1988, 81]. For the 18th century, Roger Burton has been able to quantify the well known practice, by the surrounding parishes, of using the uplands of Exmoor, and specifically within the bounds of Exmoor Forest, as commons for grazing, especially for sheep. Of the Carhampton manors at this period, Oare, Exford and Porlock sent sheep into the Forest, while Exford, Porlock, Oare, Stoke Pero, Luccombe, Culbone and Selworthy sent bullocks [Burton

1989, 42-44][7]. Chadwyck Healey prints a 16th century rental of Porlock showing that tenants of that manor enjoyed the right to stint sheep flocks on Porlock Moor, the number dependent on the size of their tenement [Chadwyck Healey 1901, 412-422]. This picture is a late one but it is certain that this activity goes back to a period well before the afforestation of Exmoor in the post-Conquest period, probably covering a far larger area than that within the later Forest as a documented legal entity [Burton 1989, 29-30], with all the implications that has for the nature of emerging field arrangements in the surrounding communities on the moor's lowland fringes.

Finally, we have already noted that infield-outfield systems, perhaps in a variety of types, are likely to have been prevalent among Carhampton's isolated medieval farms and hamlets, but is it possible to demonstrate their existence archaeologically? Hound Tor, on the eastern side of Dartmoor, provides a 'classic' model of how this arrangement might manifest itself in the landscape [Aston 1985a, 86-87], and there are indications from within Carhampton that the arable of at least some of the isolated communities was similarly disposed. At the deserted medieval hamlet of Sweetworthy in Luccombe parish, "a small field forms part of the northern edge of the settlement. A clearance heap lies to the north of this field; vegetation in this area may mask other features concerned with clearance and enclosure. The small fields depicted on an early 19th-century map may well be the remains of a field system associated with this settlement site" [Wilson-North & Riley 1996, 5]. The medieval settlement at Ley Hill, in the same parish, possessed a contemporary, well-preserved and apparently quite dynamic field system that was almost certainly operated along infield-outfield lines [Wilson-North and Riley 1997, 7]. We have already noted the extensive and well-preserved enclosed infield blocks on North Hill, Minehead Without (above), attached to two deserted medieval farmsteads. And although technically just over the county boundary in Devon, the large deserted hamlet at Badgworthy, in Brendon parish, offers a 'classic' example of an exceptionally well-preserved medieval Exmoor settlement in its landscape context. The occupation site itself is closely associated with well-defined indications of ploughland, consisting of strip lynchets on steeper, south-facing slopes, with ridge and furrow where gentler gradients permit. The lynchets themselves, "at 300 m above OD......provide the most elevated example of medieval arable cultivation on Exmoor" [Wilson-North 1996, 6]. The surveyor of Badgworthy is clear that these features together represent the remnants of an infield arrangement, and that "the remains of field boundaries [that] extend up the more sheltered combes around Badgworthy, for several kilometres", constitute "the outlying fields......[of] large irregular enclosures, presumably an extensive outfield" [Wilson-North 1996, 5].

---

[7] I am grateful to Paul Pickering for drawing Burton's work to my attention.

Chapter Eight

Shape and Society: Settlement Patterns, Settlement Morphology and Tenure

Introduction

Whitley hundred again takes centre stage here, with briefer reviews of Chew and Carhampton serving to highlight the particular nature of developments in the main hundred. In this, the final chapter of the main text, we confront the theme that lies at the centre of this study, in which the arguments and ideas outlined in the preceding sections are brought together and made to contribute, to varying degrees, to an overall synthesis. We will see that this is a far more complex matter than would be implied by a crude and indeed probably unworkable division between dispersed, nucleated and hybrid types of medieval rural settlement; for although at the most basic level it would certainly be possible to pigeon-hole each of the hundreds in those terms, such a scheme is unsatisfactory in that it takes no account of the nuances of variation, some subtle, others less so, in settlement types that exist within each of the study areas.

Conceptual Background

Notwithstanding what has just been said, the perceived dichotomy between nucleation and dispersal has been arguably the most persistent thread informing conventional views about the nature of medieval rural settlement in England. From the time of Maitland onwards scholars have by and large approached this question from the perspective of separate phenomena rather than two sides of the same coin [Maitland 1897, 38-40]. There has now, though, been a discernible reaction against this received orthodoxy, the debate over which is regarded increasingly as sterile and unhelpful. General dissatisfaction is fuelled by the twin problems of chronology and definition of types which have beset medieval settlement studies [Austin 1985a, 1988; Roberts 1987, 6]. As knowledge has improved, it is being progressively supplanted by the idea of a settlement continuum, in which dispersal and nucleation are treated as a mutually dependent totality. Neither is any longer seen as an *absolute* condition, but scholars now speak of, and indeed have attempted to map, degrees or intensity of nucleation and dispersal [Roberts and Wrathmell 1998, 2000, 2001][1]. We have already noted how this approach is increasingly espoused by archaeologists engaged in prehistoric settlement research. While we continue to acknowledge that regions may display distinct tendencies

towards one or the other, it is also clear that many medieval settlement patterns, where they can be recovered, are hybrid types constructed from a complex web of *both* conditions; so that, for example, even in Lindsey in Lincolnshire, "a region where nucleation was perceived to be the dominant form of medieval settlement, there was also a sub-structure of dispersal" [Taylor 1995, 27]. It is now customary strongly to emphasise that in any given area, the two are likely to be intimately related, and that, the correct interpretation of one will depend directly on a proper understanding of the other [Hooke 1985; Taylor 1995; Dyer *et al* 1997; Durham 1997, 350-352]. Paradoxically however, advancing knowledge has also increasingly brought with it for scholars in this field a sometimes painful awareness of the enormous obstacles to be overcome in establishing the extent and nature of medieval settlement at any given point in time. These questions have been discussed recently by Dyer *et al* [1997, 1-30; and 92-98], and turn chiefly upon issues of dating. The East Midlands, for example, typifies the dilemma [Dyer *et al* 1997, 111], and the most pessimistic view is that without major, long-term campaigns of historic landscape study such as the Shapwick Project, the task is effectively impossible [Magnus Alexander, *pers comm*]. It is, then, against this very dynamic conceptual background that we must set our perspectives on the nature of the medieval rural settlement patterns in the three study hundreds.

Chew Hundred: An Overview

Nowhere in Chew hundred presents us with the kind of arrangement where a nucleated settlement lies at the centre of an otherwise almost empty (in settlement terms) parish, as at Shapwick. We can cite Chew Magna itself to illustrate this point. The 1334 Lay Subsidy lists several settlements in that parish from which a return was recorded: Littleton; North Wick; North Elm (alias North Chew); Stone; and Knowle Hill. The location of Stone is unidentified (but see further below). Chew itself, as a diocesan property, was exempt from the subsidy and therefore does not appear [Glasscock 1975, 267]. Knowle is now reduced to three dwellings (two farms and a 'farmhouse'), but in 1327 no fewer than 14 tax payers are recorded from it. Some of the surnames are also highly suggestive. Richard and Cristina "atte Mulle" reveal the existence of a mill at this date (perhaps at Hollow Brook, marked on the 2½" map). "Johanne atte Wode" paid 12d, but there is no woodland near Knowle Hill today [Dickinson 1889].

We have already noted, in Chapter Two, Kemp's work on the nature of the medieval settlement pattern in parts of the Chew Valley [Kemp 1983; 1984]. But Kemp's

---

[1] Although we should note that at least one landscape historian has concerns over the validity of the approach adopted by these two workers; witness the sceptism implicit in Tom Williamson's remark that "the widespread assumption that settlement forms and patterns existing in the nineteenth century can in any simple or direct way inform us about the early medieval landscape is at least questionable.......settlement did not stop changing in the period after 1550". Williamson 2000a, 116.

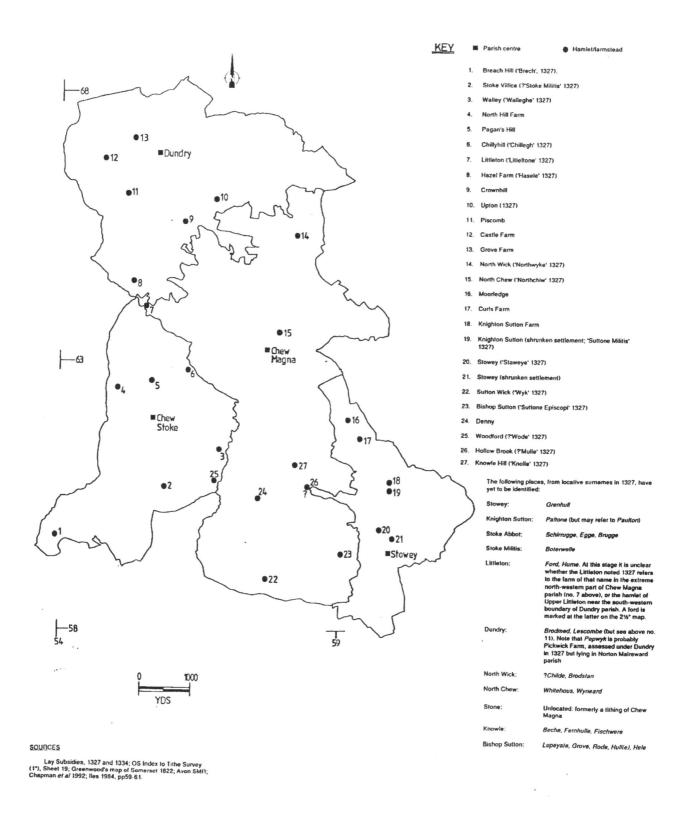

SOURCES

Lay Subsidies, 1327 and 1334; OS Index to Tithe Survey (1"), Sheet 19; Greenwood's map of Somerset 1822; Avon SMR; Chapman *et al* 1992; Iles 1984, pp59-61.

Figure 31: Map showing suggested *minimum* extent of medieval settlement in Stowey, Chew Magna, Chew Stoke and Dundry.

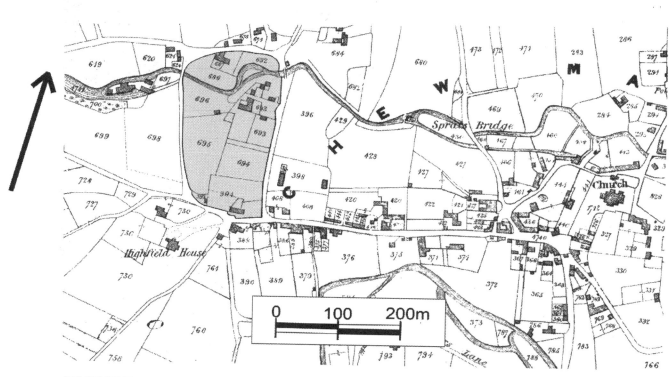

FIGURE 32

Extract from Chew Magna tithe map, SRO D/D/Rt 285, 1840, showing (shaded) the area suggested as a planned manorial enclosure representing the centre of the tithing of Stone. It seems as though the northern end of the loop has been laid out so as to bring within it a stretch of the eastwards flowing stream that separates it from the southern part of the enclosure, perhaps to service a proprietorial mill the site of which is now lost. The enclosure is bounded by Dark Lane to the west, and Battle Lane to the e a s t ,   b o t h   o f   w h i c h   a r e   d e e p l y   c u t   h o l l o w   w a y s .

Map 7 [1983], showing the medieval landscape of his study area, can now be developed and Figure 31 here is the result, collating various disparate sources in an attempt to represent the absolute *minimum* of medieval settlement as it might have appeared on the eve of the Black Death. The 1327 and 1334 Lay Subsidies show several more separate, tax-paying communities in existence in the early 14th century than Kemp allows for. From 1334 for example, he excludes Littleton, Stone and Knowle. All lie in his study area, although, as we have already noted, Stone's location is problematic. Nonetheless, this would actually have supported his case regarding the relationship between Roman and medieval sites, especially in the instance of Knowle, which he identifies only as a Roman site [Kemp 1984, 36 fig 1, and 38 fig 3]. It would also have confirmed his suggestion about the nature of the earthworks which he found on Breach Hill in Chew Stoke as those of a deserted settlement [Kemp 1983, 67-68; Avon SMR 7709] which was in existence at least by the high middle ages [Dickinson 1889, 137]. Breach is palpably a 'colonising' name, as a simplex used generally of the intaking of new arable from open waste [Gelling 1984, 233-234, and *pers comm.*; and *cf* Costen 1987a, 24, for further local examples]. We should, though, note that it could be used in conjunction with other words to take on the specific meaning of a woodland assart: thus *La Wudebrech* at

Ditcheat [Stokes 1996, 59]. In the case of Chew Stoke, there is no evidence to show that the name is not being used in its usual sense, and refers to what is probably post-Conquest intaking activity on a small, elevated plateau just above the 130m contour, in an isolated position in the extreme south-western corner of the parish. Breach was in existence by 1327; the field pattern around Breach Farm is one of small, highly irregular enclosures, and the earthworks of possible house-platforms have been noted in the area of Breach Hill [Kemp 1983, 67-68]. Likewise Chillyhill, a small Domesday manor and also in Chew Stoke, now represented by a farm and a single house (2½" OS, ST563629). In 1327, three taxpayers described by the epithet "de Chillegh" are noted [Dickinson, 138].

Figure 31 specifically excludes settlements known from medieval documentation, but which remain unlocated. The two most notable examples in this latter category are Bychewstoke and Stone. The first is recorded in 1350 and earlier [BL Charters 171; Wood 1903, 119], and it is clear that this is the same place discussed by Thorn and Thorn [1980, 352 and 366], from a variety of published works which obviously mistranscribe the original medieval sources. Stone survived as a tithing of Chew Magna into the 19th century, to which Wood was able to ascribe a precise area [Wood 1903, 80], and from its position in the 1327 list can probably be placed between

North Chew and Knowle. [Dickinson 1889, 136-139]. A reference in an early 17th century land schedule quoted by Wood equates Stone with 'West Chew' [Wood 1903, 35], and mentions a tucking mill there. A few hundred metres to the west of Chew church, a large sub-rectangular enclosure extends north of the main east-west road through the village, bounded by deeply-cut lanes to east and west that seem to serve no purpose other than to provide a boundary for the land which they delimit (Figure 32). The enclosure has been extended just far enough northwards to take in a short length of a stream, at this point flowing east-west, which is a minor tributary of the River Chew. Within the enclosure lies Chew Manor, an imposing Victorian edifice which yet almost certainly stands on the site of a far earlier, medieval house [Pevsner 1958, 159-160; Durham I and M 1991, 25-26]. Without more detailed work one can only speculate, but superficially at least this area conveys a marked impression of being a high-status enclosure and may well be worth considering as a candidate for the 'manorial' centre of Stone/West Chew tithing[2].

Figure 33 attempts to project what we might expect as the minimum settlement pattern as it existed in the late Anglo-Saxon period, using, again, a variety of sources. This represents a purely preliminary exercise, and is more a statement of ignorance than anything else; much of the 'empty' space is doubtless more apparent than real, but it does at least make the point that much more detailed work remains to be done in Chew than is possible here before the gaps can be even partially filled.

The Form of Medieval Settlement

It is immediately clear that Chew hundred is overwhelmingly an area of hamlet and farmsteads rather than of nucleated villages. To an extent this is reflected even at the level of the parish centres, for while Chew Stoke could reasonably be called a village, and Chew itself has at least the appearance of a small market town, Norton Malreward, Norton Hawkfield (intermittently regarded as a parish in its own right [Wood 1903, 67]) and Dundry are hamlets, and Stowey today consists merely of a manor house adjacent to a church. Indeed, nowhere in the core area of the hundred has nucleation reached its maximum point, to give rise to a single compact village at the centre, and the sole occupier of, its parish. Chew Stoke, for example, can perhaps best be described as a loose, irregular agglomeration [Roberts 1987, 76-77] in a parish of otherwise dispersed settlement. Dundry consists of the main hamlet, containing the church, and the quite separate settlement of East Dundry, a second hamlet cluster some 2km away to the east. Even Chew Magna itself, although undoubtedly an agglomeration in the strict sense, nonetheless displays a distinctly amorphous plan, although here at least it may be possible to discern at least two different elements: loose, straggling rows on either side of

the main east-west road into the settlement from the west [*cf* Roberts 1987, 34-35], and around the church, a more compact, agglomerated but still irregular cluster of plots and buildings. Only a single settlement displays clear and unequivocal topographical evidence of *planned* origins, an impression strongly reinforced if not actually confirmed by its toponymy. New Town (Figure 34) is a small roadside hamlet within Chew parish, and directly abutting Chew's eastern boundary with Stowey. The right-angled, zig-zag form of the boundary here suggests strongly that the house plots were laid out over an existing sub-divided field system, the whole unit perhaps taking in an entire furlong. Virtually nothing is known of New Town's history: Wood [1903] makes no mention of it whatsoever, and it is not identified by name on the county maps of either Day and Masters (1782) or Greenwood (1822), although conversely, both depict what may be intended as representative buildings in approximately the correct position [Dunning and Harley 1981]. However, New Town is sufficiently striking to prompt Roberts to comment upon it, and his assessment is that it represents "a clear example of a small parish-edge planned hamlet" [Roberts 1987, 198]. This, of course, tells us nothing about the circumstances of its origin, and without reliable documentary evidence and/or archaeological intervention, dating is entirely problematic. In form it certainly does not look like post-medieval, common-edge or roadside squatter occupation, which is usually highly irregular, 'organic' and 'straggly' in nature [Roberts 1977, 194-195; Rackham 1986, 278; Dyer *et al* 1997, 127-132]. It is also often characterised by small dwellings with gable-ends facing the road, associated with long, narrow garden plots running parallel with the road and representing encroachments on it. There seems to be the hand of overarching control at work here, and we can only speculate that perhaps New Town represents a (possibly failed?) medieval or late-medieval 'colonising' settlement founded and underwritten by seigneurial authority, in an obscure and under-exploited part of Chew Magna, in the hope of generating revenue from new rents. As we will see a little later on, parallels from Whitley hundred, with both Butleigh Wootton and Compton, in Dundon parish, suggest themselves, although in both these other cases the evidence is rather better and we can be reasonably confident of their pre-Conquest origins.

That the settlement pattern in the hundred as it appeared in the mid 19th century had been subject to contraction, is clear from the evidence of desertion that survives. At Stowey, Chapman *et al* [1992] record house platforms in the hamlet of Knighton Sutton; although the banks of crofts behind existing houses along the main street through the settlement might suggest a high degree of both boundary stability and continuity of occupation of individual plots. Desertion also clearly affected isolated farmstead sites. Pickwick, in Norton Malreward [Williams 1982, 55-56] was abandoned only in the mid 19th century, probably in favour of the newly-built

---

[2] Fieldwork within the enclosure revealed no obvious signs of earlier activity in terms of earthwork features, although the northern part of the site, bounding the stream, is extremely overgrown. I am grateful to the Sisters of the Order of Our Lady of the Missions for their permission to conduct this work.

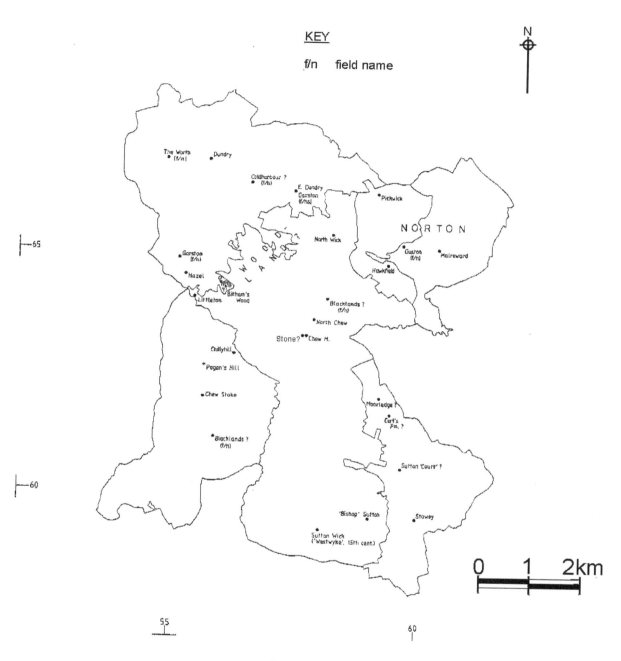

CHEW HUNDRED: LATE ANGLO-SAXON SETTLEMENT

Figure 33

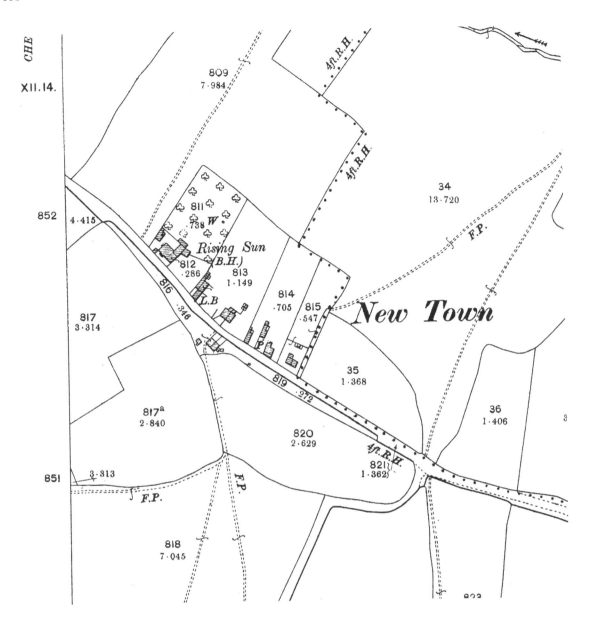

Figure 34: Reduced extract from OS second edition 25" map (1904) showing plan of New Town, on the extreme south-eastern corner of Chew Magna. The angularity of the parish boundary (Chew Magna to west, Stowey to east) may suggest that the settlement enclosures were taken in from pre-existing open arable field furlongs.

Model Farm, on a lower, more advantageous site [Aston 1987, 104; Foot 1994, 51]. Kemp has identified a possible deserted farmstead site in the area around Breach Hill Farm, in the south-western extremity of Chew Stoke [Kemp 1983, 67-68 and 74], and we have already noted the likelihood that Breach represents a post-Conquest foundation on newly-broken land; a context for which is most plausibly to be found in the early-mid 13th century, when population pressure was underpinning a rapid expansion of rural settlement in many areas [Bolton 1980, 82-118; Campbell 1990, 70-77].

Antecedents: The Examples of *Garston* and *Wick*

One major task facing students of settlement is the

identification of what Brian Roberts calls 'antecedent' cores; that is, areas where the occupation of a given site was initially concentrated [Roberts 1987, 22]. This very early stage may well have been generally common to both nucleated and dispersed settlement, with divergent paths of development only taking effect as the interacting complexity of local circumstances began to influence the physical nature of occupation. It may be possible to identify some antecedent medieval cores by the occurrence of the names 'Old Field' or 'Old Land(s)', references, it is suggested, to an early type of arrangement based on the operation of an infield-outfield regime appropriate only to relatively low population levels and settlement densities, the latter in the form of dispersed farms or extended-kin hamlets [Taylor 1975, 68-69; Rackham 1986, 161; Hooke

1995, 109-110; Aston 1985, 127-130]. There are, unfortunately, no such names known within the main body of Chew hundred (ie excluding the parishes of Timsbury and Clutton).

Another name though, Garston, holds out rather more promise, since it occurs four times in the study area, in each case in association with a slightly different settlement type. Superficially, Garston is an unprepossessing word, and as a field-name is usually taken to derive from OE *gærs-tun*, 'a grass enclosure, paddock', with no particular topographical significance [Field 1993, 123]. However, Chris Thornton, developing earlier suggestions, has made a close study of the topographical context of a Garston name at Rimpton in Somerset. From this, he has proposed that it in fact represented the earliest phase of Anglo-Saxon land-use, effectively an infield or "ancient core arable unit, perhaps associated with the putative early seigneurial farm and the first-phase curtilages", and from which other, later elements of the settlement plan took their cue [Thornton 1988, 70].

The main theme of Thornton's idea certainly seems to be borne out directly in the case of two of the four Chew hundred Garstons, for they both occupy positions either centrally within or immediately adjacent to their respective settlements. These lie at Upper Littleton, in the south-western corner of Dundry parish, and at East Dundry (Figures 35 and 36). The distinction may be crucial in formulating ideas to account for the differences we can see in the morphology of the four places. In the other two examples, at Norton Malreward ('Gaston') and Stowey ('Hengarson') (Figures 37 and 38), the name occurs in isolation from cartographically-recorded settlement. Hengarson lies in an isolated corner of Stowey, close to its western boundary with Chew Magna, directly atop a small but locally very prominent knoll at 97m OD. Topographically therefore, the first element of the name makes best sense as OE *hēah*, 'high' [Ekwall 1960, 234-235 for related examples; Smith 1956, I, 237-239]. In contrast to Rimpton however, neither of the first two cases are directly associated with a *parochial* centre, but rather, are applied to an outlying hamlet (East Dundry) or, in the case of Upper Littleton, to a loose grouping of dispersed farms that, superficially at least, could not be termed a hamlet. Nonetheless, it appears, as Thornton suggested, that Garston and its derivatives have strong and very specific associations with *early* settlement cores; and the implication may well be, where these names are now applied to isolated locations, that we can add them to the list of field-names in –worth, -tun, -hay and -croft, to enable us to identify sites from which earlier settlement has now vanished or shifted [Corcos 1983, 51]. In this instance, it does seem as though the tendency with the Garston names in Chew is towards an association with hamlet-type settlement.

The significance of –wick names we have already noted in the context of their likely Roman connotations. Here, we can set them against the Garston names to show that, by contrast, they are applied in differing forms to dispersed farms. Bearing in mind what we have already said about the nature of the known -wick sites in the rest of Somerset, this is exactly what we should expect. While in eastern England there seems to have been a marked discontinuity between Roman (but not necessarily *late* Roman) and Migration Period settlement [Powlesland 1997, 102-103], it is likely that in the west, not only may -wicks have direct Roman antecedents, but they may also straddle the transition from Late Roman to Post-Roman conditions as continuously occupied, dispersed settlement sites.

Whitley Hundred

Before looking in more detail at settlement patterns and morphology, it may be useful to note very briefly something of the environmental background to these developments, in order to appreciate their significance in the wider landscape context, and also in terms of the intensity of agriculture that was being practised, at least on the dryland fringes of the Brue Valley. Yet again, the evidence is provided by the Meare Heath pollen diagram [Beckett and Hibbert 1979], which runs well into the Anglo-Saxon period. Dark summarises the sequence by highlighting "increases of grasses and ribwort plantain at approximately the end of the Roman period, after which cereal pollen occurs more abundantly than at any earlier point.........this suggests an expansion of the area of open land and flourishing arable activity in the fifth to eighth centuries" [Dark 2000, 143]. An environmental model which, as here, suggests a scale of post-Roman arable farming which was actually *more* intense than that obtaining in the Roman period, *must* have implications for the way we view both levels of indigenous British population, and density of settlement, in the period before the transition to Anglo-Saxon political control from about the mid 7th century onwards.

The most striking point of comparison between Chew and Whitley lies in their 'hybrid' nature: for at least in part they both share the particular quality of supporting a range of settlement types from isolated, individual farmsteads that we can show to have been in existence in the medieval period, through to strongly nucleated villages. In this last respect however, Whitley is markedly different: for unlike Chew (with the sole of exception of Newtown), some of its villages are certainly planned, and may also represent almost the only settlement in their parish. On closer inspection, at the sub-hundredal level, it is possible to discern in Whitley what appear to be distinct areas which admit of crude definition by the settlement type(s) most prevalent within them. Even within these regions though, there is variation according to what criteria we use to identify them, and for the purposes of clearer discussion, it is convenient to break the hundred down and to look briefly at the settlement pattern in each of the various topographical units of which it is composed - this method has the advantage over definition by type that each area can be treated as a totality, and due consideration given to all kinds of settlement which we might encounter.

149

Figure 35

Garston field-names at Littleton in Dundry

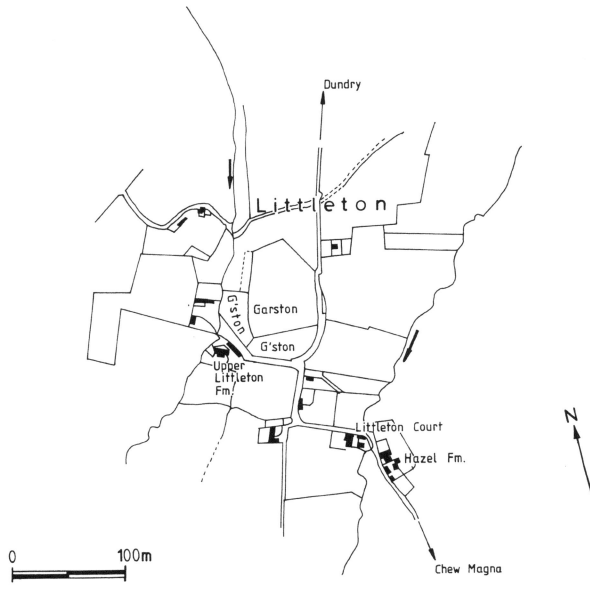

0   100m

Redrawn from tithe map, 1841
(SRO D/D/Rt 320)

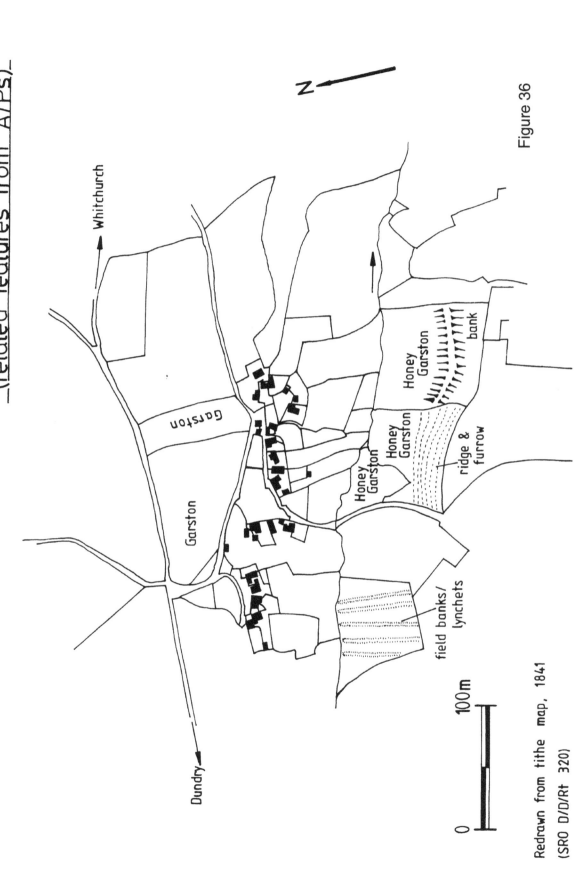

Garston field-names at East Dundry.
(related features from A/Ps).

Figure 36

Redrawn from tithe map, 1841
(SRO D/D/Rt 320)

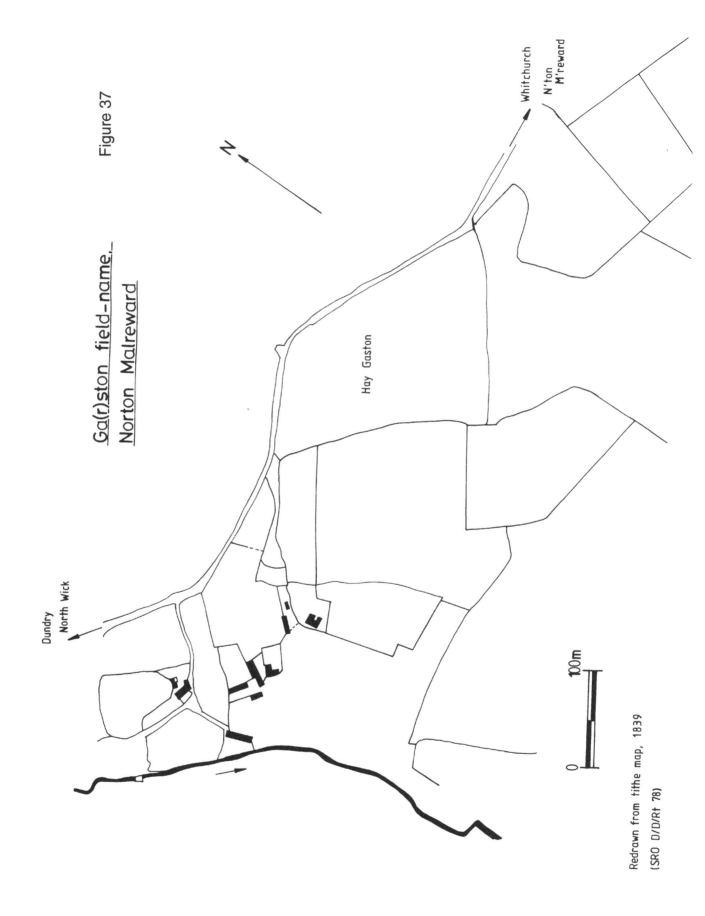

Figure 37

Ga(r)ston field-name,
Norton Malreward

Whitchurch

N'ton
M'reward

N

Hay Gaston

Dundry
North Wick

100m

0

Redrawn from tithe map, 1839

(SRO D/D/Rt 78)

Figure 38

GARSTON FIELD
NAMES, STOWEY

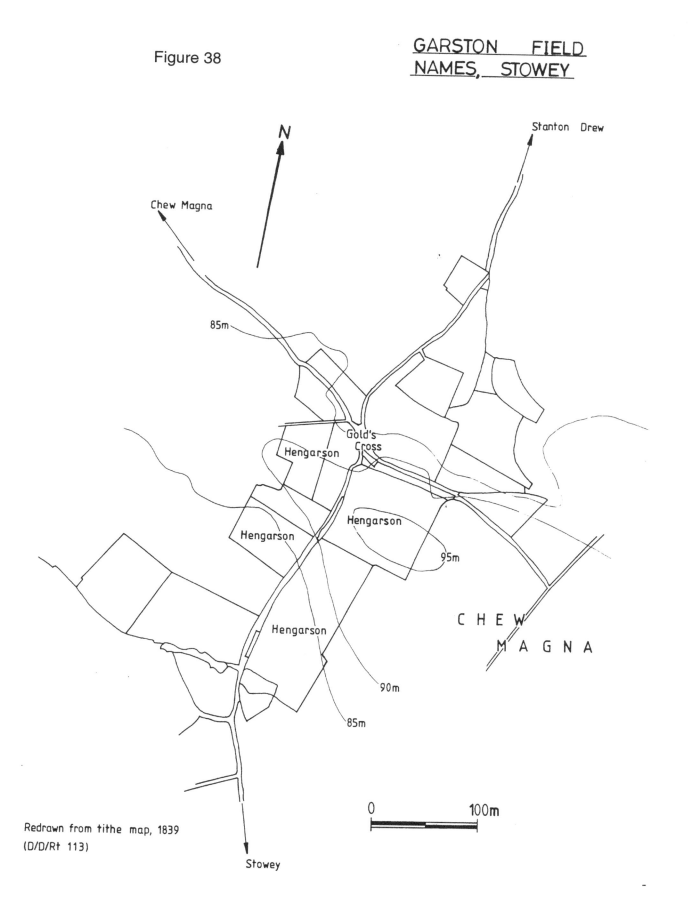

N

Stanton Drew

Chew Magna

85m

Gold's
Cross

Hengarson

Hengarson

Hengarson

95m

Hengarson

C H E W

M A G N A

90m

85m

Redrawn from tithe map, 1839
(D/D/Rt 113)

Stowey

0   100m

The geographical extent of the hundred imposes its own constraints, and the discussion that follows is of necessity taken across a broad canvas. For this reason also, it seemed best to look rather more closely at a 'case study' area, and fill out the wider picture, in the rest of the hundred, in less detail. The Polden ridge suggests itself for this purpose for a number of reasons. We have already seen, in earlier contexts, that the work of the Shapwick Project provides an invaluable frame of reference against which the usefulness, or otherwise, of the much sparser evidence from its immediate neighbours can be considered. We have also noted previously Polden's distinct topographical cohesiveness; and I will suggest later on that developments in settlement patterns in the centuries on either side of 1066, took place *within* this very bounded framework. Polden therefore provides a conveniently delimited laboratory within which models of settlement development can be applied. Further, it also contains within it just that wide range of settlement types, within such a relatively small compass, which presents us with so many problems of interpretation – in western Polden the striking contrast in the form of settlement between the northern and southern flanks presents a particular challenge, as does the apparent increase in the degree of dispersal, and decrease in the evidence for wholesale systematic planning, east of Shapwick. It is also *specifically* Polden through which runs the north/south boundary dividing the 'old' hundreds of Loxley and Ringoldsway. I hope to suggest that the reasons behind this are recoverable, and that from them flows an understanding, at least in outline, of the nature of medieval settlement along the entire ridge. These ideas form the overall Conclusion to this study. I intend, therefore, to concentrate chiefly on the Polden ridge proper (in two sections, divided west and east), and then to fill out the wider picture in a sketch overview of some of the other places in the hundred.

Settlement in Western Polden

Even at the crudest level of definition, it is not difficult to see that settlement north and south of the Polden ridge is dominated by nucleation. However, I have suggested elsewhere that the majority of those villages on the northern margin of the ridge stand as a group because they display characteristic signs of deliberate planning. Here, this is taken to mean the presence of a distinctive orderliness and regularity in the relationships between such elements as house plots and street layout [Corcos 1983]. This is certainly true of Shapwick, but also, to varying degrees, of Catcott, Edington, Cossington, Woolavington and possibly Puriton. Catcott, in fact, shows distinct traces of shrinkage, a large paddock immediately south of the church containing well-preserved earthworks, at least some of which certainly marking the sites of houses, since dwellings are depicted here on a map of the village dating to 1771 [SRO DD/PR 56]. Indeed, at Catcott there are strong indications, in the form of S-shaped field boundaries which appear to be cut by one of the main east-west lanes, of secondary expansion over existing open-field strips.

Catcott gives all the appearance of at least two phases of development, with a rather 'organic', irregular arrangement at the southern end, around the church, and a more regular, northerly element bounded by twin parallel north/south lanes. If this latter was an attempt at planned expansion over open field arable, perhaps in the 11th or 12th century, it was not entirely successful, since the focus of settlement has remained the looser, southern agglomeration.

The planning theme continues west of Puriton, where the small, 12th century, failed medieval new town of Downend is associated with the castle site there [Aston 1986, 67; Beresford and Finberg 1973, 155; Prior 1999]. The close relationship between the members of this distinctive group become even more apparent when mapped at a small scale [Roberts 1987, 182-183], although I do not agree with Roberts's assessment that there were greens present in these places, or at least, not as part of the original plan. Roberts further proposes that, on the basis of *recent* (ie mid 19th century onwards) cartography, both Ashcott and Chilton can be assigned layouts that were originally grids. It is certainly true that the tithe plans appear to show vestiges of regularity in these places, although greatly decayed by the 19th century; and Chilton, falling as it does in that group of villages west of Shapwick, and lying at the centre of a parish with a highly regular shape, is *prima facie* very likely to be founded on a systematic plan if we could but recover it. This is far less likely at Ashcott for reasons to which we will return shortly.

Edington in particular is of exceptional interest in this respect, since 'tacked on' to its main grid, immediately to the north, it possesses what appears to be a large, highly regular, sub-square 'extension' defined by parallel lanes running north-south and east-west (Figure 39). The enclosure occupies the eastern side of a small inlet or embayment of moor defined by the 10m contour, and internally, the shape and disposition of field boundaries as revealed on both OS and tithe maps (SRO D/D/Rt 37; nd but probably 1838) display distinct signs of an origin as strips within a pattern of open-field furlongs. By the late 18th century, the southern part of this unit, closest to the main village, was occupied by houses on long, narrow tenement plots running north south. Although skewed slightly, giving the appearance of a parallelogram, the feature is nonetheless sufficiently regular in shape to allow some idea of its internal area to be calculated from the map. It is almost exactly 500m square, giving an area of 25ha or just under 62 acres. In fact the true area is actually rather smaller than this, since both corners at the southern end are slightly truncated. Even more telling may be the fact that these figures, when converted to customary units of measurement, reveal that, if the southern truncations are 'straightened out', the enclosure had sides of almost exactly 100 perches (or rods) in length (using the formula 1 perch/rod = 5½ yds = 16½ ft)³. The apparent 'exactness' of the measurement when expressed in terms of the statute

---

³ I am grateful to Jem Harrison for his advice concerning the use of customary measures on the Glastonbury Abbey estates; and *cf* Foard 1992, 4-5.

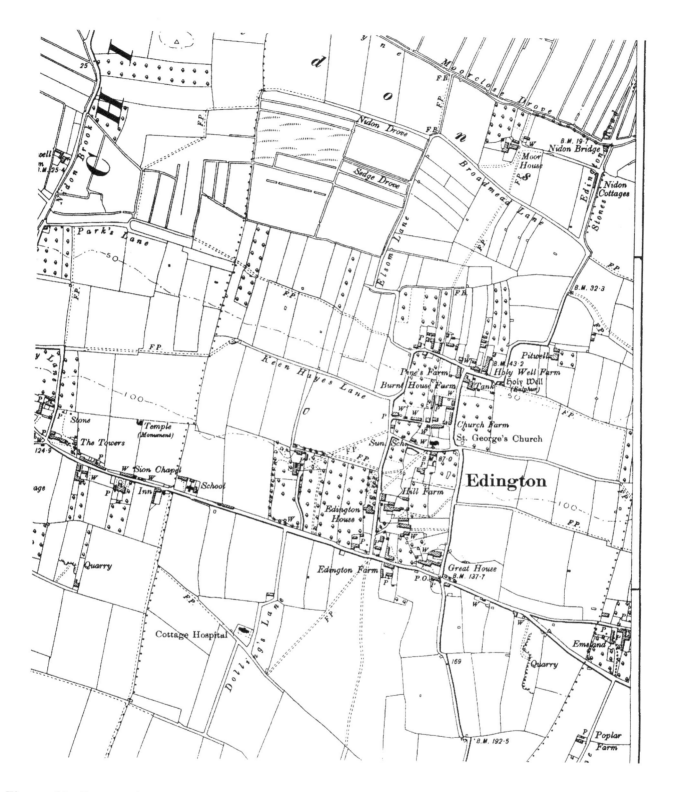

Figure 39: Extract from OS second edition 6" map (1904), showing the large trapezoidal enclosure attached to the northern end of the Edington village plan, containing what appear to be fossilised arable strip boundaries. The feature effectively forms a 'bridge' across a tract of low-lying ground between the field system proper to the south, and the slight rise of the Nidons to the north. Chilton parish is to the west, Catcott to the east.

perch may imply that the enclosure dates from some point *after* the end of the 12th century, when "at the Assize of Measures in 1196 the old perch of 20 'natural' feet became the perch of 16½ modern, standardised feet" [Fleming 1994, 112].

What, then, is the nature of this unusual feature? I suggest that it represents an attempt to extend the area of land under cultivation, involving drainage and reclamation activity, rather than being a planned *settlement* unit. It was clearly the result of a single, systematic and probably rapid act of enclosure. Its essential 'separateness' is indicated by the impression, from the disposition of the field boundaries within it, of its having been operated as a field unit in its own right, perhaps even outside the cropping regimes which operated on the rest of Edington's arable land. By the late 18th century, Edington had three open fields, South, East and West. There is no mention of a 'north' field, and it is likely that the South Field is a later development, created from an 'island' of surviving open field land that was left isolated when the southern parts of the East and West fields immediately south of the Broadway, became enclosed. A South Field that from the start occupied all the land from the Broadway south to the main ridge road, would have been disproportionately large compared to the East and West Fields.

While it does not appear to have been a part of the original (late Anglo-Saxon?) plan, the square enclosure is nonetheless sufficiently well integrated into the overall layout to be a relatively early addition, perhaps of the 11th or 12th century; and on Polden and elsewhere, David Musgrove has shown how it is precisely areas such as this, where an inlet of wetland forms an 'embayment' against the flank of higher ground, that were subject to the earliest reclamation activity in the post-Conquest period, since they "were easy to reach from dry land and [the] natural topography would have reduced the amount of enclosure required to prevent inundation in flood" [Musgrove 1999, 44]. We can also suggest that the occupation of its southern side was a later development, involving the extension of house crofts over open-field strips, giving a deceptively regular appearance, and rather in the manner that Susan Oosthuizen has recently described in Cambridgeshire [Oosthuizen 1997].

A splendid map of the manor of Edington and its associated survey book dating from 1794 [SRO DD/WG c/924; and DD/WG 11/19 respectively] allow us to suggest a possible sequence of events that links the creation of the square enclosure with the northward expansion of Edington's arable lands, and expressed here as Figure 40. It is likely that as originally cast, Edington's East and West fields extended only as far north as the northernmost cell of the main village plan. However, the 1794 map shows a block of open field arable, divided into strips and called East and West Nythons, occupying slightly higher ground, and separated from both the village and the main open field system by a short stretch of low-lying moor ground. The names suggest that, although physically divorced from them, these Nythons (the equivalent of the Nidons at Shapwick: Costen 1993, 90), may in the middle ages have

been operated as extensions of the East and West fields. It also seems possible that at least a part of the Nidons arable may have been worked from an isolated farmstead on the ridge itself[4]. Viewed in this light, the square enclosure assumes a logic as an attempt to take advantage of the very distinctive topography here by bridging the intervening moor ground and joining the two field systems together. By 1794 the enclosure was itself fully divided up by internal boundaries, but as we have already noted, and as the 1794 map makes doubly clear, there can be no doubting its origin as a 'conventional' block of open-field land worked in strips and furlongs. Whether by accident or design, it is also probable that, as time progressed, the enclosure acted as a focal point and catalyst for further reclamation and enclosure of the remaining low-lying land immediately adjacent to east and west, perhaps in phases – again, although totally laid down to pasture closes by 1794, the field boundaries here betray their open-field arable origins, and it is very noticeable that the much larger block to the west is divided in half by a continuous east/west boundary that may mark a division between stages in the process of reclamation and enclosure.

We can hardly doubt that in at least some cases the plans of the north Polden villages are intimately related to the shapes of their respective parishes. This is less true of Shapwick than it is of the central block containing Chilton, Edington and Catcott, all of which consist of a long, relatively narrow strip extending from the ridgeway down onto the wetland [Aston and Costen 1994a, 75, fig 11.1], and it seems clear that as originally cast, the northern boundaries of these parishes were marked by the east/west course of the River Brue. This is the clearest example in Whitley, and indeed within this study as a whole, of the regular, systematic subdivision of a block of land, with the parish bounds cast at right angles to the contour to take in the full range of resources offered by the natural topography. While much less regular in shape, and less recognisably the result of deliberate division of a larger unit (which nonetheless it probably once was, with Ashcott), it must be the case that allocation of a viable range of resources also provides the rationale behind the layout of Shapwick parish. Equally however, is it clear that Shapwick's somewhat truncated northern boundary, as compared to its eastern neighbours, arises from the proximity of Meare island to its north, which, perhaps precisely because of its topographical 'boundedness', seems to have been recognised as an autonomous estate as early as the late 7th century [Abrams 1996, 169-171]. By 1515 it is apparent that a line along the course of Shapwick's present northern boundary had at least been established, since it was noted that "the more and marsh is divided between Shapwyke and Mere by the boundary of the Twelve Hides of Glastonbury Abbey and that part of the moor which is outside the Twelve Hides belongs to the manor of Shapwyke" [Costen 1990, 43]. Indeed, the bounds of the Twelve Hides themselves recorded in the

---

[4] Moor House is depicted on the 1794 map in a position on the ridge symmetrically between the two blocks of arable represented by the 'Nythons'. The site is still occupied by a house of the same name.

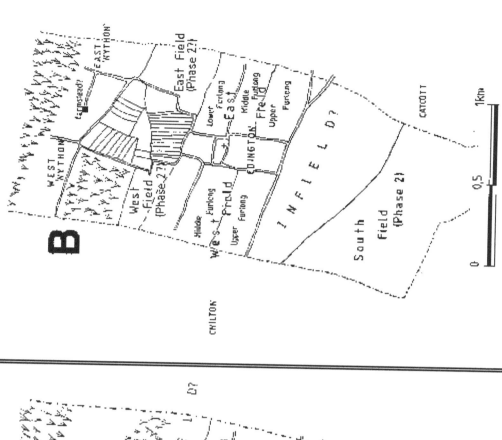

A: Late Anglo-Saxon period, associated with the establishment of a planned settlement, two formal common arable fields, East and West, with, to north and south, two further areas of occasionally-cultivated outfield. The high ground of the Nidons, further north, may already have been brought under the plough by this time, but was separated from the northern outfield by a belt of moor ground. To the south, a major boundary may mark a discontinuity between the southern outfield and a belt of non-arable land (woodland/ pasture?) at the southern extremity of the estate.

B: 11th/12th century. The southern outfield has now been brought f ormallywithin the regular field system, as has the previously unploughed belt further south which now forms a named South Field. To the north, a new trapezoidal enclosure has been attached to the northern end of the settlement, containing an independently-worked arable field system and forming a link across the low-lying moor ground between the East and West Fields and the Nidons ridge. The development of the enclosure has also acted as a catalyst for a second phase of expansion of the main field system northwards. It is possible that the Nidons arable may have been worked from an isolated farmstead sited on the ridge itself.

FIGURE 40 A model for the development of Edington's medieval field system

same source, going eastwards, took the surveyors "through the middle of the moor to the boundaries of Mere and Polden [ie Shapwick] where now boundary marks of willows are fixed". This is presumably a reference to trees planted along a fixed line in the otherwise featureless moor, probably alongside a rhyne. Morland observes that "the present boundary between Meare and Shapwick is the straight South Drain (which became the Glastonbury Abbey Canal) dug soon after 1800. A map of 1782 shows the same straight line. *The drain must have been dug along a recognised boundary*" [my emphasis; Morland 1984, 49]. This line seems, in fact, to have been in place by the mid 13th century [*ibid* 1984, 52-53]. The point is an important one since although still in 1515 Shapwick's *formal* manorial boundary may have lain further south [Costen 1998, 160-163], its share of the moor, commonable for its tenants, had probably long been allocated and marked on the ground. The same is likely, then, to have been true of Shapwick's western neighbours, and the high degree of regularity in terms of parish shape and size cannot be attributable to late-established boundaries, with earlier allocations stopping merely at the limit of the usable arable. The boundaries which come through on the tithe maps, encompassing land extending out into the moors, were probably recognised and marked in their entirety from an early date; although there may well have been occasions when the moors on the southern side of the Brue Valley, usually commonable, were 'annexed' temporarily into manorial severalty by their respective communities for their own use.

The three westernmost parishes, Cossington, Woolavington and Puriton, although perhaps lacking the absolute regularity of their three eastern neighbours, nonetheless would have lain easily together as a coherent antecedent unit. It is problematic whether we should interpret these various blocks as the result of a single phase of fragmentation and replanning or a series of phases, but we can at least say from topographical evidence that there was a major dichotomy in the nature of territorial arrangements between the eastern and western parts of this area (below).

In terms of settlements and their territories, the southern side of Polden stands in stark contrast to the northern, and it is worth reminding ourselves that this seems to have been a pattern established at least by the Roman period. As members of the 8th century *Pouholt* estate, it seems very likely that, again as in the Roman period, the settlements which became established on the southern side of the ridge at some as yet unknown date in the pre-Conquest period, were in some way dependent on those to the north; in the case of Sutton, such a link, to Shapwick, was made explicit in 1086 [Aston and Costen 1994a, 75, fig 11.1]. We have already seen that Moorlinch was also intimately associated with Shapwick. The communities from Stawell in the west, eastwards through Sutton Mallet and Moorlinch, to Greinton in the east (but with the exception of Pedwell), did develop into parishes, and by the early 14th century could clearly muster resources enough to furnish subsidies equal to or

exceeding those of most of their northern neighbours [Glasscock 1975, 273-274; Dickinson 1889, 118-123]; however, it is likely that this was a post-Conquest development related to drainage and reclamation activity in Sedgemoor [Musgrove 1999], and certainly in the late 11th century they appear to have been generally smaller [Aston and Costen 1994a, 75, fig 11.1]. It was probably the growth of these communities on the southern side of Polden, severing the northern estates from their traditional access to the summer grazing grounds on Sedgemoor, that necessitated the allocation of detachments in Sedgemoor to Shapwick and its western neighbours up to and including Woolavington [Corcos 1983, 52-53; I am grateful to Dr Harold Fox who originally suggested this to me].

However, it is the internal topography of the settlements themselves which most immediately distinguishes them from those estates to the north; for in not a single case by the mid 19th century was there any obvious intimation of regularity of plan layout, and the overall impression is of overwhelmingly 'organic' development (Figure 41). How far this picture would be altered by detailed topographical, archaeological and cartographic work, beyond the scope of this study, is another matter; and indeed what little evidence there is presents intriguing hints that any perceived irregularity in the plans of the settlements themselves may stand in stark contrast to what looks very much like a degree of 'conventional' *regularity* in at least some of the associated field systems, which compares very favourably with arrangements in the northern settlements. At Greinton, for example, in the early 14th century, the demesne arable was split between East and West Fields in the ratio 65 acres to 68 acres respectively [BL Egerton 3321, fos 32v-33r][5]. And even a grant of just a two-acre holding at Moorlinch in the mid 13th century included what looks like a careful and *equal* distribution of land: *unam acram terre arrabilis singulis annis in campo boriali et aliam acram in campo occidentali* [Watkin 1952, II, 387]. One possible inference is that, while perhaps the imperatives for planning and regularity of *settlements* were not as forceful on this side of the Polden ridge, the efficiency and close regulation of *agrarian* production was as much a central concern here as it was in those estates on the northern flank. An alternative explanation can be put forward, however. For whereas the very systematic regularity of the northern villages and their field systems invites the suggestion that such arrangements

---

[5] Although it is worth noting that at least by the end of the 18th century, the appearance at Greinton of a third sub-divided field (known as North or Hill Field) had disrupted the original medieval symmetry. As at Shapwick though, this was almost certainly a post-medieval development, attributable to the progressive disintegration of the open-field system through the exchange and consolidation of strip holdings prior to enclosure. SRO DD/CC 200751 (1773), An Account of Common Field Lands in Greinton, Diocese of Bath and Wells, sub-deanery estates. For this and subsequent occasional references to other medieval field systems on and around Polden, the original document (BL Egerton 3321) was consulted on microfilm. Ian Keil provides tabulated information, with furlong names, for *some* of the same demesne arable arrangements using the same document as his source, *except* for Walton. See Keil 1964, Appendix II, 210-216, and 221-222, for Street, Walton, Ashcott, Greinton and High Ham.

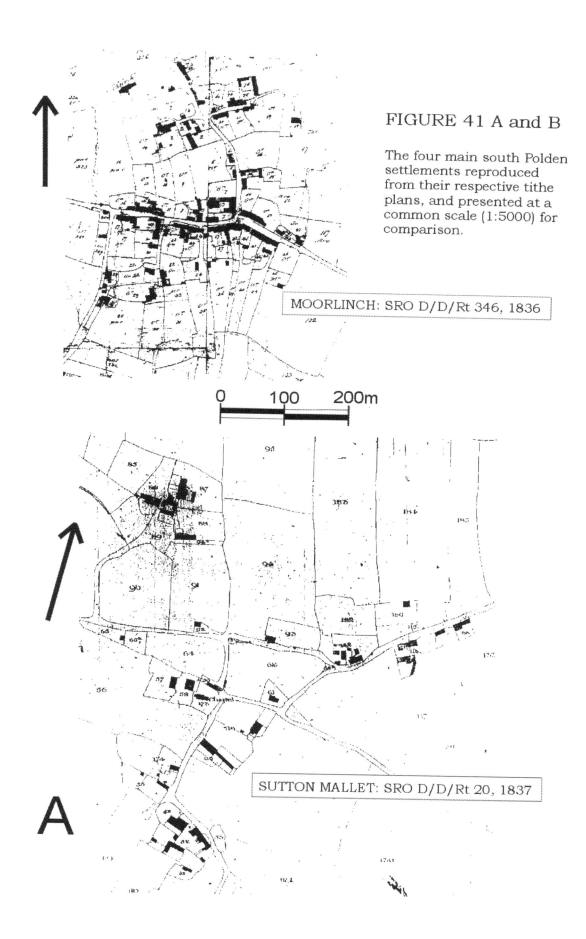

FIGURE 41 A and B

The four main south Polden settlements reproduced from their respective tithe plans, and presented at a common scale (1:5000) for comparison.

MOORLINCH: SRO D/D/Rt 346, 1836

SUTTON MALLET: SRO D/D/Rt 20, 1837

A

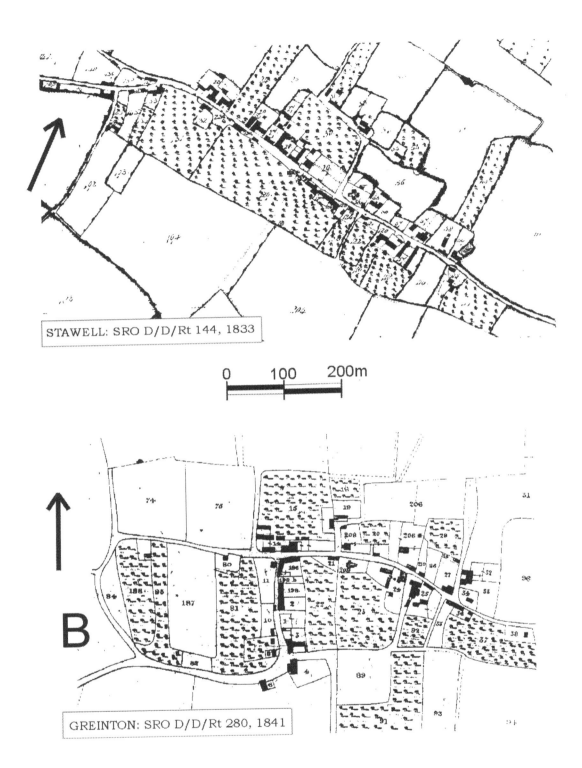

STAWELL: SRO D/D/Rt 144, 1833

0   100   200m

B

GREINTON: SRO D/D/Rt 280, 1841

are the result of deliberate planning, even if in a series of phases, so also is it possible that the adoption of regular field systems on the southern side of the ridge is the result of nothing more than simple mimicry. This is a process by which the transmission, or the diffusion, of fashion and ideas, in a rather haphazard way and without the catalyst of any systematic outside interference, may occur within a group of estates, linked perhaps by both common ownership and straightforward propinquity [*cf* Dyer *et al* 1997, 175]. Indeed, we may be able to set the south Polden villages in a far wider context, since as Dyer *et al* have recently highlighted in the East Midlands, it seems that this pattern of *regular* field system associated with *irregular* settlement is more widespread than we might suppose: "the existence in so many places of amorphous clusters of tenements rather than neatly planned rows suggests that we are dealing with many cases where the village accumulated at its site in a gradual and uncoordinated fashion, as a result of a series of decisions rather than a single act.........often the field system was more orderly than the village, and it seems likely that the nucleated village was really a by-product of the agricultural changes that encouraged the formation of the fields" [Dyer *et al* 1997, 204]. A separate, detailed review of the Northamptonshire evidence leads Brown and Foard to a similar conclusion: "the creation of regular settlements was not the inevitable corollary of the laying out of planned field systems" [Brown and Foard 1998, 89].

In any event, it is these southern communities, together with a consideration of the distribution of potential resources, which, as I will suggest, hold the key to understanding at least the outlines of the development of settlements and their territories on Polden in the mid to late Anglo-Saxon period. This western half of Polden appears to be *par excellence* a sub-region of intense nucleation, and so it is, but even here there are vestiges of dispersal, both surviving and vanished, and the importance of which in the context of the overall settlement pattern is probably completely disproportionate to both its extent and the very little we know about it. At Shapwick, an accumulation of ten years evidence from field-names, intensive field walking, detailed topographical and botanical studies, soil analysis and selective excavation, is building up a picture of late pre-Conquest dispersal and subsequent, and possibly phased nucleation dated tentatively at present to the 10th and/or 11th centuries [Aston and Penoyre 1994, 27-44; Aston 1998, 237-243; Aston and Gerrard 1999, 27-29]. Even at Shapwick however, a single isolated site, at Kent Farm, was occupied in the middle ages, as indeed it remains today [SSAVBRG 1990, 76-77]. The current view is that Kent was probably established as a late Saxon or early post-Conquest mill site [Aston 1993a, 12], to which specialist function it may well owe its survival; however, the occurrence of scatters of early medieval pottery from a site immediately to the south [Gerrard and Gutierrez 1997, fig 5.1, 40-41; 50; and fig 6.23, 80] indicates at least the possibility that Kent does indeed represent a tenacious remnant of an earlier settlement pattern.

If, then, in terms of evidence for specifically dispersed settlement, Shapwick is regarded as the template

for this part of Polden, how far can we identify any of its attributes among its western neighbours? In tackling this question we are immediately confronted with a paucity of evidence which the riches from Shapwick serve merely to throw into sharp relief. Little is known from archaeology, apart from the few brief glimpses afforded by the Polden pipeline campaign (Chapter Two). The results from Shapwick should allow us to point to a faded but distinct pattern of early medieval dispersal tightly interwoven into the fabric of nucleation, and also to say that the former is likely to have preceded the latter. It is all the more frustrating, then, that, always excluding Shapwick itself, physical indications of medieval dispersal are both pitifully few and ill-understood. Just outside the hundred the isolated and deserted medieval hamlet at Crook, in Bawdrip parish (North Petherton hundred; but see also fn 29, above), was a Domesday community and therefore almost certainly a late Saxon one. It is also one of the very few such sites in this area which has been the subject of a detailed earthwork survey to modern standards [Aston 1985, 9-10; Thorn and Thorn 1980, 363, note 24.7]. However, in the western Polden parishes proper (northern and southern settlements), a grand total of two isolated, deserted medieval farmsteads are known or suspected: at Cossington [SMR 11184], close to its eastern boundary with Chilton, and another to the south-west of Moorlinch, on the 5m contour on the very edge of Sedgemoor [SMR 11258]. For the purposes of this study, then, it is field names which must be placed centre stage, since at present they alone provide the kind of overview that is needed to enable us to discern wider relationships, even if we know that those patterns are inevitably flawed. And indeed, even a very broad survey of a part, only, of this evidence, which is all that can be attempted here, suggests intriguing possibilities.

The number of *possible* habitative toponyms that might be taken as indicative of former occupation sites is extensive, but any working list would certainly need to contain elements such as *-worth*, *-wick*, *-tun*, *-cot*, *-croft*, *-hay* and *-huish* [Ford 1979, 156; Corcos 1983, 51; Costen 1992b]. As we have already seen in the specific case of Sladwick, at Shapwick, the occurrence of these as field and furlong names in the middle ages has been one means of 'targetting' areas for closer study, in the search for an antecedent, pre-Conquest settlement pattern [Costen 1993, 94-100][6]. Even if and when they *are* discovered, however,

---

[6] The use of soil chemical techniques, developed and to some extent pioneered by the Shapwick Project, is another extremely important application in this respect. See Aston and Martin 1998a, b and c. It is highly intriguing that, as Keil remarks, in the medieval period "the best arable at Walton in the Eastfield was a close called "Worthy" and this remained in cultivation, almost continuously until 1493"; Keil 1964, 84, n15. If the Walton *worthy* does indeed mark a pre-Conquest occupation site, we can speculate that its marked fertility arose directly from an accumulation, perhaps over the course of centuries, of organic material generated by the pre-existing farmstead. It seems that the results of the Shapwick soil chemical work serve to confirm what was already well known to contemporaries. It also suggests that future work on *compoti* which looks systematically at land values of open-field furlongs (*not* just those with habitative names), may prove valuable in tracing former occupation sites. This, again, is something which Keil has studied, but *not* from a settlement perspective; *ibid*, Table B, Appendix II, 207-222.

only archaeology can provide secure dating for such sites, and the validity of this technique loses nothing in the light of recent excavations in Devon, which failed to locate any evidence of pre-12th century occupation on the site of a - *worth* at Roadford [Hooke 1998, 168]. It may indeed be, as Svensson has suggested, that, for very specific reasons, - *worthy* in Devon is overwhelmingly a *post*-Conquest name [Svensson 1991-92].

For Cossington and Greinton, lists of topographical names have been abstracted from both published and primary sources by David Musgrove as part of his wider study of the medieval exploitation of the Somerset Levels [Musgrove, *pers comm*]. At Cossington, in the mid 13th century, *Berecrofte* may suggest a former occupation site by then associated with the growing of barley [*cf* Field 1993, 96]. At Greinton, for which Musgrove's listings are far more detailed, still, only two names might be classed as potentially habitative, *Childeston* and *Yakeworthy,* both from 14th century sources. For the other western Polden parishes, a list compiled by Michael Costen from the mid-19th century tithe surveys provides the chief source. No certain habitative names survived to this period in any of the northern Polden villages west of Shapwick, with the major exception of Puriton. Here, interestingly, those habitative names which *do* occur are characteristic of, and can be safely associated with, the known Roman occupation there, rather than with early medieval settlement (above). *Blackland, Chisland* and *Crockland* all occur on the tithe map, as does *Bannick*, and the latter, as we have already seen, is almost certainly a –*wick* (Figure 42). On the southern side of the ridge, the toponymic evidence for abandoned occupation sites, while equally sparse, is nonetheless not entirely absent. *Blackland, Wadborough, Smolton* and *Tompenton* occur at Stawell; *Yeoton* and *Righton* at Sutton Mallet; and *Sidelington, Blacklands* and *Sharpington* at Moorlinch.

It is of course quite likely that a systematic trawl through even the published medieval sources, such as those produced by the Somerset Record Society, would reveal names which could be added to, or which would reinforce the authenticity of these 19th century examples. However, even at this level, it is possible to form certain general impressions. The largest parish in this group by far is Shapwick itself, whose tithable area in the mid 19th century was 3,781 acres (just over 1,530 ha) [Kain and Oliver 1995, 446]. A list of all the certain or probable habitative field-names that we know about at Shapwick (but which have *not* all necessarily been located on the ground), *including* those with connotations of occupation (such as *Blacklands* and *Abchester*), would include:

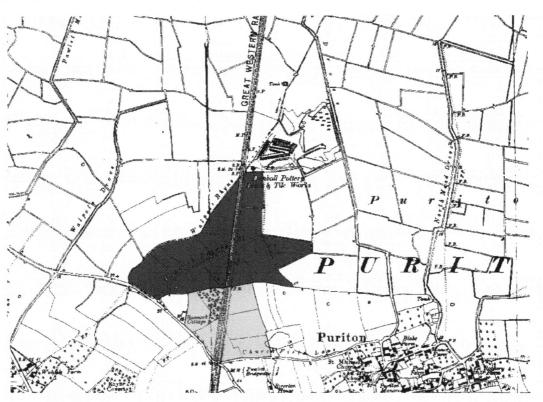

Figure 42

Extract from OS second edition 6" map (1904), showing (shaded) indicative field names north-west of Puriton: Bannick (dark grey), and Crockland (light grey). The line of the Great Western railway passes through both sets of enclosures, and the area has revealed substantial archaeological evidence for extensive settlement in the Roman period. Source: Puriton tithe map, SRO D/D/Rt 384, 1842.

Abchester
Blackland
Buddle
Grasshay
Henry
Sladwick
Worthie
Chestell

Purycroft
Ludcrofte
Bassecastell
la Grange
Snadwick
Abofehaies
Manycrofte

[Sources: Costen 1993; Aston *et al* 1998d; Ecclestone 1998]. This produces a density of one habitative name for about every 252a [102ha]. We can compare this with the other parishes in this group which have produced evidence of habitative field names [tithable areas from Kain and Oliver 1995]:

PARISH	HABITATIVE NAMES	TITHABLE AREA	DENSITY OF NAMES
Cossington	1	1381a [560ha]	1/1381a [560ha]
Greinton	2	845a [342ha]	1/422a [171ha]
Moorlinch	3	1122a [455ha]	1/374a [151ha]
Puriton	4	1577a [639ha]	1/394a [160ha]
Stawell	4	974a [395ha]	1/243a [98ha]
Sutton	2	879a [356ha]	1/439a [178ha]

This is of course a rather crude measure and there are good reasons why these densities should be regarded as absolute minima. One is merely the unknown incidence of loss of names due to the vagaries of differential survival. The figures are heavily weighted in favour of Shapwick *in part* (but *not*, I would argue, entirely) simply because it has been studied in such depth, and probably therefore represents as complete a corpus of habitative names as we are ever likely to recover. Their virtual absence in the 19th century in all the parishes west of Shapwick *except* Puriton may well to some extent be misleading: witness the case of *Beerecrofte* at Cossington, attested, as we have seen, in the 13th century but absent by the 19th; more detailed documentary work that is outside the scope of this study would be needed to confirm or refute this on any systematic basis. However, from the very survival of such names at Shapwick into the 19th century, I would infer as a *general* principle that their apparent absence from its western neighbours does indeed reflect a genuine scarcity.

We must also bear in mind that in those parishes in which we find habitative toponyms in western Polden, the densities of survival will in fact be higher than shown because in virtually all cases the area available for settlement would have been *smaller*, sometimes considerably so, than the 19th century tithable area; since the later parishes included large areas of formerly low-lying moor ground which in the early medieval period would not have been suitable for anything other than seasonal occupation. In the case of Shapwick itself, for example, we can subtract the 1000-odd acres [just over

400ha] of Heath Moor on the southern side of the Brue Valley, which underwent enclosure by parliamentary act after 1784 [Tate 1948, 41]. Taking this fact into account increases the density of known habitative names at Shapwick to 1 about every 185 acres [75ha]. To a greater or lesser extent, the same is true of every parish in this group, although more difficult to quantify since outside Shapwick, parishes tended to be grouped together for the purposes of moorland enclosure in the 18th and 19th centuries [*cf* Tate 1948, *passim*]. However, if we take the 5m contour as the likely limit of occupiable land in the early medieval period, then, for example, on north Polden, the available settlement area of both Catcott and Chilton is reduced to about a third of the later tithable area, and that of Edington to about two thirds; since the northern third of the latter contains Burtle island which was a known focus of medieval settlement, in the form of the small religious house of Burtle Priory, from at least the late 12th century [Bond and Horner 1991, 155], just as its favourable position, in terms of access to resources, is likely to have made it in the pre-Conquest period. In none of these parishes did habitative field names survive in the 19th century. At both Cossington and Woolavington the potential reduction in the habitable area is closer to a half, but only at Cossington do we have a single field name with habitative connotations; and the specifically 'Roman' affinities of the names at Puriton, we have already noted.

Already in this chapter we have applied, briefly, the evidence of the 1327 Lay Subsidy to Chew hundred. An examination of this source for Whitley reveals a comparatively low incidence of locative surnames from most of the manors within the hundred, all of which it seemed best to include here in one place. The inference may be that by the early 14th century, most members of these communities lived at some central location and did not need to be more specifically identified by the use of a locative epithet. This is particularly true of the settlements north and south of the Polden ridge. In by far the majority of instances, I have taken the Middle English preposition *atte* to indicate surnames that are likely to have been derived from sites actually in occupation in 1327; a very few other forms are also included, as for example where a 1327 surname can unequivocally be equated with a modern local place-name, or where it simply seems reasonable that we should infer the existence of an occupied site. The results are as follows:

ASHCOTT   atte Grove, atte Orchard, atte Brigge, atte Wynke, Bythemore.

BUTLEIGH   atte Hole, atte Mulle, atte Moore.

CHILTON   Bythemore, atte Broke, atte Welle.

COMPTON DUNDON   atte Orchard.

COSSINGTON   atte Broke.

GREINTON   atte Berne, atte Niche.

MIDDLEZOY	atte Drene, atte Grove, atte Sloo, atte Mere, atte Lupyete, Greylake, atte Chaumbre.
MOORLINCH	Greylake.
OTHERY	atte Kethene, atte Streme, atte Wothete, atte Grove, atte Combe, atte Watere, atte Mere.
STAWELL	atte Pole, atte Mulle.
STREET	atte Yete, atte Brighende.
WALTON	in the Hele, Bythemore.
WESTON ZOYLAND	Greylake, atte Weye, atte Tynyng, atte Mere
WOOLAVINGTON	atte Solere.

Shapwick, Catcott and Edington are noticeable by their absence from this list, and we may also note that both Cossington and Woolavington are distinguished by only a single locative surname each. Sutton, although taxed, is also absent here, as is Puriton (taxed as a manor in its own right, apparently outside hundredal jurisdiction: Dickinson 1889, 253), while Ham is not included in the returns at all. While we must be cautious in applying more weight than the immediate evidence can bear, nonetheless it is worth remembering that, *apart* from Sutton, these are also *precisely* those places which display the clearest evidence of being planned settlements. Conversely, if applied to Chilton, we might take this evidence to undermine slightly the case for placing it too in this category; although the recurrent epithet 'bythemore' may reflect nothing more than the late (ie post-Conquest) occupation of land newly won through the individualistic drainage, reclamation and enclosure activity that, as we have already seen, we know to have been in operation around the moorland fringes at least from the 13th century (see 'Sowy', below). As with field names, we must be at least aware that many circumstances may have combined to influence the way in which locative surnames have survived. However, the case of Ashcott, with five names in 1327, is especially interesting, and as a possible remnant of a pattern that did not survive in its neighbouring villages into the medieval period, may indicate a rather different (arrested?) line of development, emphasising yet again that the Shapwick/Ashcott boundary seems to represent a clear discontinuity in the nature of settlement east and west of it.

Shapwick alone excepted therefore, we are faced with the need to explain why, apparently, there should be a denser pattern of survival of habitative field names in those smaller parishes on Polden's southern flank, than there is in the larger, more topographically favoured, putatively 'primary' settlements on the northern side west of Shapwick. An attempt to answer that question, to synthesise the disparate strands of evidence and establish a *tentative* 'unifying theory' for the origin of the medieval

settlement pattern on Polden, is the purpose of the Conclusion which forms the final section of this study. Now though, we need to turn our attention briefly to the eastern part of the ridge proper, and the territory occupied chiefly by the parishes of Walton and Street.

Eastern Polden

East of Shapwick lie Walton and Street, the latter marking the eastern extremity of the Polden ridge proper. As the name suggests, Street is primarily linear in shape, with, in the 19th century, by far the greatest concentration of settlement lying along the main road through the village towards Lower Leigh, south-west of the church. Traces of regular plot layout are apparent from the tithe map in the properties either side of the stretch of the main road closest to the large triangular market place, immediately to its south-west. This is particularly true of the plots on the western side [see maps in McGarvie1987]. Further south, an area of apparently very regular plots extends both east and west of the street giving the impression of a coherent, planned unit. If so, it is certainly a post-Conquest development, since the main settlement in the parish, Street itself, grew up along a new road constructed in the late 12th century [McGarvie 1987, 36-37]. What is significant about Street is the persistence right through the medieval period of a dispersed settlement pattern of considerable antiquity. Michael McGarvie has shown that the single Old English place-name *Lega* in 1086 disguises the existence of at least three separate entities which emerge in the medieval period as Lower, Middle and Over Leigh [McGarvie 1987, 29 and 33-35]. In addition, by the late 12th century, there existed a holding centred on Ivythorn, at the southern end of the parish, which survives as an isolated farm and which in the medieval period was regarded as a separate manor [McGarvie 1987, 43]. Blackgrove Farm, on an isolated fen-edge site at the eastern extremity of the parish, was in existence by the 13th century [Gathercole 1997a, 13], and as I will argue later on for Sowy Island, may have originated as a pre-Conquest colonising farm designed to exploit systematically an important resource-interface. The Street tithe award contains no field names with connotations of settlement. Early 19th map evidence gives little hint of the same highly regular arrangement as regards the distribution of land between open fields, with the village placed dead centre between them, that was still so striking a feature at Shapwick even at that late date [McGarvie 1987, map of Street, 1821; Aston 1994b]. There can be no doubting the regularity of Street's *core* field system, with the demesne arable balanced almost evenly between the two main fields, East (239 acres) and West (249 acres) [BL Egerton 3321, ff60v-61v]. Whether such order extended over the entire estate is, though, quite another matter. What is now the main settlement at Street is strongly 'offset' in the north-western quarter of its parish, a considerable distance from the higher land at the southernmost part of the estate, which is where by the early 19th century most of the arable land had become concentrated. In terms of operational convenience, such an arrangement is probably best interpreted as evidence that, outside the area of the East and West fields, the disposition of arable was less regular, based instead on autonomous field 'systems' surrounding each of the three Leighs, and farmed partially or wholly in severalty [*cf* Brown and Taylor, 1989].

Walton, another 'street' village lying east-west along the main A39 road between Puriton and Glastonbury Abbey, displays considerable regularity in the plot layouts on either side of the road, particularly along the south side, which is marked by a distinct, common boundary at the southern end of the plots, and in the eastern end of the north row. Likewise, a southern extension along a north-south road at the eastern end of the main settlement contains regular plots running east-west, more marked on the western side [SRO D/D/Rt 428, 1843]. It is possible that this part of the village marks a separate phase of expansion at some date in the early post-Conquest period.

Settlement in Whitley Beyond Polden

Butleigh, by contrast, shows little sign from the tithe map of regular plan elements. The main body of the settlement in the early 19th century lay in a disjointed and discontinuous line along either side of the minor road curving around in a north-south arc south of the church. While many of the plots have straight boundaries, it is difficult to discern any overall uniformity in terms of their size and disposition. The clear relationship between the church of St Leonard and Butleigh Court, a Victorian mansion on a medieval site, strongly suggests a 'classic' church-manor complex. A site in the centre of the village has revealed evidence of occupation dating from the 12th century, but not earlier [Hollinrake C and N 1995, 177]. In stark contrast to Ham (below), there are few hints in Butleigh that much of any antecedent pattern of dispersed settlement survived into the post-Conquest period, something of a surprise in view of their strong similarity in terms of extensive woodland coverage. This is the more so since there are certainly indications that a pattern of at least semi-dispersal existed at Butleigh before 1066. Archaeologically, only a single deserted farmstead is known; unexcavated apart from an associated dovecote it is nonetheless probably medieval in date [Aston 1976, 74; SMR 23181]. We have already noted the field name Oldbury, in the north-western quarter of the parish, in relation to the Butleigh Anglo-Saxon charter S270a. The furlong names Easterworth and Westerworth were recorded in the early 14th century [BL Egerton 3321, 109r and v], and a field-name *worthey* appears in 1627 [SRO D/D/Rg 186]; it is probably their successors which survived into the mid-19th century as a group of tithe names of this form [Costen 1992b, 75, for names and tithe numbers]. The boundary clause of the Butleigh charter itself, as we have already seen, furnishes some evidence that isolated farmsteads at the edge of the estate were in existence by the very early 9th century, and yet a further example of a 'Gaston' field name, the suggested settlement context of which will by now be familiar, occurs on the tithe map a few hundred metres to the south of, and therefore well outside, the present village core (Figure 43).

The field layout was clearly based on a two-field arrangement: in the early 14th century there was a West Field, but its partner is described simply as *"utroque campo"*, which in the context can only be translated as 'the other field' [BL Egerton 3321, *ff*109v and 110r]. It would be perfectly reasonable to attribute this to nothing more than scribal ignorance or laziness, since from the late 13th century there survive clear references to an East Field and a West Field [Watkin 1952, II, 418-419]. The name Westfield survives to the present day attached to a lane; however, it is possible that this represents part of a *separate* field system associated with Butleigh Wootton. Revd Synge publishes a map showing a West Field at Wootton, and observes that "there are slight indications that it may have had three fields", but without, unfortunately, elaborating on exactly what these 'indications' are or his source(s) for them [Synge 1974, 6-7]. Within its parish, Butleigh is offset very strongly to the east, and a field layout such as suggested by Synge would make topographical sense as it would place Butleigh far more centrally between its East and West Fields. Synge suggests that the Butleigh East Field/West Field boundary was the main road running NW/SE from Wootton, through Butleigh, and then SSW up to the Polden ridge road. The line of the northern boundary, he maintains, was "where the cedar avenue now runs". Although logical, this is by no means certain, and in any event there is an additional problem of which we need to take account. The field name Oldbury, as we have already seen, occurs in the northern extremity of Butleigh parish, northeast of Wootton, and in the early 14th century, it was held to be in the 'West Field' [BL Egerton 3321, 109v]. It is always possible that, while perhaps being included within Butleigh's overall resources, field arrangements at Wootton were dealt with separately. However, in view of the topographical difficulties here, this is unlikely. The relevant entry in Egerton 3321 relates specifically to the Butleigh demesne and almost certainly refers to that community's own West Field. There is indeed no separate mention of Wootton at all, but the known position of Oldbury makes it difficult to fit into the context of a 'West Field' for either Butleigh *or* Wootton. One possible solution would be to postulate that Butleigh's *original* field system extended only as far northwards as a line running NW/SW, roughly represented by Rowley's Farm, and that even by the late Anglo-Saxon period, the north-western quarter of the estate remained heavily wooded, as indeed it had been in the early 9th century; so much is clear from the charter evidence. Later on, the establishment of Wootton (?10th/11th century; see further below), may have led to the creation of a separate field system which for a time was operated independently of Butleigh's, but which was later incorporated into it as a north-westward extension of the original West Field, Oldbury included.

Butleigh Wootton lies well away from the main village, just under 2km to the north-west. We can only speculate about its origins, but its straightforward Old English name is 'the wood tun' [Gelling 1984, 227], tending to reinforce the impression that it was founded as a late pre-Conquest, woodland-edge, 'colonising' farmstead,

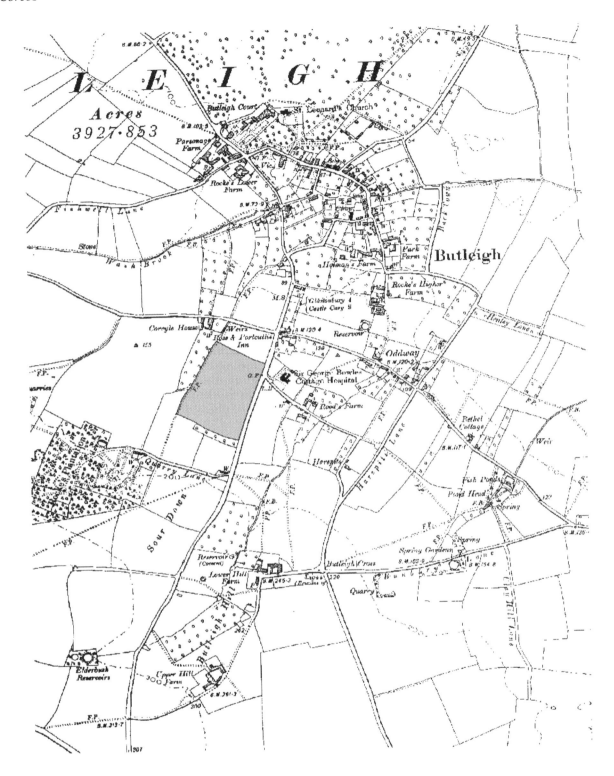

FIGURE 43

Extract from second edition OS 6" map (1904), showing (shaded) the position of Garston field name in relation to Butleigh village. Source: Butleigh tithe map and award, SRO D/D/Rt 434, 1843.

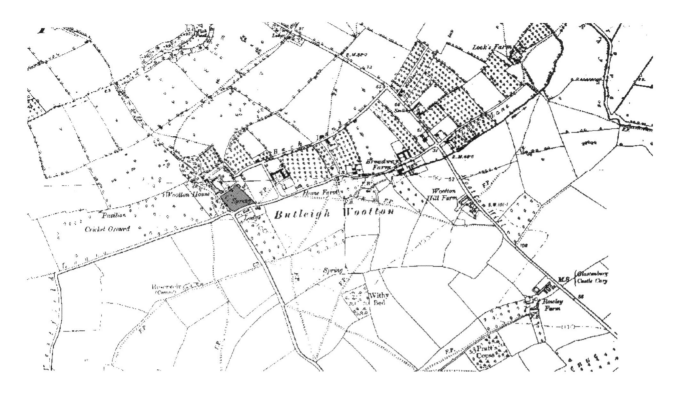

FIGURE 44

Reduced extract from OS first edition 6" map (1885), showing Butleigh Wootton. Chapel Hays lies in the orchard immediately north of Wootton House, and the (?Roman) road forming the southern side of the suggested grid plan runs south-westwards, its line continued by a footpath heading straight towards the Roman villa at Marshall's Elm (Street) immediately west of the map edge. The shaded area represents a Ga(r)ston field name, immediately adjacent to what is suggested as the initial late Saxon/early post-Conquest 'manorial' site probably marked by Wootton House, and from which a regular grid plan layout of streets and house plots extends eastwards. Source: Butleigh tithe map and award, SRO D/D/Rt 434, 1843.

which prospered and became important enough perhaps for a time to enjoy a status as a manor in its own right, with its own fields carved partly from the adjacent woodland. It is most likely at this stage, probably in the fifty years or so on either side of the Conquest, that we should expect the present, very regular plan to have been established (Figure 44), although it should be said that there is no firm evidence for this, and comparison with evidence from Compton may suggest a rather later date (below). However, the fact that it is known specifically as *Butleigh* Wootton indicates an origin as a dependency of the main settlement, perhaps with the specific purpose of opening up the northern part of the estate to more systematic exploitation, although *not* necessarily, at first, to expand the area under arable; since, as Margaret Gelling points out, "settlements so named perhaps had a special function in relation to the wood and its products" [Gelling 1984, 227]. Alternatively, while originating as a totally autonomous settlement, it may later on have lost its independence and been brought firmly within Butleigh's manorial orbit; certainly by the late 12th century, a holding there could be described quite specifically as *"apud Wotton' infra manerium de Buddeclegh'"* [quoted by

Weaver 1910, 63], and this also appears to be the earliest documentary reference to the place. Yet again though, the appearance of a 'Ga(r)ston' name immediately adjacent to Wootton House on its southern side, might seem to strengthen the case for the existence of an early (ie late Saxon) 'manorial' core in this area probably *prior* to the laying out of the regular grid plan.

Wootton's significance is that it is one of only two examples in Whitley (the other being Compton in Dundon, below) of what are clearly subsidiary, sub-parochial *planned* settlements, but different in form, and almost certainly earlier than, New Town in Chew Magna. Wootton itself displays a simple, but nonetheless clearly defined arrangement of two parallel east/west lanes closed on the east by the main road between Butleigh, Street, and Glastonbury Abbey, and on the west by a minor road originally forming a north/south through route to the west of Wootton House, but which was closed off in the early 19th century to take traffic away from the front of the mansion [SRO Q/SR roll 408, midsummer 1818]. Indeed it is highly likely that the *southern* side of the proposed plan layout is likewise based on the line of an antecedent road. Running east/west, this was once clearly an important route, and its status as a probable medieval 'Broadway', comparable with the secondary east/west route along the Polden ridge (above) is suggested by the farm of that name which fronts onto it [*cf* Room 1992, 14 and 20]. It is possible even that we should consider a Roman origin for this road, since its dead straight western section is aligned precisely on the site of the villa at Marshall's Elm; the present right-angled bend to the south could be a later diversion. At its eastern end this track would have run right out to the fringes of the Brue valley wetland, and we can easily envisage a use as a drove for stock being taken out to the summer grazing grounds there.

Wootton therefore provides yet a further example of a plan framework apparently taking its cue from *pre-existing* routes, a theme with which we are already well familiar from the north Polden settlements; the basic rectangular outline thus formed was almost certainly divided internally into several rectilinear 'cells' by a number of short north/south lanes, but only one of these survives, at the western end of the plan. The tenacity of this particular element of the layout may not be due merely to chance; for it is here in this westernmost cell that we find Wootton House, in its present form apparently dating from the early 18th century [Bush 1994, 54], but almost certainly the successor to a medieval house on the same site. This supposition receives strong support from the known existence, in the medieval period, of a chapel hard by on the north side of the mansion, in an enclosure known in 1843 as Chapel Orchard [SRO D/D/Rt 434, t469], and even more significantly, as Chapel *Hay* Orchard just over twenty years earlier [SRO Q/SR roll 408, midsummer 1818]. The suspicion of some kind of early 'manorial' core in this area is reinforced by yet another occurrence of the name Gaston attached to an orchard adjacent to the southern side of Wootton House [t467]. We can reasonably speculate that the original pre-Conquest 'wood *tūn*' lay somewhere here, and that subsequently a small, planned settlement was laid out immediately to its east. This is a similar sequence of development to that which has been tentatively proposed for Compton in Dundon, and although at Wootton, dating is problematic, parallels with Compton, for which archaeology suggests a date in the 12th century, are unavoidable.

By the early 19th century Dundon had the appearance of a regular 'street' village, aligned along a north-south road, which had undergone shrinkage. This is indicated particularly in a series of regularly-sized plots on the eastern side of the road, clearly once occupied by dwellings but largely deserted at the time of the tithe map. The church lies at the northern end of the settlement and there is an intriguing hint of a pre-village manorial core here in the form of a continuous boundary following a curving alignment south and south-east of the church. A straight road leading south from the church goes through this boundary and joins the main road south through the village. It might, then, be reasonable to see an antecedent settlement focus, with the church, to the north, followed in a later phase by a planned extension to the south [Aston 1994, 225; Ellison 1983, 114-116]. An evaluation excavation at a site in the village core produced pottery which "ranged in date from the late 10th to early 11th through to the 20th century......the majority......dated from the late 12th to the 14th century" [Hollinrakes 1989, 172]. While we should be cautious in the use of pottery *alone* to date plan layouts (and always depending on the context in which it is found), the proven occupation of a village-centre site in the late Anglo-Saxon period is at least suggestive.

Within Dundon parish, about 1km or so away to the north-east, lies Compton, which appears to be a sub-parochial planned settlement [Bush 1994, 70-71; Ellison 1983, 114-116]. Again, however, dating is highly problematic. Despite difficulties of interpretation and identification, Lesley Abrams tends to the view that Compton probably *is* the same 5 hide estate of that name which came into Glastonbury Abbey's hands in the mid 8th century, and which survived obviously intact for just over 300 years to be recorded in Domesday [Abrams 1996, 94-96].

As I have already suggested, we can draw certain parallels between Butleigh Wootton and Compton. Unlike Compton, Wootton is not attested as an estate in pre-Conquest sources. As I have proposed for Wootton, however, so also has it been suggested for Compton that an antecedent 'manorial' site, with its own chapel, and located at one end (in this case the northernmost) of the planned block, probably represents the original Anglo-Saxon *cumb tūn*, the 'farmstead/estate/settlement in the valley' [*cf* Gelling 1998, 85-89]. Bush has suggested that the planned element at Compton may be linked with a charter for a market and fair granted in the late 13th century [Bush 1994, 70-71; CCR II, 340, 17 Edw I]. As Christopher Taylor has shown, there is certainly strong evidence that such grants did indeed have a direct and demonstrable effect on settlement form, and Compton accords well in terms of both the date of its grant, and its layout, to the examples which he quotes [Taylor 1982]. Ellison, however, highlights the strong likelihood that despite appearances, Compton's is *not* a coherent, unified plan, but a phased development of at least two parts [Ellison 1983, 114]; even if the grant were responsible for one of these, it is clearly not the whole story, for what archaeology there is shows that Ellison's suggested first-phase plan, stretching along Compton Street southwards from the putative 'manorial' site, probably dates from the 12th century, and cannot therefore be associated with the market grant [Hollinrakes 1996, 165]. It is more likely to be Ellison's second-phase development, whose plots are on a markedly different alignment than the first, and which clusters around the main crossroads and the (?market) cross, that is specifically linked to the later grant [Ellison 1983, 114-116]. The overall pattern, as between Dundon, Compton and Wootton, again, therefore, invites comparison. The parochial settlement at Dundon (whether planned or otherwise) was in existence on or near its present site by the 10th century, followed by 12th and 13th century planned elements tacked on to a *pre-existing*, and clearly (from the historical evidence) early 'manorial' core. At Butleigh the evidence is altogether poorer, and will not bear too much weight, but Wootton's striking resemblance to Compton might well set us thinking along similar lines, and points up both Butleigh and Wootton as places inviting much more systematic topographical, archaeological and documentary study.

High Ham reveals a plan quite unlike anything else we have seen so far [Ellison 1983, 38-39]. The core of the settlement is formed by a large open 'square', with access roads leading in to each of the four corners. The rectangular churchyard enclosure, far from being integrated easily into the plan, sits uncomfortably in the north-west corner of the square, jutting out into it, and has the distinct appearance of an intrusive (later?) element, disrupting an otherwise perfectly symmetrical arrangement. Around the square itself there does not appear to be any evidence of regular plot layout, with the exception of the eastern side where a block of very long tenements, of varying widths, runs north-south. However, on the western side of the road leading north from the north-east corner of the square, a block of tenements, with plots running back to a common boundary, displays clear evidence of regularity in terms of size and shape, even allowing for both amalgamation and subdivision. There appear to be at least two planned elements here: the square itself (again, possibly an original manorial core, or a successor to one), and the northern 'extension'. The square has been called a 'green' [Aston 1988, 80; Bush 1994, 115; Ellison 1983, 38], but difficulties surrounding the exact definition of that term, and continuing uncertainty about the original functions of such areas, may make its use in this case inappropriate [Roberts 1987, 24].

The modern 2½" OS map shows High Ham surrounded by individual farms, although clearly not all of these will be medieval in origin. However, excluding Low Ham, High Ham also contains at least three hamlets which were probably in existence in the medieval period: in 1841, Beer was described as a tithing, and Henley, mentioned in the High Ham charter of 973, as a hamlet. Both places still survive [Dickinson 1889, 334]. In addition, Collinson [1791, III, 444] mentions Hays, like the other two hamlets, lying "under Ham-hill, and on the borders of King's-Sedgemoor". It may also be significant that immediately west of High Ham village lies an area referred to on the modern map as 'Beer Field'. Certainly by the 14th century at least, field arrangements at Ham do not seem to indicate a need in the minds of contemporaries to distinguish a few large, sub-divided fields by assigning them cardinal epithets; since at that time, Ham's demesne arable was recorded as merely a single list of furlong names with acreages given for each [BL Egerton 3321 *ff*39r and v]. This impression is heightened by a reference from a century or so earlier to a 3-acre plot in "*Cliflond in uno campo*" [Hobhouse 1891, 164]. We might, then, be excused for thinking that the names East Field and West Field, which survive today, clearly associated with High Ham itself, are post-medieval coinings. But this would probably be a mistake: for there is a further reference, also from the early 13th century, to a 12-acre arable holding belonging to the vicar of High Ham which was divided

exactly in half between two fields, explicitly named as East and West [GC I, 1944, x-xi, Introductory Documents]. Ham then, seems, during the medieval period, to have supported elements of both regular and irregular field arrangements. We can suggest that the East and West fields by this time formed a 'core' of formality around the main settlement, and their origins may, as at Shapwick, be closely linked with those of the nucleated village itself. Further out there presumably lay an encompassing ring of less orderly fields, their character underpinned by the presence of extensive belts of woodland. But the modifying influence of the woodland may have been sufficient to shape developments in the regular core area as well: there seems no other way to explain why, apparently, by the early 14th century, the demesne had been withdrawn entirely from the East and West fields. Indeed instability in the central, common field system may have been inherent – with outward attacks through assarting on the woodland fringes mirrored by inward attacks, through consolidation and piecemeal enclosure, on the *outer* edges of the open fields. More detailed topographical and documentary work in the future might usefully resolve this question.

In general though, there is a clear impression of pervading irregularity here, and it raises the obvious question of whether, as we have already suggested for Street, each of the hamlets was directly associated with, and operated a discrete, clearly defined block of open field arable, or whether they simply participated with High Ham in the working of its fields. Parallels from elsewhere strongly suggest that, even in areas where the Midland system of arable farming prevailed, the usually-accepted pattern of centrally-located, nucleated settlements working two or more open fields, in the complete absence of dependent hamlets, was by no means an invariable one; and that 'peripheral' hamlets such as Henley, Hays and Beer could quite well have been operating modified, autonomous, small-scale adaptations of more 'conventional' open-field regimes [Brown and Taylor, 1989].

If, then, High Ham is accepted as a planned village, one must also ask whether, as has been suggested for Shapwick, it may be associated with a contemporary, highly regular open-field system. It is clear that the western and northern sides of the parish have been subject to vigorous assarting activity, and must once have carried an extensive area of woodland. Beer (given as 'Beare' on Greenwood's 1822 map of Somerset) is almost certainly from OE *bearu*, a grove or wood, and the second element in Henley is OE *leah*, 'a wood, a woodland clearing'; so much is clear from its inclusion in the High Ham charter of 973 as *Henleighe* [Grundy 1935, 120]. There is other sound 'woodland' evidence from High Ham, such as the two 'wotton' field-names noted on the tithe award [T356 and 360; SRO D/D/Rt 25, 1838], and denoting early medieval dispersed settlement in the form of 'the farmstead/estate/settlement in/by the wood'; and the furlong name *worthley*, from the early 16th century [*ex inf* Dr M D Costen], with much the same meaning although probably indicating a rather smaller, lower status, individual farmstead[7]. The topographical evidence, for example, even from a map as late as Greenwood's, is telling, for at that date, running all the way down the western side of the parish, lay a belt of woodland; the 'inner' and highly indented eastern side of which, facing High Ham, has palpably had large blocks carved out of it, with the name Breach Wood on the modern 2½" map, a clear indication of former assarting. A reliable medieval spelling of the minor place-name Hays may suggest an origin in OE haga, 'a hedged enclosure'. Michael Costen has observed that "these hagan are usually very large dense hedges and they are associated with woodland or areas which were once wooded. They were probably formed by leaving a thick line of trees and bushes along the line of the boundary when the woodland was cleared. Such hedges were probably a common feature of wooded estates....." [Costen 1988, 44]. In south-eastern Northamptonshire, Brown and Foard have noted that a "less systematic approach to landscape planning was probably [due to] the presence of substantial, yet discrete, blocks of woodland" [Brown and Foard 1998, 90]. Indeed, closer to home, Harrison's recent study of another of Glastonbury Abbey's Somerset estates, the composite manor of Brent, has revealed a very similar pattern of semi-dispersed settlement linked to a field arrangement that never quite seems to have achieved the systematic regularity of the classic midland system – even in the high middle ages, documents relating to the four Brent manors give merely lists of furlong names, and never any indication of equal divisions of demesne arable between two or more large fields with cardinal nomenclatures [Harrison 1997, 123-173]. Harrison suggests that the origins of such a flexible and "pragmatic field system" [ibid, 173] are probably to be sought in the availability of large areas of pasture in the surrounding moors, which may have had the effect of releasing pressure on arable fallowing regimes. So also then for Ham might its origin as a very heavily wooded estate account at least in part both for the very strongly dispersed element in its medieval settlement pattern, and for the apparent lack of evidence that its arable land was based solely on a 'classic', highly-regulated open-field system. Another indication of this may be the large number of smallholders (21) relative to the number of villeins (22) recorded on the main manor there in 1086 [Thorn and Thorn, 1980].

Carhampton Hundred

Preceding chapters have already suggested the fundamentally dispersed and small-scale nature of the medieval settlement pattern in Carhampton hundred, from a variety of perspectives; and we have noted the likelihood that at least the basic framework of this pattern may already have been in place by the end of the Romano-British period. Domesday Book, again as we have already seen, clearly demonstrates its persistence into the late 11th

century, but how tenacious was it subsequently? Aston 1983 took as its starting point the Middle English toponymic personal names listed in the 1327 Lay Subsidy, a record which has the great benefit of identifying the specific manor or parish in which a taxpayer was resident, making it far easier to locate toponymic surnames from later map or documentary evidence. In this chapter, I have already attempted to extend this approach, although in a far less detailed way, to various places in Whitley Hundred. Nonetheless, since the publication of that article, a new source of these names has become available for Carhampton (and other areas of Somerset) which may in any future research make it possible to expand considerably the corpus of medieval settlement names within the hundred, and to check and confirm the bona fides of those already known or suspected. This is a coroner's roll covering various parts of Somerset, including Carhampton hundred, in the years 1315-21. In each separate case, the names of the jurors are given, and although there is no specific note of the tithing or parish to which each belonged, it should prove possible in some cases to locate the place which was the origin of their surname. A couple of examples, one involving a surname, the other a passing reference to a minor name, will serve to indicate the potential of this source [Stevens 1985]. A case in 1317 mentions a place called *Bynneworthe* bridge. The editor of the document puts the location in Minehead tithing at Cowbridge by the River Avill (SS 957427), but does not give his reason(s) for doing so [Stevens 1985, 459]. The name is highly significant, for it means "the new enclosure or farmstead", and may indicate the site of a late pre-Conquest farm. At present no other reference to this place is known, and the SMR for Minehead has no record of any features at that location. By coincidence, a juror at the same inquest was called John de *Hywysh* of Lynch (probably either West Lynch, near Bossington in Porlock parish, although itself in Selworthy; or East Lynch, in the extreme south-eastern corner of Selworthy). Again, this is important since, as Costen has suggested, these pre-Conquest estates, whose name is closely related to the word giving rise to 'hide', may represent "agricultural [units] which [were] self-contained, if not self-sufficient", perhaps cultivated by a single extended-kin group [Costen 1992a, 72-73]. Costen himself [65] notes only Rodhuish in Carhampton in this category, but if the 'huish' of John's surname was indeed derived from his place of residence, it may prove possible to identify it. In fact, it is difficult to resist the temptation to identify either John himself, or a kinsman, with that John of *Hiwyssh* noted in the 1327 Lay Subsidy under Allerford [Aston 1983, 99].

Neither does this by any means exhaust the available supply of such evidence; for example, so far as they relate to Exmoor and those places in Carhampton hundred which were at one time or another within it, the records arising from the proceedings of the Forest Court in eyre are an especially rich source of toponymic surnames [Macdermott 1911, esp 79-103]. Witness lists in local secular charters, particularly those from the extensive archive of the Honour of Dunster, may also prove rewarding for future research; recording, for example, in

---

[7] In addition, scattered throughout the Ham tithe award are a whole series of field names in 'Breach', and no fewer than twenty separate enclosures called 'Hurst'; Gelling 1984, 197-198.

the mid 12th century, an otherwise unknown -*worth* name in the form of Nigel de *Dilesword* [Maxwell-Lyte 1917-18, no 2]. Since most of those noted in such lists would have been drawn from a relatively small area within the Mohun barony, close to Dunster itself, it is likely that Nigel was resident in Carhampton [Frank Thorn, *pers comm*].

Archaeology is beginning comprehensively to dismantle the notion of a putative 'post-Conquest colonisation of marginal lands' as a catch-all explanation for medieval settlement in upland areas, and the antiquity of some of these sites is rapidly becoming apparent [Aston 1985a, 86-90]. We have already seen, in Chapter Five, increasing unease on the part of many scholars about the usefulness of the concept of the 'margin' and 'marginality'. The places noted in Domesday in Carhampton we can reasonably interpret as pre-Conquest foundations or re-occupations: although one must be wary of the presumption that a modern or medieval farmstead is inevitably on exactly the same site as its Domesday predecessor, nonetheless settlement in the upland areas of the south-west appears to be characterised by a high degree of stability [Astill 1988a, 47]. However, the converse is not true: it is unsafe to assume that places mentioned in documents only after 1086 must be post-Conquest foundations; and even less so automatically to assign such places to that general expansion of medieval settlement onto so-called 'marginal' fringes, during the land-hunger of the 13th and early 14th centuries, which has so often been used to explain settlement patterns in upland regions [*cf* Miller and Hatcher 1978, 85-87 for the 'orthodox' view]. This, indeed, is precisely the argument, even down to the dating, offered by the excavator of Hurscombe in Brompton Regis parish on the Brendon Hills, one of only two west Somerset upland farmsteads so far to have been the subject of even *limited* archaeological assessment. And it is perfectly true that the results of archaeology in other parts of the south-west uplands must restrain our eagerness to assign early dates for isolated medieval farmsteads on and around Exmoor: of Dartmoor for example, where the archaeological evidence is much better, John Allan remarks that "none of the excavated [medieval] settlements......has yielded pottery firmly dating before *c*1200" [Allan 1994, 145]. Despite this, even at Hurscombe, the case for an earlier foundation cannot be entirely discounted, since the main occupation site itself was not accessible for investigation [Leach 1982, 49-50].

That such a movement did indeed take place is not disputed: in some areas this would have been a genuinely pioneering trend, a first-use of resources by a permanently settled population. In the lowlands, woodlands such as the Kentish Weald [Everitt 1986, 52-57], or the Warwickshire Arden [Hooke 1985, 138-145] were a particular target. In both upland and lowland, however, medieval colonisation was frequently associated with the increasing permanence of seasonal settlements [Hooke 1997, 85-90; Fox 1996; Ward 1997], that may have been in use for many generations *before* 1066, often as detached grazing lands for settlements many miles away [Austin 1985, 73]. The other Somerset site which has been explored archaeologically falls within Carhampton

Hundred. We have already noted Ley Hill, Luccombe (Horner Wood) in the context of its associated field system (Chapter Seven); in contrast to Hurscombe, no buildings survive, but early indications are that it was a medieval settlement which had been abandoned by the end of the 14th century. Two buildings only have been investigated, but crucially, pottery from one of them *may* indicate a foundation date before the 13th century. The ceramic evidence is still being assessed [*pers comm* Isabel Richardson; Richardson 1998-9, 56, and 1999-2000; Grace and Richardson 1999, 208-209], but it may eventually prove possible to show that Ley Hill originated as a pre-Conquest single-farmstead which expanded to a hamlet in the 12th and 13th centuries.

There are several places in the hundred for which we can suggest pre-Conquest upland settlement within or close to woodland. Perhaps the most obvious example is Broadwood, an isolated farm on the 150m contour (492ft) in Carhampton parish. The name itself is suggestive, but as a Domesday manor with a large tract of woodland attached to it, Broadwood was clearly a pre-Conquest foundation. Nor was this resource detached, for the local topography is such as to show that the farm was created by the assarting of adjacent woodland. Even the modern 2½" map shows it surrounded by a patchwork of irregular fields, small close by the farm buildings, much larger further away, which have clearly 'eaten' into the woodland. Although now at the centre of a modern plantation, it is suggested that Broadwood and its fields still give a very good impression of the landscape effects of assarting.

Elsewhere in the hundred, there are indications of woodland clearance in much higher areas, but which, unlike Broadwood, do not support modern farms. The extreme south-western corner of Timberscombe parish is occupied by an area called Harwood Brakes, originally a detached part of Luccombe [Aston 1983, 74], which extends all the way to a noticeably curvilinear part of the parish boundary where it abuts on the neighbouring parishes to the west, Cutcombe and Wootton Courtenay. The significance of the second element of the name is self-evident, and Harwood was in existence by at least the early 14th century [Aston 1983, 100]. Two farms, East and West Harwood, survive. Admittedly, the fields here are generally large, straight-sided and regular in shape, and give no obvious indication of woodland clearance. Nonetheless, it seems highly likely that 'brakes' is a 'breach' name [Field 1972, 27], and a reference to assarting activity which may find a direct parallel with the 'Breach' name in Chew Stoke, Chew hundred, which we have already noted. Did Harwood Brakes originate as a piece of detached woodland belonging to Luccombe, first used only seasonally, as a source of timber, fuel and wood pasture, and later settled permanently and cleared from Harwood? Harwood Brakes is doubly interesting for being the site of an enclosure (at SS928410) on the 300m contour (984ft), which the county SMR [34132] lists as 'prehistoric'. We should note the fact that the idea of widespread woodland regeneration in the post-Roman period has recently been subjected to serious criticism [*eg* Cleary 1995, 14-15; Dark 2000, 132-133]; nonetheless the inference must be that the Harwood Brakes enclosure was constructed on an open hillside which had been cleared of woodland, but which subsequently, probably at some point before the late Saxon period, fell down again to woodland. This has clear implications for our view of the extent of continuity of land use in Carhampton hundred between the prehistoric period and the early middle ages. The name Timberscombe itself means 'the valley where timber can be got' [Gelling 1984, 93], and the notion of an origin as a pre-Conquest steading based primarily on a woodland economy is hard to avoid. The tithe map shows the layout of Timberscombe village to have been highly irregular, with no discernable order in the disposition of house plots and roads, and a surrounding scatter of small, shapeless enclosures close to the village. The constraints of the valley topography, and a woodland-edge location in which expansion was possible only by assarting, may have combined to produce this plan.

Old Brakes, north of Hindon Farm in Minehead Without, is another 'breach' name, and Hindon itself was certainly in existence by the early 14th century [Aston 1983, 95]. Holt (OE 'a wood', Gelling 1984, 196-197) is noted in Exmoor Forest records in 1270 [Macdermott 1911, 86], and again in the 1327 subsidy; it may now be represented by either Holt or Holt Ball farm, both in Luccombe parish; and Carhampton has at least three names probably derived from OE *hangra*, 'sloping wood' [Gelling 1984, 194-196]. These are Birchanger in Porlock and Wychanger in Luccombe, both associated with surviving farms but for which at present no medieval documentary evidence is known; and Harthanger, now only the name of a wood near the western boundary of Luxborough parish. The name Oaktrow, in the north part of Cutcombe parish, is self-explanatory, and as a Domesday manor, the surviving farm here may have pre-Conquest origins as an isolated steading [Aston 1983, 91; Gelling 1984, 211-222]. Such examples could be multiplied, but the overall impression is that a concerted attack on the hundred's woodland resources, for the purposes of settlement, was in full swing well before 1066, and had probably run its course by the time of Domesday Book: such we can at least infer from Hallam's assessment of Somerset's share of the area covered by the Exmoor National Park [Hallam 1978, 47]. Indeed, a more recent survey stresses that following their initial clearance between about 3000BC and the early Iron Age, and partly as a result of climatic deterioration thereafter, the Exmoor uplands were permanently to remain largely devoid of natural tree growth [Essex 1995, 69-70].

Conclusion: Tenure, Landholding and Settlement: A Review of the Problem and of the Three Hundreds

The question of how far, if at all, the nature of the pattern of landholding and tenure had a direct, causal impact upon both settlement patterns, and the morphologies of *individual* settlements, is arguably one of the most crucial, and at the same time probably the most frustratingly elusive element in the overall framework of medieval settlement history. The quality of the evidence required conclusively to prove its influence, let alone to make out at least a plausible case in its favour, must be unimpeachable, and material of this nature is consequently extremely scarce. Even given copious documentation and high-quality morphological information, there is still an *interpretational* minefield to cross. It is one thing to show that a village has at some point in its development been given a highly regular plan of lanes and tenement plots. It is quite another *effectively* to link that certainty to matters of tenure and landholding. Even where the planning aspect can be proven, the *absolute* date of the layout cannot be known without archaeological intervention, and there is no guarantee that the surviving plan is the only one that ever existed [Austin 1985a, 1988]. Even where detailed documentation exists, therefore, it may be impossible to relate its tenurial information directly to the contemporary morphology, so far as that can be reconstructed. The most extensive study of medieval settlement patterns yet undertaken, in the East Midlands, found no discernible, straightforward, causal relationship between the strength of lordship and the intensity of nucleation and dispersal, or of the incidence of village planning [Dyer *et al* 1997, 204-213].

How true is it generally, as Aston and Gerrard have recently observed of Shapwick in the late medieval period, that "social status was etched into the village plan and could be 'read' from it by any observer"? [Aston and Gerrard 1999, 34]. The whole question of the relationship between settlement form, lordship, tenure and social status has recently been subjected to detailed review by Ros Faith, who devotes an entire chapter to it [Faith 1997, 224-244]. Faith is clear that where the evidence is good enough, it *is* possible quite conclusively to prove a direct link between settlement plan and tenure, and perhaps the most telling of her quoted examples concerns work carried out by Lucille Campey on the estates of the Bishop of Durham [Faith 1997, 228-229]. Faith's analysis of Campey's work provides a telling synthesis, but it is perhaps possible to go further than she was able to do in stressing the importance of this particular study. The effect of Campey's survey is to demonstrate unequivocally, in her case-study villages, the primacy of tenure over all other factors which may have had some influence on the morphology of those places reconstructed as it was around 1400. She is able to explain virtually every aspect of village form in *tenurial* terms, and to show that, in those of her villages which were clearly also demesne or 'capital' settlements, complexity of plan is a direct consequence of the diverse tenurial status of the different nuclei, and furthermore that the spatial relationships defining the various elements can be deduced with precision.

Neither are Campey's reconstructions mere static snapshots of the situation at one point in time, for the attraction of her thesis, again as she clearly demonstrates, is that a tenurial explanation of settlement form can also be made to account for episodes of expansion and replanning, so informing perspectives on, and providing a context for, the *dynamics* of village morphology through time [Campey 1989, 85]. It is usual in all branches of historical study to treat with suspicion, or indeed to reject out of hand, any conceptual framework which is or which appears to be built on mono-causal foundations; and this is exactly as it should be. Nonetheless, Campey has effectively established the tenurial basis of the morphologies of her case-study villages[8].

We must concede the exceptional quality and range of Campey's sources. However, while Faith remarks that these relationships were revealed "in a way which cannot often be done", she is careful to add that "the different elements [which Campey] investigates are widely found. It is not an exaggeration to speak of 'servile villages' resembling her 'bond settlements', elsewhere in medieval England" [Faith 1997, 229-230]. In Somerset itself, this topic has yet to undergo systematic review, but there are intriguing hints of its potential to inform our ideas on village form in the county, the best example to date certainly being the work of Chris Thornton on the Winchester manor of Rimpton, also cited by Faith [Faith 1997, 232-233]. And on a more general level, Aston had previously suggested that the obvious 'polyfocal' form of some Somerset villages can be traced directly to their status as multiple manors, under distinctly separate lordships, by the late 11th century; a development apparently related at least in part to a post-Conquest loss of 'free' status among the landholding class of Anglo-Saxon thegns [Aston 1985, 83-92].

I must state from the outset that a detailed appraisal of this question within the three hundreds under scrutiny here, is beyond the scope of this study, and indeed might itself provide the basis of an entirely separate survey. All that we can attempt here is a somewhat anecdotal review, but while we may permit considerations of interpretation rightly to intervene, nonetheless, there *are* intimations of an iceberg's tip. For future workers, the most promising case study of the three will undoubtedly be Whitley, if only because of its wealth of potentially crucial Glastonbury Abbey documentation; and within Whitley, Shapwick provides an inevitable springboard, by simple virtue of its possessing what is to date the most minutely dissected village plan in the entire county. We have already noted that current interpretations of Shapwick favour a staged development over several phases of expansion [Aston 1994b], and this model is reproduced here as Figure 45. Straight away, it is possible to follow Faith's lead and to view these morphological processes from an essentially social perspective. Indeed, one of the proposed models (number 3) goes some way towards this, allocating different parts of the village to villeins and bordars respectively [Aston 1994b, 43], based on the very marked disjuncture in terms of plot size and plan alignment between the northern and southern halves of the settlement. On balance, it does seem likely that the larger cells, at the southern end of the settlement close to the spring and to the putative (although as yet unproven) 'primary' manorial

site, are indeed likely to be earlier, and that subsequent expansion ran northwards, as proposed in model 2. The larger plots of Aston's phase 1 might suggest occupation by tenants of some substance, perhaps associated with the first stages of nucleation when late Anglo-Saxon farmers of relatively free status were being moved by the Abbey from isolated farmsteads into a new, spacious, grid-plan settlement extending ultimately as far north as Aston's road 'b' [Aston 1994b, fig 4.11, 42; for an indication of the kind of people who might have occupied the phase 1 settlement by the early 11th century, Faith 1997, 126-152]. As Aston himself notes, "these still appear too large to be just village cottage plots" [Aston 1994b, 43]. Such a plan bears a striking resemblance to what I have proposed, for Butleigh Wootton, with a putative pre-Conquest seigneurial site located immediately to the west of a regular grid, although even at Shapwick dating remains a problem. However, Aston's phases 2a and b show not only a marked change of alignment, perhaps deliberately following a slight change of direction in the flow of the stream north of road 'b', but also apparently much smaller plot sizes. And rather than respecting and indeed taking its cue from the pre-existing through routes, as the southern cells assiduously do, the northern grid completely disrupts and disregards the line of *its* east-west road, giving the impression of an attempt to fit the maximum number of plots into a restricted area. At this point the existing model can be developed by invoking the social dimension to provide a context for these observed morphological characteristics. Aston's model 3 has already suggested a distinction between villeins and bordars for the post-Conquest period [Aston 1994b, 43]. And it is tempting to develop this argument and to ask whether the dichotomy between north and south at Shapwick is actually a chronological as well as a social one. Ros Faith has made the point that after 1066, Norman overlordship brought about changes not only in the conditions of the peasantry, overwhelmingly for the worse, but also in perceptions about the ways that estates should best be managed: "from the point of view of manorial lords, the key factor in increasing the value of a manor was to increase its population" [Faith 1997, 205]. We are entitled, then, to ask whether the clear north/south divide at Shapwick may not represent, at least in part, a morphological expression of post-Conquest developments in both the nature of landholding and a change in the social status of those tenants occupying the 'new' northern sector. By this view, a degree of chronological depth becomes possible by proposing that Aston's phase 2 plan elements, 'a' and 'b', represent a post-Conquest settlement of peasantry, in larger numbers, with smaller holdings and of a reduced social status as compared to their southern neighbours. Likewise, the condition of the latter, formerly relatively 'free' tenants, would also have deteriorated, to become, as Aston has suggested, villeins subject to varying degrees of personal unfreedom [Faith 1997, 245-265]. A link between morphology and the pattern of landholding in some medieval nucleated communities has long been part of received orthodoxy [Sheppard 1976]; and Faith is quite

---

[8] A subsequent, although less detailed study adopts a similar perspective on the question of the origins of the planned medieval settlement at Borrowby, North Yorks, another estate of the See of Durham. See Harrison 1990. For an explanation of medieval settlement planning, and the tightly controlled manipulation of space, as underpinned by the social relationships and tensions between peasants and seigneurial authority, see Saunders 1990.

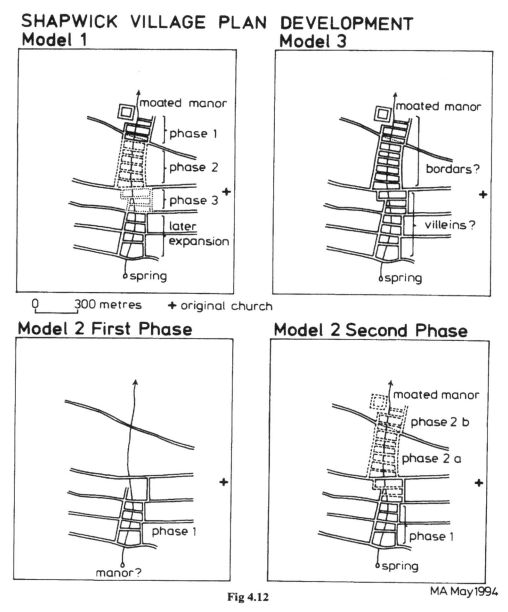

Fig 4.12

Figure 45: Aston's model for the phased development of the Shapwick village plan, from Aston and Penoyre 1994. Reproduced with the kind permission of Prof M A Aston.

clear that, although not always easy to prove, enough evidence has now accumulated to indicate very strongly that morphology and the systematic allocation of new holdings are intimately related. Perhaps most importantly, "planned villages seem to have been most common on large estates" [Faith 1997, 227]. Faith's views in this respect are, as we have already seen, borne out both by studies elsewhere, already cited, and by the other north Polden settlements, Shapwick's neighbours. However, as I hope I have shown, evidence for planning is by no means universally evident from the rest of Whitley hundred, which represents in effect Glastonbury Abbey's core, 'home' estate; and this fact may lead us reasonably to infer that even in large baronies, it was only certain holdings and

lands that were deemed suitable for the wholesale, systematic planning of settlements, although individual settlements elsewhere might show similar evidence (below). A further inference from what has already been said about Shapwick is that at least on this part of the Glastonbury Abbey barony, the tendency towards 'manorialisation' had begun before 1066, and was merely reinforced and accelerated afterwards. Again, this ties in with current thinking on the pre-Conquest origins of at least some (but by no means all, and questions of interpretation remain) of the features which in the medieval period would be viewed as distinctly 'manorial' in nature [Faith 1997, 57-59; 173-177].

Far more work needs to be done along the lines of

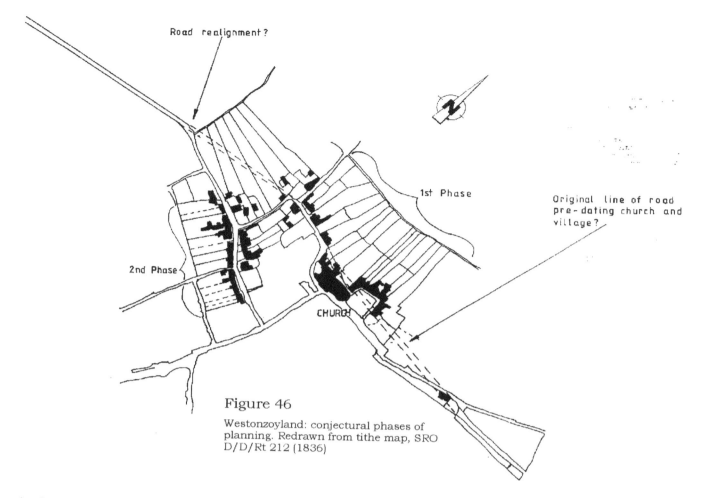

Figure 46

Westonzoyland: conjectural phases of planning. Redrawn from tithe map, SRO D/D/Rt 212 (1836)

that by Gardiner in Sussex, Prosser in north Somerset, and Campey in Durham, on obvious, close-knit groupings of planned settlements under major lordships, secular or ecclesiastical, to determine what, in each particular context, might have made a particular tract of countryside, and the people in it, a proper subject for closely-controlled topographical regulation (ie both settlements and their associated field 'systems'). We will return to this point again briefly in Chapter Nine.

However, while Whitley can show north Polden as such a grouping, elsewhere in the hundred, once our 'eye' for the possible influence of tenure and social status is used to the light, at least one other, more isolated, example suggests itself. The plan of Westonzoyland in the mid 19th century was far less overtly regular than that of Shapwick; but hints of both a *phased* development, and of the disruption of at least one pre-existing communications route, are features which it shares in common with its north-easterly neighbour (Figure 46). Is it possible to extrapolate from Westonzoyland's plan to suggest social and tenurial distinctions here, as there may be at Shapwick? The honest answer would be no, or at least, not yet, and again, the total lack of even the coarsest dating evidence from any part of the settlement is a major barrier to understanding the evolution of its morphology. Nonetheless, we can usefully remember that certainly in the post-Conquest period, and probably before 1066 as well, the area of moor around Westonzoyland was the

focus of frenetic drainage and reclamation activity that almost certainly offered opportunities for enterprising individuals to increase existing holdings or establish entirely new ones. If these were men brought in by the Abbey with the specific task of 'opening up' the moor, but over whom the Abbey would still wish to exercise at least a degree of social control and *from* whom it would require some level of rents and services, albeit perhaps on very favourable terms, the obvious solution would be to integrate them into the existing community, but in a separate part of it, on newly-planned tenements. Perhaps, then, the plan of Westonzoyland carries morphological and social echoes of this very dynamic period in the history of Sowy island in the years on either side of the Conquest.

In this context, a particularly interesting toponym unearthed by Musgrove, from 1308, is *Cotsetlemede*, whose exact location on Sowy Island cannot at present be pinpointed [Musgrove 1999, 38]. This name carries strong connotations of occupation in isolated dwellings, by smallholding cottagers owing relatively heavy labour-services to the manorial lord in return for their small tenancy. Crucially, *Cotsetla* is an Anglo-Saxon word associated with specific 1997, 56-57]. Here, in its early 14th century form, the name may refer to an actual settlement site, abandoned to meadow but its former use still well-known to local tradition; or to a meadow reserved for the exclusive current or former use of this class of tenant. This may, perhaps, be a clue in Sowy to the means

175

by which reclamation was achieved in some cases, with seigneurial encouragement to potential colonists to settle peripheral holdings close to the moor, aimed at men that might otherwise have survived merely as landless labourers[9]. Initially, these new tenements would be let on very favourable terms for a period of years before labour services came into effect, and would be associated with a sliding scale of exemptions from either labour services or rents, or both; since, as Stenton observes for the *cotsetla*, "an origin can easily be found for him among the younger sons of *ceorls* whose holdings were too small to support more than a single family" [Stenton 1971, 475]. This was a device well-known and used in other parts of Europe in the high middle ages when lords needed to attract colonists to open up formerly unproductive tracts of land [Bartlett 1993, 117-132]. There may be direct parallels here with the way that marshland reclamation and settlement progressed in the moorland fringes around Kingston Seymour (below), and in neither case is there any reason to suppose that it need necessarily be an entirely post-Conquest development; indeed, on Sowy, the incorporation of an Anglo-Saxon word in a post-Conquest minor toponym, a practice which might otherwise be viewed as highly anachronistic, strongly suggests otherwise.

Middlezoy, the chief settlement of the island, displays distinct signs of regularity [*cf* Broomhead 1997, 5-6]. Even at the scale of the modern 2½" map, the ladder-like layout is very apparent, with two parallel main streets running north-south, and joined at right-angles by at least two shorter cross-lanes (the tithe map showing the northern one blocked at its western end). Even given that, by the time of the tithe map, there was little regularity in the size, shape and disposition of the individual tenement plots, the resemblance in general terms to the plan of Shapwick is still striking. And as at Shapwick, there are strong indications that at least one pre-existing routeway has been disrupted by the layout out of the plan. The line of a track can be followed from Thorngrove eastwards, initially as a sunken green lane and then as a curving hedgeline. Its course is lost underneath the southern part of the grid, but is immediately picked up again as a footpath on the eastern side of the village, still going eastwards (Figure 47; Plate 10). If this track did indeed originate as an access to Thorngrove, then it is clear that the farmstead there must *pre-date* the village plan.

The arrangement at Middlezoy has probably taken its cue from the church and the natural topography, with the former occupying the highest, most prominent site in the village, at its northern end, and the village proper extending southwards down the slope away from the church (Figure 48). It is noticeable also that the main road from Westonzoyland, now the A372, makes a sharp right-angled bend just as it strikes the northern extremity of the village, to which it then gives a wide berth, and continues round to the south-east. This 'bypass'-like detour looks suspiciously like a deliberate displacement, and it is possible that originally the road continued southwards and

formed what is now the easternmost of the two parallel main streets of the village. If the church has not moved, one might postulate a pre-Conquest settlement in its vicinity, with the road passing straight through, and a later replanning resulting in the shifting of the main road to the east. The reason for this is unclear at present, although perhaps, as the contours reveal, replanning might have provided an opportunity to move the road on to a course with a gradient far easier than that straight downslope through the centre of Middlezoy; and the evidence of Day and Masters's map shows that the present line of the main road was certainly that followed by the late 18th century. A very small amount of Roman and early medieval pottery has been turned up in the gardens of properties in the village core [*pers comm* Dr M D Costen], and a small-scale evaluation excavation at a site in the south-eastern quarter revealed indications of structures associated with pottery of the 12th and 13th centuries [Broomhead 1997]. However, significantly, when more recently another site very close by, but immediately to the south, underwent trial excavation prior to development, late Saxon pottery was recovered, some of it associated with substantial ditches which "could have functioned as boundary and/or drainage ditches". Structural remains dating to the Roman period were also identified [Exeter Archaeology 2000, SMR 44935].

An early manorial centre at Middlezoy may indeed be suggested by the appearance of a 'Ga(r)ston' name, noted by Grundy [Grundy 1935, 118], and attached to a series of enclosures about half a kilometre downslope from, and at the opposite end of the village from the church, outside the putative planned core of the settlement. An enhanced aerial photograph described by Dick Broomhead reveals what are apparently structural traces directly associated with the Garston enclosures [Broomhead 1997, 5-6]. We can here make direct comparisons with those similar examples of this name already described from Chew hundred, which taken together strongly reinforce the impression of an association with an antecedent occupation focus that has subsequently *become* peripheral, sometimes by a significant degree, to the later medieval village core.

Perhaps Glastonbury Abbey's rationale at both Weston and Middlezoy was similar; however, as we have already seen, the nucleated villages shared the island territory in the middle ages with a respectable scatter of isolated (colonising?) farmsteads, raising the question of whether this betrays differential social status within the same township. One possible model for this might be that originally suggested for a Norfolk manor by F G Davenport, by which personal *un*freedom increased towards the manorial centre, and vice versa [cited in Faith 1997, 230]. Future work, to confirm or refute this suggestion, would require detailed examination of the documents with specific reference to the nature of the individual rents and services owed, inheritance customs, personal obligations and so on (to try to discern the varying degrees of 'freedom' described by Faith), and also, of course, topographical analysis perhaps coupled with selective archaeological investigation.

---

[9] Men whom we can perhaps equate in terms of status with the post-Conquest *garciones* of the Glastonbury Abbey estates, so vividly brought to life by Harold Fox recently; see Fox 1996b.

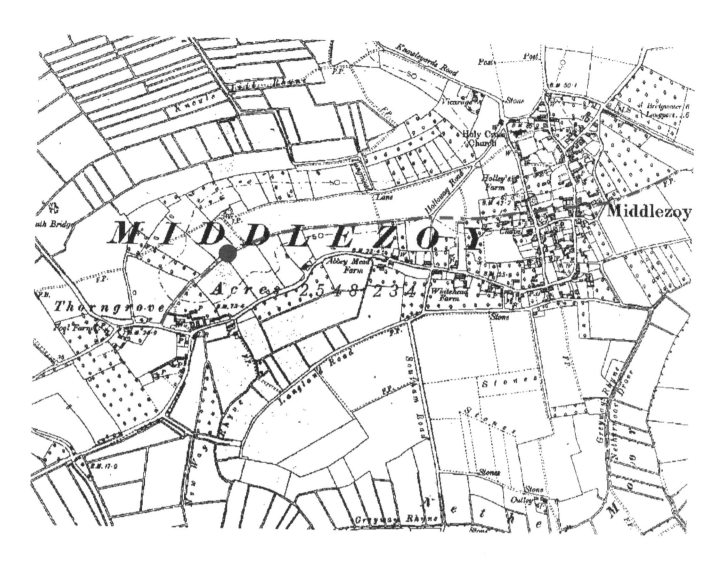

Figure 47

Extract from OS Second Edition 6" map (1904) showing suggested line of
pre-existing routeway (grey dashed line) leading eastwards from the
(?Anglo-Saxon) farmstead site at Thorngrove, its course towards Sedgemoor
(and perhaps specifically another pre-Conquest site at Greylake) having been
disrupted by the *later* establishment of the grid plan of Middlezoy village. The
approximate position from which Plate 10 was taken, looking south-west
along the hollow way leading to Thorngrove, is marked by a grey dot.

Plate 10: View looking roughly south-west along the now-disused, but deeply-cut hollow way that runs down to Thorngrove from Middlezoy. The approximate position from which this view was taken is indicated in Figure 47.

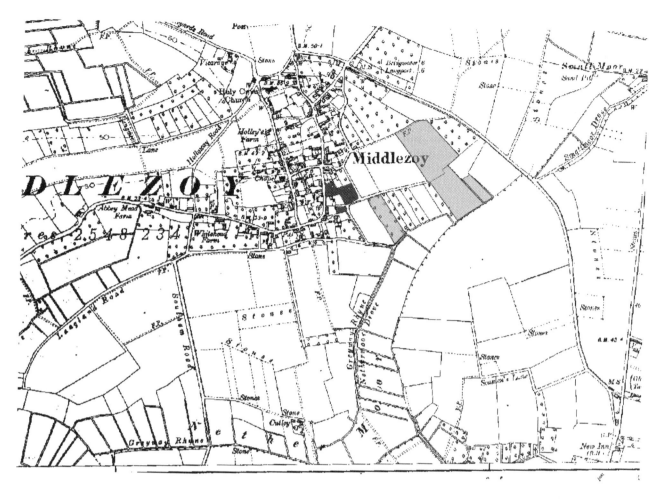

FIGURE 48

Extract from OS first edition 6" map (1885), showing surviving Garston field names at Middlezoy (shaded light), in relation to the present village plan. It is likely that the blank enclosures separating the two shaded areas also once carried this name. Sites recently subjected to archaeological investigation, revealing indications of late Anglo-Saxon occupation, are shaded dark for comparison. Sources: SRO DD/GC 85 (estate map of Middlezoy, 1787); D/D/Rt 480 (tithe map and award, 1854); Broomhead 1997; Exeter Archaeology 2000.

Even without such evidence we might, though, draw useful parallels between Sowy and another area, in a different hundred, which was also subject to reclamation activity probably throughout roughly the same period. We have already seen how at Kingston Seymour, a detached part of Chewton hundred in the Northern Levels, the settlement pattern in the medieval and pre-Conquest period shows evidence of a far greater degree of dispersal outside the central, nucleated village, and less regularity in the latter's plan, than does Weston. And yet presumably, the processes at work in the two places in terms of the recovery of wetland for agriculture, would have borne at least superficial similarities. Part of the explanation may lie in the different ownership histories of these places. The

whole Island of Sowy had been a Glastonbury Abbey possession since at least the early 8th century; and I have already suggested that Kingston, while *originating* as an ecclesiastical holding, remained relatively underdeveloped until its acquisition by the crown probably in the early 10th century. What we see in the contrasting settlement patterns may reflect at least in part a difference of approach by the respective landlords in terms of the degree of their intervention in and control over both the economic management of the estates, and their relationships with their tenants. The crown may have adopted a far more *laissez faire* attitude, interested only in revenues, tribute and resources rather than social manipulation, and allowing its tenants relatively free reign in exactly where they settled. We might, then, expect that the more independent and enterprising at Kingston would prefer to set up their holdings as ring-fence, isolated farms on lands newly-won from the moor by their own toil, where they would have a chance from the outset to establish dynastic, long-term interests in the land, heritable intact through successive generations. As we have already suggested, in the medieval period, such tenants might appear in the documents as enjoying a relatively high degree of personal freedom in terms of rents, services and manorial customs, but again, this could only be tested by far more detailed work than is possible here. Nonetheless, Faith reinforces this point with a telling description of how even as late as the late 14th century, a kind of *gestalt* folk memory allowed the peasantry a clear view of how they themselves perceived the traditional advantages of having a royal, rather than an ecclesiastical lord: "they associated [their] earlier freedom with being tenants of the king, their present serfdom with being tenants of the church. The era of better times, as they saw it, was that of the tenth-century kings of Wessex" [Faith 1997, 266].

The topographical implications of this are enormous, especially in terms of our ability to explain settlement arrangements on estates with known ownership histories. We must exercise caution, however, where evidence relating to tenure is poor or absent, and indeed we have now come full circle since this is precisely the case for virtually the whole of the study area except Whitley. As Dawn Hadley has shown in the Danelaw, it is clear that a whole variety of complex, dynamic forces is at work; a straightforward equation of ecclesiastical = control + unfreedom, and royal = *laissez faire* + freedom, simply will not answer. We have noted, for example, how on the Ham plateau in Whitley, a Glastonbury Abbey holding from at least the late 10th century, High Ham village shows signs of plan regularity, but the overall settlement pattern is one of very emphatic dispersal. I have put forward reasons for this, but it must yet remain an open question whether the occupants of those farmsteads and hamlets which probably originated as late Anglo-Saxon or early post-Conquest woodland assarts, enjoyed a greater degree of personal 'freedom' in the middle ages, as expressed in rents, services and manorial customs, than their counterparts living within High Ham village itself.

Chew Hundred offers a particularly sobering caveat in this respect. Immediately to the north, as we have already seen, Prosser has revealed the likely operation of systematic settlement planning on the 'home' estates of Keynsham Abbey [Prosser 1995, 162]. And yet Keynsham's southern neighbour, from the early tenth century in the hands of a powerful ecclesiastical overlord, displays barely *any* indication, on present evidence, of the same thing. We have noted the single example of New Town, in Chew parish, which provides a clear exception to this rule and precisely for that reason should ideally be the subject of more detailed work in the future [Roberts 1987, 196-198].

In any event, this is unlikely to be due to late acquisition, since scholars now focus very much on the 10th-12th centuries as the 'village moment' [Dyer *et al*

1997, 227-244]. Perhaps antiquity of possession enters the equation? The Bishop of Wells 'inherited' Chew hundred from the crown relatively late; it may be that an existing pattern of strong dispersal, already long established under that antecedent lordship, possessed an inertia which tended to act against any movement towards major intervention in terms of settlement replanning, and which the bishopric had neither the means nor the will to overcome. Intimately associated with such a pattern, and perhaps reinforcing the difficulties faced by anyone attempting to make fundamental changes, may have been a social structure springing from a set of traditional customs and tenurial obligations established, again, under *royal* overlordship, and the combined effect of which was to emphasise personal freedom – a condition that Faith has termed "honourable dependence" [Faith 1997, 267]. As at Ham, at least part of both the topographical and the social patterns may have been moulded by woodland colonisation. Conversely, we have already seen how in Whitley hundred, it is precisely those Polden lands which were among the very earliest in Glastonbury Abbey's possession which display the strongest evidence of settlement regulation. Even here though, while it may have played a rôle, antiquity of lordship will clearly not answer in every case, since Keynsham Abbey was founded only in the 12th century [Knowles and Hadcock 1971, 161-162], but still appears to have been able to intervene topographically and, by extension, socially, in the communities under its control.

As the hundred containing, of the three we are considering here, the most marked extremes of climate, relief and difficult terrain, the upland parts of Carhampton might anyway be expected to display a tendency towards dispersed settlement: Faith herself, indeed, acknowledges that "the landscape imposed its own constraints on settlement" [Faith 1997, 233]. But a question we must now ask, even if we are not yet in a position to provide an answer, is how far this pattern is a reflection of overlordship, and of varying degrees of lordly interference in both the topography of settlement, and in the social status of the dwellers on the land. The landscape constraints mentioned by Faith, especially in Carhampton's more isolated uplands, must surely, in themselves, have led to a considerable degree of tenurial independence and personal freedom for the occupants of farmsteads and hamlets in the pre-Conquest period. As Alan Everitt has shown for both the Downland and the Weald of Kent, the almost invariable corollary of a colonising, pioneering movement among peasant farmers is a strong, indeed almost fierce spirit of independence, self-reliance and resistance to authority [Everitt 1986, 52-57; 172-180]. On the eve of 1066, many, perhaps even the majority of inhabitants dwelling on and working the land of Carhampton's countless hamlets and ring-fence farmsteads, may have been of this ilk.

However, only for Carhampton itself is it yet possible to offer some plausible speculation in this respect. It seems to have been the only royal holding in the hundred to which it gave its name [Thorn and Thorn 1980], and it is also, as we have seen, the only settlement which displays indications of planning and regularity. Connotations of royal defensive strategies may carry with them an implication that Carhampton was distinctly out of the 'normal' run of late Saxon planned rural settlements such as we now think Shapwick is. Its affinities may, indeed, turn out to be far closer in both concept and execution to those of an Alfredian *burh*, and this in turn affects the way we should view the social status of its occupants, in terms of their degree of personal freedom, the nature of their relationship with their overlord, and their obligations in terms of services, rents and tribute. Having passed to the crown after initial ownership by an ecclesiastical foundation, it may have been intended to develop Carhampton as a town, which subsequently failed. But we know that the kings of Wessex, and others, were actively engaged in the promotion of a sound economic base in many of their urban foundations, an important element of which involved attempts to attract to them a wide range of craftsmen and traders, to establish markets and to regularise and control the commerce which took place in them [Abels 1998, 216-217; Atkin 1985; Haslam 1988; and Hodges 2000 for the earlier evidence from both England and the Continent, esp 69-92]. Stenton highlights the existence of a large number of smaller boroughs, especially in the south-west, which "had arisen on royal manors, where a king, wishing to improve his property, could offer the protection of the special peace around his house to such traders as might be willing to take plots from him" [Stenton 1971, 533]. Such nascent urban centres often enjoyed special privileges and concessions, and these would, at least in part, have devolved upon *individual* inhabitants as well as the town itself as a legally-constituted entity. An important aspect of this would be a far greater degree of personal freedom than, for example, was probably enjoyed by the tenants of the Abbot of Glastonbury on his north Polden manors. In Carhampton's case therefore, I suggest that the regularity of its topography probably does not express the tenurial *un*freedom of its occupants, but in fact rather the reverse. Although on the basis of the available evidence its claim to urban status is probably no stronger than Chew Magna's, Chew, as we have already seen, cannot show any overt indication of a regular layout, and Carhampton may therefore be the only example within the three study areas of a pre-Conquest planned town.

Chapter Nine

Conclusion and Synthesis:
Medieval Settlement on Polden and Beyond

What stands out above all else in relation to Polden is the *topographical* basis, emphasising the ridge's position as a low but locally very prominent watershed separating two extensive tracts of wetland, Sedgemoor to the south, and the Brue Valley to the north. I would argue very strongly that the settlement pattern on Polden was defined by, on one level, the symbiotic affinity between the moors and the higher ground, and on another by the relationship between the northern and southern flank of the ridge. This is precisely the kind of 'convex' territory which Glanville Jones has used to construct hypothetical models of multiple estates as they might have appeared in the 11th century [cited in Fleming 1998, 48-50]. In Cornwall, Herring has shown that the boundaries of four of the ancient hundreds are arranged so as to give communities *equal* access to the summer grazing grounds on Bodmin Moor [Herring 1996, 41-42]. So also is the likelihood of the Polden ridge as the core of an early territory supported by the way in which its hundred boundaries are so disposed as to emphasise a common resource – they are carved roughly east-west through the Brue Valley and Sedgemoor wetlands, not along the ridge crest.

For reasons which I have already sketched, it seems always to have been the northern slope which was the more favoured, but until far more work is carried out, dating will always remain a problem. It would, though, be useful to propose a *relative* chronology, within which provisional framework the various events can be set, and which can be tested and refined as knowledge increases.

It seems clear, for example, that the southern settlements must already have been in existence at the time that at least this part of the old *Pouelt* estate was breaking up, otherwise the boundaries of the northern settlements would surely have extended south into Sedemoor as well as north into the Brue valley. It is equally likely, indeed, that this was once the case, and if an arbitrary (but probable) timespan of 10th-12th centuries is assigned to the fragmentation process, to see this in the context of time-depth we need to look back to suggest what the settlement and territorial pattern might have looked like at an earlier period. The late 8th century seems a good place to start, since by this time it looks as though the surviving series of charters affecting land in *Pouelt*, whatever the difficulties of their detail, had transferred most or all of the old estate into the hands of Glastonbury Abbey Abbey [Abrams 1996, 204-205]. I have already suggested that Shapwick itself may only be a chance survivor to indicate the internal workings of the earlier entity, and that the 'manorial' toponyms of some of the other northern settlements may represent later changes which disguise other, earlier names denoting functional specialisms. By the late 8th century, therefore, the first stage of our model might consist of a series of loosely-defined territorial units focussed on the

northern slope, and including within their probably rather fluid outlines, continuous tracts of land to both north and south of the ridge. These might be akin to the 'proto-townships' which Fox has proposed for Midland England at this period, and in which "the occupiers of groups of neighbouring farms might associate one with another through kinship or.........the sharing of some types of resources" [Fox 1992, 38-39]. So also for Polden can we be confident that at least non-arable resources would have been exploited in common, especially woodland (such as Loxley itself almost certainly was) and summer grazing on the wetlands north and south. The importance of the latter cannot be overemphasised, and its antiquity, although ultimately unprovable, can hardly be doubted. The recent discovery of a Bronze Age barrow on the crest of the ridge between Puriton and Woolavington, related above, may, though, have a bearing here [Appendix1]; since on Mendip Jodie Lewis has suggested that the siting of at least some of the extensive barrow cemeteries there was particularly significant in the "wider pattern of seasonal land exploitation, involving the low-lying Somerset Levels and the Mendip uplands" [Lewis 1996, 24-25]. This perspective takes on a particular resonance in the light of ideas sketched briefly below.

If early medieval 'proto-townships' existed on Polden, the question of what relationship they may have borne to Roman predecessors is something that future research would need to address. Certainly, on a rather higher level in the territorial hierarchy, Fleming's work in Swaledale shows very forcefully that on occasion it *is* possible to demonstrate the survival of early post-Roman polities over very long periods of time [Fleming 1994a; 1998a]. Indeed, at least in terms of agrarian practices it is doubtful, according to Fowler, whether the arrival of the English actually had much of an impact on any indigenous regimes that they may have found already in operation [Fowler 1997, 248]. Cleary takes a similar perspective [Cleary 1995, 16 and 24], and the same point has been reinforced and indeed extended even more recently by both Dyer [1997, 59] and Dark [1996, 53-57; 1998, 9]. Fowler's suggested general chronology may be extremely relevant for *Pouelt*: he argues for "a pattern of arable continuing broadly within existing landscape arrangements (from prehistoric and/or Roman and/or sub-Roman times) in southern and Midland England until the late seventh/early eighth century. Thereafter, we can discern a response to increasing demands from an increasingly large elite and infer improved management of often newly-integrated estates embracing a range of resources for successful farming" [Fowler 1997, 252-253]. This would have been especially so in the west which was largely unaffected by the earliest, and most disruptive of the migration-period incursions; and in the context of *Pouelt*, these views take on an added significance, since it is in precisely this period that the series of Glastonbury Abbey charters for the old estate begins [Abrams 1996, 204-205]. This also raises the question of the structure of the entity that seems to have been progressively acquired by Glastonbury Abbey from the early 8th century onwards. What actually comes through in the historical record is a series of extensive, and for all we can tell, homogeneous blocks of land: we have absolutely no view of their *internal* structure or dynamics, or of whether these units were themselves composed of smaller building blocks. If the latter, should we view them, perhaps, as "'tithings' made up of the different types of land, attached to each farmstead/hamlet within or part of the larger units"? [*pers comm* M A Aston]. It should be said that, at this early date, there is not a shred of hard evidence for our Polden 'proto-townships'; the only place which is named as a (presumably) independent estate before 1066 is Cossington, which appears as a bound in S253, the Glastonbury Abbey charter of 729. The date of these bounds, although apparently of early form, is problematic [Abrams 1996, 98; and *cf* Lowe 1998], but nonetheless the relatively early form of the place-name [Costen 1992a, 115-116], together with its appearance in a document of this date, should give us pause for thought that even in the 8th century, it is inherently unlikely that *Pouelt*, whatever its extent, had not *already* undergone at least a degree of internal subdivision, or indeed had actually been assembled from smaller, *pre-existing* units.

We have already reviewed the problem of the internal structures of early territories, and concerns being increasingly expressed about the validity of their theoretical basis, in particular the notion of the 'multiple estate'. The implications for our understanding of the true nature of *Pouelt* are clear, but more detailed work would be needed to identify any internal framework of smaller landed units veiled within the inclusive, formulaic terms of the 8th century Glastonbury Abbey charters. Whatever the wider territorial context however, the settlement pattern itself would have been one of dispersed, isolated farmsteads and hamlets, for which we can reasonably extrapolate the Shapwick archaeological and field-name evidence, and to a much lesser extent whatever of the same evidence there is from the other northern parishes, across the whole northern flank. If Shapwick *is* merely the iceberg's tip in toponymic terms, the entities to its west may also have been functionally discrete, their individual rôles now lost with their putative specialist place-names. Common field farming is highly unlikely at this stage, the ring-fence farms probably being surrounded by their own autonomous, enclosed fields, perhaps along the lines of infield-outfield regimes. This certainly appears true at least for Shapwick, where arrangements of this type are inferred from "the halo effects of early medieval pottery around identified sites" [Aston and Gerrard 1999, 27]. Indeed, Harold Fox, developing existing ideas in this respect, has proposed recently that the sharing of non-arable resources may in part have been a precursor to, and have paved the way for, the *phased* development of the fully-fledged, common arable open-field system [Fox 1992, 43-45]. This at present is speculation; as Fowler has observed, "if we

ask what sort of fields did the Anglo-Saxons cultivate?, the only sensible answer would now seem to be lots of different sorts, depending on where you are in the British Isles and where you are in the Anglo-Saxon period" [Fowler 1997, 252]. Presumably, the arable fields of a 'Barton' or 'Whatton' would have been geared for more intensive production than those of a 'Shapwick', but the internal economic dynamics hinted at by specialist place-names are still very ill-understood, and indeed, some scholars question whether, in this respect, the toponymic evidence is not being made to bear more weight than it can reliably sustain. Thus, while Ros Faith seems to support the idea of specialist production centres [Faith 1997, 47-48], John Blair is more sceptical: "such 'defining' place-names may......refer to specialist tribute obligations rather than to an exclusively specialised economy: the township which owed renders of goats may still have produced other goods for local consumption" [Blair 1991, 30]. The truth, as always, is probably highly complex and lies somewhere between the two extremes: it might at first seem almost perverse if at least *some* specialist place-names did not indeed reflect a genuine former concentration on a particular livestock or crop; but not all will, and furthermore, the need to demonstrate both membership of a federative estate, *and* active participation in a system of inter-settlement exchange, would add considerably to the burden of proof [Fox 1981; Fleming 1998, 46-47; Aston 1985, 32-36]. We will return to this point a little later with specific regard to Shapwick and its relationship with its neighbouring settlements.

How, by the late 8th century, the settlement pattern on the *southern* side of Polden may have appeared, is problematic, but it is hardly likely that this area was devoid of occupation sites, and as a working hypothesis we can envisage here, I think, a series of secondary, minor farmsteads which were in effect dependent upon those on the northern flank, and of whose 'proto-township' territories, at this time, they remained an integral part. In terms of origin perhaps we can see these southern occupation sites with a rôle as pastoral outstations, established initially from the northern farms as short-distance summer shielings to exploit the massive grazing resource of Sedgemoor, and allowing flocks to be kept conveniently close to the moor without the necessity of a twice-daily drove up and down the steep gradients of Polden's southern face. Whether or not this activity constitutes transhumance is a moot point; Fox observes that "such movements of stock in highland Perthshire......fully qualify for the term transhumance, even though distances between wintertowns and shielings were not great, many being no more than two miles apart. Clearly, movement over great distances and altitudes is not a prerequisite for transhumance" [Fox 1996, 3]. The same writer, however, questions whether stock movements *within* township boundaries, such as might have been at least an element in the early medieval Polden economy, should properly be labelled transhumance [Fox 1996, 10-11].

It is at this point that we can make an attempt to place Shapwick in its proper landscape and economic context, for it, we can suggest, was effectively the fulcrum upon which turned the early medieval economy of at least the western part of *Pouelt*. By the time of Domesday, Shapwick had clearly become something considerably more than a mere 'sheep wick' [Corcos 1983, 51], and we have already reviewed the significant body of evidence to suggest that, in relation to its western neighbours (and, indeed, to Ashcott), Shapwick in the pre-Conquest period had held a position of pre-eminence. We have also noted John Blair's argument about the nature of 'specialist' place-names, and his belief that such names may have a *tributary* basis. This is the line of reasoning which I wish to pursue and develop here, since I believe that in many, if not most cases, it is this explanation that should inform our view of the nature of these names, and not an interpretation of 'farm/estate/settlement where commodity *X* is exclusively produced'. Shapwick emerges in the medieval period with a field system based on high-quality arable land; and following Richard Hodges, I consider it inherently unlikely that whatever its nature and extent, such an estate should not earlier on have been largely self-sufficient in terms of cereal production, at a time of relatively low (but expanding) population, and before the growth of towns in the later Anglo-Saxon period tended to skew local economies towards market specialisation [Hodges 1989, 130 and 150, and 2000, 107-125; Fox 1992, 54-55].

These ideas can be reconciled if we view Shapwick before the 10th century as in effect little more than a glorified corral, to which, perhaps several times a year, sheep from all over the western part of *Pouelt* were taken for general 'processing' (shearing, slaughtering, butchering and so on), with the various products then finding their way as tribute to a centre or centres of consumption and/or redistribution. Milking would be a daily activity carried out on the subsidiary estates, but again, we may easily imagine surpluses from local cheesemaking being taken on a regular basis to the 'sheep wick' for onward transmission; providing a local context, perhaps, for the ten cheeses referred to in Ine's Laws as an element of the food tribute due from every ten hides, leaving aside our ignorance of exactly what quantity we should infer from the term 'cheese' [Whitelock 1979, 406, item 70.1]. In any case, part of Shapwick's function would by default contain a strong *administrative* element, involving perhaps some record-keeping and overall control of produce and stock flowing into and out of its purview. Before the early 8th century this would presumably have constituted part of the *feorm* which flowed into royal *capita*, Glastonbury Abbey later taking over that rôle with its progressive acquisition of *Pouelt* [*cf* Faith 1997, 16-25 and 38-41]. It is the shadowy remnant of *this* link which manifests itself in the late Anglo-Saxon and early post-Conquest period in the form of Shapwick's tenurial, administrative and, I would argue, ecclesiastical superiority in western Polden, the first two so clearly attested in Domesday Book.

It is unclear at present how the area later known as Shapwick should have acquired this role, whether by accident (perhaps of long tradition?) or design. We know,

with Richard Coates, that the *–wic* name itself means "'farm specialising in some product' or 'in animals yielding produce'" [Coates 1999, 97]. As we have seen, for sheep, this is certainly what Shapwick ultimately became. The secondary sense of 'dairy farm', again as espoused by Coates [1999, 99], could also be understood, since at the time the name was coined, the primary source of dairy produce was sheep, not cattle [Finberg 1972, 410]. However, a further sense noted by Coates for *–wic* "is 'camp, temporary encampment'" [Coates 1999, 105], an idea which, if extended and applied to an economy with a transhumant element, might give a sense of 'shieling or temporary camp occupied on a seasonal basis for summer pasturage' [inferred from Coates 1999, 106-107].

If Shapwick was indeed rooted in such beginnings, it is reasonable to ask if the transhumant practices of which it may have formed the focus were a development of the early medieval period, or whether they could claim a greater antiquity. This is a question to which we will return later on. The central point in this model, however, is that Shapwick acted as the 'railhead' through which a very significant proportion of *Pouelt's* render of the products of pastoralism was channelled. And herein lies the key to Shapwick's pre-eminence. Harold Fox has argued that, before the widespread adoption of common multi-field systems in England, probably in the 10th and 11th centuries, it was the pastoral element in farming regimes, and the wide range of products to which it gave rise, which was overwhelmingly regarded as the most important and the most valuable, with arable very much relegated to a secondary rôle [Fox 1992, 56-60]. Indeed, the open-field system was probably *itself* "an innovation designed to accommodate more sheep, for their fleeces, milk and meat. It may marginally have brought improvements in arable farming" [Fox 1992, 59]. And Faith has noted that "in what scanty references we have to actual food renders, mutton and bacon [are] much the most common forms of meat" [Faith 1997, 47]. The 'proto-Shapwick' was probably not itself necessarily a centre of pastoral production (ie breeding, rearing, grazing) any more important than any of its neighbours. However, it is hardly surprising if a part of an ancient estate which enjoyed a rôle as the ultimate source of highly-prized pastoral products flowing as tribute first to the crown, and then to Glastonbury Abbey, should be regarded as an asset of the highest importance, and the reason why Shapwick remained a Glastonbury Abbey demesne manor right up to the Dissolution. Among the most telling threads of evidence are a significant, and probably ancient tax exemption in 1086 [Abrams 1994, 72-74; Costen 1994b, 76-78] which Faith would see as confirmation of an origin in early royal *inland* [Faith 1997, 40-41 and 48-53]; and the likely existence of an early (ie at least 8th century) primary church on or close to the site of what we have suggested (Chapter Two) is probably a Roman ritual complex of some kind, a rural shrine probably associated with the Old Church spring; and which in turn may have had a direct link with the large villa site recently discovered on the Nidons a little distance to the north. The latter may well bring us full circle and open a window on the organisation of the Roman landscape. For if, as we have already proposed, we would be right to expect at least a degree of functional continuity in farming practice in some areas, should we also ask whether the economy of the Nidons villa was geared largely (but by no means exclusively) towards large-scale sheep-processing? With subsidiary, dependent 'satellite' villas to the west, working their own estates and supplying it with livestock for this purpose, and its products being exported along the newly-engineered ridge road, westwards to the Bristol Channel via Crandon Bridge, and eastwards to the Fosse Way and Ilchester. This model presents the attractive notion of economy and religion linked by an east/west communications network: pilgrims to and from the spring-shrine [Aldhouse-Green 1999 and 2000], livestock to and from the villa estate. Does the villa site itself represent the Anglo-Saxon 'sheep wick'? Whether or not it continued as the focus of this regime, in whatever shape or form, in the 5th and 6th centuries or later, it is unlikely that its survival was an absolute pre-requisite for the perpetuation of the agricultural framework which had once supported it. What is important here is the possibility that economic inertia generated by long tradition imparted at least a degree of *functional* continuity that was tenacious enough to weather the social and economic displacement of the post-Roman period; a time when, as Aston [*pers comm*] has suggested, it is precisely pastoral economies which are likely to have been most important and to have displayed most resilience.

We can imagine, then, that the first English speakers in the area, probably around the mid-7th century, were confronted with a pre-existing and continuing activity whose nature they instantly recognised, whose operation they may well have assimilated, and which is reflected in the name they bestowed on this district.

Looking back at the northern settlements, we need for a moment to consider the nature of their relationship with the grazing lands to the south, on Sedgemoor; because there is the ironic possibility that it may have been the way in which this exploitation was managed that led ultimately to their access to that crucial resource being severed. Since we can now further suggest, moving forward through time, that perhaps by the end of the 9th century at the latest, the southern settlements were not only permanently occupied, but had become largely, if not fully autonomous entities, perhaps to the extent of enjoying some kind of notional existence as 'proto-townships' in their own right, with all that meant for the establishment of boundaries, however fluid and tenuous they may initially have been. This proposal carries with it connotations of independence in terms of economic (ie agrarian) regimes as well; and in the wider context, as a related development, this period may also have marked the appearance of the first fault lines in the territorial and economic integrity of the old *Pouelt* estate.

It is worth stressing again that the chronology of these processes is extremely blurred. But we might envisage a situation involving the growing independence of the southern settlements, and the parallel dissolution of the economic links which had previously bound this part of *Pouelt* into a coherent entity. Harold Fox has summarised

the likely nature of the diverse centrifugal forces which in the later Saxon period seem to have acted in concert to drive some ancient estates to the point of collapse [Fox 1992, 60-62]; and it may be possible to apply this principle to the situation on Polden. On the northern flank, where, as we have already seen, lay the best plough land, it may well have been the case that expanding arable in these communities, coupled with increasing difficulty of access to Sedgemoor through its progressive 'annexation' by the southern settlements, was causing problems in terms of the availability of year-round grazing. This may have constituted something close to Fox's "crisis in the provision of pasture [which] lay behind the introduction of the Midland system (and by extension the village)......" [Fox 1992, 60]; a mechanism that is now also being given serious consideration by some continental scholars confronting similar questions [*eg* Fallgren 1993, 73]. The southern Polden communities, smaller and much less demanding in terms of agricultural resource, would not have been affected to the same extent. It is at this point that Glastonbury Abbey, as overlord, may have decided to take a hand in an attempt at least to influence the *outcome* of a chain of events the genesis and prevention of which was largely outside its control. What little is known about the administration, organisation and exploitation of the Abbey's holdings in the pre-Conquest period is outlined by Abrams [1996, 266-272], one of whose points is to highlight disagreement about the nature and extent of the Abbey's interest in its own estates at this time [Abrams 1996, 269, n18].

Whatever the detail in this respect, I would argue that the very nature of the north Polden settlements finds its most logical explanation in the hand of seigneurial authority. It is becoming increasingly fashionable to stress the active involvement, and perhaps even the initiative, of the 'community of the vill' in matters of settlement planning [*eg* Fox 1992, 50-52], a position most recently restated by Dyer [1997, 58 and 1997a,167]; and there can be little doubt that continuing work in this field will increasingly reveal the participation, at many different levels and in many different ways, of peasant, agrarian communities, expressing "an idea about how people should live and organise themselves" [Dyer 1997, 58]. A thought-provoking perspective on this debate is provided by Astill, who sees the argument as essentially split between two camps, historical and archaeological [Astill 1988, 84]. Far more work needs to be done on the particular circumstances of landholding, economy, regional society, agrarian practices and so on, in which we might reasonably expect either the community or the manorial lord to take the lead in this respect. However, when we are confronted, as we are on north Polden, with a systematic series of highly regular, planned villages, side by side, in parishes clearly carved almost symmetrically from larger units, on an ancient estate of a powerful overlord, it seems almost perverse to eschew the 'seigneurial' explanation for the sake of historical political correctness. Dyer implies that such related village groups could develop "alongside one another through imitation of models" [Dyer 1997, 58], a possible process that we have already noted, and again, the operation of which will no doubt be increasingly demonstrated. Such an explanation, however, carries with it connotations of gradual diffusion and adoption rather than the relatively short-term, wholesale reorganisation which seems to characterise at least part of north Polden: Chilton, Edington and Catcott were manifestly created in a single, sweeping episode. They are production-line settlements occupying regular, closely-mensurated parishes. And while, as Fox argues, individual communities may well have been the prime movers behind the reorganisation of their particular township, we need to ask whether, on the estate of a major lord, they would also have had the wide-ranging executive authority to initiate radical change, such as the subdivision of pre-existing blocks of land, across large tracts of countryside encompassing several, or indeed many communities. Certainly, in clear cases of systematic landscape and settlement manipulation on a large scale, Ros Faith's recent review of the evidence leads her to lean very heavily towards the seigneurial explanation [Faith 1997, 234-237]. And of recent commentators, Oliver Rackham has perhaps summarised this side of the debate most cogently: "regularities in the landscape normally imply somebody's philosophy or ideology of how land ought to be divided; if on a large scale, they imply the existence of a higher authority capable of imposing that ideology on those who did the work" [Rackham 2000, 105].

Much more work needs to be done in this field, over wide areas with a variety of tenurial and ownership patterns, to see if there is any firm, quantifiable relationship between estate size and lordship, and the appearance of settlement planning. In the east midlands, where such work has been carried out, there does not appear to be any systematic correlation, although as the authors concede, "the problem……is that we are insufficiently informed about the nature and powers of lordship in the crucial period" [Dyer *et al* 1997, 206]. The equation is a highly complex one with many sometimes conflicting elements [*ibid* 204-210], but enough precedent has now accumulated for us to be confident at least that extensive, large-scale settlement planning *did* take place on major estates, lay and ecclesiastical, and that "those lords who enjoyed continuous possession of their estates in the whole period from the tenth to the thirteenth century can be shown from their later records to have a secure grip over their tenants" [Dyer *et al* 1997, 206]. Such long-term seigneurial interest was exactly the situation prevailing on Polden. Elsewhere, on the Sussex High Weald, Mark Gardiner has observed how "planned settlements are only found within the manors of the larger lords, and in particular those belonging to monasteries" [Gardiner 1997, 68]; Lucille Campey has, as we have already seen, demonstrated from 14th-15th century documentary evidence, planning involving the systematic segregation of different social groups on the estates of Durham Cathedral Priory, almost certainly pre-Conquest in date [Campey 1989]; and closer to home, albeit from a slightly later period (largely the 12th century), Lee Prosser's study of Keynsham hundred in north Somerset leads him to conclude that "there is clearly a link between the

morphology of the hundredal villages, and the tenurial pattern. Those settlements which are known to have been possessed, in part or whole by Keynsham Abbey……seem to have experienced a radical reordering along structured, planned lines" [Prosser 1995, 162].

At the present state of knowledge then, the balance of probability must be in favour of Glastonbury Abbey as the driving force behind the re-organisation of its north Polden lands that has left such a clear topographical mark. At least an element in this may have been a need to address an increasing problem of a shortage of pasture in these communities [Corcos 1983]. The more topographically-favoured northern settlements may have appeared to present to the Abbey a suitable opportunity to apply recently-introduced ideas on social intervention and manipulation, and agrarian organisation, on some of its own best agricultural land. Among the more prominent reasons for this we can suggest a drive for greater efficiency, the need for closer control of its tenants, and the increasingly burdensome and systematic military and tax obligations to the state [*cf* Faith 1997, 153-177; Prosser 1995, 171-175]. The allocation of bounded lands to the southern settlements may have been a part of the same process, although here the contrasting lack of evidence for deliberate reorganisation makes it likely that what occurred was merely the formal codification, in landscape terms, of much less regular pre-existing arrangements. However, the need to make the northern communities self-sufficient in agricultural terms, I would argue, was crucial, and that *resources*, and access to them, played a central role.

We have seen how it is Shapwick and its western neighbours which display the most overt signs of systematic manipulation in terms of settlement layout, and parish size and shape, but while the Roman road along the ridge may already to some extent have been recognised as a continuous boundary, why, as we have also seen, does the boundary suddenly part company from the road to march northwards, between Shapwick and Ashcott, as the hundred boundary? The one element that seems to tie these disparate threads together is the wetlands, north and south. Travelling eastwards, Shapwick is the last village on north Polden whose access to Sedgemoor is compromised by a southern neighbour (Moorlinch). Immediately east, Pedwell, although a manor in the post-Conquest period, failed to attain full parochial status and therefore Ashcott, by contrast, enjoyed freedom of access to both north *and* south. The same is true of both Walton and Street. There may therefore have been less urgency for the Abbey to provide a remedial solution to any pasture 'crisis', in the form of a midland-type, open-field system, in these communities, than in those to the west, a corollary of which would be that there would also be less immediate need to reorganise the settlement pattern. I should stress that there is no suggestion here that the southern communities represented by any means a total block between the northern settlements and Sedgemoor. So much is clear from the allocation of detached portions of the southern wetlands to the northern communities at the time of the enclosure of Sedgemoor by Act of Parliament in the late 18th century [Tate 1948, 44], a development arising from their long tradition of commonable use of the moor. But there can be little doubt that the growth of the southern Polden communities would have placed an additional burden on Sedgemoor's seasonal grazing resources, and this may well have been sufficient to prompt Glastonbury Abbey to seek a solution that would make the northern communities far more self-sufficient in terms of their pastoral resources.

Also, in view of the findings from the Swale Valley in Kent which we have already noted (Chapter Two), it is no longer beyond the bounds of possibility that the Abbey simply took over a series of relict Roman estates such as I have postulated on Figure 8, and when, probably in the later Anglo-Saxon period, social and economic conditions made it expedient to do so, used this pre-existing territorial framework as the basis of their own experiment in landscape and social intervention by placing a planned village at the centre of each unit.

Ashcott and Walton are of course now nucleated settlements, had open fields in the middle ages, and do both seem to display at least indications of some planning. But if so, it was on a far more limited scale, less systematic and radical in nature, and probably later in date than that to the west. And it was not thorough: we have already seen that Pedwell, in origin an isolated, pre-Conquest thegnage farm, survived as a dispersed element in Ashcott's settlement pattern, and indeed at Street 'nucleation' was a post-Conquest development with the three original, isolated settlement foci surviving as recognisable entities into the post-medieval period. Parish shapes and sizes east of the Shapwick/Ashcott boundary are also far more irregular. Likewise, the southern settlements may have been barely touched, if at all, by the same processes which so extensively changed their northern neighbours: the relatively high incidence of habitative field names present even by the mid 19th century, may indicate a tenacious thread of dispersal surviving from an earlier pattern that persisted well into the medieval period; much more detailed toponymic work along the lines of that at Shapwick [Costen 1993] might well resolve this question, and should form a central element of any future research.

There is a problem of chronology here, since it is likely that Shapwick and Ashcott were still a single unit when the northern flank reorganisation took place - the boundary between them has clearly been carved through an existing subdivided field system, whereas those further west are for the most part straight, suggesting that they pre-date or were laid out at the same time as, the open-field arrangements in those communities. The most plausible explanation at this stage is that at the time that the Shapwick/Ashcott unit underwent re-organisation, with the laying out of at least elements of the present village of Shapwick and the recasting of the field system, Ashcott was a relatively minor place, perhaps a thegnage farm sharing Shapwick's new field system. But it had also probably already acquired its own chapel, and had become sufficiently well-established to resist complete assimilation into the new Shapwick unit; a very similar situation, indeed, to that in which Ashcott's own dependency of Pedwell found itself later on. For a time then, Ashcott

could have participated in the operation of a joint field-system with Shapwick; and in this respect we have already noted the view of some scholars that in many cases, episodes of replanning focussed first and foremost on the field layout, with settlement arrangements being addressed only later in a secondary phase, or even being left, effectively, to take care of themselves [Chapter Eight; and *cf* Taylor 1995]. How long the Shapwick/Ashcott unit survived after the upheavals further west is entirely problematic. However, it is difficult to see that it could long resist the centrifugal forces which elsewhere were tearing *Pouelt* apart, and practical considerations may also have played a rôle. Unlike Pedwell, it seems as though Ashcott was able ultimately to achieve full independence. Perhaps its population had expanded sufficiently to enable it to survive as a viable economic entity in its own right, with the advantage to Glastonbury Abbey that it would provide an additional taxable unit, perhaps supporting a thegn and thus making a contribution to the Abbey's military obligations. The day to day operational difficulties presented by the joint cultivation of what must have been an unusually extensive field system may eventually have become untenable, and indeed it is quite likely that well before any formal division, the two communities had 'annexed' areas of the field system to themselves but *worked* them in close co-operation: we have already noted some topographical evidence for close ties between the two, and Harold Fox has highlighted "cases of two adjoining townships going to some trouble to ensure that their fallowing cycles synchronized so that their fallow fields adjoined every second or third year, creating vast, inter-commonable prairies between the settlements" [Fox 1992, 57]. Detailed work on the Shapwick/Ashcott annual cropping regimes, as revealed in Glastonbury Abbey's medieval *compoti*, would provide a sound empirical basis for an informed perspective[1].

In due course, Ashcott was elevated to the status of an independent manor endowed with its own territory, the boundaries to both west and east, with Shapwick and Walton respectively, carved through existing field systems, yet further evidence that east of Shapwick, territorial, field and settlement patterns were far less uniform, more 'organic' in nature, and more likely to have embedded within them elements of earlier arrangements; although we should note that certain elements of Shapwick's own internal framework of boundaries are themselves clearly extremely ancient. During excavations in 1999, a Bronze Age ditch was found directly underneath one of the field boundaries that contribute to the framework of the southern part of Shapwick's village plan. This feature clearly represented a seminal boundary at the time it was established, and was important and tenacious enough not only to survive episodes of major agrarian re-organisation, but to influence the nature of later arrangements (Plate 11; Figure 49). So much is demonstrated from its association

---

[1] This is, for example, exactly the kind of exercise which Ian Keil has already carried out for a few selected Glastonbury Abbey manors (namely Walton, and Longbridge and Monkton Deverill in Wiltshire), but not, unfortunately, for Shapwick and Ashcott. Keil 1964, Appendix III, Tables A, B and C, 225-229.

Plate 11: A trackway immediately east of Shapwick forming a major element of the village plan and associated field arrangements, under excavation. This proved that it lay on top of a boundary 'feature', probably a ditch, that was at least Bronze Age in date, and was associated with two later, parallel ditches. View looking west.

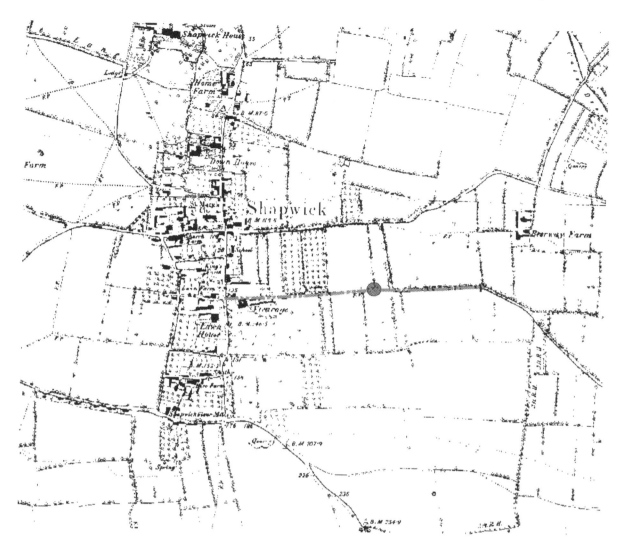

Figure 49

Extract from First Edition OS 6" map (1885) showing, with a grey dot,
location of trial trench depicted in Plate 11. The site marks the position of
an east-west ditch (probable course shown by a grey dashed line) containing
Bronze Age pottery, and demonstrates both the importance and the high
antiquity of this boundary, which survived long enough to have a major
influence on both the layout of the village plan, and the arrangement of
furlongs east of the village.

with two other parallel ditches, "one Roman and one post-medieval.........suggesting contiguity if not continuity of its east-west alignment" [Aston and Gerrard 1999a, 42].

It seems very likely that the formalisation of the Shapwick/Ashcott boundary may be closely related to the process of hundredation, and if so it is also clear that the *position* of the boundary was chosen with considerable care. For this is far more than merely an administrative and agricultural divide between two adjacent townships; perhaps even more significantly, the hundred boundary also marks a line of major ecological imbalance in terms of access to resources between those places to the west of it, and those to the east. That the profound importance of this dichotomy was clearly recognised by contemporaries we can be sure, and it is one which, I would suggest, ultimately underpinned the way in which Glastonbury Abbey organised its Polden settlements and their estates, and gave rise to the markedly contrasting level of its intervention, in topographical terms, on either side of the boundary.

Chew, Carhampton, and Whitley: Comparisons and Contrasts

This, then, is the model that I offer for the nature, origins and development of medieval settlement on Polden, which has been the central concern of this study. But where do the surveys of the other two hundreds fit into this picture, and how do they inform our view of some of the questions that this study has been trying to address?

It must by now be clear that a common thread is the importance of ecology and natural environment as important considerations in shaping the nature of medieval settlement, and by extension, the nature of the human communities occupying these areas, in all three hundreds. This is *not* a 'deterministic' conclusion, but one which accepts and indeed celebrates the extraordinary adaptive abilities of pre-industrial societies, and the fully symbiotic relationship between them and their ecological resource-base. In this respect those who point up the tenacious thread of human ingenuity in turning sometimes apparently intractable landscapes to account, and the the often prodigious expenditure of effort and skill required to achieve this, are absolutely right to do so. This is not the place to indulge in extended polemics about this profoundly important argument. However, at least partly on the basis of this survey, I must in all conscience disagree with that mode of thinking, so cogently but, in my opinion, misguidedly expressed by the late Professor Bronowski [1973, 19], that makes man total master of his environment, able to bend it to his purpose with complete impunity and without, apparently, the least reciprocal effect. Neither am I alone in this; for there is increasing disquiet among professional scholars, and particularly geographers, about the general unhelpfulness and sterility of such extreme views. We have already noted Faith's careful but firm remarks in this context. As long ago as 1985, Coones mounted a robust and sustained attack on those who would divorce the development of pre-industrial

societies from the natural environments which they occupied [Coones 1985][2]. More recently, Butlin and Roberts, geographers both, have been equally trenchant: "recent ideas in cultural geography, which emphasize the significance of the cultural construction of landscapes by human imagination and agency, are now being questioned in relation to their apparent underestimation of the role of physical environments in people-environmental relations" [Butlin and Roberts 1995, 10][3]. Indeed, even some of the most forward-thinking landscape theoreticians are now beginning to acknowledge that the pendulum has swung too far towards an almost exclusively humanist approach and that a proper understanding of the natural landscape context is crucial [McGlade 1999]. In the case of Shapwick therefore, and indeed of the Polden ridge as a whole, it is absolutely true that "it is the landscape itself which is manipulated on an impressive scale" [Gerrard 2000, 37]. But *I* would add the crucial qualification that that manipulation was shaped by and has taken place firmly within the framework of constraints imposed and opportunites offered by the natural landscape and its resources.

In all three of the study hundreds, the influence of natural topography and availability of resources is clear. The point is well made on Polden itself – the inference of the model I have already proposed is that in the early medieval period, the nature of the large-scale landscape and social manipulation which undoubtedly took place was largely dictated by ecological considerations, although the underlying causes and driving forces spring probably from far wider and deep-seated developments that were taking place in English society as a whole. Likewise was settlement and land-use in Chew Hundred, and indeed beyond, shot through with a relationship with landscape that, if not causal, was at the least pivotal. I have suggested that Chew's status as a recurrent and persistent seminal place in the landscape can probably be attributed to a range of underlying causes, among them its location at a river crossing and as a communications nodal point. But I have also suggested that not the least of these is that Chew constitutes an island in the middle of a small 'sea' of high-grade arable land. It may help to put this suggestion into a wider, continental perspective, in order to emphasise the sometimes central role that land quality and natural topography played in settlement and population dynamics. Thus van Ossel and Ouzoulias, drawing on their survey of settlement in northern Gaul in the late and post-Roman period, remark that "the mediocre quality of the soils and the low level of occupation during the High Empire explains in part the depopulation of certain lands in the 4th [century]. This is the case for the Hunsbrück, where the decline had become more marked since the Iron Age, and

---

[2] I am grateful to Jodie Lewis for this reference.
[3] After a long professional career as one of the most eminent authorities on English toponymy, and especially in regards to her work in demonstrating that topographical elements belong to the earliest stratum of Anglo-Saxon place-naming, Margaret Gelling has remarked recently that "I am.......an unrepentant geographical determinist"; Gelling and Cole 2000, xvii. Professor Philip Rahtz has expressed similar sentiments. Rahtz 2000, 6.

the uplands of Belgian Ardennes………to the west of Arlon, the division between deserted and populated areas coincides roughly with the limit between the schist plateaux and the more fertile sandstone or limestone fringes of the Gaume" [van Ossel and Ouzoulias 2000, 139]. And in the central Greek province of Boeotia, John Bintliff's long-term, multi-period landscape survey, leads him to conclude that the overriding considerations governing settlement and land-use patterns were "the distribution of fertile agricultural land, ergonomic work constraints on territorial size, social factors affecting the dispersion of communal groups, and limited locational possibilities for settlement micro-location" [Bintliff 2000, 148].

We see similar affinities in the argument I have adduced to account for Chewton hundred's acquisition of its detached pastures to the west, which turns on the notion of the importance of access to a particular resource, and the subsequent development of the settlement pattern within that resource 'enclave'. This also highlights, although as inference rather than proven fact, the economic integrity (again specifically as regards its *internal* resource-base) of the suggested Chew/Chewton 'river estate' before the endowment of the new See of Wells in 909 led to its break-up. By this view, the loss of resource for what became Chewton hundred was considered serious enough for the imbalance to be rectified (whether voluntarily or under royal duress) by a compensatory land transfer by the episcopate. Also in Chew Hundred we might point to the semi-dispersed nature of the settlement pattern, especially in the northern half, for which we find at least a partial explanation in the likely persistence there of an extensive tract of woodland in the Roman and early medieval periods, the evidence coming from place-names, the tortuous boundary between Chew and Dundry, and surviving ancient woodland located on that boundary. At High Ham in Whitley Hundred, too, a similar reason seems to underpin the dispersed and small-scale settlement that can found particularly to the west and north of the present High Ham village.

Nowhere are the constraints of nature more apparent than in Carhampton hundred, and although it has not been possible to say how far lordship and tenure played their part, as undoubtedly they did, there can be no doubt that ultimately the pattern of dispersed settlement, of hamlets and isolated farmsteads, is borne out of a society draping itself thinly across an unforgiving landscape, as I have said in Chapter Eight, of "marked extremes of climate, relief and difficult terrain". Witness the number of small Domesday manors that never became parishes. Apart from Carhampton itself, there is little evidence of settlement planning, and little to betray the hand of overarching lordship in terms of social and topographical manipulation, as there so palpably is in Whitley. But we must be careful here, for we need to recognise that planning is implicitly a result of conscious choice, and whether acted out through lordship or the 'community of the vill', or the two in concert, its absence may be as much a deliberate decision as would probably be its presence. In Carhampton, there may not have been those social and

economic imperatives whose presence in western Polden made landscape manipulation on a large scale worthwhile, particularly as regards rectifying ecological imbalances. As we have seen (Chapter Seven), generally, outside valleys and the lowland coastal strip, the economic affinities of Carhampton were overwhelmingly pastoral, although with sporadic episodes of upland ploughing visible from the archaeological and environmental record. But if, as seems likely, the greater part of the settlement framework was in position long before 1066, Carhampton may to some extent bear comparison with Chew hundred, in so far as both may have been locked into a tradition of locational inertia that brooked no interference (Chapter Eight). The reasons for this are problematic. Chew alone demonstrates that the presence of overarching lordship is not invariably a recipe for the existence of systematic planned rural settlement. There, this may have had as much to do with estate 'policy' on the part of the nascent See of Wells as the potential difficulty and expense of reorganising an entrenched and ancient settlement pattern, and the social structures that went with it. But in this respect it is Whitley which may also help to illuminate both Chew and Carhampton. For unlike Whitley, neither of the latter hundreds can show within its compass a geographically bounded entity such as Polden where, as I have suggested, the development of a distinct hierarchy of settlement, primary on the northern slope, secondary on the southern, had led to differential access to resources. If the hand of Glastonbury Abbey is to be seen pulling the settlement strings here, it was interested in doing so only on western Polden, where the problem lay. In Chew, by contrast, the See of Wells does not seem to have faced any such dilemma. It inherited instead a highly diverse framework of mixed settlement, part nucleated, part dispersed, a hybrid pattern that does not appear to have presented any difficulties or challenges in terms of access to associated resources. Presumably the increasing exactions of the state in the 10th century, especially in regards to the obligations of military service, fell as heavily on Wells as they did on Glastonbury Abbey, and the tendency towards a more rigid, closely-defined and hierarchical social structure would have been as apparent on the estates of one as they were on the other. For Glastonbury Abbey we can reasonably suggest that these were both among the chief factors which led the abbey into the experiment in large-scale landscape change that resulted in the north Polden villages. In Chew, however, the See must have followed a different path in confronting those very same demands and pressures, perhaps on the basis that one should never attempt to mend something which is not broken. If the settlement and social structure inherited by the See in Chew could meet its obligations without potentially expensive, disruptive and perhaps unpopular tampering, then so much the better. Likewise for Carhampton, whose pastoral economy was in no sense 'marginal' (Chapter Seven), but simply 'different' than that towards which Glastonbury Abbey was working on western Polden, creating highly regular, subdivided arable field systems worked from tightly planned nucleated villages. But again, an increasing body of evidence is making it clear that we are misguided to restrict our conceptual view of planning to large, nucleated villages. For we are beginning to appreciate that the principles of planning, in terms of regularity of layout and the use of repetitive elements or cells, could be and were applied with just as much vigour in areas of dispersed hamlets and farmsteads [Dyer *et al* 1997, 127-132; Taylor 1995]. Far more detailed work than has been possible here would be needed to show whether there are parts of Carhampton supporting this kind of small-scale settlement planning on a systematic basis, and future research along these lines would, I suggest, contribute much to the wider debate about the whole nature of dispersed settlement and its economic, social and topographical affinities. But even at the crudest level of analysis, the very fact of its existence should give us pause that planning could very easily be accommodated within existing social and settlement frameworks. What we need to work towards is a far greater understanding of the kinds of criteria which informed the thinking of those making the choices and decisions about whether existing settlement should be left well alone, re-organised on a small-scale, or swept away wholesale to be replaced with entirely new forms.

It is crucial that from the outset of this kind of work, the rôle of the church, especially in its wider, territorial sense, should form a central element in our thinking. It is beginning increasingly to look as though many territories allocated to ecclesiastical houses through charter grants, or which we can reconstruct with confidence through the *parochiæ* of early minsters, may preserve within their compass far older structures, such as, for example, I have suggested for the antecedents of Whitley hundred. Likewise for Chew, it seems that, among other things, the pattern of ecclesiastical dependencies there may reveal the outline of the original *parochia* attached to the probable minster church of St Andrew, after its split from the far larger, and more ancient 'river estate' of which it may have been part. Both Chew Magna and the village of Carhampton appear to be able to show examples of churches which fit into that category of superior foundations identified by John Blair as being characterised by groupings of structures, although at both the existence of subsidiary churches awaits absolute proof. I am particularly confident, however, about the nature and position of St Mary's at Chew Magna, and would suggest that its location within the churchyard should be made a priority for future work. Arising out of this, a wider, systematic topographical and archaeological survey of churchyard chapels in Somerset would add greatly to our ideas about the nature of these sites, and fluctuations in relative status. A review of the documentary evidence has already begun [*pers comm* M D Costen]. This has the potential to be extremely important work with implications far beyond the borders of the county; since, as Gervase Rosser has reminded us recently, subsidiary chapelries for which the documents appear to suggest an origin only in the medieval or late medieval periods (as at Chew Magna), may well mark ritual sites (perhaps even pre-Christian) of far deeper antiquity [Rosser 1996, 76-79].

This work would integrate well with the topographical survey of church sites that I have suggested in Appendix 2, and which springs out of my suggestion that, although Whitley cannot apparently show church groups in the same way that both Chew and Carhampton probably can, the possibilities are equally intriguing. For Shapwick and Moorlinch, I have put forward a model of landscape perception which, firstly, ties these two sites together as a liturgical group, even though at some distance, and which secondly attempts to explain the psychological perspective of the traveller through the landscape in terms of his cognitive relationship with Moorlinch church. This is a deliberate attempt, in a limited way, to use phenomenology to fix churches, in their topographical context, firmly in the landscape as ritual monuments fully integrated with 'secular' settlement. This approach originated, and has served its apprenticeship with the prehistorians, and as I have shown in Chapter Six, has not emerged entirely unscathed. However, along with my own suggestion, recent papers by Williams and Altenberg, cited in that chapter, together with Phythian-Adams's fascinating examination of 'topographies of superstition' in the early modern period, should encourage more medievalists that the rewards in this perspective are potentially very significant.

In this context, Carhampton's ecclesiastical pattern may well illuminate those of both Chew and Whitley, but especially the latter. Carhampton possesses far more surviving chapels and churches below parochial level, and at least some of these may be survivals of a very old, perhaps even pre-English pattern of hermitages and small field churches, some of which fell out of use, some of which through time developed into full parish churches, or which simply persisted as sub-parochial foundations. I have suggested that this may also have been the original pattern in Whitley, but that it was swept away, at least in those areas, particularly western Polden, affected by later large-scale landscape manipulation. Again, this has far wider implications, the inference being that the late medieval pattern of ecclesiastical provision in so-called 'planned' landscapes, with one church per village, may disguise a far denser network of smaller churches, now lost. But even in planned landscapes, there may be hints of a persistent and tenacious thread of earlier arrangements. In Whitley itself, and bearing in mind Rosser's recent survey, cited above, we can legitimately question whether, for example, the known chapels at Butleigh Wootton and Pedwell (both sub-parochial settlements) are really medieval foundations, or whether they actually represent far older sites that simply emerge into the documentary light in the post-Conquest period?

Be this as it may, comparison between the three hundreds tends to reinforce the impression of workers such as Teresa Hall and others that ecclesiastical arrangements developed very much within a topographical framework. The Chew/Chewton entity that has been suggested was based around a river basin, Whitley had at its core a marked watershed (the Polden Hills). And in both areas there emerge in the post-Conquest period a series of distinct, systematic and recoverable relationships between what appear to be primary churches, and their dependent chapelries – Chew Magna and Chewton, and Shapwick/Moorlinch in Whitley, with, in the latter, what seems to be a number of rather lower status 'mother' churches with perhaps one or two dependencies, such as High Ham, Middlezoy, Street and Butleigh. What is so striking is that, when topography is made a central element in the equation, the pattern of ecclesiastical provision becomes almost predictable. In other words, given just a relief map which also indicates land quality and the positions of churches, we might have a reasonable attempt at identifying the pattern of relationships as between 'higher' and 'lower' status churches, at the level of individual sites. The Ham plateau and Sowy Island are distinct, geographically bounded entities both of whose mother churches lie quite centrally, and on elevated sites. The suggested relationship between Shapwick and Moorlinch as a mutually-dependent liturgical pair relies to a large extent on the remarkable topographical affinities of the site of Moorlinch church. And Chew Magna St Andrew stands at a communications nodal point, a river crossing, on a slightly elevated bluff bounded on three sides by water, and at the centre of a large tract of Grade 1 agricultural land. In the cases of both Chew and Whitley, I have argued that these relationships are crucial in reconstructing the primary territorial units which, I suggest, formed the basis of the later hundreds.

In Carhampton, by contrast, these relationships are far more difficult to discern, and their significance far more difficult to deduce. Carhampton gives the strong impression, unlike Chew and Whitley, of possessing little internal 'cohesiveness'. Links between 'superior' and dependent churches are notably thin – indeed there seems to be only a single example of a dependent church (Luxborough) gaining full parochial independence from its 'mother' (Cutcombe). Unlike Chew and Whitley, Carhampton was never subject to early and unified lordship. Domesday renders may give some hint of a former administrative integrity. However, as I have suggested in the conclusion to Chapter Four, it is frankly impossible to believe that the nature of the terrain did not have a highly centrifugal effect on what internal links there were in the early medieval period, be they economic, administrative or ecclesiastical, and did not contribute markedly to an inherent tendency towards internal instability. For this same reason, it would be far more difficult for Carhampton to predict from topography alone the nature and status of individual churches, since the hundred is not, essentially, a bounded entity, and it is difficult to avoid the conclusion that the highly variable, broken nature of its natural landscape simply does not lend itself to the establishment of tenacious, persistent and cohesive relationships.

For Chew and Whitley it is possible to make an attempt, in a way that we cannot for Carhampton, at defining at least the bare outline of settlement patterns and relationships in the Roman period. The overall conclusion based on this comparison bears re-examination. Notwithstanding my suggestion of a major high-status site (?villa) awaiting discovery in the area of St Andrew's

church, Chew seems to show a general pattern of "a lower density of generally lower status sites" (Chapter Two) as compared to Whitley. Chew's only certain villa known to date, at Chew Park, was a small, lacklustre and prosaic affair. Neither in Chew can we see any clear pattern of differential status between the known sites, although this due in part to the much less systematic recovery of evidence from the hundred. Suggesting plausible territorial divisions with a balance of economic resources that might be taken to represent Roman 'estates' is also a highly problematic exercise in Chew. The contrast with Whitley could hardly be more striking. The Polden ridge provides a sound basis for the modelling of systematic economic entities with a balance of resources, and the hundred as a whole shows a greater concentration of large and wealthy villas than almost anywhere else in Somerset save the area around Bath, which of course is exceptional. What, I would argue, Whitley had which Chew does not, and which almost by itself could be used to account for this marked dichotomy, was an extremely resilient and diverse economy underpinned at every level by access to the Somerset Levels wetlands. The area encompassed by the later hundred effectively bisects the moors, with Sedgemoor to south and the Brue Valley to north. It can surely be no coincidence that the overwhelming majority of the known high-status Roman sites in Whitley lie at or close to the fen-edge[4]. And the enormous economic potential of this position could be tapped via the major communications artery of the re-engineered Polden ridge road. This pattern, though, was merely reinforcing and confirming an already firmly entrenched settlement framework that can with certainty be identified in the Iron Age, and probably has its basis in the Neolithic. The wider lessons are clear: the nature and development of patterns of rural settlement in the past, always depended on a complex and highly dynamic web of conflicting or mutually-reinforcing factors. But at the very centre of the structure, probably from the point at which human societies in Britain began the very slow and gradual process of becoming primarily sedentary, always lay considerations of access to and exploitation of the resources to hand. And fen-edge communities enjoyed a richer, more diverse, and consequently more robust and tenacious resource-base than those occupying almost any other type of environment.

****

In the Introduction to this study, I suggested, following Harold Fox's lead in the context of field

---

[4] This being said, it begs the intriguing question of why, apparently, Sowy Island, with access to the marshes all around it, is all but devoid of Roman occupation except on the most humble level, at the large Westonzoyland site; an important question to which as yet I can offer no plausible answer. *If* we can extrapolate backwards from later, early medieval topographical affinities and ecclesiastical arrangements, perhaps we might infer the existence of a high-status site (?villa) in the area of the church at Middlezoy? In this context it is interesting to note that a recent survey of the Humber marshlands, while generally restating accepted views regarding the overall diversity and resilience of fen-edge economies, qualifies them with the suggestion that "with the introduction of agriculture........wetland habitats become increasingly peripheral to the economy" [Dinnin and Van de Noort 1999, 69].

systems, that it is the regions of hybrid settlement types, in 'transitional' or 'boundary' areas, that may prove to hold the key to the antecedents of medieval rural settlement. This, indeed, was the stated rationale behind the major topographical, archaeological and historical study that underpins Dyer *et al* 1997, and it has been strongly reiterated recently in relation to the Arden and the Feldon country in Warwickshire, long regarded as a 'frontier zone' in terms of both settlement patterns and land-use [Roberts and Wrathmell 2000a]. However, I also hinted that the search for absolute origins may also carry with it certain, perhaps unhealthy, connotations of obsession, or at least, misguided single-mindedness, in the full knowledge that it represents something of an unattainable holy grail[5]. Empirical identification of occupation sites, their nature and date, *is* of course fundamental, and meaningful perspectives and interpretations of a whole range of related questions can spring only from the hard-won prize of a full and reliable archaeological, topographical and historical database. This would in itself present an awesome enough task; but nowhere more so than here, in western Britain, when, as we have seen in Chapter Three of this study, for the period between the 5th century and the 9th-10th, communities which we know full well to have been present in, and winning a living from the landscape, are at the moment effectively invisible to us because we cannot yet see their material culture.

However, it is also my personal view that future research strategies should expend far greater energy on considerations of the wider territorial, ecological and psychological/cognitive contexts of settlement and land-use. I would reiterate that, as medievalists, we dismiss the significance of the latter at our peril, especially since its role in shaping contemporary perceptions of landscape is now beginning to be recognised even by historians of far later periods [see for example Phythian-Adams 2000; Williamson 2000, esp at 76-77][6]. And I hope I have at least been able to suggest in this survey something of the potentially central role that my own county of Somerset could have to play in shaping our perspectives on the antecedents and affinities of medieval rural settlement in English landscapes far beyond her own borders.

---

[5] It is the stated aim of the Whittlewood Project, a recent initiative involving a major programme of historic landscape investigation in the East Midlands, to address questions concerning *not* just the origins of medieval rural settlements, but also their development, *floruit* and decline. Prof Christopher Dyer, lecture delivered to MSRG AGM, 9/12/2000. The Project's web site can be viewed at: www.bham.ac.uk/whittlewood.

[6] Even in the context of nothing more than a general recognition of the importance of this theme, there may be a very real danger of early medieval scholarship being somewhat 'left behind'. Witness the recent appeal by Ray Laurence to his fellow Romanists about the potential significance for their field of study of the ideas of prehistoric theorists such as Tilley and his colleagues: "learning from theory used by others seems all too obvious, but it should be noted that it is effective and useful.........we can learn so much from the work of other archaeologists, social theorists, and anthropologists, rather than isolating ourselves from their debates" [Laurence 1999, 389].

Appendix 1

Bronze Age Barrow, NGR ST338406
Woolavington/Puriton Parish Boundary

The feature appears to be a ditched bowl barrow of a form which is fairly typical of the Early Bronze Age, *c*2000 – *c*1600BC, and its potential significance was initially recognised by one of us (NC) in the course of fieldwork during the winter of 1998/99. It lies at the western end of the Polden Hills, on the crest of the ridge, and is bisected by the southern section of the parish boundary between Woolavington to the east, and Puriton to the west. It does not appear in the relevant parts of the listings of Somerset barrows published by Grinsell[1], and although Woolavington is known to have possessed two windmills by the early 13th century, their locations are unknown, and tithe field names here in the mid 19th century give no indication that there was ever a windmill on this site[2]. Windmills within Woolavington and Puriton parishes are depicted on the Somerset maps of both Day and Masters (1782) and Greenwood (1822), but in each case at locations well removed from the site described here[3]. The location has no known connection with hundredal arrangements or administration; it is therefore highly unlikely to fit into the apparently large category of barrow-like mounds which were artificially constructed in the early medieval period as markers at hundred moot sites[4].

Approaching from the north, the parish boundary takes a marked dog-leg to the east as soon as it strikes the ditch, and then runs over the top of the earthwork. It seems quite clear that the boundary surveyors used the barrow as a sight-line in what must have been, at least in this area, a quite open and featureless landscape. However, the boundary does not cut the barrow exactly in two. Probably about two-thirds of it lie on the western, Puriton side, and this section is relatively well-preserved. The remainder, on the eastern, Woolavington side, has by contrast been virtually ploughed out. The good state of preservation on the western side may have implications for the future management and protection of the monument. Across what seems to be its widest surviving diameter, from north-west

to south-east, the barrow is about 30m wide between the *outer* lips of the ditch. On 1st May 1999, a geophysical and earthwork survey was carried out by students from the Dept of Archaeology, University of Bristol, under the direction of Jodie Lewis and Dave Mullin. Magnetometry was adversely affected by a metal gate immediately to the south, which leads into the field in which the barrow lies, and also a metal cattle drinking trough which stands in the boundary hedge, exactly in the ditch immediately on the northern side of the barrow. However, resistivity picked up not only the well-preserved western section, but also confirmed the course of the ditch in the now-destroyed eastern section. The low resistance readings recorded from the top of the barrow itself, very similar to those taken from the surrounding ground surface, suggest very strongly that this is an earthen barrow without a stone or rubble core.

In terms of its wider implications, the monument seems to fit well into the context of a linear barrow cemetery running east-west along the Polden ridge that has recently been suggested by Aston[5]. The barrow has been entered onto the Somerset SMR as record item number 12894.

We would like to record our grateful thanks to the following people:

Heidi Dawson, a student in the Dept of Archaeology at Bristol University, for her sterling help with the survey; Mr Brian Lishman, of Goosegreen Farm, Sutton Mallet, for his work in tracing the farmer and the landowners on our behalf; the joint landowners, Mrs C K Hudson and Mrs K H Greenhill, for their support, and for permission for the survey to be carried out; the farmer Mr John House, for his helpful co-operation in the matter of access to the field; and Mr Paul Trolley, of the Bridgwater office of Greenslade, Taylor, Hunt, for his interest in the work, and his good offices as 'liaison' between ourselves and the landowners.

Nick Corcos, Jodie Lewis
May 1999.

---

[1] L V Grinsell, "Somerset Barrows, Part I: West and South", *SANHS* 113, 1969; *idem*, "Somerset Barrows: Revisions 1971-87", *SANHS* 131, 1987.
[2] C J Bond, *Medieval Windmills in South-Western England*, Wind and Watermill Section, Society for the Protection of Ancient Buildings, Occasional Publication No 3, 1995, 8, and 55-57; A J Coulthard, M Watts, *Windmills of Somerset and the Men Who Worked Them*, 1978, 58, 67-68. The tithe maps and awards for Puriton and Woolavington show a common field nomenclature here across the boundary. Puriton, SRO D/D/Rt 384 (1842), T688, 'Great Mortland'; Woolavington, SRO D/D/Rt 403 (1842), T73 & 74, 'Maitland'. See also Paul Ashbee, "Barrows, cairns, and a few impostors", *British Archaeology*, March 1998, no 32.
[3] J B Harley, R W Dunning (eds), *Somerset Maps*, Somerset Record Society 76, 1981.
[4] R Adkins, M Petchey 1984, "Secklow Hundred Mound and Other Meeting Place Mounds in England", Archaeological Journal 141. See also R van de Noort 1993, "The Context of Early Medieval barrows in western Europe", Antiquity 67.

[5] M A Aston, "Mounds, Barrows, Watermills, Windmills and Limekilns", in M A Aston and M D Costen (eds), *The Shapwick Project: The Fourth Report*, 1993, 12-13; M A Aston, C Gerrard, "'Unique, Traditional and Charming': The 1999 Shapwick Project, Somerset", Antiquaries Journal 79, fig 7, 13.

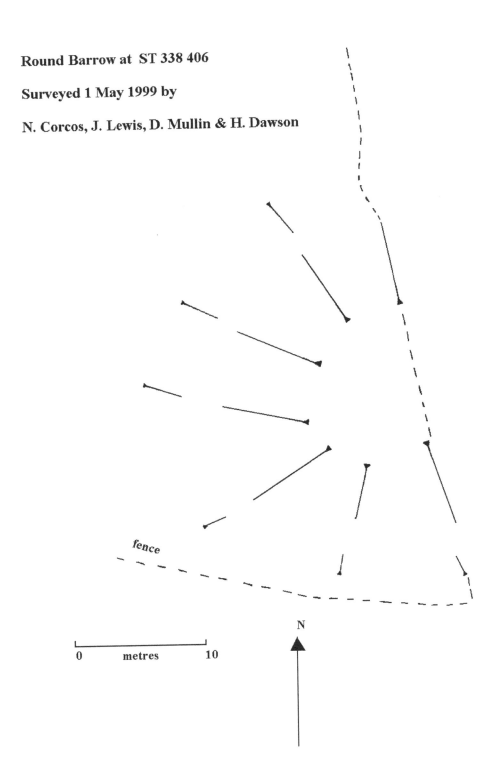

Round Barrow at ST 338 406

Surveyed 1 May 1999 by

N. Corcos, J. Lewis, D. Mullin & H. Dawson

fence

0   metres   10

N

Appendix 2

Suggestions for Further Work Arising From This Study

The preceding narrative provides a summary overview of certain aspects of the topographical basis of medieval rural settlement in selected areas of the county of Somerset. Throughout, while looking at these sometimes highly localised areas, there has been an attempt to draw out from them themes and issues which have implications far beyond the borders of Somerset itself. As essentially a work of synthesis, it has not by definition been possible to look at more than a few of the central questions and difficulties currently occupying research scholars in this field, and the treatment of those that *are* dealt with cannot by any means be said to be definitive. Nonetheless, the study has at least highlighted several key areas of interest that, I suggest, might in the future be usefully explored and developed in a far more empirical and systematic way, and made greatly to enhance and inform our understanding of the *landscape and territorial* context of medieval settlement in England; and particularly, the highly dynamic and symbiotic relationship between communities and the landscape viewed as a unified ecosystem, with both being modified by the other; the communities in a cultural, and the landscape in a morphological and ecological sense. The main points, specifically, are:

The discussion of the villages of the Polden ridge in central Somerset, suggests very strongly that there was a substantial *ecological* imperative in some cases of extensive landscape and settlement planning; in other words, that resources, their exploitation and access to them, were material considerations in what we might call 'early medieval planning decisions'.

I have also proposed a theoretical solution over a difficulty concerning the relationship between two churches on the Polden ridge. This has wide-ranging implications for the way in which we view early medieval perceptions of sacred sites, and while it is obvious that churches were essentially ritual monuments, we need to develop ways of looking at them in the *total* human landscape continuum, much as prehistorians are now beginning to discard the notion of a landscape that was partitioned between functions that were *either* 'ritual' *or* 'domestic'. Models of landscape cognition currently being used by prehistorians, although sometimes severely flawed, could, I suggest, be usefully adapted to inform and greatly expand our perspectives in this period; since it is in my opinion unequivocally the case that, intermittent documentation aside, rural settlement and territorial development in England before 1066 took place in a cultural context that was, in a very real sense, pre-historic.

As a result of this study, a number of different themes suggest themselves as potentially valuable research topics for future work:

- To look in far greater detail at the imperatives informing extensive landscape manipulation (settlements, field systems and so on), in the early medieval period in Somerset. This would involve looking at a wide variety of topographical contexts, land tenure, the role of the great landlords both lay and ecclesiastical, and very importantly, the questions of antecedent territorial structures and resource bases, among many other themes. A central concern would be to set these studies firmly in the context of an *integrated* settlement landscape, in which subjective labels such as 'nucleation' and 'dispersal', while not entirely discarded, are not allowed to dictate or prejudice the nature of the work. An important element of this work would be

- A systematic and detailed topographical, documentary and morphological survey of a selection of hamlet/farmstead settlements in Carhampton hundred, perhaps initially in a group of parishes, with a view to identifying any that give indications of deliberate planning. Selective excavation for dating purposes, on both planned *and* unplanned settlements, would be a central element of the work. This would provide a sound basis for the construction of new models, with implications far beyond the hundred, defining the nature, origins, and social and economic affinities of dispersed settlement, and its relationship with more classically nucleated forms, both planned and unplanned.

- To develop, test, and apply theoretical models of landscape cognition and perception appropriate to the early medieval period, based partly on, but not slavishly following, those currently being applied and modified by prehistorians, the more perceptive of whom are currently in the process of rejecting old and untenable models of 'ritual landscapes'. I am especially interested in this as it relates to churches and their wider topographical setting, for what it might reveal about relationships *between* churches, as I have already suggested in my own work, and how contemporaries viewed their own relationships with church sites, especially in spatial terms. Part of this would involve a detailed, systematic appraisal of the sites of large numbers of individual churches, which would then be related to other variables such as status, dedication, parish size, associated communication routes, intervisibility, indicative archaeology (ie antecedents), patronage and so on. Application of GIS techniques might be made to play a central role in this work, and I would envisage that it would greatly enhance our understanding of the territorial role of early churches, how much of the early pastoral pattern was inherited from the past, and of the dynamics of 'estate' structure before 1066.

A systematic topographical survey of indicative field names in Somerset, but with particular emphasis on names in 'Garston', empirically and rigorously to test the suggestion made by Chris Thornton that these represent early 'manorial' occupation cores in nascent settlement nucleations. Where possible this would include archaeological intervention, and use of geophysical surveying techniques. This work would have far-reaching implications, since the identification of primary settlement foci, and their relationship to later, perhaps surviving occupation sites, represents one of the key areas of difficulty currently facing scholars in this field.

Bibliography

Aalbersberg G, 1996 "The alluvial fringes of the Somerset Levels: preliminary research results", Archaeology in the Severn Estuary 7 (SELRC Annual Report).

Abdy R, 2000 "Silver Reflections of Roman Grandeur: Somerset's Shapwick Treasure", Minerva 11, No 3.

Abdy R, Brunning R A, Webster C J, 2001 "The discovery of a Roman villa at Shapwick and its Severan coin hoard of 9,238 silver *denarii*", Jnl of Roman Archaeology 14.

Abels R, 1998 Alfred the Great: War, Kingship and Culture in Anglo-Saxon England.

Abrams L, 1991 "A Single-Sheet Facsimile of a Diploma of King Ine for Glastonbury", in L Abrams and J Carley (eds), The Archaeology and History of Glastonbury Abbey.

Abrams L, 1994 "The Early Surveys of Shapwick Including the Polden Estate: An Early Anglo-Saxon Charter", in Aston M A and Costen M D (eds), The Shapwick Project: 5th Report.

Abrams L, 1996 Anglo-Saxon Glastonbury: Church and Endowment.

Additions, 1921 "Additions to the Museum", SANHS 67.

Adkins L and R, 1992 A Field Guide to Somerset Archaeology

Adkins R, Petchey M, 1984 "Secklow Hundred Mound and Other Meeting Place Mounds in England", Archaeological Journal 141.

Aldcroft D, Freeman M 1983 Transport in the Industrial Revolution.

Aldhouse-Green M, 1999 Pilgrims in Stone: Stone Images from the Gallo-Roman Sanctuary of *Fontes Sequanæ*, BAR International Series 754.

Aldhouse-Green M, 2000 "On the Road", British Archaeology 52, April 2000.

Alexander M, 1997 Portbury Hundred: Inter-Settlement Organisation in the Saxon Period, unpublished MA thesis, Bristol.

Allan J, 1994 "Medieval Pottery and the Dating of Deserted Settlements on Dartmoor" in The Archaeology of Dartmoor, Proc Devon Arch Soc 52.

Allen J R L, Fulford M G, 1996 "The Distribution of South-East Dorset Black Burnished Category I Pottery in South-West Britain", Britannia 27.

Allen N, Giddens C, 1982 Exmoor Locations: An Index of Exmoor Place-Names.

Altenberg K, 1999 "Space and Community on Medieval Dartmoor and Bodmin Moor: Interim Report", MSRG Annual Report, 14.

Anderson O S, 1939 The English Hundred-Names: The South-Western Counties.

Andrews G et al, 1997 "Geophysical Survey at 'Sladwick' (Field 1303) and Bridewell Lane (Field 7722)", in C M Gerrard and M A Aston (eds), Shapwick: The Seventh Report.

Anon, 1997 "Chew Magna", CBA South West Newsletter 126.

Applebaum S, 1975 "Some Observations on the Economy of the Roman Villa at Bignor, Sussex", Britannia 6.

Ashbee P, 1998 "Barrows, cairns, and a few impostors", British Archaeology, March 1998, no 32.

Ashley R, 1978 Essays on the History of Chew Magna.

Astill G, 1988 "Fields", in G Astill and A Grant (eds), The Countryside of Medieval England.

Astill G, 1988a "Rural Settlement - The Toft and the Croft", in G Astill and A Grant (eds), The Countryside of Medieval England.

Astill G, Grant A, 1988 "The Medieval Countryside: Efficiency, Progress and Change", in G Astill and A Grant (eds), The Countryside of Medieval England.

Astill G, Davies W, 1997 A Breton Landscape.

Aston M A, 1976 "Somerset Archaeology 1974-5", SANHS 120.

Aston M A, 1983 "Deserted Farmsteads on Exmoor and the Lay Subsidy of 1327 in West Somerset", SANHS 127.

Aston M A, 1985 "Rural Settlement in Somerset: Some Preliminary Thoughts", in D Hooke (ed), Medieval Villages.

Aston M A, 1985a Interpreting the Landscape

Aston M A, 1986 "Post Roman Central Places in Somerset", in E Grant (ed), Central Places, Archaeology and History.

Aston M A, 1988 "Settlement Patterns and Forms", in M A Aston (ed), Aspects of the Medieval Landscape of Somerset.

Aston M A, 1988a "Land Use and Field Systems", in M A Aston (ed), Aspects of the Medieval Landscape of Somerset.

Aston M A, 1989 The Shapwick Project: First Report (for 1988)

Aston MA, 1989a "The Development of Medieval Rural Settlement in Somerset", in R Higham (ed), Landscape and Townscape in the South West.

Aston M A, 1993 "Addendum: A Holy Well at Shapwick", in M A Aston and M D Costen (eds), The Shapwick Project: Fourth Report.

Aston M A, 1993a "Mounds: Barrows, Watermills, Windmills and Limekilns", in M A Aston and M D Costen (eds), The Shapwick Project: Fourth Report.

Aston M A, 1993b Monasteries

Aston M A, 1994 "Medieval Settlement Studies in Somerset", in Aston M A and Lewis C (eds), The Medieval Landscape of Wessex.

Aston M A, 1994a "Current Models and Future Research", in M A Aston and M D Costen (eds), The Shapwick Project: Fifth Report.

Aston M A, 1994b "More Regressive Map Analysis of Shapwick Parish", in M A Aston and M D Costen (eds), The Shapwick Project: Fifth Report.

Aston M A, 1994c "Introduction", in M A Aston and M D Costen (eds), The Shapwick Project: Fifth Report.

Aston M A, 1995 Review of P Rahtz, Glastonbury (1993), Medieval Archaeology 39

Aston M A, 1998 "The Development of Settlement at Shapwick: Current Ideas (1997)", in M A Aston, T A Hall and C M Gerrard (eds), Shapwick: The Eighth Report.

Aston M A, Leech R, 1977 Historic Towns in Somerset

Aston M A, Burrow I (eds), 1982 The Archaeology of Somerset.

Aston M A, Costen M D, 1990 "A Holy Well at Northbrook?", in M A Aston and M D Costen (eds), The Shapwick Project: Third Report.

Aston M A, Bond C J, 1994 "The Site of the Early Church", in M A Aston Ingle C, and M D Costen (eds), The Shapwick Project: Report

Aston M A, Penoyre J, 1994 "Analysis of the Village Plan", in M A Aston and M D Costen (eds), The Shapwick Project: Fifth Report.

Aston M A, Martin M H, Jackson A W, 1998a "The Use of Heavy Metal Soil Analysis for Archaeological Surveying", Chemosphere 37.

idem, 1998b "Soil analysis as part of a broader approach in the search for low status archaeological sites at Shapwick, Somerset", in M A Aston, T A Hall, and C M Gerrard (eds), The Shapwick Project: Eighth Report.

idem, 1998c "The potential for heavy metal soil analysis on low status archaeological sites at Shapwick, Somerset", Antiquity 72.

Aston M A, Costen M D, Hall T, Ecclestone M, 1998d The Medieval Furlongs of Shapwick: Attempts at Mapping the 1515 Survey", in M A Aston, T A Hall and C M Gerrard (eds), The Shapwick Project: Eighth Report.

Aston M A, Gerrard C, 1999 "'Unique, Traditional and Charming': The Shapwick Project, Somerset", Antiquaries Journal 79.

Aston M A, Gerrard C, 1999a "Shapwick" (Fieldwork and Excavation in 1999), MSRG Annual Report, 14.

Atkin M, 1985 "The Anglo-Saxon Urban Landscape in East Anglia", Landscape History 7.

Ault W O, 1972 Open-Field Farming in Medieval England.

Austin D, 1985 "Dartmoor and the Upland Village of the South-West of England", in D Hooke (ed), Medieval Villages.

Austin D, 1985a "Doubts about morphogenesis", Jnl of Hist Geog 11.

Austin D, 1988 "Review note: The Making of the English Village", Jnl of Hist Geog 14.

Avery B W, 1955 The Soils of the Glastonbury District of Somerset.

Bailey K, 1999 "Place-Names in –*cot*: The Buckinghamshire Evidence", JEPNS 31.

Bailey M, 1989 "The Concept of the Margin in the Medieval English Economy", Economic History Review (2nd ser) 42.

Baines A H J, 1993 "Bernwood: Continuity and Survival on a Romano-British Estate", Records of Buckinghamshire 35.

Balkwill C J, 1993 "Old English *wic* and the origin of the hundred", Landscape History 15.

Barker G, Webley D, 1977 "An Integrated Economy for Gatcombe", in K Branigan (ed), Gatcombe Roman Villa, BAR British Series 44.

Barker K, 1982 "The Early History of Sherborne", in S Pearce (ed), The Early Church in Western Britain and Ireland

Barker K, 1984 "Sherborne in Dorset", Anglo-Saxon Studies in Archaeology and History 3.

Barker P, White R H, 1998 Wroxeter: Life and Death of a Roman City.

Barlow P, 1967 "Interim report on a Romano-British site near Priddy", Annual Reports of the Wells Natural History and Archaeological Society, 77-78 (for 1965-66).

Barnwell P S, 1996 "*Hlafta, ceorl, hid* and *scir*: Celtic, Roman or Germanic?", ASSAH 9.

Bartlett R, 1993 The Making of Europe: Conquest, Colonization and Cultural Change 950-1350.

Bassett S, 1996 "The Administrative Landscape of the Dioceseof Worcester in the Tenth Century", in N Brooks and C Cubitt (eds), St Oswald of Worcester: Life and Influence.

Bates E H, 1905 "Dedications of the Churches of Somersetshire", SANHS 51.

Beaton M, Lewcun M, 1994 An Evaluation of the Archaeological Potential of the walled garden north of Chew Court and east of St Andrew's Church, Chew Magna, Avon (Bath Archaeological Trust, unpublished report).

Beckett S C, Hibbert F A, 1979 "Vegetational change and the influence of prehistoric man in the Somerset Levels", New Phytologist 83.

de la Bedoyere G, 1991 The Buildings of Roman Britain.

de la Bedoyere G, 1999 The Golden Age of Roman Britain.

Bell M, 1981 "Seaweed as a Prehistoric Resource", in D Brothwell and G Dimbleby (eds), Environmental Aspects of Coasts and Islands, BAR International Series 94.

Bell R, 1996 "Applegarth", Chew Magna: An assessment and archaeological evaluation (Bath Archaeological Trust).

Bell T, 1998 "Churches on Roman Buildings: Christian Associations and Roman Masonry in Anglo-Saxon England ", Medieval Archaeology 42.

Beresford M, Finberg H P R, 1973 English Medieval Boroughs: A Handlist.

Beresford M, 1981 "English medieval boroughs: a hand-list: revisions, 1973-81", Urban History Yearbook 1981.

Beresford M, Hurst J, 1990 Wharram Percy Deserted Medieval Village.

Bettey J H, 1989 The Suppression of the Monasteries in the West Country.

Bintliff J, 2000 "Deconstructing 'The Sense of Place'? Settlement Systems, Field Survey, and the Historic Record: a Case-Study from Central Greece", PPS 66.

Bird S, 1987 Roman Avon", in Aston M and Iles R (eds), The Archaeology of Avon.

Black E W, 1987 The Roman Villas of South-East England, BAR British Series 171.

Blagg T, 1986 "Roman Religious Sites in the British Isles", Landscape History 8.

Blair J, 1991 Early Medieval Surrey

Blair J, 1992 "Anglo-Saxon Minsters: A Topographical Review" in Blair J and Sharpe R (eds), Pastoral Care Before the Parish.

Blair J, 1995 "Debate: Ecclesiastical organisation and pastoral care in Anglo-Saxon England", Early Medieval Europe 4.

Blair J, 1996 "Palaces or Minsters? Northampton and Cheddar Reconsidered", Anglo-Saxon England 25.

Blair J, 1996a "The Minsters of the Thames", in J Blair and B Golding (eds), The Cloister and the World.

Blair J, 1996b "Churches in the early English landscape: social and cultural contexts", in J Blair and C Pyrah (eds), Church Archaeology: Research Directions for the Future (CBA Research Report 104).

Blair J, 1997 "St Cuthman, Steyning and Bosham", Sussex Archaeol Collect 135.

Blair J, 1998 "Bampton: An Anglo-Saxon Minster", Current Archaeology 160, Vol 14, No 4.

Blinkhorn P, 1999 "Of cabbages and kings: production, trade, and consumption in middle-Saxon England", in M Anderton (ed), Anglo-Saxon Trading Centres: Beyond the Emporia.

Bolton J L, 1980 The Medieval English Economy, 1150-1500.

Bond C J, 1988 "Church and Parish in Norman Worcestershire", in J Blair (ed), Minsters and Parish Churches: The Local Church in Transition, 950-1200.

Bond C J, 1994 "Forests, Chases, Warrens and Parks in Medieval Wessex", in M Aston and C Lewis (eds), The Medieval Landscape of Wessex.

Bond C J, Horner B, 1991 "Burtle, Burtle Farm", SANHS 135.

Bourne J, 1987-88 "Kingston Place-Names: An Interim Report", JEPNS 20.

Bowen H C, Fowler P J (eds), 1978 Early Land Allotment, BAR (British Series) 48.

Bowman P, 1996 "Contrasting Pays: Anglo-Saxon Settlement and Landscape in Langton Hundred", in J Bourne (ed), Anglo-Saxon Landscapes in the East Midlands.

Bradley R, 2000 "Mental and Material Landscapes in Prehistoric Britain", in D Hooke (ed), Landscape: The Richest Historical Record.

Branigan K, 1977 Gatcombe Roman Villa, BAR (British Series) 44.

Branigan K, 1989 "Specialisation in Villa Economies", in Branigan K and Miles D (eds), The Economies of Romano-British Villas.

Branigan K, Miles D, The Economies of Romano-British Villas (eds), 1989

Brayshay M (ed), 1996 Topographical Writers in South-West England.

Bridbury A R, 1992 "Domesday Book: A Re-interpretation", in The English Economy from Bede to the Reformation(collected essays).

Britnell R H, 1978 "English Markets and Royal Administration Before 1200", Economic History Review 31.

Bronowski J, 1973 The Ascent of Man.

Brook D, 1992 "The Early Christian Church East and West of Offa's Dyke", in N Edwards and A Lane (eds), The Early Church in Wales and the West (Oxbow Monograph 16).

Broomhead R A, 1997 Middlezoy 1997: An Archaeological Evaluation for Pyman Bell (Holdings) Ltd (unpublished report, Somerset County Sites & Monuments Record).

Brown A E, Taylor C C, 1989 "The Origins of Dispersed Settlement: Some Results From Fieldwork in Bedfordshire", Landscape History 11.

Brown T, Crane S, O'Sullivan D, Walsh K, "Marginality, multiple estates and environmental change: the case of Lindisfarne", in Young R, 1998 C M Mills and G Coles (eds), Life on the Edge: Human Settlement and Marginality (Oxbow Monograph 100).

Brown T, Foard G, 1998 "The Saxon Landscape: A Regional Perspective", in P Everson and T Williamson (eds), The Archaeology of Landscape: Studies Presented to Christopher Taylor.

Brunning R, 1994 "Fieldwork in the Somerset Levels and Moors 1994", in Archaeology in the Severn Estuary 5 (SELRC Annual Report).

Brunning R, Grove J, 1998 "The Romano-British Salt Industry in Somerset", Archaeology in the Severn Estuary 9 (SELRC Annual Report).

Brunning R, Webster C, "A Hoard and Villa from Shapwick", CBA 2000 South West, 4.

Bryant T C, 1984 "Burgundy Chapel", West Somerset Archaeological and Natural History Soc News, 7.

Burnham B C, Wacher J, 1990 The 'Small Towns' of Roman Britain.

Burrow I, 1981 Hillfort and Hill-Top Settlement in Somerset in the First to Eighth Centuries AD, BAR (British Series) 91.

Burrow I, 1982 "Hillforts and Hilltops, 1000 BC-1000 AD", in Aston M and Burrow I (eds), The Archaeology of Somerset.

Burrow I, 1985 "Minehead Without, Burgundy Chapel" (Somerset Archaeology), SANHS 129

Burton R A, 1989 The Heritage of Exmoor.

Bush R, 1994 Somerset: The Complete Guide

Butlin R A, Roberts N (eds), 1995 Ecological Relations in Historical Times: Human Impact and Adaptation

Caley J, Hunter J (eds), 1810-1834 *Valor Ecclesiasticus temp. Henrici VIII, Auctoritate Regia Institus* (Record Commission).

Cam H, 1963 "*Manerium cum Hundredo*: the Hundred and the Hundredal Manor", in Liberties and Communities in England (collected essays).

Campbell B M S, 1990 "People and Land in the Middle Ages, 1066-1500", in Dodgshon R A and Butlin R A (eds), An Historical Geography of England and Wales (2ⁿᵈ edn).

Campey L, 1989 "Medieval Village Plans in County Durham: An Analysis of Reconstructed Plans Based on Medieval Documentary Sources", Northern History 25.

Caseldine A, 1988 "A wetland resource: the evidence for the exploitation of the Somerset Levels during the prehistoric period ", in P Murphy and C French (eds), The Exploitation of Wetlands, BAR (British Series) 186.

Catherall P D *et al* (nd) Report on the Archaeological Site at Chew Down, Somerset, Somerset SMR 23251.

CCR Calendar of Charter Rolls, II, 1257-1300.

Chandler J, 2000 "The Discovery of Landscape", in D Hooke (ed), Landscape: The Richest Historical Record.

Chapman M *et al*, 1992 An Historic Landscape Survey of the Manors of Stowey and Knighton Sutton (Avon C C, unpublished report).

Christie N, 1995 "Italy and the Roman to Medieval Transition", in J Bintliff and H Hamerow (eds), Europe Between Late Antiquity and the Middle Ages, BAR (International Series) 617.

Cleary S E, 1989 The Ending of Roman Britain

Cleary S E, 1995 "Changing Constraints on the Landscape AD 400- 600", in D Hooke and S Burnell (eds), Landscape and Settlement in Britain AD 400-1066.

Coates R, 1984 "Coldharbour - For The Last Time?", Nomina 8.

Coates R, 1999 "New Light from Old Wicks: The Progeny of Latin *vicus*", Nomina 22.

Cole A, 1994 "The Anglo-Saxon Traveller", Nomina 17.

Coles G, Mills C M, 1998 "Clinging on for Grim Life: An Introduction to Marginality as an Archaeological Issue", in C M Mills and G Coles (eds), Life on the Edge: Human Settlement and Marginality (Oxbow Monograph 100).

Coles J M, 1978 "The Somerset Levels: A Concave Landscape", in H C Bowen and P J Fowler (eds), Early Land Allotment, BAR (British Series) 48.

Coles J M, 1982 "Prehistory in the Somerset Levels, 4000-100BC", in M Aston and I Burrow (eds), The Archaeology

Coles J M, 1989 "Prehistoric Settlement in the Somerset Levels", Somerset Levels Papers 15.

Coles J M, Orme B J, 1982 The Prehistory of the Somerset Levels.

Coles J M and B J, 1986 Sweet Track to Glastonbury.

Coles J M and B J *et al*, 1990 "Dendrochronology of the English Neolithic", Antiquity 64.

Coles J M, Minnitt S, 1997 Industrious and Fairly Civilized: The Glastonbury Lake Village.

Collinson J, 1791 The History and Antiquities of the County of Somerset (3 vols).

Collis J, 1984 Oppida: Earliest Towns North of the Alps.

Colvin H, 2000 "The Origin of Chantries", Journal of Medieval History, 26.

Coones P, 1985 "One Landscape or Many? A Geographical Perspective", Landscape History 7.

Corcos N J, 1982 Shapwick: The Enclosure of a Somerset Parish, 1515-1839 (unpublished MA thesis, Leicester).

Corcos N J, 1983 "Early Estates on the Poldens and the Origin of Settlement at Shapwick", SANHS 127.

Corcos N J, 2001 "Churches As Pre-Historic Ritual Monuments: A Review and Phenomenological Perspective From Somerset", Assemblage 6. (http://www.shef.ac.uk/~assem/issue6/index.htm).

Corney M, 2000 "Characterising the Landscape of Roman Britain: A Review of the Study of Roman Britain 1975-2000", in D Hooke (ed), Landscape: The Richest Historical Record.

Costen M D, 1979 Place-Name Evidence in South Avon", Avon Past 1.

Costen M D, 1983 "Stantonbury and District in the Tenth Century", Bristol and Avon Archaeology 2.

Costen M D, 1987 "Late Saxon Avon", in M Aston and R Iles (eds), The Archaeology of Avon.

Costen M D, 1987a "700-1500 AD", in The Natural History of the Chew Valley.

Costen M D, 1988 "The Late Saxon Landscape: The Evidence From Charters and Placenames", in M A Aston (ed), Aspects of the Medieval Landscape of Somerset.

Costen M D, 1989 "A Survey of the Manor of Shapwick in 1327", in Aston M A (ed), The Shapwick Project: 2ⁿᵈ Report.

Costen M D, 1989a "The Origins of the Rectorial Manor of Shapwick", in Aston M A (ed), The Shapwick Project: 2ⁿᵈ Report.

Costen M D, 1990 "Abbot Beere's Terrier", in Aston M A and Costen M D (eds), The Shapwick Project: Third Report.

Costen M D, 1991 "Some Evidence for New Settlements and Field Systems in Late Anglo-Saxon Somerset", in L Abrams and J Carley (eds), The History and Archaeology of Glastonbury Abbey.

Costen M D, 1992 "Dunstan, Glastonbury and the Economy of Somerset in the Tenth Century", in N Ramsay, M Sparks and T Tatton-Brown (eds), St Dunstan: His Life, Times and Cult.

Costen M D, 1992a The Origins of Somerset

Costen M D, 1992b "Huish and Worth: Old English Survivals in a later Landscape", Anglo-Saxon Studies in Archaeology and History 5.

Costen M D, 1993 "The Field-Names of Shapwick, I", and "Habitative field-names: A survey of the material for Shapwick", in M A Aston and M D Costen (eds), Shapwick: The Fourth Report.

Costen M D, 1994 "Settlement in Wessex in the Tenth Century: The Charter Evidence", in M Aston and C Lewis (eds), The Medieval Landscape of Wessex.

Costen M D, 1994b "The Domesday Book for Shapwick", in M Aston and M Costen (eds), The Shapwick Project: Fifth Report.

Costen M D, 1994c "The Population of Medieval Shapwick", in M Aston and M Costen (eds), The Shapwick Project: Fifth Report.

Costen M D, 1998 "Abbot Beere's Terrier, BL Egerton 3134: The Bounds of Shapwick", in M A Aston, T A Hall and C M Gerrard (eds), The Shapwick Project: Eighth Report.

Cox B, 1976 "The Place-Names of the Earliest English Records", EPNS 8.

Cox D, 1975 "The Vale Estates of the Church of Evesham, *c*700-1086", Vale of Evesham Historical Society 5.

Creighton J, Gerrard C, Gutierrez A, 1997 "Excavations in 1993 in Field 6987, North of Shapwick House Hotel", in M Aston and C Gerrard (eds), The Shapwick Project: Seventh Report.

Crick J, 1991 "The Marshalling of Antiquity: Glastonbury's Historical Dossier", in L Abrams and J Carley (eds), The Archaeology and History of Glastonbury Abbey

Croft R A, 1988 "Bridgwater, Wembdon Hill", SANHS 132.

Croft R A, Woods H M, "Wembdon, Wembdon Hill", SANHS 131 1987.

Croft R, 1991 "Sutton Mallet", SANHS 135.

DB Somerset Phillimore Edition of Domesday Book, edited by C and F Thorn, 1980.

Dallimore J *et al*, 1994 "Shapwick Houses and Farms: A Review of Surveys Made Up To 1993", in M Aston and M Costen (eds), Shapwick: The Fifth Report.

Dark K, 1994 Discovery by Design: The Identification of Secular Elite Settlements in Western Britain AD 400-700, BAR (British Series) 237.

Dark K, 1996 "Pottery and local production at the end of Roman Britain", in K Dark (ed), External Contacts and the Economy of Late Roman and Post-Roman Britain.

Dark K, 1998 "Centuries of Roman Survival in the West", British Archaeology, March 1998, 32.

Dark K, 2000 Britain and the End of the Roman Empire.

Dark P, 1999 "Pollen Evidence for the Environment of Roman Britain", Britannia 30.

Dark P, 2000 The Environment of Britain in the First Millennium AD.

Dark K, Dark P, 1997 The Landscape of Roman Britain.

Darvill T, 1997 "Landscapes and the Archaeologist", in K Barker and T Darvill (eds), Making English Landscapes: Changing Perspectives.

Darvill T, Gerrard C, Startin B, 1993 "Identifying and Protecting Historic Landscapes", Antiquity 67.

Davies W, 1979 "Roman Settlements and Post-Roman Estates in South-East Wales", in P J Casey (ed), The End of Roman Britain, BAR (British Series) 71.

Davies W, 1992 "The Myth of the Celtic Church", in N Edwards and A Lane (eds), The Early Church in Wales and the West

Davis K, 1993 The Glastonbury Manor of Sowy, 1086-1308, unpublished MA thesis, Leicester.

Denison S, 1999 "Christian graves around 'adapted' barrow", British Archaeology 47.

Denison S, 2000 "Regular Villas for Roman Colonists in Kent", British Archaeology 53, June 2000.

Dickinson F H (ed), 1889 Kirby's Quest for Somerset, SRS 3.

Dinnin M, Van de Noort R, 1999 "Wetland habitats, their resource potential and exploitation: a case study from the Humber wetlands", in B Coles, J Coles and M S Jørgensen (eds), Bog Bodies, Sacred Sites and Wetland Archaeology

Dixon J, 1980 Survey of the Parish of Carhampton

Dixon P, 1984 "Catastrophe and Fallacy: the End of Roman Britain", (review article), Landscape History 6.

Dornier A, 1987 Place-Names in -wich: A Preliminary Linguistic Survey", Nomina 11.

Druce D, 1998 "Late Mesolithic to Early Neolithic Environmental Change in the Central Somerset Levels: Recent Work at Burnham-on-Sea", Archaeology in the Severn Estuary 9.

Dunning R W, 1968 "Some Somerset Parishes in 1705", SANHS 112.

Dunning R W, 1974-5 "Ilchester: A Study in Continuity", SANHS 119.

Dunning R W (ed), 1992 The Victoria History of the County of Somerset, VI.

Dunning R W, Harley J B, 1981 Somerset Maps, SRS 76.

Durham I and M, 1991 Chew Magna and the Chew Valley in Old Photographs.

Durham B, 1997 Review of Dyer *et al* 1997, Medieval Archaeology 41.

Dyer C C, 1985 "Power and Conflict in the Medieval English Village", in Hooke D (ed), Medieval Villages.

Dyer C C, 1985a "Towns and Cottages in Eleventh-Century England", in H Mayr-Harting and R I Moore (eds), Studies in Medieval History Presented to R H C Davis.

Dyer C C, 1988 "Documentary Evidence: Problems and Enquiries", in G Astill and A Grant (eds), The Countryside of Medieval England.

Dyer C C, 1992 "The hidden trade of the Middle Ages: evidence from the West Midlands of England", Jnl of Hist Geog 18.

Dyer C C, 1997 "Recent Developments and Future Prospects in Research into English Medieval Rural Settlements", in G de Boe and F Verhaeghe (eds), Rural Settlements in Medieval Europe 6 (Proceedings of the 1997 Medieval Europe Conference, Bruges).

Dyer C C, 1997a "Medieval Settlement in Wales: A Summing Up", in N Edwards (ed), Landscape and Settlement in Medieval Wales (Oxbow Monograph 81).

Dyer C C, 2002 "Small Places With Large Consequences: The Importance of Small Towns in England, 1000-1540", Historical Research 75.

Dyer C C, Lewis C, Mitchell-Fox P, 1997 Village, Hamlet and Field: Changing Medieval Settlements in Central England.

Eaton T, 2000 Plundering the Past: Roman Stonework in Medieval Britain.

Ecclestone M, 1998 "Field Names in the Shapwick Court Rolls", in M A Aston, T A Hall and C M Gerrard (eds), Shapwick: The Eighth Report.

Ecton J, Willis B, 1742 Thesaurus Rerum Ecclesiasticarum.

Edwards H, 1988 The Charters of the Early West Saxon Kingdom, BAR 198.

Edwards N, 1996 "Identifying the archaeology of the early church in Wales and Cornwall", in J Blair and C

Pyrah (eds), Church Archaeology: Research Directions for the Future (CBA Research Report 104).

Edwards N, 1997 "Landscape and Settlement in Wales: An Introduction", in N Edwards (ed), Landscape and Settlement in Medieval Wales", Oxbow Monograph 81.

Edwards N, Lane A, 1992 "The Archaeology of the Early Church in Wales: An Introduction", in N Edwards and A Lane (eds), The Early Church in Wales and the West

Edwards P, 1991 Farming: Sources for Local Historians

Ekwall E, 1928 English River Names

Ekwall E, 1960 The Concise Oxford Dictionary of English Place-names (4th edn).

Ellis P, 1992 Mendip Hills: An Archaeological Survey of the Area of Outstanding Natural Beauty (unpublished report, Somerset County Council and English Heritage).

Ellison A, 1982 "Bronze Age Societies, 2000-650 BC", in Aston M and Burrow I (eds), The Archaeology of Somerset.

Ellison A, 1983 Medieval Villages in South-East Somerset.

Ely K *et al*, 1995 "Resistivity Survey in Field 0024, Shapwick", in M A Aston and C M Gerrard (eds), Shapwick: The Sixth Report.

Essex S, 1995 "Woodland in the Exmoor National Park", in H Binding (ed), The Changing Face of Exmoor.

Evans J, 1990 "From the End of Roman Britain to the 'Celtic West'", Oxf Jnl of Archaeology 9.

Everett S, 1968/69 "The Domesday Geography of Three Exmoor Parishes", SANHS 112.

Everitt A, 1986 Continuity and Colonisation: The Evolution of Kentish Settlement.

Everson P, Stocker D, 1990 "Rubbish Recycled: A Study of the Re-Use of Stone in Lincolnshire", in D Parsons (ed), Stone: Quarrying and Building in England, AD 43-1525.

Evison M, 1997 "Lo, the conquering hero comes (or not)", British Archaeology April 1997, no 23.

Exeter Archaeology, 2000 Summary Report of Archaeological Evaluation at Perhams Cottage, Middlezoy, Somerset.

Faith R, 1992 "Estates, Demesnes and the Village", in H S A Fox (ed), The Origins of the Midland Village.

Faith R, 1997 The English Peasantry and the Growth of Lordship.

Fallgren J H, 1993 "The Concept of the Village in Swedish Archaeology", Current Swedish Archaeology 1.

Farmer D H, 1992 The Oxford Dictionary of Saints (3rd edn).

Faulkner N, 2000 The Decline and Fall of Roman Britain.

Field D, 1999 "Bury the Dead in a Sacred Landscape", British Archaeology April 1999, no 43.

Field J, 1972 English Field Names: A Dictionary

Field J, 1993 A History of English Field Names

Finberg H P R, 1955 Roman and Saxon Withington: A Study in Continuity, Leicester Dept of English Local History, Occasional Papers 8. Reprinted in Lucerna (collected essays), 1964.

Finberg H P R, 1964 The Early Charters of Wessex

Finberg H P R, 1969 "St Patrick at Glastonbury", in West-Country Historical Studies (collected essays).

Finberg H P R 1969a "The Open Field in Devon", in West-Country Historical Studies (collected essays).

Finberg H P R, 1972 "Anglo-Saxon England to 1042", in H P R Finberg (ed), The Agrarian History of England and Wales, I (II), AD 43-1042.

Findlay D C *et al*, 1984 Soils and Their Use in South West England (Soil Survey Bulletin 14).

Fitton S, 1997 A Preliminary Examination of 'Wic' Sites in Somerset, unpublished certificate dissertation, Bristol.

Fleming A, 1994 "Medieval and Post-Medieval Cultivation on Dartmoor: A Landscape Archaeologist's View", Proc Devon Arch Soc 52.

Fleming A, 1994a "Swadal, Swar (and Erechwydd?): early medieval polities in Upper Swaledale", Landscape History 16.

Fleming A, 1998 "Prehistoric Landscapes and the Quest for Territorial Pattern", in P Everson and T Williamson (eds), The Archaeology of Landscape: Studies Presented to Christopher Taylor.

Fleming A, 1998a Swaledale: Valley of the Wild River.

Fleming A, 1999 "Phenomenology and the Megaliths of Wales: A Dreaming Too Far?", Oxford Journal of Archaeology 18.

Fleming 1999a "Small-scale communities and the landscape of Swaledale (North Yorkshire, UK)", in P J Ucko and R Layton (eds), The Archaeology and Anthropology of Landscape: Shaping your landscape.

Foard G, 1992 The Great Replanning?", in H S A Fox (ed), The Origins of the Midland Village.

Foot S, 1992 "Anglo-Saxon Minsters: A Review of Terminology", in J Blair and R Sharpe (eds), Pastoral Care Before the Parish.

Foot W, 1994 Maps for Family History (Public Record Office Readers' Guide No 9).

Ford M, 1998 Continuity and Change Within the Historic Landscape – An Analysis of the Micro and Macro Level Chronological Processes Around Wellow, AD 400-1066, unpublished MA dissertation, Bristol.

Ford W J, 1979 "Some Settlement Patterns in the Central Region of the Warwickshire Avon", in P H Sawyer (ed), English Medieval Settlement.

Foster S, 1987 "A Gazeteer of the Anglo-Saxon Sculpture in Historic Somerset", SANHS 131.

Fowler P J, 1971 "M5 and Archaeology", Archaeological Review 6.

Fowler P J, 1978 "Pre-Medieval Fields in the Bristol Region", in H C Bowen and P J Fowler (eds), Early Land Allotment (BAR British series 48).

Fowler P J, 1997 "Farming in Early Medieval England: Some Fields for Thought", in J Hines (ed), The Anglo-Saxons from the Migration Period to the Eighth Century: An Ethnographic Perspective.

Fowler P J, 1998 "Moving through the Landscape", in P Everson and T Williamson (eds), The Archaeology of Landscape: Studies Presented to Christopher Taylor.

Fowler R, 1935-36 "The last pre-dissolution survey of Glastonbury lands", British Museum Quarterly 10.

Fox H S A, 1970 "The Boundary of Uplyme", Transactions of the Devonshire Association 102.

Fox H S A, 1972 "Field Systems of East and South Devon", Devonshire Association, Report and Transactions 104.

Fox H S A, 1981 "Approaches to the Adoption of the Midland System", in T Rowley (ed), The Origins of Open-Field Agriculture.

Fox H S A, 1984 "Some Ecological Dimensions of Medieval Field Systems", in K Biddick (ed), Archaeological Approaches to Medieval Europe.

Fox H S A, 1988 "Social Relations and Ecological Relationships in Agrarian Change: An Example FromMedieval and Early Modern England", Geografiska Annaler 70.

Fox H S A, 1989 "Peasant farmers, patterns of settlement and pays: transformations in the landscapes of Devon and Cornwall during the later Middle Ages", in R Higham (ed), Landscape and Townscape in the South West.

Fox H S A, 1992 "The Agrarian Context", in H S A Fox (ed), The Origins of the Midland Village.

Fox H S A, 1996 "Introduction: Transhumance and Seasonal Settlement", in H S A Fox (ed), Seasonal Settlement.

Fox H S A, 1996a "Cellar Settlements Along the South Devon Coastline", in H S A Fox (ed), Seasonal Settlement.

Fox H S A, 1996b "Exploitation of the Landless by Lords and Tenants in Early Medieval England", in Z Razi and R Smith (eds), Medieval Society and the Manor Court.

Fox H S A, 2001 The Evolution of the Fishing Village: Landscape and Society Along the South Devon Coast, 1086-1550.

Francis P D, Slater D S, 1990 "A Record of Vegetational and Land Use Change from Upland Peat Deposits on Exmoor. Part 2: Hoar Moor", SANHS 134.

Francis P T H (nd), "Burgundy Chapel", West Somerset Archaeological and Natural History Soc News, 10.

Franklin M J, 1984 "The Identification of Minsters in the Midlands", in R Allen Brown (ed), Anglo-Norman Studies 7.

Frere S S, 1987 Britannia (3rd edn).

Fulford M, 1990 "The Landscape of Roman Britain: A Review", Landscape History 12.

Fullard H, Darby H C (eds), 1978 The University Atlas (George Philip & Co), 19th edn.

Gardiner M, 1997 "Trade, Rural Industry and the Origins of Villages: some Evidence from South-East England", in G de Boe and F Verhaeghe (eds), Rural Settlements in Medieval Europe 6 (Proceedings of the 1997 Medieval Europe Conference, Bruges).

Gardner K, 1985 "Apples in the Landscape: The Puxton Dolmoors", Bristol and Avon Archaeology 4.

Gardner K, 1998 "The Wansdyke Diktat: A Discussion Paper", Bristol and Avon Archaeology 15.

Garmonsway G N (trans), 1953 The Anglo-Saxon Chronicle.

Gaskell-Brown C, 1995 "Buckland Abbey, Devon: Surveys and Excavations, 1983-1995", Proc Devon Arch Soc 53.

Gater J et al, 1993 Report on Geophysical Survey: Littleton, Somerset, Geophysical Surveys of Bradford 93/20, SMR 53765.

Gater J, Gaffney C, 1993 "Prospection Using Magnetic and Resistivity Techniques During 1991", in M A Aston and M D Costen (eds), The Shapwick Project: Fourth Report.

Gathercole C, 1996 Somerset Extensive Urban Survey, Draft Archaeological Assessment: Dunster (unpublished report, Somerset County Council and English Heritage).

Gathercole C, 1997 Somerset Extensive Urban Survey, Draft Archaeological Assessment: Ilchester (unpublished report, Somerset County Council and English Heritage).

Gathercole C, 1997a Somerset Extensive Urban Survey, Draft Archaeological Assessment: Street (unpublished report, Somerset County Council and English Heritage).

Gay S, 1995 The Origin of Church Sites in North Somerset, unpublished MA thesis, Bristol.

Gelling M, 1979 The Early Charters of the Thames Valley: A Catalogue.

Gelling M, 1984 Place-Names in the Landscape

Gelling M, 1992 "Note on the place-names Cadbury and Congresbury", in Rahtz P et al, Cadbury Congresbury 1968-73: A Late/Post-Roman Hilltop Settlement in Somerset, BAR (British Series) 223.

Gelling M, 1992a The West Midlands in the Early Middle Ages

Gelling M, 1997 Signposts to the Past (3rd edn).

Gelling M, 1998 "Place-Names and Landscape", in S Taylor (ed), The Uses of Place-Names.

Gelling M, Cole A, 2000 The Landscape of Place-Names.

Gerrard C M, 1987 Trade and Settlement in Medieval Somerset, unpublished PhD thesis, Bristol.

Gerrard C M, 1995 "Excavations in the Church Field (4016), Shapwick, 1993 Preliminary Report", in M Aston and C Gerrard (eds), The Shapwick Project: Sixth Report.

Gerrard C M, 1995a "Problems and Patterns in Shapwick Fieldwalking", in M Aston and C Gerrard (eds), The Shapwick Project: Sixth Report.

Gerrard C M, 2000 "The Shapwick Project 1989-99", in C J Webster (ed), Somerset Archaeology: Proceedings of the 150th Anniversary Conference of the Somerset Archaeological and Natural History Society.

Gerrard C M, Gutierrez A, 1993 "Summary of Fieldwalking Results 1989-1990", in M A Aston and M D Costen (eds), Shapwick: The Fourth Report.

Gerrard C M, Gutierrez A, "Denying Nothing, Doubting Everything: 1997 Interpreting Pottery Distributions from Fieldwalking, 1989-1994", in M Aston and C Gerrard (eds), The Shapwick Project: Seventh Report.

Gilbert P, 1996 The North Somerset Levels, Kingston Seymour: A Study of the Pre-Conquest Landscape from AD43 - 1086 (unpublished MA dissertation, Bristol).

Gilchrist R, Morris R, 1993 Monasteries as settlements: religion, society, and economy, AD 600-1050", in M Carver (ed), In Search of Cult.

Gittos B and M, 1989 "The Evidence for the Saxon Minster at Yeovil", Chronicle (journal of the Yeovil Arch & Loc Hist Soc) vol 4, nmbr 4.

Glasscock R E (ed), 1975 The Lay Subsidy of 1334.

Grace N, Richardson I, 1999 "Luccombe, Ley Hill, Horner", in C J Webster (ed), Somerset Archaeology 1998, SANHS 142.

Grant E, 1986 "Hillforts, Central Places and Territories", in Grant E (ed), Central Places, Archaeology and History.

Gray H St G, 1939 "Excavations at Burrow Mump, Somerset, 1939", SANHS 85.

Green E (ed), 1888 Somerset Chantries, SRS 2.

Green G W, Welch F B A, 1965 Geology of the Country Around Wells and Cheddar.

Greenwood C and J, 1822 Somersetshire Delineated.

Griffith F M, 1986 "Burh and Beorg in Devon", Nomina 10.

Grinsell L V, 1969 "Somerset Barrows, Part I: West and South", SANHS 113.

Grinsell L V, 1970 The Archaeology of Exmoor

Grinsell L V, 1986 "The Christianisation of Prehistoric and Other Pagan Sites", Landscape History 8.

Grinsell L V, 1987 "Somerset Barrows: Revisions 1971-87", SANHS 131.

Grinsell L V, 1991 "Barrows in the Anglo-Saxon Land Charters", Antiquaries Journal 71.

Grove J, Brunning R, 1998 "The Romano-British Salt Industry in Somerset", Archaeology in the Severn Estuary 9 (SELRC Annual Report).

Grundy G B, 1935 The Saxon Charters and Field Names of Somerset

van de Guchte M, 1999 "The Inca Cognition of Landscape: Archaeology, Ethnohistory, and the Aesthetic of Alterity", in W Ashmore and A B Knapp (eds), Archaeologies of Landscape: Contemporary Perspectives.

Hadley D M, 1996 "Conquest, Colonisation and the Church: Ecclesiastical Organisation in the Danelaw", Historical Research 69.

Hadley D M, 1996a "Multiple estates and the origins of the manorial structure of the northern Danelaw", Journal of Historical Geography 22.

Hall T A, 2000 Minster Churches in the Dorset Landscape, BAR British Series 304.

Hallam H E, 1954 The New Lands of Elloe, Leicester Dept of English Local History, Occasional Papers 6.

Hallam H E, 1988 "Agricultural Techniques", in H E Hallam (ed), The Agrarian History of England and Wales, II, 1042-1350.

Hallam O, 1978 "Vegetation and Land Use on Exmoor", SANHS 122.

Hamerow H F, 1991 "Settlement Mobility and the 'Middle Saxon Shift': Rural Settlements and Settlement Patterns in Anglo-Saxon England", Anglo-Saxon England 20.

Hanley R, 1990 Village and Small Town in the Roman West Country, unpublished PhD thesis, Nottingham.

Hardy P, 1989 "Geological Survey", in M A Aston (ed), The Shapwick Project: Second Report.

Hardy P, 1990 "Geological Survey of the Parish of Shapwick, Interim Report, 1990/91", in M A Aston and M D Costen (eds), The Shapwick Project: Third Report.

Härke H, 1995 "Finding Britons in Anglo-Saxon Graves", British Archaeology 10, Dec 1995.

Härke H, 1998 "Archaeologists and Migrations: A Problem of Attitude?", Current Anthropology 39.

Harley J B, O'Donoghue Y, 1981 The Old Series Ordnance Survey Maps of England and Wales, III, South-Central England.

Harmer F E, 1952 Anglo-Saxon Writs.

Harris K, 1990 Glastonbury Abbey Records at Longleat House: A Summary List, SRS 81.

Harrison B, 1990 "Borrowby: Some Landscape Evidence for Early Village Planning", Medieval Yorkshire 19.

Harrison J D, 1997 The Composite Manor of Brent: A Study of a Large Wetland-Edge Estate up to 1350, unpublished PhD dissertation, Leicester.

Harvey D, 1996 "Providing a territorial framework for studying Medieval settlement patterns and early systems of landscape organisation", MSRG 11.

Harvey P D A, 1989 "Initiative and Authority in Settlement Change", in M Aston, D Austin and C Dyer (eds), The Rural Settlements of Medieval England.

Harvey S, 1988 "Domesday England", in H E Hallam (ed), The Agrarian History of England and Wales, 1042-1350 (Vol II).

Haselgrove C, 1986 "Central Places in British Iron Age Studies: A Review and Some Problems", in E Grant (ed), Central Places, Archaeology and History.

Haselgrove C, Scull C, 1995 "The Changing Structure of Rural Settlement in Southern Picardy During the First Millennium A.D.", in J Bintliff and H Hamerow (eds), Europe Between Late Antiquity and the Middle Ages, BAR (International Series), 617.

Haslam J, 1988 "The Anglo-Saxon Burh at Wigingamere", Landscape History 10.

Hassall M W C, Tomlin "Roman Britain in 1992, II: Inscriptions", R S O, 1993 Britannia 24.

Havinden M, 1981 The Making of the Somerset Landscape.

Hayes P P, 1988 "Roman to Saxon in the South Lincolnshire Fens", Antiquity 62.

Heal S V E, 1995 "Luccombe, Horner Wood", and "Luccombe, Ley Hill" (Somerset Archaeology), SANHS 138.

Heal S V E, 1999 "Exmoor National Park: Enclosure at Timberscombe", CBA South West Journal No 3, Summer 1999.

Healey C E H C, 1901 The History of the Part of West Somerset Comprising the Parishes of Luccombe, Selworthy, Stoke Pero, Porlock, Culbone and Oare.

Hearne T (ed), 1726 The Chronicle of John of Glastonbury II

Hearne T (ed), 1727 Adam of Domerham II

HE Bede's *Ecclesiastical History of the English People*, B Colgrave and R A B Mynors (eds), Oxford 1969.

Hembry P M, 1967 The Bishops of Bath and Wells, 1540-1640: Social and Economic Problems.

Herring P, 1996 "Transhumance in Medieval Cornwall", in H S A Fox (ed), Seasonal Settlement.

Higham N, 1990 "Settlement, Land Use and Domesday Ploughlands", Landscape History 12.

Higham N, 1992 Rome, Britain and the Anglo-Saxons.

Hill D, Williams M, Martin M, 1994 "Botanical Survey: A Progress Report on the Hedges", in M A Aston and M D Costen (eds), Shapwick: The Fifth Report.

Hill S, Ireland S, 1996 Roman Britain

Hindle B P, 1993 Roads, Tracks and Their Interpretation.

Hingley R, 1991 "The Romano-British Countryside: the Significance of Rural Settlement Forms", in R F J Jones (ed), Britain in the Roman Period: Recent Trends.

Hinton D A, 1997 "The 'Scole-Dickleburgh field system' examined", Landscape History 19.

Hoare P G, Sweet C S, 2000 "The orientation of early medieval churches in England", Jnl of Hist Geog 26.

Hobhouse E (ed), 1891 Rentals and Custumals of Michael Amesbury and Roger Ford, SRS 5.

Hodder I, 1974 "Some Marketing Models for Romano-British Coarse Pottery", Britannia 5.

Hodder I, 2000 "British Prehistory: Some Thoughts Looking In", review article in Cambridge Arch Jnl 10 (no 2).

Hodder I, Millett M, 1980 "Romano-British villas and towns: a systematic analysis", World Archaeology 12.

Hodder M A, 1992 "Continuity and Discontinuity in the Landscape: Roman to Medieval in Sutton Chase", Medieval Archaeology 36.

Hodges R, 1982 Dark Age Economics.

Hodges R, 2000 Towns and Trade in the Age of Charlemagne.

Hollinrake C, 1991 "Weston Zoyland: SWEB Power Line", SANHS 135.

Hollinrake C and N, 1989 "Bridgwater, Wembdon Hill", SANHS 133.

Hollinrake C and N, 1989a "Compton Dundon, Court Orchard", SANHS 133.

Hollinrake C and N, 1993 Eastbury Farm, Carhampton, unpublished report, Somerset SMR.

Hollinrake C and N, 1994 Eastbury Farm, Carhampton, unpublished report, Somerset SMR.

Hollinrake C and N, 1994a Archaeological Fieldwalking Along the Line of the Polden Villages Pipeline, Woolavington to Shapwick, Polden Villages Enhancement Scheme, unpublished report no 86, Somerset C C.

Hollinrake C and N, 1994b An Archaeological Watching Brief in the Churchyard of Holy Trinity Parish Church, Street, unpublished report no 53, Somerset C C.

Hollinrake C and N, 1994c Archaeological Fieldwalking Along the Line of the Polden Villages Pipeline, Woolavington to Shapwick, Polden Villages Enhancement Scheme, unpublished report no 71, Somerset C C.

Hollinrake C and N, 1994d Compton Dundon Parish Survey: Littleton Villa (unpublished report).

Hollinrake C and N, 1994e Archaeology on the Polden Villages Pipeline: Excavations at Edington Clover Close, Polden Villages Enhancement Scheme, unpublished Report no 65, Somerset CC.

Hollinrake C and N, 1995 "Butleigh, Perriams", SANHS 138.

Hollinrake C and N, 1995a Eastbury Farm, Carhampton, unpublished report, Somerset SMR.

Hollinrake C and N, 1995b "Archaeological Excavations along the line of the Wessex Water Pipeline in Shapwick Park in 1994", in M Aston and C Gerrard (eds), The Shapwick Project: Sixth Report.

Hollinrake C and N, 1996 "Compton Dundon, Dundon Street", SANHS 139.

Holtorf C J, 1997 "Christian Landscapes of Pagan Monuments: A Radical Constructivist Perspective", in G Nash (ed), Semiotics of Landscape: Archaeology of *Mind*, BAR International Series 661.

Homans G C, 1941 English Villagers of the Thirteenth Century.

Hooke D, 1981a "Open-field Agriculture - The Evidence from the Pre-Conquest Charters of the West Midlands", in Rowley T (ed), The Origins of Open-Field Agriculture

Hooke D, 1981b Anglo-Saxon Landscapes of the West Midlands: The Charter Evidence

Hooke D, 1983 The Landscape of Anglo-Saxon Staffordshire: The Charter Evidence

Hooke D, 1985 "Village Development in the West Midlands", in D Hooke (ed), Medieval Villages.

Hooke D, 1989 "Pre-Conquest Woodland: its Distribution and Usage", Ag Hist Rev 37.

Hooke D, 1990 Worcestershire Anglo-Saxon Charter Bounds

Hooke D, 1994 The Pre-Conquest Charter Bounds of Devon and Cornwall

Hooke D, 1995 "The Mid-Late Anglo-Saxon Period: Settlement and Land Use", in D Hooke and S Burnell (eds), Landscape and Settlement in Britain AD 400-1066.

Hooke D, 1997 "The Anglo-Saxons in England in the Seventh and Eighth Centuries: Aspects of Location in Space", in J Hines (ed), The Anglo-Saxons from the Migration Period to the Eighth Century: An Ethnographic Perspective.

Hooke D, 1997a "Place-Names and Vegetation History as a Key to Understanding Settlement in the Conwy Valley", in N Edwards (ed), Landscape and Settlement in Medieval Wales (Oxbow Monograph 81).

Hooke D, 1998 The Landscape of Anglo-Saxon England.

Hopkins P A, 1998 An Assessment of the Influence of Existing Landscapes Upon the Location of Anglo-Saxon Churches: A Study of Sixty-Five Northamptonshire Churches in Their Archaeological Landscape, unpublished MPhil thesis, Birmingham.

Hoskins W G, 1952 "The Making of the Agrarian Landscape", in G Hoskins and H P R Finberg, Devonshire Studies.

Hoskins W G, 1955 The Making of the English Landscape

Hoskins W G, 1963 "The Highland Zone in Domesday Book", in Provincial England (collected essays).

Hoskins W G, 1982 Fieldwork in Local History (2nd edn).

Hoskins W G, 1984 Local History in England (3rd edn).

Hough C, 1998 "Old English *Coppa*", JEPNS 30.

Housley R A, Straker V, Cope D W, 1999 "The Holocene Peat and Alluvial Stratigraphy of the Upper Brue Valley in the Somerset Levels Based On Soil Survey Data of the 1980s", Archaeology in the Severn Estuary 10.

Howlett D, 1998 "Literate culture of 'Dark Age' Britain", British Archaeology, April 1998, no 33.

Huish M, 1941 "The Home of a Hermit", The Field (February).

Hulbert N F, 1936 "A Survey of the Somerset Fairs", SANHS 82.

Hunn J R, 1994 Reconstruction and Measurement of Landscape Change: A Study of Six Parishes in the St Albans Area, BAR (British Series) 236.

Hurley V, 1982 "The Early Church in the South-West of Ireland: Settlement and Organisation", in S Pearce (ed), The Early Church in Western Britain and Ireland.

Hutton R, 1991 The Pagan Religions of the Ancient British Isles: Their Nature and Legacy

Iles R, 1982 "Avon Archaeology 1981", Bristol and Avon Archaeology I.

Iles R, 1984 "Avon Archaeology 1983", Bristol and Avon Archaeology 3.

Iles R, 1987 "The Medieval Rural Landscape", in M Aston and R Iles (eds), The Archaeology of Avon.

Jackson J E (ed), 1882 An Inquisition of the Manors of Glastonbury Abbey of the Year 1189

James S, 1999 The Atlantic Celts: Ancient People or Modern Invention?

James T, 1998 "Place-Name Distributions and Field Archaeology in South-West Wales", in S Taylor (ed), The Uses of Place-Names.

Johansson C, 1975 Old English Place-Names and Field-Names containing *lēah*

Jones G, 1996 Church Dedications and Landed Units of Lordship and Administration in the Pre-Reformation Diocese of Worcester, unpublished PhD thesis, Leicester.

Jones J, 1998 Some Aspects of the Clay Belt of the Central Somerset Levels During the Iron Age and Romano-British Periods, unpublished Archaeology Certificate dissertation, Bristol.

Jones M, 1986 "Towards a Model of the Villa Estate", in D Miles (ed), Archaeology at Barton Court Farm, CBA Research Report 50.

Jones M, 1989 "Agriculture in Roman Britain: The Dynamics of Change", in M Todd (ed), Research on Roman Britain: 1960-89, Britannia Monograph 11.

Jones M, 1996 "Rebellion remains the decisive factor", British Archaeology 20.

Jones M J, 1996 "Early Church Groups in the British Isles", Antiquité Tardive IV: Les Églises Doubles et les Familles D'Églises.

Jones R A, 1998 "Problems with medieval Welsh local administration – the case of the *maenor* and the *maenol*", Jnl of Hist Geog 24.

Kain R J P, Oliver R R, 1995 The Tithe Maps of England and Wales.

Keil I J E, 1964 The Estates of Glastonbury Abbey in the Later Middle Ages, unpublished PhD thesis, Bristol

Kemp R L, 1983 The Chew Basin: The Study of a Changing Landscape, unpublished undergrad. thesis, York.

Kemp R L, 1984 "Roman and Medieval Landscapes in the Chew Valley", Bristol and Avon Archaeology 3.

Keynes S, 1992 "George Harbin's Transcript of the Lost Cartulary of Athelney Abbey", SANHS 136.

Keynes S, Lapidge M, 1983 Alfred The Great.

Kitson P, 1993 "Quantifying Qualifiers in Anglo-Saxon Charter Boundaries", Folia Linguistica Historica 14.

Klingelhofer E, 1990 "Anglo-Saxon Manors of the Upper Itchen Valley: Their Origin and Evolution", Proc Hants Field Club and Arch Soc. 46.

Knight J, 1998 The Landscape Archaeology of Loxley Wood, Shapwick, Somerset, unpublished MA dissertation, Bristol.

Knowles D, Hadcock R N, 1971 Medieval Religious Houses: England and Wales (2nd edn).

Kosse A, 1963 Soils and Agriculture in Roman Somerset, unpublished MA thesis, Chicago.

Langdon M, 1986 "Wembdon, Wembdon Hill", SANHS 130.

Langdon M, 1992 "Spaxton Roman Villa" (Somerset Archaeology), SANHS 136.

Laurence R, 1999 "Theoretical Roman Archaeology" (review article), Britannia 30.

Leach P, 1982 "A Deserted Farm in the Brendon Hills", SANHS 126.

Leach P, 2000 "The South Cadbury Environs Project", CBA South West, 4.

Leach P, Leech R, 1982 "Roman Town and Countryside 43-450 AD", in M Aston and I Burrow I (eds), The Archaeology of Somerset.

Leach P, Tabor R, 1996 "The South Cadbury Environs Project", SANHS 139.

Leech R, 1977 Romano-British Rural Settlement in South Somerset and North Dorset, unpublished PhD thesis, Bristol.

Leech R, 1981 "The Excavation of a Romano-British Farmstead and Cemetery on Bradley Hill, Somerton, Somerset", Britannia 12.

Leech R, 1982 "The Roman Interlude in the South-West: The Dynamics of Economic and Social Change in Romano-British South Somerset and North Dorset", in D Miles (ed), The Romano-British Countryside, BAR (British Series) 103(i).

Leech R, 1986 "The Excavation of a Romano-Celtic Temple and a Later Cemetery on Lamyatt Beacon, Somerset", Britannia 17.

Leech R, Bell M, Evans J, 1983 "The Sectioning of a Romano-British Saltmaking Mound at East Huntspill", in J M Coles (ed), Somerset Levels Papers 9.

Lennard R, 1938 "From Roman Britain to Anglo-Saxon England", in Wirtschaft und Kultur: Festschrift zum 70 Geburtstag von Alfons Dopsch.

Lewis J, 1996 A Study of the Ashen Hill, Beacon Batch and Priddy Nine Barrow Cemeteries, unpublished MA dissertation, Bristol.

Liddle P, 1995 "Roman small towns in Leicestershire", in A E Brown (ed), Roman Small Towns in Eastern England and Beyond, Oxbow Monograph 52.

Lilley K D, 1996 "Morphologies of Medieval Market Settlements: some Warwickshire examples", MSRG 11.

Loud G A, 1989 "An Introduction to the Somerset Domesday", Domesday Book, Alecto Historical Editions.

Lowe K A, 1998 "The Development of the Anglo-Saxon Boundary Clause", Nomina 21.

Loyn H R, 1974 "The Hundred in England in the Tenth and Early Eleventh Centuries", in H Hearder and H R Loyn (eds), British Government and Administration

Lynch F, 1996 Review of Tilley 1994, Landscape History 18.

Macdermott E T, 1911 The History of the Forest of Exmoor

Macready S, Thompson F H (eds), 1984 Cross-Channel Trade Between Gaul and Britain in the Pre-Roman Iron Age

Maitland F W, 1897 Domesday Book and Beyond: Three Essays in the Early History of England.

Margary I D, 1967 Roman Roads in Britain (2nd edn).

Massey R, 1999 The North Oxfordshire Grim's Ditch: Cult, Status and Polity in the Late Pre-Roman Iron Age, unpublished MA dissertation, Bristol.

Maxwell Lyte H C (ed), 1917-18 Documents and Extracts Illustrating the History of the Honour of Dunster, SRS 33.

Maxwell Lyte H C (ed), 1931 Historical Notes On Some Somerset Manors Formerly Connected With The Honour of Dunster, SRS (Extra Series).

Maxwell-Lyte H C (ed), 1939 The Registers of Bishops King and Hadrian, SRS 54.

McAvoy F, 1986 "Excavations at Daws Castle, Watchet, 1982", SANHS 130.

McCrone P, 1993 "Carhampton, Eastbury Farm", (Somerset Archaeology), SANHS 137.

McCrone P, 1994 "Carhampton, Eastbury Farm", Medieval Archaeology 38.

McCrone P, 1995 "Carhampton, Eastbury Farm", (Somerset Archaeology), SANHS 138.

McDermott M, 1995 Sutton Mallet Church, Somerset.

McDonnell R, 1985 "Claylands Survey" (Somerset Archaeology 1984-1985), SANHS 129.

McDonnell R, 1985a Archaeological Survey of the Somerset Claylands I: North of Polden, unpublished report, Somerset

McDonnell R, 1986 Archaeological Survey of the Somerset Claylands II: South of Polden, unpublished report, Somerset C C.

McGarvie M, 1987 The Book of Street.

McGarvie M (ed), 1994 Sir Stephen Glynne's Church Notes for Somerset, SRS 82.

McGlade J, 1995 "Archaeology and the Ecodynamics of Human-Modified Landscapes", Antiquity 69.

McGlade J, 1999 "Archaeology and the evolution of cultural landscapes: towards an interdisciplinary research agenda", in P J Ucko and R Layton (eds), The Archaeology and Anthropology of Landscape: Shaping Your Landscape.

Meaney A, 1995 "Pagan English Sanctuaries, Place-Names and Hundred Meeting-Places", ASSAH 8.

Meyer M A, 1993 The Queen's 'Demesne' in Later Anglo-Saxon England", in M A Meyer (ed), The Culture of Christendom.

Miles D (ed), 1986 Archaeology at Barton Court Farm, CBA Research Report 50.

Miles D, 1989 "Villas and Variety: Aspects of Economy and Society in the Upper Thames Landscape", in K Branigan and D Miles (eds), The Economies of Romano-British Villas.

Miller E, Hatcher J, 1978 Medieval England: Rural Society and Economic Change 1086-1348.

Miller E, Hatcher J, 1995 Medieval England: Towns, Commerce and Crafts, 1086-1348.

Millett M, 1990 The Romanisation of Britain

Mills A D, 1991 A Dictionary of English Place-Names

Mills C M, Coles G (eds), 1998 Life on the Edge: Human Settlement and Marginality (Oxbow Monograph 100).

Minnitt S, 2001 The Shapwick Treasure (Somerset County Museums Service booklet).

Morland S C, 1982 "The Saxon Charters for Sowy and Pouholt and the Course of the River Cary", SDNQ 31

Morland S C, 1984 "Glaston Twelve Hides", SANHS 128.

Morland S C, 1986 "The Glastonbury Manors and their Saxon Charters", SANHS 130.

Morland S C, 1990 "The Somerset Hundreds in the Geld Inquest and Their Domesday Manors", SANHS 134.

Morland S C, 1991 Glastonbury, Domesday and Related Studies (collected papers).

Morris C, 2000 "Tintagel: Fieldwork in 1999", CBA South West, 4.

Morris R, 1989 Churches in the Landscape.

Morris R, 1991 "Baptismal Places: 600-800", in I Wood and N Lund (eds), People and Places in Northern Europe 500-1600.

Morris R, Roxan J, 1980 "Churches on Roman Buildings", in W Rodwell (ed), Temples, Churches and Religion: Recent Research in Roman Britain, BAR (British Series) 77.

Morton A, 1999 "*Hamwic* in its Context", in M Anderton (ed), Anglo-Saxon Trading Centres: Beyond the Emporia.

Muir R, 2000 "Conceptualising Landscape", Landscapes 1.

Musgrove D, 1999 The Medieval Exploitation of the Somerset Levels, unpublished PhD thesis, Exeter.

NCC, 1988 Inventory of Ancient Woodland: Avon (Nature Conservancy Council).

Nash A, 1988 "The Population of Southern England in 1086: A New Look at the Evidence of Domesday Book", Southern History 10.

Nash G (ed), 1997 Semiotics of Landscape: Archaeology of Mind, BAR International Series 661.

Neale F, 1976 "Saxon and Medieval Landscapes", in R Atthill (ed), Mendip: A New Study.

Newman J, 1992 "The Late Roman and Anglo-Saxon Settlement Pattern in the Sandlings of Suffolk", in M O H Carver (ed), The Age of Sutton Hoo: The Seventh Century in North-Western Europe.

Newman J, 1999 Wics, trade, and the hinterlands – the Ipswich region", in M Anderton (ed), Anglo-Saxon Trading Centres: Beyond the *Emporia*.

OS, 1996 Ordnance Survey UK Rainfall Wall Map (1:1,000,000)

O'Brien E, 1999 Post-Roman Britain to Anglo-Saxon England: Burial Practices Reviewed, BAR (British Series) 289.

O'Donovan M A (ed), 1988 Charters of Sherborne.

Olson L, 1989 Early Monasteries in Cornwall

Oosthuizen S, 1997 "Medieval Settlement Relocation in West Cambridgeshire: Three Case-Studies", Landscape History 19.

Orme N, 1996 English Church Dedications, With a Survey of Devon and Cornwall.

Orme N, 2000 The Saints of Cornwall.

Osborn B, 1983 Survey of the Parish of Minehead Without

van Ossel P, Ouzoulias P, 2000 "Rural settlement economy in Northern Gaul in the Late Empire: an overview and assessment", Jnl of Roman Archaeology 13.

Palliser D M, 1992 "Town and Village Planning in Early Medieval England", Pre-Printed Papers of the Conference on Medieval Archaeology in Europe, I, Urbanism.

Palliser D M, 1993 "Domesday Book and the 'Harrying of the North'", Northern History 29.

Palliser D M, 1996 "The 'minster hypothesis': a case study", Early Medieval Europe 5.

Pantos A, 1999 "Meeting-Places in *Wilvaston* Hundred, Cheshire", JEPNS 31.

Papworth M, 1997 "The Romano-British Settlement at Shapwick, Dorset", Britannia 28.

Parry M L, 1985 "Upland Settlement and Climatic Change: The Medieval Evidence", in D Spratt and C Burgess (eds), Upland Settlement in Britain: The Second Millennium B.C. and After, BAR (British Series) 143.

Parsons D, 1990 "Review and Prospect: The Stone Industry in Roman, Anglo-Saxon and Medieval England", in D Parsons (ed), Stone: Quarrying and Building in England, AD 43-1525

Pearce S, 1978 The Kingdom of Dumnonia

Percival J, 1989 "The Villa Economy: Problems and Perspectives", in K Branigan and D Miles (eds), The Economies of Romano-British Villas.

Pevsner N, 1958 The Buildings of England: North Somerset and Bristol.

Phythian-Adams C V, 1993 "Introduction: an Agenda for English Local History", in C V Phythian-Adams (ed), Societies, Cultures and Kinship, 1580-1850.

Phythian-Adams C V, 1996 Land of the Cumbrians: A Study in British Provincial Origins, AD 400-1120.

Phythian-Adams C V, 2000 "Environments and Identities: Landscape as Cultural Projection in the English Provincial Past", in P Slack (ed), Environments and Historical Change: The Linacre Lectures 1998.

Porter H M, 1971 The Celtic Church in Somerset

Powlesland D, 1997 "Early Anglo-Saxon Settlements, Structures, Form and Layout", in John Hines (ed), The Anglo-Saxons from the Migration Period to the Eighth Century: An Ethnographic Perspective.

Powlesland D (ed), 1998 "The West Heslerton Assessment", Internet Archaeology 5.

Powlesland D, 1999 "The Anglo-Saxon Settlement at West Heslerton, North Yorkshire", in J Hawkes and S Mills (eds), Northumbria's Golden Age.

Poyntz-Wright P, Barlow M, 1967 "Ashcott, Pedwell Hill", Archaeological Review 2.

Preece A, 1993 "Exmoor, Dunkery Area" (Somerset Archaeology, 1993), SANHS 137.

Preston-Jones A, 1992 "Decoding Cornish Churchyards", in Edwards and A Lane (eds), The Early Church in Wales and the West.

Prior S, 1999 An Earthwork Survey of a Motte and Bailey Castle at Downend, Puriton, Sedgemoor, unpublished MA dissertation, Bristol.

Prosser L, 1995 The Keynsham Hundred: A Study of the Evolution of a North Somerset Estate, 350-1550, unpublished PhD dissertation, Bristol.

Pryor F, 1998 Farmers in Prehistoric Britain.

Proudfoot E, Aliaga-Kelly C, 1997 "Aspects of Settlement and Territorial Arrangements in South-East Scotland in the Late Prehistoric and Early Medieval Periods", Medieval Archaeology 41.

Quinnell N V, Dunn C J, 1992 Lithic Monuments Within the Exmoor National Park, RCHME Report.

Rackham O, 1980 Ancient Woodland: Its History, Vegetation and Uses in England.

Rackham O, 1986 The History of the Countryside.

Rackham O, 1988 "Woods, Hedges and Forests", in M Aston (ed), Aspects of the Medieval Landscape of Somerset.

Rackham O, 1990 Trees and Woodland in the British Landscape (2nd edn).

Rackham O, 2000 "Boundaries and Country Planning: Ancient and Modern", in P Slack (ed), Environments and Historical Change.

Rahtz P, 1982 "Celtic Society in Somerset, AD 400-700", Bulletin of the Board of Celtic Studies 30.

Rahtz P, 1982a "The Dark Ages 400-700 AD", in M Aston and I Burrow (eds), The Archaeology of Somerset.

Rahtz P, 1987 "Post-Roman Avon", in M A Aston and R Iles (eds) The Archaeology of Avon.

Rahtz P, 1991 "Pagan and Christian by the Severn Sea", in L Abrams and J Carley (eds), The Archaeology and History of Glastonbury Abbey.

Rahtz P, 1993 Glastonbury.

Rahtz P, 2000 "150 Years of Somerset Archaeology: Looking Backwards and into the Next Millennium", in C J Webster (ed), Somerset Archaeology: Proceedings of the 150th Anniversary Conference of the Somerset Archaeological and Natural History Society.

Rahtz P, Greenfield E, 1977 Excavations at Chew Valley Lake Somerset, DOE Archaeological Reports 8.

Rahtz P, Watts L, 1989 "Pagan's Hill Revisited", Archaeological Journal 146.

Rahtz P, Meeson R, 1992 An Anglo-Saxon Watermill at Tamworth, CBA Research Report 83.

Rahtz P, Wright S, Hirst S, 2000 Cannington cemetery: excavations 1962-3 of prehistoric, Roman, post-Roman, and later features at Cannington Park Quarry, near Bridgwater, Somerset (Britannia Monograph 17).

Ramsey F (ed), 1995 English Episcopal Acta: Bath and Wells 1061-1205.

Reynolds A, 1999 Later Anglo-Saxon England: Life and Landscape.

Richardson I, 1998-1999 "Ley Hill Deserted Medieval Settlement, Horner Wood", National Trust Annual Archaeological Review 7.

Richardson I, 1999-2000 "Ley Hill Excavation", National Trust Annual Archaeological Review 8.

Riden P, 1987 Record Sources for Local History

Rippon S, 1991 "The Somerset Levels in the Roman Period", Annual Report of the Severn Estuary Levels Research Committee 2.

Rippon S, 1992 "The Exploitation of the North Somerset Levels in the Roman Period", Annual Report of the Severn Estuary Levels Research Committee 3

Rippon S, 1993 The Severn Wetlands During the Historic Period", Annual Report of the Severn Estuary Levels Research Committee 4

Rippon S, 1994 "Medieval Wetland Reclamation in Somerset", in M A Aston and C Lewis (eds), The Medieval Landscape of Wessex.

Rippon S, 1994a "The Roman Settlement and Landscape at Kenn Moor, North Somerset: Interim Report on Survey and Excavation, 1993/4", Annual Report of the Severn Estuary Levels Research Committee 5.

Rippon S, 1995 "The Roman Settlement and Landscape at Kenn Moor, Avon: Second Interim Report on Survey and Excavation, 1994/5", Annual Report of the Severn Estuary Levels Research Committee 6.

Rippon S, 1996 "Roman and Medieval Settlement on the North Somerset Levels: Survey and Excavation at Banwell and Puxton", Annual Report of the Severn Estuary Levels Research Committee 7.

Rippon S, 1996a "Roman Settlement and Salt Production on the Somerset Coast: the Work of Samuel Nash", SANHS 139.

Rippon S, 1997 The Severn Estuary: Landscape, Evolution and Wetland Reclamation.

Rippon S, 1997a "Roman and Medieval Settlement on the North Somerset Levels: the second season of survey and excavation at Banwell and Puxton", Annual Report of the Severn Estuary Levels Research Committee 8.

Rippon S, 2000 "Landscapes in transition: the later Roman and early medieval periods", in D Hooke (ed), Landscape: The Richest Historical Record.

Rippon S, 2000a "The Historic Landscapes of the Severn Estuary Levels", in S Rippon (ed), Estuarine Archaeology: The Severn and Beyond, Annual Report of the Severn Estuary Levels Research Committee 11.

Roberts B K, 1977 Rural Settlement in Britain.

Roberts B K, 1987 The Making of the English Village.

Roberts B K, Wrathmell S, 1994 "The Monuments Protection Programme: Medieval Settlements Project", MSRG 9.

Roberts B K, Wrathmell S, 1998 "Dispersed Settlement in England: A National View", in P Everson and T Williamson (eds), The Archaeology of Landscape: Studies Presented to Christopher Taylor.

Roberts B K, Wrathmell S, 2000 "Mapping Rural Settlement: Problems and Perspectives", in J A Atkinson, I Banks and G MacGregor (eds), Townships to Farmsteads: Rural Settlement Studies in Scotland, England and Wales, BAR (British Series) 293.

Roberts B K, Wrathmell S, 2000a "Peoples of Wood and Plain: An Exploration of National and Local Regional Contrasts", in D Hooke (ed), Landscape: The Richest Historical Record.

Roberts B K, Wrathmell S, 2001 An Atlas of Rural Settlement (English Heritage).

Rodwell W, 1984 "Churches in the Landscape: Aspects of Topography and Planning", in M Faull (ed), Studies in Late Anglo-Saxon Settlement.

Rodwell W, 1996 "Above and Below Ground: Archaeology at Wells Cathedral", in T Tatton-Brown and J Munby (eds), The Archaeology of Cathedrals, OUCA Monograph 42.

Rodwell W and K, 1985 Rivenhall: Investigations of a Roman villa, church and village, 1950-77, I (CBA Res Rep 55).

Rodwell W and K, 1993 Rivenhall: Investigations of a Roman villa, church and village, 1950-77, II (CBA Res Rep 80).

Rogers J, Ponsford M, 1979 "Human remains from a sub-Roman cemetery at Station Road, Portishead, Avon", in N Thomas (ed), Rescue Archaeology in the Bristol Region: 1.

Rogerson A, 1996 "Rural Settlement c.400-1200 ", in S Margeson, B Ayers and S Heywood (eds), A Festival of Norfolk Archaeology.

Room A, 1992 The Street Names of England.

Rosser G, 1996 "Cult centres new and old", in J Blair and C Pyrah (eds), Church Archaeology: Research Directions for the Future (CBA Research Report 104).

Russell J, 1999 "The Archaeology of the Parish of Clifton, With a Note on the 883AD Boundary Survey of Stoke Bishop", BAA 16.

Russett V E J, 1991 "Hythes and bows: aspects of river transport in Somerset", in G L Good, R H Jones and M

W Ponsford (eds), Waterfront Archaeology, CBA Research Report 74.

Russo D G, 1998 Town Origins and Development in Early England, c.400-950 A.D.

Samson R, 1999 "Illusory *emporia* and mad economic theories", in M Anderton (ed), Anglo-Saxon Trading Centres: Beyond the *Emporia.*

Saunders T, 1990 "The Feudal Construction of Space: Power and Domination in the Nucleated Village", in R Samson (ed), The Social Archaeology of Houses.

Saunders T, 1995 "Trade, Towns and States: A Reconsideration of Early Medieval Economics", Norwegian Archaeological Review, 28.

Savage J, 1830 A History of the Hundred of Carhampton

Savage W, 1955 "Somerset Towns", SANHS 100.

Sawyer P H, 1968 Anglo-Saxon Charters: An Annotated List and Bibliography.

Sawyer P, 1974 "Anglo-Saxon Settlement: The Documentary Evidence", in T Rowley (ed), Anglo-Saxon Settlement and Landscape, BAR (British Series) 6.

Sawyer P, 1983 "The Royal Tun in Pre-Conquest England", in P Wormald (ed), Ideal and Reality in Frankish and Anglo-Saxon Society.

Scherr J, 1986 "Names of Springs and Wells in Somerset", Nomina 10.

Schofield J, Vince A, 1994 Medieval Towns.

Scott E, 1993 A Gazetteer of Roman Villas in Britain.

Scott J (ed), 1981 The Early History of Glastonbury: An Edition, Translation and Study of William of Malmesbury's *de Antiquitate Glastonie Ecclesie.*

Scull C, 1997 "Urban Centres in Pre-Viking England?", in J Hines (ed), The Anglo-Saxons from the Migration Period to the Eighth Century: An Ethnographic Perspective.

Seebohm F, 1883 The English Village Community: An essay on Economic History

Semple S, 1998 "A fear of the past: the place of the prehistoric burial mound in the ideology of middle and later Anglo-Saxon England", World Archaeology 30.

Shaw M, 1993-4 "The Discovery of Saxon Sites Below Fieldwalking Scatters: Settlement Evidence at Brixworth and Upton, Northants", Northamptonshire Archaeology 25.

Sheppard J A, 1976 "Medieval Village Planning in Northern England: Some Evidence from Yorkshire", Jnl of Hist Geog 2.

Shilton D O, Holworthy R, 1925 Medieval Wills from Wells, SRS 40.

Silvester R, 1997 "Historic Settlement Surveys in Clwyd and Powys", in N Edwards (ed), Landscape and Settlement in Medieval Wales (Oxbow Monograph 81).

Sims-Williams P, 1990 Religion and Literature in Western England, 600-800.

Smith A H, 1956 English Place-Name Elements (2 vols).

Smith J B, 1999 "Votive Objects and Objects of Votive Significance from Great Walsingham", Britannia 30.

Smith J T, 1997 Roman Villas: A Study in Social Structure.

Smith R, 1988 "Human Resources", in G Astill and A Grant (eds), The Countryside of Medieval England.

Snyder C A, 1996 Sub-Roman Britain (AD 400-600): A Gazetteer of Sites, BAR (British Series) 247.

Snyder C A, 1997 "A Gazetteer of Sub-Roman Britain (AD 400-600): the British Sites", Internet Archaeology 3 (slightly revised and updated version of Snyder 1996).

Snyder C A, 1998 An Age of Tyrants: Britain and the Britons AD 400-600.

Sparey-Green C, 1996 "Poundbury, Dorset: settlement and economy in Late and post-Roman Dorchester", in K Dark (ed), External Contacts and the Economy of Late Roman and Post-Roman Britain.

SSAVBRG, 1990 "Farms and Farmsteads", in M A Aston and M D Costen (eds), Shapwick: The Third Report.

Stacey N E, 1971 The Estates of Glastonbury Abbey c1050-1200, unpublished DPhil thesis, Oxford.

Stenton F, 1971 Anglo-Saxon England (3rd edn).

Stevens D, 1985 "A Somerset Coroner's Roll, 1315-1321", SDNQ 31.

Stokes P A, 1996 The Organisation of Landscape and Territory on the Estates of Glastonbury Abbey: A Case Study of Ditcheat and Pennard, unpublished MA thesis, Leicester.

Strachey E, 1867 "On Sutton Court and Chew Magna", SANHS 14.

Straker V, Crabtree K, 1995 "Palaeoenvironmental Studies on Exmoor: Past Research and Future Potential", in H Binding (ed), The Changing Face of Exmoor.

Svensson O, 1991-92 "The *Worthy*-Names of Devon", Nomina 15.

Swainson B M, 1943 "Dispersion and Agglomeration of Rural Settlement in Somerset", Geography 29.

Synge, Revd E F, 1974 Butleigh: A Thousand Years of a Somerset Parish.

Szostak R, 1991 The Role of Transportation in the Industrial Revolution.

Tate W E, 1948 Somerset Enclosure Acts and Awards.

Taylor C C, 1975 Fields in the English Landscape.

Taylor C C, 1982 "Medieval Market Grants and Village Morphology", Landscape History 4.

Taylor C C, 1983 Village and Farmstead

Taylor C C, 1988 The Making of the English Landscape (annotated edn of Hoskins 1955).

Taylor C C, 1994 "The Regular Village Plan: Dorset Revisited and Revised", in Aston M and Lewis C (eds), The Medieval Landscape of Wessex.

Taylor C C, 1995 "Dispersed Settlement in Nucleated Areas", Landscape History 17.

Taylor R F, 1967 "A Romano-British Site at Woolavington", SANHS 111.

Thomas C, 1971 The Early Christian Archaeology of North Britain

Thomas C, 1994 And Shall These Mute Stones Speak?

Thompson M et al, 1997 "Fieldwalking in 'Sladwick', Field 1303", in M A Aston and C M Gerrard (eds), Shapwick: The Seventh Report.

Thomson G, 1994 All Saints' Church, Ashcott: Historical and Descriptive Notes (2nd edn).

Thorn F and C (eds), 1980 Domesday Book: Somerset

Thorn F, 1989 Map, Domesday Book: Somerset (Alecto Historical Edition)

Thorn F, 1989a "Hundreds and Wapentakes", Domesday Book: Somerset (Alecto Historical Edition)

Thornton C, 1988 The Demesne of Rimpton, 938 to 1412: A Study in Economic Development, unpublished PhD thesis, Leicester.

Tilley C, 1994 A Phenomenology of Landscape.

Tipping R, 1998 "Towards an environmental history of the Bowmont Valley and the northern Cheviot Hills", Landscape History 20.

Todd M, 1989 "Villa and Fundus", in K Branigan and D Miles (eds), The Economies of Romano-British Villas.

Todd M, 1995 "Charterhouse on Mendip: Interim Report on Excavations in 1994", SANHS 138.

Tolan-Smith C, 1996 "And then came farmers to the North", British Archaeology, Feb 1996, No 11.

Torr V J, 1974-79 "Ecclesiastical Somerset in 1563", SDNQ 30.

Toulmin-Smith L (ed), 1910 The Itinerary of John Leland

Tratman E K, 1963 "Some ideas on Roman roads in Bristol and north Somerset", Proc UBSS 9.

Turner A G C, 1952 "Some Aspects of Celtic Survival in Somerset", SANHS 97.

Turner A, 1998 "Geophysical Survey in Fields 7372, 7951, 7722 and 4016, Undertaken in 1997", in M A Aston,T A Hall and C M Gerrard (eds), The Shapwick Project: Eighth Report

Turner S, 2000 "Aspects of the development of public assembly in the Danelaw", Assemblage 5.

Van de Noort R, 1993 "The Context of Early Medieval barrows in western Europe", Antiquity 67.

Wacher J, 1995 The Towns of Roman Britain (2nd edn).

Ward A, 1997 "Transhumance and Settlement on the Welsh Uplands: A View from the Black Mountain", in N Edwards (ed), Landscape and Settlement in Medieval Wales (Oxbow Monograph 81).

Ward-Perkins B, 2000 "Why did the Anglo-Saxons not become more British?", English Historical Review 115, No 462.

Watkin A (ed), 1947 The Great Cartulary of Glastonbury Abbey, I, SRS 59.

Watkin A (ed), 1952 GC II, SRS 63.

Watkin A (ed), 1956 GC III, SRS 64.

Watts L, Leach P (eds), 1996 Henley Wood, Temples and Cemetery Excavations 1962-69, by the late Ernest Greenfield and Others (CBA Research Report 99).

Watts V, 2000 "Some Place-Name Distributions", JEPNS 32.

Weaver F W, 1890 Wells Wills.

Weaver F W (ed), 1905 Somerset Medieval Wills 1531-1558, SRS 21.

Weaver F W (ed), 1909 A Cartulary of Buckland Priory in the County of Somerset, SRS 25.

Weaver F W (ed), 1910 A Feodary of Glastonbury Abbey, SRS 26.

Webster C J, 2000"The Dark Ages", in C J Webster (ed), Somerset Archaeology: Proceedings of the 150th Anniversary Conference of SANHS.

Welldon Finn R, 1967 "Devonshire", in H C Darby and R Welldon Finn (eds), The Domesday Geography of South-West England.

Welldon Finn R, Wheatley P, 1967"Somerset", in R Welldon Finn and H C Darby (eds), The Domesday Geography of South-West England.

Whitelock D (ed), 1979 English Historical Documents I: c550-1042 (2nd edn).

Whittock M, 1987 "A Retrospective Examination of an Old English Royal Estate", Bristol and Avon Archaeology 6.

Wickham C, 1992 "Problems of Comparing Rural Societies in Early Medieval Western Europe", Trans Roy Hist Soc (6th Series) II.

Wilkinson K, 1998 "An Investigation of Holocene Peat and Intertidal Stratigraphy on Shapwick Heath, Somerset: Preliminary Results", Archaeology in the Severn Estuary 9.

Wilkinson P, 1998 "Finding Beowulf in Kent's Landscape", British Archaeology, 39 (November).

Wilkinson P, 2000 The Swale District: An Archaeological Survey Commissioned by Swale Borough Council (unpublished report).

Williams D, 2000 "Wanborough Roman Temple", Curent Archaeology 167, March 2000.

Williams E F, 1978 Survey of the Parish of Luxborough

Williams E F, 1990 Survey of the Parish of Treborough

Williams H, 1997 "Ancient attitudes to ancient monuments", British Archaeology 29 (November).

Williams H, 1997a "Ancient Landscapes and the Dead: The Reuse of Prehistoric and Roman Monuments as Early Anglo-Saxon Burial Sites", Medieval Archaeology 41.

Williams H, 1999 "Placing the dead: investigating the location of wealthy barrow burials in seventh century England", in M Rundkvist (ed), Grave Matters, BAR International Series 781.

Williams M, 1970 The Draining of the Somerset Levels

Williams M, 1971 "The Enclosure and Reclamation of the Mendip Hills, 1770-1870", Ag Hist Rev 19.

Williams M, 1976 "Mendip Farming: The Last Three Centuries", in R Atthill (ed), Mendip: A New Study.

Williams R G J, 1982 "Norton Malreward", Bristol and Avon Archaeology 1.

Williams R G J, 1983 "Romano-British Settlement at Filwood Park, Bristol", Bristol and Avon Archaeology 2.

Williams R G J, 1986 "John Strachey FRS: A Review of Fieldwork by an Early Antiquary in South Avon", Bristol and Avon Archaeology 5.

Williams R G J, 1992 "The Stratford Lane Roman Road and Other Early Routes on Mendip", Proc Univ of Bristol Speleol Soc 19.

Williams R G J, 1998 "The St Cuthbert's Roman Mining Settlement, Priddy, Somerset: Aerial Photographic Recognition", Proc Univ of Bristol Speleol Soc, 21.

Williamson T, 1998 "The 'Scole-Dickleburgh field system' revisited", Landscape History 20.

Williamson T, 2000 "Understanding Enclosure", Landscapes 1.

Williamson T, 2000a "The Rural Landscape: 1500-1900, The Neglected Centuries", in D Hooke (ed), Landscape: The Richest Historical Record.

Wilson-North R, 1996 Badgworthy Deserted Medieval Settlement (RCHME Survey Report).

Wilson-North R, Riley H, 1996 The Prehistoric Enclosures and Medieval and Post-Medieval Settlements at Bagley and Sweetworthy, Luccombe, Somerset (RCHME Survey Report).

Wilson-North R, Riley H, 1997A Medieval Settlement and Prehistoric Enclosure at Ley Hill, Luccombe, Somerset (RCHME Survey Report).

Wilson-North R, Riley H, 1997a The Field Archaeology of North Hill: An Archaeological Survey of the Exmoor National Park Holding (RCHME Survey Report).

Wilson-North R, Riley H, 2001 The Field Archaeology of Exmoor (English Heritage).

Winchester A, 1990 Discovering Parish Boundaries.

Witcher R, 1998 "Roman Roads: phenomenological perspectives on roads in the landscape", in C Forcey, J Hawthorne and R Witcher (eds), TRAC 97: Proceedings of the Seventh Annual Theoretical Roman Archaeology Conference (Oxbow).

Wood F A, 1903 Collections for a Parochial History of Chew Magna.

Woods H M, 1990 "Bridgwater, Wembdon Hill", SANHS 134.

Woodward A, 1992 Shrines and Sacrifice.

Woodward G H (ed), 1982 Calendar of Somerset Chantry Grants, SRS 77.

Wormald P, 1982 "The Age of Bede and Aethelbald", in J Campbell (ed), The Anglo-Saxons.

Yorke B, 1995 Wessex in the Early Middle Ages.

Yorke B, 1999 "The Origins of Anglo-Saxon Kingdoms: The Contribution of Written Sources", ASSAH 10.

Young A, Erskine J, 1994/95 "West Wansdyke Research Project", Bristol and Avon Archaeology 12.

Young R, Simmonds T, 1995 "Marginality and the Nature of Later Prehistoric Upland Settlement in the North of England", Landscape History 17.

9 781841 714240